Bulgaria under Communism

The book traces the history of communist Bulgaria from 1944 to 1989. A detailed narrative-cum-study of the history of a political system, it provides a chronological overview of the building of the socialist state from the ground up, its entrenchment into the peaceful routine of everyday life, its inner crises, and its gradual decline and self-destruction. The book is the definitive and the most complete guide to Bulgaria under communism and how the communist system operates on a day-to-day level.

Ivaylo Znepolski (Editor) is Emeritus Professor at the University of Sofia and Director of the Institute for Studies of the Recent Past, Sofia, Bulgaria.

Mihail Gruev is Head of the Bulgarian State Archive.

Momtchil Metodiev is Research Fellow at the Institute for Studies of the Recent Past, Sofia, Bulgaria.

Martin Ivanov is Professor at the Department of Sociology, University of Sofia.

Daniel Vatchkov is Head of the Institute of Historical Studies at the Bulgarian Academy of Sciences.

Ivan Elenkov is Full Professor at the University of Sofia, teaching the History of Bulgarian Modern Culture.

Plamen Doynov is Associate Professor at the New Bulgarian University.

Routledge Histories of Central and Eastern Europe

www.routledge.com/Routledge-Histories-of-Central-and-Eastern-Europe/book-series/CEE

1 **Hungary since 1945**
   Árpád von Klimó, translated by Kevin McAleer

2 **Romania under Communism**
   Denis Deletant

3 **Bulgaria under Communism**
   Ivaylo Znepolski, Mihail Gruev, Momtchil Metodiev, Martin Ivanov, Daniel Vatchkov, Ivan Elenkov, and Plamen Doynov

Bulgaria under Communism

Ivaylo Znepolski, Mihail Gruev,
Momtchil Metodiev, Martin Ivanov,
Daniel Vatchkov, Ivan Elenkov, and
Plamen Doynov

LONDON AND NEW YORK

First published 2019
by Routledge
2 Park Square, Milton Park, Abingdon, Oxon OX14 4RN

and by Routledge
52 Vanderbilt Avenue, New York, NY 10017, USA

First issued in paperback 2020

Routledge is an imprint of the Taylor & Francis Group, an informa business

© 2019 Ivaylo Znepolski, Mihail Gruev, Momtchil Metodiev, Martin Ivanov,
Daniel Vatchkov, Ivan Elenkov, and Plamen Doynov

The right of Ivaylo Znepolski, Mihail Gruev, Momtchil Metodiev, Martin Ivanov,
Daniel Vatchkov, Ivan Elenkov, and Plamen Doynov to be identified as authors
of this work has been asserted by them in accordance with sections 77 and 78
of the Copyright, Designs and Patents Act 1988.

All rights reserved. No part of this book may be reprinted or reproduced or utilized
in any form or by any electronic, mechanical, or other means, now known or
hereafter invented, including photocopying and recording, or in any information
storage or retrieval system, without permission in writing from the publishers.

Trademark notice: Product or corporate names may be trademarks or registered trademarks,
and are used only for identification and explanation without intent to infringe.

British Library Cataloguing in Publication Data
A catalogue record for this book is available from the British Library

Library of Congress Cataloging in Publication Data
A catalog record has been requested for this book

ISBN 13: 978-0-367-58643-0 (pbk)
ISBN 13: 978-0-8153-7279-0 (hbk)

Typeset in Times New Roman
by Out of House Publishing

Contents

Acknowledgments	x
List of abbreviations	xii

Introduction: how should we write the history of
communist Bulgaria?   1
The problem of distance: from close up and far away 1
Why the silence about communism? 4
Macrohistory; or, history from the "bottom up" 6
The trajectory of the regime: three provisionally differentiated
  periods 11
The regime and society in an interdisciplinary perspective 18
The People's Republic of Bulgaria and the Republic of
  Bulgaria: continuity or a break? 20

Historical background: the Communist Party's path
to power   28
The building of the modern Bulgarian state 28
The upswing of the end of the nineteenth century and the beginning
  of the twentieth century 29
Bulgaria's participation in wars from 1912 to 1918 and the
  subsequent catastrophe 32
The intense struggles of the interwar period 33
The initial phase of the war and Bulgarian neutrality (1939–1941) 37
Bulgaria in the orbit of the Third Reich (1941–1944) 41

PART I
The times of high Stalinism   53

1   Bulgaria in the shadow of Stalin   55
  Establishment of the Fatherland Front government in Bulgaria 55

vi *Contents*

The Moscow Truce and Bulgaria's participation in the final stage
  of World War II 60
Conflicts within the Fatherland Front and the formation of a legal
  opposition to the regime 64
The intensification of social-political struggles within the country 68
Signing the peace treaty with Bulgaria 74
Convening a Grand National Assembly and the liquidation of
  the opposition 76

2 Georgi Dimitrov and "the people's democracy"   84
Georgi Dimitrov and his diary 86
Dimitrov and Stalin 87
On the nature of "the people's democracy" 92

3 Bulgaria in the years of classical Stalinism   99
The second major wave of repression 100
Vâlko Chervenkov: the new charismatic leader 103

4 Building the communist economy in Bulgaria   106
The postwar economic crisis and the beginning of deep
  transformations within the Bulgarian economy (1944–1947) 106
The sovietization of the Bulgarian economy (1948–1953) 116
Ideas for Bulgaria's economic development as a weapon in power
  struggles (1953–1956) 121

5 The Bulgarian village under communism: collectivization,
   social change, and adaptation   126
At the crossroads between private and collective agriculture 126
Tools for imposing the Soviet kolkhoz model 130
The first stage of mass collectivization 135
The TKZSs and social change in the Bulgarian village 137
The villagers' resistance 139
The temporary lull 141
The final push toward mass collectivization 142
The villagers' strategies for adaptation 144

6 The *goryani*: armed resistance against communist repression   149

7 The sovietization of Bulgaria: a basic resource for the new
   communist authorities   156
Objective factors in the sovietization of Bulgaria 156
Subjective factors in sovietization 161
Entanglement in the totalitarian web 164

Contents vii

8 State Security within the structure of the communist
   state: ruling through violence   168
   Building State Security 168
   Political repression 170
   Organizational principles 171
   Intelligence departments 176
   Domestic security and political police 181

9 Education and culture within the system of the
   communist state   189
   The new government's educational policy 190
   The seizure and centralization of cultural institutes and independent
   *   organizations of intellectuals 193*
   Censorship institutions 195
   The imposition of socialist realism in the literature and culture of
   *   communist Bulgaria 197*

10 Communist Bulgaria's foreign policy and the Cold War   205
    The idea of a south Slavic federation and its failure 205
    The signing of the peace treaty and the official establishment of
    *   Bulgaria's status as a Soviet satellite 207*
    Bulgaria and international relations within the borders of the
    *   Eastern Bloc 208*
    Bulgaria's relations with the United States and other Western
    *   countries during the Cold War 210*
    Bulgaria and bloc-internal crises 213
    Bulgaria and the Third World 214

PART II
From sheepish de-Stalinization toward the consolidation of
the regime and its penetration into everyday life   219

11 After Stalin: political processes within "real socialism"   221
    A timid thaw in Bulgarian society 223
    The 1956 April Plenum of the Central Committee of the BCP
    *   and its consequences 228*
    Todor Zhivkov's seizure of absolute power 233
    Factional struggles and conspiracies within in the BCP during the
    *   1960s and the early 1970s 237*
    The Zhivkov Constitution of 1971 and the leader's new cult of
    *   personality 241*
    Old foreign policy with a new voice 244
    Bulgaria and the end of the Cold War 247

viii *Contents*

12 The course toward accelerated economic development
and reform of the economic model   252
In search of new economic priorities 252
Communist Bulgaria's first debt crisis (1960–1964) 254
*The first timid attempts at reforming the economic model
(1963–1968) 258*
Substitutes for reform (1968–1976) 263
The second foreign-debt crisis (1973–1978) 268
"The new economic mechanism" (1979–1980) 272
*Economic or political restructuring: Zhivkov with/versus
Gorbachev 275*

13 Sovietization in the shadow of Khrushchev and the
Brezhnev Doctrine   281

14 In search of a communist model of consumer society   289
Reasons for consensus instead of violence 290
The paths to constructing a feigned consensus 293
Disintegration of the feigned consensus 301

15 Processes within society: the division of the public and
private spheres   306

16 The ghosts of national communism and pressure on
Muslim communities   313
Pressure and survival during the 1960s and early 1970s 314
"The Revival Process" from the mid-1970s through the 1980s 319

17 The church on the periphery of society   324
Christian churches: a struggle to survive under Stalinism 324
*Elevation of the international status of the Bulgarian Orthodox
Church 328*
*The isolation of the Bulgarian Orthodox Church under Patriarch
Kiril (1953–1971) and Patriarch Maxim 331*
*The Bulgarian Orthodox Church's international and ecumenical
activities 334*

18 Processes within the culture of "real socialism"   340
*Lyudmila Zhivkova and the new cultural policy: unified long-term
cultural programs 341*
*The historicization of culture and the transformation of classical
ideological postulates 343*
Crisis and mimicry in socialist realism: discursive tension 346

Contents   ix

The alternatives: vacillation and acknowledgment 349
From the invisible turn during the 1970s and 1980s to the slow
  advance of alternatives 351

PART III
The collapse and peaceful withdrawal of communism in Bulgaria   355

19 The deepening crises and the paralyzation of the regime   357
Reform fever to the bitter end: from the July Conception to
  Decree 56 357
The foreign-debt trap 360
The collapse of the "Revival Process" and the intensification
  of Bulgaria's international isolation 364
Perestroika-*related processes in late-communist culture 367*
Socialist realism as an abandoned fortress 369

20 The limits of the communist model and an evaluation
of the regime's social policy   373
A social policy "in service of the people" 377
Sources and uses of nostalgia 381
Justice and solidarity in the communist état-providence *383*
Social benefits and the social corruption of the masses 388
Social rights and their internal erosion: an element of communist
  Bulgaria's final crisis 401

21 Gorbachev's *perestroika* and its influence on processes
in Bulgaria   407
Gorbachev's perestroika *and Zhivkov's* perestruvka *409*
The "grand era of the intelligentsia" and the late Bulgarian
  dissident movement 410
The November 10 coup and Todor Zhivkov's removal from power 414

22 The beginning of the Great Transition   418

Timeline of the People's Republic of Bulgaria   423
Leading historical figures from the period   432
Bibliography   444
Index   450

Acknowledgments

As the first comprehensive history of Bulgaria under communist rule, this book was in the pipeline for quite a while. Up until the fall of the Berlin Wall, that history had stayed virtual more than anything else as it only existed in the backstage of the communist propaganda take of the period as imposed from the top. Therefore, the unexpected end of communism originally appeared, as François Furet had put it, as a mystery of some sort. A comprehensive revision of the period was in order, with the sequence of events being placed within the context of often-inconspicuous processes taking place within the depth of Bulgarian society itself and amidst the workings of various social spheres. It was an approach that necessitated continuous research while delving into different aspects of a history still unwritten.

Given the plethora of new sources and the variety of social fields that needed a closer look, the book's design demanded multiple specializations of its authors: at least at this stage, it could have hardly been written by a single person. Hence, it took the effort of seven well-established researchers of the regime's individual periods – or of the various segments of its life (economy, society, foreign policy, culture, faith, repressive institutions, party machine, ethnic relations, etc.). Each one of these researchers already had well-received monographs on the same subjects under their belts. Yet this book is not a compendium of individual studies, nor is it a synopsis of previous publications. Its seven authors can in a sense be seen as a single research agency inasmuch as they worked within a shared – and agreed in advance – concept and design of the future book. Discussions were held around each individual chapter and over the final text. As they were mostly attended by all seven authors, the group functioned as a never-ending workshop. The criticism and proposals that were traded this way have eased our way into a shared terminology, around factual inconsistencies and into a final overall redaction by myself, Ivaylo Znepolski.

This work is a confluence of multiple sources. Among the most important ones were the unclogging of individual memories, which resulted in an exponential growth of memoir literature over the years, and the incremental relaxation of access to the archives of State Security, the Bulgarian Communist Party and the administrative branches of the regime. But that in itself was not

Acknowledgments xi

enough: as is well known, documents do not exhaust history; what is needed is their critical interpretation and verification. Bulgarian historiography had to work its way through a methodological update – and this process could not simply be spearheaded by individual researchers; instead, it had to transform the research ecosystem as a whole. Our work on the book was hugely benefited by a string of local or international academic gatherings dedicated to the communist past, with our authors actively participating in them. I remember thankfully the stimulating contacts with Jacques Revel (École des Hautes Études en Sciences Sociales, Paris), Giovanni Levi (University of Turin), Jeffrey Goldfarb (New School for Social Research in New York), Sandrine Kott (University of Poitiers), Padraic Kenney (Indiana University), Thomas Lindenberger (Center for Contemporary History, Potsdam), etc.

Besides, a host of local researchers have, directly or indirectly, been related to our subject as either contributors to previous joint projects or as having carried out exploration work on their own along similar lines. I would like to express our tremendous appreciation of the help provided by researchers such as Petya Kabakchieva, Pepka Boyadjieva, Daniela Koleva, and Kostadin Grozev from Sofia University; Hristo Todorov and Lachezar Stoyanov from the New Bulgarian University; and Evelina Kelbcheva from the American University in Blagoevgrad. We are also grateful to Blagovest Niagulov (BAS Institute for Historical Studies) and Boyko Penchev (Sofia University) as the book's reviewers. The remarks of Routledge's internal reviewer, Robert Bideleux (Department of Political and Cultural Studies, Swansea University) were also outstandingly helpful. We also owe a whole lot to Martin K. Dimitrov (Tulane University) for his useful advice on the English versions of certain concepts and his guiding us to this publishing house.

It would have been impossible to have this book either produced or published without the understanding and financial support of the America for Bulgaria Foundation, and I highly appreciate all that help. Unlike so many foundations, which are increasingly focusing on more current and narrowly pragmatic issues, America for Bulgaria should be hailed for its unfailing interest in and assistance to research into our near past. This book wouldn't have been able to reach its English-speaking readership without the invaluable help of Angela Rodel, whose talent in translation gave it the linguistic shape it needed. I am immensely thankful for this.

Ivaylo Znepolski

Abbreviations

ACC	Allied Control Commission
AMVnR	Archive of the Ministry of Interior
APK	*Agrarno-promishlen kompleks* (Agrarian-Industrial Complex)
BANU	Bulgarian Agrarian National Union
BCP	Bulgarian Communist Party
BNB	Bulgarian National Bank
BSP	Bulgarian Socialist Party
BWP	Bulgarian Workers Party
BWP(C)	Bulgarian Workers Party (Communists)
BWSDP	Bulgarian Workers' Social Democratic Party
BWSDP(U)	Bulgarian Workers Social Democratic Party (United)
CFM	Council of Foreign Ministers
Comecon	Council for Mutual Economic Assistance
CPSU	Communist Party of the Soviet Union
DSO	*Dârzhavni stopanski obedineniya* (state economic unions)
GDR	German Democratic Republic
GNA	Grand National Assembly
IBEC	International Bank for Economic Cooperation
IMF	International Monetary Fund
NKVD	*Narodniy komissariat vnutrennih del* (People's Commissariat for Internal Affairs)
NOVA	*Narodoosvoboditelna vâstanicheska armiya* (National-Liberational Insurrectional Army)
NTR	*Nauchno-technicheska revolyutsiya* (Scientific-Technological Revolution)
OCA	Orthodox Church in America
OSCE	Organization for Security and Co-operation in Europe
PAK	*Promishleno-agraren kompleks* (Industrial-Agrarian Complex)
PGU	*Pârvo glavno upravlenie* (First Main Department)
PRB	People's Republic of Bulgaria

Abbreviations xiii

RMS	*Rabotnichesko-mladezhki sâyuz* (Workers Youth League)
TKZS	*Trudovo kooperativno zemedelsko stopanstvo* (Labor Cooperative Agricultural Economy, cooperative farms)
UDF	Union of Democratic Forces (*Sâyuz na demokratichnite sili*)
WCC	World Council of Churches

Introduction

How should we write the history of communist Bulgaria?

This book offers an account of one part of the most recent history of the Bulgarian state, known as "the people's republic," covering the forty-five-year period of the communist regime (September 9, 1944–November 10, 1989). At the same time, in order to clarify the preconditions necessary for establishing communist rule and the subsequent circumstances and mechanisms that led to its bankruptcy and peaceful withdrawal, as well as to be able to examine the mimicry of communist-style nomenclature within the conditions of emerging democracy, this book takes the liberty of slightly overstepping the chronological boundaries backward and forward in time. In carrying out this task, the authors faced a series of specific difficulties, which had to be overcome in the research process itself, since this is the first Bulgarian undertaking of its kind, and, as far as we are aware, one of the first in the former Soviet satellite states in Eastern Europe.

The problem of distance: from close up and far away

The first and perhaps most difficult problem to overcome was that of distance. It appears in two completely different yet connected cases. In the first, problems arise from the relatively short temporal distance separating the end of the communist regime from the moment its history is being written. This presents a challenge to historians, who must find a fitting approach for dealing with the difficulties resulting from strongly emotional evaluations of the recent past. In the second case, the problem arises from the way the previously written history of the regime has been received and results from the greater temporal distance separating the generations who grew up under late socialism or those whose childhood coincided with the democratic transitions from the radical phase of the regime (1944–1956), when it established itself through mass terror and everyday violence. Over its nearly five decades in power, the regime changed its façade several times and for each new generation, its countenance has shifted slightly – a process made possible due to the total absence of freedom of opinion and to deliberate disinformation regarding the regime's past practices. This made the transfer of experience between generations and the formation of personal opinions impossible. For

2 Introduction

these younger generations, there is no memory of the repressive practices and the criminal aspects of the regime. Time has washed away all traces. Each new generation lived in the pure present of the regime, hence they now judge it based on the familiar grimaces of late, exhausted communism and its covert violence imbued in petty restrictions and deficits, yet tolerable to some degree. Moreover, there are also contemporary factors that disseminate and encourage the opinion that despite the unjustified repression and undesirable distortions of the social project, the communist years remain a time of social equality and security, marked by tangible improvement in the lives of the poorest of the poor. It is also asked why are we constantly digging up the negative sides of the past? Let's look at its good, constructive aspects as well. In this context, lacking personal experience and given the absence of a principled and responsible assessment of the regime on the part of society itself, whole generations are growing up without a clear idea of communism's essence, yet also with a distorted understanding of what constitutes "normal life." The majority of foreign observers also find themselves in a similar position, having only a very general idea of the nature of communism but not having experienced life in a communist country and also lacking knowledge of the basic events outlining the Communist Party's trajectory in any one particular country. Finally, this situation also presents an additional problem for historians of the period, who must recount and interpret the same history for different audiences. The young and foreigners seem to be the best prepared to calmly accept a history of communism as the history of its collapse. This is not the case with those whose lives passed under communist rule and for whom the encounter between emotions and research approaches is often highly problematic.

And so we return to the question: Is two decades sufficient distance to begin an assessment of a historical period? Many tend to answer this question negatively, arguing that to guarantee a fair evaluation more time must pass, generations must change, emotions must die down. I will leave aside the old methodological debate about the possibility of "objective" history. A historical narrative, even concerning the most distant periods, is always the product of a particular viewpoint, strongly marked by particular cultural or political traditions. This is a problem that Bulgarian historiography does not face alone. During the 1990s, a historiographical debate about the possibility of a *Histoire de temps present* arose in connection with breaking the silence around the nature of the Vichy Regime, French collaboration and the destruction of French Jewry. Almost fifty years had passed since the end of the war, yet most of the actors from that time were still alive. Historians found themselves facing the problem of the impossibility of reaching consensus within the collective memory – varying levels of agreement, as well as tensions, exist within this memory. Against the backdrop of the ongoing battle between differing memories, the evaluation of events always risks being disputed. It is very difficult for the historian of the present to secure non-biased distance and to define the border between subjective and objective moments in the transition from memory toward historical narrative. In the fields of power occupied by competing political and ideological discourses, he or she faces the risk of being reduced to simply one of many voices, to being one witness too many, whom everyone expects to act as corroborating witness in support of his own testimony. This is why historians have reached the conclusion that in order to escape the pitfalls of memory, historical research must shake off memory and orient itself toward understanding and interpretation.

In the Federal Republic of Germany, historians of the present have faced fewer difficulties than their French counterparts. National Socialism collapsed at the height of its criminal practices – testimony about the death camps, about mass killings and the pillaging of occupied territories, about destroyed cities and the millions of victims on the battlefields was an immediate reality. Both the active as well as the passive complicity of the German population in Nazi crimes is beyond a doubt, thus this has allowed for both the moral and political delegitimization of Nazi memory about the war period. Yet despite the fact that there is internal resistance to facing the reality of the regime (most Germans felt themselves to be accomplices in what happened and hence fearful of retribution), in historical studies the process of judging the Nazi period began from a much closer distance. In France, for a long time after the end of the war, the Vichy Regime was looked upon as an incident placed in parentheses outside the continuity of the French democratic tradition, which, embodied by the French Resistance, should construct the dominant image of the country during the period of the occupation. For this reason, many functionaries of the Vichy Regime took up positions in the postwar French administration undisturbed. Only a half-century of distance from the crime of collaboration made a debate about responsibility and guilt possible. This means accepting that the French defeat in the war and the establishment of a pro-Nazi regime constitutes a historical break, a disruption of democratic continuity, with all the evaluations that follow from this.

Those writing the history of Bulgarian communism find themselves in a position closer to that of their German counterparts. Regardless of the short temporal distance, the necessary conditions for studying the period are at hand, since it is framed distinctly enough by bounding events that entail a radical change of perspective. Such framing events for Germany include the collapse of the Weimar Republic and the defeat of Nazism in World War II. For Russia, such events are the October Revolution and the fracturing of the Soviet Union. For Bulgaria, the framing events constituting radical breaks are the communist coup of September 9, 1944, with the support of the Red Army, and the toppling of the communist dictator Todor Zhivkov through an internal coup on November 10, 1989, and the opening of the path toward democratic development. At the same time, elements of the French situation can also be noted. The peaceful transfer of power and the established democratic consensus have not only allowed many former communist functionaries or heirs of the former nomenclature to actually recreate power positions (in administration or politics) but have also fed their ambitions to work toward imposing a politics of continuity between communism and post-communism.

4 *Introduction*

In other words, the struggle over the evaluation of the communist period has not ended even today.

Why the silence about communism?

The clash between differing memories of communism is the key reason that public debate about its crimes has been blocked. Political analysts, not only in Bulgaria, have discussed "the silence about communism" with good reason. But in searching for an explanation for that silence, hypotheses have arisen that threaten to further feed this tendency. Motivated by common features between national socialism and communism, some scholars have looked toward the rich existing literature on the Nazi past and how to overcome it. At a press conference in Sofia on the occasion of the release of the Bulgarian edition of *The Black Book of Communism*, Stéphane Courtois, reflecting on the reasons for Bulgarians' passiveness vis-à-vis their communist past, suggested that those emerging from communism are in the same situation as Jews emerging from Nazi concentration camps. The suffering was so great that people are not in a condition to speak about it. This explanation is a typical example of the mechanical introduction of external viewpoints. For everyone who has an adequate view of the reality of the European post-communist countries, such a notion of a trauma blocking memories of the past holds no explanatory value. No matter how oppressive late communism may have been, no matter how justifiable the metaphor of the *socialist camp* as a *camp* may be, the comparison with the Nazi death camps is at odds with the truth and further hinders making an assessment of it. Communism left deep trauma in its wake, but the question of its nature must be discussed on a different plane. A large percentage of the people who lived under its conditions and who struggled for survival and personal realization in such a context were inescapably drawn into the practices of regime; they lived with compromises and for this reason they feel guilty and to a certain extent vulnerable today and hence strive to avoid conversations about their own behavior. In building new identities, they do not have the courage to face their own image, expecting reproaches, which, incidentally, no one is in a position to make . . . On the other hand, people who were repressed by the regime, entire generations of scarred people, met the changes of November 10, 1989, not only with relief but more with euphoria, something which to a certain extent blurs the objective evaluation of what really took place.

The silence about communism, or, to put it another way, the reluctance to talk about it, the difficulty of making an overall assessment and evaluation of the period, and hence the difficulty of writing its history, can also be partially explained by the confusion caused by the clash between two alternative approaches to interpreting it. We can discover these two approaches both in the West, as well as in Eastern Europe. After the fall of the Berlin Wall, most analysts viewed communism as a phenomenon that had run its course in an already closed cycle and which lent itself to an overall assessment and

Introduction 5

historical evaluation. This evaluation was inevitably extremely negative and could not be otherwise, since the focus of research interest tended toward the period that best reveals communism's essence – Stalinism and the classical totalitarian model, which crystallized in the generalized violence of Soviet history. The individual Eastern European communisms stayed in the shadow of Russian communism, where they were considered copycat phenomena of no particular interest, which condemned them to a dearth of specialized research interest. Certain moments of crisis within the system constituted exceptions: the Hungarian Revolution of 1956, Prague Spring of 1968, or the activities of the Solidarity trade union in the 1980s. But there is almost no interest in the practices of late Eastern European communism, or so-called *real socialism*. The reduction of the communist past to a theoretically sufficient notion of the regime's political nature completely ignores its internal evolution and the evolution of the people existing within it, which distorts the picture and prevents analysis of it. Many apparatchiks who participated in the government at various levels during the later periods of the regime refuse to take responsibility for the deeds of their predecessors and to share the guilt for the regime's historical burdens.

The other approach focuses on late socialism and its peaceful withdrawal, on the communist leaders' unexpected resignation to the project's failure and their relinquishment of the monopoly on power – after businesslike negotiations, however, which carefully prepared the groundwork that would guarantee the erstwhile communists a place within the democratic system's political life. The emphasis placed on change and on emergence from the totalitarian model definitively blocks the condemnation of communism due to the simple fact that people are not reacting to the phenomenon as a whole but only to its late modifications. In this understanding, the regime's internal development atones for its early transgressions, which people are prepared to admit; however, they more likely see them as inevitable, instead of condemning them. This position situates itself as a balanced compromise between gradual change and waning continuity.

Each of these two approaches raises problems and hinders the development of historical studies. To overcome their one-sidedness, we must familiarize ourselves with the history of the period in its totality and also acquaint ourselves in detail with the regime's trajectory. To this end, the two approaches must not be juxtaposed as alternatives, since combining them can be useful for revealing the actual dynamics of the regime. If we remain only within the boundaries of either of the two competing discourses, we will be forced to accept the existence of a gap between the realities they delineate, making the change that occurred in 1989 difficult to comprehend. Not only would the true subject of our research – communism – disappear into this gap, but also the lives of several generations, who in the end made this change possible.

Over the course of its history, the communist regime preserved its political nature yet at the same time it had no single form. A series of important transformations took place within its policies and the practices that resulted

6   *Introduction*

from them. The claim that totalitarian communism was not frozen but rather possessed certain dynamics has also been found in the writings of some of the classical scholars of the phenomenon: Hannah Arendt, Carl Joachim Friedrich, and Raymond Aron. With the deepening of the process of de-Stalinization, some of the characteristic features constituting the basis of totalitarian theory were substantially modified or disappeared. Mass terror disappeared (the practice of sweeping purges and of large political trials was ended), while during the 1960s concentration camps were also shut down in Bulgaria (although in certain cases this form of mass repression was used periodically until the mid-1980s), pressure on everyday life and the private sphere decreased considerably, while the conditions for a parallel economy arose. The atomization of society continued, but there is also evidence of the establishment of a certain routine and predictability on the part of the government, as well as the stabilization of existence based on a partially coerced consensus around the norms of the regime. Ideology was drained of content and its weight in public life decreased; and although propagandistic rhetoric continued to bombard people's consciousnesses, they had acquired a certain immunity, hence the wooden language of Marxism-Leninism became instead a marker of official speech. With the disappearance or modification of one or other of its characteristics, the totalitarian model itself is brought into question, raising doubts about its compatibility with the changes that occurred. This hybridity in part explains the scant scholarly literature about late communism.

To the external observer, many of these changes understandably go largely unnoticed, due to the lack of a concrete basis for comparison, and perhaps are even evaluated as not sufficiently crucial so as to force a reevaluation of the research perspective. This is not the case for people whose lives passed under the communist regime, however; they were sensitive to even the smallest changes, since such changes directly affected their own existence. "Compared to norms within pluralistic societies, the psychological (and overall social) change in communism appears small and unimportant [. . .] However, compared with the classical period of Leninism-Stalinism, the changes that have taken place – both in reality as well as in the spiritual realm – are nevertheless incredible." This observation was offered to us by a Bulgarian philosopher who emigrated to West Germany in the 1970s.[1]

Macrohistory; or, history from the "bottom up"

Today there is an ever-increasing number of personal stories of communist times. More and more individuals and groups insist upon sharing their own experiences and their own assessment of the past.[2] How is that related to the general history of communism and what are the methods that can organize and conceptualize that colorful mosaic of often-contradictory testimonies? We face the problem of how to write the history of communism in Bulgaria – from the "top down" or from the "bottom up," i.e. from the point of view of major historical events and structural characteristics, of the government and society – in other words, via overarching processes or via the lived experience of individuals and groups. This also brings us face to face with the problem of how both points of view can coexist – not be reconciled but, precisely, to coexist.

In his volume on *The Constitution of Society*, Anthony Giddens emphasizes the dynamic nature of social life. He introduces the term "structural contradiction" to describe the specific ambivalence of social structures (or political regimes). They are incessantly rearranged to limit the individual social actor and its inherent voluntarism. Having said that, social structures are the product of a series of individual actions. Assuming society is something *external* to us is wrong. It is external for *each* individual but in its essence it cannot be external to *all* individuals. Structures do not exist independently. No matter what the level of competence or awareness of social actors is they are at the same time subjects and agents in the reproduction of social practices. Political regimes function because humans in the course of their daily experience take an active role in the establishment and the maintenance of social structures. Indeed, *structural contradiction* and the dynamics of the *structuration* process defy the "correct" reproduction of social practices. Social agents have the potential to direct and manipulate social change to accommodate specific contexts. Social change is not an immediate product of single individual actions. The real subject of the *theory of structuration* is neither social totality nor the private experience of social actors but the accumulation of social practices performed and prescribed in a certain time and space (Anthony Giddens).[3]

Giddens' understanding of power rests on the same principles. As far as human individuals have the capacity to intervene in the course of events, power is never absolute. Dominating social groups possess the resources to enforce their norms and achieve their goals, yet at the same time dominated social groups still retain opportunities to resist or reduce the control imposed upon them. Thus, systematic relations of power are formed in the struggle between control and autonomy.

A bid in the same direction is Michel Foucault's concept of *the microphysics of power*, which refutes the hypothesis that society is organized around the bipolar relation dominator–dominated. Power cannot be localized in only one institution or agent; power in its essence cannot be detached from the multiplicity of social bonds. It originates from and is executed in the uncountable intersections of dynamic and perhaps unequal relations in which resistance from below is not without significance.[4] Theories of *structuration* and *micropowers* as well as the history of everyday life contributed considerably to recent studies of late-communist societies, which called themselves "real socialism." There are authors who insist on the existence of individual autonomy even in Soviet society in the 1930s during the forced collectivization or during Nazism (Nicolas Werth, Ian Kershaw, Alf Lüdtke, Sheila Fitzpatrick).[5]

From a global perspective, late communism creates the impression of a homogeneous and stable structure, but from a closer view on an everyday

8 *Introduction*

level it is not difficult to recognize the cracks in its monumental façade. The regime's appetite to totally control the human factor runs aground. The facts of life disagree with ideological representations. Individual life still manages to imitate some forms of "normality" by both resisting and accommodating the system. In this respect we can define three directions in studying regime–society relations.

The first direction relates to the theory of *network societies* (Manuel Castells, Bruno Latour, Vincent Lemieux, B. Karseni, Stein Ringen). Its proponents outline two types of networks depending on the principles and the intensity of connectivity among individuals. The first type are social networks that pervade the entire community, while in the second we think about bonds within specific groups and their own private principles. Relations in the second type of networks are characterized by a chain of interactions, in which each social agent is treated as equal and indispensable. Each network participant possesses something or does something which is not accessible to or lies outside the competence of the rest. This private aspect of the network theory, the *actor-network* aspect (Bruno Latour), was adapted by some recent analyses of Eastern Europe into a kind of *historical sociology of communism*.[6] The latter imposed strict controls over all formal organizations but could not impose such controls over private relationships. Individuals learned how to dodge official structures under a variety of pretexts. Researchers have described various contexts and methods whereby this is done: colonization of the state by family clans (Ivo Možný, Czech Republic), coping with the shortage economy (János Kornai, Hungary), gift-giving and mutual dependence translated into everyday life terms as "give to be given" (Deyan Deyanov, Bulgaria), redistribution of capital as a homogenizing factor and the advancement of a middle class (Andrei Raytchev, Kantcho Stoytchev, Bulgaria), the growing importance of social capital and its crucial role in the process of capital exchange (Dariusz Stola, Poland).[7] Despite various nuances, these analyses share common ground in the assumption that individuals are involved in certain activities behind the authorities' backs, establishing and keeping private zones that elude systematic control, and using social channels and resources to meet their narrow group interests, very often to the detriment of general public welfare. It is not hard to conclude that networks are not only a tool for survival but also a mechanism for the accumulation of various types of capital and power. A result of individual or group initiatives, these alternative networks jam the top-to-bottom mainstream and conserve the premodern and backward state of society.

The second direction of our research scrutinizes the processes of the emancipation of private life away from the dominating party and ideology – a trend related to the fact that during the 1960s the regime relinquished its aspiration to control every aspect and space of everyday living. This gave significant portions of the populace the opportunity to retreat from mandatory modes of action into their hidden-away, although not entirely surveillance-free, parallel world. Social energies were shunted into private spheres promoting a special type of consumerism. This analytical context gave rise to the theories of *social niches* (Günter Gaus), *internal emigration, the parallel economy, the second society*, etc. The same concepts are palpable in recent studies of the German Democratic Republic (GDR) regime and society, although somewhat modified and readjusted. They claim that if the late totalitarian society cannot be depicted as entirely absorbed by the regime, then it is equally wrong to depict it as something independent and separate from the same regime. This situation is conceived as a project for *social exchange*. Individual actors and groups act and represent themselves through the system structures and through the official language, pretending to follow the prescribed modes of behavior but at the same time pursuing their own agendas. This integration of private and official programs resulted in the gradual transformation of norms as well as in their successful internalization. The procedures of appropriation (including material appropriation) would not have been possible if they were recognized as subversive. Only when attained in an agreement with the regime, they became tolerated in order to preserve the societal equilibrium. These "negotiations" are nothing more than symptoms of the existence of a partially autonomous society, but they also stress its unorganized, fragmented character (Thomas Lindenberger, Richard Bessel, Ralph Jessen, Sandrine Kott, Esther von Richthofen).[8]

As it turned out, the system's reproduction did not entirely clash with social change. On the contrary, organizational sociology claims that changes are vital for the system's perpetuation. Karl Marx uses two notions to describe this: *regular* and *extended reproduction*. Obviously after de-Stalinization the *regular* reproduction of the communist regime was no longer viable. Networks, regime–society accommodations on the local level, and social exchange were practices within the scope of the *extended reproduction* of the communist regime. A crucial element in this process is the routine negotiated between individual social actors and official institutions. For both sides, routine proved to be a source of certainty and a guarantee for successful reproduction. This consensus can be interpreted as a process of mutual corruption: The regime corrupts the masses by compelling them to succumb to indoctrinated modes of survival or careers, but, despite the prescriptions of its ideology, it is forced to ease its radical and revolutionary stance in order to sustain its grip on the masses. The communist regime lasted so long due to its ability to cut a public figure of a tolerable and acceptable system for the majority of its subjects. Why risk upsetting the equilibrium and pursuing revolutionary change if you are able to address most issues through mutual compromises? Political indifference is a by-product of this arrangement. Corrupt paths toward a measure of private autonomy are profoundly conservative and contribute to stabilizing the regime at least as much as they erode it. Freedom constitutes your ability to find ways to adapt to the regime without making big compromises with your own principles and interests (Dariusz Stola).[9] Part of the established networks proved so effective (we should not forget the active participation

10   *Introduction*

of different-level party nomenclature in them) that they outlived the system and continued to operate throughout the Transition years, when they became a primary generator of political, bureaucratic and criminal corruption.

Scrutinizing the process of constant accommodation between society and regime reveals that the transformations that led to the collapse of communism were not irreversible. Throughout its mandate, the regime sustained all the necessary mechanisms for violent repression. The defeat of the Hungarian Revolution in 1956, the Warsaw Pact's occupation of Czechoslovakia in 1968 and the introduction of martial law in Poland in 1981 benchmarked severe repression and political intransigence. For "ordinary people," the incremental change of the regime was clearly felt, but *the skeleton of the communist system remained intact.* Nobody in the GDR or any other country of the "socialist camp" was able to dodge the party–state altogether. Individuals faced the limits of their relative autonomy across the board, even within their families. In this sense we can define "real socialism" as the *dictatorship of constraints.*

The third direction is the so-called *sectoral research.* Two separate trends emerge here. The first one of them is along the lines of social anthropology and the related fieldwork, while the other relies on the analysis of case studies or archival resources. I will list a few examples: (1) family relations in Bulgaria vis-à-vis *the postulates for a socialist way of life*;[10] the social consequences of collectivization in one Romanian village (David Kideckel);[11] ideology and cultural policy in the times of Ceaușescu (Katherine Verdery);[12] the "domestication" of the revolution in a Bulgarian village or how the tenets of cooperation evolve to meet the peasants' private interests (Gerald Creed);[13] mass organizations in Czechoslovakia (Sandrine Devaux);[14] the life of industrial workers in GDR (Sandrine Kott);[15] the traditions and culture of the German proletariat (Alf Lüdtke);[16] public utilization of the communist past in the Czech Republic (Françoise Mayer), etc. (2) Good examples of the second trend are provided by the publications of the Institute for Studies of the Recent Past, Sofia: the economic crisis and the efforts to reform the socialist planned economy (Martin Ivanov);[17] the role of the State Security services in the communist state (Momtchil Metodiev);[18] government policies toward the Turkish minority in communist Bulgaria (Michail Gruev, Alexei Kalionski);[19] "cultural front" communist policies (Ivan Elenkov);[20] collectivization and social change in the Bulgarian village (Michail Gruev);[21] the repression of the Bulgarian Orthodox Church and its integration within the regime (Momtchil Metodiev).[22]

Some sectoral studies of the first type offer a close focus on the apparently minor but repeated everyday experiences leading to the somewhat unexpectedly "normalized" social practices under communism that contribute to the system's perpetuation. The studies in the second trend, based on archival work and official documents, zero in on the grand structural characteristics of the regime and describe the functions or malfunctions of its institutions.

The concepts of social change, as well as their applications in various historical contexts in our project, show that communism was not a rock-solid and

Introduction 11

entirely stagnant reality. Instead, it underwent considerable transformations –
some of which were very crucial. Our current academic efforts still lack solid
knowledge of the chronology of these changes and the logic they followed.
The relative significance of what went on in the 1960s, 1970s, and 1980s still
has not been a matter of serious scientific debate.

The studies of everyday life and culture, of networks, of local-level
regime–society accommodations, of social exchanges or parallel economies
push our understanding of communism further, but, given their mostly
descriptive character, they still do not sufficiently address the main question
we are interested in: how to write and understand the history of communist
Bulgaria from its beginning till its end? They are tied to various forms of
microhistorical analysis or, to put it more broadly, respresent a history
written from the "bottom up." These kinds of historical studies are situated
between social history and social anthropology.

In terms of genre, the present book belongs rather to macrohistory, even
though at different times various personal examples are woven into the historical narrative in order to provide specific illustrations of the more general
constations. The most basic difference between macrohistory and history
"from below" is not reflected in the subject of the research but rather in
the choice of perspective and materials included. Macrohistory (event-
based and political history) organizes its discourse around facts and events
related to the society as a whole, which are the result of conscious and deliberate actions and arguments on the part of leaders and institution, while
microhistory and social anthropology are more interested in individual
cases, in separate social groups, as well as in the unconscious conditions
of social life, whose effects are only seen much later. History written "from
below" needs the context of macrohistory; without this framework, the
picture of the times could be easily distorted, as has happened, incidentally, in some of the nostalgia-tinged publications about the period. The
macrohistory of Bulgarian communism in turn will be continually enriched,
fleshed out and corrected by the interpretation and revision of various
microhistorical narratives. Thus, we cannot be content merely with a history
of events but must also weave into it social practices, attitudes, and discursive strategies that do not come from immediate lived experience but rather
are experiences confirmed by numerous sources, generalized experience, or
experience transformed into historical knowledge. Without this, it will be
difficult for communism to be understood from the outside.

The trajectory of the regime: three provisionally differentiated periods

In order to avoid leveling the picture and raising doubts as to the validity
of the assessment offered by one or another theoretically preconditioned
approach, we need a periodization of the regime, which will allow us to
trace and make sense of its historical trajectory. One prerequisite for

12 *Introduction*

such a periodization is the provisional distinction between a strictly historiographical approach and an approach based on political science. For political science, communist rule in Eastern Europe represents a clearly demarcated object whose life cycle is marked by a constant ideology and the practices imposed by it. For the historian, this half-century is more likely seen as heterogeneous in its homogeneity. It is the historian's task to study and describe the various modes of existence of the PRB. The regime remained the same, but, under pressure from various factors arising from the conditions of lasting peace, the society imperceptibly changed, which in turn provoked shifts in the regime's practices as well as in the forms of everyday life.

What are the criteria for the periodization proposed here? The basic reference point is the appearance of new practices within the functioning of the regime and changes in the relationship between the regime and society. However, this does not exclude recidivism, or throwbacks to older practices, whose existence until the very end of the regime confirms the constancy of its political nature. In so far as this change over the years was due to multiple factors, the periodization takes into account the dynamics of various parts of the system, as well as the ways in which they were combined. Here are some of the basic elements determining the regime's mutations: changes in society's social structure, the general elevation of the educational level, the introduction of new communication technologies (telephone, television, video, computers, despite the lack of access to the Internet), changes in the relationship between the public and private spheres, processes within culture and the reduction of pressure on the arts, the change of generations, increased consumer standards, and so on. On the other hand, changes in Eastern Europe and above all in Bulgaria were also largely determined by external factors, by processes in the imperial center (the generational turnover and political changes in Moscow), by directives (which since the time of Stalin had been carried out almost to the letter), and by the advancement of the peace process between the two superpowers. Over the course of time, processes on the empire's periphery also took on an ever-greater significance (the clearest example of this is the founding and activity of the Solidarity trade union in Poland), which weakened the center's power, provoking repercussions that were capable of shaking its very foundations. From 1987 to 1988, Mikhail Gorbachev, in the face of rising internal opposition within his own party, sought arguments supporting *perestroika* in the changes in Eastern Europe, which he himself encouraged through all possible means. Taking all of this into account, it is fitting for the trajectory of Bulgarian communism to be divided into three broad periods, each of which had its own dominant feature. The first two periods are lengthier and contain one or several sub-periods, which, without changing their general character, additionally underscore the real political and social dynamics of the regime and of society.

The first period begins with the Communist Party seizing power and gradually imposing a classical Stalinist regime. On September 5, 1944, despite the

Introduction 13

existence of diplomatic ties between the Soviet Union and Bulgaria throughout the whole war and despite the new "democratic" Bulgarian government's announcement of its break with Germany, the Soviet Union declared war on Bulgaria (the country had been a regional ally of the Reich mainly due to old territorial disputes with its neighbors but without confessing national socialism as its official political doctrine) and invaded the country three days later. On September 9, 1944, with the support of the Red Army and taking advantage of full institutional paralysis, the Bulgarian Communist Party (BCP) seized control of the main state institutions and the practical levers of power. The end of the first period spans the interval between Stalin's death in 1953 and the disclosures made in Khrushchev's report at the Twentieth Congress of the Communist Party of the Soviet Union (CPSU) in 1956. These events shook up the BCP as well, causing some changes in party leadership and setting off a hesitant process of de-Stalinization. The party was headed – temporarily, as many erroneously assumed – by a man who was not the most distinguished in battle, nor the best prepared, nor the most popular among the party membership: Todor Zhivkov. This first period is full of dramatic events: a military coup and the subduing of towns and villages around the country by partisan detachments and illegal communist groups, the revolutionary purging of society and mass terror, the People's Court (*Naroden sâd*), political show trials, nationalization, the collectivization of land, and Soviet-style forced industrialization. Yet it is also characterized by many acts of resistance against the regime, which continued into the early 1950s and whose clearest expression came in the so-called *goryani* or mountaineers' movement (armed groups operating in the mountains or in border regions), which led to radical changes in all sectors of society. The battle cry of fighting fascism or "the enemy with the party ticket" served as an excuse to eliminate or marginalize the old elites and any potential political opponents to the accelerating sovietization of the country. Society fell into the iron cage of the totalitarian state. The direct result of all this was that the process of widespread social mimicry and the rapid mass expansion of the Communist Party was set into motion. The communists disseminated effective propaganda, which, combined with brutal censorship and the complete isolation of the country, helped in creating broad support for the "new leadership." The changes stirred broad strata of impoverished rural and urban populations into action and directly involved them in social and political life. Signs of enthusiasm over the prospect of a "new society" and the fanaticism of the communist activists and their new converts were combined with rustic shrewdness and a striving for social revenge. This feeling of "includedness" on the part of broad strata of the population would for some time lend legitimacy to what was occurring and partially justify its brutality.

Within the first period, we can conditionally identify a subperiod covering the first years of the regime (1944–1947), marked by the stillborn concept of "the people's democracy," which was imagined as a specifically Bulgarian form of the dictatorship of the proletariat. We can find evidence of this in

14 *Introduction*

Georgi Dimitrov's diary, which pedantically documents his correspondence with Stalin on this question.[23] Some contemporary Bulgarian historians view "the people's democracy" as something different from the Soviet-style regime and express regret that, under pressure for Moscow, the Bulgarian communists were forced to abandon this emerging form of socialism with a pluralistic tinge.[24] However, from these arguments, it remains unclear how this form differed from already familiar historical examples of a transitional period to the totalitarian domination of society (a process observed both in Germany and in Russia). This basic line of argument points to the multiparty profile of the Fatherland Front government, but the actual picture is quite different. The Fatherland Front (a formula fabricated in the laboratories of the Kremlin and Comintern), was created on the initiative of the Communist Party after Germany's invasion of the Soviet Union and included a series of left and left-centrist parties dominated by the communists. However, its leadership was essentially single-party in nature, since its politics depended solely on the Communist Party. During this period, one can speak conditionally about political pluralism (but not about the presumed democratic guarantees and freedoms that normally accompany it) only for a short period of time when part of the Agrarian Union, led by Nikola Petkov, left the Fatherland Front and participated independently in the last "free" elections. The cat had released the mouse for a moment so as to savor the game more fully. After the communists' "triumphant" victory, representatives of the opposition were driven out of Parliament, their party was banned, and their leader was executed after a brief show trial.

The upheaval of social strata destroyed thousands of human destinies, while a new political elite took shape, one that was charged with carrying out the sovietization of the country and guaranteeing unquestioning loyalty to the Kremlin. The Soviet model of a planned and centralized state economy was imposed: forced industrialization on a low technological level and with an orientation toward a self-sufficient economy suited to the conditions of international isolation; in other words, the Bulgarian economy became a complete appendage to the Soviet economy. Thus, even the last illusions as to what was happening were dispelled, if any such existed at all.

A new stage in the exercise of power began, which expressed itself in the consolidation of the party-bureaucratic apparatus – the nomenclature, a model introduced by political emigrants returning from the Soviet Union as well as by the progressively increasing number of Soviet advisers. Policies were developed that combined compulsion with the seduction of the lower classes. Within a single decade, complete control over society was achieved and the feeling of "inclusiveness" that had existed in the beginning for the regime's rank-and-file supporters gradually melted away, becoming ritualized and formalized. The proletarianized classes that had been roused to action by the "revolution" were turning into an enormous and passively obedient mass.

During the *second period* (1956–1986), the trajectory of the regime is marked by movement away from a sheepish de-Stalinization toward a certain normalization of everyday life within the context of a lack of basic rights and freedoms, intensified "socialist construction," a search for a way out of economic difficulties, and not particularly successful attempts to reform the economic model. During this period, which can conditionally be called "peaceful," violence and pressure on the individual did not disappear, nor did the principle of the total mobilization of society subside, but rather these phenomena were modified, becoming more perfidious, installing themselves as a permanent backdrop to life and reinforced by fresh memories of terror. Overt drama decreased: the camps, despite being resurrected several times at specific political moments, were closed in 1962, there were no show trials; there were still political prisoners, but their numbers were not large and they were no longer demonstratively brought to society's attention but rather were kept hidden. The authorities even created the impression of a transition from a mobilized to an administrated society. But even this "bloodless violence" was sufficiently effective: it was indicative of the internal drama of people forced to don the mask of loyalty. The regime's norms successfully infiltrated everyday life and dictated people's behavior. Something like a consensus was established, albeit coerced, around the regime's norms and goals (which was referred to in propaganda materials as "the unity between the party and the people"). This consensus is tied to a feeling of predetermination in a society that clearly did not possess particularly large capabilities for resistance. With the gradual emergence from the Cold War period and the deepening of the process of "peaceful coexistence" between the systems, as well as the nor-malization of the West's relations to the regimes in the Soviet Union and Eastern Europe, the last hopes for a possible change coming from the outside died out. No one believed any longer, as they had during the 1950s, that "the Americans are coming." The defeat of the Hungarian Revolution in 1956 and of Prague Spring in 1968 definitively confirmed the belief that the regime was alive, unshakable, and eternal, in so far as it was intimately tied to the "mighty Soviet Union." All of this was crystallized in the widespread slogan: "USSR – friendship for centuries past and for centuries to come!" Thus, fully aware that their lives would pass under this regime, people began searching for various strategies for entering into the frameworks it had defined. The process of the pacification of society is marked by most of the population retreating into pri-vate life. The character of society in so-called real socialism can be defined as a society of niches. This was an almost imperative condition for the younger generations, whose conscious life took shape entirely within the conditions of communist reality.

Late Bulgarian communism is a regime without history, if we do not count the pseudo-events chronicling an official life formalized and ritualized to the extreme: congresses and plenary sessions of the only party, the Five-Year Plans, ribbon-cuttings at newly built factories, official celebrations and holiday demonstrations, changes in leadership, the cyclical relaxation and tightening of party vigilance and control over one or another sphere, propaganda about economic "achievements," decisions about economic reforms, concerns about the life of "the working class" and so on. Distinctly structured, late-communist

16 *Introduction*

society was a society without events, at least in the sense imbued in the concept *event* by historical sociology: something unexpected and unforeseen, which results from the usual course of things and which changes the prospects for certain positions and interests.

There is evidence that both sides – those in power, as well as most of their subjects – were truly afraid of the *event* (treated as a synonym for "scandal"). Everything possible was done to prevent this from happening or, if it did, to cover it up. The list of the nomenclature had already been established, and changes to it were carefully calculated. The regime's central political actors remained on the scene for a long time; despite the constant reshuffling of cadres, they changed places but rarely left the game. These processes developed in the shadow of Todor Zhivkov, who, over the course of thirty-five years, unreservedly controlled the Communist Party and the state apparatus, becoming an emblem of the regime.

Everyday life under communism locked onto the prescribed tracks and grew monotonous and repetitive in the shadow of a certain routine. Society grew ever more closed: activeness and advancement in a profession or administratively (i.e. a change of statute) were possible only through a party career. People not only adapted themselves to the established conditions of their existence but also learned how to scheme, how to further their own ambitions and interests without entering into open confrontation. This occurred thanks to the ever-more-prevalent system of corruption.

The only real event during this period was the physical relocation of large streams of people, caused by the drive toward forced industrialization that had been undertaken. The process was exceptionally painful, its drama stems largely from the mass acculturation that accompanied ambitions to build a communist-style industrial society. Migration processes waned toward the end of the 1970s, yet they left a lasting mark on the nature of Bulgarian socialist society until its very end and even thereafter. With certain caveats, a series of phenomena in intellectual life could be defined as micro-events; under communist conditions, intellectual life alone managed, by the power of its specific characteristics, to deviate from the strict regimentation from time to time. Due to this, even small deviations from official topics or styles within this sphere enjoyed wide resonance. Writers, filmmakers and philosophers were among the primary critical figures of the period.

At the end of this period, a more palpable generational shift among the ruling elite can also be noted. The poorly educated, partisan commanders were gradually pushed aside by new party cadres who had received their higher education at party schools in Moscow and Sofia and who had not directly contributed to seizing power. Technocrats and managers took up prominent positions, having been recruited into the government with the hope that they might improve its economic efficiency. However, the economic reforms did not achieve the desired effects due to the simple fact that they ran up against one insurmountable barrier: the Communist Party's unwillingness to part with full control over the economy and the system of distribution. All

Introduction 17

of this led to an upsurge in careerism and cynicism within society, while ever more frequently ideological speech was devoid of any real content. Here we find the definitive dwindling of the communist ideal. "The people's government" openly took on the character of the government of the party bureaucracy, clinging to the status quo. The shadow of the "de-ideologization" of behaviors was spreading among ever-wider social strata, including a majority of party members as well.

The third period in the trajectory of the communist regime in Bulgaria is relatively short (1987–1989) and covers the regime's final crisis and its peaceful, yet carefully orchestrated withdrawal, which allowed the most adaptive part of the nomenclature to retain control over economic activity and the court system. The negative consequences of this weigh heavily on the country's progress even today. The deepening economic crisis and the emergence of a timid civil society, encouraged by Gorbachev's policy of *glasnost* (openness) and *perestroika* (restructuring), brought to light the system's deep internal contradictions. Society was gripped by some vague expectation of change, while the leadership of the Communist Party feverishly sought an escape from the situation while sinking ever deeper into a morass of problems. It resorted to reforms (such as Edict No. 56, regulating private initiatives in the economic sphere, discussing the idea of turning over ownership to workers' collectives, and orienting state enterprises toward the market), which until then had looked like a retreat from the principles of socialism. But instead of meeting with approval, these waves of reform-minded efforts, combined with jealously guarded centralization and the overwhelming attitude of mass disinterest and distrust among the people, as well as their lack of initiative and inability to take responsibility, led to even greater confusion and destabilization. The parallel implementation of differing legal reforms led to deepening chaos in production. It became obvious that no competent actors existed to engage in an alternative type of economic behavior. One indication of this was how few people took advantage of the opportunities offered in Edict No. 56; the isolated few who dared to do so came from the ranks of the nomenclature, people who were prepared for what was coming and who after the Transition would become the "new capitalists." The communist regime entered an openly defensive phase in its existence.

This period is marked by the return of the event. First and foremost, the regime's poorly hidden repression, which was directed at a collective object – the large minority of Bulgarian Turks – came to a head. In searching for an exit from the crisis, the leadership of the BCP did not hesitate to play the nationalism card, hoping that national communism would compensate for the communist idea, which had lost its mobilizing force. At the end of the second period (1984–1985), Zhivkov and his circle undertook a venture known as the "Revival Process" (a change of Turkish names under the pretext that this population, which was supposedly forced to accept Islam under Ottoman rule, must be returned to its "Bulgarian roots"), expecting this to lead to an upsurge in patriotism and to become a new source for legitimizing the government.[25] The exact opposite occurred: the Turkish minority offered

18 *Introduction*

considerable resistance, while the initiative was not unambiguously accepted by a series of groups within society, nor by the Bulgarian population in the affected regions. In the spring of 1989, this caused a huge wave of migration to Turkey, known by the name "The Grand Excursion."

To deal with the unrest, the government reopened the concentration camp in Belene, and activists from the Turkish minority were sent there. There was also increasing stagnation in the country's intellectual life, yet, despite this, fear was waning, and under the auspices of various causes (ecological and economic causes, in support of Gorbachev's *glasnost* and *perestroika*), dissident behaviors and movements were activated. Thus, for the first time since 1944, the source producing events changed its address: the pressure was now bottom-up rather than top-down. The civil sector timidly gained strength, building its platform around legally regulated civil rights stemming from documents the regime had signed in connection with the so-called Helsinki Accords and policies for guaranteeing human rights; the new activists also took advantage of the existence of an international mechanism for monitoring whether such rights were observed. The communist rulers had been hoping that the promulgated rights would remain simply on paper, as they had until then. Fortunately, they did not grasp the rapidly changing domestic and international context. The result was a more and more uncontrollable splintering of the communist elite in the face of a clearly emerging dilemma: a return to an openly repressive political regime of a neo-Stalinist type or a deepening process of democratization, which would inevitable lead to a challenge to the single party's monopoly on power. The position of the reformist wing of the Communist Party was strengthened and encouraged by the Soviet Union's renunciation of the Brezhnev Doctrine. The countries in Eastern Europe were shaking off Soviet tutelage, since the empire itself was in deep crisis and could not longer afford to rule its vassal states through terror or economic support. Having lost its external mainstay, the communist regime in Bulgaria's chances for maintaining the status quo were growing ever smaller. The Berlin Wall fell in early November 1989, thus marking the end of a historical era. This was a time for gradually undermining the consensus that had been achieved around the norms of the regime. This consensus could also be seen as the result of certain negotiations – the regime would make changes X, Y, and Z in return for behaviors A, B, and C on the part of the people. This was precisely what was put into question at a certain point. The Round Table from the beginning of 1990 represented one way of renegotiating this consensus. The consensus of "real socialism" was replaced by the consensus of a transition to democracy and a market economy.

The regime and society in an interdisciplinary perspective

The trajectory of communist rule outlined by this periodization shows that the history of the PRB cannot be fully understood on the level of a history of events alone. Remaining on such a level runs an immediate risk of falling into the trap of the recent official historiography of the regime, even when the evaluation of what happened was negative. This historiography examines the history of the PRB as the history of the Communist Party (the party–state) and the policies it imposed on various spheres of life – the economic sphere, the social sphere, the spheres of international relations, education, culture, and religion – with the full support of the population. After the retreat of communism, a tendency can be noted in anti-communist historiography toward reducing the period to the total enslavement of the people by the regime and their passive submission. It could be said that for different reasons both of these diametrically opposed viewpoints present society as swallowed up by the regime. In one case, the masses are presented as complete supporters and hence participants in the regime, while in the other they are presented as completely passive victims of the regime. These two grand narratives completely ignore society, creating the misleading impression that with the retreat of the regime, society was automatically reborn out of the void.

Society during the communist period neither enthusiastically supported the regime nor was it a passive victim. Yet it was deeply marked by communism. After the first free elections in the GDR, the dissident writer Stefan Heym exclaimed, "The history of the GDR will be nothing more than a footnote to world history."[26] This statement was disputed with good reason, since "the masses" had not simply been innocent victims, nor could the consequences of a half-century of life under the conditions of a totalitarian regime be erased so easily. In post-communist everyday life in Bulgaria, features inherited from communism are becoming ever more clearly discernible: in civil and interpersonal relationships, in work ethics, in attitudes toward the government, and so forth. The system collapsed politically; however, it did not automatically retreat psychologically but rather left deep traces in that which social psychologists call "the people's experience."[27] Including this aspect in the history of the regime is an important aspect of the historian's work and one of the prerequisites for understanding the period. Over recent decades, critical revisions of the classical theory of totalitarianism, based on opened archives, on expanding oral histories or on newly discovered written evidence, have taken the classical formulation to task for not paying attention to the very dynamics of society, the various forms of coexistence with the regime, and of passive or active resistance. This means that in order to understand what exactly happened during the period of communist rule we must expand the scope of our research and alongside political and economic history we must also turn our attention to social history, intellectual history, and the history of everyday life. This is why this book does not see the regime and society as identical but rather as phenomena of different orders. The fictional world created by George Orwell in the novel *1984* represents one extreme which totalitarian ambition can reach, but luckily this was not achieved in the real political practice of the communist regime, not even in its most radical phase. Even in its parched ground, sprouts of preserved individuality and resistance managed to spring forth.

20   *Introduction*

The People's Republic of Bulgaria and the Republic of Bulgaria: continuity or a break?

On top of all the other difficulties involved in writing a history of the PRB, we must also add the context of the Transition, the difficulties and distortion that have accompanied the path toward democratic reform and the establishment of a market economy. Behind the façade of a pluralistic model, the economic transition, which was manipulated by the communist nomenclature ("You want capitalism? Fine, we'll be the capitalists!"), has put a number of social groups in a very difficult situation: elderly people and retirees, the unemployed, the young, everyone suffering the effects of rising crime levels and the lack of rule of law . . . The political use of such difficulties is at the root of nostalgia for the past and its clouded evaluation, which aims to rehabilitate past practices by discrediting the democratic project and to impose certain political actors from the past. Thus, the narrative of the communist period, which unfolds in the two types of discourse already described above, takes on new connotations, whose goal is not only to reassess the communist past but also to define the political nature of the Transition. On the one hand, it is a discourse of continuity; that is, it insists that the peaceful transition presupposes a smooth flowing of the old into the new, that it is not a question of turning one's back on the preceding years but rather of building on what was achieved in them. It suggests that the troubles of the Transition stem from abandoning the positive things that were achieved during communism. On the other hand, there is also a discourse of *breaking* with the past, of the conviction that there must be a new beginning, which draws its strength from revealing the totalitarian nature of the old regime and condemning it.

The discourse of continuity uses various arguments, but first and foremost it draws support from the fact that the BCP was one of the primary actors in the peaceful political transformation, setting off the changes with an internal coup against Todor Zhivkov and unleashing the process of Bulgaria's "velvet revolution." This fact legitimates the place that many of the BCP's old leaders have assumed in politics or in the new democratic administration, while others have transformed themselves into key economic players. Their individual fates in large part have depended on the successful establishment of a close connection between late communism and early democracy. The communist leaders' strategy was clearly announced as early as the Round Table (January 3–May 15, 1990), where the conditions for a peaceful transition had to be negotiated, while the BCP was still the ruling party. In statements by leading party figures, we can clearly see a lack of awareness of the totalitarian character of the communist regime and an attempt to direct processes toward a "democratic socialism," nurtured by the resurrected myth of Prague Spring '68 and by Gorbachev's *perestroika*. The concept of totalitarianism and a theory of totalitarianism were absent from the PRB's dictionaries and encyclopedias and this can be easily explained: in a logocentric regime, naming serves as the only guarantee that something exists, and vice versa. The

Introduction 21

regime's ideologues saw these words as a tool for ideological sabotage, used by the class enemy to slander and discredit socialism by comparing it to national socialism, and simply tossed them out of the dictionary. The concept "totalitarianism" freely appeared for the first time in Bulgarian public space during the Round Table's political clashes, but it functioned not as an academic concept but as an extended metaphor that expressed the parties' emotional relationship to the communist domination that was ending. Here is what Andrey Lukanov, a powerful figure in the party and a key strategist in transforming the nomenclature's political power into economic power, had to say:

> Detaching ourselves from the totalitarian system [. . .] is a goal that unifies all participants in the National Round Table. We clearly declare that [. . .] as a party, as the ruling party, we started down the path toward democratization and we will follow it decisively, with the goal of completing a transition toward democracy together with all well-intentioned forces in Bulgaria, but also [with the goal] of safeguarding our society against any possibility for the revival and recreation of the totalitarian system [. . .] According to the BCP delegation, one fundamental question which we must clarify in this regard is the question of a socialist foundation and a socialist future for our society. This question was not mentioned in the statements made yesterday by the leaders of the Union of Democratic Forces. They touched on numerous other questions [. . .], but they forgot about socialism. We are convinced that this question, even when one is not a supporter of socialism, cannot be forgotten and omitted in the PRB, since it is a question that interests millions of Bulgarians. Without this question, without answering it, we cannot answer the other question – what have we done, and not merely where and how we have done wrong during those forty-five years after September 9, 1944. The BCP has decisively broken with the Stalinist model of socialism and with its totalitarian methods of governing. It is precisely this kind of pseudo-socialism, and not socialism as a whole that is today undergoing a historic collapse before our eyes. But we, with even greater conviction, will proclaim ourselves as the defenders of socialism, of a democratic and humane socialism.[28]

This position allows us to clearly trace the dramaturgy of the Round Table, which was founded upon a fundamental disconnect in the evaluation of the past, as well as upon a lack of clearly defined, generally accepted concepts that could serve as the basis for such an evaluation. Lukanov essentially declared that totalitarianism and the communist regime are two different things, that totalitarianism is a result of the distortions of Stalinism and of its later throwbacks, implicitly localized in the deposed leader, or, to use Aleksandr Solzhenitsyn's expression, the *egocrat*, Todor Zhivkov. He further said that totalitarianism and the Communist Party cannot be arbitrarily connected, since the party found the strength within itself to reject the pseudo-socialism that had existed to that

22 Introduction

point and to declare itself in support of a democratic and humane socialism. In other words, an internal dividing line exists within the trajectory of the Communist Party, just as in the history and practices of the regime established by it. On the one side, we find the terror, the distortions, the discrimination, and the lack of rights and freedoms, while on the other there are the successes of socialist construction, the social benefits enjoyed by millions of ordinary people. One must look at "what we have done, and not only where and how we have done wrong" – this position rejects the question of the regime's crimes or rather sweeps them under the rug. For Lukanov, criticism of communism must be understood as an act of purifying self-criticism, which allows for the eternal relevance of the socialist perspective to once again be revealed.

Beneath the façade of democratic rhetoric, this policy of rehabilitating the practices of the old regime has been carried out with surprising consistency over the past two decades – as demonstrated by opposition to lustration laws, the long delay in opening State Security dossiers or pleading for a series of limitations to be placed upon the procedure, the defense of regular officers from the foreign or military intelligence services, and furious opposition to the government's decision to remove all diplomats who had collaborated with the communist secret services from their posts. However, the politics of continuity is far from exhausted by this alone. I will offer an example that demonstrates the drive toward recycling the old regime's entire ritual system (as well as the spirit of the regime itself), in so far as our young democracy is still extremely inexperienced in creating its own rituals.

On June 2, 2009, the day commemorating the anniversary of the death of Hristo Botev, the poet-revolutionary from the second half of the nineteenth century who perished in the Balkan Mountains near Vratsa in a battle against numerically superior Ottoman forces, Bulgarian National Television broadcast directly from the central square in Vratsa, where a solemn commemoration was being held for "those who had fallen for the freedom and independence of the fatherland." The place, as well as the figure of the poet, is imbued with deep symbolism. The entire ritual celebration (a parade inspection of military subdivisions and a roll-call of those fallen in battles for national freedom) was developed during the time of the communist state as an operation for appropriating national history by equating the national with the social and by including all previous heroic moments from Bulgaria's national history in the pantheon of its martyrology. This was a gesture marking the logic of succession, allowing the Communist Party's struggles and its government to be presented as the natural culmination of national aspirations. From this point of view, the preservation and literal reproduction of the ritual in question in a changed political and social context not only allows emotions tied to certain moments in national history to be exploited but also transforms them into a refusal to break with the communist past. Not only is the form of the ritual a nostalgic and vengeful throwback, but its contents are as well.

Here is what was broadcast directly on the state television channel during prime evening viewing time. On the city's central square, several military companies as well as a "battalion" of university students and a "battalion" of children stood at attention around the imposing monument to Hristo Botev. After speeches by high-ranking politicians and statesmen, it came time for the official evening roll-call. At the beginning, the military commanders reported to the parade leader using a formula well known from communist times: "Mr. Lieutenant-Colonel, sir, this is the commander of the first company reporting. During the inspection conducted all soldiers were present, with the exception of those who have fallen in . . ." And here the names of the following are called out in successions: Botev and the members of his rebel detachment, the heroes from the 1876 April Uprising against Ottoman rule, those killed in the Bulgarian–Serbian War of 1905, defenders of the country's unification, and so on. With this, it would seem that the similarities with celebrations from the time of the old regime should come to an end, but the continuation of the ceremony shows otherwise. The commander of the students' "battalion" approaches the parade leader and reports: "Mr. Lieutenant-Colonel, sir, during the inspection, all students were present, with the exception of those who have fallen for the freedom of the Republic of Bulgaria." After this, the commander of the children's "battalion" also reports: "All children were present, with the exception of those who have perished for the freedom of the Republic of Bulgaria." Thus, in essence, they once again broadcast the old message of praise and gratitude to the communists who died in the struggle against "fascism and capitalism" and honor the deliberate self-sacrifice of the mythologized child-partisan Mitko Palauzov and the brutal killing of the children from the village of Yastrebina due to their families' participation in the armed uprising against the government before 1944, i.e. the symbolic capital through which the communist regime upheld its political legitimacy and which some wish to use again today to the same ends – except that the Republic of Bulgaria dates from 1990 and no students or children have sacrificed themselves for its freedom. The conclusion which follows is that just as the form of address "comrade" can easily be replaced with "Mister," in the same way, for the Speaker of Parliament, the ministers and the MPs from the Socialist Party, which was the ruling party at that moment and who were present at the celebratory demonstration/military review, there exists only a formal difference between the People's Republic of Bulgaria and the Republic of Bulgaria, in so far as for them the latter is an unacceptable, but forcibly imposed version of the former. Although they hesitate to express this attitude directly, preferring to keep such remarks parenthetical, they still have found a way to express it, and in a sufficiently categorical manner at that.[29]

The strategy of imposing the idea of historical continuity is also indirectly supported by processes within the mass consciousness, by staunch stereotypes that were pedantically imposed over the course of decades. "The people's experience" and inertia-driven processes within social psychology, encouraged by the confusion of the Transition, have turned out to be a source for political and ideological mimicry. Such processes reproduce everyday practices and behavior from the era of "real socialism" – extreme individualism bordering

24 *Introduction*

on anti-sociality, lack of interest in common actions and projects, striving to be close to power and to use it for personal ends, weak participation in civic causes, a lack of a disciplined work ethic and distrust in others. This continuity in "the people's life," which preserves it just as it was cultivated by communism, appears less often and not as openly on the level of public, political speech, but it is especially visible in the everyday behavior of political actors, sometimes independent of their political stripes.

The question that must be answered by anyone dealing with the history of the Transition is: "Is there continuity between the People's Republic of Bulgaria and the Republic of Bulgaria?" The way "the story is told" determines whether the Transition period will be seen as an inevitable link in a chain of preceding and subsequent states, or whether it will be presented as something that possesses as a particular guise, that characterizes it as a break within the course of society's development. There are sufficient arguments available showing that the temporal boundaries of the communist regime were clearly marked by two radical breaks. Let us recall them: they were: (1) the forcible seizure of power by the Communist Party in 1944 and the resulting socialist transformation of the country; and (2) the "velvet revolution" of 1989 and the unleashing of the democratic process. These two breaks lend the history of the communist regime the character of a clearly defined phenomenon. This is why, even when examined formally, from the point of view of political systems there should not be any institutional continuity or succession in terms of values between the first and the second republic. But when it comes to the abovementioned inertia-driven processes, to internal attitudes and mentalities not only among the masses but also among the political elite, *making a break* turns out to be a painful internal problem. Yet despite such objective preconditions for the blurring of the two epochs, the Republic of Bulgaria is and cannot be anything but the result of a drive for a radical break with the communist past and from such a point of view an understanding of the history of the PRB as a clearly delineated period, as a closed cycle that can be described and evaluated, also follows. Thus, the principle behind the writing of the history presented here is that of a radical break with the communist period.

The basic tasks the authors of this book faced were: (1) to tell a story of the communist state and regime – the historical contexts and means used to establish it, the factors in its consolidation and continuation, as well as the reasons which forced it to withdraw peacefully; (2) to study the processes within society which were restricted by the political nature of the regime and which resulted in the establishment of a series of practices of mutual adaptation and compromise, which found their expression in the "consensus" of real socialism, but also in the later, slowly emerging civil activeness and practices that sought legal frameworks for resistance. The history of society and individuals is an important component in the history of the PRB. In this history, there are things that change (the framework and the context within in which power is exercised, as well as the motives and strategies employed by

Introduction 25

individuals and groups), but there are also things that do not change (the structure of the regime and the place of the single party within the life of society). These two factors together outline the contours within which the history of the PRB unfolds. It is important for this complexly composed history to be written because without it, it will be more difficult to understand not only the historical period dominated by communism but also contemporary Bulgarian society. The communist past of the country (and of particular individuals) is still a part of the present. Anyone who questions what is happening today (the difficulties and distortions of the Transition, the recycling of old ideological clichés, the displays of nostalgia by part of the population or the behavior of major actors in the Transition, etc.) must know the past and must understand its mechanisms. One's position in narrating the past is the key to understanding the present.

Notes

1 Assen Ignatow, *Psychologie der Kommunismus*, Munich: Johannes Bergmans Verlag, 1985. Cited in the Bulgarian edition: *Psihologiya na komunizma*, Sofia: Arges, 1991, p. 127.
2 Ivaylo Znepolski, *Kak se promenyat neshtata: Ot intsidenti do Golyamoto sâbitie. Istorii s filosofi i istoritsi*, vols. I and II, Sofia: Ciela/Institute for Studies of the Recent Past, 2016; Georgi Gospodinov and Yana Genova (eds.), *Az zhivyah sotsializma: 171 lichni istorii*, Sofia: Ciela, 2006; Ivaylo Znepolski (ed.), *Tova e moeto minalo: spomeni, dnevnitsi, svidetelstva (1944–1989)*, vols. I–III, Sofia: Ciela/Institute for Studies of the Recent Past, 2010–2015.
3 Anthony Giddens, *The Constitution of Society*, Cambridge and Oxford: Polity Press, in association with Basil Blackwell, 1984.
4 Michel Foucault, *Histoire de la sexualité*, vol. I: *La Volonté de savoir*, Paris: Gallimard, 1976.
5 Nicolas Werth, "Les Formes d'autonomies de la 'société socialiste,'" in Henry Rousso (dir.), *Stalinisme et nazisme: Histoire et mémoire comparée*, Paris: Éditions Complexe, 1999; Ian Kerschaw, *Popular Opinion and Political Dissent in the Third Reich*, Oxford: Oxford University Press, 1983; Alf Lutdtke, *Des ouvriers dans Allemegne du XXéme siècle: Les Quotidien des dictatures*, Paris: L'Armattan, 2000.
6 Bruno Latour, *Nous n'avons jamais été modernes*, Paris: La Decouverte, 1991; *Changer de société, réfaire de la sociologie*, Paris: La Decouverte, 2005.
7 Ivo Mozny, *Proc tak snadno . . .*, Prague: SLON, 1999; János Kornai, *Contradictions and Dilemmas: Studies on the Socialist Economy and Society*, Cambridge, Mass.: MIT Press, 1986; Deyan Deyanov, "Obshtestvoto na mrezhite i sotsioanalizata na dara," *Sotsiologicheski problemi*, 1–2 (2003): 72–86; Andrey Raychev, Kolyo Kolev, Andrey Budzhalov, and Liliya Dimova, *Sotsialnata stratifikatsia v Bâlgariya*, Sofia: LIK 2000.
8 Sandrin Kott, *Le Communisme au quotidien: Les Entreprises d'État dans la société est-allemande*, Paris: Éditions Belin, 2001, p. 17. See also: Thomas Lindenberger, "Alltagsgeschichte und ihr moeglicher Beitrag zu einer Gesellschaftsgeschichte der DDR," in Richard Bessel and Ralph Jessen (eds.), *Die Grenzen der Diktatur: Staat und Gesellschaft der DDR*, Göttingen: Vandenhoeck/Rupzecht, 1996, pp. 298–325.

26 *Introduction*

9 Dariusz Stola, "The Communist Regime as a Process: 'People's Poland' – from Imitation to De-totalitarization," *Divinatio*, 31 (2010): 161–169.

10 Ulf Brunnbauer, *"Die sozialistische Lebensweise": Ideologie, Politik und Alltag in Bulgarien, 1944–89*, Vienna: Böhlau, 2007; Ivan Elenkov and Daniela Koleva (eds.), *Detstvoto pri sotsializma: Politiki, institutsionalni i biografichni perspektivi*, Sofia: Riva/Center for Advanced Studies, 2010; Ina Pachamanova, *Predishniyat prehod: zhenata i semeystvoto pri sotsializma*, Sofia: Ciela, 2015; Daniela Koleva (ed.), *Lyubovta pri sotsializma: obraztsi, obrazi, tabuta*, Sofia: Riva/Center for Advanced Studies, 2015.

11 David Kideckel, *The Solitude of Collectivism: Romanian Villagers to the Revolution and Beyond*, Ithaca, NY: Cornell University Press, 1993.

12 Katherine Verdery, *National Ideology under Socialism: Identity and Cultural Politics in Ceausescu's Romania*, Berkeley, Calif.: University of California Press, 1991.

13 Gerald W. Creed, *Domesticating Revolution: Socialist Reform to Ambivalent Transition in a Bulgarian Village*, University Park, Pa.: Pennsylvania State University Press, 1997.

14 Sandrin Devaux, *Engagements associatifs et postcommunisme: Le cas de la République tchèque*, Paris: Belin, 2005.

15 Sandrin Kott, *Le Communisme au quotidien: Les entreprises d'État dans la société est-allemande*, Paris: Belin, 2001.

16 Lutz Niehmmaer, "Approcher le changement: À la recherche du vécu populaire spécifique dans la province industrielle de la RDA," in Alf Ludtke (dir.), *Histoire du quotidien*, Paris: Éditions MSH, 1994.

17 Martin Ivanov, *Reformi bez reformi: Politicheskata ikonomiya na bâlgarskiya komunizâm*, Sofia: Ciela/Institute for Studies of the Recent Past, 2008.

18 Momtchil Metodiev and Mariya Dermendjieva, *Dârzhavna sigurnost: Predimstvo po nasledstvo – Profesionalni biografii na vodeshti ofitseri*. Sofia: Ciela/Institute for Studies of the Recent Past, 2016.

19 Metodiev and Dermendjieva, *Dârzhavna sigurnost*.

20 Ivan Elenkov, Kulturniyat front. *Bâlgarskata kultura prez epohata na komunizma – politichesko upravlenie, ideologicheski osnovaniya, institutsionalni rezhimi*, Sofia: Ciela/Institute for Studies of the Recent Past, 2008.

21 Mihail Gruev, *Preorani slogove: Kolektivizatsiya i sotsialna promyana v bâlgarskiya Severozapad 40-te i 50-te godini na 20ti vek*, Sofia: Ciela/Institute for Studies of the Recent Past, 2009.

22 Momtchil Metodiev, *Mezhdu vyarata i kompromisa. Pravoslavna tsârkva i komunisticheskata dârzhava v Bâlgariya 1944–1989*, Sofia: Ciela/Institute for Studies of the Recent Past, 2010.

23 Georgi Dimitrov, *Diary of Georgi Dimitrov, 1933–1949*, New Haven, Conn.: Yale University Press, 2003. Bulgarian edition: Georgi Dimitrov, *Dnevnik 9 mart 1933– 6 fevruari 1949*, Sofia: St. Kliment Ohridski, 1997.

24 Mito Isusov, *Politicheskite partii v Bâlgariya, 1944–1948*, Sofia: Professor Marin Drinov/St. Kliment Ohridski, 2000; Evgeniya Kalinova and Iskra Baeva, *Istoriya na Bâlgariya: Uchebnik za 11. klas, dyal VI*, Sofia: Planeta, 2001; Evgeniya Kalinova and Iskra Baeva, *Bâlgarskite prehodi, 1939–2002*, Sofia: Paradigma, 2002.

25 Mihail Gruev and Aleksey Kalionski, *Vâzroditelniyat protses: Myusyulmanskite obshtnosti i komunisticheskiyat rezhim – politiki, reaktsii, posleditsi*, Sofia: Institute for Studies of the Recent Past/Ciela, 2008.

26 Hans Ulrich Wehler, *Deutsche Gesellschaftsgeschichte*, vol. V: *Bundesrepublik und DDR, 1949–1990*, Munich: C.H.Beck, 2008.

27 Pierre Kende, "Un retour a quelle tradition?," *Vingtième Siècle*, 36 (1992): 81–88.

28 Rumyana Kolarova and Dimitâr Dimitrov (eds.), *Krâglata masa: Stenografski protokol 3 yanuari–15 may 1990 g.*, Sofia: BIBLIOTEKA 48, 1998, pp. 123–129.

29 The insistence on this continuity is demonstrated in two major ways: by the reproduction of the communist governing elite based on the class/family principle and through open expression of a preference for the economic and social model of communism, in opposition to the basic principles of a liberal democracy. A very characteristic illustration of the first is an anecdote told by ex-Prime Minister Sergey Stanishev, not without a certain smugness, in an interview in the tabloid newspaper *Weekend*: "They asked Radio Yerevan: if November 10, 1989, hadn't happened, who would be the Prime Minister, the Speaker of Parliament and the Attorney General of Bulgaria? The answer: Sergey Stanishev, Georgi Pirinski and Boris Velchev (all three men's fathers held posts within the highest ranks of the communist party)." Thus the transition itself has been put into parentheses. The second line can be illustrated with an advertisement distributed by BCP activists in some Sofia neighborhoods on the eve of the parliamentary elections of July 5, 2009. Under the title "BCP and Its Role in National Politics," we find, "During the past two decades, the Bulgarian economy has undergone a shocking transition from central planning towards a market-based economy, tied to fundamental changes in the production structures and relations of production. High-tech and structurally defining enterprises were shut down. As a result, production forces have been set back by decades. Now a market economy exists in the country that strongly stimulates the maximization of profits, and in which incomes and quality of life lag significantly behind average European levels."

Historical background
The Communist Party's path to power

To better understand how the Bulgaria Communist Party seized power, we must be well acquainted with the situation in the country during the years preceding this event. Bulgaria's political, economic and social development in the period between the two world wars was marked by numerous internal crises that seriously undermined society's foundations and that, at a certain moment, brought it to the state of latent civil war.

The building of the modern Bulgarian state

At the end of the fourteenth century, Bulgarian lands were conquered by the Ottoman Turks, putting an end to the medieval Bulgarian kingdom, which, over the course of the seventh to the fourteenth centuries, had experienced a series of periods of political and cultural ascendancy. Over the following five centuries, Bulgarians were part of the enormous Ottoman Empire, which established itself on three continents. The majority of Christians did not have the right to participate in the administrative and military institutions of the Ottoman state. Their basic social status was as a population of producers. In the eighteenth century, under the influence of Enlightenment ideas and as a result of ongoing economic changes connected with the empire's gradual economic opening toward Central and Western Europe, Bulgarians began to form a national consciousness. The Bulgarian intelligentsia, small in number yet inspired by these new ideas, initiated popular movements for spiritual and political independence. In 1870, Bulgarians were granted the right to form their own independent church as an exarchate, freeing themselves from the guardianship of the Greek patriarchate in Constantinople. Struggles for national liberation also intensified. In the spring of 1876, a widespread uprising against Ottoman rule enveloped Bulgarian territories.[1] Its bloody suppression set off a major wave of discontent against the Ottoman Empire across all of Europe. Giving Bulgarians their political freedom became an agenda item in international relations. The following year, with the consent of the Great Powers, Russia declared war on the Ottoman Empire. Romania, Serbia, and Montenegro joined the Russian side. After the successful end of the war, the Treaty of San Stefano was signed on March 3,

1878, reestablishing the Bulgarian state. Concerned that Russia had greatly expanded its influence in the Balkans, in the summer of that same year the Western Great Powers called an international conference in Berlin, where the borders of the Balkan states were redrawn.[2] Bulgaria included only the territory between the Balkan Mountains and the Danube River, plus the Sofia region. It had the status of a vassal kingdom to the Ottoman sultan. Great swaths of territories inhabited by Bulgarians remained outside the borders of the reestablished Bulgarian state. The territory to the south of the Balkan Mountains became an autonomous province within the confines of the empire and was called Eastern Rumelia, while Macedonia was returned to the sultan's direct control.

Despite their lack of governing and administrative experience, in the spring of 1879 in Turnovo (the medieval capital of Bulgaria), Bulgarian representatives created a modern and liberal constitution following the Belgian model. The foundation was laid for the creation of a democratic political system. Following Russia's suggestions, the Hessian nobleman Alexander of Battenberg, who was nephew of the Russian emperor Alexander II, was selected as the first Bulgarian prince.

The reestablished Bulgarian state set itself two major goals: to begin a rapid process of modernization that would help the country "catch up" to other European nations and to unite all the Bulgarians living on the Balkan Peninsula. These ambitious goals, which significantly outstripped the small principality's actual economic, political and cultural potential, became the reasons behind the intense social struggles during the first few years of its independent development. Wanting to improve the functioning of state institutions, to improve the quality of administration and to protect political life from populist pressures, Alexander I suspended the liberal constitution in 1881 and began governing by special authority. However, this unconstitutional regime did not receive serious support from Bulgarian society. The prince soon found himself in conflict with the new Russian emperor Alexander III as well. St. Petersburg was highly suspicious of the Bulgarian prince's modernization efforts, seeing in them an attempt to free Bulgaria from Russia's political orbit. Lacking external and internal support, in 1883 the prince was forced to reinstate the constitution and shortly thereafter turned power over to a government elected by the people and headed by the Liberal Party. This put a decisive end to the heated debate around the state constitutional structure that had raged for several years and the political system took on a broadly democratic character.[3]

The upswing of the end of the nineteenth century and the beginning of the twentieth century

Relatively soon after its reestablishment, the Bulgarian state achieved an impressive foreign-policy success. In September 1885, unrest began in the autonomous region of Eastern Rumelia, and on September 6, in Plovdiv, the

30 Historical background

province's unification with the principality of Bulgaria was proclaimed. This caused a serious international crisis, since the Bulgarians had dared to revise a treaty signed and guaranteed by the Great Powers. Russia declared its opposition to the unification, seeing in it an attempt on the part of Prince Alexander to strengthen his position within the state and to reorient it toward Western Europe. Upon learning of the Russian position, Great Britain decided to support the unification between Northern and Southern Bulgaria, seeing in this an excellent opportunity to weaken Russian influence in the Balkan country.[4]

While a diplomatic solution to the crisis was being sought, Serbia, unhappy about Bulgaria's territorial expansions, declared war on November 2 and began advances into Bulgarian territory. The Bulgarian army, fueled by enormous patriotic fervor and led by Prince Alexander I, stopped the Serbian advance 30 kilometers from the capital city, Sofia, undertook a counteroffensive and soon pushed the military actions into Serbian territory. The Great Powers intervened to put an end to the war, but it became clear that an acceptable solution for recognizing the unification of the principality of Bulgaria and Eastern Rumelia had to be found. With the British acting as diplomatic intermediaries, a compromise was suggested that would both reflect the new status quo while at the same time not formally violating the Berlin Treaty: Eastern Rumelia remained as a separate territory but from then on it would be governed by the Bulgarian prince. In this way, the unification of Northern and Southern Bulgaria was achieved through a personal union.

The unification's success caused Russia to increase its political pressure on Bulgaria, aiming at the removal of its uncooperative prince. With Russian support, a group of Bulgarian officers staged a coup on August 9, 1886, and forced Alexander I to abdicate. However, serious resistance to the coup arose, led by the Stefan Stambolov, the Speaker of Parliament, and only four days later the junta's government was toppled, and some of the officers involved in the coup were arrested. Prince Alexander I was invited to return to the country, but, faced with Russia's decisively negative attitude toward him, he decided that it was in Bulgaria's best interest for him to voluntarily abdicate, which he did. For more than a year, the country was governed by a regency led by Stambolov.[5] This Bulgarian government was dominated by politicians who called for opposition to the Russian guardianship over Bulgaria. They rejected the insulting Russian suggestion that a provincial Georgian noble with a bad personal reputation be selected as the new Bulgarian prince. This attitude did not change even when St. Petersburg threatened Bulgaria with Russian military occupation. Great Britain and the Austro-Hungarian Empire were categorically against such a possibility and encouraged Sofia's governors to resist Russian pressure. Seeing that its policy in Bulgaria had failed, in November of 1886 Russia cut diplomatic ties with Sofia.

Given the entangled international relations around the Bulgarian dynastic crisis, it turned out to be difficult to find a candidate for the shaky

Bulgarian throne. In the end, Prince Ferdinand Saxe-Coburg-Gotha declared his willingness to govern the state. In the summer of 1887 he was chosen by the Grand National Assembly (GNA) and in early August swore his allegiance to the constitution. Under pressure from Russia, Sultan Abdul Hamid II refused to recognize his selection as legitimate. Bulgaria found itself in a complicated political situation: its head of state was not recognized internationally.

Prince Ferdinand appointed the energetic and decisive politician Stefan Stambolov as Prime Minister. Over the course of seven years he implemented an active policy aimed at modernizing the country economically and culturally. With the support of the state, the foundations for Bulgarian industry were laid, intensive work on railroads and roadways was undertaken, and tenuous trading relations were established with states in Central and Western Europe. All attempts by the Russian-supported illegal opposition in Bulgaria to destabilize the situation in the country via terrorist attacks, assassinations and conspiracies were harshly deflected by the government. In his foreign policy, Stambolov took up a course of orienting Bulgaria toward Western Europe and protecting the country from Russian pressure. Even though he was a former revolutionary himself and one of the main organizers of the 1876 uprising, as Prime Minister, Stambolov sought to bring the country closer to the Ottoman Empire. As a result of this, he managed to expand the activities of the Bulgarian Exarchate in Macedonia – many Bulgarian schools and churches were opened in the region.[6]

The following government led by Konstantin Stoilov continued Stambolov's policies in terms of modernization but changed positions vis-à-vis Russia. Under the new emperor, Nicholas II, he managed to reestablish diplomatic relations with St. Petersburg in 1896, which in turn led to the international recognition of Prince Ferdinand.[7]

In the early twentieth century, Bulgaria experienced an impressive economic upturn. Despite being the last country to be liberated, Bulgaria, judging by macroeconomic indicators, outstripped the other Balkan nations of Serbia, Greece and Montenegro, as well as the remaining European provinces of the Ottoman Empire. Industrial and agricultural production rose at a rapid rate. Foreign and domestic trade doubled in comparison to the 1890s.[8] The country's basic railway network had been established, cities were developing public services, and the banking sector was being modernized. State finances were stable, while the level of foreign debt was very tolerable. The country's rapid development during this period gave grounds for some European observers at the time to use the term "the Bulgarian miracle." The declaration of Bulgaria's full independence from the Ottoman Empire on September 22, 1908, came as a natural result of this upward developmental trend. The Bulgarian state reclaimed the title of "Kingdom," which it had traditionally held in the Middle Ages, while the Bulgarian ruler became a king.

32   *Historical background*

Bulgaria's participation in wars from 1912 to 1918 and the subsequent catastrophe

In the meantime, there was also an upsurge in Bulgarians' struggles for national liberations in Macedonia and Eastern Thrace (also known as Odrinsko Thrace, after the largest city Odrin – modern-day Edirne), which had remained under Ottoman control. In 1893, a group of local Bulgarians in Thessaloniki established a revolutionary organization that quickly set up a wide network of rebel groups in the two Ottoman provinces. The structure, which later came to be known as the Internal Macedonian–Odrinsko Revolutionary Organization also worked closely with organizations of Macedonian Bulgarians inside the principality of Bulgaria. In the summer of 1903, it organized a mass uprising in Macedonia and Eastern Thrace. This led the Ottomans, under pressure from the Great Powers, to introduce reforms in Macedonia, but they did not lead to the establishment of true autonomy and hence to the pacification of the rebellious province.[9] More and more, the idea that Macedonia and Thrace could be liberated through military action began finding support within Bulgarian society.

Achievements in the economic and financial spheres, as well as a new rapprochement with Russia, gave grounds for Ivan Geshov's Russophile government to undertake an initiative in late 1911 to create the Balkan Alliance against the Ottoman Empire. In 1912, the alliance took shape and included Bulgaria, Serbia, Greece and Montenegro. In the autumn of the same year, war broke out with the Ottoman Empire. Within several months, the Balkan allies won important military victories and forced the empire, in the London Peace Treaty of May 30, 1913, to retreat from all European territories, retaining only a small hinterland around the capital of Istanbul.[10]

But at the end of the military actions, it turned out that most of Macedonia, which had been Bulgaria's main reason for taking part in the war, was occupied by Serbian and Greek forces. They refused to cede these territories to Bulgaria, thus in June 1913 the Second Balkan War broke out. While the Bulgarian army was fighting in Macedonia, Romania began to invade from the north, and Romanian troops reached the outskirts of Sofia without encountering any resistance. The Ottoman Empire also took advantage of the situation to reseize its territories in Eastern Thrace. Attacked on all sides, Bulgaria was forced to surrender. In the Bucharest Peace Treaty of August 10, 1913, Bulgaria ceded Southern Dobrudja to Romania, while Macedonia was divided between Serbia and Greece. Bulgaria received only 10 percent of the whole of Macedonia: the Pirin region. For good reason, the results of the Balkan Wars were seen by Bulgarian society as a national catastrophe, leading to a strong desire for revenge.

The outbreak of World War I in the summer of 1914 gave Bulgarians the sense that perhaps the time had come to right the wrongs of the Balkan Wars and to finally achieve Bulgarian national unification. Over the course of a year, Vasil Radoslavov's liberal government held intense negotiations with the various military alliances to clarify the conditions under which Bulgaria would enter the war. In the end, Germany was the winning bidder, promising to hand over the whole of Macedonia to Bulgaria. This promise, as well as Germany's military successes in the east in the summer of 1915, was the reason for the Bulgarian government to decide to ally with the Central Powers. This choice proved fatal, however.[11]

Four years later, in Paris, Bulgaria was forced to accept a harsh peace treaty. It lost strategic territories such as southern Dobrudja and western Thrace, the latter of which had secured the country's access to the Aegean Sea. The Bulgarian state was also forced to pay excessive reparations in cash as well as goods, while also being deprived of the right to maintain a standing army.[12] The postwar economic crisis, made worse by the wave of 300,000 Bulgarian refugees flooding into the country from Macedonia and Thrace, created the grounds for the growing influce of radical leftist movements such as the agrarians and communists within Bulgarian society.

The intense struggles of the interwar period

The politics and actions of Aleksandâr Stamboliyski's agrarian regime, which was established after 1919, not only did nothing to pacify the country but aggravated social tensions even further.[13] As a result of growing conflicts, a bloody military coup took place in the summer of 1923. A government made up of the oppositional democratic parties was formed, but the leading role was given to representatives of the military union. The new government declared that it was returning the country to the norms of the Târnovo Constitution, which had been trampled by Stamboliyski's agrarian government. In reality, Bulgaria was transformed into an arena for fierce political struggles. Following orders from the Comintern, the Bulgarian communists organized an armed uprising in September of the same year, centered in regions close to the border with Yugoslavia. After the brutal suppression of the revolt, the Communist Party, which was subsequently banned by law, focused on daring acts of terrorism, the most sinister of which was the bombing of St. Nedelya's church in Sofia in April 1925, which killed more than 150 people.[14] The government and especially the so-called non-responsible factors (the military union and the Macedonian organization) responded to these attacks with ruthless brutality: hundreds of people with ties or suspected of having ties to the Communist Party were tortured and killed.

From early 1926, with the formation of a new, more liberal government, social tensions gradually began to subside. The urgent problem of Macedonian and Thracian refugees was solved – with the help of the League of Nations, they were permanently settled and granted land – while financial and economic stability was achieved, which led to a rise in living standards for most of the population. However, the positive processes within Bulgarian society were abruptly interrupted by the effects of the Great Depression (1929–1933). The deep crisis that the economy found itself mired in, combined with ineffective

34   *Historical background*

action on the part of the ruling coalition of centrist and left-centrist parties, once again strengthened the influence of radical ideas within Bulgarian society. Alongside the traditional communist and agrarian movements, various pro-fascist organizations underwent significant growth. Thus, in the context of the deepening economic, political and moral crisis, a new military coup took place in May 1934. This time, the military announced that parliamentary democracy was not capable of ensuring the people's prosperity and progress; thus, it abolished the constitution, outlawed political parties and established an authoritarian government characterized by strong state interference in the economic and social spheres.

Despite its grand ambitions, however, the military regime proved quite unstable. Its inability to cope with the country's problems, its lack of even minimal public support, as well as internal dissent within the military union caused the military soon to be removed from power. After a succession of short-lived cabinets in the autumn of 1935, a nonparty government of experts was created, headed by the professional diplomat Georgi Kyoseivanov as Prime Minister.

Despite having removed the coup participants from power, the new regime did not hurry to reinstate constitutional freedoms and categorically refused to allow the banned parties to restart their activities. Similar to most Eastern and Central European states during that period, Bulgaria, too, established a form of authoritarian rule. The monarch King Boris III began to play a leading rule in the newly imposed political system of nonparty cabinets. His control over the country's foreign affairs was particularly substantial. The political and economic stability the country achieved in the second half of the 1930s also further added to his public prestige.

The stabilization of the regime gradually allowed for the reintroduction of certain elements of parliamentary democracy; in 1938, elections were held, and, despite the fact that parties were not allowed to exist, a quite politically diverse representative body took shape in Parliament. Alongside the majority, which supported the nonparty model, there were also supporters of classical democracy, as well as champions of radical leftist ideas.[15]

The significant improvement of economic conditions during these years was due to deepening trade relations with Germany. The broad opening of the German market to Bulgarian agricultural goods offered opportunities not only for individual producers but also for the state as a whole to reap substantial profits. On the other hand, the clearing agreements that had been made allowed Bulgaria to import a significant quantity of industrial goods from Germany, without needing to have the normally obligatory currency reserves at its disposal. Slightly more than two-thirds of Bulgaria's entire foreign trade was with Germany. Although this produced quite positive economic results, the Bulgarian economy's overly close trade relationship with Germany was a source of concern for the government in Sofia. On several occasions, Prime Minister Kyoseivanov appealed to the representatives of Great Britain and France to take greater interest and be more active in their trade with

Bulgaria.[16] However, these Western partners' insistence that payment be made in stable currencies (pounds sterling or dollars) limited the development of such diversified economic contacts.

During the two decades after World War I, the basic foreign-policy goal of all Bulgarian governments, independent of their political orientation, was a peaceful revision of the terms of the Treaty of Neuilly. The first success in this regard was the abolition of the economic clauses. As early as the 1920s, reparation payments were reduced, and, in the course of the global financial crisis, they were definitively terminated. The dynamic changes taking place on the international stage during the 1930s also opened up some (albeit vague) prospects for changes to the remaining onerous terms of the peace treaty. With the abolition of military restrictions on Germany in 1935, conditions were ripe for those treaty terms to be dropped for the other conquered states as well. Thus, in July 1938, Bulgaria signed an agreement with the countries from the Balkan Pact (Yugoslavia, Romania, Greece, and Turkey), which gave it the right to freely modernize and develop its army.

Of course, the issue that most interested Bulgarian society was the possibility of redrawing its territorial borders. Hitler's policy of destroying the Versailles status quo gave rise to expectations that the moment was drawing near when Bulgarian national aspirations would also be recognized and satisfied. In 1938, the political map of Europe underwent serious changes. In March, Germany effected *Anschluss* with Austria, while in September, with the official consent of the Western European powers, it annexed the Sudeten region of Czechoslovakia, which was inhabited by Germans. These events in Central Europe were met in Bulgaria simultaneously with hope and fear. On the one hand, Bulgarians rejoiced at the first signs of the collapse of the political system built after World War I, which they considered highly unfair, but on the other hand, apprehensions grew with each passing day that Hitler, with his aggressive behavior, was pushing the world toward a spectacular new conflict, which a small country like Bulgaria could not hope to safeguard itself against and would again bear the brunt of its onerous consequences. These gloomy outlooks intensified when, in March 1939, in violation of the Munich Agreement, Hitler's Germany seized the Czech Republic and made it into a protectorate of the Third Reich. It became clear that the policy of appeasement, which the Western democracies (and, above all, Great Britain) had followed and which had consisted of making significant concessions to Germany, had already failed. The guarantees that London and Paris gave to Poland, Romania, and Greece, which were all threatened by Nazi aggression, appeared to be too little, too late.

On the eve of the impending war, the Bulgarian government felt that the moment had come to present Bulgaria's territorial aspirations more clearly to the international community. The government accepted the idea of a more moderate approach, realizing that it could not make maximum demands on all of its neighbors. For this reason, its aspirations were mainly focused on the return of territories that had belonged to the Bulgarian state in the recent

36 *Historical background*

past, since even the Treaty of Neuilly itself contained (albeit minimal) possibilities for reconsidering their status. Thus, the goals of the peaceful revision of the treaty were focused on the return of Southern Dobrudzha from Romania and of Western Thrace from Greece, which would secure the economic outlet to the Aegean Sea which Bulgaria had been promised in the peace treaty. Concerning Yugoslavia, the Balkan state with which Bulgaria had the closest relations at the time, the Bulgarian government intended to raise the question of returning the western outlands to Bulgarian control. As for the most painful topic for Bulgarian society – Macedonia – the government decided that it was unrealistic to demand its unification with Bulgaria and that the only possibility was to insist that the population in that region receive rights as a national minority.[17] At this stage, the Bulgarian government hoped to achieve its ends solely through diplomatic means, without resorting to the use of military force.

Besides the potential for satisfying some of Bulgaria's territorial aspirations, the approaching war also held the threat of the country falling under the political influence of one of the Great Powers, which would wholly predetermine its social development for the foreseeable future. At the end of the 1930s, the prospects of a radical change to the political and economic system in Bulgaria, and especially the establishment of a communist-style regime, were practically nonexistent. From the point of view of classical Marxist theory, in an agrarian state with weakly developed industry, a low concentration of capital, a minimal industrial proletariat and a society consisting largely of petty and mid-sized proprietors, the preconditions did not exist for socialist revolution to break out, for the dictatorship of the proletariat to be imposed, and for the full nationalization of the means of production to be implemented. The conditions for social transformations in the communist spirit also cannot be found in Lenin's theory, which seriously revises Karl Marx's claims and which insists that proletarian revolution will break out where there are sharp social contradictions and where a revolutionary situation exists. On the contrary, in Bulgaria during the second half of the 1930s, there was a marked improvement in the state of the economy and its effects, along with measures taken by the nonparty cabinets in the social sphere, significantly reduced social conflicts – in comparison to the years immediately following World War I, the social situation was far calmer. Moreover, to speak of the existence of certain symptoms of a revolutionary situation is absolutely unfounded. Thus, it turns out that the establishment of a communist regime in Bulgaria could be implemented only under the influence of a powerful external factor, which would, in fact, counteract and neutralize Bulgarian social impulses toward development.

During the spring of 1939, developments in the international situation unexpectedly increased the political significance of the Soviet Union, creating the first preconditions for its transformation into the factor anticipated by the European communist parties that would influence sociopolitical processes on the Old Continent. In diplomatic preparations for the impending world war, the Soviet Union ever more tangibly began to be seen by the European powers as a possible political and military partner. In April 1939, French–British–Soviet negotiations began, but progressed rather slowly. The USSR, however, gave signals that it had still not chosen sides among the warring parties. The replacement of the long-standing Commissar for Foreign Affairs, Maksim Litvinov, who was of Jewish descent and a supporter of the idea of collective security, with Vyacheslav Molotov was a sign to Berlin that the Soviets were prepared to negotiate with Hitler's Germany as well. Even though they began later, Soviet–German negotiations progressed much more dynamically, and, on August 23, they concluded with the signing of the German–Soviet Nonaggression Pact.[18] Having secured an alliance with Moscow, Hitler gave the order for a German invasion of Poland on September 1, 1939. World War II had begun. Two weeks later, in accordance with the pact's secret clauses, Germany and the USSR divided up Poland and established a common border between the two countries.

The initial phase of the war and Bulgarian neutrality (1939–1941)

On September 15, Kyoseivanov's government announced that Bulgaria was abiding by a policy of neutrality with respect to the military conflict that had broken out in Europe. This position reflected a sincere desire, on the part of both the government as well as a large majority of Bulgarians, to remain out of the war. Despite the strong drive to settle territorial disputes with Bulgaria's neighbors, the fear of repeating the catastrophe of World War I, which had resulted from a mistaken choice of allies, made Bulgarian foreign policy exceptionally cautious. The government in Sofia knew very well that a policy of neutrality would be very difficult to maintain if one of the warring parties undertook more aggressive actions in Southeastern Europe. In this situation, the goal of the government was to maintain neutrality, if not until the end of the war, at least for as long as possible, and thus to spare society and the economy the ravages of war.

At the beginning of the conflict, the general circumstances still looked favorable for Bulgarian interests, since all the Great Powers had declared their intentions for the Balkans to remain outside the theater of active military operations at that stage. For its part, the Bulgarian government was also very careful not to take up viewpoints that could call the country's neutrality into question or that would provoke the displeasure of powerful external factors. In this respect, Sofia refrained from making condemnatory declarations both regarding the partitioning of Poland in September 1939, as well as about the Soviet attack on Finland in December of the same year. During this time as well, Bulgaria continued to follow the line of categorically refusing to participate in alliances and coalitions aimed against any one state. This was also the main reason why the Bulgarian government turned down London's invitation for the country to join the Balkan Pact, which had existed since 1934. British diplomacy's attempts to incorporate Bulgaria into its Balkan policy were dead

38   *Historical background*

on arrival, however, since the Bulgarian position had long since been made clear: until the question of borders was reexamined, Bulgaria would not join into any sort of alliance whatsoever with the remaining Balkan states. The problem was that Neville Chamberlain's cabinet, and later that of Winston Churchill, was not in a position to force the governments in Bucharest and Athens to make the necessary concessions to Bulgaria and in this way to ensure the conditions for cooperation and mutual aid among the countries in the region.[19]

With a view to the complex and unclear military situation in Europe, as well as the need to react in a timely manner to the rapidly changing circumstances at the end of 1939, the regime in Sofia took steps whose aim was to bring about internal consolidation and to rally society around certain basic foreign and domestic policy questions, such as the policy of neutrality, the peaceful settlement of Bulgarian territorial aspirations, and continuation of the processes of modernization within the economic and social spheres. In connection with this, special parliamentary elections were held in December 1939 and January 1940, which secured a striking majority in support of the government, while the regime's opposition was left with extremely weak representation in Parliament.

Changes to the executive power soon followed. In February 1940, the longtime Prime Minister, Kyoseivanov, was removed by the country's government and was sent to Bern as Minister Plenipotentiary. A cabinet headed by archeology professor Bogdan Filov was formed. The replacement of an experienced statesman with a scholar uncorrupted by politics revealed King Boris III's drive to strengthen his control over the state government and to take the leadership of the country's foreign policy into his own hands.[20] Moreover, despite the fact that Bulgaria continued to strictly follow the policy of neutrality, the replacement of Kyoseivanov, who passed for an anglophilic politician, with a sincere adherent of German science and culture such as Bogdan Filov, could also be taken as a sign that Bulgaria was counting primarily on German support in achieving its territorial aspirations.

Indeed, beginning in the spring of 1940, the development of the military situation in Europe created an enormous advantage for Germany; at that moment, it was the key factor in solving political and territorial disputes on the Continent. After several *blitzkrieg* campaigns in April, the Wehrmacht conquered Denmark and Norway. On May 10, 1940, the invasion of France also began. French–British resistance was quickly overcome. British troops were forced to evacuate French territory at Dunkirk, while the French government was forced to sign the country's surrender on June 22, 1940.

On the eastern part of the continent, the Soviet Union also took advantage of the Western European powers' failures in order to begin annexing wide swaths of territory. In the spring of 1940, in the course of a quite humiliating but ultimately successful war with Finland, the Soviets expanded their holdings to the northwest. During the summer of the same year, the USSR swallowed up Bessarabia, Bukovina and the Baltic states: Lithuania, Latvia, and Estonia. Regardless of the various preexisting political and economic particularities, wherever the Red Army moved in, deep social transformations took place and Soviet rule was established.

With the military collapse of Finland, the final power that could defend the territorial status quo in Eastern Europe dropped out of the picture. The former French allies in this area of the continent found themselves in a critical situation. This was truest of Romania, which was under pressure from most of its neighbors to return territory it had seized after World War I. The process of reclaiming such territories began with the Soviet ultimatum to the Romanian government to withdraw its troops and administration from Bessarabia and Bukovina. Shortly thereafter, Hungary also demanded that Bucharest return Transylvania. The government in Sofia decided that the moment had come for Bulgaria, too, to declare its territorial aspirations over Southern Dobrudzha. Bulgarian diplomats posed the question to the leading European powers and received categorical support from Germany and the USSR. Great Britain was also in no condition to dispute the reasonableness of Bulgaria's request. The general international approval of Bulgaria's demand was a major success for the policy of a peaceful revision of the Neuilly Treaty that the country had been following, as well as for its policy of taking a neutral stance on the global conflict.

Nevertheless, support from Berlin proved to be the most substantial, as Germany insistently encouraged Bucharest to open negotiations with Bulgaria to settle the problem of Dobrudzhda. In the second half of August, bilateral Bulgarian–Romanian discussions began in the Romanian city of Craiova, which ended on September 7, 1940, with the signing of an agreement stating that Romania would return Southern Dobrudzha to Bulgaria.[21] Bulgarian society was euphoric over the end of what they saw an unjust situation created after World War I and expressed their hopes that other Bulgarian demands would also be satisfied.

The events of autumn 1940, however, complicated the situation in the Balkans, making the prospects for maintaining Bulgarian neutrality hazier. On September 27, 1940, the Axis powers of Italy, Germany, and Japan consolidated their forces, creating the Tripartite Pact. They openly declared their ambition to establish a new world order dominated by fascist ideology. To achieve these goals, pressure increased on the central European states to accept German domination and to join the Tripartite Pact. In November, Hungary, Slovakia, and Romania joined the pact. The desire for complete domination soon extended to the Balkans as well, putting an end to illusions that the region could escape the cataclysms of the war. With the intention of responding to the stunning German victories and thus taking up an equal position in the newly formed bloc, Mussolini decided to attack Greece and establish predominant Italian influence in the Mediterranean basin. On October 20, Italian troops began their invasion of Greek territory. Knowing of Bulgaria's aspirations toward Aegean Thrace, Rome suggested that Bulgaria also join in the military campaign. The Bulgarian government announced, however, that

40   *Historical background*

it would remain true to its policy of neutrality and declined to take part in the conflict.[22]

In addition to the countries from the Tripartite Pact, the Soviet Union, too, demonstrated its particular interest in the Balkans and especially Bulgaria. In his visit to Berlin in November, Molotov expressed the desire that his country's special rights in Bulgaria be recognized.[23] This suggestion, however, did not meet with Hitler's approval and the first open signs of disagreement between Berlin and Moscow since the signing of the Soviet–German pact arose over the question of Bulgaria.

Such Soviet activity undoubtedly inspired Bulgarian communists with great hopes, which increased all the more when the Soviet Union also made an official diplomatic overture to the Bulgarian government. Moscow suggested to Sofia that the two countries sign a pact for mutual aid, in which the Bulgarian side would allow the USSR to use several Black Sea ports as bases for the Soviet Navy. The agreement was extremely similar to those which the Soviets had made with the Baltic states shortly before annexing them. To convince the Bulgarian government of the benefits of the pact, Deputy Commissar for Foreign Affairs Arkadiy Sobolev arrived in Sofia in November 1940. His visit offered an opportunity for Bulgarian communists to organize broad public campaigns in support of the agreement. Many petitions were signed, demonstrations were organized, numerous letters and telegrams were sent from all over the country demanding that the government accept the Soviet offer. Despite the Soviet representative's assurances that after signing the pact Bulgaria's aspirations toward Eastern and Western Thrace would be satisfied, the Bulgarian government cited its policy of neutrality and refused to sign the agreement. Besides not wanting to complicate its relations with Germany, as well as with its Balkan neighbors and Great Britain by signing an agreement with the USSR, the Bulgarian government clearly did not believe Soviet promises that the pact would not interfere with the political regime in the country.[24]

The Bulgarian government's ability to adhere to its policy of neutrality grew ever more limited as a result of Italy's unsuccessful military activities in Greece. To erase the shame of the humiliating defeats his ally had suffered in the Balkans, Hitler planned a powerful offensive by the German army that would crush Greek resistance and put an end to the hesitation of the Balkan states that remained outside the Tripartite Pact – Bulgaria and Yugoslavia. These two countries were informed that the Wehrmacht would have to fly over their territory and to this end it would be advisable for them to establish allied relations with Germany. But even under such circumstances, the Bulgarian government attempted to hew to the policy of neutrality it had been following, pleading its military unpreparedness to Berlin. With the goal of demonstrating that such neutrality would be wholly favorable toward Germany, the Bulgarian government undertook measures that brought the regime closer to the new world order proclaimed by Germany. In December 1940, the government introduced and Parliament adopted two laws of an undemocratic nature: the Law on the Organization of Bulgarian Youth and the Law in Defense of the Nation. Under the first law, the Brannik (or "Defender") organization was founded to allow the state to exercise control over the education of young people so as to imbue them with the spirit of nationalism and loyalty to the crown. The second law had an anti-Semitic nature. It imposed a series of limitations on Bulgarian Jews, barring them from marrying Bulgarians, from holding government jobs, and levying an additional high tax on their property. The law's stipulations did not apply to Jews who had already accepted Christianity, nor to those who had participated in the wars between 1912 and 1918 as volunteers in the Bulgarian army, nor did it affect those who had been awarded medals for bravery.[25]

Despite these moves by the government in Sofia, as of early 1941, German pressure on Bulgaria to abandon its policy of neutrality and join the Tripartite Pact increased. Despite the fact that the King and some members of the government were not at all convinced that Germany would emerge as the ultimate victor, it was already clear to everyone that Bulgaria no longer had any freedom of choice. Great Britain's appeal to the country to put up armed resistance against Germany was seen as a doomed campaign that would only lead to catastrophe – all the more so because Bulgaria saw no reason to heed London's calls, since the latter had shown absolutely no interest in solving Bulgaria's territorial disputes. Given this situation, Prime Minister Filov had no choice but to sign Bulgaria's accession to the Tripartite Pact on March 1, 1941, at the Belvedere Palace in Vienna. Nevertheless, the Bulgarian government managed to secure the condition that the country would not actively participate in military activities.[26] The direct consequence of this act was that Great Britain and the United States broke off diplomatic relations with Bulgaria.

Bulgaria in the orbit of the Third Reich (1941–1944)

Representatives of the democratic opposition led by Nikola Mushanov protested vehemently against Bulgaria's joining the Tripartite Pact and insisted on continuing the police of neutrality, while not denying that such a move would mean German occupation of the country. The communists' position was strikingly passive. Even this fateful step, which had brought Bulgaria closer to more active engagement in the war, was still not reason enough for them to fundamentally change their behavior toward the international conflict or toward the regime in Sofia. Following directives from Moscow, Bulgarian communists continued aiming their criticism primarily at Great Britain and France, blaming them for fomenting the world war. In the evolving situation, only the leader of the Pladne, or "Noonday" Bulgarian Agrarian National Union (BANU), G. M. "Gemeto" Dimitrov, declared himself an anti-fascist, and even before the country officially joined the Tripartite Pact, he attempted to organize an anti-governmental conspiracy with the cooperation of British diplomats. After his plans became known to the Bulgarian police, in March,

42   *Historical background*

G. M. Dimitrov managed to leave the country with the help of the British legation.[27] Most of the conspirators were caught, brought to trial and given heavy sentences, including capital punishment. Later in Jerusalem, and after that in Cairo, Gemeto organized a center of resistance, broadcasting radio programs criticizing the Bulgarian government's pro-German orientation and exhorting the people to fight against the nondemocratic state government.

But in actuality preconditions for increasing the prestige of the regime in Sofia arose in spring of 1941. At that moment, the dynamically developing military situation allowed Bulgaria to realize its boldest territorial aspirations. On March 25, Yugoslavia, which until then had enjoyed friendly treatment from Hitler, joined the Tripartite Pact; however, two days later there was a pro-British coup in Belgrade, and the new leadership announced that the country was leaving the alliance with Germany. This gave the Wehrmacht cause to launch a new *blitzkrieg* on April 6. Yugoslavia surrendered on April 18. The German offensive against Greece began, and resistance in the continental part of the country was quickly crushed.

In the course of these military victories, Germany allowed Bulgaria to establish its own administration in Vardar Macedonia and Aegean Thrace. On April 19 and 20, Bulgarian troops entered these territories. Most of the population in Macedonia greeted the Bulgarian army warmly, hoping that this would put an end to the policy of de-nationalization that the Serbian regime had first imposed in 1913. However, the situation in Aegean Thrace was quite different than it had been prior to World War I. Under the population-exchange agreements that had been made, most of the Bulgarian population in the region had already been dispelled to Bulgaria in the 1920s, replaced by an enormous number of Greek refugees who had arrived from Asia Minor after the catastrophic war with Turkey (1919–1920).[28] This was why establishing Bulgarian rule over Aegean Thrace faced a series of difficulties. To achieve lasting Bulgarian control over the region, the country had promoted a campaign to repatriate Bulgarian refugees from Aegean Thrace. However, the initiative did not meet with much enthusiasm. By 1944, only slightly more than 50,000 Bulgarians had taken action to return to their ancestral homes. However, what impressed Bulgarian society at that moment was the fact that the regime, without engaging in any military actions, had managed to achieve Bulgaria's long-dreamed-of national unification. The problem was, however, that unlike the return of Southern Dobrudzha, which had occurred when Bulgaria was still following a policy of neutrality and which had received the approval of all the warring parties, the unification with Macedonia and Aegean Thrace occurred when Bulgaria was already an ally of the Third Reich.

The German attack on the Soviet Union on June 22, 1941, was a fateful moment not only in the development of the war but also for subsequent events in Bulgaria. Despite being a member of the Tripartite Pact, the Bulgarian state remained true to its policy of not participating actively in military operations and refused to take part in any way in the German campaign in the

Historical background 43

east. It did not even break off its normal diplomatic relations with Moscow. Furthermore, at the end of July, when the Soviet Union's position was critical, Molotov turned to the Bulgarian Minister Plenipotentiary with a request to play an intermediary role in negotiating a truce between the USSR and Germany.[29] The initiative did not come to fruition, but the very idea of it sufficiently demonstrates that on the whole, good relations existed between Sofia and Moscow. The behavior of the Bulgarian communists underwent a fundamental change, however. They sharply condemned the German invasion and only then began denouncing Bulgaria's alliance with Germany, which had already been a fait accompli for several months. Again following orders from Moscow, they organized armed resistance, including the formation of sabotage groups as well as partisan guerrilla detachments. At first, their basic activity consisted of acts of sabotage as well as show assassinations of prominent generals and public figures known for their pro-German statements. This resistance was entirely supported by the USSR, which used secret channels to funnel people (Bulgarian political emigrants), as well as weapons, explosives, and other such supplies to Bulgaria. The illegal Hristo Botev radio station began broadcasting from Moscow.

At this stage, the scope of the communist resistance movement posed no threat whatsoever to the regime in Bulgaria. Beside the partisans' small numbers, the other reason for this was affective action on the part of the police, who in most cases nipped the communists' plans in the bud. Many of the functionaries sent from Moscow were caught before they were able to undertake any action whatsoever. In the summer of 1942, the government even captured the top leadership of the illegal Communist Party. Some of the activists from the Central Committee were arrested and later sentenced. Among those executed was the talented Bulgarian poet Nikola Vaptsarov.

At the end of 1941, new, significant events occurred to which Bulgaria could not help but respond. On December 7, Japanese forces attacked and destroyed Pearl Harbor, the US Navy's largest base in the Pacific Ocean. As a result, the United States abandoned its policy of nonintervention in the conflict and declared war on Japan. Despite being nonplussed by Japanese actions, Hitler honored his obligations under the Tripartite Pact and declared war on the United States. The German satellites in Europe were also forced to take a stance on the emerging problem. Via a parliamentary decision on December 13, Bulgaria also declared war on the United States and Great Britain. In Sofia, this declaration was taken as a purely symbolic act, in light of the fact that, geographically, Bulgaria was far too distant from the two countries and thus would never reach the point of undertaking real military action. This feeling of "symbolic war" was also deepened by the fact that for quite some time Washington did not respond to the Bulgarian position; only in June 1942 did Congress declare war with Bulgaria.[30]

The first year to year and a half of the German–Soviet conflict unfolded very unfavorably for the USSR, but even during this period tendencies arose that foreshadowed a possible reversal in the course of the war. Despite having

44 *Historical background*

advanced deep into Soviet territory, the German army had not yet won strategic battles that would secure a final victory. Furthermore, with the United States' entrance into the war, the military and economic potential of enemies of the Tripartite Pact grew considerably. In the following year, 1942, the Anti-Hitler Coalition definitively took shape, which not only made the fight against the Rome–Berlin–Tokyo Axis far more effective but also legitimized the USSR as one of the major factors in politics writ large while also consigning Soviet activities from the first two years of World War II to oblivion.[31]

In the summer of 1942, under such conditions – the war's progress was very difficult and its outcome still uncertain, while at the same time Soviet authority was growing – the exiled Bulgarian communist leader Georgi Dimitrov sent Bulgarian communists a directive from Moscow to begin building a broad coalition of non-fascist organization in Bulgaria, to be called the Fatherland Front. This program was announced on July 17, 1942, on the illegal Hristo Botev radio station broadcast from Moscow. At this stage, the stated goals were connected solely with the struggle for reestablishing democratic freedoms in Bulgaria and decisively breaking with the policy of close ties to Germany. The program contained no hint of instigating deep social changes and of establishing a political regime based on the Soviet model – a goal which the BCP had consistently been striving toward since its founding in 1919. Now the idea was to unify within the Fatherland Front a maximally broad range of democratically minded politicians, who, on the basis of pan-democratic principles alone, would cooperate with the Communist Party.

Despite the democratic character of the proposed alliance, over the following several months the leaders of the opposition in Bulgaria responded to the communist initiative with reserve. They believed that the prerequisites were still not in place for a radical change in Bulgaria's foreign policy, while as straightforward democrats they did not approve of the communist methods of armed resistance against the government. Besides this, many of them harbored serious suspicions that the Fatherland Front was merely a smoke-screen for the communists whose real goal was to seize control of the country.

As a result of this attitude, over the following months approximately 100 local committees of the Fatherland Front were created, which in practice included primarily communists and leftist agrarians.[32] However, in the summer of 1943, it was becoming ever clearer that a total reversal of the war was at hand. After its defeat at Stalingrad, the Wehrmacht again suffered catastrophic losses on the Eastern Front at the battle of Kursk, while the war in North Africa had been definitively won by Anglo-American forces, which had also begun an offensive on the Continent in southern Italy. Benito Mussolini's fascist regime had also collapsed. Bulgaria's "symbolic war" with Great Britain and the United States began to take on ever-more-real dimensions at that time with the bombings of Sofia. The military successes of countries from the Anti-Hitler Coalition created opportunities in Bulgaria for the creation of a political alliance that included the active participation of the communists. On August 10, 1943, the National Committee of the

Fatherland Front was founded. It included representatives of the following political forces: the Bulgarian Labor Party (Kiril Dramaliev), the Pladne BANU (Nikola Petkov), the Bulgarian Labor Social Democratic Party (Grigaor Cheshmedzhiev), Zveno or "Link" (Kimon Georgiev), and one independent (Dimo Kazasov). It is striking that the most prominent leaders of the democratic opposition – Nikola Mushanov (Democratic Party) and Dimitâr Gichev (Vrabcha BANU) – did not join the Fatherland Front, which was announced as a broad, anti-fascist coalition. Thus, from the very beginning, the Fatherland Front took shape as an alliance of leftist and left-centrist forces.

The noncommunist politicians had various reasons for joining the Fatherland Front, but the most general of them was the growing sense of an impending change which would provide an opportunity for them to take part in the government. With certain individuals, such as Kimon Georgiev and Dimitâr Kazasov, who had previously taken part in all manner of political combinations, their strong ambition for power is completely obvious, while for others the coalition offered them a chance to take center stage not only in the political life of the country but also within their own parties (for example, Nikola Petkov's influence within Pladne BANU still paled considerably in comparison to that of the organization's main leader, G. M. Dimitrov). Of course, most of the participants in the Fatherland Front hoped that a future joint rule with the communists, even though it would mean Bulgaria's total reorientation toward the Soviet Union, would nevertheless allow them to preserve some measure of freedom in domestic politics and even to direct the development of social processes within the country. Some official measures taken by Stalin gave them grounds for such expectations: the USSR's adoption of the principles of the Atlantic Charter and most of all its recognition of nations' right to self-determination, as well as the dissolution of Comintern in 1943, which had always been seen as a basic tool for imposing Soviet political influence in European states.

As German failures in the war grew more frequent, so did the pressure from Berlin on the Bulgarian government for the country to participate more actively in real military operations. King Boris III staunchly refused German demands that Bulgarian divisions be sent to the Eastern Front, citing the threat of a Turkish attack on Bulgaria on the one hand, as well as the Bulgarian people's sympathies to its liberator, Russia (as a result of the Russo-Turkish War of 1878, the Bulgarian state was founded after five centuries of Ottoman rule) on the other. Thus, Bulgaria continued to be the only German ally whose troops did not fight on the battlefields of World War II.[33]

Bulgaria also categorically opposed another German demand: the deportation of Bulgarian Jews to death camps. In connection with implementing the so-called Final Solution, a special German envoy on European questions, Theodor Dannecker, arrived in Sofia in March 1943. He insisted that preparations begin for the deportation of 20,000 Jews from Bulgarian territory to Poland. However, his mission met with serious opposition from the whole

46 *Historical background*

of Bulgarian society. Deputy Speaker of Parliament Dimitâr Peshev organized a petition signed by MPs both from the opposition and the ruling party. It sharply protested plans to send Jews out of Bulgaria.[34] The petition provoked a serious, albeit short-lived, parliamentary crisis. After the intervention of Prime Minister Filov, Peshev was removed from his leadership position in Parliament, while majority MPs were forced to toe the official government line. However, the action that had been taken resonated widely with the Bulgarian public. Numerous prominent figures from Bulgarian academic and cultural spheres, as well as leading clerics in the Bulgarian Orthodox Church, including Bishops Kiril and Stefan, announced their support of Bulgarian Jews.[35] Many ordinary people also joined in such public expressions of support. Of course, the communists also actively joined in the campaign to save Bulgarian Jews. King Boris III, who absolutely did not share in the anti-Semitic hysteria of the Nazi regime, ordered that all activities for deporting the Jews be ceased. In this way, Bulgaria is counted among one of the few states (along with Denmark and Finland) which did not allow its Jewish citizens to be liquidated. In those critical times, the Bulgarian public displayed an exceptional sense of tolerance and commitment. Unfortunately, this policy of protecting the Jewish population was not imposed on the new territories of Macedonia and Aegean Thrace, from whence more than 11,000 Jews were deported to death camps.

In the late summer of 1943, the political situation in Bulgaria grew even more complicated: on August 28, King Boris III died. With his death, the regime lost its basic authority both with the Bulgarian public as well as in its contacts with the outside world. On September 8, the Twenty-Fifth Ordinary National Assembly appointed a regency council consisting of Bogdan Filov, General Nikola Mihov, and Prince Kiril (the late King Boris III's younger brother) to rule until Boris's young son Simeon turned eighteen. A government was appointed, led by Dobri Bozhilov, who had previously served as Minister of Finance. Those in power found themselves ever more urgently facing a painful dilemma: should they continue the alliance with Germany and subsequently suffer all the catastrophic consequences that would follow from its eventual defeat, which was looking entirely likely, or should they reoriented themselves toward the Anti-Hitler Coalition, knowing that this would mean giving up their recently achieved national unification with Macedonia and Aegean Thrace? Furthermore, Bulgarian politicians had no doubt that any change in their foreign policy would lead to German military occupation, as had occurred in Italy and later in Hungary when these countries had attempted to leave the war. The increasing diplomatic and military pressure on German allies (bombings of Sofia grew more frequent) on the one hand, and the constant German threats of occupation on the other, made the Bozhilov government's foreign policy completely indecisive.[36]

The reversal on the war's fronts, as well as the political crisis in Bulgaria, created preconditions for the expansion of communist resistance. During the summer of 1943, it developed a higher level of organization, known by the bombastic name of the National-Liberational Insurrectional Army (whose acronym in Bulgarian, NOVA, spells the word "new"), headed by a general staff. The country was divided into operative zones, which were led by members of the Central Committee of the Communist Party. Significantly expanded mass participation in partisan detachments and brigades could be noted in the summer of the following year, when, according to government intelligence, the number of communist fighters had grown to approximately 4,000.[37] They engaged ever more frequently in battles with a special gendarmerie that was created to fight the partisans. Regardless of this significant expansion, until Soviet troops entered Bulgaria in September 1944, the communist resistance movement did not manage to achieve a scope capable of truly threatening the mainstays of the regime. Despite this, the movement turned out to be an important means for the communists to exercise a certain influence over the population in Bulgaria, especially the rural population. In fact, the significance of the partisans grew palpably after September 9, 1944, when the cadres who would run the country on the local and mid-levels – and who would also carry out the new government's repressive policies – were selected mainly from their ranks.

Despite active official government propaganda, the Bulgarian public's sense of an impending military catastrophe grew ever more tangible as a result of the heavy bombing campaigns suffered by the capital Sofia (25 percent of the city's historical center was destroyed), as well as certain cities in the provinces (Dupnitsa, Vratsa). Besides their strong psychological effect on the population, the aerial attacks by the English and American air forces seriously disrupted life as a whole in Sofia, which was the country's main financial, industrial and administrative center. Part of the citizenry and some institutions were evacuated, while the government ever more frequently convened in Chamkoriya, a location 60 kilometers outside Sofia (the present-day mountain resort of Borovets).[38] The destruction, as well as the drastically reduced volume of imported goods from Germany already gave a foretaste of the serious economic crisis that was looming.

In the spring of 1944, Soviet diplomats issued an ultimatum that their consulate in Varna be reestablished and that two new ones be opened in Ruse and Burgas, causing a new change of government in Bulgaria. As a result of this diplomatic note, Bozhilov's cabinet submitted its resignation to the regents, throwing the country into a protracted governmental crisis. On May 24, Ivan Bagryanov received a mandate to form a government. A former agricultural minister in Georgi Kyoseivanov's and Bogdan Filov's cabinets, he had left the government shortly before the country had joined the Tripartite Pact. This moment in his political biography gave him the image of a statesman who was not directly involved in tying Bulgaria to Germany and who could effect a smooth change in Bulgaria's foreign policy. The fact that Bagryanov held talks with the Communist Party through its representative Dr. Ivan Pashov as part of his consultations about forming the government and defining its platform is indicative of the growing political influence of the Bulgarian Workers Party (BWP) as a result of the Soviet army's offensive. An agreement was

48 Historical background

reached for the communists to cease armed resistance, while the government, on its part, was required to reinstate democratic freedoms, to begin releasing political prisoners, and to break the alliance with Germany. Bagryanov also held talks with the Soviet Minister Plenipotentiary in Sofia, Alexander Lavrishchev, who expressed his support for the government's platform. The diplomat assured him that the Soviet Union had no intentions of changing the regime in Bulgaria and impinging on the rights of the ruling dynasty.[39]

Having received the necessary approval for his governmental aims both from the regents and from the communists, on June 1, Bagryanov formed a government that included individuals who were politically unconnected with the former government and who instead held the status of experts. One communist also was included in the executive power: Doncho Kostov, who headed the Ministry of Agriculture and State Property. Unexpectedly, however, the Communist Party abruptly changed its attitude toward the cabinet before it could undertake any action whatsoever. This time, too, instruction came from Moscow via Georgi Dimitrov, who on June 5 announced that Ivan Bagryanov's government was fascist and that it would not break with Germany.[40] Several days later, Kostov tendered his resignation. Once the situation was "clarified" to them, the Bulgarian communists again took up the course of armed resistance. It is obvious that the Soviet government's tactic was to refuse to allow the government to effect an abrupt reversal in Bulgaria's politics, which would make finding a reason for Soviet troops to enter the country more difficult. This policy can be clearly seen in Moscow's quite categorical opposition to attempts on the part of Bagryanov's cabinet to sign a truce with Great Britain and the United States. For various petty reasons (for example, the Soviet side was offended because the Bulgarians had not sought it as an intermediary when beginning negotiations with Great Britain and the United States), Soviet diplomacy did not allow Stoycho Moshanov's efforts in Cairo to end in success with the signing of a truce. For their part, diplomats for the Western allies also did not insist on negotiating a truce without Moscow's approval, which shows that they had already accepted the idea of predominant Soviet influence being established in Bulgaria. The first symptoms of the politics of compensation for the huge Soviet efforts and sacrifices made in the war with Germany in terms of ceding spheres of influences can be found as early as 1943. Precisely then, the USSR, supported by the United States, rejected Churchill's suggestion that the second front in Europe be opened in Balkans, essentially leaving this region within the operational plans of the Red Army. Thus, with the failure of Moshanov's mission, the government in Sofia's last hopes of escaping Soviet military intervention died.

The only possible move was to form a government made up entirely from the ranks of the opposition, which would immediately break the alliance with Germany and begin the reestablishment of constitutional rights. On September 2, 1944, a cabinet was formed with Konstantin Muraviev as Prime Minister. During talks to define the government's composition, four ministerial posts were offered to the Fatherland Front coalition, which would have

Historical background 49

created a truly broad coalition government. But the communists and their allies in the Fatherland Front turned down the invitation.[41] Of course, the ministers in Muraviev's cabinet were consistent opponents of pro-German policies from the very beginning of World War II, and their struggle to reinstate the Târnovo Constitution dated from May 1934, when precisely one of the current leaders of the Fatherland Front, Kimon Georgiev, had suspended it. Regardless of the indisputably democratic character of the new executive power, Fatherland Front activists did not wish to join a government that they did not fully control. And the Soviet troops already in Romania were a sufficiently clear guarantee that the Fatherland Front would very soon have the opportunity to take full control of the country.

Finding itself in an exceptionally difficult situation due to a lack of clear domestic and foreign support and having practically no time at its disposal, Muraviev's government took measures to change Bulgaria's foreign-policy orientation.[42] On September 4, it definitively announced that Bulgaria was breaking its alliance with Germany and would begin the disarmament of German military units found within Bulgarian territory. It also decided to release political prisoners. These actions were not seen as sufficient by the Soviet leadership, however, and on September 5, the Soviet Union declared war on Bulgaria. Despite the fact that during the whole period when Bulgaria was an ally of Germany in the Tripartite Pact, the various Bulgarian governments had not broken off diplomatic relations with Moscow, now, without any serious grounds, the Red Army began invading Bulgarian territory. The official order for Soviet troops to enter Bulgaria was issued the morning of September 9, but, in fact, by that date all of northeastern and parts of southeastern Bulgaria (including Burgas) had been seized by subdivisions of the Third Ukrainian Front.[43]

Notes

1 D. Strashimirov, *Istoriya na Aprilskoto vâstanie*, Sofia: Prof. Marin Drinov Academic Press, 1996.
2 K. Kosev, *Bâlgariya i knyaz Bismarck*, Sofia: Zahariy Stoyanov Press, 2013.
3 S. Black, *Ustanovyavane na konstitutsionno upravlenie v Bâlgariya*, trans. R. Genov, Sofia: Open Society Press, 1996.
4 Ilcho Dimitrov, *Predi 100 godini: Sâedinenieto*, Sofia: Septemvri State Press, 1985.
5 R. Popov, *Bâlgariya na krâstopât: Regentstvo 1886–1887*, Sofia: St. Kliment Ohridski University Press, 1991.
6 D. Marinov, *Stefan Stambolov i noveyshata ni istoriya*, Part 2, Sofia: Bulgarian Writer Press, 1992.
7 S. Radev, *Dr. Stoilovata vânshna politika i pomirenieto s Rusiya*, Sofia: St. Kliment Ohridski University Press, 2012.
8 Martin Ivanov, *Brutniyat vâtreshen produkt na Bâlgariya 1870-1945 g.*, Sofia: Ciela, 2012.
9 *Natsionalnoosvoboditelnoto dvizhenie na makendonskite i trakiyskite bâlgari 1878–1944*, vol. II. Sofia, Macedonian Research Institute, 1995.

50 Historical background

10 Georgi Markov, *Bâlgariya v Balkanskiya sâyuz sreshtu Osmanskata imperiya 1912–1913*, Sofia: Zahariy Stoyanov Press, 2012.

11 Georgi Markov, *Golyamata voyna i bâlgarskiya klyuch za evropeyskiya pogreb 1914–1916*, Sofia: Prof. Marin Drinov Academic Press, 1995.

12 *Nyoyskiyat dogovor s obyasnitelni belezhki ot Dr. B. Kesykov i D. Nikolov*, Sofia: Martilen, 1994, pp. 30–33.

13 Dimitrina Petrova, *Samostoyatelno upravlenie na BANU 1919–1923*, Sofia: Nauka i izkustvo, 1988.

14 Georgi Naumov, *Atentatât v katedralata "Sv. Nedelya,"* Sofia: Partizdat, 1989, p. 152.

15 Ilcho Dimitrov, *Bâlgarskata demokratichna obshtestvenost, fashizma i voynata 1934–1939 g.*, Sofia: St. Kliment Ohridski, 2000, pp. 258–259.

16 Martin Ivanov, Tsvetana Todorova, and Daniel Vachkov, *Istoriya na vânshniya dârzhaven dâlg na Bâlgariya 1878–1990. Vtora chast*, Sofia: Bulgarian National Bank, 2009, p. 178.

17 Nikolay Genchev, *Vânshnata politika na Bâlgariya prez nachalniya period na Vtorata svetovna voyna*, GSU, FIF, 63 (3) (1970): 42–43.

18 Jean-Baptiste Duroselle, *Histoire diplomatique de 1919 a nos jours*, Paris: Dalloz, 1978, pp. 244–252.

19 Ilcho Dimitrov, *Angliya i Bâlgariya, 1939–1941*, Sofia: St. Kliment Ohridski, 1996, pp. 138–140.

20 Statelova, Elena, and Stoycho Grâncharov, *Istoriya na nova Bâlgariya*, Sofia: Anubis, 1999, p. 585.

21 Antonina Kuzmanova, *Ot Nyoy do Krayova: Vâprosât za Yuzhna Dobrudzha v mezhdunarodnite otnosheniya 1919–1940*, Sofia: Nauka i izkustvo, 1989, pp. 256–280.

22 Ilcho Dimitrov, *Bâlgaro-italianski politicheski otnosheniya 1922–1943*, Sofia: Tilia, 1996, pp. 322–327.

23 Henry Kissinger, *Diplomacy*, New York: Simon & Schuster, 1994. Cited in the Bulgarian edition: Henri Kisindzhâr, *Diplomatsiyata*, Sofia: Trud, 1997, p. 317.

24 Evgeniya Kalinova, *Pobeditelite i Bâlgariya 1939–1945*, Sofia: St. Kliment Ohridski, 2004, pp. 81–84.

25 Evgeni Yochev, *Zakonodatelstvoto v tsarstvo Bâlgariya (1879–1944 g.)*, Sofia: Fondatsiya "Otvoreno obshtestvo," 2006, pp. 598–607.

26 Bogdan Filov, *Dnevnik*, Sofia: Otechestven front, 1990, p. 270.

27 Stoyan Rachev, *Chârchil, Bâlgariya i Balkanite (1939–1945)*, Sofia: 1998, St. Kliment Ohridski, pp. 107–108.

28 According to data from the official census conducted in 1940 in Greece, 84,751 "Slavophones" lived in Aegean Macedonia, making up only 4.8 percent of the region's total population. Some Bulgarian scholars argue that the actual number of Bulgarians was around 236,000, or 13.4 percent of the total population. Despite these significant differences, in both cases it is clear that on the eve of World War II, the Bulgarian element had been reduced to a minority with respect to ethnic Greek immigrants who had arrived. See Georgi Daskalov, *Bâlgarite v Egeyska Makedoniya: Mit ili realnost*, Sofia: Macedonian Scientific Institute, 1996, pp. 229–230.

29 Dmitriy Volkogonov, *Stalin: Triumf i tragediya – Politicheskiy portret Y. V. Stalina*, vol. II, Moscow: Novosti, 1990, p. 258.

Historical background 51

30 Vitka Toshkova, *SASht i Bâlgariya 1919–1989: Politicheski otnosheniya*, Sofia: Sineva, 2007, p. 167.
31 Norman Davides, *Europe at War, 1939–1945: No Simple Victory*, London: Macmillan, 2006.
32 Kalinova and Baeva, *Bâlgarskite prehodi, 1939–2002*, p. 23.
33 Vitka Toshkova, Nikolay Kotev, Roumen Nikolov, Nikolay Stoimenov, Zheko Kiossev, and Yordan Baev (eds.), *Bâlgariya: svoenravniyat sâyuznik na Tretiya rayh*, Sofia: Military Publishing House, 1995, pp. 124–125.
34 Gabriele Nisim, *Chovekât, koyto sprya Hitler: Istoriyata na Dimitâr Peshev, spasil evreite na edna natsiya*, Sofia: Ivan Vazov, 2003.
35 *Borba na bâlgarskiya narod za zashtita i spasyavane na evreite v Bâlgariya prez Vtorata svetovna voyna (Dokumenti i materiali)*, Sofia: BAS, 1978.
36 Statelova and Grâncharov, *Istoriya na nova Bâlgariya*, p. 627.
37 Doncho Daskalov, *Zadgranichnoto byuro i antifashistkata borba v Bâlgariya*, Sofia: St. Kliment Ohridski, 1991, p. 233.
38 Filov, *Dnevnik*, pp. 654–656.
39 Ilcho Dimitrov, *Ivan Bagryanov: Tsaredvorets, politik, dârzhavnik – Istoricheski ocherk*, Sofia: Professor Marin Drinov, 1995, p. 56.
40 Kalinova, *Pobeditelite i Bâlgariya 1939–1945*, p. 132.
41 Ilcho Dimitrov, *Burzhoaznata opozitsiya, 1939–1944*, Sofia: Hristo Botev, 1997, p. 196.
42 Konstantin Muraviev, *Sâbitiya i hora*, Sofia: Bâlgarski pisatel, 1992, pp. 358–391.
43 Ilcho Dimitrov, *Burzhoaznata opozitsiya*, p. 228; Veselin Angelov, *Tretata natsionalna katastrofa*, Sofia: Aniko, 2005, p. 179.

Part I
The times of high Stalinism

1 Bulgaria in the shadow of Stalin

As the Soviet invasion of Bulgaria began, it became ever more imperative for the Fatherland Front to undertake immediate action to seize power, so as to avoid creating the impression abroad that it had been directly installed by Soviet military leadership. In the plot against the government – which incidentally did not indicate that it intended to put up any serious resistance (the Defense Minister in the Cabinet, General Ivan Marinov, even went over to the Fatherland Front's side) – the officers who were members of the *Zveno* political circle and communists played a crucial role: Damyan Velchev, Petâr Iliev, Petâr Vranchev, Stoyan Trendafilov and others. In the early hours of September 9, military units seized the more important ministries and established control over communications. The change in government was achieved with complete ease. In Sofia, it took on the characteristics of a typical military coup.[1] In the provinces, control over local governments was seized by Fatherland Front committees and partisan detachments which descended from the mountains, giving the unfolding events the appearance of involving more mass participation.

Establishment of the Fatherland Front government in Bulgaria

At 6:25 a.m., Radio Sofia announced that the country had a Fatherland Front government headed by Kimon Georgiev from the political circle Zveno. The rest of the executive power was made up of four representatives each from the BWP, the Pladne BANU, and Zveno, as well as two social democrats and two "independent intellectuals." A week later, on September 17, Georgiev officially announced the new cabinet's program. It set itself purely democratic tasks tied to the reestablishment of constitutional rights and the implementations of a series of economic transformations whose basic goal was to raise the population's living standards. Again, intentions to construct a communist system in Bulgaria were not mentioned at this time. However, the program did state that the country would be purged of "anti-popular (*protivonarodni*) elements."[2]

A large portion of the Bulgarian population accepted the coup of September 9 as a positive development. The need for a change from the

56 The times of high Stalinism

desperate situation the country had found itself in for the past year had become ever more closely tied to the need for a complete reorientation of foreign policy toward the countries of the Anti-Hitler Coalition. The Bulgarian people's traditionally strong sympathies toward Russia also were at the root of the euphoric welcome Soviet troops received in the country. At that time, very few people in Bulgaria were aware of the true situation in the Soviet Union and had no idea of what would happen in the future. Moreover, the changes that had occurred in the ten years after 1934 played a crucial role in the direction taken by political processes in the country and in the possibilities for constructing a democratic system in Bulgaria. Despite the fact that positive economic, financial and social results had been achieved in the second half of the 1930s, the nonparty regime dealt heavy and irreversible blows to Bulgarian society's democratic attitudes. During that whole period, a targeted campaign was led against the traditional champions of democratic principles: the political parties. Also, by calling attention to the parties' weaknesses and failures in the preceding years, the nonparty regime created the public sentiment that, in Bulgaria, classical parliamentary democracy did not function effectively. The policy of intensified state control in all spheres of economic and cultural life had accustomed society to the exercise of strong governmental power on the one hand, while on the one hand it had also made the business and cultural elite insufficiently proactive and quite passive in their civil attitudes.[3] On the whole, Bulgarian citizens did not have a strong tradition of standing up for their rights and freedoms. From this point of view, at the end of World War II, the public positions held by the champions of liberal democracy could not be defined as strong. Thus, in the struggle against the authoritarian nonparty regime, the radical opposition took the lead, which included primarily leftist political forces: agrarians, communists and left-leaning social democrats, which did not represent a true democratic alternative for the country. In Bulgarian society, which was nearly 80 percent rural at that time, just as the necessary prerequisites were not in place for constructing a communist system, likewise the prospects for establishing a democratic system based on a Western European model were also slight. At the time, it seemed that domestic tendencies were tending most favorably toward the establishment of a populist agrarian regime similar to that of Aleksandâr Stamboliyski after World War I.

Having come to power with a program of reestablishing constitutional rights, the Fatherland Front government set to work abolishing a series of repressive and restrictive laws (the Law in Defense of the Nation and the Law on the State Gendarmerie, as well as anti-Semitic legislation). They also outlawed all activities of Brannik, or "Defender," the official youth organization of the old regime. At the same time, legal ordinances were adopted for granting amnesties, for equal rights for persons of both sexes, and other public acts which were, in principle, democratic. In practice, however, the country did not move toward true democratization. Besides the parties making up the ruling coalition, others were not allowed to participate in political life, not even pro-Western parties such as the Democratic Party, the Radical Party, or Vrabcha BANU, all of which had no connection to fascist ideology and practice. Alongside the communists, the other partners in the government also declared their opposition to the restoration of parties outside the Fatherland Front. In actuality, this meant that forming an opposition to the government was not permitted.

Quite quickly it became common practice for the new regime to violate the Târnovo Constitution on both important and petty questions. Thus, for example, in violation of constitutional regulations, a regency council was appointed to perform the functions of the head of state in place of the underage Simeon II without being selected by a GNA. The regency council included Todor Pavlov (a communist), Tsvyatko Boboshevski (a democrat), and Venelin Ganev (a radical). This institution was reduced to a mere formality and was stripped of any real power.

In fact, the most sinister violations of constitutional norms occurred in connection with the persecution of people connected, to greater and lesser degrees, to the old government, which was unleased after September 9. Mass arrests began, in which no official charges were brought against the detainees. Without the opportunity to prepare themselves whatsoever, victims were dragged from their homes, locked up in buildings and premises which had been quickly converted for such purposes, transported from one location to another – all without the scantest of information being provided to their families as to whether they were alive, where they were and what they had been charged with. A great number of detainees were killed without ever reaching the courtroom. Most often, mass executions were carried out at night in some wooded location, and the corpses were thrown into mass graves, rivers, wells and shafts.[4] Foreign journalists passing through Bulgaria at the time were categorical that the repression here was one of the most brutal in comparison to other Eastern European countries occupied by the Soviet army.[5] Victims of this burgeoning terror were people from extremely varied social and professional backgrounds: from the police and members of the gendarmerie to the lowliest clerks in the local and central government, merchants, entrepreneurs, priests, lawyers, teachers, journalists, scholars, and cultural figures, most of whom had not committed any crimes but who had participated in the old government or had expressed support for it and for the national unification that had occurred. In more than a few cases, such murders were the result of settling personal scores.

The wave of repression unleashed upon the country was carried out through several separate channels. One was through the Communist Party's military units. It was precisely these structures that exercised the most crucial power at the lowest level in both the provinces as well as in the capital. They typically decided who would be arrested, relocated or fired. They were simultaneously the inspiration behind and the direct participants in executions. They also actively took part in the confiscation and plundering of property belonging to "enemies of the people." At certain moments, their activities were so extreme

58   *The times of high Stalinism*

that the leadership of the Communist Party was forced to appeal to them for more moderation and even for a cessation of the indiscriminate "revolutionary purge."[6] Despite these criticisms, the Central Committee of the BWP looked favorably on what was happening in the country. The whole orgy of lawlessness was defined as "revolutionary activity by the masses of the people."

Another way the policy of "purging fascist elements was carried out" was via the *narodna militsia*, or "the People's Militia." Immediately following September 9, the staff of the Interior Ministry (which was in charge of the police) was completely changed. The entire leadership and most of the rank-and-file officers were replaced by former partisans and political prisoners. Of the former employees, only some working in the crime unit retained their posts.[7] This state institution actively participated in reprisals against figures from and supporters of the former regime. In its police stations, people who had been detained without being formally charged were often beaten to death. One of its leaders, Lev Glavinchev, earned a particularly sinister reputation for methodically killing arrestees.[8] Such police activity had an enormous effect on the general population. The institutions which should be responsible for protecting public order and constitutional rights not only failed to curb the lawlessness but, on the contrary, actively took part in it, and in so doing sowed deep fear in most of society.

The political violence in the country was legally legitimated on September 30, when the government adopted a legal ordinance allowing those guilty of dragging Bulgaria into the war to be tried before the People's Court (*Naroden sâd*). The court was designed to try the regents, ministers, MPs, high-ranking administrative, legal and military officials, palace advisers, and many private individuals who had taken part in the development and implementation of Bulgaria's official policies. The stipulations in this ordinance also strongly contradicted the Târnovo Constitution, especially the clause that the creation of such a court must occur through a parliamentary decision. An enormous number of defendants – 11,122 people – were brought to the subsequent trials, which took place between December 1944 and April 1945. The government placed extraordinary pressure on the members of the so-called People's Court. Almost all of the judges and prosecutors appointed to the court were absolutely devoted to the Communist Party. The Fatherland Front press called for the strictest sentences possible, while the Communist Party organizations in Sofia and around the country organized noisy street demonstrations demanding heavy sentences. Later, some of the judges who showed leniency were themselves convicted of taking bribes or interceding on behalf of certain defendants.[9] In the end, the results of the People's Court's activities earned it a top-ranking in terms of the number of convictions in comparison to other such tribunals created in other countries that truly bear responsibility for starting the war, such as Germany and Japan.[10] A total of 9,155 sentences were handed down, of which 2,730 were death sentences and 1,305 life in prison.[11] The remaining sentences ranged from one to twenty years in prison. Those executed by firing squad include the regents, all the ministers from Filov and Bozhilov's cabinets, and four ministers from Bagryanov's cabinet. Death sentences were also meted out to prominent intellectuals such as Professor Boris Yotsov, Professor Aleksandâr Stanishev, and Dimitâr Shishmanov. Professor Mihail Arnaudov, Konstantin Muraviev, Vergil Dimov, and others were given life sentences in solitary confinement.[12] The People's Court also handed down death sentences to people who had already been executed. Victims of the People's Court also included the person who had contributed greatly to saving Bulgarian Jews: Dimitâr Peshev. As deputy speaker of the Fifteenth Ordinary National Assembly, he was sentenced to fifteen years in solitary confinement.[13]

Western observers were shocked at the huge number of convictions and at the exceptionally harsh sentences. They saw the trials as a sweeping political purge that could create a vacuum in Bulgaria's public life, which could be used by the one-party government to establish a dictatorship in the country. Another thing they found worrisome was that the excesses committed by the People's Courts in Bulgaria could serve as a precedent for other European countries as well, where war criminals were expected to be tried.[14]

In these violent days of political retribution, another means for crushing the opposition was also institutionalized, one that would sow terror in the Bulgarian public for the next twenty years. On December 20, 1944, following a suggestion by Interior Minister Anton Yugov, who was a communist, the Council of Ministers adopted a legal ordinance creating labor-reeducation camps. There, people with criminal backgrounds, as well as those posing a "threat to public order" would be imprisoned without being officially sentenced. They could be held in the camps for up to six months; however, this term could be extended by an order from the Interior Minister. The ordinance was approved by all participants in the session, including the noncommunist ministers.[15] Soon the first camps appeared: in the town of Sveti Vrach (present-day Sandanski) and near the Rositsa Reservoir in the Sevlievo region. As early as the spring of 1945, more than 3,000 people considered opponents of the regime were already imprisoned there.[16]

The Legal Ordinance for the Defense of the People's Government, an openly repressive law that contradicted elementary constitutional norms, was adopted on January 28, 1945. Besides stipulating harsh punishments for all activities directed against the established government, including various forms of violence and subversion such as sabotage, attacks and deliberate damage of public property, heavy sentences were also introduced for the founding of anti-governmental organizations and for spreading rumors and untrue information, which in actuality meant that freedom of speech, of the press and of free association were seriously restricted, making possible the completely arbitrary treatment of citizens at the hands of the police.[17]

Significant violence was also committed by Soviet troops stationed in the country. Besides the economic burden stemming from the fact that the Bulgarian population was forced to constantly furnish enormous quantities of food and all sorts of provisions without any payment whatsoever, Soviet

60 *The times of high Stalinism*

military agents actively participated in the application of political pressure. In more than a few cases, Soviet officers and soldiers participated directly in the organization of purges, which only served to further embolden the Bulgarian military units and Fatherland Front committees.[18] Besides providing "assistance" to the new government, in many places drunken Soviet soldiers committed purely criminal acts and engaged in lawless behavior. Cases of brazen theft, rape and even murder began to multiply. The problem clearly grew so serious that on September 22, 1944, Georgi Dimitrov was forced to personally appeal to Stalin and Molotov in a letter in which he begged them to take measures to stop such incidents, again reminding them of how joyfully Soviet troops had been welcomed in Bulgaria.[19]

The Fatherland Front's actual seizure of power on September 9 took place almost bloodlessly, but in the following weeks and months a terrible wave of terror engulfed the country, and an enormous number of people fell victim to this repression. With the exception of those convicted by the People's Court, historians do not have precise data on all those who were killed extrajudicially, those who died in prisons and camps, and those who disappeared without a trace. Most scholars studying the period agree that the figure must range from 20,000 to 25,000 people – a colossal number for a small country like Bulgaria.[20] It is clear that this repression surpasses anything known in post-liberation Bulgarian history – and, unfortunately, it must be noted that in terms of violence this history is quite rich in tragic examples. In fact, the horrors committed after the establishment of the Fatherland Front government is largely comparable only to the massacres committed in Bulgarian territories by the Turks after the suppression of the April Uprising in April and May 1876.

The Moscow Truce and Bulgaria's participation in the final stage of World War II

One of the most important political problems the Fatherland Front had to solve at this early stage after seizing power was signing an armistice with the countries from the Anti-Hitler Coalition, which would allow Bulgaria to join in the ultimate military defeat of Germany. The previous government led by Muraviev had already declared war on Germany on September 8, 1944, during a moment of growing political crisis when Soviet troops had already begun their deep advance into Bulgarian territory. The new cabinet, formed on September 9, showed its fierce determination for the country to actively take part in combat operations, using all the military capabilities at its disposal. The government in Sofia wanted to show that it had categorically rejected Bulgaria's old foreign policy and that the country was sincerely joining in the Allies' efforts to destroy Nazism in Europe. Additionally, the country's leaders clearly hoped that by participating in the war, Bulgaria would be treated more favorably at the subsequent peace conference.

The Bulgarian desire to actively join in the war against Germany faced a series of serious hurdles related to foreign policy. London was openly opposed to eventual Bulgarian participation in military operations. The British government shared the concerns of the Greek government-in-exile and of the local Greek opposition, that under the pretext of battling German troops the Bulgarian army would not withdraw from Aegean Thrace, which had belonged to Greece before the war. Moreover, London was worried that if Bulgarian administration in those territories was not quickly terminated, this would also indirectly strengthen Soviet influence in the region. This is why the main British condition on the impending truce with Bulgaria was for Sofia to immediately withdraw its divisions from captured Greek territories.[21] The Yugoslav resistance movement also had definite reservations about Bulgarian military operations in Vardar Macedonia and Serbia, having previously declared Bulgarian troops in those regions as one of its main enemies. For its part, Moscow fully supported the idea of the Bulgarian army taking part in the Soviet offensive on the Balkan Peninsula, while even London could not deny the need for new forces in the fight against Germany.

Disagreements within the Anti-Hitler Coalition regarding Bulgarian participation were one of the main reasons Bulgarian troops did not launch any military operations during September. Moreover, a redeployment of troops was necessary, since until that time significant military power had been concentrated on the Bulgarian–Turkish border. Such a troop transfer to the west was severely complicated by the fact that the Bulgarian railways were already entirely occupied with the transportation of Soviet troops. Another factor that negatively affected the Bulgarian army's fighting capacity was the brutal persecution that most of the Bulgarian officer corps had been subjected to immediately following September 9. Even Soviet correspondents noted this phenomenon, declaring in their reports that such repression had a negative effect on the overall morale of the army at a moment when it was expected to undertake a successful offensive.[22] In Bulgaria, the noncommunist parties within the Fatherland Front were also alarmed by the scope of the repression aimed at the officer corps. The Defense Minister, Damyan Velchev, saw an opportunity to protect officers from constant political attacks by sending them to the front. It was in this spirit that the Decree No. 4 was later adopted by the Council of Ministers; however, the communists were categorically opposed to it and repealed it with Soviet assistance.

The unsolved diplomatic questions concerning whether to allow the Bulgarian army to undertake military operations in the former Yugoslav and Greek territories allowed German divisions to advance in the region and capture stable positions in Macedonia, disarming some of the Bulgarian units that had been stationed there. A strong front took shape in the region, which would allow the German forces located in the Balkans to retreat north through the Morava River Valley. These developments made it imperative that a joint offensive to clear the peninsula of German forces be undertaken as soon as possible. Bulgarian commanders announced their readiness to begin the offensive on September 25, but it was delayed due to the failure to receive permission from the allies and from the Balkan resistance movements.

62   The times of high Stalinism

In the beginning of October, the leader of the Yugoslav National Liberation Army, Josip Broz Tito met with high-ranking Soviet representatives and agreed to let Bulgarian troops undertake military operations within the borders of Yugoslavia – under the condition that they withdraw to their own territory immediately after the successful conclusion of the operation.

Only after the necessary approval had been given did Bulgarian troops begin the long-awaited offensive on October 6, 1944. The Second Army advanced into Yugoslav territory toward the Niš Valley. After several days of fierce attacks, it managed to drive back German forces and seized the city of Niš on October 15. Once this position had been captured, the Wehrmacht's retreat route along the Morava River was cut off. The First Army, deployed to the south of the Second, advanced against fortified German positions in Northern Macedonia. It liberated Kriva Palanka, smashed German defenses in the region of Stratsin, and turned its attack toward the city of Kumanovo. The Fourth Army, which performed auxiliary functions, was active in southernmost part of the war theater. Its forces captured the city of Strumitsa and helped in the general Bulgarian advance toward the Vardar River Valley. The German divisions, suffering heavy losses at the hands of the advancing Bulgarian troops, were forced to retreat toward Kosovo. The Second Army pursued and defeated them at Prishtina.[23]

In the middle of October, when the Bulgarian army had already launched military operations against Germany, negotiations for concluding a truce with Bulgaria began. Soviet diplomacy managed to impose its demand that the agreement be signed in Moscow, which was an unambiguous sign that the USSR was insisting on taking a leading role in defining the conditions of the truce and most of all in exercising control over its implementation. British Prime Minister Winston Churchill clearly understood the political consequences for the Eastern European states following the Red Army's incursion into their territory, and for this reason he attempted to guarantee some sort of political influence for the Western countries, while at the same time recognizing the Soviets' dominant presence in certain regions of the Balkans. To this end, he, accompanied by Foreign Secretary Anthony Eden, arrived in Moscow, where on October 9 and 10 personal meetings were held first between Churchill and Stalin, and then between Eden and Molotov, in which the Allies' respective percentages of political influence over the Balkan countries was decided.[24] The British Prime Minister announced his readiness to accept the USSR's leading position in Romania and Bulgaria in return for Moscow acknowledging Great Britain's position in Greece. For Yugoslavia, a fifty-fifty split was agreed upon.[25]

In the spirit of these agreements, British diplomacy consented to the Allied Control Commission (ACC) (which would exercise control in Bulgaria) being led by a Soviet representative, while the remaining Allied members would have limited, almost formal functions. President Roosevelt's diplomatic corps was not informed of the details surrounding these Soviet–British negotiations, as a result of which the American Ambassador in Moscow found himself isolated.

His suggestion for an "equal voice" within the ACC, which came if not from the very beginning, but at least after the end of the war with Germany, did not meet with Soviet approval and was rejected.[26]

After the Allies' most important questions had been clarified in their basic outlines during the preliminary discussions, the Bulgarian delegation was handed the Truce Agreement and was given twenty-four hours to accept it, after which the document was signed on October 28. The agreement imposed a series of military and economic conditions on the government. The country was required to actively join in the war against Germany (something which had long since been under way) and after the end of military actions to withdraw its troops located beyond the previous borders of Bulgaria within a certain period and to demobilize them under the control of the Allied Commission. Most of the body of the agreement specified the Bulgarian state's numerous engagements regarding the upkeep of Soviet occupying forces. In practice, these clauses in the agreement are openly reparative in nature.[27]

By the end of November, almost all of Macedonia and Serbia had been liberated and cleansed of German units. The Bulgarian army is largely responsible for achieving this goal. A military contingent of more than 450,000 troops participated in the campaign. Even though the Bulgarian offensive was undertaken with the cooperation of the Yugoslav Liberation Army, as all observers at the time noted, the latter's forces were absolutely insufficient and without Bulgarian participation, defeating the enemy would have been impossible. Another thing noted at the time was the wholly upright behavior of Bulgarian troops in Macedonia and Serbia. After conquering a given territory, the army turned over control to the new administration that was being formed from the ranks of the Yugoslav opposition. In contradiction to preliminary expectations, it was found that on the whole the local population, especially in urban areas, calmly accepted the Bulgarian military presence in the region.[28] This generally positive attitude was connected to the idea of a future federation between Yugoslavia and Bulgaria that was beginning to be promoted.

In the beginning of December 1944, Bulgarian military forces needed to regroup with the aim of continuing the pursuit of German forces, now beyond the borders of Yugoslavia. The First Army was formed out of the most war-ready divisions and was to take up the left flank in the joint offensive undertaken by the Third Ukrainian Front. General Vladimir Stoychev, who enjoyed the communists' full confidence, was placed at the head of Bulgarian forces. Accounts from most foreign observers note, however, that for the Bulgarian troops, 80 percent of whom were villagers, the idea of fighting far from the homeland was unpopular. A Bulgarian government delegation was even forced to visit the troops in order to raise morale.

Indeed, for the first time in their recent history, Bulgarians were forced to fight thousands of kilometers from their homeland, and, despite initial expectations, they performed the military tasks assigned to them extremely well. Bulgarian successes were noted several times in official Soviet and American military communiqués. The official British position remained more

64 *The times of high Stalinism*

reserved toward Bulgarian military participation.[29] During the first half of March 1945, the First Army engaged in fierce battles with German elite forces in the region of the Drava River, with the aim of liquidating the established beachhead and not allowing the enemy to launch a counterattack. At the end of the month, Bulgarian troops began the Nagykanizsa–Körmend Offensive, which was part of the Soviet army's Vienna Offensive. The German's Margit defense line was broken. Germany's surrender on May 8 found Bulgarian forces in the region of the Austrian Alps, where they had already established contact with the Eighth British Army.

The number of victims and scope of material losses incurred over the course of active military operations confirm Bulgaria's serious participation in the final stage of the war. The total number of killed, disappeared and wounded exceeded 40,000, while the expenses incurred by the state exceeded 133 billion leva, which was almost equal to the country's entire national revenue for 1945.

The Bulgarian government's strict adherence to the conditions in the Truce Agreement and most of all the Bulgarian army's considerable contribution to the liberation of Yugoslavia provided grounds for Foreign Minister Professor Petko Staynov and the Bulgarian representative in Moscow, Professor Dimitar Mihalchev, to raise the question of giving Bulgaria status as an allied country, as had been done for Italy, several times to high-ranking Soviet diplomats. The Soviet leadership's response was that formally Bulgaria had no need for such recognition and that it was sufficient that Moscow had full confidence in the Bulgarian government, which had shown its commitments to the Allied cause through its actions. The country's harsh punishment of its former government and its diligent implementation of the necessary social transformations, and not so much its military contributions, were emphasized as examples of this commitment.[30] The position of the other Allies was also used as justification for refusing to grant Bulgaria its desired status. The goal was once again to drive home the fact that Bulgaria would not receive understanding from the West and the only power that supported it was the Soviet Union. And while it is true that Great Britain did not agree to grant Bulgaria the status of an allied country, it is also a fact that the Vice-Chairman of the ACC, General Biryuzov, did not even pose this question to the Allies for discussion.[31] It is obvious that the USSR also did not want Bulgaria to receive any serious international recognition of its participation in the war against Germany that might strengthen the Bulgarian position on the eve of signing the peace treaties and that might create prospects for greater independence for Bulgarian foreign policy.

Conflicts within the Fatherland Front and the formation of a legal opposition to the regime

When the new government was formed on September 9, the principle of equality between the parties participating in the Fatherland Front coalition was formally preserved. The communists, however, controlled two of the most important institutions – the Interior Ministry and the Justice Ministry – which, along with the commencement of nationwide purges, allowed them to establish significant control over the state apparatus as well as over society as a whole. At that time, the activity of the *militsia* headed by communist functionaries acquired particular authority, and in practice there was no institution in the country that was in a position to effectively oppose it. It turned out that no one could curb the arbitrary violence on the part of the police and protect the personnel of any institution. It reached the point where even Defense Minister Velchev was forced to issue an order requiring officers to sleep in the barracks and to leave them only in well-armed groups so as not to fall prey to attacks by armed units and illegal arrests by the military police.[32]

The other important mechanism for strengthening the real influence of the Communist Party within the government was the process of total politicization of state employees that had already begun. In contradiction to tendencies that had developed in Bulgaria in the second half of the 1930s, now government posts were filled entirely according to political recommendations by local Fatherland Front committees, where members of the BWP(C) predominated.[33] Appointments were not made due to the candidates' knowledge or their ability to govern but rather due to their demonstrated loyalty to the Fatherland Front and, most often, to the Communist Party. To this end, one of the first things the new government did was to abolish educational requirements for government employees. There were many cases in which the noncommunist ministers admitted that their authority to make appointments was severely limited and even usurped by the lower structures of the Fatherland Front. By creating an active party core within state institutions, the BWP(C) also acquired a powerful means for controlling the one important ministry that it did not directly govern: the Defense Ministry. Through the creation of a so-called Assistant Commanders Institute, it guaranteed that party policy would be carried out in the army as well. The assistant commanders were political commissars, usually former partisans, who were assigned to each detachment to observe the behavior and actions of the commander and the whole officer corps.

Besides having many levers at their disposal with which to pressure their partners, the communists also resorted to openly rejecting decisions approved by the majority in the Council of Ministers when necessary. A typical example of this is Decree No. 4 by the Defense Ministry of November 23, 1944. It announced that officers brought to trial before the People's Court would be freed from prosecution if they actively took part in the war against Germany. The main goal of this ordinance was to limit persecution of the Bulgarian officer corps. Shortly after its adoption, however, the Communist Party categorically opposed this decision and organized massive street demonstrations. The direct intervention of the Soviet representative on the ACC (General Biryuzov) followed, forcing the government to repeal the decree.[34] As a result of this, many officers who were heroes from World War II and who had just

66　The times of high Stalinism

been awarded metals for bravery were interrogated, thrown into prison, and even sentenced to death upon their return to the country.

The mass expansion of the ruling parties was also a key moment in the struggle for dominant influence in the government. After the coup of September 9, all the political forces from the Fatherland Front began furiously increasing their membership numbers. This process did not unfold uniformly, however; the membership ranks of the BWP(C) expanded the most rapidly. From around 14,000 during September 1944, in little more than a year, by October 1945, its membership had swelled to over 400,000 new communists.[35] This was in some degree due to the fact that in the preceding era, when all parties had been banned, the communists, thanks to their experience and ability to adapt to operating illegally, had managed to preserved a major part of their party structures, which in the current situation gave them a decisive advantage over the other participants in the coalition. The main reason for the sharp rise in communists in the country, however, is that the party fully controlled the repressive bodies and thus within society the opinion took hold ever more clearly that the BWP truly held the reins of power. This feeling was also strengthened by the open support it received from the Soviet occupying forces. Thus, alongside the people who sincerely believed that communism meant the creation of a just social system, many Bulgarians, frightened by the wave of repression that had been unleashed, joined the ranks of the BWP. Of course, they were also joined by openly power-hungry office-seekers.

While supporters of the communist idea multiplied greatly, the BWP(C) leadership devoted serious efforts to limiting the growth of the other Fatherland Front parties. It constantly accused its coalition partners of accepting numerous undercover enemies of the people's government into their party structures. Despite technically being equal participants in governing the country, the other parties were seriously restricted in their public appearances. Thus, for example, any significant public gatherings or demonstrations, as well as statements broadcast on the national radio, had to be authorized by Interior Minister Anton Yugov and hence the Communist Party. The most heavy-handed tactics included the BWP(C)'s interference in the struggles between various wings of the agrarian and social-democratic parties. The goal was to remove the older and more authoritative leaders of these parties in favor of lesser-known activists who were striving for closer relations with the communist leadership. The actions of the noncommunist ministers in the government were frequently subject to attack.[36]

The unequal relations between those in power, on the one hand, and the lack of a legal opposition that would unify the forces within the government on the other, made the outbreak of conflict within the Fatherland Front inevitable. The first attempts to oppose the communists' established dominance within the government were made by the Agrarian Party, which had traditionally been the strongest party in Bulgarian society. On September 23, 1944, after nearly four years of exile, the authoritative leader of the Pladne branch of the party, G. M. Dimitrov, returned to the country. He soon began to openly denounce what was going on within Bulgarian society and the restrictions that were imposed on the Agrarian Union. His behavior made him the communists' primary enemy, and a vicious campaign against him began in December of the same year. In the struggle for the political elimination of G. M. Dimitrov, internal conflicts within BANU were used in addition to blunt external interference. By openly supporting left-centrist agrarians in high-level bodies within the union, the Communist Party aimed to establish an agrarian leadership that was absolutely obedient to the communists. The intervention of General Biryuzov proved decisive, however; on January 17, 1945, in connection with the upcoming BANU conference, the general categorically announced to Comrade G. M. Dimitrov that the communists did not want to work with him and that he would have to withdraw from his post as General Secretary of the Agrarian Union.[37] This declaration made it perfectly clear who was actually governing Bulgaria at the time. With the Agrarian Party under threat of being banned and dissolved, the union's supreme council selected Nikola Petkov as their leader. The attacks against Dr. G. M. Dimitrov did not end with that, however. In April 1945, he was placed under house arrest, where he was kept under strict watch. On May 23, he nevertheless managed to escape from his home, first seeking refuge in the British diplomatic mission, and shortly thereafter he established himself within the safer residence of the American political representative, Maynard Barnes. In the meantime, with the approval of the Soviet occupying forces, the Bulgaria *militsia* arrested G. M. Dimitrov's secretary, M. Racheva, and killed her in a particularly brutal manner, suspecting her of having aided Dimitrov in his escape. The Vice-Chairman of the ACC, General Biryuzov, demanded that the American mission immediately hand G. M. Dimitrov over to the Bulgarian authorities. Barnes categorically refused to comply with the Soviet demand, even declaring that he was prepared to defend him with the small number of soldiers at his disposal. After a three-month stay in the American residence, G. M. Dimitrov was taken out of the country in early September.[38]

The communist attack also took aim at the other significant partner within the Fatherland Front: the Bulgarian Workers' Social Democratic Party (BWSDP). The BWP(C) also interfered quite heavy-handedly in this party's internal life, supporting its left wing, which was headed by Dimitâr Neykov, and attempting to discredit the social democrats' authoritative leaders through all possible means. The communists' initial attack was aimed at Krâstyo Pastuhov, who, as a deeply convinced democrat, criticized the Fatherland Front's domestic policy and the unscrupulous politicization of state institutions. As the result of strong internal and external pressure on the BWSDP, the party leadership strengthened the role of its left wing.[39] Taking a centrist position, Grigor Cheshmedzhiev and Kosta Lulchev attempted to preserve the party's independence, a task that proved very difficult. Beginning in early 1945, the BWP(C) had already mobilized its numerous structures not only against "fascist elements" but also in an attack on anyone who expressed dissatisfaction with the regime.

68 *The times of high Stalinism*

Despite leadership changes in the agrarian and social-democratic parties, beginning in the spring of 1945, the atmosphere in the government grew ever tenser. Disagreements and mutual accusations over matters of principle grew ever more frequent. A serious problem arose on March 31, when the police, along with a group of communist activists, used brutal force against a BANU demonstration that had not been approved by the communists, leading to bloody clashes.[40] During May, the agrarians in Aleksandâr Obbov's circle, supported by the BWP(C), took over the leadership of BANU, and, shortly thereafter, Nikola Petkov was removed from the post of General Secretary.

Sharp dissension broke out concerning the parliamentary elections, which had been scheduled for August 26. Agreement could not be reached during negotiations to prepare the Fatherland Front's lists of candidates. The communists' tactic was for the candidates to be selected so as to guarantee the election of ninety-five communist MPs, while from the ranks of the coalition partners, people close to the Communist Party would be selected. Under these circumstances, guided by the feeling that under the conditions of a full communist dictate it would be impossible to work together, in July and August 1945, most of the agrarian ministers and several of the independents left the government. Soon an opposition was formed to the September 9 regime, consisting of two main parties: Nikola Petkov's BANU and Kosta Lulchev's BWSDP(U). Officially, the Fatherland Front continued to be a coalition, but only groups wholly subservient to the BWP(C) remained within it: Zveno members, Obbov's agrarians, and Neykov's social democrats.

By leaving the government, the leaders of the opposition believed that they could preserve the authenticity of their parties and create a relatively democratic alternative to the communist-dominated Fatherland Front government. They were clearly aware that as far as foreign policy was concerned, the postwar realities in the world were such that the USSR would exercise predominant political influence in Bulgaria, but they hoped that at least in domestic policy they would be able to secure greater independence for Bulgarian state institutions. Furthermore, they planned to champion an economic policy that would reduce the enormous burden resulting from the fulfillment of the Moscow Truce Agreement and that would accelerate the revival the Bulgarian economy.

The intensification of social-political struggles within the country

Given that agrarians and social democrats were severely restricted in their political expression even while serving as partners in the ruling coalition, now that they had officially formed an opposition it was clear that their political activities would face even greater difficulties. The government's power structures, state propaganda, and local committees of the Fatherland Front – all controlled by the BWP(C) – would not create space for the normal functioning of an opposition. Under such circumstances, the only hope for securing elementary democratic freedoms in the country lay with the American and English

Bulgaria in the shadow of Stalin 69

representatives on the ACC. Expectations that external pressure might reduce the authorities' arbitrariness arose from the declaration made at the meeting in Yalta of the three leaders of the Anti-Hitler Coalition. It stated that the peoples of Europe must have the right to freely choose their national government through democratic elections.[41] However, the means that the Western members of the ACC had at their disposal to influence processes within the country were severely limited. As they themselves admitted, and as foreign journalists noted, their ability to visit various locations in the country and to freely interact with Bulgarian citizens faced serious difficulties in practice. In Sofia, they were only allowed to move along a specifically designated route, and if they decided to go beyond its borders or to visit provincial regions in Bulgaria, that could only happen with the express authorization of the Deputy Chairman of the ACC, General Biryuzov, and under the condition that they were accompanied by a Soviet officer. Decisions were constantly being made in the name of the Commission, without the Western representatives even being familiarized with the issues under discussion.[42] The American representative on the Commission, General Crane, turned to his superiors in Washington several times, requesting that they demand that the Soviet Foreign Ministry give greater freedom of action to the Western representatives in Bulgaria. In fact, the not-particularly-energetic diplomatic maneuvers undertaken in Moscow did not change the situation on the commission at all. It was clear that the State Department did not wish to confront its ally; the United States expected the Soviets to continue their powerful offensive on the Eastern Front and even to soon join in the final defeat of Japan. From this point of view, the problems in Bulgaria seemed far less important. The full Soviet domination of the ACC, which continued after the war as well, allowed the USSR to control and direct political processes within Bulgaria. In addition, it created the impression among the Bulgarian population that the Western countries did not care enough about the political situation in the country and that Bulgarian society could not expect substantial support from them against the increasing communist pressure.

After the end of the war, American diplomacy in Sofia began to more openly express its dissatisfaction with the way political freedoms were being trampled in Bulgaria. Conversely, the USSR demonstrated its full approval of what was happening in the country and on August 14 announced that it would reestablish its diplomatic relations with Bulgaria. Moscow made it clear to the Bulgarian communists that the United States and Great Britain would not be allowed to observe and control the preparation and implementation of the upcoming elections.[43] Nevertheless, instructions were sent to the government to Sofia to take a more flexible stance and to formally make some concessions to the opposition – without, however, giving up control over the situation in the country.

Following this approach, the government accepted the opposition's demand, which was also supported by the Western representatives on the ACC, that the parliamentary elections be delayed. On September 7, a

70 *The times of high Stalinism*

decision was made to allow for the legal existence of an opposition. Along with Nikola Petkov's BANU and the BWSDP(U), the Democratic Party and Vrabcha BANU were also reestablished – the latter shortly thereafter fused with Nikola Petkov's agrarians. A leftist opposition also formed, creating the Anarcho-Communist Federation; however, its influence in Bulgarian society was insignificant. Opposition parties were also allowed to publish their own newspapers. Thus, in the autumn of 1945, some rudiments of democratic life began to spring up in Bulgaria.[44]

But the real situation in the country could not be described as democratic by any stretch of the imagination. The opposition did not have access to the radio, while state-owned means of transportation were used solely by candidates from the Fatherland Front. Local communist activists subjected opposition parties to particularly fierce harassment. Organized armed groups of communists and members of the Workers Youth Movement – known as *remsisti* from the organization's Bulgarian acronym RMS (Rabotnichesko-Mladezhki Sâyuz) – periodically attacked the opposition's public events, broke up their meetings and parties, and openly threatened opposition activists and supporters with brutal mob violence. With the goal of sowing fear among the population, the post-September 9 killings and torture were recalled.[45] Despite the fact that, officially, the central leadership of the Communist Party distanced itself from such actions by its rank-and-file members, in fact, the tactic of pressuring the opposition originated within the highest levels of the party. Georgi Dimitrov, who had returned from Moscow on November 4, also took part in the pre-election struggles. General Velchev, the Defense Minister, also appealed to Bulgarian officers and soldiers to vote for the Fatherland Front.

Given the total absence of normal conditions for political activity, the opposition decided not to take part in the elections and to boycott them. They were held on November 18, and the only participant in them – the Fatherland Front – won a decisive victory. Not appearing at the polling station was tantamount to declaring oneself an opposition activist – something that was quite dangerous given the pre-election terror, and this was the reason for the exceptionally high rate of voter participation (nearly 85 percent). Thus, the Twenty-Sixth Ordinary National Assembly did not contain a single MP who opposed the government's policies. As early as 1945, it was clear what the legislative body would look like in the state system the Bulgarian communists were striving to establish. The Soviet Union declared the elections fully legitimate, while the United States and Great Britain considered them undemocratic and unfree. Despite the fact that, according to official data, Parliament had received the overwhelming support of the people, Georgi Dimitrov announced that the main bulwark of the government continued to be the Fatherland Front, which was a clear sign that the basic democratic institutions would not even formally be respected.[46] In the meantime, Parliament rapidly and easily passed numerous laws (in a nine-month period 250 laws were passed), creating the system of the so-called

Bulgaria in the shadow of Stalin 71

people's democracy.[47] First, all the actions taken by the Fatherland Front since September 9, 1944, were legalized. Overall, Parliament's activity greatly expanded state interference in the economic, social and cultural life of the country.[48] Under the pretext of fighting speculation and profits made from the war, the legislative conditions were created for serious attacks against private property and citizens' economic initiatives.

The exclusion of the opposition from the country's political life, as well as the unrelenting pressure on that opposition, provoked a negative reaction in democratic countries. At a meeting of the foreign ministers of the victorious countries in Moscow on December 16–25, 1945, the topics discussed also included the situation in Bulgaria. The US and British representatives demanded a restructuring of the government in which the Foreign Ministry would be taken out of the communists' hands and two opposition figures would be included in the cabinet. Despite these quite moderate demands, the Soviets strongly opposed them. Given that since September 9, 1944, Moscow had fully controlled the situation in Bulgaria, issuing instructions to the Bulgarian communists on even the smallest of political questions, now it brazenly declared that the Anglo-American demands constituted a heavy-handed interference in the internal workings of a sovereign state. Nevertheless, it was agreed that two representatives of the opposition would be invited to participate in the government.

The negotiations held between the ruling party and the opposition in order to implement the decisions from the Moscow Conference did not produce results. Opposition leaders were in practice offered insignificant and secondrate posts in the government in return for demands to acknowledge the legitimacy of the elections of the Twenty-Sixth Ordinary National Assembly. For their part, the opposition representatives, encouraged by the United States and Britain's firmer stance, presented a series of important conditions: that the communists relinquish the foreign and justice ministries, thus creating the necessary prerequisites for the preservation of civil freedoms in the country; that they cease the politicization of the Bulgarian army; that they close down the concentration camps; and that they give the opposition access to the radio. Their demands were categorically rejected. Stalin, from Moscow, issued personal orders not to negotiate with the opposition but simply to declare that it had to identify two individuals who would join the cabinet. If it refused, it could "go to hell."[49] Andrey Vishinski, Deputy Foreign Minister of the USSR, arrived in Sofia on January 9 to implement the Soviet decisions, meeting with the regents and with representatives of the government. At two o'clock in the morning, he invited the leaders of the opposition to talks. While the terror-stricken Soviet Union was perhaps used to late-night political meetings and making reports at all hours of the day or night, in Bulgaria such a practice had not yet been established. Nikola Petkov arrived to see the Soviet representative in the morning on the next day. Again, the opposition refused to formally participate in the government. The negotiations continued for the following two months, but an agreement was never reached.[50]

72   The times of high Stalinism

On March 31, 1946, Kimon Georgiev again headed the second Fatherland Front government. The cabinet consisted of five communist ministers, four agrarians, four members of Zveno, two social democrats, one radical and one "independent." In fact, there were only four new ministers: one communist, one agrarian and two Zveno members. Despite the fact that the parties participating in the Fatherland Front were publicly declared as fully equal coalition partners, in reality the process of the complete obliteration of noncommunist political forces within the government continued. They were not in any condition to undertake any independent political initiatives, nor could they take up a position on social processes that was different to that of the BWP(C). Their merely formal presence in the government was well understood by the population, an understanding that was reflected in the completely unbalanced growth of the various Fatherland Front parties' membership ranks. As of mid-1946, the BWP(C) had 421,559 members, which was twice as many as all of the other Fatherland Front parties combined: BANU had 150,756; Zveno had 34,196; the BWSDP had 31,529; and the Radical Party, which had recently joined the Fatherland Front, had 3,873. Given the open threats and repression, it was natural that the number of opposition party members significantly declined. Thus, Nikola Petkov's BANU had 51,361 members, the BWSDP(U) had 2,214, and the Democratic Party had 2,214.[51]

Just as during the negotiations, after the formation of the new government the struggle against the opposition continued just as fiercely. Arrests and beatings of opposition activists grew ever more frequent. The oppositions' publications (*Narodno zemedelsko zname* [*National Agrarian Banner*], *Svoboden narod* [*Free People*], and others) were periodically suspended; most often the reason for this was their publication of anti-Soviet and anti-Yugoslav articles. This gross violation of the constitutional right to freedom of the press was framed by the government as a refusal on the part of the workers in the printing houses to publish newspapers that slandered the USSR or the people's government.

During the spring of 1946, trials against emblematic opposition figures began. G. M. Dimitrov, who had already left the country in September 1945 and who was now in the United States, was sentenced *in absentia* to life in solitary confinement. The authoritative and long-standing leader of the Bulgarian social democrats, Krâstyo Pastuhov, was also put on trial. Because of two articles in which he had declared his opposition to the politicization of the Bulgarian army and its subordination to the communists' party interests, he received a sentence of five years in solitary confinement. In August 1949 he was strangled in his cell in the Sliven Prison. The editor-in-chief of the newspaper *Svoboden narod*, Tsveti Ivanov, also suffered harsh retribution. He was sentenced to ten months in prison but after serving his sentence he was sent to the camp in Belene, where he fell gravely ill and later died.[52] The prominent writer and poet Trifon Kunev also fell victim to the communist terror. As a result of the numerous feuilletons he had written in the *Narodno zemedelsko zname*, on June 8 he was severely beaten at the newspaper's editorial office and then thrown in the Central Prison, where he was held for five months without a sentence having been pronounced against him. At this time, show trials were also held against the secret military organization Tsar Krum and the Internal Macedonian Revolutionary Organization.[53] In the first case, without providing definitive evidence that such an illegal organization even existed, one death sentence and several prison sentences of varying lengths were meted out. Activists from the Internal Macedonian Revolutionary Organization, who had opposed the denationalization policy imposed by the Fatherland Front in Pirin Macedonia, also received harsh sentences.[54] In all of these trials, the prosecutors and judges went out of their way to try to prove the defendants' connection to the Bulgarian opposition.

The purges also continued within the structures of the central and local government, as well as in the army, the court system, education, healthcare, and cultural organizations. Suspicions of having expressed sympathy for the opposition was reason enough for a state employee to be fired. The removal of unreliable politicians from within the ranks of the coalition partners took place even at the highest levels in the government. Since the Zveno minister Professor Stancho Cholakov was not included in the new government, now the communists' attack was focused on another inconvenient Zveno minister: General Velchev. The Defense Minister's attempts to shield the army from total subjugation to the Communist Party drew him into conflict with the true rulers of the country. He was soon forced to take sick leave and never returned to the ministry. At the end of September 1946, he was sent to Bern as the Bulgarian Minister Plenipotentiary in Switzerland. He was later recalled, but he refused to return to Bulgaria.

Given the BWP(C)'s full control over state institutions, the tight restrictions on the opposition's public statements, and the Soviet troops that were still stationed in the country, an important step toward changing the governmental structure in Bulgarian was taken. Parliament passed a law to abolish the monarchy through a public referendum. The procedure undertaken was in complete violation of the Târnovo Constitution, which stipulated that any governmental changes of the sort could occur only with the approval of a GNA. Such an assembly, however, could only be convened by the King, who at that time was still underage. (Simeon II was barely nine years old.) Besides not conforming to constitutional norms, the referendum was organized and carried out in a deeply nondemocratic fashion. First, the formulation of the referendum (abolition of the monarchy) gave voters a completely clear political message. In addition to this, the country lacked even a formal defender of the monarchy. The opposition, which in large part (the agrarians and social democrats) supported republicanism as well, could not take a position that radically differed from that of the governing party. It could only object to the way in which the monarchy was abolished, pointing out that this was yet another gross violation of the constitution. In any case, in the situation that was taking shape, the opposition, lacking a better option, called upon its

74 *The times of high Stalinism*

supporters to vote for a republic.[55] Conversely, the Fatherland Front government could use this unchallenged contest as proof of broad public support for the people's power.

The referendum was held on September 8, 1946. Official statistics reported that 4,132,107 out of a total of 4,509,354 eligible voters participated in the referendum, which is more than 91 percent voter participation. A total of 3,833,183 votes were cast in favor of a republic. The total number of votes in support of the monarchy, as well as invalid or blank ballots, slightly exceeded 676,600, or around 15 percent of voters. The results were absolutely categorical in favor of a republic. Taking into account the overall atmosphere in the country since the end of World War II, as well as the crisis the institution of the monarchy had found itself in following King Boris III's death, it can be presumed the public attitudes were indeed overwhelmingly in favor of a republic. However, on the other hand, the possibility could not be discounted that in a freely organized referendum, Bulgarian society might express not so much its attitude toward the monarchy but rather its attitude toward the repressive policies of the Fatherland Front regime. This was the reason that the referendum was organized in such a way as to rule out the possibility of surprises. On September 15, the National Assembly declared Bulgaria a people's republic. The royal family was forced to flee the country the very next day, temporarily taking up residence in Egypt.

Signing the peace treaty with Bulgaria

Immediately following the end of military operations and the capitulation of the last member of the Tripartite Pact, Japan, in September 1945, the leading countries in the Anti-Hitler Coalition began preparations for the organization of a peace conference and for drawing up agreements with the conquered nations. To this end, a special body called the Council of Foreign Ministers (CFM) was created, which included the respective ministers from Great Britain, the United States, France and the USSR and which held its first meeting in London during September and October 1945. In December, a new conference was convened in Moscow, where it was decided that the United States would not participate in negotiations with Finland.[56] By the time the peace conference was convened in Paris in the summer of 1946, the CFM had already held over fifty meetings. Some of the frequently debated topics included the question of reparations and the peace treaties' economic clauses. Two basic factors determined the crystallization of the victors' positions on these issues. The first was the emerging decision to not impose harsh political and economic sanctions on the Reich's former satellites, while the other was the growing disagreements between the USSR and the Western countries. From the very beginning, the victors took the standpoint that, on principle, the conquered countries should not be forced to pay the full sum of losses suffered, which provided a favorable basis for Bulgarian reparations to be reconsidered in the future.[57]

Bulgaria in the shadow of Stalin 75

The peace conference began on July 29, 1946, in the Luxembourg Palace in Paris. At first, a new spirit reigned; unlike the conference in 1919, where the conquered countries were not allowed to present their viewpoints during the sessions, now their representatives were officially invited to take part in the discussions on drawing up the peace treaties. On August 11, the Bulgarian delegation led by Prime Minister Kimon Georgiev arrived in the French capital. It also included Vasil Kolarov, who was already in Paris, as well as Foreign Minister Georgi Kulishev, Finance Minister Professor Ivan Stefanov, and other high-ranking officials. During the conference, the Bulgarian delegation enjoyed the support of the USSR, which unambiguously treated Bulgaria as part of its sphere of influence in Europe; from this point of view, it did not wish to allow the treaty to weaken its "client state" militarily and economically. Given the established Soviet influence in Eastern Europe, Bulgaria could also count on the support of countries such as Poland, Czechoslovakia, and Yugoslavia.[58] Conversely, the political conditions in Bulgaria were the reason that the Fatherland Front government did not receive any sympathy on the part of the Western democracies and their allies. Thus, in Paris a serious conflict took shape among the victors regarding the drawing of up the peace treaties, and not just that with Bulgaria.

The basic demands – but far from the only ones – were presented to the Bulgarian delegation by the Greek government. It accused Bulgaria of aiding Italian and German aggression against Greece after occupying Greek territory, where Bulgarian troops and administrative structure had committed serious crimes and inflicted large material damages on the local population. Athens demanded that Bulgaria pay damages of US$700 million and also that the Bulgarian–Greek border be shifted 50–60 kilometers to the north, thus transferring a significant amount of Bulgarian territory to Greece. The Greeks relied mainly on the support of Great Britain. Bulgaria, for its part, not only rejected the Greek territorial aspirations as absolutely in contradiction to the principle of nationalities but in turn demanded that Bulgaria be given the Aegean Sea outlet that had been discussed at the Paris Conference of 1919 and stipulated in the Treaty Neuilly as an economic outlet. Now, too, the Bulgarian viewpoint was based on the claim that an Aegean outlet would have an exceptionally favorable effect on its economic recovery. Particularly well-grounded arguments were offered in support of the idea of transforming the city of Kavala into an important trade port connecting eastern and northeastern Europe with the Mediterranean region.[59] However, neither Greek nor Bulgarian proposals for border changes influenced the political commission's decisions in any way, since the Great Powers had already decided among themselves not to change the existing Bulgarian–Greek border. This position was categorically upheld by the United States and the USSR, while even Great Britain did not actively support Greek territorial claims.[60]

The Great Powers also did not back Greek demands that Bulgaria pay maximal reparations. On the one hand, Athens' arguments concerning the scope of losses suffered under the Bulgarian occupation were not the least

76 *The times of high Stalinism*

bit convincing, while on the other hand there was a prevailing attitude that the mistakes made in the peace treaties after World War I should not be repeated and that damages should not exceed the conquered countries' financial and economic capabilities.[61] The initial amount that Bulgaria was to pay in reparations was set at US$125 million, but later this was further reduced to $US70 million ($US25 million to Yugoslavia and $US45 million to Greece).

Another important element of the treaty was the military restrictions placed on Bulgaria. The Bulgarian armed forces were allowed to number 65,000, including all types of troops, and they should carry out "tasks of a domestic nature" and "defense of the country's borders." Bulgaria was forbidden from possessing strategic weapons and from maintaining permanent fortifications along the Greek border.

The peace treaty with Bulgaria, as well as with Germany's other former allies, was signed on February 10, 1947, in Paris. The most important thing for Bulgaria was that the borders of the country would remain as they had been on January 1, 1941 – that is, there were no territorial changes along the border with Greece, while at the same time the unification with Southern Dobrudzha from September 7, 1940, was officially recognized.

Convening a Grand National Assembly and the liquidation of the opposition

After the referendum had been held and Bulgaria had been declared a people's republic, the communists shifted their focus to drawing up and adopting a new constitution which would reflect the changes that had taken place. To this end, a GNA had to be convened. Despite finding themselves on fully unequal footing, both the government and the opposition prepared for a serious political battle. As part of the election campaign for the GNA, the Fatherland Front presented a draft of a constitution that would give Parliament sweeping authority. It was decided that the Fatherland Front parties would participate in the election with common candidate lists, but with different colored ballots. The opposition appealed to the people, criticizing the Fatherland Front government's dictatorial regime and declaring itself in favor of creating a system that would guarantee the population's civil and political rights. The main opposition parties – Nikola Petkov's BANU and the BWSDP(U) – united into a common block called the Federation of Rural and Urban Workers.

The pre-election struggle was accompanied by a new wave of political violence. The *militsia* began arresting the opposition MP candidates. Many of its most active figures, such as Trifon Kunev, Asen Stamboliyski, and Dr. Petâr Dertliev, were already in prison or interned in camps. The opposition's public events continued to be attacked and broken up. In response to the Bulgarian government's actions, the American Secretary of State James Byrnes sent a letter to Prime Minister Georgiev, demanding that the conditions for a free election campaign be secured. The basic points included freedom of the press and the radio, freedom of assembly for the opposition, noninterference by the *militsia* in the political process, the freeing of political prisoners, and a cessation of threats of post-election repression on political grounds. The Soviet representative on the ACC, General Biryuzov, under the pretext that it was beyond the purview of the ACC, blocked all attempts to limit government pressure on the population and the opposition.[62]

Alongside openly brutal activities, the ruling party also resorted to brazen manipulation of public opinion, making pre-election promises that it had no intention of keeping. In contradiction to the Communist Party's true intentions, on October 26 in a campaign speech given in Sofia, Georgi Dimitrov categorically announced that the regime would not resort to liquidating the private property of farmers, craftsmen, and people involved in physical and intellectual labor.[63]

Overshadowed by numerous violations of the campaign process, on October 27, 1946, elections were held for the Sixth GNA. The most fundamental distortion of the election process stemmed from its very organization (the handing out of voter cards), which allowed many Fatherland Front activists to vote at several different precincts simultaneously. Conversely, a large number of opposition supporters were not even allowed to cast their votes. In many places, no representatives of the opposition were present during the vote counting, elections records were falsified, and so on.

The official results indicated a major victory for the Fatherland Front, which received around 2,980,000 of the total 4,250,000 votes cast in the election. This assured the ruling coalition a stable majority in the GNA – 366 out of a total of 465 seats. The internal distribution of votes within the coalition block showed that the process of reducing the profile of the noncommunist parties within the Fatherland Front had had the desired effect. BANU, Zveno, the BWSDP and the Radical Party combined received just over 16 percent of all votes. Those who voted for the Fatherland Front very rightly realized that the only true power in the coalition was the BWP(C), thus it captured the greater part of the vote – 53 percent of all votes cast.[64]

Considering the political repression that had been taking place in the country for more than two years, the opposition won a surprisingly large percentage of the vote (nearly 29 percent) – or approximately 1,205,000 votes. The basic opposition party was Nikola Petkov's BANU, which won ninety seats in the GNA. The remaining opposition representatives included eight MPs from the BWSDP(U) and one from the group of independent intellectuals, bringing the total of opposition MPs to ninety-nine.

The GNA began its work on November 7, 1946. It was immediately clear from the ruling and opposition parliamentary groups' opening statements that they would be engaged in an irreconcilable political struggle. Post-electoral violence against those who had voted for the opposition, which was carried out both by bodies within the Interior Ministry, as well as by local communist organizations, reached terrifying proportions. Even the BWP(C)'s coalition partners, such as Zveno members and social democrats, were forced to call on communist leaders to control their local organizations.[65]

78 *The times of high Stalinism*

On November 23, the third Fatherland Front government was formed, this time headed by the communist leader Georgi Dimitrov as Prime Minister. The formal parity in making up the cabinet was abandoned: half of the ministers were communists, while the remaining ten posts were divided up between the agrarians, the social democrats and one "independent."

In addition to launching a propaganda campaign to spread the communist ideology among the people and to accustom them to Soviet political attitudes, the new government launched a powerful offensive against the opposition. They were branded as "anti-popular" and "reactionary," while their actions were characterized as weakening and dividing the Bulgarian people. Under the pretext that they were constantly obstructing parliamentary activity, the opposition MPs' opportunities to speak in Parliament were severely restricted. They were very often removed from sessions, and there were even cases in which quaestors or *militsioneri* openly beat MPs on the floor of Parliament itself. As early as the end of 1946, the publication of the Democratic Party's flagship newspaper *Zname* (*Banner*) was banned, and during the following months other opposition publications were stopped under the pretext that the country was suffering a paper shortage or that again the workers had refused to print them. For its part, the opposition openly accused those in power of establishing a terroristic regime in Bulgaria.[66] They rejected the government's domestic, economic and cultural policies. They lent support solely to the foreign-policy course that the country had been following to date: that of maintaining good relations with the countries that had been victorious in World War II.

The main reason that the Sixth GNA had been convened – the drawing up of a new constitution – was also the object of heated political struggles. In May 1947, discussions of the draft constitution proposed by the Fatherland Front began. Besides this proposal, other draft constitutions were also submitted by the opposition, as well as individually by the lawyers Professor Venelin Ganchev and Professor Stefan Balamezov. The basic disputes centered on questions of the separation of powers, the head of state's prerogatives, the future of private property, and the guaranteeing of political and civil freedoms. Despite failing to receive the support of a two-thirds majority in the GNA, on June 20 the Fatherland Front's draft constitution was passed on first reading. The constitution of the PRB was definitely adopted on December 4, 1947.

In many of its clauses and accepted principles, it resembled the Soviet constitution of 1936. It contained openly ideological statements and offered political evaluations of events from the country's recent past. Thus, for example, even in Article 1 it declared that the people's republic was a result of the "victorious people's uprising on September 9, 1944," hence the regime established after that date was raised to the level of constitutional norm.[67] The National Assembly was declared the supreme body of the republic. In practice, no separate presidential institution was formulated in the constitution. The Presidium of the National Assembly was something resembling a presidency but without fulfilling the typical functions of a head of state. In

Bulgaria in the shadow of Stalin   79

fact, this elevation of the role of the collective bodies within the government and the strong devaluation of the personal institutions within the context of the one-party system that was already establishing itself was a clear signal of the full subordination of state structures to the party. What's more, the constitution instituted the principle of state control over the economy, which must be developed according to plan, while domestic and foreign trade must be carried out by the state. Private property was allowed; however, the conditions imposed on its existence (that it must be acquired through honest labor and must not be used to the detriment of society) allowed it to be confiscated completely arbitrarily.[68] In the section on civil rights and responsibilities, the social aspects of the topic predominated: Bulgarians had the right to labor, rest, social compensations, a pensions, education and so on. Purely political rights – freedom of speech, of the press, and of assembly – were briefly mentioned in Article 88. Bulgarians also had the right to unite within organizations, as long as they were not opposed to the established state order and they did not "infringe upon the rights and freedom of the Bulgarian people won through the people's uprising of September 9, 1944," which in actuality meant that real opposition to the regime could not exist. The inviolability of one's person was also declared. No one could be held for more than forty-eight hours without the permission of judicial bodies or a prosecutor.[69]

Although it reflected certain elements of the Stalinist system of socialism that was taking shape in the country, the constitution of 1947, called the "Dimitrov Constitution" in the propaganda, also proclaimed classical democratic freedoms. They did not pose any problem whatsoever to the ruling party, however, since prior as well as subsequent practice in Bulgaria would show that given the party's total control over judicial bodies, Bulgarian society, which was deprived of the possibility for creating independent organizations, did not have any mechanisms at its disposal for controlling the government or for defending its constitutional rights.

In fact, even before the constitution come into force, which occurred on December 6, the BWP(C) had already established a complete monopoly over the country's political and social life. This process, which had already begun in September 1944, definitively ended with the complete liquidation of the opposition in Bulgaria. The authorities' decisive attack began immediately following the signing of the Paris Peace Treaty on February 10, 1947, and the subsequent reestablishment of diplomatic ties with Great Britain and the United States. Once the regime had been officially acknowledged, there was no longer any need to keep up the charade of even formally democratic governance. Moreover, in 1947, there was an abrupt deterioration in relations between the former allies in the Anti-Hitler Coalition, which marked a new epoch in the world's postwar development: the Cold War era. Given the sharp international conflict, the Bulgarian government, which was wholly subservient to Moscow, not only had no intention of taking the Western countries' objections into consideration but even felt it was necessary to take a firm stance against the Soviet Union's new enemies.

80   *The times of high Stalinism*

Retribution against opposition leaders began with a series of show trials against organizations which had been declared illegal and whose goal was the armed overthrow of the Fatherland Front government. The organizations "Neutral Officer" and "Military Union" were put on trial, while the prosecutors' main task was to demonstrate a connection between the officers accused of conspiracy and the leaders of the opposition. By using brutal torture methods borrowed from the Soviet Union and constant, round-the-clock interrogation, fabricated confessions were wrenched from the defendants that implicated opposition figures in anti-state activities.[70] On the basis of the "evidence" that had been gathered, on June 5, 1947, Interior Minister Anton Yugov submitted a request to the GNA that Nikola Petkov be stripped of his parliamentary immunity and that he be handed over to judicial bodies. An exceptionally heated debate following in Parliament, during which Prime Minister Georgi Dimitrov directed exceedingly harsh threats at Petkov and the entire opposition. The debate ended with the opposition MPs being beaten by plainclothes *militsia* officers. The majority in Parliament voted to strip Petkov of his parliamentary immunity. During a search of Petkov's home the next day, signed letters of resignation from some of the opposition MPs were found. This was an old party practice, used even before 1944, in which those MPs elected through a certain party list gave their signed letters of resignation to the party leader in advance as a guarantee that they will observe party discipline. The authorities now used them to immediately remove twenty of the opposition MPs.[71]

The trial against Nikola Petkov began on August 4, 1947. He was accused of instigating conspiratorial activities, writing articles aimed at reducing the military preparedness of Bulgarian troops, and spreading untrue rumors and communications. The trial ended on the sixteenth of the same month with a death sentence.

While all serious newspapers in Western Europe and the United States condemned the trial against Petkov, calling it a juridical farce and political retribution against the opposition, in Bulgaria the communists organized "nationwide approval" of the sentence, including mass demonstrations demanding that the opposition BANU party be banned. The authorities insisted that Petkov admit his guilt publicly. Despite intense pressure, he stood his ground. Alarmed by the broad international response the case had evoked, the Temporary President of the Republic (the constitution still had not been definitely adopted), Vasil Kolarov, suggested that the death sentence be commuted to life in prison. However, Georgi Dimitrov, who was in Moscow at the time, reported that Stalin had agreed that the sentence should stand.[72] Thus, shortly before midnight on September 23, the sentence was carried out at the Central Sofia Prison and Nikola Petkov was hanged.

In the meantime, the liquidation of the opposition continued in full force. In August, the GNA voted to ban the opposition Agrarian Union. Its MPs were thrown into prison or sent to camps. The authorities definitively crushed the remnants of the opposition in 1948, when, again through a series

Bulgaria in the shadow of Stalin 81

of scandalous trials, Dimitâr Gichev (life in prison), Kosta Lulchev (fifteen years in solitary confinement) and a series of other opposition activists were convicted and imprisoned.[73]

Notes

1 Lyubomir Ognyanov, *Dârzhavno-politicheskata sistema na Bâlgariya 1944–1948*, Sofia: BAS, 1993, p. 11.
2 *Ustanovyavane i ukrepvane na narodnodemokratichnata vlast (septemvri 1944–may 1945)*, *Sbornik ot dokumenti*, Sofia, Partizdat, 1969, pp. 133–136.
3 The topic of the distorting effect of state interference in the economy for the period before 1944 is developed and discussed in detail by Rumen Avramov. See Rumen Avramov, *Komunalniyat kapitalizâm*, vols. I–III, Sofia: Fondatsiya "Bâlgarska nauka i kultura"/Center for Liberal Strategies, 2007.
4 Ognyanov, *Dârzhavno-politicheskata sistema na Bâlgariya*, p. 27.
5 Volfgang Bretholts, *Vidyah sgromolyasvaneto im*, Sofia: Bâdeshte/Tilia, 1944, pp. 67, 80–84, 162–168.
6 Mito Isusov, *Stalin i Bâlgariya*, Sofia: St. Kliment Ohridski, 1991, pp. 172–173.
7 Dimitâr Ludzhev, *Grad na dve epohi: Istoriya na obshtestvenite grupi v bâlgarskite gradove v sredata na XX vek*, Sofia: St. Kliment Ohridski, 2005, p. 73.
8 *Bâlgariya, nepriznatiyat protivnik na Tretiya rayh*. Sofia: Military Publishing House, 1995, p. 139.
9 Ognyanov, *Dârzhavno-politicheskata sistema na Bâlgariya*, p. 36.
10 The Nuremberg trials ended in twelve death sentences and the Tokyo trials in seven.
11 Petâr Semerdzhiev, *Narodniyat sâd v Bâlgariya, 1944–1945*. Sofia: Makedoniya pres, 1998, p. 406.
12 For interesting information about retribution against certain academic and cultural activists, see Sashka Milanova, "Razmisli vârhu prisâdite na VI sâstav na Narodniya sâd – 1945 g.," in *Istoriyata – profesiya i sâdba. V chest na chlen-korespondent d.ist.n. Georgi Markov*, Sofia: Tangra Tanakra, 2008, pp. 510–514.
13 In his memoirs, Dimitâr Peshev described the unbelievable physical and psychological torture that those convicted by the so-called People's Court were subjected to. Dimitâr Peshev, *Spomeni*, Sofia: Gutenberg, 2004.
14 *Bâlgariya nepriznatiyat protivnik*, pp. 222–225.
15 Ognyanov, *Dârzhavno-politicheskata sistema na Bâlgariya*, pp. 47–49.
16 Penka Stoyanova and Emil Iliev, *Politicheski opasni litsa: Vâdvoryavaniya, trudova mobilizatsiya, izselvaniya sled 1944 g.*, Sofia: Sv. Kl. Ohridski., 1991, pp. 13–14.
17 Ognyanov, *Dârzhavno-politicheskata sistema na Bâlgariya*, pp. 50–51.
18 Bretholts, *Vidyah sgromolyasvaneto im*, p. 165.
19 Veselin Angelov, *Tretata natsionalna katastrofa*, Sofia: Aniko, 2005, pp. 143–144.
20 Georgi Markov, *Kâm brega na svobodata ili za Nikola Petkov i negovoto vreme*, Sofia: Informatsionno obsluzhvane, 1992, p. 57; Georgi Markov, *Bâlgarskata istoriya vkrattse*, Sofia: Svyat, 1992, p. 267. We can accept the figure of 18,000 people killed or disappeared without a trace as the most well-founded, since it was deduced from a report by Interior Minister Anton Yugov during November 1944. See Polya Meshkova and Dinyo Sharlanov, *Bâlgarskata gilotina: Taynite mehanizmi na narodniya sâd*, Sofia: Agentsiya "Demokratsiya," 1994, p. 49.

82 The times of high Stalinism

21 Stoyan Pintev, *Bâlgariya v britanskata diplomatsiya 1944–1947*, Sofia: Professor Marin Drinov, 1998, pp. 47–48.
22 *Bâlgariya nepriznatiyat protivnik*, pp. 49–54.
23 *Bâlgariya nepriznatiyat protivnik*, pp. 183–184.
24 Iskra Baeva and Evgeniya Kalinova, *Sledvoennoto desetiletie na bâlgarskata vânshna politika (1944–1955)*, Sofia: Polis, 2003, pp. 63–66.
25 Hungary was also included in the negotiations; the USSR was acknowledged as the dominant influence there.
26 Vitka Toshkova, *SASht i Bâlgariya 1919–1989: Politicheski otnosheniya*, Sofia: Sineva, 2007, pp. 205–206.
27 This topic is examined in more detail in the section devoted to the country's economic development.
28 *Bâlgariya nepriznatiyat protivnik*, pp. 176–178.
29 Baeva and Kalinova, *Sledvoennoto desetiletie*, p. 51.
30 *Bâlgariya nepriznatiyat protivnik*, pp. 198–199.
31 Officially, Marshal Fyodor Tolbukhin was the Chairman of the ACC but in practice it was led by General Sergey Biryuzov.
32 Zhoro Tsvetkov, *Sâdât nad opozitsionnite lideri*, Sofia: Kupesa, 1991, p. 13
33 After September 9, 1944, the Bulgarian Worker's Party officially added *komunisti* or "communists" in parentheses and the party's acronym was henceforth written as BWP(C). As is noted below, in December 1948 at the Fifth Party Congress, the party officially changed its name to the Bulgarian Communist Party (BCP). Mito Isusov, *Politicheskiyat zhivot v Bâlgariya 1944–1948*, Sofia: Sv. Kliment Ohridski/ Professor Marin Drinov, 2000, pp. 24–25.
34 Evgeniya Kalinova, *Pobeditelite i Bâlgariya 1939–1945*, Sofia: Sv. Kl. Ohridski, 2004, p. 194.
35 Isusov, *Politicheskiyat zhivot*, pp. 33, 150.
36 Ognyanov, *Dârzhavno-politicheskata sistema na Bâlgariya*, pp. 56–57.
37 Ludzhev, *Grad na dve epohi*, p. 67.
38 Charles Moser, *Dimitrov of Bulgaria: A Political Biography of Dr. Georgi M. Dimitrov*, Ottawa: Caroline House, 1979. The Bulgarian edition is cited here: Charlz Mozer, *D-r G. M. Dimitrov: Biografiya*, Sofia: Military Publishing House, 1992, pp. 180–189.
39 Isusov, *Politicheskiyat zhivot*, p. 44.
40 Ludzhev, *Grad na dve epohi*, p. 70.
41 *Teheran, Yalta, Potsdam: Sbornik dokumenti*, Sofia: Izdatelstvo na BKP, 1968, pp. 152–153.
42 Toshkova, *SASht i Bâlgariya 1919–1989*, pp. 204–206.
43 Kalinova, *Pobeditelite i Bâlgariya*, p. 338.
44 Isusov, *Politicheskiyat zhivot*, pp. 123–143.
45 Ognyanov, *Dârzhavno-politicheskata sistema na Bâlgariya*, pp. 78–80.
46 Tsvetkov, *Sâdât nad opozitsionnite lideri*, p. 16.
47 The concept of "the people's democracy" is discussed in detail in a separate chapter of this book.
48 Ognyanov, *Dârzhavno-politicheskata sistema na Bâlgariya*, p. 85.
49 Sashka Milanova, "Moskovskoto reshenie ot 1945 g. za predstavitelnostta na bâlgarskoto pravitelstvo – diplomaticheski izhod ili politicheski kamuflazh," in *Bâlgariya v sferata na sâvetskite interesi*, Sofia: Professor Marin Drinov, 1998, pp. 28–29.

Bulgaria in the shadow of Stalin 83

50 Ognyanov, *Dârzhavno-politicheskata sistema na Bâlgariya*, pp. 94–99.
51 Isusov, *Politicheskiyat zhivot*, p. 246.
52 Tsvetkov, *Sâdât nad opozitsionnite lideri*, pp. 58–68.
53 The VMRO was the revolutionary organization of the Bulgarians in Macedonia. Founded in 1893 in Thessaloniki, it worked towards the autonomy of Macedonia, which was still under Ottoman rule at the time of its founding.
54 As part of the negotiations and preparations for the Bulgarian–Yugoslav Federation championed by Moscow, the Bulgarian part of Macedonia was to join the Republic of Macedonia. Following a request by Tito, the Bulgarian authorities began a forcible campaign to change the national self-identity of citizens of southwestern Bulgaria; at times this campaign met with armed resistance.
55 Ognyanov, *Dârzhavno-politicheskata sistema na Bâlgariya*, pp. 120–123.
56 Jean-Baptiste Duroselle, *Histoire diplomatique de 1919 à nos jours*, Paris: Dalloz, 1978, p. 441.
57 Pintev, *Bâlgariya v britanskata diplomatsiya*, p. 147.
58 Baeva and Kalinova, *Sledvoennoto desetiletie*, p. 96.
59 AMVnR, PMK, op. 1, a. e. 167, l. 21–61.
60 AMVnR, PMK, l. 102, 112.
61 Daniel Vachkov and Martin Ivanov, *Bâlgarskiyat vânshen dâlg 1944–1989: Bankrutât na komunisticheskata ikonomika*, Sofia: Ciela, 2008, pp. 38–39.
62 Isusov, *Stalin i Bâlgariya*, pp. 180–181.
63 Nikolay Genchev, *Nauchni trudove*, vol. I: *1961–1972*, Sofia: Gutenberg, 2003, p. 128.
64 Isusov, *Politicheskiyat zhivot*, p. 247.
65 Ognyanov, *Dârzhavno-politicheskata sistema na Bâlgariya*, p. 138.
66 Ognyanov, *Dârzhavno-politicheskata sistema na Bâlgariya*, pp. 154–155.
67 *Bâlgarski konstitutsii i konstitutsionni proekti*, Sofia: Petâr Beron, 1990, pp. 37–38.
68 *Bâlgarski konstitutsii i konstitutsionni proekti*, p. 39.
69 *Bâlgarski konstitutsii i konstitutsionni proekti*, pp. 49–52.
70 Tsvetkov, *Sâdât nad opozitsionnite lideri*, pp. 96–97.
71 Petâr Semerdzhiev, *Sâdebniyat protses sreshtu Nikola Petkov 1947 g.*, Sofia: Trud, 1990, pp. 181–184.
72 Isusov, *Stalin i Bâlgariya*, pp. 190–191.
73 Tsvetkov, *Sâdât nad opozitsionnite lideri*, pp. 180–191.

2 Georgi Dimitrov and "the people's democracy"

The totalitarian regime initially arises in response to particular social and political circumstances in the form of a project that may or may not succeed in establishing itself. Its success depends on a series of circumstances. Thus, the totalitarian personality precedes the totalitarian system and in that sense the latter is a product of the former. At the same time, however, once having established itself, the totalitarian system mass-produces totalitarian personalities, without which it could not survive. These are personalities created by and adapted to live under the conditions of a totalitarian system and to reproduce its principles. The particularities of the Bulgarian case suggest that we should differentiate between local adherents of a utopian project who were to some degree naive revenge-seekers, on the one hand, and individuals who came of age under the conditions of totalitarian rule and who had absorbed its rules into their very being, on the other. The political emigrant returning from the Soviet Union fit the role of the totalitarian personality perfectly. Almost without exception, not only were their passports Soviet but they themselves were deeply marked by life within the Soviet system. Some of them arrived in Bulgaria having just been released from concentration camps, and once on the ground in their home country they had to prove their trustworthiness. In terms of their internal mindset, they belonged to another reality, that of Bolshevik terror, of the Great Purges, in which they had mastered the art of survival. They took up important posts in Bulgaria, but they were not the only ones: they were joined by the core leadership of the local Communist Party, which had long been strictly following orders from the Moscow foreign bureau of the Central Committee. This is why we cannot say that the processes in Bulgaria unfolded spontaneously; rather, they were orchestrated by the totalitarian personality following a carefully refined formula for establishing total control over society and for its complete transformation in accordance with the model (i.e. the Soviet Union).

Undoubtedly, the towering figure of Georgi Dimitrov took the lead, followed by Vasil Kolarov, Vâlko Chervenkov, Vladimir Poptomov, Ferdinand Kozovski, and hundreds of others. They would not only form the top of the pyramid but would also provide a model for the behavior of its promising foot soldiers. Of course, full responsibility for what happened cannot be placed

Georgi Dimitrov and "people's democracy" 85

squarely on the shoulders of one or another particular individual, no matter how much he may have towered over the others. However, it is worth noting that Georgi Dimitrov, given the image he had acquired, possessed the potential to be transformed into a model, or better yet, into a composite image, an embodiment of the totalitarian personality – a status solidified in party jargon by his clichéd epithet – *leader and teacher of the Bulgarian people.* Precisely Georgi Dimitrov is interesting in this case, since he as an individual combined what is exceptional with what is typical in the character and fate of the totalitarian personality. Without a doubt, Georgi Dimitrov was a clearly distinguished figure on the provincial Bulgarian stage, one whose personal history and position within the international communist movement further fed his charisma. Yet beneath this whole brilliant façade lies a second, hidden and worried face: the face of the potential victim from Stalin's inner circle, striving to master and neutralize the totalitarian leader's arbitrariness. Let us once again recall what Hannah Arendt says about the anthropological changes that occur within people living under totalitarian conditions: they are ideally prepared for two equally possible roles: that of the executioner and that of the victim. Bulgarian political emigrants in the Soviet Union enjoyed privileges and at the same time were hostages. They were Moscow's dependents and had to uphold its policies, while their ability to impose Soviet influence on the Bulgarian political stage was the basic capital that could guarantee their survival. Georgi Dimitrov was no exception. He had to show great talent in order to convince Stalin of his loyalty and usefulness.[1] Many of those around him did not succeed in doing so. Communist political emigrants, not just Bulgarians but from various countries, sent him hundreds of requests for assistance, for intercession before various repressive bodies, yet he could never shake his sense of helplessness in the face of caprice, even when he managed to help. Having survived, unlike many other emigrant-activists from various communist parties, Georgi Dimitrov and his inner circle had no choice but to be on the side of the executioners, thus turning themselves into executioners as well. This psychological split was also transferred to the Bulgarian context. The destruction of "enemies" is understood as an inescapable condition for one's own survival – only a dead enemy cannot himself become an executioner. But in the end, acting as an executioner first by sending instructions from afar and later in his actual deeds and actions after his return to Bulgaria, Georgi Dimitrov nevertheless did not manage to escape the victim's fate. According to unsubstantiated rumors, when Dimitrov fell seriously ill, under the pretext of concern over his health and the need to provide him with competent medical treatment, he was summoned to Moscow, from whence his dead body returned to Bulgaria in order to take part in the organized ritual of national mourning. But even if such rumors of his Kremlin-orchestrated demise are completely unfounded, Stalin and Moscow's attitude toward him even before that had essentially turned him into a political corpse, into an ordinary agent fulfilling their orders, without any particular value of his own in their eyes. The myth of the influential, creative figure from Comintern had

86 *The times of high Stalinism*

been buried in hidebound Bulgarian reality, where there was room only for obedient servants.

Despite the fact that during the years of communist rule, Georgi Dimitrov's body, which lay in a mausoleum in the center of Sofia, constantly kept his memory alive (at the very least because from the tribunal of the mausoleum, his heirs greeted the obligatory mass demonstrations organized in praise of the regime and of the leaders themselves), his place within the rhetoric of party propaganda grew ever more modest and formalized. "The Dimitrov Principles," which were often cited as precepts to be followed, did not contain any real content that would make them relevant within the changing context, besides as a parallel meant to ape the call that had arisen in the USSR for a return to the "pure sources" of the revolution and for following "The Lenin Principles" of party life.

With the passing years, Georgi Dimitrov's legacy became less and less relevant, and, despite the volumes written about him as part of mass party propaganda, the only thing time sifted out was the cliché of the hero of Leipzig. Even today, no complete, objective, documentary and convincingly argued study of his life and work has been undertaken – a study that would be based on the Comintern archives, the Moscow party archives and KGB archives, the archives of the Yugoslav Communist Party, on memoirs and testimonies from collaborators and brothers-in-arms from the international communist movement, as well as on existing Western studies of the period. This is an important and enormous task, which we mention in passing, without pretending that we are capable of even partially compensating for it. To elucidate the place and role of Georgi Dimitrov in one limited period of time – the regime established after September 9, 1944 – we will rely on an accessible and reliable source, his own diary, which was published twenty years ago yet which went practically unnoticed during the turbulent Bulgarian Transition. In his diary, Georgi Dimitrov speaks in the first person and situates himself within the epoch in a way which he himself considered fitting.

Georgi Dimitrov and his diary

Clearly guided by a sense of his own importance following the end of the Leipzig Trial, Georgi Dimitrov kept a pedantically detailed diary, which was nevertheless exceptionally cautious.[2] For him, especially once he was elevated to the head of Comintern, keeping a diary was not an entirely wise and safe undertaking. He must have realized perfectly well that were it to fall into the hands of Stalin's secret police, parts of the diary could be used as arguments against him, turning him into a target of repression. Despite this, he continued to keep a highly detailed diary, whose content is undoubtedly selective, and only addresses things that concerned him personally. This diary is not only a unique testament to a life and an epoch, it is also a unique phenomenon, in so far as it belongs to a functionary of such high rank within the international communist movement who spent long years close to Stalin and who was privy to details at the very heart of Kremlin politics. It is very rare for a person of his stature and biography to leave behind such a document – normally such people take everything they know with them to the grave. This does not mean that we will find something sensational in the diary, something that might pique morbid curiosity. Undoubtedly it contains far less than what Dimitrov knew, but we still find quite a bit.

His undertaking was possible thanks to his talent for maintaining a carefully selected presentation style. We find before us hundreds of pages covering almost three decades, offering recorded facts written dispassionately, without a hint of emotion, even in critical situations, and devoid of any commentary. If commentary does slip in somewhere, it is in the name of the collective subject: the party, the people, the movement, the class . . . This factological neutrality is preserved even when the circumstances being described are far from favorable for Dimitrov himself, as often happened in his relations with Stalin after the end of the war and especially after his return to Bulgaria. This is precisely the reason that the diary did not provoke Stalin's distrust in any way but remained hidden for decades in the archives of the BCP. And it is believable precisely for those reasons.

Dimitrov and Stalin

Georgi Dimitrov, in his capacity as a high-ranking functionary within the international communist movement, was entirely Stalin's creation. He knew this very well and was grateful and loyal until the end of his life. Everything began with the Leipzig Trial, when Moscow and Comintern decided to roll out a massive propaganda campaign against national socialism around the court proceedings. All Comintern's forces were mobilized, the most talented and influential activists and supporters around the world were engaged in the campaign. The clash around the defendants turned into an occasion to measure the strength of the two totalitarian giants' propaganda strategies. In this propaganda war, which was the first of its kind, the side with more experience won out: the communist camp. Georgi Dimitrov found himself at the center of the conflict, given that he played the role assigned to him with a certain amount of talent. The media made him exceptionally popular, and, after the end of the trial, Stalin saw the opportunity to use the symbolic capital amassed by his image as a fighter, transforming him into an emblem of the struggle against fascism and of proletarian solidarity. Georgi Dimitrov appeared to be an exceptionally suitable candidate to lead Comintern. Above all, he was not Russian, so this would deflect insinuations that the Communist International was a puppet in Moscow's hands. Furthermore, in his capacity as a representative of a small party that held no international positions or theoretical ambitions, the choice of Dimitrov would on the one hand be proof of the equality and democratism within the ranks of the international communist movement, while, on the other, Dimitrov himself would not be as hard to manipulate as would a representative from a large and strong party such

88   *The times of high Stalinism*

as the French, Italian or German communist parties. Thus, the elevation of Georgi Dimitrov looked like a reward for his heroic behavior, but, in fact, it was a well-calculated move: he was an impressive figure who would not create problems. Stalin's hunch proved correct: he had found a fitting person, and Georgi Dimitrov was equal to the task entrusted to him.

We can speak of two periods in the relations between Stalin and Dimitrov. The first covers the time of Comintern while the second begins with the Red Army's invasion of Bulgaria, Dimitrov's return and his campaign to establish communist rule in the country. Dimitrov's attitude toward Stalin remained constant, but Stalin's attitude toward Dimitrov changed significantly during the second period. The reason for this is rooted in the different roles he assigned to Dimitrov and the latter's differing ability to fulfill them. In Comintern, Dimitrov strictly carried out Stalin's wishes; he was something like Stalin's unofficial mouthpiece, possessing a certain personal charm and flair for communication. In his informal contact with Stalin, he was informed of the course policy would follow, which allowed him to be the first to publicize the leader's viewpoint, most often speaking in his own name. Thus he managed to impress the leaders of the international communist movement for his farsightedness, since what he said was later confirmed by the supreme authority. Reflecting the leader's hidden light, Dimitrov gradually made a prominent name for himself within the communist movement. He was in constant personal contact or conspiratorial correspondence with the most important figures in the movement at the time, sending instructions and advice everywhere from America to China regarding the accepted strategy. His everyday life included both constant contact with the Kremlin elite as well as family lunches at his villa outside Moscow with the likes of Maurice Thorez, Palmiro Togliatti, Walter Ulbricht, Mátyás Rákosi, Soviet ministers and generals, and so on. All of that could not have failed to inspire self-confidence about his own significance and influence – a self-confidence he never for an instant revealed to Stalin. His diary shows him as an irreproachably devoted, trustworthy person, who constantly feels the need to confirm his position as vassal. The congratulatory telegrams he regularly sent on the leader's birthday are a model of the flattery and obsequiousness that was established etiquette at the totalitarian court. Upon his return to Bulgaria, Dimitrov sent a farewell letter to Stalin on November 3, 1945, which unambiguously showed his awareness of the relations between them:

> Dear Comrade Stalin, as I leave for Bulgaria in connection with the parliamentary elections, I would like to express to you my deepest gratitude for the fact that I have had the opportunity to work under your immediate guidance for many years and thus to learn so much from you, and also for the trust you placed in me. Of course, I will make every effort to justify that trust in the future as well. But I beg you to grant me the opportunity to benefit from your exceptionally necessary and valuable advice in the future as well.[3]

Georgi Dimitrov and "people's democracy" 89

In fact, this "request" to benefit from the leader's advice in the future as well was essentially an assurance that he would continue to carry out the instructions he was given. In this way, he himself defined his status – both past and future – as one of dependence and complete subservience.

As compensation, he was left with the external trappings of such status – the privileges that the highest stratum of the Soviet nomenclature enjoyed. During his stellar period at Comintern, Georgi Dimitrov ranked sixth in the list of the highest Soviet nomenclature and enjoyed all the benefits granted to this category of people. Upon his departure, he kept all the perks he had been enjoying in Moscow until then: his apartment in the so-called house of government (where the highest-ranking Soviet leaders lived), his villa in Meshcherino near Moscow, and the special treatment. He also transferred his established lifestyle to Bulgaria. The Soviet secret services surely prepared the way for his arrival, selecting and securing a place for him to live in Sofia, as well as assuring the necessary comforts. In postwar Bulgaria, a Stalinesque living standard and Soviet protection were secured for him.[4] In Bulgaria, Dimitrov led not so much a double as a divided life – the reason for this lay not only in his dual citizenship but also in his inability to choose between his two homelands. His devotion to the Soviet nation and his taste for life there were obvious. Until his death, his apartment in Moscow and the dacha in Meshcherino were maintained and inhabited as if they were his own home. When he was in Moscow, he would receive guests there and hold receptions for members of the Bulgarian delegations who were visiting the Soviet capital. Georgi Dimitrov traveled to Moscow very frequently, sometimes incognito, and maintained his contacts with the supreme Soviet leaders, to whom he had direct access, and also underwent medical treatment in the famous Barvikha sanatorium. And when he was in Bulgaria, Soviet doctors would go there to treat him. This was a person with two countries and two duties, which he hoped in vain to combine. His behavior at times gave the impression that he felt as if he had been sent to Bulgaria on a business trip.

Upon their return from the Soviet Union, Bulgarian political emigrants did what was necessary to reproduce this familiar model of privileges in Bulgaria. Given the conditions of postwar deprivation, Georgi Dimitrov personally recommended that a system of "special supply" be introduced for high-ranking party and government figures, thus laying the foundation for the system of privileges for the communist nomenclature that was already taking shape in Bulgaria. Initially, this behavior on the part of the newcomers evoked considerable bewilderment and discontent in the ranks of the local communists and former partisans. We have access to the later testimony of one of them, Rusi Hristozov, who was interviewed by the documentary film director Malina Petrova during November 1989:

> At the Sixteenth Plenum during June 1948, a huge argument broke out in the Politburo. Traycho (Kostov) demanded that Dimitrov engage in serious self-criticism for violating the collective method, for living cut

90   *The times of high Stalinism*

off from the party, from the people and so on. He wanted Dimitrov's report for the Sixteenth Plenum to be revised. A serious argument broke out and Traycho said: 'If you don't revise the report, I'll come out with a co-report.' There was also another such moment at the beginning of the Plenum – Nikola Pavlov and Stefan Bogdanov provided information about Roza Dimitrova, that she was acting like a queen, going around to orphanages and giving out presents, and that Dimitrov was living in the palace.[5]

Of course, not all local communists expressed such discontent, while these accusations against Dimitrov were later used as an argument to vilify Traycho Kostov – he was accused not only of anti-Sovietism and factionalism but also of leftist sectarianism. The crucial thing in this case is that Dimitrov and his Moscow suite created a model to be imitated, a model that proved to be exceptionally attractive and which during the 1960s developed into generalized corruption.

In Sofia, Dimitrov could flatter himself that he was no longer playing second fiddle, but in fact his rank had changed substantially for the worse. After occupying the grand international stage, he had ended up in a small province on the periphery of the Soviet empire that was taking shape; he was out of his element in a situation he did not appear fully equipped to handle. His new situation nevertheless had one advantage: far from the leader's watchful eye, he had room for more independence, especially with respect to the endless specific tasks the situation thrust upon him. He was one of the few Bulgarians known throughout Europe and even the world, and that, along with his close contact with the most powerful person in the world at the time, could not fail to impress the provincial public. In Bulgaria, he was "number one" and was flattered with the title *vozhd* or "leader," even though he would never be able to forget that the expression "the long arm of Moscow" was more than just an empty phrase. Still, he missed the Comintern stage. In other words, his native stage proved too small for him. This drove him to make certain unapproved and immoderate moves that irritated Moscow. On his visits to one or another of the "brotherly" countries in Eastern Europe, where he was received as the former General Secretary of Comintern, he took the liberty of improvising on the theme of their common future and possible joint initiatives. Since his close ties to the Kremlin were well known, many thought that he continued to express the official Soviet position, but this was no longer the case. Georgi Dimitrov was not sufficiently conscious of the new role that had been assigned to him. He was not expected to theorize but rather to successfully carry out one particular dirty deed: to clear the communists' path to absolute power and to guarantee Soviet hegemony in Bulgaria. Almost every one of Dimitrov's international initiatives met with hostility from Stalin.

During an official visit to Romania, Georgi Dimitrov, without the "center's" approval, took the liberty of stating his desire to build a federation or confederation between Eastern European countries and to form a customs union.

Georgi Dimitrov and "people's democracy"   91

This statement was considered damaging, and Stalin, not sparing Dimitrov's ego, wrote him directly: "It is difficult to judge what could have moved you to make such a hasty and unadvised announcement at the press conference."[6] One month later (February 9, 1945), Georgi Dimitrov was summoned to Moscow for talks concerning plans to create a federation with Yugoslavia. This was an old idea championed by Stalin himself, who wanted to build a strong communist country in the center of the Balkans. This time, Georgi Dimitrov's mistake was his failure to recognize the seriousness of the conflict between Moscow and Belgrade, which was rooted precisely in the nature of relations between the two countries: Belgrade insisted on equality and did not accept direct dictates. Stalin had organized a comradely mini-trial for him:

> It seems to us that Comrade Dimitrov is getting carried away to a certain extent with press conferences and interviews [. . .] We have to take up a position, because everyone – both our enemies and our friends – thought that was our viewpoint [. . .] You are a political figure and you have to think not only about your own intentions, but also about the results of your statements.[7]

Molotov, who was also present at the meeting, added: "In the future, Comrade Dimitrov must spare both himself and us the danger of such statements."[8]

Stalin's harshness in his relations with Dimitrov was demonstrative. He was trying to show him his true place in the contemporary communist movement and who defined the borders of his competency: "You shouldn't give interviews so often. Do you want to say something new and puzzle the whole world? You speak as if you are still General Secretary of Comintern [. . .] All of you are either inexperienced people, or else you let yourselves get carried away like Komsomol members, who fly right into the flame like moths."[9] Dimitrov knew perfectly well which flame Stalin meant; thus he did not attempt to defend his ideas for a instant or even his right to speak in his own name. And this corresponded perfectly to the state of affairs in Bulgaria. He immediately capitulated in the face of any criticism, curled up in his shell, acted like a guilty schoolboy, and promised that "such declarations will not be made in the future."[10] After being criticized for his statements in Romania, he immediately replied with a telegram: "I accept your criticism with gratitude. I will draw the necessary conclusions."[11] However, he then decided that this was insufficient and six days later sent a new letter:

> I consider it superfluous to try to persuade you that someone in our party, least of all myself, would consciously take any measure in our domestic or foreign policy that would contradict the positions of the BWP(C) and which would be to the detriment of our common work [. . .] Regarding my unfortunate statements, I have already learned a sufficient lesson from your criticism and you can rest assured that such carelessness will not happen again.[12]

92   *The times of high Stalinism*

Moscow's harsh pressure and the sick man's meekness and weak character are first-hand evidence of the decline of the myth of the hero of Leipzig, of the myth of the important, independent figure of the activist in the international communist movement. Dimitrov awkwardly took up his new role, which was quite humble in comparison to his ambitions.

On the nature of "the people's democracy"

In recent years, one concept that had been forgotten by chroniclers and theoreticians of the history of the BCP has returned to historical publications and even high-school textbooks: *the people's democracy*. A tendency has been taking shape within historiography that resembles an emerging revisionism. The claim has been revived that between 1944 and 1947 a form of government existed in Bulgaria that was different both from the overthrown monarchy and from the subsequent communist regime. This intermediary, transitional form of government is presented as combining parliamentary democracy and the leading role of the Communist Party as well as multiple forms of ownership and a policy of social solidarity, with the decisive interference of the state in economic life. However, Soviet hegemony and Stalin personally, supported by his marionettes within the party, demanded that this form of government be sabotaged and that the country be put the track toward Soviet totalitarianism. Why did the post-communist situation after 1989 revive this long-forgotten episode from the country's development and in the history of Bulgarian communism? Undoubtedly, this revival was due to the formal analogy with the Transition the country underwent following the change of November 10, 1989, whose vicissitudes and failures created the impression among part of the population of some missed opportunity for improved social benefits, for the combination of the best aspects of democracy and socialism. It was as if it were a question of a repeated near-miss; hints of disappointment over squandered opportunities during the second Transition slip into the narrative about the failure of the people's democracy.

In the debate over how to evaluate the half-century of communist rule, this early episode is also used to defend the hypothesis of the regime's contradictory trajectory and of the various possibilities it contained. We are faced with the question, "Does this episode from the history of the country truly constitute some independent stage, an isolated period, which, even if only hypothetically, could have resulted in an outcome different from that which actually occurred?" Today it is perfectly clear that such a claim contradicts the very logic of the processes within Bulgarian society after the end of the war. *The people's democracy* was the stillborn child of the Fatherland Front's mutation of so-called communist antifascism. Dimitrov's diary helps us reconstruct the history of the concept.

The diary contains indisputable facts that can be traced chronologically, showing that the concept of the people's democracy was a product of the Kremlin's ideological laboratory. Stalin promoted the concept as a

Georgi Dimitrov and "people's democracy" 93

simultaneously propagandistic and tactical move, without ever believing in its true value even for an instant. Of course he did not admit this publicly but in confidential conversations and in briefings in the form of suggestions to people who were sent "to work" in the new territories where the empire intended to establish its influence. He did not look upon his interlocutors as equal partners who could be privy to his innermost intentions or who were in a position to understand the complexity of the game. He would reveal the truth to them bit by bit. He likely believed that for his plan to succeed his agents themselves had to believe in the idea of the people's democracy to a certain extent. This is why he allowed them to present themselves to their own countrymen as the creators of the idea.

Why did Stalin resort to this strategic move? Because he needed time to take full control of his postwar acquisitions, a process that could be hindered by local communists, who were eager to experience and consume at first hand the benefits of total, undivided power. The transitional form was intended to play a dual role: on the one hand, it would delude the allies as to Moscow's true intentions (until the peace treaty was signed and Soviet influence was consolidated), while on the other hand, it would keep the local communist forces' impatience in check. Following Stalin's recommendation, Georgi Dimitrov, acting from Moscow, exercised the full measure of his authority to cool the local communists' impatience to undertake a hasty course toward the dictatorship of the proletariat and the expropriation of bourgeois property. On September 9, 1944, Dimitrov sent the following telegram to the Central Committee:

> We have learned that in Varna *soviets* [councils] have been formed and are disarming the police. Take the quickest and most decisive measures for the immediate cessation of such activities. Soviets should not be formed anywhere, nor should the police be disarmed. Such actions are nothing but grist for our enemies' mill, the enemies of our people. Maintain a strictly democratic position.[13]

This position made possible the establishment of two Fatherland Front governments, in which the coalition was ever more openly dominated by the communists. Nevertheless, the urge to quickly settle scores with competitors and opponents was continually growing. This led to a meeting at the Kremlin in February 1946 (the formal pretext was to approve the new constitution that had been prepared for the country), at which Georgi Dimitrov, speaking in the name of the party rank-and-file, expressed dissatisfaction at the slow pace of the changes. The Bulgarian delegation's position caused Stalin to be extremely frank, explaining the rules of the game to them as if they were slow-witted schoolchildren. (The conversation was taken down in shorthand by Traycho Kostov and subsequently included by Dimitrov in the diary.) He even accused them of sectarianism and recommended that they make an attempt to recruit Bulgaria's large rural population to the cause.

94   *The times of high Stalinism*

Your constitution must be a people's constitution; with fewer details, if possible; the constitution of a people's republic with a parliamentary regime; don't frighten the non-working classes; create a constitution that is more right-leaning than Yugoslavia's [. . .] It is not advantageous to have a Workers' Party but nevertheless to call it communist [. . .] You need to unite the working class with the other laboring classes on the basis of a minimal program, the time will come for the maximal program [. . .] The party will be communist in its essence, but it will receive wider support and a convenient mask for the time being. This will help you in the transition toward socialism along a special path – without the dictatorship of the proletariat.[14]

Stalin's final words deserve special attention: "without the dictatorship of the proletariat." It is difficult to believe that they were uttered a year and a half after taking control of the country. But in these Moscow briefings Stalin played a dirty trick on Dimitrov, who clearly found it difficult to interpret the leader's intentions precisely. This became clear two years later, when, in connection with the concept of the people's democracy, the following clash arose between the harsh teacher and the vain, slow-witted student.

At the end of 1948, during yet another visit to the Barvikha sanatorium, Georgi Dimitrov spoke with another patient there, Wille Kuusinen (Chairman of the Presidium of the Supreme Soviet of the Karelo–Finnish Soviet Socialist Republic). In their discussion of the situation in Bulgaria, they touched on the problem of the people's democracy. Dimitrov recorded their conversations almost literally in his diary. Together, the two men reached the conclusion that the people's democracy is a means for establishing socialism, alongside the dictatorship of the proletariat. Under then-current conditions, thanks to the help of the USSR, it was possible to transition from capitalism to socialism without the dictatorship of the proletariat. "The means are different, but the end is the same," the two men concluded.[15] According to Dimitrov's definition, the people's democracy is "a government of the great majority of the people under the leadership of the working class," which establishes an economic monopoly (through nationalization, the liquidation of capitalistic elements – that is, through terror). Stalin's theory of the intensification of class struggle can even be found in Dimitov's notes. In other words, for him the people's democracy means "the constant reinforcement of the position of the working class led by the Communist Party in all spheres of governmental, economic, sociopolitical and cultural life." The transition to communism without "the creation of a Soviet regime," that is, without the formation of *soviets* or "councils," is possible, since "the people's democracy can and even must in particular historical circumstances, as experience has already shown, successfully carry out the functions of the dictatorship of the proletariat."[16] The people's democracy is a strategic move for establishing control over society by other means, which are not so radical but which also result in the elimination of the class enemy. Inspired by these conversations, which once again offered him an opportunity to theorize about a general issue in complete agreement with Stalin's hints from the preceding years and encouraged by a high-ranking Soviet functionary's interest in the problem, Dimitrov decided to attempt to rehabilitate himself as a theoretician. This can be seen as a desperate attempt to once again take up the pose of a theoretician from the international communist movement which was elaborating Marxist-Leninist teachings within their contemporary context. On November 1, 1948, he sent a letter to Stalin familiarizing the latter with his ideas: "Following instructions from the Central Committee of the [BCP], I turn to you with the urgent request that you acquaint yourself with our viewpoints on the questions discussed here and that you help us with your advice to correctly orient the party in its forthcoming difficult and complex activity."[17] There is no evidence that anyone within the Central Committee of the BCP was informed of this initiative, or that anyone shared his theoretical anguish.

The time was not right for this, however, and Stalin, seeming to have forgotten what he himself had said on such questions, brutally dashed Dimitrov's hopes of returning to the international stage as an independent figure. His answer reads:

> The people's democracy does not carry out the functions of the dictatorship of the proletariat, rather it is a form of the dictatorship of the proletariat. In the history of Marxist thought, two possibilities or forms of the dictatorship of the proletariat have emerged [. . .] One form is the democratic republic, which Marx and Engels saw in the Paris Commune [. . .] After that, Lenin discovered the Soviet form of the dictatorship of the proletariat, which was more suitable and expedient in our circumstances [. . .] In your case, where power was seized not by the working class through an internal uprising, but through outside aid from Soviet troops, i.e. easily, without particular efforts, it can occur without the Soviet form, returning to the form which Marx and Engels spoke of, i.e. the people's republic parliamentary form [. . .] but this regime will implement the functions of the proletarian dictatorship.[18]

This is exactly what Georgi Dimitrov himself had been saying. But while he was laying out his arguments about the people's republic, the whole game was already up: Bulgarian society was already completely dominated by the Communist Party and was undergoing an intense process of sovietization. His musings are completely inadequate both in terms of the actual state of affairs in the country, as well as in terms of the historical moment – at least in the eyes of Stalin, who had grown very distrustful after the incident with Tito and who likely suspected that some pretensions to autonomy lay behind Dimitrov's theorizations, which were completely pointless from Stalin's perspective.

96 *The times of high Stalinism*

The moment when the Cold War was intensifying was not the time to emphasize differences from the Soviet system. In the following years and decades, Marxist-Leninist theoretical thought would fully accept the Stalinist viewpoint on the question of the transitional period. "Between the capitalist and the communist society, there exists a period of revolutionary transformation of the former into the latter. A politically transitional period also corresponds to this period and the state during this period cannot be anything but a revolutionary dictatorship of the proletariat."[19]

Dimitrov's own party was not particularly adamant in its support of his theoretical variations on the theme of the people's democracy. Before the Seventh Congress of the BCP, Todor Zhivkov offered this clarification: Despite the fact that after the victory a multiparty system was established in the country, the party had never shared power. He further declared:

> The Central Committee has always believed that the revolution in our country, which took the form of the people's republic, from its very beginnings and in its objective laws was a repetition of the main essence of the Great October Socialist Revolution, that it was a continuation of the work of the October Revolution in the Bulgarian context, that it was part of and a manifestation of the great international march from capitalism toward socialism, which began with the revolution of the Soviet workers and villagers in October 1917, that from its very beginnings it possessed a socialist character.[20]

Here is what is said in the fourth edition of the official *History of the Bulgarian Communist Party*:

> The participation of other parties as well in the victorious uprising of September 9, 1944, under the given historical conditions was a great success for Marxist-Leninist policy, carried out by the avant-garde of the proletariat. Even on the day of its victory, the new government began to carry out the functions of the dictatorship of the proletariat. The existence of the Fatherland Front did not replace, but rather consolidated the party's leading role. The primary, crucial posts within the state power were in the party's hands.[21]

On July 22, 1949, Georgi Dimitrov died in Moscow after a long illness, humiliated and isolated. Yet his corpse turned out to be exceptionally useful and necessary, once turned into a symbol of the indivisible unity of the working people. Claude Lefort finds at the bottom of the totalitarian project precisely this imaginary drive for the restoration of social unity as a body, where again the embodiment of power within the figure of the leader, his cult of personality, plays a definite role. Such personalization was effected in the Soviet Union by Stalin and in Bulgaria by Georgi Dimitrov, who, despite having lost all of his historical authority, was canonized as "leader and teacher of the Bulgarian people." His figure in the transformed ideological *mise-en-scène* successfully replaced the figure of the King. It is not at all a coincidence that the Bulgarian people, with equal outpourings of grief and tears at their untimely deaths, accompanied both the King and their party secretary to their graves (regardless of how orchestrated the manifestations of grief may have been in the second case). Thus, the mausoleum of Georgi Dimitrov came into being. It housed and preserved the physical body of the leader, guaranteeing his continuing, tangible presence in the life of the community. The leader's mummy, sunk into mystical silence and far from the temptations and dangers of real politics, offered proof that there had been no break, that the community's identity had not been called into question, since there was a body personifying it.

Notes

1 A story circulated among the circle of Bulgarian political emigrants that after the Leipzig trial, when Stalin met Georgi Dimitrov in Moscow, the Soviet leader surprised him with the question of why he thought he hadn't been convicted in Germany. Dimitrov replied that he had been acquitted because he had defended himself successfully and the whole international progressive community had risen to his defense, for which he was personally grateful to Comrade Stalin. Stalin shook his head and cryptically replied that Hitler simply hadn't learned how to hold trials yet. Georgi Dimitrov must have remembered this statement well.

2 The diary, which was preserved in the archives of the Bulgarian Communist Party, was classified until the mid-1990s. Its first edition was published by the St. Climent Ohridski University Press in 1997. In the following years, due to its enormous historical value, it was published in the major European languages. See the American edition: Georgi Dimitrov, *Diary of Georgi Dimitrov, 1933–1949*, New Haven, Conn.: Yale University, 2003. Bulgarian edition: Georgi Dimitrov, *Dnevnik 9 mart 1933–6 fevruari 1949*, Sofia: St. Kliment Ohridski, 1997.

3 Dimitrov, *Dnevnik*, p. 510.

4 Dimitrov, *Dnevnik*, p. 508.

5 Rusi Hristozov, "Entsiklopediya na zloto 4 (intervyu s Malina Petrova)," *Glasove*, 27 (July 28–August 3, 2006). After the referendum of September 8, 1946, regarding the impending reform of state government which abolished the monarchy, Georgi Dimitrov settled into the Vrana Palace, the residence of the royal family.

6 Dimitrov, *Dnevnik*, p. 595.

7 Dimitrov, *Dnevnik*, p. 597.

8 Dimitrov, *Dnevnik*, p. 597.

9 Dimitrov, *Dnevnik*, p. 598.

10 Dimitrov, *Dnevnik*, p. 598.

11 Dimitrov, *Dnevnik*, p. 595.

12 Dimitrov, *Dnevnik*, p. 595.

13 Dimitrov, *Dnevnik*, p. 320.

14 Dimitrov, *Dnevnik*, p. 534.

15 Dimitrov, *Dnevnik*, p. 633.

98 *The times of high Stalinism*

16 Dimitrov, *Dnevnik*, p. 639.
17 Dimitrov, *Dnevnik*, p. 638.
18 Dimitrov, *Dnevnik*, pp. 644–645.
19 *Filosofskaya entsiklopediya*, vol. II, Moscow: Miysl, 1969.
20 *Istoriya na Bâlgarskata komunisticheska partiya*, Sofia: Partizdat, 1967, p. 212.
21 *Istoriya na Bâlgarskata komunisticheska partiya*, p. 441.

3   Bulgaria in the years of classical Stalinism

From September 22 to September 28, 1947, a meeting took place in the Polish city of Szklarska Poreba, which brought together the communist parties from the countries occupied by the Soviet army plus two from Western Europe: the Italian and French communist parties. In the reports, which were coordinated in advance with Stalin, it was noted that the political situation in the world required an accelerated transition toward the building of socialism in Eastern Europe. In practice, this meant destroying the few remaining freedoms in the political, economic and cultural spheres and shifting toward the establishment of full control over society and state institutions by the communist parties in each country. All the communist leaders had to acknowledge the USSR as the leading example and strictly follow its governmental-political model.[1] In terms of foreign policy, this entailed these countries giving their full and unconditional obedience the Soviet Union. To be able to coordinate the activities of the various communist parties, a decision was made to create a constantly functioning information bureau, the Communist Information Bureau (known as "Cominform"), headquartered in Belgrade.

The BWP(C) was soon informed of the new course set by Moscow by Vâlko Chervenkov, who read a report before the Central Committee. The report sharply criticized the party's policy over the previous years, accusing it of allowing an opposition to form and of giving the "reaction" too much space for public expression and taking the party to task it for not carrying out social transformations in the socialist spirit from the very beginning.[2] To the leadership of the BWP(C), this report was a clear signal that they needed to mount an offensive in all spheres of social life. As a first step in response to this pointed appeal, mass nationalization in the industrial and financial sector was undertaken in December 1947. By liquidating private ownership over production, the economic independence of most of the population was abolished, leaving it wholly dependent on the government.

However, the most important changes at this stage continued to be changes within the political system. Their basic goal was to do away with any political party that differed from the Communist Party and that might in some way be able to present an alternative course of development for Bulgaria. After the brutal defeat of the opposition, they were left with the far easier task of eliminating the parties within the Fatherland Front, which had already been completely stripped of any distinct identity. Since it was ideologically quite close to the communists, the BWSDP was organizationally swallowed up, with the majority of its members joining the ranks of the BWP(C). The other two Fatherland Front parties – Zveno and the Radical Party – decided to dissolve themselves at the beginning of 1949. The situation with BANU was slightly different. After its leadership was taken over by Georgi Traykov, who was completely loyal to the communists, in the autumn of 1948, the Agrarian Party officially announced that it was adopting the BWP(C)'s program in full and would actively join in the building of socialism.[3] This allowed it to formally preserve its independent existence, which also permitted the regime's propaganda to claim that there was not a one-party system in Bulgaria. Of course, BANU remained under the constant control of the communists, who even set quotas on its acceptance of new members.

This fate of the Fatherland Front is not at all surprising, either. In February of the same year, it decided to transform itself into a mass social organization. As a result of this restructuring, it completely lost its political significance and ceased to be even formally a coalition. Its structures were already openly under the direct and total control of the communist apparatus.[4] The General Workers' Professional Union was absolutely subservient to the Communist Party. It, too, became a mass organization for workers through which the ruling party's economic goals were implemented. Party control over the young generation, which had to be brought up entirely in the communist spirit, was deemed particularly important. In addition to transformations within the educational system, communist indoctrination was also implemented through the ever more mass structures of the organizations Young Septembrists (for children) and the Union of the People's Youth (for teens and young adults), which in 1949 began to be called the Dimitrov Union for the People's Youth.

The second major wave of repression

In December 1948, the Fifth Congress of the BWP(C) was held. The main task formulated by the Congress was the transition toward building socialism as a total social system. In other words, this meant establishing the structures of the totalitarian state. At the Congress, the party abandoned its old name of the Bulgarian Workers Party (Communists) and rechristened itself the Bulgarian Communist Party. The fact that an opposition no longer existed and that all social, professional, cultural, academic, athletic and other organizations were under strict party control did not mean that political persecution in Bulgaria ceased. On the contrary, in response to Cominform's conclusion that at that political moment "the class struggle was intensifying," terror in the country increased. In 1948, the number of inmates in camps reached record levels; on the island of Belene alone there were more than 4,500 prisoners, most interred for political reasons. The number of Bulgarians forced from their homes and places of birth also reached record levels: more than 6,600 families, which meant nearly 30,000 people.[5] Given the fact that the official opposition had been totally liquidated, it was inevitable that opponents would begin to be discovered within the ranks of the ruling party. The directive was given to search out "the enemy within the party." Thus, what was new in comparison to the preceding period in Bulgaria was that the full force of violence was also aimed at activists from the Communist Party.

As in most processes within the country, the signal for this was again received from outside. With the aim of fully subjugating the countries from the Eastern Bloc and eradicating even the most insignificant expressions of independence among the European communist parties, Moscow undertook a powerful campaign against the Yugoslav leader, Josip Broz Tito. Besides wanting to eliminate a statesman who behaved far too independently, Stalin's idea was that with the destruction of such an authoritative communist figure like Tito, he would be giving a clear example to all the other Eastern European leaders of what their fate might be – especially since none of them enjoyed the public influence of their Yugoslav counterpart. Soviet accusations were formulated in the spring of 1948 via Cominform. Tito was branded a nationalist who did not defend the principles of communist internationalism (that is, he refused to submit to the Soviet Union), the authoritarian leader of the party and so on. The Yugoslav communists were called upon to remove their party leader. When this did not happen but instead the precise opposite occurred – Tito strengthened his position by challenging the pro-Soviet communists – the rupture between the USSR and Yugoslavia was complete. This conflict was used to begin mass purges within the Eastern European communist parties with the goal of eliminating all communist functionaries who were inclined to demonstrate more independence in implementing the domestic policy of their countries.[6] Besides replacing the communist leadership with people completely loyal to Moscow, the trials against "supporters of Tito" all over Eastern Europe were part of the intense power struggles raging within the communist parties themselves.

In Bulgaria, the attack was aimed at the Organizational Secretary of the BCP, Traycho Kostov. Besides that fact that, as the party's second-in-command after Georgi Dimitrov, his elimination would have a strong social effect, he was chosen because he had refused to provide confidential information about Bulgaria's foreign trade to Soviet specialists. The dispute was touched off by Stalin personally, who on December 5, 1948, at a meeting with the Bulgarian delegation in Moscow, harshly attacked Traycho Kostov, who was present at the meeting, accusing him of nationalism and anti-Sovietism. After seeing the clear opinion of the "leader of the international proletariat," the leaders of the BCP began feverishly distancing themselves from Kostov's activities and obligingly "discovering" new transgressions committed against the USSR by their fellow communist functionary who had fallen out of favor.[7] Vasil Kolarov was especially militant about these denunciations, since in the situation taking shape he saw an excellent opportunity to eliminate a rival in the struggle to identify a replacement for Georgi Dimitrov, who was already clearly quite ill.

102   *The times of high Stalinism*

Tryacho Kostov engaged in deeply repentant self-criticism, but this was not sufficient to dispel the threat hanging over his head. In March 1949, he was removed from the Politburo of the Central Committee of the BCP and from the government. This punishment, of course, was not sufficient, thus a court case was opened against him as well. The same tactic that had been used to crush the opposition was again employed. First, trials began against lower-ranking public figures, in which it was "proven" that an entire conspiracy against the people's power had been created, personally led by the main suspect – Traycho Kostov in this case. Such a trial also mounted against the industrialist/communist Kiril Slavov. After horrifying torture, the defendant made a "confession" in which he accused Kostov of creating an anti-revolutionary organization that carried out directives from the English secret service.[8] Now armed with such solid "evidence" against him, in the summer of 1949, forces from the Interior Ministry arrested Kostov. In September of the same year, again on the basis of evidence provided by Slavov, who had died in investigative detention, almost all the economic ministers, deputy ministers, and directors of economic and financial institutions were arrested by the *militsia*. The trial against Traycho Kostov took place in December 1949 and ended in a death sentence, which was carried out the same month. In the trial against him, numerous high-ranking economic and government leaders were also convicted, many of whom had undertaken specialized studies or completed their university education in Western Europe. The most prominent such figures included the Finance Minister, Professor Ivan Stefanov; the Minister of Electrification, Waters and Natural Resources, Manol Sekelarov; and the Director of the Bulgarian National Bank (BNB), Tsonyo Tsonchev. They were all harshly sentenced to years in solitary confinement.

The growing hysteria to find enemies within the party engulfed not only the economic sphere but all important state institutions. A vigorous purge was carried out within the army, where, alongside the total elimination of royalist officers, people who had until then been considered loyal party followers were also subject to investigation. The trials involved many generals who had participated in the preparation and execution of the coup of September 9, as well as a series of former partisans who had assumed high ranks within the army's political leadership. Not even the repressive bodies within the Interior Ministry and State Security were passed over. Some of the executioners from the preceding period now fell victim to the very same machine they had so fervently created. Blows also reigned down on rank-and-file members of the BCP. Under the pretext that many enemies of the people had hidden by joining the party's ranks, detailed investigations into the family lineage and past of communists accepted into the party after September 9 were launched. Mass expulsions from the party followed (nearly 20 percent of the rank-and-file membership), and such individuals were fired from their jobs and not infrequently sent to camps as well. Within only a few short years, the number of persecuted communists surpassed 100,000.[9]

Vâlko Chervenkov: the new charismatic leader

While the dispute with Traycho Kostov was unfolding, the ground was being prepared for significant leadership changes within the BCP, and hence within the Bulgarian state. In March 1949, Georgi Dimitrov left for medical treatment at Barvikha, the sanatorium for high-ranking Soviet party nomenclature. Despite official reports that his condition was improving, he never returned to Bulgaria; after his death on July 2, the struggle for party leadership began, which was skillfully stoked and guided by Stalin. After the removal of Traycho Kostov as the most serious contender for the post of First Secretary, Vasil Kolarov, who had long experience as a communist functionary, emerged as a potential choice. Stalin, however, did not support Kolarov, preferring instead Vâlko Chervenkov, who was far more devoted to him and whose common-law wife was Georgi Dimitrov's youngest sister (even though they were never officially married). Soviet representatives in Bulgaria made Stalin's preferences known to the communist leadership; as a result, in July Kolarov was not allowed to head the party but only to assume leadership of the Council of Ministers. In practice, from that moment on, Chervenkov took up the leading role within the BCP. In subsequent meetings with Bulgarian communists, Stalin let it be understood ever more openly that he considered Chervenkov the future leader of the country.[10] The question of who would be Georgi Dimitrov's successor was ultimately solved without dramatic twists, since the elderly Vasil Kolarov soon died on January 23, 1950.

The overall construction of Vâlko Chervenkov as a communist functionary took place within conditions that had allowed him to acquire exceptionally valuable skills and that had opened his path not only to the supreme leadership of the party but also, more importantly, had secured him the support and trust of the omnipotent ruler of Eastern Europe – Stalin. Born in 1900, Chervenkov had joined the Communist Party already in the extremist phase of its development (after 1919) and thus did not experience the ideological qualms felt by activists familiar with its more normal and moderate period from the time of narrow socialism.[11] Thus, without any doubts or pangs of conscience, he took part in organizing the Septembrist Uprising in 1923 and subsequently helped establish the terrorist course of action for the illegal BCP by acting as the contact between the party leadership and its military groups. He participated in the preparations for a series of murders, for which he was condemned to death *in absentia*. In 1925, he emigrated to the USSR, and over the course of twenty years he was able to observe and study at first hand the construction and functioning of the Soviet Union's communist totalitarian system. In Moscow, he began diligently studying Marxist-Leninist dogma, and his effort soon paid off: he became a teacher and later director of the International Lenin School. Unlike the vast majority of Bulgarian communists, Vâlko Chervenkov was highly educated. Moreover, he had exactly the right education acquired exactly in the right place.

104 *The times of high Stalinism*

Of course, being head of the international school allowed him to establish numerous contacts with communist figures all over the world, which soon brought him to the attention of the people's commissariat of internal affairs (the Stalinist police, known by the Russian acronym NKVD). Actions were undertaken for his arrest, but, having been forewarned, Chervenkov managed to escape from his home and immediately sought help from Georgi Dimitrov. While the Comintern Chairman may not have managed to save hundreds of other blacklisted Bulgarian communists, when it came to his brother-in-law, Dimitrov was clearly more convincing. In the end, the charges against Chervenkov were dropped.

During World War II, Chervenkov strictly carried out Moscow's orders, and, via Hristo Botev radio station, where he was editor-in-chief, he gave Bulgarian communists rigorous instructions for action that were thoroughly subordinated to Soviet policy in the region. Thus, as head of the state and party in Bulgaria, Vâlko Chervenkov could be nothing but what he had always been for the greater part of his life: an agent who unwaveringly carried out Stalin's will.

As in every totalitarian model, which demands the establishment of total submission to the party and state leader, in Bulgaria an impressive cult of personality began to form around Vâlko Chervenkov. It began in September 1950, when his fiftieth birthday was celebrated. The ceremony became a national event, exceeding the scope of such celebrations of the royal family from the previous period many times over. An exhibit was organized displaying the hundreds of gifts he had received. Local party structures organized mass visits to it by labor collectives in Sofia and the provinces. This well-coordinated campaign was presented as a spontaneous demonstration of the people's full support of "the great successor to the work of Georgi Dimitrov."

Having assumed full power within the party and the state, Chervenkov became the basic political factor in the country. His statements and conclusions immediately received the support of the entire high-ranking party leadership and were turned into resolutions and laws. Propaganda in the country outdid itself praising his political wisdom, his glorious communist past and his dedication to the ideas of Marxism-Leninism-Stalinsism. Like other totalitarian leaders, Vâlko Chervenkov was credited with genius that expressed itself in a wide variety of spheres: politics, economics, culture, and science. Everything he said or wrote was the subject of ecstatic commentary on the part of the labor collectives in state enterprises as well as within academic and cultural institutions. Factories, power plants, agricultural collectives and schools were named after him.

Notes

1 Draganov Dragomir, *Komunisticheskoto dvizhenie sled Vtorata svetovna voyna*, Sofia: Sv. Kl. Ohridski, 1990, pp. 36–39.
2 Ognyanov, *Dârzhavno-politicheskata sistema na Bâlgariya*, pp. 192–193.
3 Isusov, *Politicheskiyat zhivot*, pp. 368–375.

Bulgaria in the years of Stalinism   105

4 Aleksandâr Vezenkov, *Vlastovite strukturi na Bâlgarskata komunisticheska partiya 1944–1989*, Sofia: Institute for Studies of the Recent Past/Ciela, 2008, pp. 295–296.
5 Stoyanova and Iliev, *Politicheski opasni litsa*, pp. 63–66.
6 Soulet, Jean-François, *Histoire de l'Europe de l'Est de la seconde guerre mondiale à nos jours*, Paris: Armand Colin, 2006. Cited in the Bulgarian edition: *Istoriya na Iztochna Evropa ot Vtorata svetovna voyna do nashi dni*, Sofia: Lira print, 2007, pp. 127–134.
7 Mito Isusov, *Poslednata godina na Traycho Kostov*, Sofia: Hristo Botev, 1990, pp. 36–52.
8 Gospodinka Nikova, "Dramatichnata promyana na partiynoto râkovodstvo prez 1949 g.," in *Prelomni vremena: Yubileen sbornik v chest na 65–godishninata na prof. Lyubomir Ognyanov*, Sofia: St. Kliment Ohridski, 2006, p. 523.
9 Kalinova and Baeva, *Bâlgarskite prehodi, 1939–2002*, pp. 101–102.
10 Nikova, "Dramatichnata promyana na partiynoto," pp. 526–527.
11 At the beginning of the twentieth century, the social democrats in Bulgaria were divided into two groups: the doctrinarians who closely adhered to Marxist ideas and who were called the "narrow" socialists, and the reform-minded group known as the "broad" socialists. In 1919, the narrow socialists adopted Lenin's theses and began calling themselves "communists."

4 Building the communist economy in Bulgaria

The postwar economic crisis and the beginning of deep transformations within the Bulgarian economy (1944–1947)

On September 17, 1944, a week after seizing power through a military coup, the Fatherland Front government announced its governing platform, which included a series of economic initiatives. Their primary focus was to increase state intervention in and control over production, trade and finances, under the pretext of securing all basic necessities for the population. However, the government's declaration did not mention the main factors determining the immediate tasks and goals of the economy – namely, the drive to materially and financially secure Bulgaria's participation in active military operations and to maintain Soviet troops in the country. These two circumstances had a fundamental effect on the development of the economic situation in Bulgaria over the next three years.

The economic dimensions of Bulgarian participation in the war

Bulgaria took part in the final phase of the war – between October 1944 and May 1945 – and although this period may appear quite short, the payments made from the state budget and the burdens the war placed on the economy and the population were quite significant. The upkeep of more than 450,000 troops, some of whom were fighting in territories more than 1,000 kilometers away from Bulgaria, required a huge mobilization of the country's financial and economic forces. The amount of goods, materials, weapons, and money spent not only for the Bulgarian army's needs but also provided to the Third Ukrainian Front and the National Liberation Army of Yugoslavia was particularly substantial. When all the various expenditures are combined, we arrive at the colossal sum of 133,280,719,447 leva, which represents the total amount of expenses incurred by Bulgaria's participation in the war against Hitler's Germany.[1]

With a great degree of certainty, the figure can be said to approximate US$310 million. In any case, it is clearly a question of a burden that was beyond the strength of Bulgaria's financial and economic capabilities and which was incurred over an extremely short period at that – in less than nine months. For example, according to official statistics, the country's entire national income for 1945 amounted to 141.8 billion leva, while in terms of the regular budget, the amount spent was three times more than revenues generated (43 billion leva).[2]

While the generation of enormous expenses is understandable at a moment when a country is engaged in actual military operations, the heavy payments Bulgaria was saddled with as a result of the Truce Agreement in Moscow on October 28, 1944, appear absolutely unjustified, given that the country had not actively fought any of the powers within the Anti-Hitler Coalition. The Truce Agreement contained numerous clauses imposing various financial obligations on Bulgaria. The Bulgarian state was obliged to fully assume the cost of transporting Soviet troops within its territory on land, sea, and air. It also stipulated that the liberation and repatriation of German prisoners of war would occur at the Bulgarian government's expense. Article 9 imposed the principle of reparations that Bulgaria would have to pay in the future. The government was obliged to restore all property belonging to the United Nations and its member states, including Yugoslavia and Greece, and to pay reparations for all losses and damages they had suffered. Bulgaria also undertook the obligation to restore in perfect condition all valuables and materials removed from the territories of the USSR, Yugoslavia, Greece and other members of the United Nations by Germany and Bulgaria during the war. The following clauses required all weaponry belonging to Germany or its satellite states to be surrendered to the USSR, and that all vessels located in Bulgarian ports be turned over to the Allied (Soviet) High Command, regardless of whose control they were under at the end of the war against Germany and Hungary. Trade vessels also came under the operative control of the Allied (Soviet) High Command. Article 13 required the Bulgarian government to safeguard German and Hungarian property in the country while the regulation in question prepared the future surrender of that property to the Soviet Union. Particularly large expenses were later incurred under Article 15, which stipulated that the Bulgarian government regularly make cash payments in Bulgarian leva and provide goods, resources, and services to be used by the Allied (Soviet) High Command in the fulfilling its functions.[3]

According to the 1944 Truce Agreement, deliveries of significant quantities of good and even cash payments were to begin immediately and continue for an unspecified period. It also required the transfer of ownership over significant assets and property belonging to German subjects and firms in Bulgaria, a stipulation that led the rise of numerous technical and financial problems.

The implementation of Article 3 from the Truce Agreement constituted a serious expense for the state budget. The transport of Soviet troops through Bulgaria continued until the end of 1945; to this end, nearly 100,000 wagons were consigned to the Allied (Soviet) High Command, while the expenses incurred by the Bulgarian State Railways amounted to 1.6 billion leva.[4]

The Bulgarian government undertook an exceptionally energetic campaign to restitute items and valuables taken from United Nations member states,

108 *The times of high Stalinism*

especially Greece and Yugoslavia. To this end, as early as November 1944, the cabinet sent a memorandum to all state and autonomous institutions, as well as to private firms and individuals, requiring them to declare everything that had been looted from occupied Greek and Yugoslav territories. By the end of that year, military and civil objects had been returned and were loaded onto 105 wagons – not counting mobile railway equipment. The BNB calculated that expenses incurred in the restitution of Yugoslav property amounted to 140,729,176 leva.[5] During February 1946, a Greek commission arrived in Svilengrad to begin accepting restituted items. From February 12 to February 14, sixty-five wagonloads of civil and military property were handed over, not counting mobile railway equipment.[6]

Article 15, which required the Bulgarian state to provide resources, goods and services for the needs of the Allied (Soviet) High Command, turned out to be the most destructive to the Bulgarian economy. The delivery of enormous sums of money, goods, weapons, as well as renovations undertaken and all the materials needed for them, began immediately after Soviet troops entered Bulgaria and was fulfilled without complaint by the Bulgarian government long after the cessation of military operations, despite the critical state of government finances and the Bulgarian economy. Despite the repressive nature of the regime, the population expressed its dissatisfaction – in the spring of 1945 villagers protested against the policy of requisition. The communists blamed Nikola Petkov's Agrarian Union for inciting the demonstrations.[7]

The expenses incurred under Article 15 alone amounted to the colossal sum of 35,952,618,192 leva. When implementation of all the clauses of the Truce Agreement are taken into account, it turns out that for the period from October 1944 to May 1947, the country provided the Soviet command with money, goods, and services totaling 38,935,523,344 leva.[8]

It is obvious that in fulfilling the Truce Agreement, Bulgaria was burdened with making exceptionally large payments, which reflected extremely negatively on its economic development. The total amount of nearly 39 billion leva is comparable to the enormous debt of 38 billion leva that Germany accrued in its clearing trades with Bulgaria for the period of 1941–1944. Despite the fact that the lev underwent significant devaluation following 1944, we can conclude that Bulgarian expenditures made to the victors' advantage do not differ greatly from those made to Germany's advantage – with one major difference, however: Bulgarian expenses incurred by trade with Germany took the form of an absolutely official debt, while those incurred by the Truce Agreement were made entirely without compensation.

The country's economic development was also determined by the peace treaty signed in Paris in February 10, 1947. The topic of reparations and restitutions was included in Part V of the treaty, which consisted of a total of two articles: 21 and 22. The first determined the amount of the reparations Bulgaria had to pay: US$45 million to Greece and US$25 million to Yugoslavia. Payment had to be made not only in cash but also in kind in accordance with international market prices from 1938, adjusted to reflect an increase of 15 percent for industrial products and 10 percent for all remaining goods. The deadline for paying off this debt was eight years from the moment the treaty entered into force.[9]

Unlike in the Treaty of Neuilly, now the problem of reparations was far more manageable. First of all, the total amount was nearly ten times smaller than that levied after World War I. Soon this burden was additionally lightened by Belgrade's refusal to accept reparations from Bulgaria. This gesture was inspired by the preparations for the creation of a South Slavic federation between Bulgaria and Yugoslavia that were under way in 1947. Besides the less onerous reparations, another important difference from the post-World War I situation was the fact that the Paris Peace Treaty stipulated payment to be made in kind, rather than in cash, which made reparations far less of a threat to the financial stability of the state and hence of the whole Bulgarian economy.

Article 26 was the most damaging to Bulgarian finances, since its Paragraph 4 required Bulgaria and Bulgarian subjects to drop all claims against Germany and German subjects for debts that were incurred during the war: from September 1, 1939 until May 8, 1945.[10] This applied mainly to the significant German debt which had accrued through bilateral clearing. According to data from the BNB, the total amount of German debt to Bulgaria as of the summer of 1946 was 38.6 billion leva (US$105 million).

On the whole, the Paris Peace Treaty did not saddle the country with significant financial payments in the future; this undoubtedly provided an opportunity for Bulgaria to achieve a successful economic recovery. The disadvantageous clauses in the treaty are those that denied the Bulgarian state and its citizens the right to raise justified demands for compensation for at least part of the enormous expenses accrued abroad. In fact, Bulgaria accrued its major war-related expenses before even signing the peace agreement and transferred any rights to compensation to the Soviet Union, which Bulgaria had never actually fought and which had not suffered any damages whatsoever as a result of Bulgarian military activities.

Such financial expenses and losses, placed in chronological order, include:

- German debt to the Bulgarian state and its citizens, which the peace treaty required Bulgarians to forgive (38.5 billion leva);
- materials and objects left behind, as well as investments made by the state budget, Bulgarian banks and private companies in the newly unified territories, which were not restored to the Bulgarian economy (28 billion leva);
- expenses for the maintenance of Bulgarian troops until September 1944, taken from state budgets and military allocations (84 billion leva);[11]
- destruction caused by the bombings of Sofia and other Bulgarian cities (more than 50 billion leva);[12]
- expenses incurred by the Bulgarian army's participation in the final phase of the war (133 billion leva);

110   *The times of high Stalinism*

- raw materials, goods and financial resources provided in accordance with the Truce Agreement (upkeep of the Allied Command and Soviet troops) (39 billion leva).

Thus, to make very rough estimate, the scope of war-related expenses amounted to approximately 372.5 billion leva. The dollar equivalent of this sum can be estimated only provisionally at best, due to the fact that the lev in 1940 was significantly stronger than in 1946. Nevertheless, if we accept that the average exchange rate for the period was approximately 450 leva to US$1, then the resulting amount exceeds US$825 million, or around 2.7 billion gold francs.

The scope of the economic and financial crisis

The impossibility of covering the constantly mounting war-related expenses with regular revenues from the budget allowed for the rapid growth of the state's domestic debt. In 1939, the government took a loan of 4.2 billion leva from the BNB, bringing the total domestic debt to 7.6 billion leva. Over the following two years, it nearly doubled, reaching 14.4 billion leva. In 1942, the government began issuing treasury bonds with a yield of 3 percent, thus managing to finance its ongoing payments. However, the debt continued increasing. In 1943, the debt had already reached 31.3 billion leva, but it truly skyrocketed in 1944, growing to 59.2 billion leva, while in the first seven months of 1945 alone it reached 91.4 billion leva.[13] To secure the necessary resources and to avoid setting off runaway inflation, the government resorted to compulsory domestic loans: the *Naroden zaem*, or "National Loan," in 1943, and the *Zaem za svobodata*, or "Loan for Freedom," in 1945, which citizens and companies were required to support. In this way, some of the financial burden was directly transferred to company and family budgets. Thus, from the beginning of the war until its end, the snowballing national debt increased twelve-fold.

The amount of money in circulation also grew from 2.8 billion leva in 1938 to 43.7 billion leva in 1945, a development that was also extremely dangerous for the stability of the lev, as it represents an almost sixteen-fold increase.[14] As of the middle of 1945, Bulgarian currency began to be printed at Gosbank in Moscow, where the BNB could not exercise effective supervision. The largest order was for currency with a face value of 30 billion leva, but whether more was printed and if so, exactly how much more, no one can say.[15] Despite the policy of maintaining a fixed exchange rate, which was strictly followed by the central bank, the devaluation of the leva became absolutely inevitable. In 1938, the official exchange rate was 132 leva to US$1, while in 1945 a new rate was determined: 288 leva to US$1. In fact, however, according to admissions made by governmental and bank representatives, an exchange rate of 450 leva to the dollar was closer to the truth, while some analyses have even deemed normal an exchange rate of 1,000 leva to the dollar.[16] All of these monetary processes inevitably provoked inflation. According to official statistics, the retail price index grew from 100 in 1938 to 560 in 1945. In practice, however, the prices of certain crucial food products, such as cooking oil, for example, increased more than tenfold. Yet despite the leva's headlong plunge the rate of inflation fell behind the rate of its devaluation and the increase in the money supply, since at the end of the war and in the years following, the Bulgarian population's purchasing power declined abruptly (due to the periodic seizure of monetary resources from the population), and thus it could not apply natural inflationary pressure. Furthermore, the rationing system also did not allow for a swift increase in product prices.

The financial crisis also continued after the end of military operations. Implementing the state budget in 1946 turned out to be a particularly tense process. Even after maximally levying tax revenue sources, budget revenues barely reached 39 billion leva – an amount that fell far short of covering expenses, which had reached 65 billion leva, not counting the budget for the Bulgarian National Railways. The looming budget deficit of 26 billion leva could not be covered in any other way except by continually mounting public debt and again increasing the amount of unbacked currency in circulation.[17] The government recognized that the population's difficult financial straights would not allow for the issuing of yet another domestic loan, especially since the Loan for Freedom from the previous year had secured the maximum possible amount of 22 billion leva as a result of intense pressure from state bodies.

The political events connected to the change of government also had an extremely negative effect on the development of the economic situation in Bulgaria. The coup of September 9, 1944, was taken by communists around the country as the cue for beginning deep economic transformations as well. In most mills, factories, and institutions, Fatherland Front committees and pro-communist labor unions took control, forcing the company directors to reduce the work day and lower labor quotas while increasing wages and immediately improving working conditions. In many places, they even began directing the personnel and production policies of a given enterprise. The introduction of numerous social benefits without the necessary economic preconditions for them not only stimulated inflationary processes but also threw the economy into administrative chaos. In a few short days, labor discipline collapsed. It has been found that workers failed to appear at work en masse or did not fulfill their professional duties. These processes soon generated serious losses for the companies and threatened to paralyze national production. Some of the BWP(C)'s political partners, especially Zveno, warned of this danger and criticized the local Fatherland Front's structures' interference in the economic sphere. Facing a growing crisis, at the end of 1944, the BWP(C) leadership called for the management of such enterprises to be left to "patriotic" industrialists and exhorted the local factory committees to assist in restoring labor discipline.[18]

The enormous expenses incurred by the war and the fulfillment of the peace treaty were the reasons for the substantial reduction of real capital investments in the industrial sector, which also contributed to the deepening of the economic crisis. The outflow of a huge quantity of goods, materials

112 *The times of high Stalinism*

and even cash from Bulgaria and the lack of a corresponding inflow of consumer goods or raw materials for industry, as well as the ever more decrepit equipment used in the agricultural sector, the less effective cultivation of the land, and the fact that part of the country's labor resources were tied up in the army led to a severe collapse in production in the country. Bulgaria's economic activity registered a significant drop of 15 percent even in 1944. The real national income, calculated according to 1939 prices, amounted to 55.2 billion leva in 1943, while in 1944 it had further fallen to 46.9 billion leva. The situation took on the dimensions of a true crisis in 1945, when the real national income barely reached 26.6 billion leva, which, in comparison to 1943, represents a more than a 50 percent contraction in production.[19]

The official Bulgarian–Soviet trade relations that were established in 1945 reflected the unequal footing Bulgaria found itself on during that period with respect to the Allies and especially the USSR.[20] There is no doubt that the conclusion of such a trade agreement was of particular importance for Bulgaria, since it would secure the external placement of the country's production and in this way avoid a collapse in Bulgarian production at a moment when the country's main trading partner from the past decade, Germany, was completely excluded from international trade. Moreover, the national economy could thus receive supplies, raw materials and machines so vitally necessary for its normal functioning. In reality, however, with the signing of the agreement on March 14, 1945, Bulgaria was obliged to export goods worth 13.4 billion leva, while in return to import only 9.3 billion leva worth of goods, which means that the Bulgarian state was to a large extent financing the USSR's exports – and that at a time when Bulgaria's economic and social situation required stronger imports. Despite the Bulgarian delegations' protests, the Soviet side imposed extremely disadvantageous prices – the Bulgarian goods were devalued twofold with respect to international prices, while, on the contrary, the value of Soviet goods was increased by the same proportion.[21] It soon became clear that the actual results of these trade relations were even less advantageous than those that had been agreed. By the end of November 1945, Bulgarian exports had reached 11.4 billion leva, while Soviet imports barely amounted to 6.1 billion leva – a positive trade balance of 5.3 billion leva for Bulgaria. In a report, the manager of the BNB noted that the difficult state of Bulgarian finances and the danger of the complete collapse of the lev required that a way be found to cover this imbalance as soon as possible. This was supposed to come about by asking the Soviet Union to send the BNB a sum in the amount of 1.9 billion leva in hard currency or gold to cover its delayed import for 1945, while the import of Soviet goods into Bulgaria should be accelerated in the beginning of 1946 to cover the rest of the imbalance. In closing, it insisted that the Soviet state bank accept a more favorable exchange rate for the lev against the ruble, which was at that time 1 ruble–19.30 leva. The BNB considered 4–5 leva to the ruble a more acceptable exchange rate.[22] Despite taking the country's interests into account and demonstrating a professional approach to the problem, given the political relationships that had been established and the Soviet authorities' behavior in Bulgaria, making such a suggestion to Moscow sounds extremely naive and even dangerous for the one making the suggestion.

The requisitions and quotas levied by the government on agricultural products, especially at a time of a significant drop in agricultural production, made overcoming the crisis even more difficult and did not help motivate agricultural workers to participate more actively in economic activities.[23] Attempts on the part of individual politicians and financiers (Petko Staynov, Vasil Kolarov, and Professor Ivan Stefanov) to procure concessions related to Bulgaria's external payments on the whole ended in failure. The country was under pressure to strictly fulfill its obligations under the peace treaty, despite the difficult state of the agricultural sector and the economy as a whole.

The Fatherland Front government's tax policy also had a very negative effect on the country's economic development. Guided on the one hand by its class-based understanding of private capital as predatory and exploitative and by its drive to cover large deficits in the state budget on the other, the communist-dominated government introduced additional tax laws. Under the pretext that indirect taxes are injust and weigh heavily on the whole population, an almost eight-fold increase in direct taxes was adopted, without indirect taxes being reduced.[24] The changes to the tax code introduced in 1945 sharply reduced normative costs and increased the tax rates. Private trade and industrial enterprises were subject to particularly high tax rates. In this way, the policy of the Fatherland Front cabinet accelerated the process of decapitalization of private firms.

In order to avoid the impending collapse in state finances due to enormous expenses, the authorities resorted to drastic measures that no previous regime in Bulgaria had ever imposed. The idea was to sharply limit the amount of currency in circulation, in this way overcoming the inflationary spiral and creating conditions favorable to easing the state's domestic debt. All of this would occur entirely at the expense of the population's leva-denominated resources.

Once it had signed the peace treaty, the government felt that it now had a free hand to begin implementing its radical monetary policy. Under conditions of complete secrecy, preparations were made to replace all banknotes in circulation, without resorting to redenomination: i.e. the money had the same face value, the old bills were simply withdrawn from circulation. Between March 10 and March 16, 1947, all banknotes with denominations of 200, 250, 500, 1,000 and 5,000 leva were withdrawn from circulation, as well as all 3-percent treasury bonds. The conditions under which this exchange was carried out were exceptionally harsh for citizens. An individual could only exchange up to 2,000 leva of old bills and treasury bonds (the equivalent of a laughably tiny amount – around $4), while any remaining money was placed in a frozen account in the individual's name, at which point the frozen accounts were taxed under the Property Tax Act, which had been adopted especially for this purpose.[25] The tax rates the law imposed in actuality constituted a seizure

114 *The times of high Stalinism*

of a significant part of the population's money by the state. Amounts up to 15,000 leva were not taxed, but the tax percentages levied on amounts above them increased quickly. Thus, for example, deposits of more than 200,000 leva (approximately $400) were taxed at a rate of 25 percent, while those above 2 million were taxed at 70 percent.[26]

The result of this financial operation was that most of the population's cash reserves were forcibly collected by the banks. Treasury bonds, which previously had been used as a form of tender due to their ubiquity, were also taken out of circulation, while the money supply in circulation was severely restricted. The BNB's official statistics attest to the scale of this liquidation of society's monetary resources. Before this exchange, there was a total of 39 billion leva in banknotes and 31 billion leva in 3-percent treasury bonds in circulation. Out of this total of 70 billion leva, 69 billion leva were seized from the population and from state and private enterprises. After this exchange, the entire amount of money in circulation was reduced to 21 billion leva, consisting only of the new bills. The burden of this exchange primarily fell on ordinary citizens, as 49.5 billion leva was forcibly collected from them alone.[27] The main effect of this governmental policy was to create conditions for the stabilization of state finances at the expense of brutally liquidating the population's savings and sharply reducing its purchasing power. The population's tangible impoverishment as a result of the devaluation of the lev, the exchange of banknotes, the imposition of enormous taxes, as well as the sharp deficit in mass consumer products virtually destroyed all possibilities for the development of private initiatives within production and trade long before the governmental policy of nationalization was undertaken.

Changes in the management and structure of the Bulgarian economy

The implementation of important changes to the management and ownership of a significant portion of the Bulgarian economy had already begun at the end of World War II. They were related to the agreements reached within the Anti-Hitler Coalition, which held that all enterprises with German capital or capital from other members of the Tripartite Pact located in the Eastern European countries conquered by the Red Army would become the property of the Soviet Union under the form of compensation for the damages inflicted by the German army and losses suffered by the Soviet economy.[28]

Immediately upon establishing itself in Bulgaria, the Soviet command demanded that the Bulgarian government provide it with information about all enterprises with German and Hungarian capital, which were placed under the control of the supervising administrative officer. On May 31, 1946, a law was promulgated transferring German property to the Soviet Union.[29] On July 10, General Biryuzov and Minister Kulishev signed a plan for the seizure and handover of enterprises held by predominantly German interests. The document included forty-one enterprises with a total share capital calculated to exceed 1.5 billion leva.[30]

Besides allowing the Soviet government to exercise considerable control through this large number of companies in the industrial, trade, insurance and banking sectors, through these firms it also continued to inflict financial losses both to the state budget as well as to various Bulgarian economic organizations. New clashes which arose in 1947 were related to the Soviets' claims resulting from the 1946 law that arranged the transfer of former German property to the USSR. According to the leadership of Bureau of Soviet Property in Bulgaria, Article 10 of the law transferred only the assets of the former German companies to the USSR, and not their liabilities. On this basis, they refused to honor debts owed to the Bulgarian state, banks, companies and individuals.

Another serious problem that gave rise to deep differences of opinion was Moscow's demand that the Soviet companies be exempt from any sort of taxation. Besides the fact that significant amounts of revenue owed to the state budget were at stake, it also was a question of creating an impermissible precedent before the remaining economic enterprises, which were burdened with large tax obligations.

These topics were also at the center of the discussions the Bulgarian governmental delegation held with Stalin in the spring of 1947 and which Traycho Kostov joined in 1947. Nevertheless, the Bulgarian position was generally reflected in the agreement of January 10, 1948, which stipulated that all Soviet companies that had not functioned would be exempt from taxes (old and new), while the rest, which had undertaken economic activity, would pay the taxes owed but without the interest and fines foreseen in the law.[31] However, contradictions related to the planned transference of German property seized by the USSR as reparations to the Bulgarian state continued. The most sensitive question related to Soviet demands that the Bulgarian state pay damages for damages inflicted on former German property during the war. Here they meant confiscated property, goods, furniture, and money (such damages were incurred primarily by Soviet troops after September 9, 1944).

The other substantial change, which had lasting and negative consequences, was the elimination of most of the management personnel in the Bulgarian economy. In the days immediately following September 9, many of the country's most prominent industrialists, traders and financiers were declared "enemies of the people" and were subject to investigations. They were removed from leadership positions in enterprises and firms, and in many places, management was taken over by representatives of the Fatherland Front or workers' committees. As the crisis deepened and economic life was paralyzed at the end of 1944, the Communist Party was forced to soften its stance toward prominent capitalists and appeal to some of them to once again take up economic activity, assuring them if they worked for the good of the people, this would be taken into account. In connection with this changed attitude, the Fatherland Front regime began using the terms "patriotic" industrialists and businessmen ever more frequently (i.e. entrepreneurs who were prepared to cooperate with the new

116 *The times of high Stalinism*

government).[32] Despite everything, such people remained under suspicion and at the tiniest hint of disloyalty they were removed from leadership positions. Specialists who had received their education or work experience in Western Europe and especially Germany roused particularly strong suspicions.[33] The communist authorities saw them as potential foreign spies. Over the following years, their role in managing the economy was reduced to a minimum. Some were repressed in the course of the subsequent political show trials against the opposition and Traycho Kostov; others were fired from their jobs, while still others were assigned economic duties of secondary importance. As a result of these changes, the Bulgarian economy was deprived of a large number of competent specialists (engineers, economists, lawyers, and financiers), whose knowledge and experience constituted valuable capital that was not used to restore the country's postwar economy.

The most significant transformation the Bulgarian economy underwent in this initial stage of the Fatherland Front government's rule was the nationalization of industrial enterprises and banks, which was carried out at the end of December 1947. The attack on private property, which had begun as early as the fall of 1944 under the form of confiscations of property belonging to those convicted by the People's Court or of property declared to have been acquired through speculative activities, as well as through the levying of extremely onerous taxes on private firms, reached its natural culmination at the end of 1947. The signal for sweeping nationalization of capital and the means of production came from outside. At the meeting of communist parties in the Polish city of Szklarska Poreba in September 1947, the Soviet leadership (i.e. Stalin) expressed the viewpoint that the socialist transformations in Eastern Europe had been groundlessly delayed. The Soviets accused the communist parties in various countries of having allowed the old capitalistic relations within the economy to continue functioning for too long and called for an end to that situation. The BWP(C) and the Fatherland Front government undertook new activities to implement the directives received from Moscow. On December 23, 1947, a law for the nationalization of industrial and mining enterprises came into force. Over the next two years, nearly 7,000 enterprises were nationalized, most of which were small and medium-sized industrial structures.[34] The last traces of the market economy in the country were wiped out. Almost all of Bulgaria's economic capacity was under the control of the Communist Party, which could now turn toward realizing its grandiose economic plans.

The sovietization of the Bulgarian economy (1948–1953)

The beginning of industrialization in Bulgaria

The collapse of relations between Stalin and Tito in 1948 and the powerful campaign Cominform undertook against the Yugoslav Communist Party's policy were a clear signal to the remaining Eastern European communist parties that Moscow would not allow them to build a political and economic model of socialism that differed from the Soviet one. This forced the party and state leaders in countries with "people's democracies" (including Bulgaria) to begin assiduously applying Soviet economic experience. Besides the basic postulates of socialist economic theory concerning the nationalization of the means of production, the liquidation of private property, competition and the free functioning of market mechanisms, and the establishment of a centralized, planned economy that was directly commanded by the government, the notion of the accelerated development of industry was also adopted, giving priority to the production of the means of production and not to the means of consumption. Thus, it was necessary to begin zealously developing heavy industry: mining, metallurgy, machine-building, the energy industry, the chemical industry and so on. To the classical formulations were added those developed by Soviet economists under the direct directions of Stalin – those necessary for building an economic system of the autarchic type. The idea was that for a "people's democracy" to be truly independent, it would have to develop all the necessary industries and to satisfy most of its economic needs on its own. While this theory sounds dubious even for a large country rich in natural resources such as the USSR, it is patently absurd for a small country like Bulgaria with scarce deposits of ore, oil and other resources.

Despite the fact that the prerequisites (capital, technology and natural resources, qualified specialists, workers, and, last but not least, a market) were lacking for the rapid development of a series of industries, a course of wide-scale industrialization was the main goal of economic activity in the country from the very first Five-Year Plan (1949–1953). These ideas underlie the basic decisions made by the Fifth Congress of the BCP in December 1948. In approximately five years, the respective proportions of agricultural and industry within the economy were expected to shift from 70:30 to 55:45. Following this policy, the plan calls for 83 percent of all investments earmarked for industry to be invested in heavy industry.[35]

To complete these grandiose economic tasks, the party and the press (which was completely subservient to the BCP) undertook a massive propaganda campaign targeting the entire society. Workers at firms were pressured to promise to fulfill the Five-Year Plan early, to take on an enormous amount of additional work, and to create more products for the national economy. The Stakhanov initiative for surpassing daily work quotas that had been applied in the Soviet Union was introduced across Bulgaria. The propaganda was particularly aimed at the young generation, emphasizing that they had been called upon to build the new life and to secure a bright future for the country and for their children. The enormous enthusiasm that gripped a large portion of Bulgarian youth found its expression in the brigadier movement, which grew to impressive proportions. During 1949–1950, nearly 300,000 brigadiers worked on various construction sites

118 *The times of high Stalinism*

(railroads, passes, reservoirs, and Dimitrovgrad). This unique "army of workers" not only guaranteed the communist regime cheap labor but was also a serious public force for applying pressure to other social groups. The BCP set great store by juxtaposing the generations and by its strategy of influencing parents to accept the socialist transformation of the economy through their children.

Despite numerous expressions of youthful enthusiasm and heroic feats of labor, industrialization in the late 1940s and early 1950s was carried out through a huge exertion of strength and serious deprivation on the part of the whole population. The production quotas were set exceptionally high, and fulfilling them was often a strenuous task that required working beyond one's regular shift. The "wage scale" introduced in 1948, which aimed to introduce some differentiation in pay, in actuality led to a decrease in most workers' salaries.

One natural result of the deteriorating material conditions was a high turnover rate among workers at most of the factories and mills. Dissatisfaction also took on more open forms, such as a certain collective's refusal to work overtime to fulfill the plan, for example. In May 1953, something unprecedented in totalitarian communist reality occurred: several hundred tobacco workers in Plovdiv declared a strike to protest against the new production quotas.[36]

During these years, which party propaganda declared a turning point in the economic development of the country, numerous industrial enterprises were built and new productive capacities were created. A series of thermal power stations were built near Sofia, Pernik, Dimitrovgrad and elsewhere. Large-scale industrial complexes such as the metallurgical factory in Pernik and the chemical works in Dimitrovgrad also appeared. Numerous reservoirs and water-supply systems were also completed. Ore output and mining activities also increased significantly.

According to official data, in 1952 industrial production was four times greater than prewar levels. It was trumpeted far and wide that Bulgaria had transformed from an agrarian into an agrarian-industrial country.[37] But in reality the foundation was laid for an industrial sector that swallowed up capital and energy, that could only exist thanks to the import of raw materials and energy from abroad (primarily the USSR), and that could partner up only with the highly administrated and strongly propped up economies of other communist countries.

The roots of Bulgaria's economic and financial dependence on the USSR

In order to achieve the goals of the first Five-Year Plan – to change Bulgaria's economic structure within a short time frame and to transform the state from an agrarian to an agrarian-industrial state – the country's own capital, which had in any case been drained by the war, was not sufficient; thus, significant external financing was necessary. This was necessary both for postwar reconstruction as well as for the massive industrial construction that had been undertaken.

After Moscow ordered the Eastern European countries to refuse financial aid provided under the Marshall Plan, a system for mutual financing that would correspond to their investment projects had to be developed. Moreover, the Eastern European economies' dependence on the Soviet Union was brought about not only through the rapidly expanding trade contacts but also through extended commodity and investment loans.

On July 5, 1947 (exactly one month after the Marshall Plan was announced), in a special agreement, the USSR granted Bulgarian a commodity loan of $US20 million, which it had to repay within four years at an annual interest rate of 3 percent via the export of Bulgarian goods, primarily tobacco, ore, spirits, and foodstuffs. The loan was intended to cover the import of machines, equipment and materials for reservoirs, railroads, and industrial enterprises.[38] Over the next several months, the USSR also granted Bulgaria two new investment loans totaling $US65 million.[39]

The Council for Mutual Economic Assistance, known as "Comecon," which was created in January 1949 in Moscow, offered Bulgaria additional opportunities for securing significant loans for the development of its industrial base and for infrastructure projects. In the initial phase of Comecon's development, large-scale processes for economic integration were not envisioned; rather, its task was expanding trade between the countries in the Eastern Bloc and regulating economic contacts with Western countries, as well as organizing the boycott against Yugoslavia.[40] Thus, in the first years of its existence, Comecon was above all a means for the USSR to establish control over its satellites in Europe. Nevertheless, through Comecon, Bulgaria received several commodity credits worth nearly 60 million rubles as early as 1949.

It is indisputable that the purely financial parameters of the loans agreed upon were favorable for Bulgaria: low annual interest rates, an initial grace period, and servicing the debt through the export of Bulgarian goods. In reality, however, repaying these investment loans caused some serious problems, while their economic and political effect did not turn out to be particularly positive. It has been established that some of the Soviet machines were not on a satisfactory technological level and did not correspond to then-current requirements.[41] Attempts by Bulgarian representatives to make some claims failed due to the Soviet alliances' refusal to discuss such questions.

The enormous quantity of exports to the USSR limited Bulgaria's ability to export goods to the international markets. This is one of the reasons (along with the deterioration of East–West political relations in connection with the Korean War, 1950–1953) that the share of Bulgaria's foreign trade with Western countries rapidly contracted in the early 1950s. While in 1949 this share had been 17.9 percent, in 1950 it was 12.6 percent, and in 1951 it had fallen to 6.9 percent.[42] In this way, the loan agreements further bound the Bulgarian economy and its trade to the Soviet Union and distanced it from the Western countries. Bulgaria's contacts with Western countries were subject to particularly strict Soviet control. After each contact with a Western

120   *The times of high Stalinism*

firm, Bulgarian ministers had to obediently give explanations to the Soviet diplomats and advisers in Bulgaria.

The strongly inflated ruble exchange rate also became a serious problem with trade with the Soviet Union. Officially, US$1 was equal to approximately 5 rubles, which, according to Bulgarian specialists, inflated the value of the Russian currency sixfold. Or, in other words, for each unit produced, in order for the Bulgarian side to receive the value it would hold on the international markets, it would have to sell six times more of the same product in the Soviet Union. Thus, for example, Bulgarian tobacco was exported to the Soviet Union at a price much lower than its international value. The case was similar for other Bulgarian items, such as rose oil, lead-zinc concentrates and so on. Alongside this, Bulgarian trade representatives reported that certain Soviet goods were offered to Bulgaria for an international price higher than what the same product cost in Western countries.[43] From this point of view, paying off Soviet loans with Bulgarian goods cannot be called advantageous for Bulgaria. And in the years after the signing of the Paris Peace Treaty, in the sphere of financial-economic relations, the USSR continued to treat Bulgaria as a conquered country, bluntly imposing its solutions to contentious questions and forcing the authorities in Sofia to take on quite unsound economic commitments.

Disbalances in the communist economy

During the first Five-Year Plan (1949–1953), the Bulgarian economy underwent enormous transformations. An industrial base began to be built that was significant with respect to the economic traditions of the times and the country's capabilities, while radical changes were made in the structure of the national economy. As a result of the policy of accelerated industrialization, industry's contribution to Bulgaria's national income sharply increased. In 1952, with its 47.1 percent share, industrial production accounted for nearly half of the country's economic output. This fast rate of economic development was achieved at the price of exceptionally large industrial investments; for example, more than one-fourth of the entire national income was set aside for the accumulation fund. Besides direct deductions from the state budget, the government also resorted to issuing domestic loans in 1951 and 1952, through which more than 973 million leva (or more than 24 billion old leva) were collected from the population.[44]

The administratively planned organization of the economy guaranteed the state huge resources through which it could induce and control economic processes in the country. The redirection of significant investment and labor streams from one sphere into another allowed for the rapid development of branches which otherwise, under normal market conditions, either would not have arisen or would have developed at a much more moderate pace. Precisely this particularity of communist economics allowed the regimes to claim impressive successes in industrialization, mining and construction. But

Building the communist economy in Bulgaria   121

having developed outside market imperatives, communist industry worked for and by itself, primarily satisfying its own needs and not the direct needs of the population. In the planned system, measuring output produced was of fundamental importance, while the ultimate use of what was produced was of far lesser significance. Thus, communist enterprises only took into account indices of quantity, without taking any interest in raising the quality of the products. The emphasis on quantitative indices in implementing the plan led to numerous products that did not meet the necessary requirements or which were not applicable to the economy or to the population's everyday life. A large part of stocks were primarily unused, defective or out-of-style products.

Bulgarian enterprises' grave financial state seriously threatened to paralyze the country's production and banking systems. According to bank data, the state and cooperative sector had accumulated 1.2 billion new leva worth of goods which, in their present state, could not be released either on the foreign or on the domestic market. In comparison to 1952, at the end of 1953, intercompany debt grew from 604 million leva to 938 million leva, a more than 50 percent increase within a single year. Increasing thefts, primarily in rural cooperatives, also became an economic problem. Losses, including oversupply, diverted funds, deficits, abuses, and thefts amounted to more than 2.386 billion leva.[45]

The financial crisis also deepened considerably due to the monetary policy conducted by the government and the central bank over the next several years. From the late 1950s, an increase in the money supply could be noted, which did not, however, correspond to the growth of the national income. The main reasons for this are low labor productivity and the large quantity of defective goods in production. Due to the failure to secure income from the necessary quantity of goods and services, more than 25 percent of the money released did not return to banks. Despite this, the BNB continued issuing banknotes, which increased the money supply.[46] This increase in income beyond the ultimate production capacity indirectly made Bulgarian goods more expensive, while the intensified exports meant increases losses for the budget. This situation gave rise to one of the most difficult issues facing monetary policy in a planned economy: striking a balance between income and the national output that was produced. In fact, the lack of such a balance is one of the main reasons for the existence of a constant commodity shortage in the socialist economies.[47]

Ideas for Bulgaria's economic development as a weapon in power struggles (1953–1956)

The death of Stalin in March 1953 marked the beginning of gradual yet important changes, first in the Soviet Union and later in the other countries in the socialist system. The political struggles between the deceased leader's heirs played a leading role in how the situation developed, while one of the

122 *The times of high Stalinism*

arenas where the conflict was most intense was precisely the economic sphere, where substantial ideological dissension arose. The desire to discredit a rival or to survive in the new political landscape was the reason for the frequent conceptual changes concerning the development of and priorities within the socialist economy. At first, the new leadership in Moscow turned its attention to distortions in the economic structure that had led to a serious deterioration in the ability to supply the population with basic consumer goods. Criticism of this situation and growing dissatisfaction was aimed at some of Stalin's would-be successors who had taken up some of the strongest positions, such as Lavrentiy Beria. Decisions to develop agriculture and light industry were then made. This change in economic course allowed Nikita Krushchev to begin his rise to power – he officially took up the post of First Secretary of the CPSU in September 1953. He shared power with Georgiy Malenkov, who retained control over the executive power as Chairman of the Council of Ministers. But little more than a year later, in February 1955, accusations that he had violated the basic economic principle of socialist development – the expansion of heavy industry – provided grounds for Malenkov's removal from his leadership position and allowed Krushchev to take full control of the government.[48]

Similarly, the economic problems in the Eastern European satellites were also used as an excuse to clear the path to power for new party leaders. In Bulgaria, Vâlko Chervenkov, aiming to show his devotion to the new masters in the Kremlin and to demonstrate his own ability to accept innovations, quickly introduced a "new course" in economy policy that supported light industry and agriculture.[49] This abrupt change in state priorities did not lead to a rapid solution to existing problems. Failures continued to mount in agriculture and animal husbandry, even though new measures had been adopted to increase the rural population's income. Serious errors in planning production, inefficient organization, and poor harvests due to adverse weather conditions were the reasons that the expected results were not achieved.[50] In fact, no visible improvement was made on another important economic and social issue – improving the population's food supply – due not only to the poor harvest but also as a result of the increasing export of Bulgarian agricultural products to the USSR and other socialist countries.

The change in signals coming from Moscow, combined with economic goals that had clearly not been met, offered Todor Zhivkov a good opportunity to launch a new assault on state power. Just one month after Chervenkov was removed from the post of Prime Minister, in May 1956 at a Comecon session, Todor Zhivkov insisted that the rapid pace of Bulgarian industrialization be resumed.[51] Of course, given the command economy in Bulgaria and when processes are not defined by natural market forces, sufficient arguments can be found to support any number of approaches to the economy. Thus, for example, arguments citing the lack of raw materials, technology, qualified personnel, a production tradition and, above all, markets for the development of heavy industry could easily be countered by the need to overcome growing

Building the communist economy in Bulgaria   123

unemployment, by the theoretical Marxist view on the leading role of the production of the means of production and by other such noneconomic arguments. In the end, the prevailing ideas in Moscow determined which particular economic conception was imposed.

Despite the fact that the Soviet leadership returned to the classical socialist ideas about the development of heavy industry in 1955, within the community of "people's democracies," Bulgaria was assigned the special role of supplying agricultural products and light industrial goods. Given such products' low prices on the Comecon market, their lack of prestige from a theoretical point of few, and also due to certain economic reasons (the significant investments in industrialization that the country had already made, the increase in income for those working in industry, the creation of new jobs), the Bulgarian government and party leaders did not greet the economic suggestions coming from Moscow with enthusiasm.[52]

Despite such objections, the Bulgarian government nevertheless used the Soviet leaders' new vision for economic divisions within Comecon to secure significant new loans for the Bulgarian economy, this time for the modernization of the agricultural sector. On February 3, 1956, the prime ministers of both countries, Nikolay Bulganin and Vâlko Chervenkov, signed an agreement for aid from the USSR to the PRB for the further development of agriculture and the mineral fertilizer industry. The document provided for the USSR to export a large number of tractors, combines, balers, cargo trucks, backhoes, agricultural equipment and spare parts between 1956 and 1959, while for this equipment the Bulgarian government would be granted a loan of 300 million rubles at a 2 percent annual interest rate to be repaid within ten years.[53]

After the prolonged depletion of Bulgarian agriculture and animal husbandry due to World War II and its second-tier status in the socialist government's investment policy, this agreement and the loans it entailed secured more auspicious conditions for the modernization of this sector and for increasing its productivity. For the first time since the socialist regime had been established in Bulgaria, significant foreign investment resources were allocated toward this important branch within the national economy, which continued to constitute the basic part of the country's exports and remained the only stable source of freely convertible foreign currency.

The state's increase in purchase prices is the other important factor that contributed to a notable upsurge in the development of agriculture in the second half of the 1950s. By 1960, official data show a 41.7 percent increase in comparison to prewar levels.[54] Regardless of such positive quantitative indices, however, Bulgarian agriculture continued to face serious problems; to a considerable extent, they were only just beginning to accumulate as a result of mass collectivization. The imposition of administrative-command management methods, the alienation of farmers from ownership, and the elimination of market stimuli for their activity led to lasting negative results, whose impact would be felt until the end of the century.

124 *The times of high Stalinism*

Notes

1 AMVnR, PMK, op. 1, a. e. 25, l. 10; according to Mito Isusov, who also adds that considerable indirect payments and damages suffered, Bulgaria's expenses during the war amounted to an ever greater sum: 159,719,446,661 leva. See Mito Isusov, "Stopanskite razhodi na Bâlgariya v Otechestvenata voyna," *Istoricheski pregled*, 1 (1) (1969): 52–67, p. 67.
2 AMVnR, PMK, op. 1, a. e. 42, l. 5; op. 1, a. e. 278, l. 18.
3 AMVnR, PMK, op. 1, a. e. 12, l. 6–8.
4 AMVnR, PMK, op. 1, a. e. 39, l. 3.
5 TsDA, f. 132, op. 3, a. e. 14, l. 3.
6 AMVnR, PMK, op. 1, a. e. 629, l. 62.
7 Evgeniya Kalinova, *Pobeditelite i Bâlgariya (1939–1945)*, Sofia: St. Kliment Ohridski, 2004, p. 245.
8 Daniel Vachkov and Martin Ivanov, *Bâlgarskiyat vânshen dâlg 1944–1989. Bankrutât na komunisticheskata ikonomika*, Sofia: Institute for Studies of the Recent Past/Ciela, 2008, p. 24.
9 *Dârzhaven vestnik*, 201, August 30, 1947, p. 8.
10 *Dârzhaven vestnik*, 201, August 30, 1947, p. 14.
11 This amount has been calculated on the basis of data presented in Lyudmil Petrov, *Voennata ikonomika na Bâlgariya 1919–1945*, Sofia: St. Kliment Ohridski, 1999, pp. 91–96.
12 AMVnR, PMK, op. 1, a. e. 299, l. 43.
13 AMVnR, PMK, op. 1, a. e. 278, l. 34.
14 AMVnR, PMK, op. 1, a. e. 278, l. 15.
15 Veselin Angelov, *Tretata natsionalna katastrofa*, Sofia: Aniko, 2005, p. 133.
16 AMVnR, PMK, op. 1, a. e. 278, l. 14.
17 AMVnR, PMK, op. 1, a. e. 278, l. 17.
18 Ludzhev, *Grad na dve epohi*, pp. 187–190.
19 Asen Chakalov, *Natsionalniyat dohod i razhod na Bâlgariya 1924–1945*, Sofia: Knipegraph, 1946, p. 117.
20 Gospodinka Nikova, "Vânshnoikonomicheskite otnosheniya na Bâlgariya sled Vtorata svetovna voyna (1945–1960)," in *Stranitsi ot bâlgarskata istoriya. Sâbitiya, razmisli, lichnosti*, vol. II, Sofia: Prosveta, 1993, p. 133.
21 Mito Isusov, *Stalin i Bâlgariya*, Sofia: Sv. Kl. Ohridski, 1991, pp. 114–116, 119–120.
22 AMVnR, PMK, op. 1, a. e. 74, l. 3.
23 Vladimir Migev, *Problemi na agrarnoto razvitie na Bâlgariya (1944–1960)*, Sofia: K&M, 1998, pp. 16–17.
24 Z. Zlatev, *Stopanskata politika na bâlgarskite pravitelstva (1944–1949)*, Sofia: Kota, 2007, pp. 66–68.
25 TsDA, f. 132, op. 3, a. e. 11, l. 14.
26 *Dârzhaven vestnik*, 80, April 8, 1947, p. 4.
27 Vachkov and Ivanov, *Bâlgarskiyat vânshen dâlg*, pp. 48–49.
28 For a more detailed discussion of the transfer of German property to the USSR and the resulting difficulties for the Bulgarian economy, see Gospodinka Nikova, "Likvidiraneto na germanskata sobstvenost v Bâlgariya sled Vtorata svetovna voyna," in *Problemi na stopanskata istoriya*, Sofia: UI "Stopanstvo," 2000; Evgeniya Kalinova, "Pobeditelite vinagi imat pravo (Sâdbata na germanskite imushtestva v

Building the communist economy in Bulgaria 125

Bâlgariya i na bâlgarskite pretentsii spryamo Germaniya sled Vtorata svetovna voyna)," in *Collegium Germania*, vol. III, Sofia: Gutenberg, 2000, pp. 201–226.

29 *Dârzhaven vestnik*, 120, May 31, 1946.

30 AMVnR, op. 1p, a. e. 293, l. 1–9.

31 AMVnR, PMK, op. 1p, a. e. 488, l. 2.

32 Ludzhev, *Grad na dve epohi*, p. 189.

33 Gospodinka Nikova, "Bâlgarskoto stopanstvo mezhdu Germaniya i Sâvetskiya sâyuz," pp. 70–112.

34 Ludzhev, *Grad na dve epohi*, p. 211.

35 Iliyana Marcheva, "Problemi na stopanskata politika v Bâlgariya – krayat na 40-te i nachaloto na 50-te godini," in *Moderna Bâlgariya*, Sofia: St. Kliment Ohridski, 1999, pp. 273–291, at p. 275.

36 Ludzhev, *Grad na dve epohi*, pp. 386–397, 425.

37 *Istoriya na Bâlgarskata komunisticheska partiya*, Sofia: Partizdat, 1981, p. 486.

38 Zlatko Zlatev, *Bâlgaro-sâvetski ikonomicheski otnosheniya (1944–1958)*, Sofia: BAS, 1986, p. 63.

39 AMVnR, op. 2ap, a. e. 30, l. 27–28, 29–35.

40 Jozef Van Brabant, *Economic Integration in Eastern Europe*, New York, London, Toronto, Sydney: Harvester Wheatsheaf, 1989, pp. 31–32.

41 Zlatev, *Bâlgaro-sâvetski ikonomicheski otnosheniya*, p. 65.

42 Gospodinka Nikova, *Sâvetât za ikonomicheska vzaimopomosht i Bâlgariya 1949–1960*, Sofia: BAS, 1989, p. 141.

43 AMVnR, op. 1ap. a. e. 313, l. 5.

44 Iliyana Marcheva, "Politikata na bâlgarskoto pravitelstvo za finansirane na industrializatsiyata 1949–1953," *Istoricheski pregled*, 4 (1990): 5, 8.

45 Vachkov and Ivanov, *Bâlgarskiyat vânshen dâlg*, p. 82.

46 Avramov, *Komunalniyat kapitalizâm*, pp. 83–87.

47 Kornai, János, *Economics of Shortage*, Amsterdam: North-Holland, pp. 265–271.

48 Michael Voslensky, *Les Maîtres de la Nomenklatura*, Paris: Pierre Belfond, 1989, pp. 142–143.

49 Iliyana Marcheva, *Todor Zhivkov: pâtyat kâm vlastta – Politika i ikonomika v Bâlgariya 1953–1964 g.*, Sofia: Kota, [2000], pp. 78–79.

50 Vladimir Migev, *Problemi na agrarnoto razvitie na Bâlgariya (1944–1960)*, Sofia: K&M, 1998, p. 56.

51 Evgeniya Kalinova and Iskra Baeva, *Bâlgarskite prehodi, 1944–1999*, Sofia: Paradigma, 2000, p. 84.

52 Marcheva, *Todor Zhivkov*, pp. 92–93.

53 TsDA, f. 132, op. 2, a. e. 115, l. 171.

54 Migev, *Problemi na agrarnoto razvitie na Bâlgariya*, p. 243.

5 The Bulgarian village under communism

Collectivization, social change, and adaptation

At the crossroads between private and collective agriculture

Studying the process of collectivization, as well as defining and analyzing its various direct and indirect effects, is exceptionally difficult. This is due above all to the fact that collectivization was in reality an enormous project whose goal was not only to change the structure of ownership but also to bring about total social engineering – a kind of "genetic modification" of society. It laid the foundation for a complete economic and social transformation of the Bulgarian village and the lives of millions of people, whose mentality also underwent a fundamental change. Overall, collectivization was an essential part of the BCP's integral policy for reconstructing the country, and its implementation was the most wide-ranging of all "initiatives" undertaken by the regime at that time.

The coup of September 9, 1944, found the Bulgarian village and the country's agriculture as a whole in quite a dismal state. As of 1946, approximately 76 percent of the population was still rural, while 68 percent earned a living from agriculture, animal husbandry and forestry.[1] The process of dividing land between heirs into ever smaller parcels, which had begun after Bulgaria's liberation in 1878, had been gathering steam. This became particularly visible after World War I, when the practice of women inheriting up to 50 percent as much land as her brothers inherited also began to be adopted.[2] Thus, by the 1940s, arable land was split between almost a million farms which were scattered across nearly 13 million plots (fields). The vast majority of them were exceptionally small: according to official statistics, 712,000 such farms possessed up to 50 decares, constituting 37.5 percent of all arable land; 254,000 farms had between 50 and 100 decares; and only 200 such farms possessed more than 500 decares.[3] This made the modernization of agricultural production, such as the introduction of mechanization, agricultural technology, etc., extremely difficult. Attempts made by a series of governments during the interwar period to provide relief to Bulgarian villagers by forgiving a large number of farm debts, introducing state protectionism in agriculture, instituting the partial consolidation of land in some villages and so on led to modest results on the whole and were not capable of

The Bulgarian village under communism 127

bringing about a qualitative leap in modernization. The serious underdevelopment of Bulgarian agriculture, as well as of the village and the peasantry as a whole, was indisputably one of the factors that eased the imposition of the Soviet *kolkhoz* or "collective farm" model. This precondition should not be taken as absolutely necessary, however, since for Stalin's regime and its epigones in Eastern Europe the actual state of landownership and the specific agrarian characteristics of each of the conquered countries were not of particular importance. For them, collectivization constituted an obligatory part of the overall transformation of the political systems and thus it began to be implemented everywhere.

Even in the years before World War II the collectivist model existed in latent form in parallel, alongside the evolutionary project for rural development. Among the welter of variations, the communist one was by far the most consistent. Through their propaganda machine, the two organizational mouthpieces for this movement – the legal Workers' Party and the illegal BCP – actively popularized the USSR and the Soviet lifestyle among the Bulgarian population. The *kolkhoz* system in the Soviet Union occupied a prominent place in this propaganda and was recommended – directly or indirectly, depending on the audience – as a panacea for solving the Bulgarian village's problems as well. Influenced by this propaganda, in around 1939 steps were taken toward founding the first three experimental farms in northern Bulgaria for the collective cultivation of the land, whose working principles to a great extent resembled those of the Soviet *kolkhoz* model. Although their organizational structure inarguably bore the stamp of the Communist Party, it must be emphasized that in their essence they upheld the principles of voluntary cooperation, which preserved private ownership of the land.

The abbreviation TKZS (*trudovokooperativno zemedelsko stopanstvo* or "labor cooperative agricultural enterprise") first appeared in public space in the middle of September 1944, when the Decree for TKZS was being drafted. The first TKZSs were already being created then, but before the autumn of 1948 the number of such collective farms in the country did not exceed 400, in which approximately 8 percent of farmers participated.[4] On the whole, the participants in such early TKZSs were primarily communists and their supporters, who freely contributed their land, livestock and inventories. At the beginning of 1945, the National Committee of the Fatherland Front announced a month-long "collectivization campaign" in the country, whose goal was to attract villagers into the TKZSs en masse.[5] Communists were the most active participants in this drive, noisily proclaiming that, by spring of 1945, all the villagers in twelve villages had already joined cooperatives.[6] Even though this announcement was greatly exaggerated, it nevertheless reflects to a certain extent the attitude of a number of local functionaries, who began forcing the process "from the bottom up." After a quite lengthy delay and debate, the Council of Ministers finally adopted the legal ordinance on TKZS on April 13, 1945.[7]

128   *The times of high Stalinism*

Despite the fact that historiography until now has established a narrative according to which the imposition of forced collectivization measures did not begin until after 1948, it must be noted that they also existed during this initial period in villages where farms were being built. When determining the borders of the cooperative blocs and influencing farmers to enter the cooperatives, the forms of pressure employed were no different than those used in the following years. Those who refused to cooperate were given other plots of land – scattered, of course – usually on the periphery of the village lands and whose quality as a rule was not equal to that of the lands seized. These "exchanges," as they were known in the jargon of the time, constituted one of the widely used tools for pressuring villagers to join collective farms.

The BWP(C) itself and the coalition it led realized that, given Bulgaria's unsettled international standing, the moment was not ripe for mass forced collectivization and that any hasty further steps in that direction would only turn the great majority of the peasantry against them. Thus, in the fall of 1945, the first wave of pressure on private farmers died down, while priority was given to purely propagandistic efforts. Initiatives were undertaken that showed a certain continuity with the agricultural policy of the nonparty cabinets before the coup. Thus, in February 1946, Parliament passed the Law on the Sanitation of Villages. In accordance with it, standard plans for residential and public building were popularized, annual contests were held for the development of public services in villages, for cleaning villages and homes, and for raising the sanitation standards of their residents.[8] In July of the same year, the law for agricultural education and improving living standards in the village was also passed. It created a special bureau within the Ministry of Agriculture and State Property for the improvement of the rural population's living standards. It was charged with the task of coordinating the efforts of the separate universal cooperatives, public committees, associations and so on with those of the state for the opening of bakeries, *bitovi kombinati* (general enterprises uniting small-scale firms offering local services), vacuum-packing canning workshops, drying houses for fruits and vegetables, etc.[9] Efforts to supply villages with electricity also continued.

The government's next important step in the sphere of agricultural policy was the preparation and adoption of a Law on Labor Land Ownership, in which it declared its intention to undertake agrarian reform. It was prepared as early as the end of 1945 and was passed on March 12, 1946, by the Twenty-Sixth Parliament after a brief discussion.[10] The very name of the law, as well as many of the clauses within it, make it clear that it demonstrated continuity with the reformist policy of the agrarian leader Aleksandâr Stamboliyski in the sphere of agriculture from the beginning of the twentieth century. This can be traced in both the similar maximum amount of *trudova pozemnlena sobstvenost*, the technical term for private plots owned and worked by the owner's family alone, without hired labor (in the 1921 law that limit was 300 decares, while in 1946 it was 200 or 300 for the Dobrudzha districts), as well as in the even stricter limitations on so-called *netrudova pozemlena sobstvenost*,

The Bulgarian village under communism   129

or plots held by rural capitalists who hired outside laborers to work the land.[11] Analogously, the law also stipulated the formation of a state land fund and also specified the types of land that would be vested in it: land from owners who exceeded the abovementioned limits, state land, and lands held in various funds (such as land belonging to municipalities, the church, *vakif* charitable endowments, schools, community centers, and so on). It must be taken into account that the law was passed during an upswing of opposition attitudes within society. During this period, the original BANU split into two "branches": the BANU controlled and manipulated by the communists and BANU–Nikola Petkov (the name of the leader under whose banner the opposition members and sympathizers gathered). In this context, the two wings of the Agrarian Party were waging an intense struggle for the symbols and principles of agrarian ideology. The Communist Party definitely had an interest in demonstrating to society that the "real" BANU was in the coalition that it dominated and that the Communist Party also stood behind the principles defended by the BANU. On the other hand, the law was also passed with the goal of dispelling villagers' suspicions about the impending introduction of a Soviet *kolkhoz* system. Of course, in the spirit of the new times, the law also introduced a series of conditions on the acquisition and preservation of private property and, in fact, aimed to create the preconditions for expanding the network of TKZSs. This was precisely where the major differences lay between the agrarian reform designed and only partially realized by Stamboliyski and this later variant, which likewise remained only in the initial phase of implementation. Analogously, the law also stipulated that those who received land through it would be forgiven the cost of the land received (up to 50 decares) upon their entrance into a TKZS, while still guaranteeing that they could retain 5 to 10 decares for their personal use, which was the only land they were required to pay for under the alleviated conditions. At the same time, however, one of the law's clauses states: "Those who receive land and who become members of a cooperative for cooperative land management receive ideal shares of the land stock designated for them, without it being divided into lots." Thus, it was a question of fictitious land grants; the only true benefit they offered to such new TKZS members was the rent received (up to 40 percent of the profit per decare), which slowly but surely decreased, until later it was abolished as well. The benefit was more tangible for so-called landless persons, who were given up to 10 decares (subsequently reduced to 5) of land for personal use, and they, in fact, were the only ones who acquired (albeit temporarily) something real.

In this form, however, even if it had been thoroughly implemented, the Law on Labor Land Ownership was in no condition to lead to a real and relatively just redistribution of agricultural land in the country. Even the motivations for the bill calculated that in order to fully grant the 50 decares maximum stipulated for landless or indigent villagers, approximately 10 million decares would be needed.[12] Nearly 564,000 decares had been confiscated from the 3,600 large landowners affected by the law. When confiscated municipal,

130   *The times of high Stalinism*

school, community center, ecclesiastical and *vakif* lands were added to this amount, the total reached 2,437,810 decares, or approximately one-fourth of the land needed.[13] Since it was more than clear that agrarian reform was an exceptionally propagandistic move and its implementation was impossible, the government did not rush to put the law into practice. As Titko Chernokolev, the architect of the Communist Party's agricultural policy, admitted in September 1948, the actual numbers of those who received land were 11,000 landless and 29,000 indigent villagers. In reporting this data, he himself conceded that the government had failed in its attempt to solve the problem in this way.[14] It is striking that similar agrarian reforms or attempts at such reforms were made between 1945 and 1948 in all the countries that fell under the Soviet sphere of influence. Their general parameters were also quite similar in terms of the maximum amount of land owners could possess and which grantees could receive, who could be a claimant, the time frame for payment, the stipulated compensations, etc.[15] These comparisons unambiguously indicate that the Law on Labor Landownership in Bulgaria resulted not from the country's actual conditions and needs but from the overarching strategy for establishing Soviet control in Eastern Europe. The failure to complete these wide-ranging reforms due to the collectivization that had meanwhile begun is another shared feature.

Tools for imposing the Soviet *kolkhoz* model

If the promise of carrying out land reform and justly distributing land constituted the crux of the regime's propaganda strategy at this stage, the quota system (or the so-called compulsory state deliveries) was at the heart of the actual imposition of the new agrarian model and was the basic tool for pressuring the rural population. It was inherited from the war years but was gradually refined so as to be transformed into a form of overt plundering on a scale unseen before that time. As of the autumn harvest of 1947, the quota system was established in its classical form, which essentially introduced a colonial regime for draining villagers' output and resources. A decree by the Council of Ministers stipulated the confiscation of producers' entire grain harvest, leaving them only 600 grams per family member per day, as well as 200 grams of corn per person per day. And since the regime anticipated difficulties in collecting the requisitioned goods, it introduced compulsory threshing at a common threshing floor, where farmers first had to fulfill their quota to the state, after which they could keep anything that remained.[16] The official name of this campaign was "compulsory purchasing," but in fact the rural population was truly "squeezed dry," since the prices paid for grain, corn, milk and meat by the state purchasing organizations ranged between one-fourth and one-third of their market value. In the following years, the system of compulsory state deliveries gradually expanded to include ever newer crops.[17] This practice by the communist regime in Bulgaria, which was borrowed directly from Stalin's rural policy, would become the main tool for

The Bulgarian village under communism 131

forcing villagers into the TKZS. In 1948, the quota system was expanded to include wheat, rye, barley (a separate decree was issued for corn), oats, vetch, beans and sunflowers. With respect to fodder crops, hay and straw were also subject to compulsory purchasing. Potatoes were also not spared. The quotas for meat and animal products – skins, wool, and milk – were particularly onerous. The basic principle was the progressive increase of in-kind taxation depending on the amount of arable land.[18] Thus, according to some cursory calculations, in real terms, this draining system of compulsory state deliveries plundered between 50 and 70 percent of the fruits of rural labor. For this reason, villagers were left with few options for escape from the situation that had arisen: joining the TKZS or migrating to the city. The practice over the following years showed the first option to be a likely interim stage toward the second.

The other tool for applying pressure, which was closely tied to the quota system, were the so-called sowing plans. Under the new conditions, they began to play the role of a guarantee of sorts that a given private farmer would fulfill his obligations to the state. In accordance with the purchasing plan, the state would release sowing plans to the districts, which the corresponding district agricultural bureaus would in turn distribute to the municipalities. The latter, for their part, through local "functionaries" – village mayors, party secretaries, chairmen of TKZSs and so on – would relay them to the relevant land owners. The accounting plans for deliveries would be developed based on the sowing plans. Over the subsequent years, this practice also underwent evolution, in which the so-called *kulaks* (the term, which literally means "fist" in Russian, was a negative label used to refer to wealthy farmers) were saddled with large sowing plans, while failure to fulfill them was grounds for the confiscation of their property. Natural disasters and cataclysms, which constitute a basic risk in agriculture, were not planned for in principle and usually such costs were again born by the peasants.

A key tool in the regime's creeping advance toward collectivization was strict social stratification and segregation. It is well known that in the Bulgarian context, the borders between small, medium-sized and large land holdings were quite relative and that the differences between them generally did not lead to visible differences in the landowners' way of life and living standards. It must also be noted that in the different regions of the country, depending on whether the terrain was flat, semi-mountainous or mountainous, there are differing criteria for whether a given farm should be defined as "small," "medium-sized" or "large." The actual social stratification of these three categories was to a large extent an ideological construct, the result of Bulgarian communists' striving to firmly abide by Lenin's teachings and Soviet political practice from the 1920s and 1930s.

The attitude toward wealthy peasants was especially negative, and they were subject to all manner of economic, political, and psychological pressure. Since in the earliest years the state depended on some such farmers to fulfill its plans, the interim category of "wealthy peasant" was introduced into the political language of time to indicate farmers who possessed more than 100 decares of land and who at the same time showed a certain loyalty to the government. In such cases, the pressure on this category of farmer was primarily economic, but conditions were constantly ripe for such individuals to be permanently labeled as "enemies."

Indisputably, the most extensive pressure was directed at so-called *kulaks*. In speeches by communist functionaries from that period, the term was directly borrowed from Soviet political jargon – and it turned out to be ill defined and quite broadly applied. Communist Party ideologues themselves used it primarily with the ideological and political connotation of "class and ideological enemies of the new state." The definition of *kulak* relevant to the Bulgarian context was that given by the Council of the People's Commissars of the USSR in May 1929: "A *kulak* is someone who uses hired labor, owes a mill, saw-mill or equipment which he rents out, engages in trade and usury and in general has other sources of non-labor income, including priestly income."[19] Clearly, this image was constructed as the antithesis of the "laboring peasant," a particular model of the exploiter, the rural capitalist and bloodsucker. Over the course of time, this definition proved narrow for the people who were labeled with it for various reasons. Initially, it included people who did not fulfill the compulsory state deliveries. After that, the definition was expanded to include all former members of the oppositional Agrarian Union, provincial functionaries of the old political parties, grocers, merchants, publicans and so on. Thus, in practice, it came to include a large number of people uninvolved in agricultural labor who became the target of a systematic campaign. Beginning with the Law on Nationalization from December 1947, creameries, carding machines, soda-water and lemonade factories, etc., were seized from such individuals. The law for reducing the number of pubs and limiting drunkenness left one pub for every 700 residents, the first of which obligatorily had to be municipal. This law, however, had an ulterior motive: along with introducing a monopoly on spirits, it was of vital significance in the gradual marginalization and eventual abolition of the private trade in alcoholic beverages.[20] The effect was that the state took control of yet another important arena for economic and personal independence.

The American anthropologist Katherine Verdery, who studies collectivization in Romania, has turned attention to the fact that in everyday practice in the village, "class struggle" constituted part of the constant process of constructing the image of the *kulak* in the local community through labeling certain villagers in this way and of deconstructing it, i.e. removing the label from a given individual after he demonstrated active cooperation with or a desire to cooperate with the government – which she calls the *making and unmaking process*. There are also cases in which, under certain circumstances, an individual or a group that has already been "labeled" once again falls into the category of *kulaks*, a situation Verdery calls *remaking*.[21] Thus, in fact, a permanent contrast between individualization (or decontextualization) on the one hand, and communalization (or contextualization) on the other is established.[22] In all cases, the imaginary construction of a status group stigmatized by the official authorities is achieved. *Kulaks* as a rule are blamed for all agricultural difficulties and failures in governmental initiatives, while poor results on farms are attributed to the "*kulaks* who have infiltrated them." One of the important aspects of party politics is the creation of public intolerance toward such people. This is achieved primarily through pointing them out: naming them in lists specially displayed in visible locations, condemnatory "graffiti" on their houses, and so on. We can call the second stage "segregational." It is expressed via a refusal to serve such individuals in stores, pubs and cafés, through publicly demonstrated reluctance to speak to them and so on.

The other method allowing the state to seize resources from wealthier peasants was the regime's tax policy. In 1946, a progressive income tax was adopted that freed from taxation any farmer with up to 30 decares sown with grains and 20 decares with intensive crops, one cow and up to five sheep.[23] Clearly, this law was meant to stimulate small and mid-sized farmers, upon whom the state had placed its hopes for fulfilling the quota system and for feeding the population in general. It directly encouraged grain production, which in the first years after the war turned out to be one of the country's few sources for acquiring hard currency. The new law for income tax, passed in 1950, introduced an even steeper scale for taxing private farmers. At the same time, symbolic taxes were levied on TKZS members only for "land for personal use." The income tax was particularly restrictive with respect to the so-called free professions as well: craftsmen, grocers, etc. By and large, its general message was to indicate the only possible path open to the peasant – joining the TKZS.[24]

One of the important tools for pressuring the peasantry was pricing policy. The restriction of market mechanisms in this sphere was brought about through regulating not only the prices of agricultural goods but all goods in the country in general. So-called limit prices were introduced as early as 1945. The strict regulations and the government's broad powers under the law against speculation were undoubtedly instrumental in controlling prices. However, despite the large number of criminal prosecutions under the law, a parallel black market continued to function. Thus, in actuality three pricing levels were established within agriculture. The first was the so-called quota system. As mentioned above, under this system the price of agricultural products was completely symbolic, often half of the "limit price" and a quarter or sometimes even less of the product's real value. The very existence of such farcical prices can be explained by a "courtesy" of sorts: the state's plundering of the peasantry was formally hidden behind some form of "selling." Only after fulfilling their quotas could farmers sell any surpluses on the market. This occurred at the abovementioned "limit prices." These prices were also used by the state for its "free purchasing" of agricultural products: meat, skins, eggs, etc. The term "free purchasing" must be understood quite conditionally, since very often the motivations behind such sales were not economic. The whole propaganda and administrative apparatus was harnessed to fulfill the state plans; thus, in many cases, "free purchasing" became compulsory. The category of "limit prices" also applied to so-called industrial goods, which could only be purchased with ration coupons. Such coupons could only be obtained once a given peasant had received a certificate showing that he had fulfilled his deliveries to the state. Due to the chronic shortage of such goods, Bulgarians frequently resorted to in-kind bartering of agricultural products calculated in terms of "limit prices" and manufactured goods.[25] Thus, the peasant found himself in a situation in which he was selling his own output to the state cheaply but also buying products from the state at prices lower than their actual value. The third category of prices consisted of the actual market prices. They were officially classified as "black market," but the state frequently turned a blind eye to the existence of such a market. Normally, such deals took place "out of sight" via direct negotiations between the producer and the buyer.[26] Even though the state undertook showy campaigns against black-market participants from time to time, the functioning of this market in fact guaranteed the continued functioning of the quota system. It was typical practice for peasants who had produced less than they owed to the state to compensate for this lack precisely through purchases from the black market.

The functioning of the rationing system in the country was also based on the social and class differentiation officially postulated by the Communist Party. Since according to its ideology, the working class was seen as the "avant-garde" of the society that must be built, it was quite officially favored. This can be seen in norms adopted in government documents guaranteeing the minimal subsistence requirements of various groups of Bulgarian citizens. Thus, for example, the daily amount of wheat flour a peasant should receive was calculated at 300 grams, while a worker received a card for bread equal to 1 kilogram a day.[27] Even when peasants began fleeing to industrial sites in the cities, initially as temporary and seasonal workers, the government decreed that they should be relieved of their agricultural compulsory state deliveries only for the time they were engaged in construction and industry, and accordingly they would receive larger rations only for that period.[28] Of course, not all peasants received the same rations. Thus, for example, local agents could use their own discretion in allotting rations – the wealthier a farmer was, the less he needed rationed goods. As far as *kulaks* were concerned, one of the regular measures employed against them was to totally deprive them of ration coupons. Thus, peasants essentially fell into yet another type of dependence on their local leaders, as the latter held "both the bread and the knife." This tool was one of the most actively used in the course of collectivization. Officially, the ration system was partially lifted in 1951 and completely abolished in 1953; hence it ceased to be a factor in the final phase of the collectivization process. As is well known, however, the socialist economic system constantly creates shortages, thus the old practice of rationing was frequently revived for certain products in various periods.

The last but certainly not the least important tool the regime used to force peasants into the TKZS was direct psychological and physical pressure. It took on various forms and inevitably accompanied the other coercive tools. In the context of the arbitrariness on the part of the *militsia* and the courts which had swept the country and due to all manner of pressure, fear slowly but surely gripped the rural population. Through systematic beatings of the most stubborn opponents of collectivization, as well as arrests, forced resettlements, and show trials, this fear deepened, in the end transforming into a surefire agent for change. Perhaps the most effective means of psychological pressure on peasants was tying their entrance into collective farms to their children's future. The threat hanging over peasants' heads that their sons and daughters would not be able to continue their education (and in some cases were actually hindered from doing so) and to make something of their lives turned out to be the most powerful weapon communist agitators possessed to force open even the most stubbornly locked doors.

The first stage of mass collectivization

From the beginning of 1948, the regime openly let it be known that "the socialist reconstruction of agriculture" was inevitable and allowed for no alternatives. The government's next step was in keeping with this: the law for buying heavy agricultural equipment from private owners, which was passed on February 18, 1948.[29] This law in practice nationalized heavy agricultural machinery, for which the former owners were compensated with securities for which they ultimately received almost nothing. In this way, the authorities definitively put an end to the competition between the private and cooperative sectors in rural Bulgaria, since the former completely lost its ability to modernize and was left armed only with the wooden plow to compete against the tractor, the combine and so forth. This blow was aimed not only at *kulaks* and capitalist landowners but especially at mid-sized farmers, those who owned between 50 and 100 decares. It was obvious that no matter how numerous his household might be, without machinery and with only hand labor and draft animals, a private farmer was in no condition to work such an amount of land.

On March 4, 1948, the law for amending the legal ordinance on TKZS was passed.[30] It legitimated the Ministry of Agriculture and Forestry's supervisory-directorial functions over the collective farms in the country, giving it the right to approve newly founded farms, to issue compulsory orders to them, and to reverse decisions made by their governing bodies. These new amendments required TKZS members to surrender all of their land to the collectives, as well as their livestock and agricultural tools. In this way, a clearer boundary was drawn between collective and private farmers. Those who had joined the collectives up until that moment faced a dilemma, as they had harbored hopes of retaining at least part of their lands and of being simultaneously semi-cooperative, semi-private farmers. Indisputably,

136 *The times of high Stalinism*

all of these amendments represented a crucial turning point in bringing the TKZS closer to the Soviet *kolkhoz* system, as the differences between the two steadily melted away. Formally, no move was made toward nationalization of the land, but, in fact, peasants lost their ownership over it.

On August 26, 1948, dogmatically following Soviet experience, the Politburo entrusted Agriculture Minister Titko Chernokolev with the task of preparing a series of measures that would give the green light to implementing the next stage: the mass expansion of collectivization. Despite concentrated governmental efforts supported by the Communist Party at all levels, only approximately 7 percent of the land was farmed cooperatively at that time.[31]

At the very end of 1948, the GNA passed a law banning rental agreements for sharecropping and other contracts.[32] In reality, it abolished private land-lease agreements in rural Bulgaria and opened space for the TKZS and hence for the state as the sole and unchallenged leaseholder and hence exploiter of agricultural labor.

This policy was temporarily and partially amended after May 1949, when private farmers were allowed to breathe a bit more easily. This was due to the strict copying of the Soviet model, according to which before the final drive to force peasants into collectives, a *peredyshka* or "short break" was allowed. Stalin himself gave his approval.[33] Softening the course of collectivization became the official party position at the June Plenum of the Central Committee of the same year. In this spirit, the Council of Ministers issued corresponding decrees that took steps toward a certain decrease in compulsory state deliveries and at the same time increased the purchase prices of agricultural goods.[34] Governmental committees were also formed to investigate abuses that had occurred in forming the collectivized blocs of land within the TKZS.[35] This was taken by peasants as a sign that the noose had been loosened, and they began lodging complaints en masse regarding fields wrongly seized from noncooperative farmers, unequal exchanges or simply the usurpation of property. The total number of such plaintiffs in 1949 was 61,854. Ten of thousands of requests to leave the TKZS were submitted.[36] Thus, this *peredyshka* confirmed one of the communist leadership's basic conclusions: that further collectivization would be unfeasible if pressure on peasants were to let up.

From the beginning of 1950, the pace of forced collectivization abruptly increased. The implementation of a sweeping plan for its mass expansion began with a new decree issued by the Council of Ministers and the Central Committee of the BCP, which defined the Ministry of Agriculture's duties, the size of deliveries and the steps to be taken toward the impending mass expansion of collectivization.[37] It called for 2.5 million decares to be newly incorporated into cooperatives, bringing the total amount of collectivized land to 8 million decares – approximately half of the country's arable land. The stipulated deliveries for milk and wool saw particularly steep increases.[38]

On April 4, 1950, the Central Committee of the BCP held its next plenum, which was dedicated to the course of collectivization. Its goal was

The Bulgarian village under communism   137

to definitively confirm the so-called model statutes for TKZS, which would unify the mechanisms for the functioning of the individual farms, as well as establishing the size of lands and number of animals allowed for "personal use" in the various parts of the country. The adoption of these statutes strongly restricted the working of land "for personal use" – which ranged from 2 to 5 decares (including a house and yard), depending on the district's geographic particularities. It also restricted the possession of livestock to one draft animal (horse, donkey, mule), one head of large horned livestock (a cow or buffalo, or in exceptional cases, a goat), and up to five sheep.

At the same time, the regime adopted a new correction to the delivery requirements on milk. It introduced a tax on every single head of large horned livestock; in other words, the compulsory delivery system was extended to include barren cows and oxen.[39] All of this closed the vicious circle: in order not to be forced to buy milk to pay off their debts to the state, farmers had no choice but to give up their oxen. Without oxen, they could not work their land. In short, there was again only one escape: joining the TKZS.

The TKZSs and social change in the Bulgarian village

Initially, TKZS arose as production units of the village universal cooperatives. Very soon in their development, however, the TKZS began to show certain signs of the "Cuckoo Syndrome": having invaded a foreign "nest," the TKZS began to take over ever newer functions from the older cooperatives, extending their prerogatives over secondary production activities, trade, services, and little by little shoving aside the other economic actors in the village. First of all, they took over existing village (municipal) stock-breeding farms, in this way gaining control over private farmers' animal husbandry, as the latter were forced to resort to the TKZS's services to breed their large livestock. The TKZS also seized village stills from consumer cooperatives, thereby gaining not only new resources but also control over the production of every household's alcohol. Some of the collective farms also began creating stores, bakeries, public baths, and so on for their members. They also extended loans in the form of cash and materials for the building of new houses. The creation of the Central Cooperative Union in April 1947, which in practice nationalized cooperative work, rendered the village universal cooperatives, which had grown particularly popular in Bulgaria in the previous fifty years, irrelevant. Under the new conditions, the older cooperatives were ever more frequently reduced to local centers for state purchasing and trade. The authorities essentially nationalized the cooperative trade network and took steps toward creating one of its own only where no other such network existed.[40] Thus, at the very end of the 1940s, through duplicate structures, the primary one being the TKZS, the totalitarian state in practice wiped out the authentic cooperative movement. The private sector, not only in agriculture, but also in trade and services, grew ever more dependent on the insatiable economic form of the TKZS, which very soon swallowed up the entire system.

138　*The times of high Stalinism*

The American anthropologist Gerald Creed likens the gradual "softening" of the peasants and the developing mass expansion of collectivization to "a rolling snowball due to the thick network of connections between them."[41] Inarguably, there is something reminiscent of a snowball in the social nature of the phenomenon. To start the snowball rolling, however, a critical mass is necessary – in this case, a critical mass of peasants who transform from a minority core into a dynamic majority. In different local communities – ethnic and religious groups, various settlements, regions and so on – this "critical mass" varies, being strictly individual and subjective. Since in the months of mass collectivization, radio rediffusion sets typically announced how many and whom of the villagers had joined the collective, the rough psychological boundary was between a quarter and a third of the villagers. Here the identities of those joining was of decisive importance. Typically, the poorer peasants waited for the wealthier, more industrious and authoritative people in the village to join. Thus, drawing on Creed's metaphor, we can liken mass collectivization to a rockslide or avalanche, in which first the top layer grows unstable, beginning to "weigh" on those beneath it. Due to the dense network of family-kinship and neighborly ties, those who subsequently joined would themselves "weigh upon" the most stubborn and staunchly resistant members of the local community. This hastened the avalanche-like process but at the same time increased its destructive power and the consequences for its staunchest opponents. After the definitive capitulation of the masses, they were completely crushed in the literal sense of the word and/or cast out as unneeded fragments that had no place in the village. They were usually looked upon with hostility not only by the authorities but also by their fellow villagers who were not like them. In this dynamic process, the role played by the so-called loyalists in the village collective was particularly significant. They constituted the majority of the people, who had no well-formed political convictions but who, following established traditions and a well-honed instinct for self-preservation, supported the government and who turned out to be very important in building up the abovementioned "critical mass." Here we must introduce yet another concept that expresses relatively precisely the social processes of that time: namely, skeptical collaboration. In other words, most people had no choice but to collaborate with the regime, without, however, any particular individual possessing the corresponding personal or ideological motivations. It was precisely this that helped erode the classical socialist system from the inside out, when conditions eventually made this possible.[42] A series of accompanying economic and socio-psychological phenomena developed in parallel to skeptical collaboration, forming a specific mentality and attitude toward the world. This also created another problem: that of public and individual identity and the behavioral models behind them. Individuals were forced to speak and act in one way in public, while at home, in the intimate space of the family, they spoke and acted in a completely different manner. Of course the phenomenon being described here is not characteristic only of the village: it is a general characteristic of the social nature of the whole communist system. In the village, however, in the context of the enormous changes taking place, it created a particularly sharp contrast. Precisely due to the necessity to situationally take up different roles in the private and public spheres, a fault line appeared in the social and political identity of the average person, in whom duplicity was permanently ensconced. In the beginning, the basic agent of these processes was fear. In the first years, fear was evoked by absolutely concrete, physically tangible causes, but it slowly and surely was replaced by a vague and depersonalized feeling that gave rise to new social and moral norms. These general tendencies also presuppose numerous exceptions, which, however, do not cast doubt on these tendencies' relevance in the majority of cases.

The villagers' resistance

Pressure on villagers was so intense that joining the TKZS became their only possibility for survival. By the end of 1950, more than 50 percent of Bulgarian villagers were already members of collective farms. However, dissatisfaction, both among those "inside," as well as among those who were still "outside," was so strong that spontaneous rural unrest broke out in many places in the country. It is striking that all of these were exclusively female uprisings. Indisputably, female resistance in Bulgaria had serious historical roots, primarily in the demonstrations against the war and hunger in the period of 1913–1918. It is also well known that women were also the keepers of tradition to a much greater extent than men, who frequently sought means of supporting their families outside of their villages. Since in the traditional person's imagination, collectivization meant the "destruction of tradition," it is completely natural that women should be much more categorically opposed to it. One of the main reasons, however, is tied to the shared fear (on the part of both men and women) of the inevitable repression that would follow and the hope that the authorities, for purely humane reasons, would look upon resistance by the "weaker sex" more indulgently.

Such unrest began on July 3, 1950, in the large Catholic village of Bârdarski Geran, whose residents were resettled Bulgarians from the Banat region. The uprising was even better organized in the Orthodox village of Stavertsi in the Oryahovo Region. Four days after the incidents in Bârdarski Geran, the residents of Kozloduy also rose up in protest. The female rebellions both in the villages mentioned above, as well as in five others in the same region of northern Bulgaria, essentially remained on the level of publicly demonstrated dissatisfaction with the TKZS and governmental policy; however, participants' behavior did not overstep a certain invisible boundary, and when things went so far as to involve the use of firearms, this had a paralytic effect on the majority of protestors and the authorities gradually reestablished control over the situation. The subsequent public trials against the most active participants, which were framed more as instructive examples, further sowed hesitation and confusion in the villagers' souls and thwarted their desire

140   *The times of high Stalinism*

for further resistance. The uprisings in villages in the Vratsa district during 1950 were not the only such outbreaks in the country; at the same time, such disturbances arose in the Asenovgrad, Plovdiv and Pârvomay regions and in individual settlements in other regions.

The hunger thousands of farmers found themselves facing in the winter of 1950–1951, thanks to the system of state deliveries and the increasing pressure to join the TKZS, was ground for a new wave of unrest to break out in dozens of villages in the spring. This time the resistance was centered in the Vidin and Kula regions in northwestern Bulgaria. The immediate cause of the new wave of village uprisings was the course taken "from above," allowing for a certain easing of pressure. This, incidentally, was Stalin's latest piece of "advice" to his Bulgarian proxy, Chervenkov. This new approach was taken up by the whole Bulgarian communist leadership and was one reason for the general softening of their attitude toward the peasantry. One of the main initiatives in this spirit was aimed at distancing the central leadership from the "grassroots" violence and arbitrariness and placing it in the role of arbiter and fair judge in the conflict between the villagers (but not the *kulaks*) and upstart local authorities. Following this line, on March 12, 1951, an Extended Plenum of the Central Committee of the BCP was called in Sofia to discuss and condemn "distortions in party policy." A week later, on March 19, a joint decree was issued by the Council of Ministers and the Central Committee of the BCP renouncing "distortions in rule of law in the people's democracy." This new course was noisily announced by the party mouthpieces, in brochures printed specifically for that purpose, as well as broadcast over village radio diffusion sets, so that it would reach the entire populace. The anticipated effect was that it would calm unrest in the villages. The real reaction, however, proved to be exactly the opposite. This move was interpreted by the villagers as a "green light" to leave the collective farms and to reacquire the fields, gardens, vineyards, animals and equipment that had been taken from them. In many cases, a true rural revolution broke out. The clash between villagers and the authorities was particularly dramatic in the Plovdiv and Asenovgrad regions, where thirteen and twelve villages, respectively, rose up against the regime.[43] The situation in Pleven was similar – this region was the first to suffer the loss of human lives as a result of direct clashes with government forces.[44] In this respect, the Kula and Vidin districts also followed suit. Just as in the preceding year, the unrest took the form of spontaneously organized protests with the goal of collectively deserting the cooperative farms, returning confiscated livestock and equipment to individuals' personal barns, and submitting petitions en masse to leave the TKZS and so forth. From the Kula district, unrest spread into the neighboring Vidin district. Indisputably, the proximity of the two districts to the Yugoslav border, at a time when bilateral relations were at their most hostile point, played a significant role in the mass rural uprisings. A series of illegal groups formed within Yugoslav territory that raised the morale of the rebels and promised them armed support. This was also the reason why hundreds of villagers fled across the border. The authorities took

The Bulgarian village under communism 141

all the necessary measures so as to thwart the spread of unrest to other areas of the country. As a supreme representative of the government, the Secretary of the Central Committee of the BCP, Todor Zhivkov, who at that time was in charge of agriculture, arrived in the region. Hundreds of *militsioneri*, State Security agents, and full-time and part-time political workers were mobilized. An enormous number of people were arrested. Some of them were convicted in public political trials in their home villages, while others were sent to prisons and concentration camps without ever having been officially sentenced. Mass campaigns to forcibly resettle relatives and loved ones of participants in the uprising or those who had fled across the border were also organized. A total of 3,500 people from that region were interned in camps in other parts of the country. Approximately the same number was imprisoned. The measures taken by the authorities indeed managed to paralyze rural resistance and to hinder the further spread of unrest, but at this stage they were in no condition to force the villagers back onto the collective farms. However, the regime decided to forgo further experiments and temporarily halted the mass imposition of collectivization.

The temporary lull

Following established Stalinist tradition, such unrest had to be explained also by "hostile activity" within the ranks of the Communist Party. This was the reason that the leadership of the district committees of the BCP in Vidin and Kula to be replaced, while some of their members were convicted and sent to prison. A scapegoat was sought at the highest levels: in the very Politburo of the Central Committee of the BCP. Such a victim was found in the person of the Minister of Agriculture, Titko Chernokolev. Although he had staked his entire political career on collectivization, he still never managed to win the trust of the party leader, Chervenkov. He had been accused several times at various party forums, at one point for unrealistically optimistic plans released by the Ministry for creating new collective farms, at another for failing to fulfill various types of compulsory state deliveries.[45] Despite the fact that he had been banned from issuing orders related to the progress of collectivization during the previous year, on June 15, 1951, he circulated a memorandum in the name of the Ministry of Agriculture and Forestry permitting private harvests for those villagers who had planted their fields before joining the collective farms.[46]

The party leader's reaction was exceptionally harsh. In a telephoned telegram, he personally repealed Chernokolev's "memorandum," while the Minister himself was stripped of all posts, excluded from the BCP and arrested.[47] The ex-Agriculture Minister spent seven months in detention at a State Security prison, where they were clearly hesitant as to exactly what charges to bring against him. The model of behavior used with respect to Chernokolev as well as the evaluations and epithets employed were highly reminiscent of the drama that had flared up two years earlier around the

142   *The times of high Stalinism*

Communist Party's second-in-command, Traycho Kostov. However, most likely the Kremlin was refusing to give the green light to a similar unfolding of events. The Chernokolev case is particularly emblematic of the logic of decision-making, the interrelations and vicissitudes at the top of the party–state pyramid. It also serves as an epilogue to the second stage of collectivization, when pressure was temporarily discontinued.

All periodizations of collectivization in Bulgaria to date have noted the tangible cessation in pressure on villagers to join collective farms during the second half of 1951. It was precisely then that the third period began, which could be called a stage of "delayed waiting" and which continued until the beginning of 1956. Calls to "obey the people's republic/socialist rule of law" led to the practical discontinuation of pressure immediately following the end of the unrest. It can be said that in the wake of the events of March and April 1951, the authorities' efforts were above all concentrated on "defending the ground they had already won." This was the case with regard not only to efforts to maintain the overall amount of collectivized land but also to measures for the economic, financial and personnel-related stabilization of already existing farms. Between the villagers and the state, a truce of sorts was established, which transformed into a dynamic equilibrium that was primarily expressed in a "game of nerves." The suspension of mass collectivization, however, did not at all translate into reduced pressure on the private farmer. On the contrary, the regime was worried that a stabilization of the private sector might ensue, thus it increased pressure via compulsory state deliveries. Although the quotas for grain remained the same in 1952 as they had been the previous year, fulfilling them became more onerous due to the exceptionally harsh winter and the poor harvest. Deliveries of animal products were also drastically increased.

One of the reasons for the difficult state villagers found themselves in during this period was related to the reductions in the prices of basic foodstuffs and industrial goods imposed by the government several times. This cheap propagandistic trick on the part of the regime resulted in extremely harsh consequences for agricultural producers, whose output was further devalued. This was true both for the products they sold on the free market as well as for those sold at purchase prices determined by the state. According to some calculations, these steps reduced prices of agricultural goods almost twofold in comparison to 1950.[48]

The final push toward mass collectivization

The fourth and final stage in the collectivization of the Bulgarian village, also known as the "period of the second mass collectivization," began at the beginning of 1956, which was a crucial year for the political system. This fact in and of itself is indicative of how relative this border is in the history of the regime and of the deep continuity between the waning Chervenkov and the rising Todor Zhivkov in terms of their long-term strategy, tactics

The Bulgarian village under communism 143

and forms of influence employed. Krushchev centrally issued the directive to continue and complete mass collectivization wherever possible to all the satellite states.[49] This was the reason why the forced completion of the processes in Bulgaria, Hungary, the GDR, Romania, and Czechoslovakia coincided.[50] Exceptions to this model included Yugoslavia, where the regime gave up on collectivization as early as 1953, and Poland, where the process ended in 1956 with barely 11 percent of the land collectivized. The concurrence in all the remaining countries, however, unambiguously shows that this was a directive from Moscow and that its fulfillment was a test of the loyalty and suitability of the new political leadership in the respective countries.

Shortly following the "de-Stalinizing" April Plenum of the Central Committee of the BCP in 1956 and the subsequent change of the supreme leader, a new Central Committee Plenum completely dedicated to agricultural questions was convened during July of the same year. There the decision was made for collectivization in the country to be completed within one to two, or at the most three, years. What was new in this case was that a system of measures was developed that would lead to a tangible improvement in the quality of life for villagers in the cooperative farms. The first such measure was the exemption of "land for personal use" from state deliveries. A more serious step taken to strengthen the entire cooperative sector, however, was related to the so-called agricultural pension, which members of such farms would have the right to receive from the beginning of the following year, 1957.[51] Indeed, such pensions were quite modest, but for villagers this act held enormous symbolic significance. The other important decision made at the plenum was to allow so-called *kulaks* to become members of the cooperative farms, without, however, being able to take up leadership positions within them.[52] The goal of these changes was to publicly demonstrate the new face of the government in order to reassure the most stubbornly anti-collectivist villagers. Thus, during 1958 and the beginning of 1959, collectivization reached even the last and most remote mountain villages and huts, spreading throughout all of rural Bulgaria. The final chords in the process coincided with the most intense wave of mass desertion of the mountainous regions and of radical changes in occupation.

One of the important characteristics of the final phase of collectivization was the increase in centralized state budget support for weak and economically ineffective TKZS. Their gradual bureaucratization, the fact that they eventually became "overgrown" by activities that were unsuitable and generated net losses, as well as their ever-more-remote administration were only some of the reasons for their poor economic performance. These findings forced the government, in parallel with putting the finishing touches on collectivization in 1959, to begin the so-called consolidation of cooperative farms. This continued over the next two years as well, its goal being to create larger-scale and more sustainable agricultural organizations by eliminating most of the administrative officials within them. As a result, the acronym OTKZS

144 The times of high Stalinism

appeared, standing for *Obedineno trudokooerpativno zemedelsko stopanstvo* or "United Labor Cooperative Agricultural Enterprise," whose headquarters would be located in a more central town, while the structures within the smaller neighboring farms would be fused with it. In most cases, the latter continued to exist as separate grain-producing or animal-husbandry brigades within the newly consolidated cooperative. The effects of this bombastically implemented campaign were temporary. It resulted in a certain reduction of the bureaucratic stratum that had formed in the agrarian sector, but by the end of the decade this bureaucracy had re-entrenched itself.

The villagers' strategies for adaptation

Government decrees reducing compulsory state deliveries offered a certain freedom for sales at unregulated prices. It can definitely be said that this led to the strengthening of private producers in the village despite active counter-pressure from the state. A comparison of the private and cooperative sectors in terms of economic results, productivity and motivation is categorically unflattering for the latter. This is clearly illustrated even in official statistics on cooperative members' so-called auxiliary farming (their working of plots granted "for private use") in the late 1950s. Such land constituted 9–11 percent of the total area of the TKZS but produced nearly a third of the sector's output, including two-thirds of yield of animal products.[53] This data, extracted from official statistics, shows that such auxiliary farming was at least three times more efficient than the TKZS's remaining activities. It would be an exaggeration, however, to characterize this form of production and existence as "proto-capitalist" and "free market." It must be noted that this form of production was precisely parasitic to the classical system of cooperative agriculture from which it drew resources (machines for tilling, seeds for sowing, animals for breeding and offspring, etc); it also promoted the development and flourishing of abuses and theft and guaranteed farmers placement of their goods, without incurring any risks or losses.

The partial "loosening of the noose" that was noted above failed to put a stop to the continuing alienation of the villager from the land and the ever-growing distance between him and the economic institution interceding in the cultivation of that land. Attempts by the government to compensate for this by giving some freedom to the semi-private farmers who gradually cropped up via a series of decrees and sub-normative acts along the lines of what was called "self-satisfaction" only led to the improvement of certain individuals' and families' economic situations but did not give rise to collective economic and social engagement in state-cooperative agriculture on the part of the peasantry. This tendency further increased during the next reorganization of the sector in the early 1970s, when the *Agrarno-promishlenite kompleksi* (APK, agrarian-industrial complexes) were created. They further intensified the concentration and centralization of agriculture, while those producers

The Bulgarian village under communism 145

who remained in the village definitively ceased to consider the land they worked "their own."

All of this led to a deep crisis in the Bulgarian village. Life there became ever less attractive against the backdrop of the opportunities the city and the urban lifestyle offered. These demographic tendencies and attempts to "soften" or at least slow them through purposive state policies affected not only the villages but the cities as well – and in practice influenced the whole of Bulgarian society. The situation can be generally characterized by two processes that took place in parallel and which were mutually interdependent: that of the depeasantification of the villages and the rustification of the cities. The first phenomenon was first described by two American sociologists, Irwin Sanders and his student Roger Whitaker, who, over the course of half a century, from the 1930s until the early 1980s, studied the Bulgarian village (and the case of Dragalevtsi in particular). They characterized depeasantification as a process of the gradual disappearance of traditional peasants through their transformation into cooperative members and in the end into state wage workers on their own land or proletarians, in the Marxist sense of the term.[54] Depeasantification also has a broader meaning: the loss of specific older worldviews and moral values, the change in daily life and occupation, and, last but not least, drawing closer to the conditions of urban life. In parallel to this phenomenon, in the cities the opposite process of rustification was taking place. At the root of the phenomenon lay the huge migrational flow to the city that continued unabated for decades. As a result, the time-honored mechanism for "assimilating" to city stereotypes, for the gradual integration of villagers into the urban economy and culture was nullified precisely due to the lack of gradualness and smoothness in the transition and due to the fact that the usual proportions in the process of this acculturation were upset. In fact, the precise opposite occurred: the migrational wave from the village to the city was so significant that after 1960s we have witnessed the gradual engulfment of old city culture, which was eroded by its ideological devaluation and by the new migrants' more vital and adaptive milieu. Of course, here again we are not talking about the peasantry in the classical sense of the term. Uprooted from its natural environment and placed within new economic conditions, it had already lost some of its stereotypical characteristics and was inclined toward adaptation. As a result of these complexly interacting processes, a new type of "citizen" (in the literal sense of "city-dweller") was created, who is named as such more thanks to official terminology (including legislation) that designates an individual as a citizen and not because he is a representative of a certain occupation, certain social characteristics and cultural attitudes. Inside, he remains a peasant, having lost, however, a significant portion of the traditional virtues of his former social category. Thus, the depeasantification of the villages and the rustification of the cities, working in parallel, would eventually bring the two former strata very close together and lead to the creation of the average "new socialist person," who would combine within himself characteristics of both constituent parts, without being identical to either one of them.

146 *The times of high Stalinism*

Notes

1 Veska Zhivkova, *Bâlgarskoto selo prez vekovete*, b. d. i., Sofia: Nauka i izkustvo, 1985, p. 46.

2 The initial attempts to abolish this inequality were made during Stambolov's first government. However, since the legislation was drastically at odds with centuries-old tradition, these regulations were not applied in practice. This necessitated the adoption of a new Law on Inheritance in 1906, which gave sisters the right to inherit property half the size of that of their brothers. In the great majority of cases, however, they continued to voluntarily give up their shares over the following decades as well.

3 Boris Mateev, *Dvizhenieto za kooperativno zemedelie v Bâlgariya v usloviyata na kapitalizma*, Sofia: Partizdat, 1967, p. 12.

4 Vladimir Migev, *Kolektivizatsiyata na bâlgarskoto selo (1948–1958 g.)*, Sofia: Stopanstvo, 1995, p. 23.

5 Mincho Minchev, *Bâlgariya otnovo na krâstopât (1942–1946)*, Sofia: Tiliya, 1999, p. 118.

6 *Otechestven front* 196 (April 25, 1945); Ivan Marinov, *Za dobroto na horata*, Sofia: Zemizdat, 1991, pp. 127–130.

7 It was published in the *Dârzhaven vestnik* on April 25, 1945.

8 *Rabotnichesko delo* 21 (February 1, 1946).

9 Rima Kanatsieva, "Sotsialno-ikonomicheskata politika na BRP (k) po otnoshenie na seloto (9 septemvri 1944 – 1948 g.)," in *Izvestiya na Instituta za istoriya na BKP*, vol. XLVIII, Sofia: BAS, 1983, p. 146.

10 *Dârzhaven vestnik*, 81 (April 9, 1946).

11 *Dârzhaven vestnik*, 31 (May 12, 1921).

12 *Stenografski dnevnitsi na XXVI ONS, 1 red. sesiya, 22 zasedanie*, p. 125.

13 TsDA, f. 1B, op. 13, a. e. 111 (1), l. 84–90.

14 Titko Chernokolev, *Dokumenti, publitsistika i spomeni za nego*, Sofia: Partizdat, 1989, p. 125.

15 Nikola Popov, *Agrarnite otnosheniya pri sotsializma*, Sofia: Partizdat, 1976, pp. 82–84.

16 *Dârzhaven vestnik*, 158 (July 11, 1947); Vladimir Migev, *Problemi na agrarnoto razvitie na Bâlgariya (1944–1960)*, Sofia: K&M, 1998, pp. 17–18.

17 This term replaced *naryadite* ("quotas") beginning in 1950, but in fact they refer to one and the same thing.

18 Migev, *Problemi*, p. 23.

19 Robert Konkvest, *Chemerna zhetva: Sovjetska kolektivizatsija i teror gladi*, Belgrade: Filip Višnjić, 1988, p. 70.

20 Nikolay Mihov, "Kapitalisticheskite selski stopanstva v Bâlgariya i tyahnoto likvidirane (September 9, 1944–1958 g.)," unpublished doctoral dissertation summary, Sofia: Sofia University, 1988, p. 18.

21 Katherine Verdery, "Dialogic Collectivization: 'Rich Peasants' and Unreliable Caders in the Romanian Countryside, 1948–1959." Working paper, University of Michigan, 2004, p. 4.

22 Verdery, "Dialogic Collectivization," p. 9.

23 *Dârzhaven vestnik*, 234 (October 12, 1946) (*Law for Taxation of General Income*); Chernokolev, *Dokumenti*, p. 84.

24 DA – Vidin, f. 180, op. 1, a. e. 31, l. 58–61; f. 332–b, op. 2, a. e. 4, l. 367.

The Bulgarian village under communism   147

25 Kanatsieva, "Sotsialno-ikonomicheskata politika na BRP (k) po otnoshenie na seloto," p. 130.

26 Migev, *Problemi*, p. 121.

27 TsDA, f. 172, op. 1, a. e. 15, l. 192 (Accounting reports from the Department of State Supplies and State Reserves).

28 TsDA, f. 136, op. 5, a. e. 2374 (Decree of the Council of Ministers No. 2454, September 8, 1950).

29 *Dârzhaven vestnik*, 48 (February 28, 1948).

30 *Dârzhaven vestnik*, 63(March 18, 1948).

31 Minka Trifonova, *BKP i sotsialisticheskoto preustroistvo na selskoto stopanstvo (1944–1958)*, Sofia: Partizdat, 1981, p. 103.

32 *Dârzhaven vestnik*, 304 (December 27, 1948).

33 *Dârzhaven vestnik*, 304 (December 27, 1948), p. 48.

34 Migev, *Problemi*, pp. 109–111.

35 TsDA, f. 1B, op. 18, a. e. 50, l. 3.

36 TsDA, f. 1B, op. 18, a. e. 50, l. 3.

37 *Rabotnichesko delo*, 18 (January 23, 1950).

38 TsDA, f. 136, op. 5, a. e. 439, l. 1–9.

39 TsDA, f. 136, op. 5, a. e. 599, l. 80–84.

40 Nadya Manolova, "Obedinenie i reorganizatsiya na bâlgarskoto kooperativno dvizhenie v sredata na 40-te godini," *Istoricheski pregled*, 2 (1990): 16–33, p. 28; Hristo Ganev, *Moyat zhiznen pât: Razvitie na kooperativnoto dvizhenie v Bâlgariya mezhdu dvete svetovni voyni*, Sofia: Zahari Stoyanov, 2006, pp. 178–225.

41 G. W. Creed, *Domesticating Revolution: From Socialist Reform to Ambivalent Transition in a Bulgarian Village*, University Park, Pa.: Pennsylvania State University Press, 1997. Cited in the Bularian edition: *Opitomenata revolyutsiya: Ot sotsialisticheskite reformi kâm protivorechiviya prehod v edno bâlgarsko selo*, Sofia: Apostrofi, 2005, p. 79.

42 For a more detailed discussion, see Mihail Gruev, *Preorani slogove: Kolektivizatsiya i sotsialna promyana v Bâlgarskiya severozapad (40-te–50-te godini na XX vek)*, Sofia: Institute for Studies of the Recent Past/Ciela, 2009.

43 AMVR, f. 1, op. 1, a. e. 1795, l. 85–89; a. e. 1873, l. 2 (Reports on the agent-operative work of the State Security division within the Plovdiv and Asenovgrad regional office of the Interior Ministry for 1951).

44 Migev, *Kolektivizatsiyata*, pp. 123–125; Yosifov, *Totalitarnoto nasilie v bâlgarskoto selo (1944–1951) i posleditsite za Bâlgariya*, Sofia: Sv. Kl. Ohridski, 2003, p. 186.

45 *Rabotnichesko delo*, 126 (May 6, 1950); Gyurova, "Kooperirane na selskoto stopanstvo v Plevenski okrâg 1949–1951 g.," in *Izvestiya na muzeite v Severozapadna Bâlgariya*, 15 (1989): 165–168.

46 TsDA, f. 1B, op. 5, a. e. 160, l. 80. (Obsâzhdane v otdel "Selskostopanski" na TsK na BKP).

47 Migev, *Kolektivizatsiyata*, pp. 141–142.

48 Migev, *Kolektivizatsiyata*, p. 151.

49 This thesis was expressed orally by Professor Dariusz Jarosz, who has worked in the archives of the Central Committee of the BCP (b), at a conference on collectivization in eastern Europe organized by the Central European University in Budapest: "The Collectivization of Agriculture in Communist Eastern Europe: Comparison and Entanglements from the 1930s to the 1980s," Budapest, June 22–23, 2007. He claimed that he was not allowed to make notes and that

148 *The times of high Stalinism*

documents were brought to him selectively, but one of them was a protocol from precisely such a meeting at the Kremlin.

50 For more details, see Ch. (Hg.) Boyer, *Zur Phisionomie sozialistischer Wirtschaftsreformen: Die Sowjetunion, Polen, die Tschechoslowakei, Ungarn, die DDR und Jugoslawien im Vergleich*, Frankfurt: Max Plank Institut fuer europische Rechtsgeschichte, 2006; see also Karl Eugen Wädekin, *Agrarian Policies in Communist Europe: A Critical Introduction*, ed. Everett Jacobs, The Hague and London: Martinus Nijhoff Publishers, 1982.

51 Notice from the Presidium of Parliament, No. 1 (January 2, 1957) (Law for Amending the Law on Pensions); Angel Tanov and Vasil Mishev, *Agrarnata politika na BKP na sâvremenniya etap*, Sofia: Partizdat, 1981, pp. 177–178.

52 *BKP v rezolyutsii i resheniya na kongresite, konferentsiite, plenumite i na Politbyuro na TsK*, vol. IV, Sofia: Partizdat, 1955, pp. 31–40.

53 *BKP v rezolyutsii i resheniya na kongresite, konferentsiite, plenumite i na Politbyuro na TsK*, pp. 198–199; Marcheva, *Todor Zhivkov*, p. 235.

54 Irwin Sanders and Roger Whitaker, "Tradition and Modernization: The Case of Bulgaria," in J. Lutz and S. El-Shaks (eds.), *Tradition and Modernity*, Washington, DC: Washington University Press, 1982, pp. 62–70.

6 The *goryani*

Armed resistance against communist repression

In the Transition years after 1989, the topic of *goryani* (literally "mountaineers") was loaded with an enormous emotional and moral charge. Authors critical of socialism regularly used the armed *goryani* movement (1945–1955) as an antidote against weighty (self-)accusations that Bulgaria was the only country in the former Eastern Bloc that had submissively accepted the Soviet regime that had been imposed on it. "Traditional Russophilia" and "communist attitudes" that had dominated before 1944 were most often pointed to as an explanation for the lack of Bulgarian analogues to the Hungarian Revolt, Prague Spring, and Polish Solidarity.[1] Attempts to "rehabilitate" Bulgaria's image, on the other hand, cited mass support for the opposition (1945–1947) and particularly the armed resistance of the *goryani* (1945–1955).[2]

After the anti-communist opposition was crushed and its leader Nikola Petkov was executed (in 1947), the possibilities for legally challenging the usurpation of power and communist oppression were exhausted. The mass terror, the subsequent forced resettlement of families of the "disappeared," and the system of concentration camps through which tens of thousands of individuals passed, however, did not succeed in smothering the broad discontent in the country. At the end of the 1940s and the beginning of the 1950s, Bulgaria was gripped by various forms of open resistance. The *goryani* movement was only one of the visible tips of the iceberg of widespread discontent. Alongside this movement, we also must mention the uprisings against collectivization in western Bulgaria, the so-called "conspiracies" (attempts to resurrect the outlawed BANU – Nikola Petkov and other patriotic and right-leaning organizations), the creation of illegal anti-communist organizations, the growing popularity of Radio Goryanin, and so on.

The basic "catalytic mechanisms" for transforming the latent, hidden discontent into open forms of resistance were the collectivization of land, the attempt to artificially construct a Macedonian nation in southwestern Bulgaria, and mass repression (known as *divo pravosâdie* or "wild justice").[3] For a nation in which two-thirds of the population still lived in villages and made their living working the land (according to the 1946 census), the collectivization of this land and its inclusion in TKZS had the destructive effect of an atomic bomb. One of the basic institutions stabilizing traditional village society that had dictated the rhythm of economic and daily life for centuries was obliterated. The decision to "build" a Macedonian nation had more regional reverberations (primarily in southwestern Bulgaria), but it blatantly trampled the right to self-definition of a considerable portion of the Bulgarian population, which had spent the past few decades in a constant struggle to defend its identity. However, the wave of red terror that washed over the country in the first few days following September 9, 1944, and which escalated after the legal opposition was crushed, was the basic catalytic mechanism setting off armed resistance. When even supporters of the regime (declared "enemies with a party ticket") could be subjected to harsh inquisition, sent to concentration camps without a trial, or simply executed and buried in mass graves which they themselves were forced to dig beforehand, there were no guarantees that you would not be the next one called in for a "short questioning." In many cases, individuals turned to desperate (and doomed measures) – going underground and joining the armed resistance – as a defensive reaction to the ubiquitous terror. One of the first armed groups, the G. M. Dimitrov Brigade, arose in 1945 with "the goal of self-defense." The future commander of the detachment, Ivan Leshnikov, was arrested immediately after September 9, 1944, on false charges that he was a former police officer. During an attempt to execute him without trial outside of Kyustendil, he managed to break free and flee into the mountains. His brother-in-arms, Bogdan "Boncho" Tsekov, had similar motives for joining the resistance. His father had been killed as early as September 7, 1944, while he himself was sent to the Bogdanov Dol concentration camp. Boncho managed to escape and hid in the woods. In his testimony before the court, another member of the G. M. Dimitrov Brigade admitted, "We were in the Balkan Mountains to hide and were armed with the goal of self-defense."[4] In a letter to the communists from his home village, Gerasim Todorov, commander of the Sixth Pirin Detachment, noted that he had left his family, relatives, and friends "purely and solely to save my life."[5]

Perfectly in keeping with folktales, the mountains were seen as a sort of parallel world, where one whose life was in danger could hide, save himself and wait for help from some external "superpowers." Thus, more than once the *goryani* would claim that, in fact, they were in the mountains "waiting for the Americans." The primary motivation – to save themselves for repression and terror – filled the forests with staid, middle-aged people with established livelihoods, families and children. They represented a wide variety of social backgrounds and ideological predilections (anarchists, agrarians, disappointed communists, nationalists, fascists). This made coordination between the separate formations difficult and rendered the emergence of a unified central leadership impossible. Thus, unlike the Lithuanian *gorski bratya* ("mountain brothers") and the Polish Armia Krajowa ("Home Army"), in Bulgaria the movement consisted of a collection of numerous fragmented local centers of resistance without an ideological framework to knit them together, a structure or a visible external enemy in the form of an occupying army.

In fact, perhaps the closest parallel to the *goryani* are the Romanian *haidci*. Despite the considerably larger geographical and temporal reach (up until 1961) of their activities with all of their ideological diversity, the *haidci*'s lack of visible coordination and their choice of defensive tactics is very reminiscent of the way the Bulgarian anti-communist resistance recruited, was structured and developed.[6] Unlike them, Draža Mihailović's Serbian guerrillas, the Croatian crusaders *križari*, the Slovenian *Matjaž Army* and the Albanian *balists* had military experience and established networks from World War II. All branches of the Yugoslav armed resistance (perhaps with the exception of the *balists*) had clear ideological (anti-communist) profiles, while the Croatians, who could rely on the hidden, yet powerful support of the Catholic church, used proactive tactics, often attacking small government targets and police patrols, or organizing punitive campaigns against local party leaders deemed guilty.[7]

Understanding the *goryani* movement as a desperate attempt at self-defense will also help us explain the illegal groups' passivity, which seems strange at first glance. Despite being armed, the detachments almost never undertook punitive or subversive actions. Instead, they were content with propagandistic and explanatory activities among the population and with the distribution of leaflets.[8] Given the enemy's crushing military superiority, its proven brutality, and the inability of most of the rebel groups to cross the border into foreign territory, the refusal to undertake armed resistance appears to be a more reasonable strategy for survival.[9] Isolated attempts on the part of some *goryani* groups to undertake more active initiatives led to their splintering (for example, the Goryani Resistance Movement in Kazanlâk, the National Christian Cross in the Asenovgrad region, or the First Sliven Band) or disgusted the local population.[10] The support of a wide network of *yatatsi* or "associates" is vital to the survival of every illegal group. Individual terrorist acts or retribution against brutal local BCP activists or *militsia* members attracted unwanted attention from the government, which would immediately concentrate its resources in the region in order to root out the threat that had arisen. The first victims of such operations were precisely the *goryani*'s relatives and *yatatsi*, who were often subjected to inhuman torture. This also explains why, after several individual acts of revenge, the G. M. Dimitrov Brigade in Kyustendil, the Union of Free Warriors in the Pazardzhik Region, and the Second Sliven Band lost their broad popularity and the population gradually distanced itself from the *goryani*.[11]

If until the beginning of the 1950s going underground was primarily an attempt to survive amidst the mass terror that had gripped the country, with the beginning of the Korean War (1950–1953), hopes for an impending American–Soviet clash that would also affect Bulgarian territory seemed ever more realistic.[12] This motivated opposition "sleeper" cells that had managed to survive despite the repression to "activate" and to create bases that could offer support to an eventual American invasion. During this second period of struggle, the number of *goryani* increased significantly. From 173 fighters in 1945 and 780 at the end of 1948, in 1950 their numbers reached 1,520, while in 1952–1953, the security services spoke of 3,130 *goryani*.[13] The Ruse Regional

152   *The times of high Stalinism*

Agrarian Illegal Center, the First and Second Sliven Bands, the Committee for Resistance in the Sliven Region, and other groups that arose in 1950 had a clear ideological profile. At the same time, other ideologically motivated "conspiracies" also sprang up in Karnobat, Zvezdets, the Lovech and Asenovgrad regions, the villages of Dragana, Brezhanovo, Vâlchedrâm, and others, which did not manage to create armed wings or which did not aim to do so.[14] In most cases, these more clearly formulated *goryani* units also followed the wait-and-see tactic employed by the earlier armed groups, refraining from more decisive attacks against local authorities.

The resistance groups generally enjoyed serious support from the local population. According to Marian Gyaurski and Konstantin Kasabov, researchers studying the movement, the ratio between *goryani* and *yatatsi* was 3:1. This data is based on information from trials after the armed groups had been crushed.[15] Given that the average family had approximately five members, I feel that Gyaurski and Kasabov's estimates are far too low. It must be kept in mind that besides the *goryani*'s relatives and loved ones their supporters also included more than a few *yatatsi* who were not blood relatives. Circles of friends, familial ties, and former party networks were successfully mobilized in support of the resistance. Most detachments were backed by illegal organizations whose task was to deliver food, weapons, funds, and information to the *goryani*. New fighters for the detachments were also recruited through such channels. Given all this, a ratio on the order of 1:5 or 1:6 seems far more likely. Thus, given the nearly 7,000 officially registered *goryani*, their supporters numbered at least 40,000–50,000. This serious "rear guard" in practice made *goryani* "supply raids" on dairies and alpine sheep-pens unnecessary; such actions had been frequently undertaken by partisans from the communist resistance before September 9, 1944, who clearly did not enjoy such support from the local population.

Broad public support for the *goryani* was admitted more than once in official documents for internal use. A report by the Deputy Interior Minister from 1949 emphasizes that "the population in the region where the band is active . . . offers more support to the detachments than to the authorities," while an inquiry conducted by State Security in the early 1950s confirmed that "the local population actively assists them . . . and hides them."[16] It is highly likely that this wide public support for the *goryani* frightened the regime far more than the *goryani* groups themselves, who avoided direct clashes with the authorities. In order to neutralize this threat, the government and the security services attempted to construct a dense network of undercover agents that would reach even the most isolated corners of the country. As early as 1948, in a specially issued set of instructions, the government declared that the fight against the *goryani* must be waged not with force (blockades, mobilization of the army, or special units) but rather through gathering insider information and planting agents within the bands. Experience had shown that the use of physical force often backfired and led to new defections into the mountains.[17] In staking its bets on a network of agents, the Bulgarian government adopted

The *goryani*   153

the NKVD practice, which had already proved successful in the struggle against the *gorski bratya* in the Baltic region.[18] Of course, the quality of the agents did not always meet the necessary standards, and in more than a few cases such networks turned out to be "unfit for such work and traitorous."[19] A report from 1951 notes, "Many former agents had gone underground and become bandits."[20] On the whole, however, this practice proved to be successful, and with the help of insiders most of the *goryani* groups were broken up. Again thanks to undercover agents and despite the widespread popular support that such detachments enjoyed, the average active duration of such groups barely exceeded seven or eight months. The only units that managed to survive for a year or slightly longer were Gerasim Todorov's Sixth Pirin Detachment, the two Sliven bands, and the Illegal Patriotic Organization in the Trân region.

Given the extremely brief period during which *goryani* bands managed to survive, and given the passive, wait-and-see tactics they adopted, the question arises as to what extent we can speak of resistance and mass discontent in Bulgaria at all. The *goryani*'s refusal to engage in radical opposition to the communist regime (through individual terrorist acts, sabotage, and open threats) should not be interpreted as a sign of fear. The waiting tactic they chose was the result of a sober and realistic analysis, which showed that without external reinforcements, entering into open confrontation with the authorities would put their network of *yatatsi* at risk and would lead to a loss of the population's support. The expressions of discontent, which grew ever more widespread during the first half of the 1950s – the uprisings against collectivization in the Kula, Vidin, Vratsa, Bela Slatina and other regions of the country, the "conspiracies," and the second wave of the *goryani* movement – show that tension continue to build, making it ever easier to cross the invisible border between passive and active resistance.[21] It also should not be forgotten that this wave of open opposition to the communist regime came after several years of strenuous legal struggles on the part of the Fatherland Front opposition (1945–1947). Although it did not take up the path of open conflict, the Bulgarian resistance against communism managed to sustain widespread discontent over time, something that the significantly more radical movements in Poland and Lithuania, for example, failed to do. The Armia Krajowa was disbanded in the summer of 1945, while the ranks of the nearly 30,000-strong Lithuanian *gorski bratya* abruptly shrank to only 4,000 only a year later, and to 2,000 by 1948. At the same time, the culmination of the *goryani* movement in Bulgaria was significantly later: between 1950 and 1953.

After the end of the Korean War and following the West's clear reluctance to support the rebellions in Berlin (1953) and Budapest (1956), hopes faded that a Soviet–American war would break out that would lead to the fall of the communist regime in Bulgaria. Given the geopolitical positioning of forces, armed opposition began to appear ever more pointless even to the most uncompromising anti-communists. The collapse of hopes for external aid came at a moment when the government was ever more successfully rolling out its strategy for "corrupting the masses" with the help of various social benefits.[22]

154 *The times of high Stalinism*

Notes

1 According to Iskra Baeva, "The popularity of the system of soviet-style state socialism adopted from the Soviet Union was due to the Bulgarian people's *traditional Russophilism*" [my emphasis]. I. Baeva, "Aprilskiyat plenum: predpostavki, problemi i posledstviya," *Novo vreme*, 81 (6–7) (2006): 137–146. In his monumental, yet quite provocative study, Roumen Avramov insists that due to "deeply rooted *egalitarian and communal traditions . . .* which came together more organically within Bulgaria than in many other places in Eastern Europe . . . here, forcibly imposed communism was accepted with significantly *more subdued resistance*" [my emphasis]. Roumen Avramov, *Komunalniyat kapitalizâm: Iz bâlgarskoto stopansko minalo*, vol. III, Sofia: FBNK i TsLS, 2007, p. 433.

2 See, for example, D. Sharlanov, *Goryanite. Koi sa te?* Sofia: Prostranstvo i forma, 1999, p. 185: "It is true, that [in Bulgaria] there were not the events of 1953 in Berlin, it is true that there was no Hungarian Uprising of 1956, it is true that there was also no Prague Spring of 1968, but it is also true that we did have ten years of armed struggle (1945–1955) against the sovietization of Bulgaria, in defense of the Bulgarian national tradition." In their still unpublished study, Marian Gyaurski and Konstantin Kasabov also claim, "in reality, the security services . . . found themselves facing a series oppositional movement that took on a mass character at certain times." Gyaurski and Kasabov, *Vâorâzhenata sâprotiva sreshtu komunisticheskiya rezhim v Bâlgariya – Goryanskoto dvizhenie (1944–1955 g.)*, in Ivaylo Znepolski (ed.), *Da poznaem komunizma*, Sofia: Institute for Studies of the Recent Past, 2012, pp. 9–57.

3 Roger Petersen of the Massachusetts Institute of Technology has recently offered a brilliant analysis of the "causal mechanisms" for shifting from passive to open resistance against the communist regime. Roger Petersen, *Resistance and Rebellion: Lessons from Eastern Europe*, Cambridge: Cambridge University Press, 2001, see especially pp. 7–15.

4 AMVR, II sâd. 2636, l. 105 and following, cited in Ivanov, *Goryanskoto dvizhenie*, p. 120.

5 AMVR, III raz. 1713, vol. 5, l. 16. Cited in Gyaurski and Kasabov, *Vâorâzhenata sâprotiva*. Numerous similar exampes are given by other authors, such as Sharlanov, *Goryanite*, p. 119; P. Ogoyski, *Zapiski po bâlgarskite stradaniya*, vol. II, Sofia: Jusautor, 2008, p. 182.

6 For more on Romanian *haidci*, see D. Dobrincu, "Historicizing a Disputed Theme: Anti-Communist Armed Resistance in Romania," in V. Tismăneanu (ed.), *Stalinism Revisited: The Establishment of Communist Regimes in East-Central Europe*, Budapest and New York: Central European Press, 2009, pp. 284–305; A. Miroiu, *Romanian Counterinsurgency and Its Global Context, 1944–1962*, Basingstoke: Palgrave McMillan, 2016.

7 D. Tasić, "Violence as Cause and Consequence: Comparing of Anticommunist Armed Resistance in Yugoslavia and Bulgaria after the Second World War," Research Project at Centre for Advanced Studies, Sofia, 2016; Z. Radelić, *Križari: Gerila u Hrvatskoj 1945–1950*, Zagreb: Hrvatski institut za povijest, 2002; M. Premk, *Matjaževa vojska, 1945–1950*, Ljubljana: Društvo piscev zgodovine NOB Slovenije, 2005.

8 In his testimony, one of the arrested *goryani* described this propaganda: "I told [the villagers] that in the Holy Bible it was written that the number 666 meant

Stalin and that the communist symbol, the five-pointed star, was made from it ... Besides that, it meant that the communists would be in power only three years and six months or forty-two months total." AMVR, II sâd. 28, l. 6–18. Cited in M. Ivanov, "Goryanskoto dvizhenie v Kyustendilsko i Gornodzhumaysko po sâdebni dokumenti ot Arhiva na MVR," *Demokraticheski pregled 9*, 27 (1994): 119–140, p. 136.

9 With the exception of Turkey and Greece, where a civil war raged until 1949, Bulgaria's remaining neighbors were also firmly tethered within the Soviet orbit. Even after the break with Tito's Yugoslavia, Yugoslav authorities very often handed Bulgarians who had crossed the border directly over to State Security.

10 For more on the conflicts that arose from differing views of what the armed groups' activities should entail, see Gyaurski and Kasabov, *Vâorâzhenata sâprotiva*, pp. 18, 22; and Sharlanov, *Goryanite*, pp. 107–109, 140. Some of the Romanian *haidci* groups also undertook proactive campaigns. For example, in 1948 members of the National Defense Front–Haidci Corps attacked and robbed the tax agency in the village of Teiuş in Transylvania. Miroiu, *Romanian Counterinsurgency and Its Global Context*.

11 Sharlanov, *Goryanite*, pp. 89, 131, 147.

12 The hope that "the Americans would come" soon was among the basic motivations for both the Croatian *križari* and the Romanian *haidci*. In Romania, the phrase "Vin americanii!" (The Americans are coming!) was particularly popular. Disillusionment in Romania came later, only after the crushing of the Hungarian Revolution in 1956. This perhaps explains the longer duration of the armed anti-communist resistance north of the Danube, which lasted until the end of the 1950s and the beginning of the 1960s. See https://en.wikipedia.org/wiki/Vin_americanii! (accessed July 9, 2017).

13 Gyaurski and Kasabov, *Vâorâzhenata sâprotiva*.

14 Ogoyski, *Zapiski*, pp. 136–153, 247–248, 251–252, 309.

15 Gyaurski and Kasabov, *Vâorâzhenata sâprotiva*.

16 Cited in Sharlanov, *Goryanite*, pp. 158, 164.

17 Sharlanov, *Goryanite*, pp. 60–61, 77.

18 Petersen, *Resistance and Rebellion*, pp. 19–20.

19 Sharlanov, *Goryanite*, p. 70.

20 Cited in Sharlanov, *Goryanite*, p. 70.

21 From position 0 towards positions +1, +2 and +3 according to Petersen's scale, which is well known in the literature. See Petersen, *Resistance and Rebellion*, pp. 7–15.

22 Ivaylo Znepolski, *Bâlgarskiyat komunizâm: Sotsiokulturni cherti i vlastova traektoriya*, Sofia: Institute for Studies of the Recent Past/Ciela, 2008, pp. 221–254.

7 The sovietization of Bulgaria

A basic resource for the new communist authorities

The reasons for the swift sovietization of Bulgaria are numerous and complex. By schematizing the picture to a certain extent, we can divide them into objective and subjective reasons. More has been said about the objective reasons, while the subjective ones have remained in the shadows. The main objective reason is indisputably the occupation of the country by Soviet troops – in accordance with agreements made between the countries in the Anti-Hitler Coalition, Bulgaria was left within the zone of Soviet influence. As a result of this, it was relatively easy to establish a communist government, which, lacking the solid support of Bulgarian society, could not have remained in place without the military threat on the part of the Soviets. The fear of this external force headed off civil war and was the basic guarantee backing the regime.

Objective factors in the sovietization of Bulgaria

Another important objective precondition for the sovietization of Bulgaria was the nature and state of the BCP. Although initially quite small in terms of membership, it was a well-constructed conspiratorial organization, which even before September 9, 1944, had infiltrated various sectors of society, including the army and the educational system. This gave it an enormous advantage over the traditionally leftist and centrist parties from the Fatherland Front coalition, which were of a more purely electoral type. This is also why after the coup the Communist Party easily took control of the entire state apparatus from within, despite the fact that certain ministries were formally headed by noncommunist politicians. Yet at the same time, the party was extremely dependent and incapable of making important decisions, since it had grown deeply accustomed to relying on and being led by external directives, which it never discussed or questioned. In fact, its central leadership bodies had been transferred outside of the country long before the war and the launching of the resistance movement. The foreign office of the BWP(C) in Moscow and Comintern exercised direct control over the party. Directives, which were coordinated in advance with Soviet institutions, were issued within Bulgaria, and the party's domestic bureau saw to their practical implementation.

The sovietization of Bulgaria 157

Thus, even after seizing power, the Bulgarian communists continued to look toward Moscow, all the more so since their supreme leader Georgi Dimitrov continued to live there for a year after the "victory" and, in direct contact with the occupying forces, he gave them instructions via encoded telegrams written in Russian. The party's entire normative basis for action and for building the new state was developed in Moscow. The second Fatherland Front government was discussed and confirmed in Moscow, as were the subsequent personnel changes within it. Bulgaria's new constitution was also developed and approved there. Church business and the elevation of the Bulgarian Exarchate into a patriarchate was also decided by the Kremlin. It even got to the point that party membership booklets were printed in the Soviet Union, which, incidentally, also supplied the paper for the BCP flagship newspaper *Rabotnichesko delo* (*Workers' Cause*).

In order to understand the nature of this process, we must differentiate the concepts of "communization" and "sovietization," even though in a certain geostrategic context they seem to overlap. A communist regime in and of itself does not necessarily have to take on the form of Soviet government – a theoretical possibility, which, as already mentioned above, Stalin himself did not hesitate to toy with in the first few months after the war. Nevertheless, the difference between communization and sovietization is real, and it can be demonstrated by comparing Tito and Georgi Dimitrov, or rather by comparing the respective regimes established under their guardianship. The difference in the behavior and the destiny of these two prominent communist leaders reflects the difference in their positions, the degree to which they could rely on their own forces, and hence the difference in their personal self-confidence and pride. Tito possessed the self-confidence of a person who had fought and achieved something on his own, while Dimitrov's support was top-down. He was an envoy without roots in the party base, who had been assigned the mission of acting as spokesman for the great country's interests. This is why at any sign of displeasure from the supreme leader, Dimitrov castigated himself and immediately rectified his behavior, while Tito rejected Big Brother's direct control over his activities and refused to appear in Moscow for explanations and briefings.[1] However, the difference between the two of them did not end there. It is also true that the two men would not suffer an equal defeat in an open conflict with Moscow. The threat of physical retribution hung over Dimitrov's head, as he was uncertain and likely fearful of treachery within his close circle of associates (indirect evidence of this exists), while Tito in practice showed that he was in a position to safeguard himself from the long arm of Stalin. However, for Dimitrov, who was familiar with the mechanisms of the Moscow trials, the threat of his symbolic death had to be every bit as frightening as that of his physical demise. Conflict with Moscow would destroy him on the international level; he would risk losing his mythological image, while he still nursed hopes of being an actor on the broader political stage. This is also an expression of pride, but one that made him more rather than less dependent on Moscow.

158　*The times of high Stalinism*

Yugoslavia established a communist regime par excellence even before Bulgaria, yet the former could not be called a sovietized country. Despite the fact that mass repression in Yugoslavia was every bit as intense as in Bulgaria, if not more so, given the Yugoslavs' dual targeting of the bourgeois as well as party circles designated as "Muscovite agents" with ties to the Soviet Union and Comintern. Sovietization is a multilayered process, which, on the one hand, expresses itself in Soviet infiltration of all levels of the governmental structure, while on the other, goes so far as to apply pressure on and pervade even the most intimate forms of everyday life.

The indisputable agents in this process were the Bulgarian political emigrants returning from the Soviet Union, who automatically took up key posts in the Communist Party and state administration, transferring to them the oppressive psychological atmosphere of Soviet reality. Having worked mainly in the army, the police, the propaganda agencies or the Comintern apparatus, they possessed no experience of (or taste for) political life in a democratic, pluralistic environment. For them, anyone who was different could not be anything but an enemy – present or future. They transferred their Soviet attitudes and gradually transformed political life in Bulgaria into a conspiratorial drama – they continued to use encoded telegrams, special couriers, pseudonyms, and to weave networks of secret agents and to cultivate Trojan horses to infiltrate the ranks of allies and enemies alike.

Here, too, of course, Georgi Dimitrov played a leading role. He returned to Bulgaria with his enormous authority as a heroic anti-fascist, with his international reputation, with his close contracts with the Soviet leadership and even Stalin himself – all of which was dazzling to the provincial party milieu. His every word or gesture was taken as an indisputable maxim, he acted as and possessed the status of the leader of the country long before he took up any official post. His advice and public statements constructed the image of the Soviet Union as a model to be followed and as the only sure bulwark on which Bulgaria could depend to overcome postwar difficulties. His position resulted both from his personal devotion to the Soviet state, to which he owed so much, as well as from the obligations he had taken on. It was not a question merely of obligations to an external power whose representative he was, but also of a deep tie to the communist idea and the international proletarian revolution, whose basic mainstay was this same power.

Just like his Moscow patrons, Dimitrov believed the Leninist idea that the crisis that had gripped the capitalist system during World War II had created the necessary conditions for the global change that could not be realized after World War I. Thus, his actions were guided by principles deriving from a more global strategy, which was being successfully implemented before his eyes in a large part of the European continent. Using his contacts in Moscow, Dimitrov immediately began weaving a wide network of direct contacts between similar state institutions in Bulgaria and the USSR. Human resources flowed in both directions: hundreds of BCP activists went to the Soviet Union for training and to familiarize themselves with "Soviet vanguard experience," and to establish the necessary connections.

For their part, numerous Soviet advisers, agents, and specialists were installed at all levels within the Bulgarian state apparatus: the army, the police, the judicial system, governmental bodies . . . They introduced and defended Soviet standards and practices everywhere. They indicated who should be arrested, initiated the newly formed police into the techniques for wrenching the necessary confessions from detainees, and prepared charges in the political trials. Such overzealousness in introducing Soviet experience led to paradoxes. In a telegram from Moscow even before his return to Bulgaria, Georgi Dimitrov, following Soviet experience for overcoming the production crisis, recommended that the Bulgarian agricultural sector "sow Soviet buckwheat so as to feed the population," despite the fact that buckwheat is absolutely foreign to Bulgarian agriculture and customs and requires different climactic conditions.[2]

The other real factor contributing to sovietization was Bulgaria's ever-increasing international isolation, which it was pushed toward due to its blind following of Stalinst policy. Under pressure from "Big Brother," Bulgaria cut almost all diplomatic and economic ties to the allies from the Anti-Hitler Coalition. Bulgaria was also harshly dragged into a serious conflict with the country which until recently had been its closest ally within the communist bloc: Yugoslavia. This brought Bulgaria face to face with serious economic problems, which could only be escaped by ever-closer bonds with the Soviet Union. Thus, Bulgaria's complete economic dependence also made it completely politically dependent. In early 1945, Georgi Dimitrov relayed Mikoyan's words from Moscow: "The USSR can give Bulgaria all basic things it needs for its agriculture and industry. In this respect, it could get by without any particular trade relations with America and England."[3] All the signs of a loss of national sovereignty are in evidence. The process of sovietization spread from public to private life: from party and state symbols, slogans for mobilization, mass songs, education, culture, the food supply and language, to strict prescriptions regarding personal behavior. Brigadiers, shock workers, and Stakhanvites became an indelible part of the "labor front." Strange abbreviations adopted from the Soviet Union were called upon to organize life: Narmag (short for *naroden magazin*, or "people's store"), Agitprop, Rabfak (from *rabotnicheski fakultet*, a special department designed to prepare workers for higher education), Glavlit (the censorship institution for literature and publishing), and so on. Language was transformed into a tool for the transfer of reality. Cities and mountain peaks with centuries-long histories were renamed for Stalin, as well as boulevards, factories, and schools, among other things. Other prominent Soviet officials were similarly honored, including generals in the occupying army. After Georgi Dimitrov, Vâlko Chervenkov would also be called "the Bulgarian Stalin."

The final significant objective factor contributing to the sovietization of Bulgaria was the existing illusions concerning the nature of Soviet reality and

160 *The times of high Stalinism*

the communist utopian ideal of a just and peaceful society. Such illusions were truly believed by a considerable portion of the impoverished rural and urban population, as well as by the proletarianized intelligentsia. Such ideas were tied not only to deference to the Soviet Union's power but also to the enormous prestige the USSR enjoyed at the end of the war. Years later, the social democrat Petâr Dertliev, who was imprisoned during the 1950s, would note this fact: "That was a time when a significant portion of our people and the West looked toward the advance of Soviet troops with sympathy and hope. Only far-sighted and well-informed politicians harbored fears about how events would development, but they, too, remained unarticulated."[4] To this we can also add arguments about the stable state of the Soviet economy, whose growth had accelerated during the Great Depression that had seized capitalism during the 1930s. The combination of these two factors exercised a powerful influence and confirmed opinions about the superiority of the Soviet planned economy over the destructive chaos of the capitalist market. In fact, such opinions held sway even beyond small and occupied Bulgaria:

> After the rout of Germany, in Europe the opinion arose that the future belonged to some sort of leftist political system, something halfway between Western capitalism and Soviet-style socialism. When you think about it, during 1944–1945, people's impressions of capitalism, especially in Europe, were derived primarily from the crash of 1929 and the subsequent global crisis, which led to widespread unemployment and created fertile soil for the rise of fascism and its aggressive foreign policy. The Soviet Union was considered the only country which had escaped such damage and economic decline [. . .] After the war, people believed that the end of capitalism as they knew it had arrived. No one could have imagined the successful capitalism that appeared during the 1950s and 60s. Thus, it was inevitable that people would think that some leftist political system was necessary.[5]

In Bulgaria, these arguments were rounded out with another, specifically Bulgarian one: the masses' traditional Russophilia, whose as-of-yet-unexhausted roots lay in the revival period, and the belief that in the name of Slavic solidarity, the Soviet Union would best defend Bulgaria's national interests when concluding the peace treaty. To a great extent, this prestige also carried over to the BCP, which was the direct link with the Soviet Union and which served to guarantee the benevolence of this huge, infuriated bear. However, the Communist Party itself had also managed to earn its own prestige, thanks to its behavior during the period of resistance and its readiness to take risks and make sacrifices. The seizure of power on a local level and the party's organizational capacity, which was based on Soviet formulas and which arose in the postwar context, caused the population, which was weary of war and social difficulties, to see in the party a sure means for overcoming insecurity and chaos.

The sovietization of Bulgaria   161

If we move slightly farther west in Europe, we will see that far more developed societies were also susceptible to similar illusions. The whole plan for the GDR, which arose based on the Soviet occupation zone, was interpreted by many Germans as an expression of the intention to build a "new" democratic Germany which had radically broken with the Nazi past and which would be based on a democratic "noncapitalist" society. Many émigré intellectuals settled in the GDR, believing in the possibility for a new social project. This project also attracted a series of world-famous and influential intellectuals, who returned from the United States, including Bertolt Brecht and Ernst Bloch. This idea also garnered wide responses that spread beyond class and political antagonisms. "The truth is that in 1945, the appearance of radical antifascism was welcomed not only by those close to the new rulers' leftist parties, but also by the bourgeoisie . . . Such ambitions were crushed by the Soviet authorities, concerned for their hegemony."[6]

To all of this, we must also add one consideration of a strictly theoretical nature.

> The October Revolution not only created a historic division of the world, but it also established the first State and the first post-capitalist society, it also separated Marxism from the socialist political movements . . . After the October Revolution, socialist strategies and prospects began to be based more on a single political example than on an analysis of capitalism.[7]

The truth is that in Bulgaria, even if the true situation had been recognized, there was no one in the mid-1940s or later who could have performed an analysis of the mutations within postwar capitalism to assess the opportunities that the Americans were offering to Eastern Europe as well through the Marshall Plan, and to draw the necessary conclusions and create work plans for future development.

Subjective factors in sovietization

Precisely at this moment, we arrive at the extremely fundamental subjective reasons for the encroaching sovietization. The core leaders within the party and the state did not possess any governing experience, while those who came from the Soviet Union were not familiar with any public practices besides Soviet ones; thus, in both cases they depended above all on external help and literally copied Soviet governing techniques. The situation concerning local leadership (i.e. party members who remained in Bulgaria before and during the war) was particularly alarming. Such local leaders were numerically dominant – some of them even occupied top party and state positions, but they constituted the majority of the party's middle echelon and served as the local face of the party. It was most often a matter "our people," i.e. Communist Party sympathizers or their relatives, who lacked not only any leadership

162   *The times of high Stalinism*

qualities but also educational credentials.[8] After the communists seized power, the old Bulgarian elites in all spheres, which had formed slowly and with much difficulty, were methodologically destroyed or marginalized to the periphery of society. In terms of qualified personnel, an enormous vacuum arose. This was the reason why some established officials or specialists in the economic sphere were allowed to retain their jobs for several years, but after that the communists' increasing appetite for positions and privileges sealed their fate as well, at least for those who had not managed to change horses in time. Ignorant people with limited intellectual capacity were leading the state, and they could give the appearance of competence only when they followed and propagated norms and rules issues from above, without being capable of independent thought and decisions.[9]

The problematic lack of qualified personnel was recognized above all by Soviet-trained party leaders and was the basic motivation behind the adoption of measures for creating their own workers' intelligentsia.

> In our national economy, we unconditionally should have used and should use the old specialists who were trained earlier in the bourgeois spirit, helping them to reeducate themselves and to join socialism. But here we made a serious mistake, in my opinion: we uncritically used some old specialists, who ostensibly presented themselves as being *on our side*, and we trusted them too much; not only did we trust them too much, but we left them fully in charge of a series of crucial sectors in the national economy . . . We were late in arriving at a viewpoint and a solution to the question of the preparation of specialists from the ranks of the working class for various branches of our economy, and for economic and state leadership. It is sufficient to recall that it was only last year that we established by law the requirement that only the sons and daughters of laborers can study in institutes for higher education.[10]

The true picture can be discovered in documentary studies on the partisan movement in Bulgaria conducted during the 1970s and 1980s on the initiative of the party itself, which, with the self-confidence of one stably ensconced in power, was eager to reconstruct its historic path to that power, and in such a way to reconfirm its legitimacy. Lengthy publications appeared detailing the histories of most of the regional partisan organizations, whose activities also included leading the local partisan movement. "Precisely [these studies] provide an opportunity via quantitative analysis to trace almost completely the rural social profile of the communist movement during the war years, from which the first generation of the new state elite would be recruited."[11] According to the authors of one such study covering the partisan movement in the Plovdiv region, approximately 20 percent of the partisans in the region were uneducated or had only an elementary education; while overall, 71 percent of the partisans had no more than a primary education. In terms of the social characteristics, the statistics are as follows: 75 percent of the partisans

The sovietization of Bulgaria   163

are defined as villagers, while 83 percent were born in a village. In the category of urbanites, the main representatives are people of Jewish descent, who for obvious reasons ended up in the anti-fascist resistance.[12]

Let us jump ahead to the year 1957, a time marked by "victorious socialism." The party headquarters undertook a statistical study of the educational qualifications of full-time party employees in regional and municipal committees of the BCP, i.e. they received a full picture of the party nomenclature at all levels of the system, which exercised full control over the government. The results are astonishing, due above all to the fact that so little had changed in the intervening thirteen years, after so many measures had been taken for the creation of a "proletarian intelligentsia" and hundreds had been sent for training to the Soviet Union, to newly opened party schools and Rabfaks. This shows, on the one hand, the lack of desire on the part of people who ended up in the government to waste their time obtaining qualifications and to part with the post they had taken up, while on the other, it shows the feeble dynamics of personnel change within the party. Over the course of forty-five years, until the end of the regime in 1989, public space was filled with one and the same names: of those who had turned a few months or a year in the mountains into capital they could live off their whole lives.

The results of the quantitative study show that in the regional committees of the BCP, 47.5 percent of members had not finished their elementary education or had completed elementary school but not high school; 29.3 percent had high-school diplomas, and only 16 percent possessed college degrees. Some of the full-time party employees received some form of party education – ranging from three months to a year of training in party schools. Things were even worse in the district committees: 70 percent of the personnel had not finished elementary school or had completed elementary school but not high school, and only 3.8 percent had college degrees. For the entire country, the statistics were as follows: 62.7 percent of the full-time party employees had not finished elementary school or had completed elementary school but not high school, and only 7 percent had college educations.[13] These statistics confirm that not only had the most unenlightened and uncultivated stratum of Bulgaria's population seized power but also that it continued to reproduce and maintain its control over a long period. Given this level of education and the lack of any public or governmental experience whatsoever, people from such a milieu could not be a hub or engine for new policies and strategies for development; only maintaining the status quo was within the sphere of their competence – that is, holding on to power and carrying out directives issued from above. Their basic function was to mobilize the masses and exercise control. It was precisely this which made the sovietization of society not only inevitable but, from their point of view, extremely necessary since it introduced some kind of experience, albeit inefficient, and created a sense of order and of a system.

The paradox lies in the fact that with the signing of the peace treaty in Paris, Bulgaria ceased to be occupied, and the Red Army, according to its

164 *The times of high Stalinism*

contractual obligations, was obliged to withdraw from the country. However, it was precisely at this moment that the internal, hidden occupation of Bulgaria took place, assisted most actively by the BCP. The processes set into motion during Georgi Dimitrov's time were brought to their logical conclusion by his heirs, with the basic credit going to his direct successor Vâlko Chervenkov, who enjoyed the Stalin's complete trust. Dimitrov's next heir, Todor Zhivkov, rounded out the whole process by twice suggesting during the 1970s that Bulgaria become a Soviet republic. At the same time, the process of sovietization was also the process of imposing the totalitarian model on Bulgarian society.

Entanglement in the totalitarian web

This process was set into motion by a time-tested method used by classical totalitarian regimes: terror. Widespread and arbitrary violence on September 9 and over the following weeks and months has been presented by some scholars as revolutionary violence directed at the repressive bodies of the old state and people with ties to Germany (sometimes those who had simply received their college education there) or at pro-German and pro-fascist organizations. Quite soon, however, such revolutionary violence transformed into generalized terror aimed at peaceful, unarmed people whose guilt was questionable and who did not put up any resistance but who nevertheless fell into the ill-defined category of "enemies of the people" solely due to their class affiliations or disagreement with the new regime. This terror targeted an "objective enemy," that is, an alleged enemy, individuals who were enemies not because they had committed some hostile act but because they were suspected of possible disloyalty or class affiliations. The entire bourgeoisie and even the middle class were branded as fascists. This terror even subjected individuals and groups not directly affected by it to intense psychological pressure. Uncertainty and a sense of threat gripped the whole of society: everyone felt he was a potential target until he sought individual security in the bosom of the communist movement itself. Social engineering focused on inculcating Marxism-Leninism into the consciousness of the ever more alienated masses. The Bolshevik-style party avant-garde did not tolerate ideological rivals and imposed its politics with any tools it had on hand. And all of this was crowned by the figure of the charismatic leader. Dimitrov's authority, molded in Stalin's image, was imposed through his status as "the leader and teacher of the Bulgarian people," and his commands were a mandatory imperative not only for the communists and their sympathizers but for the people as a whole.

The totalitarian regime in Bulgaria fleshed itself with all the content characteristic of such regimes as a result of the accumulating effects of several key events and administrative acts: the conviction and execution of Nikola Petkov (which meant the liquidation not only of the main political opponent but also of political pluralism); nationalization and the two-year economic plan (i.e. the establishment of a state economic monopoly); the new (Dimitrov) constitution, which was adopted on December 4, 1947, by the Sixth GNA and which promulgated the principle of the unity of the legislative, executive and judicial powers; and the reorganization of the Fatherland Front into a mass social organization during February 1948, in which membership became obligatory for all citizens. The culmination was the Fifth Congress of the BWP(C) on December 18–23, 1948, when the party finally officially changed its name to the Bulgarian Communist Party and announced its program for building a Soviet-style society. The fact that the same person occupied the posts of First Secretary of the Party and Prime Minister de facto legitimized the fusion of party and state that had already taken place. The principle of the Communist Party's leading role, which Georgi Dimitrov proclaimed upon his return to Bulgaria, was finally declared publicly, even though it was not explicitly stipulated within Bulgarian law until the adoption of the (Zhivkov) constitution of 1971. The basic levers used to maintain control were the state ideology of Marxist-Leninist propaganda and terror. (Over the years of communist rule, mass purges had been carried out in all spheres of society: the state apparatus, the economy, the army, the police, the educational system, the media, the church, etc.) Overt terror eventually gave way to psychological repression and everyday coercion. Propaganda was turned into a powerful weapon, which was intended to ward off any attempt at an independent interpretation of events and to create a framework of recommended behavior. This total organization made it possible to nip in the bud even the slightest deviation from official opinion. The culmination was the opening of "hunting season" on "enemies with a party ticket."

The chief strategist behind this new approach was the new BCP Secretary, Vâlko Chervenkov. The "unmasking" of Traycho Kostov and his circle and the subsequent flare-up of paranoia over "enemies with a party ticket" provided a suitable pretext for Bulgarian political emigrants returning from the Soviet Union to take their revenge once and for all on their local, uneducated counterparts, whom they had looked down upon, and to confirm their leading position. In this respect, Chervenkov, who had mastered these Stalinist techniques very well, did not stop even at open blackmail.

> Some of those in our ranks have passed through fascist prisons. Having done time in prison is generally a plus for communist revolutionaries, and not a minus; it is a trial, a test that toughens them up. But I'll have you know that not everyone can endure in the hands of the fascist State Security and fascist prison. The enemy is also at work in prison. We need to orient ourselves correctly here, too – [to recognize] who has really been a hero and who hasn't, who caved, who didn't hold out [. . .] From this point of view, we need to review the party ranks, beginning with the Central Committee and ending with the local party organizations.[14]

Thus, the fear that the communists had implanted within society eventually took root in the party itself as well. From that point on, no matter how much

166 *The times of high Stalinism*

an individual may have contributed to the struggle, there was no guarantee whatsoever that he was beyond suspicion, that he was safe. There was a single requirement for survival: complete submission to the cult of the regime's new, strong personality that was taking shape. "The Central Committee must be a monolithic hammer pounding a single point. It must put an end to every lack of coordination, to contradictory statements and speeches concerning the party, and to unwarranted actions. The Central Committee is responsible for everything in our country. The future of the people and the state are in its hands."[15] The "Bolshevik-style unity of action from top to bottom" that Chervenkov demanded was the necessary final flourish that gave the established political regime a classic, completed totalitarian form. The totalitarization of the Communist Party was a necessary condition for the full totalitarization of society.

Notes

1 After World War II, Evgeniy Silyanov, who worked at Radio Free Europe (Munich) interviewed Milovan Đilas and discussed this situation: "In the interview, [Đilas] mentioned only one thing concerning Bulgaria – the fact that Georgi Dimitrov had given in to Stalin and hadn't had courage, unlike Tito. He told me: *You'll forgive me in your countryman's name, but he wasn't a man with a strong character.*" Irina Nedeva, *Misiya Parizh: Razgovori s Evgeniy Silyanov*, Sofia: Semarsh, 2007, p. 363.
2 Georgi Dimitrov, *Dnevnik 9 mart 1933–6 fevruari1949*, Sofia: Sv. Kl. Ohridski, 1997, p. 569.
3 Dimitrov, *Dnevnik*, p. 509.
4 Petâr Dertliev, "Prevratât beshe izvârshen operetno leko," *Standart*, September 9, 1993.
5 Richard Crampton, "Britanski uchen za bâlgarskoto partizansko dvizhenie." Interview on BBC Radio, October 11, 1992. Cited from the BTA Bulletin "Svetât za Bâlgariya."
6 Alf Ludtke, "La République democratique Allemand comme histoire: Reflexions historiographiques," *Annales*, 1 (1998): 3–39, p. 88.
7 Goran Therborn, "Leaving the Post Office Behind," in M. Nikolic (ed.), *Socialism in the Twenty-First Century*, London: Verso, 1985, pp. 225–251, at p. 227. Cited in Eric J. Hobsbawm, *L'Age des extremes: Histoire de court XXe Siècle*, Paris: Éditions Complexe/Le Monde Diplomatique, 2004, p. 483.
8 "With his high school diploma [whose authenticity has been disputed by several scholars – Ivaylo Znepolski's note], Todor Zhivkov turned out to be the best educated among the communists of his generation. Unlike most of his comrades at the time, who could boast of only a primary, middle-school or vocational-school education [. . .] the future Interior Minister and Prime Minister Anton Yugov completed sixth grade; Georgi Dimitrov's education also lasted about as long [. . .] while the future Prime Minister, Chairman of the State Planning Committee and Speaker of Parliament Stanko Todorov had finished middle school, which meant a total of eight years' schooling." See Iskra Baeva, *Todor Zhivkov*, Sofia: Kama, 2006, pp. 13–14.

The sovietization of Bulgaria   167

9   As early as October 6, 1944, an ordinance from the Council of Ministers adopted the Decree for Temporarily Abolishing Educational Requirements that had been previously demanded under the Law on Appointments for Government Officials. This was done "so that individuals suitable for the purpose could be appointed." See: TsDA na RB, f. 136, ap. 1, a. e. 23.

10 Vâlko Chervenkov, *Za osnovnite pouki ot razkrivaneto na Traycho-Kostovata banda i borbata za neyniya razgrom. Za nedostatâtsite v partiynata rabota i nashite zadachi, Doklad pred plenuma na TsK na BKP* (January 16, 1950), Sofia: Izdatelstvo na Bâlgarskata komunisticheska partiya, 1950, pp. 27–28.

11 Mihail Gruev, "Komunisticheskiyat elit v Bâlgariya: genezis i evolyutsiya," *Razum*, 1 (2005): 15–24.

12 Donko Dochev, *Semenata na buryata*, Sofia: Partizdat, 1984, p. 125.

13 *Spravka za obrazovatelniya tsenz na shtatnite partiyni rabotnitsi v okrâzhnite, okoliyskite, gradskite i rayonni komiteti na BKP (1957 g.)*, TsDA, f. 1b, op. 15, a. e. 693, l. 1–4.

14 Vâlko Chervenkov, *Za osnovnite pouki ot razkrivaneto na Traycho-Kostovata banda i borbata za neyniya razgrom. Za nedostatâtsite v partiynata rabota i nashite zadachi. Doklad pred plenuma na TsK na BKP (16 January 1950 g.)*, Sofia: Izdatelstvo na BKP, 1950, p. 41.

15 Chervenkov, *Za osnovnite pouki ot razkrivaneto*, p. 37.

8 State Security within the structure of the communist state

Ruling through violence

Building State Security

The communist State Security (*Dârzhavna sigurnost*) system was founded in 1947, when the Security Department that had existed until then was transformed into the Directorate for State Security within the Interior Ministry. In the early years of the communist regime, the Interior Ministry was headed consecutively by Anton Yugov (1944–1949), Rusi Hristozov (1949–1951), and Georgi Tsankov (1951–1962), who became infamous as the organizers and implementers of repression and political purges. Until 1954, the system was subject to frequent reorganization, which makes it difficult to trace its history. Two significant factors played a role in its structuring: on the one hand, State Security was highly dependent on the political changes within the BCP, while on the other hand, from the very beginning State Security copied the Soviet model and especially changes within the Soviet Committee for State Security. The latter's influence was strengthened by Soviet advisers sent to Bulgaria, who played an important role in organizing and introducing in Bulgaria methods used by the Soviet security services. Especially during the first decade of communist rule in Bulgaria, Soviet advisers within the Interior Ministry, the most prominent of whom was General Filatov, played such a large role that, according to some data, they were even able to challenge decisions made by the Interior Minister. General Filatov also personally led the investigations for some of the most high-profile political show trials held in Bulgaria during that period. This was a time in which State Security in practice stood above the law, which also guaranteed it an important role in making political decisions. During the first years of communism, the repressive instincts of that system were established, which were always ready to resort to overt physical violence in times of crisis. Establishing full control over the security services was one of the Communist Party's priorities upon seizing political power. Thus, after the coup on September 9, 1944, Communist Party activists or former partisans flooded the ranks of State Security both on the central and local levels, most of them without having any specialized education.

The statistical data from 1951 shows that in 1951 the staff of State Security consisted of 5,433 employees, of which 4,181 were active. A total of 2,991 were members of the BCP, 410 were candidate BCP members, 762 were members of the communist youth organization. There were only eighteen nonparty people. A total of 102 had tertiary education, 142 incomplete tertiary education, and all the rest had varying degrees of secondary education, along with those who had primary education (197 people). The lack of clear regulations concerning the functioning of these services and the lack of professional education for the staff officers within the system led to uncontrolled political violence, whose scope is difficult to establish via archival research alone.

The basic hallmark characterizing State Security's work during the whole period from 1944 until the mid-1950s is extrajudicial political repression. At the same time, institutional instability during this decade brought political loyalty to the Communist Party to the fore in the work of State Security employees, with a tendency for such loyalty to be replaced by personal loyalty to high-ranking officials or especially to the General Secretary of the BCP. Institutional instability, as well as the lack of clear regulations governing the activity of the various departments within the State Security system offer indirect evidence of the political leaders' reluctance to curb the mass political violence.

To guarantee its grip on power, the totalitarian communist state not only relied on the political police within the country, but immediately after seizing power, it also began active intelligence work. In this sense, it is very difficult to speak of a clear demarcation between the intelligence services that worked outside the country and the political police who operated within the country. The reason for this was that all the structures within State Security had clearly delineated political functions both with respect to domestic enemies of the regime, as well as with respect to external enemies; State Security developed particularly active operations against so-called "hostile emigration."

The most important characteristic of the work of the security services was the paranoia that took hold as a result of the Soviet leadership's belief in the existence of a "unified conspiracy" between class enemies within the country and the "imperialist forces" abroad.[1] The creation of this paranoid attitude led to the formation of a vicious circle, which produced a spiral of political violence. Since State Security was dependent on the political trust of the party leadership, while at the same time the party leadership expected State Security to disarm the regime's enemies, it was in the system's own best interest not only to battle existing enemies but to invent imaginary ones as well. State Security's influence was also based on this spiral: the more enemies the regime had, the more it depended on the security services to neutralize them and the more real power these structures gained. This turned the security services into a closed society rife with paranoia and violence, whose ultimate goal was to gain access to the state's political decisions. One result of this paranoid attitude was the belief that foreign services in Bulgaria operated just as actively, centrally and comprehensively as Bulgarian intelligence services were expected to act abroad; i.e. Bulgarian counterintelligence was thought to be a mirror image of such intelligence-gathering. This vicious cycle was finally

170   *The times of high Stalinism*

broken only by the change in the party's political leadership, which for a certain period of time calmed the tension within the system.

Political repression

During the period of its construction (1944–1954), State Security actively took part in the waves of political repression that characterized the establishment and imposition of communist rule in Bulgaria. Show trials against representatives of the overthrown regime, against the opposition, and later against communist functionaries were accompanied by mass arrests and imprisonment of the defendants' supporters. The targets of such repression were detained en masse in the concentration camps which were opened during this period and which were called "labor-reeducation communities." These camps constituted an alternative to judicial retribution, since imprisonment there resulted not from a court order but from an internal order issued by bodies within State Security, who, with the same administrative order, also determined the length of time a given individual was to be detained at the camp.

The first such camp opened in January 1945 at the railway station in Sveti Vrach (the present-day city of Sandanski) and existed until March of the same year. The Council of Ministers made an attempt to regulate the activities of these camps only as late as 1949. In April 1949, the prison in Belene, located on one of the large islands in the Danube River near the town of Belene, was designated as the main prison for the regime's political opponents. This quickly made the name "Belene" a synonym for political violence during the communist era. Initially, 4,500 people were imprisoned at Belene; this number decreased to 2,323 in 1952. The camp continued to exist until January 1, 1953, when the labor-reeducation communities were officially closed. The camp in Belene, however, was reopened in the fall of 1956, when, under the influence of the Hungarian Revolution, the regime reestablished this method of control over opposition-minded citizens. This camp continued to function until August 27, 1959, when the labor-reeducation communities were officially closed by a Politburo resolution. During that time, 276 people died in the Belene camp. During this period, several smaller but equally infamous concentration camps existed within Bulgaria, such as Lovech, Kutsiyan, Bosna, Buhovo, and others.[2] After 1959, political prisoners continued to be interned in the existing prison in Belene and the camp was reopened once again in the mid-1980s during the so-called Revival process against Bulgarian Turks, which means that political prisoners were detained in Belene during the whole communist period.

The only evidence about the regime and the way of life in these camps (and more specifically in Belene) can be found in the memoirs of political prisoners who survived. They include people with "incompatible" political convictions – such as the former diplomat Stefan Bochev, the agrarian Grigor Yanev, and the former communist partisan commander Dencho Znepolski.[3] Despite their very different biographies, all of them found themselves imprisoned in the camp. They were arrested by State Security without warning and after spending a few days under arrest, without a court order and without being informed of where they were going, they were taken by train to the banks of the Danube, from whence they were transported by boat to the island of Belene.

The prison on the island consisted of several sites: Site 1, located close to the river, is where criminals were imprisoned; they enjoyed a lighter penal regime than the political prisoners. Site 2 was located on the northern bank of the island facing the Romanian shore; it housed the political prisoners serving the harshest sentences. The third and fourth sites were dedicated to agricultural work and political prisoners serving sentences of up to five years worked there, while the Site 5 was located on the smaller, neighboring island of Magaretsa. Life in the camps was characterized by harsh living conditions which made survival difficult, while the inmates were forced to perform heavy physical labor – primarily logging and building dikes, which was done solely with primitive tools. Visitation rights technically existed, but they were dependent on a given prisoner's sentence and status. Inmates with the harshest sentences had the right to one visit every three months and could receive one letter from their families during that period.[4] The daily food ration at the camp included 400 grams of bread and small quantity of other staple foods, which were generally of a low quality.[5]

Organizational principles

A turning point in the history of State Security came about in 1954 as a result of the political shockwaves within the communist system following Stalin's death. Over the following ten years, the Communist Party would actively take up the struggle to "overcome the consequences of the cult of personality." In the case of State Security, decisive changes came in the form of the imposition of strict party control, a ban on State Security getting involved in struggles within the Communist Party, a demand that the institution obey the law, as well as the replacement of direct repression with more active use of informants. Evidence for this dramatic change in State Security was party leader Vâlko Chervenkov's speech to the State Security leadership on April 17, 1954, in which he tried to distance himself from State Security practices that had existed until that moment and to impose new priorities for State Security's work. The speech confirmed the necessity that State Security be "the eyes and ears of the party and the people's government" and "the proletarian dictatorship's drawn sword." At the same time, it sharply criticized State Security's practice of placing itself "above the party and the government," which was characterized as a "hostile tendency" and a "crude and dangerous distortion."[6] It unambiguously stated that since the political opposition was already decisively crushed and since "now the laws are ours, socialist," State Security must cease to function according to "administrative measures" and to consider itself above the law and the party, and that it must take its place as a state institution subordinate to the party leadership.[7]

172   *The times of high Stalinism*

Political loyalty to the BCP was State Security's governing principle after the process of de-Stalinization. All important resolutions regarding the security services' activities were prepared by the Interior Ministry and then submitted to the respective departments of the Central Committee of the BCP for consideration; however, final approval for such proposals was given by the BCP's collective leadership – the Politburo or the Secretariat of the Central Committee.

One of the Communist Party's goals, which it implemented with partial success, was to impose political control over State Security so as to keep the organization far from the political decision-making process. The party developed several mechanisms to implement such control in practice, the most important of them being direct oversight of State Security activities by a specific department within the Central Committee; one of the Central Committee secretaries was directly responsible for this department's work. From 1965 until the end of the communist regime, party control over State Security was entirely in Todor Zhivkov's hands.

The other mechanism for controlling State Security was the Interior Minister, who was always selected from the ranks of the party nomenclature, and not from within the Ministry itself. The Minister, for his part, was obliged to report to the respective Central Committee secretary and department. The so-called collegium of the Interior Ministry also exercised political control over State Security, as it was made up of deputy ministers and other high-ranking leaders within the Ministry. It was established as the collective body governing the Interior Ministry, whose jurisdiction also allowed it to bring controversial questions directly to the party's Central Committee.

On a lower level, political control within the State Security system was ensured by party organizations within the Interior Ministry. This constant oversight covered even the most mundane details in the lives of State Security employees, including questions of moral or professional discipline. The point of all these defense mechanisms was to impose full political control over State Security and to draw a clear dividing line between the party leadership and State Security. The degree to which these mechanisms were able to fulfill this task in the end depended on the stability of the regime itself and on the political health of its leader. In fact, the relationship between State Security and the Communist Party was far from unproblematic, especially in moments of crisis when political loyalty to the party was replaced by personal loyalty to the party leader.

The second period in the history of State Security – from the mid-1950s until 1967 – is a time of active reforms to the system with the goal of "overcoming the consequences of the cult of personality." Such reforms were the reason for the decline in State Security's political influence. The third period began in 1967, when the Sixth Department was created – the regime's undisguised political police, whose official task was to fight "ideological sabotage." This laid the groundwork for a new strengthening and expansion of State Security structures, which became especially clear by the mid-1980s.

In 1962, the Politburo issued two resolutions concerning the structure, status and functioning of the Interior Ministry and of State Security.[8] These documents reformed communist Bulgaria's security services and confirmed the structure of State Security, which remained largely unchanged until the end of the communist regime. These reforms designated State Security as one of the two basic structures within the Interior Ministry, along with the People's Militia (i.e. the police). From the period between July 1965 to December 1968, State Security was removed from the Interior Ministry and became a separate ministry known as the Committee for State Security, which was directly subordinate to the Council of Ministers.[9] The pre-1965 structure, in which State Security was part of the Interior Ministry, was reestablished in late 1968, when the Chairman of the former Committee for State Security, Angel Solakov, was appointed as Interior Minister. He remained in this post until July 9, 1971, when he was replaced by Angel Tsanev (1971–1973). Both men's careers ended ignominiously, since they both lost the party leadership's trust. They were succeeded by communist Bulgaria's longest-serving Interior Minister, Dimitâr Stoyanov (1973–1988), who was followed by Georgi Tanev in the final year of communism (December 15, 1988–December 27, 1989). Under Dimitâr Stoyanov, State Security activities were directed not only by the Minister himself but also by his deputies Grigor Shopov and Stoyan Savov, with the latter in charge of intelligence services.

During Dimitâr Stoyanov's tenure, the party leadership passed a series of resolutions aimed at regulating State Security's activities in detail. During this period, State Security managed to impose a system of total, yet relatively bloodless, control over public life in Bulgaria, while also offering a helping hand to Soviet intelligence when it came to gathering information abroad or undertaking "active measures" in defense of the socialist system. At the end of this period, in the mid-1980s, State Security gradually began overstepping the bounds of this strict framework, slipping away from the party's political control and returning to methods of overt oppression. One example of this is the "Revival Process" – the most widespread wave of political violence committed by the security services since the early 1950s.

The most important document adopted during this period to regulate State Security activities was the State Council ordinance on the rights and functions of State Security; the nonclassified portion of it was promulgated in the *State Gazette* on August 20, 1974. It served as a "constitution" for the security system until the end of the communist regime and defined State Security as a "specialized governmental body included within the system of the Interior Ministry, whose purpose is to provide for the security of the PRB and to defend the socialist public and state system from criminal attacks." It also stipulated that "State Security carries out its activities under the leadership and control of the Central Committee of the BCP, under the leadership of the Politburo and the First Secretary of the Central Committee of the BCP, respectively."[10]

174 *The times of high Stalinism*

According to this document, State Security had the right to work undercover within other state institutions and also to recruit citizens "for voluntary cooperation." The number of individuals with ties to State Security by the end of the communist regime has remained one of the best-kept secrets even after the fall of the regime. To this day, archival data has not been released indicating the status and number of secret collaborators. On the basis of data from earlier periods, as well as from several indirect sources, the conclusion can be reached that by the end of the communist period, State Security had about 15,000 full-time employees, who depended annually on approximately 50,000–65,000 secret collaborators and informants.[11] (Or, to put it another way, every year approximately 1 percent of the total Bulgarian population acted as State Security informants.) In other words, the regime depended on a total of more than 75,000–80,000 people who were directly involved with State Security in one way or another. These statistics also sound plausible when compared to similar data from other countries in Eastern Europe. Approximately 90,000 officers worked for East Germany's State Security (Stasi), and, with a population of nearly 17 million, the system had nearly 150,000 informants. The Romanian analogue of State Security, Securitate, had approximately 15,000 full-time officers, who collaborated with between 400,000 and 700,000 informants, given a total population of 23 million. KGB informers in the USSR are thought to have numbered around half a million, even though such data remains a secret even to this day.[12]

Despite the trend toward professionalization of the services, the process remained incomplete by the end of communism, because educational qualification as a criterion always yielded to ideological fidelity, as evidenced by BCP membership. Of a total of 7,000–7,200 officers working for State Security in the 1972–1978 period, the nonparty (i.e. officers who were not members of the BCP or communist youth organization) constituted a small minority, their number dropping from 153 people in 1972 to ninety-two people in 1978. By the end of the 1970s, the trend toward professionalization had produced some results, because at that time the number of officers with higher education by then exceeded the number of dropouts from higher education. But this achievement was possible thanks to employees who had graduated from the school of the Interior Ministry. There was some growth in the number of staff who could speak foreign languages, but they still remained a small fraction of the total officer corps. Data for 1978 show that 2,027 officers were fluent in a foreign language (including Russian) while 5,263 could not speak any language other than Bulgarian.

Secret agents played a central role in State Security's working methods. They would relay information to their handling officers at meetings held at *yavochni kvartiri*, or "safe-house" apartments (which belonged to individuals who were recruited as *yavochnitsi* or "supporters" of State Security and who would provide secure meeting places for agents, etc.). Intelligence officers abroad used more complicated methods for receiving information from their agents.

The two basic activities within State Security – intelligence and counter-intelligence – had identical hierarchies made up of official employees and undercover agents, known as "secret collaborators."

Potential agents were recruited for both intelligence and counterintelligence using identical methods: by playing on the individual's ideological-political beliefs or by exploiting some weakness or dependency (which might involve monetary or career-related incentives or the use of compromising materials). The dossiers of secret collaborators that have been opened thus far reveal a tendency over the years for an increasing number of people to be formally recruited on an ideological basis, but their primary motivation was actually the opportunities State Security offered for advancing their career within a state institution as an undercover agent. In this sense, State Security served as a "social elevator" for its secret collaborators, which made it an important factor in forming the elite within quite a few social groups and professions even after the fall of communism.

Data gathered by undercover agents could have informational value, but it could also be used as grounds for soft or hard forms of repression against political opponents or freethinkers. In State Security internal cases, such repression could vary from softer measures such as "prophylactics" (i.e. warnings) to blocked opportunities for professional development or, in extreme cases, to an investigation and a prison sentence, once information gathered by the operative departments was turned over to the investigative services and the prosecutor's office. For their part, intelligence officers abroad were not only gathering information on the host country but were also required to keep an eye on official Bulgarian diplomatic representatives and to watch whether they upheld the law and even moral standards. The group that was most heavily affected by these repressive intelligence operations was the "hostile emigrant community." Since the communist intelligence services had almost no other channels through which to successfully influence this group, they resorted to kidnappings and murders.

Like the intelligence services, State Security divisions responsible for domestic security also had the right to organize their own station offices within Bulgaria, which were usually based within large institutions. In such cases, the personnel of these station offices were part-time collaborators, who played the role of intermediaries between the operative workers themselves and the agents. Such a structure also made it possible for State Security to quickly mobilize large numbers of agents to carry out specific, large-scale tasks.

Both main parts of State Security, intelligence and counterintelligence, not only carried out repressive functions but were also assigned the task of securing the regime's domestic and international legitimacy. In this respect, one intelligence goal was to plant State Security employees within international organizations and, in cooperation with other communist countries, to steer these international organizations' activities in the socialist camp's desired direction. The State Security division responsible for domestic security also played a role in supporting the regime's legitimacy, since their agents had to

176 *The times of high Stalinism*

be able to exercise "positive influence on a wide circle of people," as well as to "reliably control the situation and to influence its development in a direction desired by State Security bodies."[13] This network of collaborators could be mobilized when necessary to manipulate public opinion in accordance with the desires of the regime and State Security.

State Security's enormous network of agents allowed it to "take over" other state institutions, which it used as "undercover State Security institutions." The Ministry of Foreign Affairs and the Ministry for Foreign Economic Relations became "branch offices" of State Security to the greatest extent. Thus, for example, in 1988, the First Main Department of State Security had 246 full-time employees working undercover in the Bulgarian foreign service,[14] and this included only official operative workers in political intelligence and did not count State Security secret collaborators who worked within the same department. Nor did it count employees of Military Intelligence.

Intelligence departments

The intelligence departments within State Security were the darlings of the communist authorities. Created at the dawn of communism, they established themselves as one of the fastest-growing and most important structures within the secret services. By definition, they were supposed to employ the most talented officers, who had the opportunity to travel abroad frequently, which also made them one of the few groups with access to the world beyond the socialist system. To what extent did this idealized image correspond to reality? Research from recent years shows that the intelligence services not only gathered political or military information but were also involved all sorts of activities, including "extreme measures," such as the kidnapping and murder of political opponents to the regime abroad.

It is difficult to examine the activities of Bulgarian military and political intelligence during the communist period outside the context of the country's relationship to the USSR and its membership in the Warsaw Pact. Bulgarian intelligence was not an independent structure that functioned autonomously and in defense of specifically Bulgarian interests (be they national or purely party interests). Its dependence on Soviet intelligence services began with the training of the first generation of Bulgarian communist intelligence personnel, when Bulgarian intelligence officers were sent en masse for a year-long course of instruction at the Soviet intelligence school. In the context of the Brezhnev Doctrine, the concept of "defending the national interest" lost all real meaning and was replaced by the idea of "socialist internationalism," i.e. of preventing "counterrevolution" from breaking out in any of the Eastern Bloc countries.

Foreign Intelligence was incorporated as the third division within the Directorate of State Security in 1947. One of the first heads of the division was Hristo Boev, who is regarded as the true founder of Bulgarian intelligence work and who, in a relatively short period from 1949 to 1952, managed

State Security: ruling through violence   177

to fully impose the Soviet organizational system for intelligence work and to set up the first Bulgarian station offices abroad, a task aided by his own personal experience as a Soviet intelligence agent in the pre-1944 period. In 1950, the first intelligence agents began being sent to Bulgarian embassies abroad, under the cover of assuming diplomatic posts; such decisions were made directly by the Politburo.[15]

These newly appointed Bulgarian "diplomats" included Rayko Nikolov, whose name is associated with one of the greatest intelligence "successes" of that period. In 1996, the French weekly *L'Express* reported that in 1953, Rayko Nikolov recruited the French politician and future Defense Minister for the period of 1981–1985, Charles Hernu, who was subsequently passed off first to Soviet and later to Romanian intelligence. In response, Nikolov denied the accusations, while some scholars question the claim that the practice of communist states' intelligence agencies sharing agents existed during that period.[16] Archives that have been declassified up to this moment show that Nikolov was sent to Paris precisely as an intelligence agent masquerading as a diplomat and also that such "sharing" of agents was fully possible.

Despite all this, the picture of Bulgarian intelligence from the early 1950s remains contradictory. The documentation reveals the lack of clear priorities, the existence of a certain amount of overlap between the activities of Political and Military Intelligence, the lack of well-trained personnel, as well as the slow process of regulating the relationships between the intelligence bodies and other state institutions. Thus, for example, in 1948, a Bulgarian diplomat in Paris, Ivan-Asen Georgiev, wrote a letter to Foreign Minister Vasil Kolarov, in which he gave a scathing evaluation of the state of Bulgarian intelligence: "People are sent abroad as heads of intelligence station offices who are unfit for that purpose. They, in turn, recruit incompetent people as agents . . . As a result, intelligence is weak, replaced by a stream of rumors and slander, which destroy station offices abroad and the unity of Bulgarians there."[17] Later, Ivan-Asen Georgiev, who worked as a diplomat in the Bulgarian mission to the UN in New York, was arrested, sentenced to death for being an American spy, and executed in 1964.

Bulgarian intelligence developed as part of the communist countries' common intelligence system; the Bulgarian services, however, focused on certain geographical zones – primarily Bulgarian's neighboring countries of Greece and Turkey, which were both NATO members, as well as the Arab world. Documents from the communist era indicate that Bulgarian intelligence priorities were divided into three basic geographical regions, which were ranked in order of importance. In first place were Turkey and Greece, while the large capitalist countries ranked second – among these, priority was given to the United States, Italy, France and the Vatican. The third geographical zone included "poorly developed Arab and African countries" (with the Arab countries taking precedence).[18] In 1966, China and Albania were added to this list of priorities due to the strained relations between the USSR and China during this period.[19]

178 *The times of high Stalinism*

In the period of the reorganizations of State Security in the 1950s and 1960s, the intelligence division within State Security evolved into the First Main Department, known by its Bulgarian acronym PGU (for Pârvo Glavno Upravlenie). Its structure reflected the department's geographical priorities. The First Main Department also included scientific-technological intelligence, whose goal was to acquire scientific and technological information, and, above all, intelligence on new weapons systems. The importance of the *nauchno-technicheska revolyutsiya* (NTR, or "scientific-technical revolution") grew over the years, since the government pinned its hopes on this unit in order to catch up with Western countries' technological advances. The NTR's growing importance was also reflected in the frequent expansion of its personnel toward the end of communism. By 1980, it had built up its own network of agents in the United States, Japan, West Germany, England, France, Italy, Austria and Canada. The same year, certain NTR representatives were also sent to work in Sweden, Switzerland, Holland, India, and Spain. As of 1980, ninety-eight operative workers were officially employed as officers in the NTR, in addition to a ten-person technical staff. That same year, funding was released for an additional ninety-five full-time officer positions, sixty-five of whom would be stationed abroad.[20]

Despite the fact that the NTR did indeed manage to acquire certain technical secrets from the West, its great tragedy lay in its inability to discover a mechanism that would guarantee the successful incorporation of these acquired technologies into the planned economy. However, the importance of the Bulgarian scientific-technological intelligence services should not be exaggerated. As Andryu and Mitrohin conclude, within the framework of the Eastern Bloc, the German and Czech scientific-technological intelligence services were the most effective, while the Bulgarian services were significantly less effective.[21]

One strange unit called Cultural-Historical Intelligence existed within the framework of the First Main Department of State Security. It was created in 1973 as the fourteenth division within the First Main Department, and its official task was to acquire documents about Bulgarian history from abroad as well as to defend the Bulgarian viewpoint in historical disputes with neighboring states through the production of relevant propaganda materials. Due to the nature of their work, however, employees within Cultural-Historical Intelligence were also able to gather political information while posing as scholars. Dossiers that have been declassified in recent years show that Cultural-Historical Intelligence collaborators included important figures from contemporary Bulgarian politics, such as Georgi Pârvanov, who served as the country's president from 2002 to 2012, and Bozhidar Dimitrov, director of the National History Museum, who served briefly as Minister Without Portfolio.[22]

The Bulgarian intelligence services became infamous throughout the world primarily for the "extreme measures" they took against members of the Bulgarian émigré community, which official communist documents labeled as "hostile." The case that caused the largest international outcry was the murder of the writer Georgi Markov, who was poisoned by pellets shot from a "Bulgarian umbrella" on September 7, 1978, while crossing the Waterloo Bridge in London. Other less prominent emigrants who were also critics of the communist regime fell victim to the Bulgarian secret services as well.

Georgi Markov was a Bulgarian writer, who, after his defection to the West, established himself as the most prominent and eloquent critic of the communist regime in Bulgaria. Born in 1929, he left Bulgaria in 1969, when he was already an established author, dramaturg and screenwriter. He left the country legally, and, during the first few years of his emigrant period, the Bulgarian authorities nursed the hopes that he could be convinced to return to Bulgaria. However, as his public criticism of the regime increased, he was labeled a "defector" and "hostile emigrant" by State Security. These were the official grounds given in 1971 when the Sixth Department of State Security opened a case against him under the codename *Skitnik* or "Wanderer." The following year, Markov became the object-in-absentia of an investigation that was opened on the grounds that he had "placed himself in the service of foreign states" and that he had written material with "slanderous content" against Bulgaria, which had been broadcast on foreign radio stations. The investigation ended with the decision that the case be handed over to the courts, and on December 26, 1972, the closed trial ended by sentencing him *in absentia* to six years and six months in prison.

Repression against the writer took on even more drastic forms when the case against him was transferred to the First Main Department of State Security. This happened on April 9, 1976, when the department opened a case to launch operations against the writer, once again under the codename "Wanderer."

By 1977, Markov had already become the most prominent critic of the Bulgarian communist regime and of Todor Zhivkov personally.[23] That same year, the case against "Wanderer" entered a new phase, culminating in "extreme measures" to be taken for his "neutralization." Only high-ranking Interior Ministry leaders were informed about the operation: Minister Dimitâr Stoyanov; the Deputy Minister in Charge of Intelligence, Stoyan Savov; the head of the First Main Department, Vasil Kotsev, and his deputy Vladimir Todorov. According to memoirs by the head of the counterintelligence division within the Soviet PGU, Oleg Kalugin, at the beginning of 1978, the Bulgarian security services turned to their Soviet counterparts with a request for assistance in liquidating the writer. Despite some hesitation, in the end the Soviet KGB provided State Security with the poison ricin, which was later used in the assassination. However, Bulgarian intelligence was solely responsible for orchestrating the murder. The First Main Department developed several plans, one of which was carried out on September 7, 1978, when, according to the writer's own testimony, a "random" passerby bumped into him on the Waterloo Bridge in London, after which Markov felt a sharp pain and saw the man bending down to pick up an umbrella he had dropped.

180 *The times of high Stalinism*

Attempts to save the writer's life failed, and, on September 11, 1978, Markov died in a London hospital.

Several days earlier, on August 26, 1978, an attempt had been made on the life of another prominent critic of the regime, the journalist Vladimir Kostov. The attack against him took place in Paris, involving methods similar to those used against Markov. Kostov, however, managed to survive.

The murder of Georgi Markov provoked a huge media outcry in the West and became a propaganda catastrophe known as the "Bulgarian umbrella" for the regime in Bulgaria. The Bulgarian secret services fiercely denied any involvement in the murder while also circulating various propagandistic takes on the event. The case remained unsolved for years. Only in the early 1990s did the first Bulgarian anti-communist politicians begin making real efforts to uncover the truth. Over the course of the reopened investigation, it became clear that the State Security files on the writer had been destroyed or in any case had disappeared from the intelligence archives, which had been "culled" by the last communist head of intelligence, General Vladimir Todorov, with the permission of Stoyan Savov, who continued to hold the post of Deputy Minister until the end of 1989. An investigation against them was opened, which ended with the decision to turn the case over to the courts. Stoyan Savov killed himself on January 6, 1992, forty-eight hours before the opening of the trial, while Vladimir Todorov was sentenced to fourteen months in prison.

The case has officially remained unsolved until the present day, but after years of archival research and legal battles against governmental institutions to gain access to classified documents, the journalist Hristo Hristov has documentary proof that the murder was organized by the Bulgarian secret services, while the physical assassin was a First Main Department agent who went by the codename "Piccadilly" who was actually an Italian with a Danish passport, Francesco Gullino, who was recruited as an agent by the First Main Department in 1971 after the Bulgarian authorities caught him smuggling. In 1977, he was recruited to work on the "Wanderer" case, and in the years following the assassination he was paid at least $30,000. Ties with Agent Piccadilly were cut in 1990. On April 7, 1990, his handling officer, Micho Genovski, held a meeting with him in Budapest at which the agent was informed that ties with him would be "frozen" but that the secret services would continue to take care of his "stabilization." At the meeting, the officer also gave the agent $700.[24]

Hristo Hristov also uncovered the murder of another less prominent Bulgarian emigrant, Boris Arsov, who was kidnapped from Denmark by Bulgarian intelligence agents in 1974. He was subsequently sentenced to fifteen years in prison, and at the very end of December 1974 he was found hanged in his cell under highly suspicious circumstances.[25]

The other basic intelligence structure, which was located outside the State Security system and which was subordinate to the Ministry of Defense, was Military Intelligence. It developed its activities in parallel to State Security's foreign political intelligence, with a primary focus on the enemy's military preparedness, using identical structures and working methods. Military Intelligence concentrated on the military threat that Western countries and, above all, NATO posed to the socialist bloc, following priorities assigned by the USSR. Its working methods did not differ from those of foreign political intelligence as it also had the right to create its own legal and illegal station offices within the countries subject to reconnaissance.[26] Military Intelligence also had the right to use the institution of the "military attaché" as legal cover for intelligence activities. The overlap in activities and the very real competition between the Interior Ministry and the Defense Ministry on the macro-level, as well as between the various diplomatic agencies and other "undercover" departments on the micro-level makes the relationship between the two major branches of intelligence one of the most interesting and as of yet least studied questions related to Bulgarian intelligence during the communist era.

Domestic security and political police

Unlike intelligence units, the divisions for domestic security had comparatively greater autonomy from the Soviet Union, since their activities took place almost entirely within Bulgaria and were under the absolute control of the BCP. As the party saw it, the job of such divisions was to deal with real and potential political opponents of the regime in the broadest sense – from foreign citizens suspected of engaging in intelligence activities against the Bulgarian state, through the remnants of the former opposition parties and religious communities, to potential dissidents and all who harbored doubts about the communist system. The great advantage employees in these structures enjoyed was access to actual information about the state of the regime. Their other advantage was that failure inside the country was completely out of the question, while these secret services could also influence the decisions made by the political leadership to a lesser or greater degree.

The strength of domestic security divisions varied in inverse proportion to the basic legitimacy of the regime – that is, the more stable the regime was, the weaker these structures were, and vice versa. After 1954, these structures were banned from working inside the Communist Party, since by definition the party should be able to control its members on its own. However, this restriction did not last long, and with the increase in opponents to Todor Zhivkov, including those from within the ranks of the Communist Party itself, the temptation to allow these structures to function within the party itself once more proved overwhelming. Thus, in 1967, a political police in the narrow sense of the term was created – the Sixth Department of State Security, which was assigned the task of dealing not only with real and potential dissidents, but also with displays of political opposition within the party. This department gradually established itself as a personal guard unit for the First Secretary of the BCP. In the mid-1980s, the department had already established the practice of carrying out surveillance on high-ranking members of the party

182   *The times of high Stalinism*

nomenclature, including those who were closest to the General Secretary. This evolution of the Sixth Department is just one of numerous pieces of evidence attesting to the impossibility for internal reform within the regime, since by definition, State Security was created to prevent any attempts at such internal reform.

The basic counterintelligence unit within State Security was the Second Main Department, which reached the height of its powers in the mid-1960s, when it became the largest department within State Security. During the second half of the 1960s, the department gradually lost some of its functions, since the Sixth Department was formed in 1967 out of some of its sub-units, as was the Department for Economic Counterintelligence in 1986.

After the late 1960s, the Second Main Department's main task was limited to watching foreign diplomatic missions and counteracting foreign intelligence. Its agents were primarily Bulgarian citizens who worked at foreign diplomatic missions. The existing documents show that the Bulgarian secret services closely observed foreign diplomats' every step, especially those from "hostile" countries. Counterintelligence, however, maintained quite a large network of agents outside these circles as well. For example, in 1965, it was officially given the right to recruit foreign students. Besides using such agents, the Second Main Department also had the right to send agents abroad with the goal of "keeping tabs on traitors to the homeland and intelligence centers hostile to our country."[27]

The Third Department in State Security, military counterintelligence, generally did the same sort of work as the Second Main Department had done in the early period of its existence, except that the Third Department's efforts were focused on the army. It fought foreign-intelligence incursions within the army while also functioning as the political police within the armed services. The reason that military counterintelligence was under the Interior Ministry's control, unlike Military Intelligence (which was subordinate to the Ministry of Defense), can likely be attributed to the communist government's desire to establish mutual surveillance between the various power structures within the state and thus to prevent the concentration of too much power in either one of these two influential ministries.

The Sixth Department was the communist regime's political police in the narrow sense of the term. It was created in direct imitation of the Soviet example – in 1967, a new KGB director was appointed in Moscow, Yuriy Andropov, who that very same year created a specialized structure within the KGB (the Fifth Department), whose basic goal was namely the fight against ideological sabotage and the neutralization of dissidents.

The Bulgarian Sixth Department had identical goals; thus, its efforts were aimed at social groups who were the most sensitive to and potentially critical of the regime: the intelligentsia, youth, and minorities, while later BCP members were added to its jurisdiction. These were the social groups that were most likely to influence public opinion and political power, therefore keeping control over them was key to the regime's survival. The Sixth Department also kept watch over religious and national minorities, as well as the Orthodox clergy. The department was also responsible for countering "anti-state expressions" organized by "hostile emigrant centers" and "counterrevolutionary remnants." By controlling attitudes within these important sectors of society, the regime hoped to indirectly control all of society as well.

By the end of communism, the Sixth Department had a total of nine divisions covering all social groups that could potentially organize some sort of anti-communist activities.[28] After the fall of communism, the Sixth Division became the most notorious, since it was assigned the task of working within the Communist Party itself. As of the mid-1980s, the Sixth Department bore the greatest share of responsibility for counteracting "Turkish nationalism," that is, for organizing and carrying out the "Revival Process" against Bulgarian Turks.

The history of the Sixth Department shows that during the second half of the 1980s, certain structures within State Security could already violate all existing rules regarding acceptable working methods. While during the 1960s State Security was explicitly forbidden from investigating members of the party leadership, in the 1980s this activity became one of its priorities. In this sense, a precise description of this department's functions is that it was a political police force designed to secure the longevity of the party leader.

Another counterintelligence structure that appeared in the 1980s was the Department for Economic Counterintelligence. It had existed as a division within the Second Main Department since 1982, but it became an independent department within State Security during January 1986.[29] This new department's main task was to supply the regime with hard currency, which was becoming ever more limited, by controlling all the "hidden transit trade" (i.e. smuggling) that was being done by the Bulgarian secret services, including the arms trade run by the Kintex company and its daughter firms Alltrade, Sokotrade, and Inar. The Interior Ministry's official report from 1991 established that "hidden transit trade was official state policy." It involved goods "subject to particular international controls, for which the supply firms did not have the official import permits."[30] Goods smuggled with the help of State Security included gold, hard currency, home electronics, cigarettes, beverages, etc., as well as the re-export of weapons and ammunition and the import of "medications subject to control by the International Health Organization."

Within the structure of State Security, the most prestigious structures were the so-called operative departments, whose main task was gathering of information through agents and secret collaborators. Conversely, agents played only a secondary role in the work of nonoperative departments within State Security; however, this did not decrease the importance of these structures' activities.

The Department for Safety and Protection was one of the most infamous and publicly visible State Security structures during the communist era. It occupied a middle position between operative and nonoperative departments,

184 *The times of high Stalinism*

since it also used its own network of agents. Its primary task was to provide security for the party leadership, but its functions also included securing everyday privileges for the high-ranking nomenclature, including personal services, taking care of their homes and providing special supplies as well as seeing to the security and maintenance of special vacation residences and hunting lodges. The system for supplying and distributing luxury and rationed goods to the party leadership also fell under its jurisdiction. The department obtained such supplies by placing an order for certain items with the Ministry of Foreign Trade, which used its representatives abroad to purchase such goods and deliver them free of charge.

The Department for Safety and Protection also occupied a unique place within the structure of State Security. On the one hand, it was the largest department within State Security, judging from the number of its employees. On the other hand, during most of the communist period, even though it was formally considered part of State Security and fell under the Interior Minister's authority in terms of its operative functioning, the department was in fact directly subordinate to the party leader. The Department for Safety and Protection received its name and corresponding enumeration as the Fifth Department within State Security during January 1963. Within the context of the hyper-centralized communist state, its functions could be described as an enormous state-protocol department, which was responsible both for the regime's official events and for the day-to-day needs of the top communist nomenclature. This turned its directors (Dimitâr Grâbchev and Iliya Kashev) into mythological figures, since their work allowed them to have daily contact with the party leadership and assured them informal influence which few people could boast of. The Department for Safety and Protection's informal influence on the government, as well as its role in distributing consumer privileges, were precisely the reasons that it was under the direct control of the party leader.

The Scientific-Technical Department was a hyper-specialized structure whose goal was to secure the technology needed by all the operative departments within State Security. Unlike the operative departments, which depended primarily on their network of agents, this department concentrated on all forms of technical intelligence and counterintelligence. Its duties included securing the technical equipment needed for investigating certain individuals as well as activities such as the production of fake passports that were necessary for building up the intelligence agents' official biographies abroad. This department's most frequent undertakings involved bugging and wire-tapping, visual tracking and observation, intercepting telex communications, providing secret locksmith services, and exercising control over correspondence. The department was also involved in dispatching encrypted messages, spreading rumors and so on, in addition to other concrete technical tasks, such as radio counterintelligence, radio intelligence, and radio communication.[31]

The structure that brought State Security activities full circle from the initial discovery of an "anti-state" action all the way through to the levying of a corresponding punishment was the Investigative Division. It developed as one of the most sinister structures within State Security, which bears direct responsibility for extrajudicial political repression. One resolution by the Politburo, ratified on August 1, 1950, speaks to the way investigations were conducted during those years, at the height of the purge of high-ranking Communist Party functionaries. It admits to a series of "distortions" that had been permitted during investigations, specially mentioning the practice of interrogating detainees "around the clock," while the interrogations allowed for "leading questions" and the "application of measures for physical coercion."[32]

In the following decades the Investigative Division remained a separate unit within the State Security structure, while in 1979 all investigative units within the Interior Ministry were combined into the Main Investigative Department, which was known by the abbreviation GSU-MVR. This new structure had two main priorities: working on State Security investigations and People's Militia investigations. By 1984, the Main Investigative Department had a total of 1,321 full-time employees, with more than half of them working on State Security cases.[33] Investigations were divided into two basic phases: preliminary investigations and operative work. Preliminary investigation consisted of guarding and isolating detainees and overseeing their daily regime as well as processing and summarizing the information that had been gathered. The main goal of the operative work was the gathering of information from detainees, implanting secret agents among the detainees themselves. Over the whole communist period since the mid-1950s, the party leadership periodically tried to limit physical violence as a means for proving suspects' guilt, which in and of itself is proof that such methods were never fully abandoned.

All of State Security's work would have been pointless without the Filing and Archive Division, which secured all the information necessary so that the so-called operative departments could do their job. It contained files both on secret collaborators who had been recruited by various State Security departments (which made it impossible for any given individual to be recruited by more than one department), as well as files on victims of the political police.[34]

Thus, within the communist system, State Security long occupied an intermediary position between the ruling party and all the other structures in the country, including governmental ministries, official public organizations, citizens' private space, and even Bulgarian émigré organizations abroad. The relationships between these three levels were strictly hierarchical. At the top of the pyramid stood the Communist Party, which made political decisions for governing the country. Beneath it was State Security, whose job was to oversee the implementation of those political decisions. In this sense, its role within the communist state could be figuratively described as an institution that carried out the function of shock absorber for the government. Its task, on the one hand, was to soften the jolts to the regime by repressing those unsatisfied by its methods of governance, while on the

186 *The times of high Stalinism*

other hand actively furnishing the party leadership with the political legitimacy it lacked.

How did the communist State Security succeed in "protecting" the security of the regime for four decades? Of course, the stability of the regime was due to numerous factors, including external ones that cannot be ignored, but it partly has to be credited to State Security.

The answer lies in the institutionalized arbitrariness with which State Security operated, or, in other words, in its right to apply administrative measures. Just as the first repressions at the end of 1944 and 1945 were largely arbitrary, so too was the repression (albeit softer) in the late years of communism also arbitrary. With a judicial system that was firmly under external control and with a lack of any institutional corrective on the work of the secret services, this administrative arbitrariness becomes crucial for understanding the impact of State Security on society. State Security was everywhere and nowhere. There was no principle on the basis of which one could assume on whom, when and why State Security would direct their attention or where there was, it followed "the lottery principle," according to the apt expression of the Bulgarian emigrant and philosopher Assen Ignatov.

The power of State Security was based on an arbitrary mode of action, combined with its large administrative powers and the lack of any control over them. It chose its objects without any apparent principle and then was able to apply to them administrative measures such as deprivation of citizenship, dismissal from work, a transfer to a less promising and prestigious position. The activities and decisions of State Security were not subject to appeal. The anonymous and unprincipled danger of a person becoming a subject of State Security was all the more reason to feel monitored without the system really being able to monitor everyone.

Notes

1 Andryu Kristofâr and Vasiliy Mitrohin, *Taynata istoriya na KGB ili arhivât na Mitrohin*, Sofia: Trud & Prozorets, 2001, p. 41.

2 Hristo Hristov, *Sekretnoto delo za lagerite*, Sofia: Ivan Vazov, 1999. After the closure of the camp in Belene, 166 of the inmates, who were labeled as "irredeemable recidivists," were moved to the newly opened camp near Lovech, which existed until 1962, when it was closed by a Politburo decision. A total of 1,501 people passed through the camp in Lovech, of whom 147 died as a result of the inhumane conditions. The camp in Belene was reopened once, during the so-called Revival Process in the mid-1980s. During the 1950s, the member of the high-ranking party leadership responsible for the system of camps in the country was Mircho Spasov, who served as head of the Sofia Regional Department of the Interior Ministry (1954–1957) and Deputy Interior Minister (1957–1973); he was later appointed as head of the "cadres division" of the party's Central Committee.

3 Stefan Bochev is the author of one of the most detailed descriptions of camp life on the island of Belene. See Stefan Bochev, *Belene: Skazanie za kontslagerna Bâlgariya*, Sofia: Fondatsiya "Bâlgarska nauka i izkustvo," 2003. For detailed information

State Security: ruling through violence 187

and data on the camp of Belene see the excellent research by Borislav Skochev, *Konzlagerât "Belene" (1949–1987)*. Sofia: Ciela, 2017.

4 G. Yanev, *Persin, Belene – ostrovât na smârtta*, Plovdiv: Poligraph, 1998, pp. 35–36.

5 D. Znepolski, *Posmârtna izpoved*, Sofia: Hristo Botev, 1997, p. 444.

6 TsDA, f. 1 B, op. 24, a. e. 161. Speech by Vâlko Chervenkov at a meeting of the Politburo of the Central Committee of the BCP with the leaders and responsible parties from State Security, held on April 17, 1954.

7 The "reformist" ideas with respect to State Security spelled out in this speech were actually implemented in the following years. However, this program remained valid for the period of de-Stalinization, i.e. the first years of the government of Vâlko Chervenkov's successor as party leader, Todor Zhivkov. During the 1970s and 1980s, a new strengthening of these structures could be observed; with the deepening of the crisis within the communist system, they returned to their instinctively repressive practices.

8 TsDA, f. 1 B, op. 64, a. e. 301. Protocol B No. 9 from the meeting of the Central Committee of the BCP on November 3, 1962, regarding the structure and status of the Interior Ministry. TsDA, f. 1 B, op. 64, a. e. 302. Basic Activities of the Interior Ministry, November 1962.

9 TsDA, f 1B, op. 6, a. e. 5896. Politburo decision "For the Restructuring of the Interior Ministry and the 'Administrative Bodies' Division of the CC of the BKP." July 6, 1965.

10 Decree 1670 of the State Council about State Security. *Dârzhaven vestnik* (August 20, 1974), Art. 1.

11 Yordan Baev and Kostadin Grozev, *Bâlgarskite spetsialni sluzhbi prez godinite na Studenata voyna: Bâlgarska izsledovatelska grupa za Studenata voyna*, Sofia: IK 96+, 2005, p. 21.

12 Lavinia Stan (ed.), *Transitional Justice in Eastern Europe and the Former Soviet Union: Reckoning with the Communist Past*, London and New York: Routledge, 2009, p. 6.

13 AMVR, f. 22, op. 1, a. e. 71. Plan for the Work of the Sixth Department during 1979, February 5, 1979. In Baev and Grozev, *Bâlgarskite spetsialni sluzhbi prez godinite na Studenata voyna*; order from the Interior Minster G. Tanev for the activities of the organs of State Security in acquiring and using secret collaborators and trusted agents, April 11, 1989, in Veselin Angelov, *Strogo sekretno: Dokumenti za deynostta na Dârzhavna sigurnost 1944–1989 g.*, Sofia: 2007, p. 655.

14 TsDA, f. 1 B, op. 64, a. e. 891. Decision B No. 7 of the Politburo of the Central Committee of the BCP from July 21, 1988, regarding the status of intelligence agents undercover within other ministries.

15 TsDA, f. 1 B, op. 64, a. e. 106. Decision B of the Politburo of the Central Committee of the BCP No. 33 from October 27, 1950, on sending Interior Ministry employees to work abroad.

16 R. Nikolov, *Parizhki godini*, Sofia: Trud, 2004, pp. 169–174; 307–318.

17 TsDA, fond 147 B, opis 3, a. e. 1633. Baev and Grozev, *Bâlgarskite spetsialni sluzhbi prez godinite na Studenata voyna*. In 1963, Georgiev was convicted of spying for the United States and was executed in the first days of 1964.

18 TsDA, f. 1 B, op. 64, a. e. 891. Decision B No. 7 of the Politburo of the Central Committee of the BCP from July 21, 1988, regarding the status of intelligence agents undercover within other ministries.

19 TsDA, f. 1 B, op. 64, a. e. 345. A. Solakov's proposal for intelligence work against Albania and China, January 11, 1966.

188 *The times of high Stalinism*

20 TsDA, f. 1 B, op. 64, a. e. 595. Reshenie B No. 17 of the Politburo from June 25, 1980 on the improvement of NTR.

21 For more on information obtained by NTR, see Andryu and Mitrohin, *Taynata istoriya na KGB*, pp. 245–251.

22 Bozhidar Dimitrov was Minister without a Portfolio from August 2009 until December 2010, when he was forced to leave the cabinet precisely because of his past history as a State Security informant.

23 For more information about Georgi Markov's literary biography and his public influence as a dissent, see Chapter 6 of Part II of this book.

24 State Security activities relating to the investigation of Georgi Markov as well as to his murder are described in detail, based on extensive archival materials, by Hristo Hristov in *Kill the Wanderer: Bulgarian and British State Policy in the Case of Georgi Markov*, Sofia: Ciela, 2008.

25 The case is described in Hristo Hristov's book *State Security against Bulgarian Emigration*, Sofia: Ivan Vazov, 2000.

26 TsDA, f. 1 B, op. 64, a. e. 253. Decision B No. 17 of the Politburo of the Central Committee of the BCP from September 18, 1958, for the improved functioning of Military Intelligence.

27 AMVR, f. 2, op. 1, a. e. 626, list of agents sent abroad by the second department of State Security from January 1, 1958, until June 15, 1959, June 17, 1959. In Baev and Grozev, *Bâlgarskite spetsialni sluzhbi prez godinite na Studenata voyna*.

28 AMVR, Historical inventory of f. 22.

29 TsDA, f. 1 B, op. 64, a. e. 656. Decision B No.8 of the secretariat of the Central Committee of the BCP from March 18, 1982, for the creation of an economic department within the second main department of State Security; TsDA, f. 1 B, op. 64, a. e. 818. Decision B No.1 of the secretariat of the Central Committee of the BCP from January 16, 1986, for the creation of a department for economic counterintelligence.

30 "Doklad za deynostta na Dârzhavna sigurnost prez 80-te godini na XX vek," in V. Angelov, *Strogo sekretno: Dokumenti za deynostta na Dârzhavna sigurnost 1944–1989 g.*, Sofia: Simolini, 2007, pp. 658–689, at p. 687.

31 AMVR, Historical inventory of fund no. 4.

32 TsDA, Fond 1 B, opis 64, a. e. 88 Decision B No. 15 of the Politburo of the Central Committee of the BCP on the structure of the investigations department of State Security, August 1, 1950.

33 AMVR, Structural information about the main investigative department.

34 AMVR, Historical inventory of f. 8.

9 Education and culture within the system of the communist state

In the late nineteenth and early twentieth centuries, the decades of Bulgarian society's early modernization, education and the educational system attained exceptional significance. Given traditional social equalization and the fact that new classes had not yet formed, one's level of education became an essential condition for raising oneself from the "lowly ranks of the people" toward higher social strata.[1] Since that time, education and the educational system has offered a path toward prestigious social status and occupied a central place in modern Bulgarians' biographies. Despite Bulgaria's dramatic change of sides in World War II and the Soviet army's invasion of Bulgarian territory, the Fatherland Front's enlightenment-cultural policy, which was announced in the governmental plan of September 17, 1944, at first glance did not seem like an exception to the preexisting consensus:

> accessible and widespread enlightenment for the people . . . mandatory middle school education . . . encouragement of gifted children . . . intensified construction of schools . . . supplying schools with the necessary equipment . . . increasing the level of literacy and enlightenment among the broad mass of the people . . . free and universally accessible higher education.[2]

But behind these familiar-sounding educational slogans, which were championed throughout the whole first half of the twentieth century, the Fatherland Front's program also contained other, previously unseen and not completely comprehensible attitudes:

> reconstructing the whole educational system on democratic and scientific foundations in accordance with the needs of life . . . eliminating the interference of foreign factors in educational activity . . . strengthening the labor element within education . . . reorganizing the university and higher education . . . rooting out authoritarian ideology . . . instilling a scientific worldview and robust social feelings in young people.[3]

The program clearly expressed the tension between Bulgaria's educational tradition and left-wing, postwar political radicalism, which with every passing

190   *The times of high Stalinism*

day was becoming more unambiguously associated with the BWP(C)'s ideas, suggestions, positions, and actions; it was very quickly projected onto all levels of the educational system – from the structural reorganization and functioning of the Ministry of Public Education all the way to the most minor innovations in schools. This tension gradually increased, finally coming to a head during the second half of 1947 and in 1948 given the overall changes in the political context that established the absolute supremacy of Communist Party and its ideology.[4]

The new government's educational policy

According to the agreement between the coalition parties for the proportional sharing of political influence within the first Fatherland Front cabinet, the post of Minister of Public Education was entrusted to Professor Stancho Cholakov, an established scholar of finance, Rector of the Higher Institute for Statistics and Financial Sciences in Varna. The choice of such an authoritative and independent expert was in keeping with the regime's propagandistic aspirations, yet it had no intentions of allowing the new minister to conduct an independent policy. To keep Cholakov in check, the Temporary Committee for Managing Teachers, Professors and Employees of the Ministry of Public Education, ostensibly created to assist him, immediately during a session on September 16, 1944, established two new public organizational structures that exercised direct control over the Minister's activities. They were the Union of Educational Workers, which united all those working within the field of education along professional lines, and the Academic Council, an advisory body that expressed the will of teachers from all categories and levels and allowed for the direct interference in ministerial work by its representatives, who were not accidentally selected "from below." The creation of these two institutions ostensibly came about as the result of spontaneous citizens' initiatives in the name of free and democratic self-government, in opposition to the old regime's professional educational organizations, which were unambiguously labeled "fascist." Unconvincing in their extremity, these naive assurances lasted only a short time. At the First National Conference held in January 1945, Dr. Kiril Dramaliev was elected Chairman of the Union of Educational Workers; at the same time, he was head of the public-education division within the Department for Agitation and Propaganda (Agitprop) of the Central Committee of the BWP(C). And, despite the fact that according to a legal ordinance of February 26, 1945, the Supreme Academic Council was a subdivision of the Ministry of Public Education, all questions on its agenda were funneled through the Union of Educational Workers, ultimately originating in the abovementioned Agitprop Department.

Direct indications of the impending radical reorganization of the educational system included the personnel changes and punishments which were meted out to officials from all levels within the Ministry's hierarchy following an investigation and evaluation of their political past, with an eye to their

Education & culture in the communist state 191

suitability to the political present. On a purely administrative level, the process, which became widely known by its true name as a "purge," was carried out via unregulated brutal and sweeping actions on the part of Fatherland Front committees, which were remarkably successful. As early as the end of November 1944, ninety-two of the 135 high-school principals in the country were already members of the BWP(C), two were from the BANU, and one was from the BWSDP; the remaining twenty-seven had no party affiliation but had been recognized by the BWP(C) for "contributions to the anti-fascist movement."[5] The following year, this personnel replacement was fully implemented vertically throughout the entire organization of the Ministry. Out of a total of 124 inspectors within the Ministry, ninety-six were members of the BWP(C), eighteen of the BANU (Fatherland Front), one from Zveno, one from the Radical Party, three from the BWSDP (Fatherland Front), and five had no party affiliation but were proven supporters of the leading political force. Of the fourteen regional inspectors, nine were communists and five were agrarians, tried-and-true Fatherland Front supporters.

The purge of teachers was carried out on the basis of the legal ordinance for "cleansing school and university teaching personnel in the people's primary and secondary schools, teachers' colleges, and in the university, higher institutes and academies" of October 20, 1944. In fact, its actual scope covered even more than the numerous categories named in the law's verbose title. In practice, it covered everyone, from teachers in preschool nurseries to professors at institutions of higher education who were "undeniably guilty in the past and in the future of active, explicitly fascist activity."[6] On top of everything, the purge was not a one-time occurrence. In November and December of the same year, the Council of Ministers adopted new decrees that dramatically increased the lists of "old" professors who were fired or faced sanctions and also broadened the category of teaching activities labeled as "active, explicitly fascist activity."[7] In the system of lower-level schools, the "cleansing" naturally ran a wider course. In a public speech during March 1945, Prime Minister Kimon Georgiev announced that out of a total of 26,000 primary-school teachers, as a result of the commission's ongoing, intensive work, "as of now" 2,500 of them had been punished. At the same time, a parallel process arose: Following a proposal by the Politburo of the Central Committee of the BWP(C) from the beginning of the same year, former communist emigrants' diplomas from Soviet educational institutions were recognized and "individuals with valuable academic work, even when lacking the necessary qualifications" were allowed to pursue academic careers.[8] One of the Supreme Academic Council's constant demands was that the professorial positions vacated after the firing of "fascist" professors be immediately refilled by "progressive professorial and teaching personnel."[9] The normative language of such "cleansing initiatives" unreservedly adopted the post-September 9 "newspeak" opposition between the labels "anti-fascist," "pro-Fatherland Front," "communist" and "progressive" on the one hand, and "pan-Bulgarian chauvinism," "fascist," "anti-Fatherland Front," "anti-communist" and

192   *The times of high Stalinism*

"reactionary" on the other hand. Given the more complex situation after the establishment of an opposition during the summer of 1945, this wealth of accusatory labels was further enriched with "oppositional" and "apolitical." This, in fact, also emphasized the undeviating tendency in the development of this language over the following years to define as "hostile" everything that did not fit the BWP(C)'s political and ideological imperatives. At the beginning of its term in the late autumn of 1945, the newly elected Twenty-Sixth Parliament adopted all the legal ordinances issued during the extraordinary situation following the September 9 coup, including that calling for the purge of the Ministry of Public Education. Not a single one of the ordinance's paragraphs lost its punitive force even after the adoption of the Law for Public Education in 1948. Even during the first half of the 1950s there were teachers and professors who were sanctioned for "fascist and hostile manifestations."

Regulating the make-up of the student body at higher levels of education and controlling access to such institutions were the other fundamental aspects of the complete reorganization of the educational system during the years of early communism in Bulgaria and – particularly importantly – which was also directly related to the policy of the communist "social engineering" so as to create a "true people's intelligentsia."[10] In an attempt to bring about this political effect, open enrollment was announced for the 1944/1945 school year, which brought more than 25,000 new students into institutes of higher education, as opposed to the 13,574 accepted the previous year.[11] It was impossible for the educational process to follow its regular course since the available resources could not accommodate such a large number of students; thus, in early 1946, a purge was undertaken among students that was predominantly based on ideological concerns and evaluations of negative social behavior. The implementation of this campaign to institute a meticulous social selection of students was openly adopted following the party's success in the elections for the GNA on October 27, 1946. In the new cabinet appointed by Georgi Dimitrov, the post of Minister of Public Education was occupied by a communist, Dr. Mincho Neychev. Over the following year, the range of students subject to exclusion from higher education widened and included the following social categories: officers discharged from the "tsarist army" or their children; those convicted by the People's Court and their children; merchants and industrialists affected by nationalization and their descendants; Legionaries (members of a pre-1944 fascist youth organization in Bulgaria); students "demonstrating bad political attitudes"; and, finally, those with poor grades.

Control over access to higher education was expanded in parallel to the construction of a new society. Beginning in the fall of 1944, the basic criterion for access to higher education was an applicant's political reliability – not their personal qualities, previous academic success and results of competitive exams but rather their political assessment, and not only theirs but also their whole family, including more distant relatives. The specific documents epitomizing this procedure were the notorious "Fatherland Front notes" issued by the political coalition's local committees, which were the sole items allowing access

Education & culture in the communist state   193

to the university. From the moment of their introduction, their powerful, concentrated potential as a political weapon was obvious, whose goal was to build a new "people's intelligentsia" loyal to the BWP(C). In 1946, new norms for controlling access to education were officially introduced with the "Instructions for Answering the Question of University Applicants," which took on various forms but whose essence only slightly changed and which were essentially maintained until the fall of communism in Bulgaria.[12]

On February 1, 1947, a new law for the Bulgarian Academy of Sciences was adopted that established the Council of Ministers' supreme control over this authoritative research institution. With this, the academic autonomy of the university and of scientific research was rejected. On November 22, 1947, a new Law on Higher Education was adopted, separating it from the general Bulgarian educational system to which it had been intimately tied since the end of the nineteenth century. The law reaffirmed the new social functions of higher education in the creation of politically loyal personnel. To this end, the law also stipulated the creation of departments of dialectal and historical materialism in all institutes of higher education, although the subject was still disguised under the euphemistic name of "scientific philosophy." After the ratification of the new "Dimitrov" Constitution in December 1947, higher education was made subordinate to the Committee for Science, Art and Culture, which was created as the main ideological institute. This transfer also clearly and definitively expressed higher education's necessary institutional subordination to the ideological center. In the summer of 1948, yet another Law on Higher Education was adopted, in which Marxism-Leninism was now openly declared as the ideological basis of teaching in all types of institutions of higher education. On September 23, 1948, yet another law to that effect was adopted which stated that the supreme goal of public education was "the shaping of citizens of the socialist state."[13]

The seizure and centralization of cultural institutes and independent organizations of intellectuals

The drive toward full administrative centralization was at the root of the system of state institutions created in the first years after the September 9 coup in order to control Bulgarian culture. The political conviction that the reeducation of the Bulgarian people was extremely necessary via "the organization of the struggle to morally and politically root out fascism, pan-Bulgarian chauvinism, and all reactionary ideologies" tied culture to propaganda.[14] The Ministry of Propaganda, created immediately on September 9, 1944, also arose from this conviction and followed an unswerving course. It was hyper-administrative, responsible for direct control over and effective leadership of all cultural-educational institutions, departments, organizations, and free initiatives in the country, whose expressions via live speech, the press, books, radio, cinema, visual arts, photography, exhibits, theater, music, choreography, museum curatorship, production of knowledge and so on could be a

194   *The times of high Stalinism*

vehicle for propaganda. The press and propaganda directorate became its central structure, along with the radio diffusion directorate, since both possessed an enormous capacity to shape public opinion. Even though the ministerial position was given to Dimo Kazasov, who was recognized as an "independent intellectual," communists occupied the directorship posts in both of these crucial directorates.[15]

With a decree from the Council of Ministers of September 12, 1944, the directorate for cultural work and public cultivation was transferred from the Ministry of Public Education to the Ministry of Propaganda. Its duties included assisting academic associations and unions, purchasing and printing significant academic, literary and critical works to be freely distributed to community centers, libraries and schools, creating monuments and busts of deserving individuals, purchasing valuable works of art, securing budgetary resources for the pension funds of people working in the arts, etc. Last but not least, the directorate was responsible for state cultural institutions: the national theaters, as well as regional, municipal, community and children's theaters, the National Philharmonic, the symphony orchestras at the national music academy, established choirs and so forth.[16] Upon being transferred to the Propaganda Ministry, this unit was rechristened the Directorate for National Culture and gained wider, centralized authority over cultural initiatives. Its new director was the nonparty-affiliated writer Konstantin Petkanov. The "Division for Cultural Connections abroad" and the "Information Office" from the Ministry of Foreign Affairs were entirely transferred to the new Directorate for National Culture.

Under pressure from the communists, by mid-November 1944, almost all the professional associations founded by the educated and artistic elite had reorganized their activities: the Union of Bulgarian Writers, the Actors' Union, the Union of Journalists in Bulgaria, the Bulgarian Doctors' Union, the Union of Agronomists, the Union of Architects and Engineers, and the Union of Technicians with Secondary Education. On September 15, 1944, a new Union of Bulgarian Artists was founded that united the previously existing associations Native Art, Contemporary Art, the Association of Southern Bulgarian Artists, the Association of Independent Artists, and the Association of New Artists. The creation of the Union of Educational Workers and the Union of Academic Workers began during the second half of September 1944. As early as autumn of 1944, nearly all workers had joined the central trade union, which was completely dominated by the Communist Party: the General Workers' Professional Union. The Fatherland Front committees in every one of these unions received instructions from the National Committee of the Fatherland Front, while at the same time they had ties to and exerted active pressure on the ministries who had an interest in the activities of each of these unions.[17] This alone was a coup within artistic circles; by their presence alone, the Fatherland Front committees generated political attitudes by changing the creative principles upon which such associations were based. The change of by-laws and the rapid replacement of leadership bodies led in practice to the creation of new creative unions from the ground up. The new chamber for national culture represented the development of the subsequent, "higher" phase of political centralization within the construction of a system for managing and controlling intellectuals.

After the adoption of the "Dimitrov" Constitution of December 23, 1947, the Council of Ministers approved the statute for the structure and duties of the newly created Committee for Science, Art and Culture, with which the new institution independently took full control over intellectuals and their organizations. This date should be taken as the end of the deliberate political tactic of the duplicitous support for and juxtaposition of the Propaganda Ministry and its subordinate state cultural units on the one hand, and the communist-dominated chamber and its subdivisions "for the reeducation of all cultural activists" on the other. The development of cultural institutions after September 9 replicated the regime's political and ideological transformations. The history of each one of them reveals a gradually introduced system of centralized control and of institutional production of politically suitable cultural events that brooked no alternatives and that was undeviating in its ultimate administrative aim. Every such institution in and of itself was part of the overall system of bureaucratic guarantees assuring the BWP(C)'s effective political domination within culture.

Censorship institutions

The censorship practices that were developed and established in the second half of the 1940s were directly related to and invariably followed from the development of the above-described institutions, the processes of their administrative centralization, as well as the unwavering imposition of Marxism-Leninism as the sole aspect of every phenomenon within Bulgarian culture.[18] In that respect, the newly established Ministry of Propaganda played a fundamental role. Its earliest activities involving censorial restrictions can be found in its officially established, monopolistic right to distribute printing paper. Using the wartime shortage as justification, the Ministry's Printing and Paper Division also introduced the first measures aimed at establishing Fatherland Front control over ostensibly free publishing practices via requirements regarding the topics, lay out, size and press run of works to be published.[19] Out of concern over the expedient use of limited quantities of printing paper, a special ministerial order was issued on December 1, 1944, suspending the publication of all periodicals belonging to private individuals or political groups that had remained outside the governing coalition. Only the publication of the four Fatherland Front parties' newspapers, as well as that of the National Committee of the Fatherland Front and the army newspaper was allowed.[20]

In accordance with a decree from the Council of Ministers of October 6, 1944, which was in turn following instructions from the National Committee of the Fatherland Front, by the end of October and during November of

196 *The times of high Stalinism*

Table 9.1 Censorship on books.

	1945 (First list)	1945 (Second list)	1945 (Third list)	1952	1955	1957
Titles	678	284	824	2,883	755	848
Authors	360	163	520	1,435	394	564
Chrono-logical Range	1917–1944	1921–1943	1916–1943	1923–1951	1896–1951	1899–1946

Source: Ilko N. Penelov, "Tsenzurata varhu knigite v Balgaria 1944–1956," unpublished Ph.D. dissertation, 2007, Sofia University, p. 64.

the same year, the Printing-Materials Department within the Ministry of Propaganda compiled detailed lists of "fascist literature." This was the first case in Bulgarian history of organized, systematic destruction of written works. The Ministry's branches throughout the whole country coordinated the tracking down, seizure, and destruction of a total of 993 titles included on the lists.[21] And these were far from the last lists. In his study of book censorship in Bulgaria after World War II, Ilko Penelov examines the content as well as the expanding thematic and chronological scope of books destroyed following their inclusion in six lengthy lists from 1945 to 1957 (see Table 9.1).

Given the radical political changes in Bulgaria, it would seem natural for there to be intolerance toward the old regime's publications dedicated to the monarchy, royal personages and their families; toward impossible (given the new political climate) "historical arguments" for the presence of the Bulgarian army in Macedonia and Aegean Thrace; and toward works dealing with political science and law, the new government's intolerance toward religious and ecclesiastical books is not even surprising. However, alongside such works, the lists of books subject to destruction were filled with titles from Bulgarian and world literature, literary criticism, scholarly historical works, philosophical books, works on aesthetics, psychology, psychoanalysis – in short, they were filled with titles from the realm of humanitarian knowledge that are not in agreement with Marxist ideology. The subsequent expansion of the lists' scope was very much due to the unflinching Orwellian rewriting of all aspects of the past.

Establishing a state monopoly over printing, publishing, and bookselling activities was one of the exceptionally important strategic tactics related to censorship in socialist Bulgaria, which had long-term consequences with respect to the genre diversity of books published within the country even as late as the end of the 1980s. In 1950, a head directorate for publishing houses, the printing and publishing industry, and trade in printed works was created, which was directly subordinate to the Council of Ministers and which gained exceptional power within the sphere of the production and distribution of printed media. It was established with the goal of exercising general control over all firms in the printing, publishing and book-distribution sectors, regardless of what other governmental departments they might be directly subordinate to.[22]

The Committee for Science, Art and Culture also had specific censorship duties, which were carried out via the repertoire bureau, founded in September 1948. Its task was to plan repertoire and to control and supervise current theatrical, operatic and operetta productions, as well as on public performances in general by using its vertically constructed chain of subordinate links (artistic councils, directors' councils, literary bureaus, etc.).[23] Analogous structures within the Committee for Science, Art and Culture also included numerous subordinate divisions aimed at controlling the visual arts (committees and juries to select artists and content for exhibitions), divisions responsible for determining the content for and supervision of the annual cinema projections in the country, and so on.

At the end of 1952, a decree from the Council of Ministers created the first and only censorship institution officially acknowledged as such in Bulgaria, called the head office on questions of literature and publishing houses, known in socialist newspeak by the abbreviation "Glavlit."[24] The office existed for almost four years – until August 1, 1956 – and was indicative of the transition toward a new stage in censorship practices via their total centralization. Constructed absolutely in keeping with the Soviet model in the presence of Soviet instructors, who took a leading role in its creation, it had a web-like structure with a central office in Sofia and representatives (*politredkatori* or "political editors") in the regional and some of the more important district cities, on the editorial staff of periodicals, at printing presses, publishing houses and all other cultural-educational institutions in the country. Its task was to ensure constant supervision over public information of a political, economic and especially of a military nature within periodicals and the printed media as a whole, as well as in libraries, museums, radio broadcasts, theaters and all other propaganda channels and institutions. The general instructions given at the time of Glavlit's creation explicitly entrusted the office with the responsibility for preventing the publication of information constituting a "state secret." In December 1953, an enormous "list of topics constituting a state secret" was complied, which tied Glavlit's activities to the directorate of the People's Militia and the Minister of Defense in that respect. As a body designed to impose ideological and political control, Glavlit played a highly significant role in the context of the Cold War. Overzealous censorship even led to the halt of the publication of statistical yearbooks in the PRB from 1949 to 1956.

The imposition of socialist realism in the literature and culture of communist Bulgaria

The temporal overlap between the functioning of the totalitarian state and the dominance of socialist realism in Bulgarian literature and culture is not

198 *The times of high Stalinism*

merely a coincidence. Understanding the problem of socialist realism is directly tied to the question of the communist government. The beginning of the totalitarian state was also the beginning of the official enthronement of socialist realism as the "only correct method."[25] The regime's fall also marked socialist realism's definitive end. The Communist Party's unquestioned power produced and guaranteed the *exclusiveness* and *correctness* of the doctrine and the works that fit within its frame. Socialist realism itself was a product of the discourse of power. This is why not only its functioning within communist Bulgaria but also its crystallization into an official and obligatory canon after 1948 became possible thanks to the "dictatorship of the proletariat" which had been achieved.

Socialist realism was *imported* into Bulgarian during the 1930s. It is a well-known fact that socialist realism was invented in 1932 with the direct participation of the "father of the peoples" Stalin and was proclaimed as the "basic method" at the founding First Congress of the Union of Soviet Writers in 1934. The fixing of this doctrine within the union's by-laws led to the homogenization of the artistic sphere through the direct interference of the totalitarian state; in other words, socialist realism was a *post-revolutionary* "method" employed by the new communist state.[26] As would be confirmed in the subsequent life of the doctrine, the government set much greater store by the word "socialist" than the word "realism." This emphasis could be found in theory and practice both in the USSR, the "method's" homeland, as well as in countries *colonized* by the doctrine, such as the PRB.

Socialist realism's streamlined formulations and unstable criteria allowed the government to unscrupulously take advantage of its function as mentor and arbiter within the sphere of literature and culture in accordance with its specific goals in a given situation. Moreover, the role of mentor and arbiter was often played by the communist leader himself who dominated a given epoch: Georgi Dimitrov, Vâlko Chervenkov or Todor Zhivkov. Their public or behind-the-scenes meddling in literary, theatrical, cinematic and other artistic questions outlined a force field within which the hegemonic discourse could have a direct impact on the field of artistic production. The speeches of each communist leader became officially sanctioned policy statements, which were periodically recomposed in various editions, providing "catechisms" of sorts on questions of literature and culture: *Georgi Dimitrov on Literature, Art and Science* (1971), *Vâlko Chervenkov on Art and Culture* (1950), *Vâlko Chervenkov on Science, Art and Culture* (1953), Todor Zhivkov's *Art, Science and Culture in Service of the People*, vol. 1 and 2 (1965), and *Todor Zhivkov on Literature* (1981).

Literature and culture's direct dependence on the totalitarian authorities led to a decisive loss: the artistic field was deprived of autonomy and was reconfigured beyond recognition. In practice, culture fulfilled functions that served the policies of the party/state. For this reason, the complete domination of socialist realism was a sign of the fact that, in communist Bulgaria, the artistic sphere had been totally restructured and *nationalized*. Through a series of nationalization laws (affecting publishing houses, printing presses, bookstores, theaters, film studios and so on), the totalitarian state seized all possible alternatives for the public production and distribution of books, theatrical productions and films. Through the state's censorship apparatus, not only was actual production controlled, but library collections and antique stores were also purged of "harmful literature."[27] Through repressive and exploitative operations, the state destroyed entire affluent social classes, in this way reformatting the cultural market, leaving only a single patron and buyer for works of art – the state itself. Through pressures and bans, the Communist Party ensured a monopoly for a single organization within each artistic discipline: the Union of Bulgarian Writers in literature, the Union of Artists in Bulgaria in visual arts, the Union of Composers and Musicologists, and so on.

The years between 1944 and 1948 were a time of open competition between artistic tendencies, methods and stylistic trends, as was officially proclaimed by the BWP(C), the leading party within the ruling Fatherland Front coalition. Until early 1948, even the most authoritative representatives of the Communist Party declared that socialist realism "is not and cannot be a condition for accepting writers into the Union and for their common work within it," that "the very development of our literature itself will show whether our views on socialist-realist art are correct or not," and that "works of socialist realism will impose themselves not by patronage and administrative action, but rather through by demonstrating their undeniable qualities in competition with works from other democratic schools and trends."[28]

At the same time, the cultural sphere's ostensible freedom and openness to debate gradually grew ever more specious. The artistic sphere began losing its autonomy with regard to politics. Literature and art's direct engagement in topical political tasks became ever more noticeable, on both the organizational level (the participation of artistic unions in demonstrations, in campaigns for local and parliamentary elections, and for the referendum of 1946), as well as on the creative level (writing propagandistic texts, painting portraits, composing songs and cantatas for Soviet and Bulgarian leaders, etc.). State/party commissions became established as a crucial factor in the tightly orchestrated art market.[29]

This was accompanied in the beginning by a "cleansing" and "restructuring" of a large portion of the intellectual elite and with tactical moves to seize control of artistic unions and to replace their leadership with members of the Communist Party. This first phase between 1944 and 1948 laid the necessary groundwork for the institutional and normative imposition of socialist realism.

From 1947/1948, it became more and more difficult to distinguish socialist-realist narratives from political narratives. In them, transformed or newly arisen core themes for Bulgarian literature and culture (construction and the brigadier movement, fulfillment of the national economic plan, the stigmatization of "Western" capitalism) shone forth, while the cast of characters was reshuffled, with the main characters now being "the new people" (communist, workers and cooperative farmers). "The new people" were also transformed into a privileged readership (with ultimate goal of making them the *only one*), for whom Bulgarian writers created their works.[30]

In order to fulfill the party/state commissions that arose in 1947, new techniques were developed for supplying plotlines and ideas. Writers were sent on "business trips" to construction sites and factories, while labor-literary brigades were also created. The call issued by the Union of Bulgarian Writers and its mouthpiece, the newspaper *Literary Front*, was blunt: "Among the people."[31] The notion of the *business trip*, of *acquainting oneself with life* and *going out among the people* emerged as a tool with ever-increasing significance within the whole cycle of literary production in communist Bulgaria. This, in practice, constituted the development of the "method" of socialist realism in its pre-creative phase, i.e. by supplying "living material" and by securing those elements that would make a literary text believable and through which every socialist-realist work could be put to the test of "realisticness" and "proletarianness."

A campaign was undertaken to homogenize the creative "worldview" and "method," to reorganize the ideological consciousness and to introduce directly political interests into the creative process. Literary and art critics began acting ever more openly as proxies for the Central Committee of the BWP(C). They set to work illustrating the authorities' statements – they made selections and offered negative examples in literature and culture through specialized articles such as "Harmful Tendencies within Our Contemporary Literature" and through reports such as "Literary Criticism and Literary History during 1947."[32] They stigmatized artists who had been declared "reactionary" and stepped up pressure against suspiciously "neutral" expressions, and indeed, against any work that could be problematically qualified as *non-socialist-realist*.

The period between 1949 and 1956 was the epoch of "classical" socialist realism in Bulgaria. During this time, the institutional imposition of the doctrine was completed, and any possibility for the functioning of an alternative public sphere was definitively blocked. As early as March 1949, the Steering Committee of the Union of Bulgarian Writers proposed – and the general assembly approved – changes to the union's statute, namely Article 2, as follows:

> The goal of the Union is: a) to support and guide writers in mastering socialist realism as a basic method for our literature; b) to organize and guide writers' efforts to study the life of the working class and all laborers in the country; c) to work incessantly for greater mastery of Marxism-Leninism on the part of writers; d) to strive to root out and eliminate bourgeois-capitalist ideology in literature and public life by helping the Bulgarian people in their struggle to build socialism, against capitalism, for lasting peace and the people's democracy.[33]

Education & culture in the communist state 201

Thus, the subordination of writers and their union to the hegemonic BCP's program and ideology came full circle. The same process occurred within the other artistic organizations as well. Certain principles were put into intense circulation, including party-mindedness (*partiynost*) and the people, heroism and historical optimism, along with such core concepts from the political aesthetics of socialist realism such as "the typical, revolutionary romanticism," "ideological content (*ideynostta*)," "the class-party approach," "the positive hero," and so on.

The principle of party-mindedness in socialist-realist art was often reduced to a principle allowing for the communist leader's direct interference in the artistic sphere or for the evaluation of specific creative acts. It was also invoked in debates that flared up in artistic, literary or theatrical guilds. Vâlko Chervenkov's "show" injunctions are emblematic in this respect. The first was composed as a punitive action of sorts against the communist artist Aleksandâr Zhendov in 1950. Chervenkov took advantage of interpersonal tension within the Union of Artists as well as a contradictory and in places far too "open" letter to him from Zhendov to graphically demonstrate the "principle of party-mindedness." The leader characterized Zhendov's criticisms regarding "disappointment with the party leadership," "army-style discipline" and "arbitrary censorship" as "a bourgeois rebellion against party-mindedness in the visual arts, against the leading role of the party" and as a denial of "the right and competence of the Central Committee of the party to lead visual art."[34] Called upon to conduct self-criticism, Zhendov did so publicly, yet despite this he was excluded from the Communist Party, ostracized from public life and deprived of the opportunity to sell or publish his works. All artistic institutions took up a carefully orchestrated campaign "against Zhendovism" (i.e. in support of party-mindedness) in their relative spheres.[35]

The other case of Chervenkov's decisive interference in culture came during a 1952 discussion about Dimitâr Dimov's novel *Tobacco* (1951). Initially, the novel was sharply criticized by socialist-realist critics – both in the press and at a special discussion within the writers' union. But following the General Secretary's personal intercession, materials in support of Dimov and his book appeared in the press, while an editorial in *Rabotnichesko delo* (which later turned out to have been inspired and edited by Chervenkov himself) blasted the most prominent critics of *Tobacco*.[36] An ideological campaign was again rolled out, this time in support of the editorial, which ended with the critics being punished. At the same time, however, taking Chervenkov's advice to heart, Dimov reworked and rewrote his novel, adapting it yet further so as to better bit socialist-realist frameworks.[37] It was precisely this second version of *Tobacco* (1954) that became the fundamental text within the socialist-realist literary canon that was taking shape. Thus, despite having personally "saved" the author, the General Secretary's actions in fact entirely embodied the principle of party-mindedness: "introducing order" into the literary field, contributing to "more" socialist realism in art and clearly indicating who the main literary and artistic critic in the people's republic was.

202 *The times of high Stalinism*

Practices for personally modeling the new *socialist-realist artist* were developed. Artists belonging to the Communist Party were caught up in the wave of "investigations" into party organizations in the late 1940s and early 1950s, while nonparty artists had to respond to the call to "reeducate themselves" in the spirit of the new Marxist-Leninist ideology. Due to old "transgressions" or new "denunciations," many of them were forced to undertake public self-criticism – a particular procedure of ritual repentance before the party and the people, after which the self-critic could count on rehabilitation and resumption of his status as a writer or an artist.[38]

Notes

1 N. Aleksiev, *Nashata uchilishtna politika*, Sofia: n.p., 1912, pp. 295–296.
2 "Program of the Fatherland Front Government," *Otechestven front*, 8 (September 18, 1944).
3 "Program of the Fatherland Front Government."
4 The following monograph was of exceptional significance to the study in developing an outline and understanding of the changes in education during the second half of the 1940s: Vesela Chichovska, *Politikata sreshtu prosvetnata traditsiya*, Sofia: Universitetsko izdatelstvo "Sv. Kliment Ohridski," 1994.
5 Chichovska, *Politikata sreshtu prosvetnata traditsiya*, p. 100.
6 "Naredba-zakon za prochistvane na," in Vera Mutafchieva, Vesela Chichovska, Dochka Ilieva, Elena Noncheva, Zlatina Nikolova, and Tsvetana Velichkova, *Sâdât nad istoritsite: Bâlgarskata istoricheska nauka. Dokumenti i diskusii 1944– 1940*, vol. I, pp. 50–58, at p. 54.
7 Mutafchieva et al., *Sâdât nad istoritsite*, pp. 63, 70.
8 Mutafchieva et al., *Sâdât nad istoritsite*, p. 75.
9 Chichovska, *Politikata sreshtu prosvetnata traditsiya*, p. 218.
10 Pepka Boyadjieva, *Sotsialnoto inzhenerstvo: Politiki na priem vâv visshite uchilishta prez perioda na komunizma v Bâlgariya*, Sofia: Institute for Studies of the Recent Past/Ciela, 2010.
11 Chichovska, *Politikata sreshtu prosvetnata traditsiya*, p. 252.
12 Boyadjieva, *Sotsialnoto inzhenerstvo*, p. 106 and following.
13 Chichovska, *Politikata sreshtu prosvetnata traditsiya*, pp. 428–430.
14 TsDA, f. 2, op. 1, a. e. 2, l. 90. Untitled document from June 1945, arguing for changes in the Ministry of Propaganda; see also Vesela Chichovska, "Dârzhavni kulturni institutsii v Bâlgariya (1944–1948)," in *Bâlgariya 1300: Institutsii i dârzhavna traditsiya*, vol. I, Sofia: Bâlgarsko istorichesko druzhestvo, 1981, pp. 459–482, at p. 460.
15 Chichovska, "Dârzhavni kulturni institutsii v Bâlgariya," pp. 461, 478.
16 TsDA, f. 136, op. 1, a. e. 29, l. 28, 29 i 30. A report by Finance Minister Petko Stoyanov to the Chairman of the Council of Ministers regarding a reduction of funds within the budget for the Ministry of Public Education for 1944 in connection with the regrouping of departments within that Ministry and the creation of the Ministry of Propaganda. The report was approved by the Prime Minister on October 17, 1944.
17 Vesela Chichovska, "Bâlgarskata inteligentsiya v narodnodemokraticheskata revolyutsiya," in *Velikiyat October i sotsialisticheskite revolyutsii v Tsentralna i Yugoiztochna Evropa*, Sofia: BAS, 1980, pp. 222–242.

Education & culture in the communist state 203

18 The presentation of censoring bodies here owes a significant debt to the following exceptionally valuable, detailed and in-depth study by Ilko N. Penelov, "Tsenzurata vârhu knigite v Bâlgariya 1944–1956," which was brilliantly defended as a doctoral dissertation in 2007 (unpublished manuscript).

19 TsDA, f. 136, op. 1, a. e. 23, l. 11. Decree of the Council of Ministers No. 11, Protocol 194 of October 6, 1944. The distribution of existing supplies of medium-fine paper, printing paper and newsprint, which were under embargo, "was done with the permission of the Ministry of Propaganda, which determined the size and print-run of publications." It was saved for the state and municipal administration; for the office needs of all municipal and private firms and institutions; for school supplies and textbooks; for scientific, artistic and economic literature; and "for the needs of political and professional presses belonging to political and professional organizations of public significance."

20 Chichovska, "Dârzhavni kulturni institutsii," p. 456. With the formation of the political opposition and after the intercession of the Allied Control Commission in the summer of 1945, the situation changed – but not for long, alas.

21 Mutafchieva et al., *Sâdât nad istoritsite*, pp. 24–50.

22 Penelov, "Tsenzurata," p. 50

23 Ivan Elenkov, *Kulturniyat front: Bâlgarskata kultura prez epohata na komunizma – politichesko upravlenie, ideologicheski osnovaniya, institutsionalni rezhimi*, Sofia: Institute for Studies of the Recent Past/Ciela, 2008, p. 185.

24 The leading study is an article by Vesela Chichovska, "Glavlit: Formirane na edinna tsenzurna sistema v Bâlgariya (1952–1956 g.)," *Istoricheski pregled*, 10 (1991): 38–69; Penelov's work expands upon Chichovska's substantial work on the interference of Glavlit in the sphere of control over books and existing book-publishing practices.

25 This instructive formulation was announced by Vâlko Chervenkov in a report presented at the Fifth Congress of the BCP. See Vâlko Chervenkov, "Marksistko-leninskata prosveta i borbata na ideologicheskiya front," in *Za izkustvoto i kulturata*, Sofia: Bâlgarski pisatel, 1950, pp. 78–79.

26 See *Perviy Vsesoyuzniy sâezd sovetskih pisateley, 1934: Stenograficheskiy otchet*, Moscow: Goslitizdat, 1934, p. 716. There the authorized position reads: "Socialist realism, which constitutes the basic method for Soviet literature and literary criticism, requires the artist to make a true, historically concrete depiction of reality in its revolutionary development. Moreover, the truthfulness and historical specificity of the artistic depiction must be coordinated with the tasks of the ideological transformation and education of the working class within the spirit of socialism."

27 See, for example, the brochures published by Glavlit and the Vasil Kolarov State Library: *Spisâk na zabranena literatura*, Sofia: Glavlit, 1952; *Spisâk na vredna literatura: Svitâk I*, Sofia: Vasil Kolarov State Library, 1955; *Spisâk na vredna literatura: Svitâk II*, Sofia: Vasil Kolarov State Library, 1957.

28 From the statement of regent Todor Pavlov before the First National Writers' Conference in *Dokladi i izkazvaniya na pârvata natsionalna konferentsiya. 23–25 September 1945*, Sofia: Bâlgarski pisatel, 1946, p. 8; see "Todor Pavlov pred godishnoto sâbranie," *Literaturen front*, 24 (March 1, 1947); and "Rechta na Todor Pavlov pred godishnoto pisatelsko sâbranie" *Literaturen front*, 25 (March 8, 1947).

29 See numerous accounts of writers being recruited – through the use of their works or their personal presence – into specific political actions supporting the

204 *The times of high Stalinism*

Fatherland Front government: TsDA, f. 28, op. 1, a. e. 565, l. 81; "Bâlgarskite pisateli i Pârvi may," *Literaturen front*, 34 (April 27, 1946) and many others.

30 See Mladen Isaev, "Knigi za novite hora," *Literaturen front*, 27 (March 22, 1947).

31 See "Sred naroda," *Literaturen front*, 27 (March 22, 1947).

32 See Panteley Zarev, "Vredni tendentsii v sâvremennata ni literatura," *Novo vreme*, 12 (1947): 1129–1143; see the report to the assembly of the Bulgarian Writers' Union, given on February 28, 1949, and published: Stoyan Karolev, "Literaturnata kritika i literaturnata istoriya prez 1947 godina," *Rabotnichesko delo*, 58 (March 11, 1948).

33 TsDA, f. 551, op. 1, a. e. 11, l. 40.

34 See Vâlko Chervenkov, "Za partiyata i protiv partiyata v izobrazitelnoto izkustvo," in *Za izkustvoto i kulturata*, Sofia: Bâlgarski pisatel, 1950, pp. 148, 152.

35 See, for example, the reports by the Writers' Union: "On Some of the Lessons from Comrade Vâlko Chervenkov's Article 'For the Party and Against the Party in Visual Art'" and "The Literary Sector in Light of Comrade Vâlko Chervenkov's Speech 'For the Party and Against the Party in Visual Art,' given at the artists' meeting," TsDA, f. 357 B, op. 1, a. e. 20, l. 1–19.

36 "Za romana 'Tyutyun' i negovite zlopoluchni krititsi," *Rabotnichesko delo*, 76 (March 16, 1952).

37 See more on this topic in Albert Benbasat and Anna Svitkova (eds.), *Sluchayat "Tyutyun": Stenogrami, statii, retsenzii, spomeni. 1951–1952 g*, Sofia: St. Kliment Ohridski, 1992.

38 See more on this topic in P. Doynov (ed.), *Prinudeni tekstove: Samokritika na bâlgarski pisateli (1946–1962)*, Poreditsa "Cherveno na byalo: literaturen arhiv na NRB," Kniga 1, Sofia: Ciela, 2000.

10 Communist Bulgaria's foreign policy and the Cold War

Defining communist Bulgaria's foreign policy as an independent field of study is problematic. This is due above all to its total dependence on the Soviet Union and the latter's more global geostrategic interests. In this sense, communist Bulgaria's foreign policy must be examined as a structure of Kremlin diplomacy, which was directly responsible for Kremlin's policy in the Balkans, while at the same time mediating its interests to the other Eastern European countries and some Third World countries. Within the framework of the Eastern Bloc, during the communist period, Bulgarian foreign policy swung between two federative poles: from the idea of creating a unified state with Tito's Yugoslavia to the planned "increasing closeness and future merging of the People's Republic of Bulgaria and the Soviet Union." Of course, the former of these options remained valid only in the first four years of the regime, until Stalin's break with Tito. The idea of a southern Balkan federation was not new. Ever since the nineteenth century, this idea had undergone various transformations; following Bulgaria's liberation, it would periodically fade away, only to be revived again in the context of the ongoing development of the Macedonian question. After World War I, this idea enjoyed a new surge of popularity due the kingdom of Yugoslavia, which then appeared to be a successful example of such unification. It was adopted as a future prospect in various ways in the platforms of all the parties that would later make up the Fatherland Front coalition: Zveno, the agrarians, the social democrats and especially the communists. As early as April and again in August 1941, Georgi Dimitrov suggested the idea of a Bulgarian–Yugoslav Federation to Stalin.[1] Stalin preferred to wait, without excluding this possibility.

The idea of a south Slavic federation and its failure

The idea was further developed after September 1944, when the Red Army overran Bulgaria and invaded Yugoslavia. From that moment on, the prospect of a future federation became an inseparable part of the two countries' new phase of bilateral relations, which also included the Macedonian question.[2] If we were to break down this problematic process into the most general periods possible, three stages could be provisionally identified. The

206 *The times of high Stalinism*

first includes the period immediately following the creation of the People's Republic of Macedonia as a component part of Tito's Yugoslavia on August 2, 1944. It continued until the end of the same year and is characterized by strong Yugoslav pressure on Bulgarian communists to immediately hand over Pirin Macedonia to Yugoslav control as a necessary condition and prerequisite to beginning negotiations on the question of founding a unified state. This undertaking failed due to the fact that Tito and his functionaries in Skopje clearly stated their intentions to include Aegean Macedonia in their plans for unification. This seriously contradicted the agreement between Churchill and Stalin and meant that the newly formed Eastern Bloc would have an outlet on the Aegean coast. It also directly threatened Greek national interests. All of this was grounds for Great Britain to pressure Stalin to "talk some sense" into his subordinate regimes in Belgrade and Sofia and to delay all territorial changes in the Balkans until after the peace treaties had been signed.[3] Moscow advised its satellites to step back, which put an end to plans for a "quick Anschluss" between Yugoslavia's Vardar Macedonia and Bulgaria's Pirin Macedonia; however, even in this early phase the Yugoslavs emerged as an active and leading party in the negotiations, who would apply ongoing pressure to the Bulgarian communists.

The second stage in the idea of a South Slavic federation began in early 1945. The Bulgarian and Yugoslav sides exchanged several possible schemes for a federation, with basic differences emerging during the negotiations. According to Tito, Bulgaria should join the already created Yugoslav federation as the seventh republic, while Sofia envisioned a bipartite confederation between Bulgaria on the one hand and the Yugoslav federation on the other. Under pressure from Moscow, the "two brotherly parties" adopted Stalin's vision of the stages that should precede unification. According to him, it was first necessary for the two countries to restore diplomatic relations that had been broken off during the war, then they should sign a separate agreement for cooperation and mutual support, and only after that should they move toward unification into a single state.[4] At the beginning of June 1946, in his role as arbiter in the bilateral negotiations, Stalin called upon Sofia to concede "cultural-national autonomy to Pirin Macedonia" as the first step toward unification.[5] Preparations for this process also coincided with the Tenth Expanded Plenum of the Central Committee of the BWP(C) on August 9 and 10, 1946, which was devoted especially to the Macedonian question. There, party leader Georgi Dimitrov gave the main report, whose essence can be reduced to these words: "There are not three Macedonias. There is only one Macedonia, and that Macedonia now primarily consists of the already founded and developing People's Republic of Macedonia."[6]

The third and final phase in the plan to create a common federation began with the Bulgarian–Yugoslav Agreements in Bled (July 30–August 1, 1947) and ended less than a year later with the ratification of the resolution to exclude the Communist Party of Yugoslavia from Cominform on June 28, 1948. In Bled, Georgi Dimitrov and Josip Broz Tito agreed to the parameters of the

Foreign policy and the Cold War 207

"treaty for friendship, cooperation and mutual aid"; they also signed three additional agreements for economic cooperation, a customs union and for management of properties along the border whose owners now found themselves on the other side of the border.[7] It was decided that the Pirin region would become part of the People's Republic of Macedonia when the federation was officially declared and upon the return of the western outlands to Bulgaria.[8] Once again, since the "road map" for this plan had not received the Kremlin's final seal of approval, all of these agreements did not state specific deadlines. In order to facilitate their implementation, the Bulgarian government assumed the obligation to work toward "drawing the Macedonian population in Bulgaria culturally closer to the People's Republic of Macedonia," while also introducing the study of Macedonian language and the history of the Macedonian people in Bulgarian schools in the Macedonian region."[9]

The strained relations between Tito and Stalin and hence between Yugoslavia and the Soviet communist leadership began in late 1947. In practice, the decision to expel Yugoslavia from Cominform put an end to the idea of a joint federation between Bulgaria and Yugoslavia and led to the first postwar splintering of the monolithic communist system.

The signing of the peace treaty and the official establishment of Bulgaria's status as a Soviet satellite

Even during the Yalta Conference between Stalin, Roosevelt and Churchill (February 4–11, 1945), it became clear that the USSR had no intention of withdrawing from the countries its army had invaded or would shortly invade, while Stalin's "Percentages Agreement" with the British Prime Minister remained on a napkin that was tossed out after their dinner together. At this stage, however, the Allies were still not prepared to apply collective pressure on Stalin to honor his agreements, since the war in Europe was not yet over and the United States was interested in securing the USSR's active involvement in military operations against Japan. For this reason, they were content to accept the so-called Yalta Declaration on Liberated Europe, which contained humane and democratic calls for legitimate governments, representatives institutions and communities of free citizens to be created in war-ravaged countries, without, however, imposing any mechanisms whatsoever to enforce these declared aims. This was the reason Stalin signed the declaration, knowing full well that they were merely empty words.[10]

At the Potsdam Conference between the heads of state of the USSR, Great Britain and the United States (July 17–August 2, 1945), the postwar organization of the world was again discussed and preparations were made for concluding peace treaties with Nazi Germany's former allies in Europe, which included Italy, Romania, Hungary, Bulgaria, and Finland. There, the decision was made to establish a council of foreign ministers from the victorious countries which would develop preliminary plans and supervise the process of establishing legitimate and democratic governments in those countries.[11]

208 *The times of high Stalinism*

The representatives of the United States (Harry Truman) and Great Britain (Clement Attlee) again insisted on establishing effective oversight over all conquered countries in accordance with the Yalta declaration and on the immediate reorganization of the governments in Romania and Bulgaria. The Soviet side replied with the categorical stance of "nonintervention in the internal affairs of the two countries" and with a call for the urgent restoration of diplomatic ties between the conquerors and the conquered.[12] Stalin had no intention of relinquishing the territories over which he had already established control.

The speech given on March 5, 1946, by the former British Prime Minister at Westminster College in Fulton, Missouri, is usually considered by historians as the start of the so-called Cold War. In the presence of President Truman, Churchill announced the irreversibility of the division between the West and the already Sovietized Eastern Europe. He characterized this division's density and insurmountability as an "iron curtain" that had descended from Stettin on the Baltic Sea to Trieste on the Adriatic. Churchill's speech did not urge the West toward military action but toward rather a firm and categorical resolve, declaring that it should not repeat the mistake made before the outbreak of World War II. Despite being considered "academic," the former British Prime Minister's speech was above all political and held great symbolic importance in the disintegration of the now defunct Anti-Hitler Coalition and the transformation of a "hot" war into a "cold" one.

Between the signing of the peace treaty in Paris on February 10, 1947, and its entrance into force, the deep divisions in the world had already become a fact. The civil war erupting in Greece, which was linked to yet another refusal by Stalin to honor the "Percentages Agreement," accelerated this process. Since Great Britain was no longer in a position to singlehandedly support Greek government forces in their struggle against the growing communist partisan movement, it turned to the United States for help. After a series of consultations, President Harry Truman gave a speech before the American Congress on March 12, 1947, in which he announced, among other things: "it must be the policy of the United States to support free peoples who are resisting attempted subjugation by armed minorities or by outside pressures."[13] The effect of this speech was remarkable, both in the United States as well as around the world. One prominent scholar of the Cold War, David Fromkin, attests to its significance: "Thus the Truman Doctrine was born – the United States took England's place in maintaining the European balance of forces in the eastern Mediterranean, but in so doing, also claimed to lead the global ideological campaign against communism."[14]

Bulgaria and international relations within the borders of the Eastern Bloc

The first type of intra-bloc interdependence came in the form of bilateral agreements for friendship, cooperation, and mutual aid signed by each country

Foreign policy and the Cold War 209

with all of the others. Initially they were concluded for a period of twenty years and had an almost standard character – alongside mutual pledges of friendship and loyalty, they also contained clauses promising military support in the event of an attack by a third country. As mentioned above, the first such bilateral agreement concluded by Bulgaria was with Yugoslavia on November 27, 1947, and was tied to the prospects of a future joint federation. The second was with Albania, signed four days later by Georgi Dimitrov and Enver Hoxha at Krichim Palace. On January 16, 1948, an agreement was signed with Romania in Bucharest, and only then was it the Soviet Union's turn. The Bulgarian– Soviet agreement was signed on March 18, 1947, in Moscow. Agreements with Czechoslovakia, Poland, and Hungary followed.[15] This system, made up of bilateral agreements, could be compared to a crystal grid whose strongest connection was that between each country and Moscow, but which was also further strengthened by the horizontal interrelations between the satellites themselves. It turned out to be exceptionally stable, since every time any one country threatened to "stray from the correct path" it was held back both by the "umbilical cord" with Moscow as well as by the gravitational force of other countries. In 1949, when the Soviet occupation zone in East Germany was transformed into the GDR, it was also included in the already consolidated structure.

The next step toward strengthening the Eastern Bloc was the creation in 1949 of a common economic organization called the Council for Mutual Economic Assistance, which became known as Comecon in the West. The fact that the national political systems in the countries making up the council had already been transformed in Soviet-style dictatorships made this form of mutual assistance much easier. The organization of Comecon was also aided by the advanced stage of development of the centralized planned economies in all of the member countries. Comecon's founding charter declared its basic goals to include:

- the development of plans for economic relations and trade between the participant countries;
- the coordination of annual and five-year economic plans based on specialization and cooperation in production;
- negotiations concerning imports and exports of strategic significance;
- the easing of transportation ties between member countries and so on.[16]

Logically, the organization's headquarters was in Moscow. Initially, within the Comecon framework, Bulgaria's specialized areas of production included agriculture (and more specifically the production of fruits and vegetables, as well as tobacco and cotton), the mining of lead, zinc and copper ores, as well as certain branches of the chemical industry.[17]

In 1951, NATO undertook its first expansion, which was entirely focused on the Balkans, since at that time both Greece and Turkey were accepted simultaneously as member states.[18] Recently scholars of the Cold War have interpreted this move on the part of these two governments as a response to

210　*The times of high Stalinism*

the Bulgarian, Hungarian and Romanian policy during 1950–1951 to rearm and sharply increase their military potential. In practice, this meant that they essentially refused to abide by the restrictions on their armed forces stipulated in the peace treaty of 1947 and were undertaking an arms race with their neighbors. A conference of Eastern European prime ministers and defense ministers in Moscow was called by Stalin in 1951 specifically to pressure these countries into undertaking a series of measures that would lead to the rapid and overall strengthening of their military capacity.[19] One of the topics discussed in the academic literature in this respect is the planned joint military operation against Yugoslavia. Until the very end of his life, Stalin could not forgive Tito's "betrayal," and even as late as 1953 Belgrade's neighbors continued to carry out complex military exercises to prepare for a future war against him.[20] For Bulgaria, however, Greece and Turkey's entrance into NATO and the creation of the Balkan Pact of 1953 were significant in further increasing paranoia about potential hostile attacks and led to exceptional security measures being taken on the country's southern and western borders.

Bulgaria's relations with the United States and other Western countries during the Cold War

From the very beginning of the Cold War, Bulgaria emerged as one of the Soviet Union's most loyal allies and supporters in all of its foreign-affairs moves and international initiatives. This was clear both from the fury Tito's "betrayal" evoked among communists in Sofia, as well as from their categorically negative evaluations of NATO and its members. It was also evident in the country's Balkan policy. The Bulgarian authorities' militaristic rhetoric and behavior took on a particular ferocity where relations with the United States were concerned. After a six-year break during the war, diplomatic relations between Bulgaria and the United States were officially restored on October 1, 1947. Donald Reed Heath was sent to Sofia as Minister Plenipotentiary. However, his stay in the Bulgarian capital turned out to be quite short. His name first came up in early 1949 during a trial against fifteen evangelical pastors accused of spying for the United States and Great Britain. During the trial, a broad anti-American campaign was launched, which Washington responded to in kind. Bulgaria, Hungary and Romania were sent diplomatic notes for failing to uphold the provisos guaranteeing civil rights and freedoms in the peace treaties they had signed.[21] The theory that the American diplomatic mission was involved in espionage activities was revived in the indictment against Traycho Kostov published on November 30, 1949. On the very next day, the US State Department issued a denial, drawing a parallel with the analogous narrative that was developed during the trial against Laszlo Rajk in Hungary, further stating:

> The allegations concerning Minister Heath are completely fabricated. From the day of his arrival in Bulgaria during October 1947 until now,

Foreign policy and the Cold War 211

he has had no meetings whatsoever with Traycho Kostov. In fact, he has never exchanged verbal or written communications with him. This fact alone provides full grounds for judging the veracity of the indictment.[22]

In addition, the Ambassador himself also sent his own denial, insisting that it be published in the Bulgarian press. Only on December 20, after Kostov had already been executed, did Sofia newspapers run Heath's letter, accompanied by a commentary from the Bulgarian Ministry of Foreign Affairs. On January 19, 1950, the Bulgarian government declared Heath "persona non grata." The very next day, the American legation in Sofia sent a note to the Ministry of Foreign Affairs stating that if Heath were not allowed to remain in the country, the entire mission would be withdrawn and that reciprocal measures would be taken by the American side. Since the Bulgarian government, which in the meantime had been taken over by Vâlko Chervenkov, kept completely silent on the case and let the note go unanswered for a month, on February 20, 1950, the United States broke off diplomatic ties with Bulgaria. Thus it became the only country in the Eastern Bloc with which the United States did not have diplomatic relations for almost ten years.[23]

Nevertheless, the mild thaw in the international climate after Stalin's death made the Americans slightly more tolerant on the question of accepting Nazi Germany's one-time allies in Eastern Europe – Bulgaria, Romania, Hungary and Albania – into the United Nations. They finally reached an agreement with the Russians to accept a total of sixteen countries "en masse" – including those belonging to both blocs, as well as certain countries from the so-called Third World. On December 14, 1955, following a proposal by the USSR, the UN Security Council recommended to the general assembly that these countries be admitted. Their admission was voted on the very same day. In the case of Bulgaria, the United States and four other countries "abstained" from voting.[24]

Bulgaria's relations with Great Britain were also extremely strained. The decision by Professor Nikola Dolapchiev, the Bulgarian Minister Plenipotentiary to the UK, to stay in that country as a "defector" after being recalled and his transformation into one of the most prominent critics of the Bulgarian communist regime abroad also contributed to this tension.[25] Analogous to the case with Heath, the name of the British Ambassador in Sofia, John Bennett, was also mentioned in the indictment of Traycho Kostov. During the same year, three British diplomats were declared "personae non gratae." The government in London responded with reciprocal measures but did not go so far as to break off diplomatic relations. Gradually, the British capital became one of the most important centers for Bulgarian political emigrants. In January 1952, the city also was the site of the international conference on "peoples enslaved by communism," in which participants from nineteen countries took part. The Bulgarian émigré community was represented by Dr. G. M. Dimitrov, Professor Nikola Dolapchiev, Tsenko Barev and others.

212   *The times of high Stalinism*

During the Cold War years, Bulgaria developed increasingly polarized relations with Israel. Since Stalin in principle supported the plan to create an independent Jewish state, the Bulgarian diplomatic corps also took up an identical position. Georgi Dimitrov's government also theoretically allowed Bulgarian Jews to resettle in Israel if they so desired. In 1947, their so-called Great Aliyah (or "Great Immigration") began – a movement to return to their ancestral homeland, which continued intensively until approximately 1951.[26] On November 29, 1948, Bulgaria also established diplomatic relations with the young state. In their first years, the legates of both countries were almost entirely preoccupied with problems related to emigrating and resettling families, the fates of their relatives, property questions and so on. Overall, in a period of approximately five years, nearly 45,000 of Bulgaria's 52,000-strong Jewish community emigrated to Israel. As in the Soviet case, the Bulgarian government, in fact, "sold" these people, introducing a tax of $1,500 for an exit visa for each adult family member.[27] Shortly after its founding, the Jewish state found itself embroiled in conflicts with all of its Arab neighbors; thus, it seemed logical for it to fall into the American orbit. In the process of the decolonization of the Near East, newly created nations or those that had newly acquired full sovereignty by and large oriented themselves toward cooperation with or at least a willingness to "do business" with the USSR and its satellites. This development led Eastern Bloc nations to rapidly cool their relations with Israel and to engage ever more seriously with the Arab nations. This turn of events also contributed to the intensification of anti-Semitic (or alternatively, anti-Zionist) statements in the course of political trials from the late 1940s and the early 1950s in the Soviet Union, Hungary, Czechoslovakia and other countries. In Bulgaria, just as during the war, such expressions did not receive mass circulation.

In 1955, Bulgaria and Israel's bilateral relations suffered a sudden and abrupt freeze. The reason for this was an Israeli airplane that was shot down above the village of Rupite near Petrich with eighty people on board. The airplane had illegally entered Bulgarian airspace and had not responded to signals demanding that it land immediately. Worried that the plane would ultimately leave the country's borders unimpeded, Bulgaria's anti-aircraft defenses decided to shoot it down. In the end, all the passengers and the entire crew were killed.[28] This was a heretofore-unprecedented incident in peacetime. It continued to be used as an example of a completely unacceptable and simultaneously brutal act of inhumanity as late as 1983, when the USSR shot down a South Korean passenger airplane with more than 300 people on board. The Israeli side labeled this act as "coldblooded murder," a "wild, bloody attack," a "terrible slaughter committed in the heights of the sky," and so on.[29] Although the two countries did not go so far as to break off diplomatic relations, Bulgaria's positive image as "the rescuer of its Jews" suffered an abrupt change for the worse. The incident had long-lasting and exceptionally negative international repercussions.

Bulgaria and bloc-internal crises

The bloc mentality and behavior of all the Soviet satellites until Stalin's death makes it quite difficult to identify differences between them and to categorically state which of the countries was the "most loyal." However, after 1953, some countries' policies began to show faint attempts to achieve some small measure of autonomy and a more nuanced approach to the set course. In the Bulgarian case, however, nothing of the sort occurred. This provided grounds for the country to be considered by diplomats, observers and scholars as "the USSR's most loyal satellite" during the whole of the Cold War period. To quote the apt political portrait of Todor Zhivkov drawn by the writer Georgi Markov:

> It can be said that he has served the Soviet Union more zealously than the Soviet leaders themselves, he was the first in the fight against the Chinese, he was the first to support the USSR during the invasion of Czechoslovakia, the first to express his abhorrence of Eurocommunism and so on.[30]

The documents and information available at that time did not allow Markov to include at the top of his list the Bulgarian leader's position on the unrest in Poland during the spring of 1956 (especially in Poznan) and the Hungarian events during the autumn of the same year. At the September Plenum of the Central Committee of the BCP held in 1956, which was dedicated to "the results of work done so far to eliminate the cult of personality and upcoming tasks," the unrest in Poland was discussed among other questions, and concern was expressed over the turn of events in Hungary. In the discussion following the First Secretary's report, one of the members of the Central Committee, Zhivko Zhivkov, declared: "We, the members of the Central Committee, are also interested in certain other questions concerning the international workers' movement; for example, the events in Poland and Hungary and above all, how is proffered slogan for democratization to be understood?"[31] Another member of the party's supreme body, Kiril Dramaliev, also expressed concern, especially over the shortsighted way the party leader had interpreted these events, announcing before the plenum: "Not long ago, I heard Comrade Zhivkov announce with satisfaction at a Central Committee meeting, 'Comrades, State Security put up a good fight in Poznan.' This is a good thing, undoubtedly, but if we rely upon State Security alone to preserve the people's power, then woe betide us."[32]

When events in Hungary got out of control, a new plenum of the Central Committee of the BCP was called on October 31, 1956, to discuss the situation. At this session, Anton Yugov informed the Committee in detail about what was happening. As both the report and the subsequent statements show, the Bulgarian communists' main concern was that the spark of discontent would spread to Bulgaria. Todor Zhivkov, who presided over the session, even

214　*The times of high Stalinism*

offered evidence of growing domestic dissatisfaction: "On the streetcars and in lines in Sofia, they are openly saying: 'What are we waiting for? We should rise up, too, like in Hungary.' Our communists haven't put up any resistance. Some comrades have told us: some communist spoke up, but everyone started snarling at him and he backed down."[33] Another participant in the plenum, Pencho Kubadinski, recommended the following recipe for keeping things under control: "A fist in the teeth."[34]

As newly discovered documents have revealed, before the military suppression of the Hungarian Uprising, Khrushchev conducted a series of meetings with Eastern European communist leaders. They all categorically agreed that military force should be used against "the counterrevolution." At a meeting on November 2, 1956, in Bucharest, which was attended by Bulgarian and Czechoslovakian representatives as well as the Soviet and Romanian political leadership, Todor Zhivkov and Gheorghe Gheorghiu-Dej even offered to personally participate in the crushing of the Hungarian Uprising.[35] Due to a series of foreign-policy considerations, Khrushchev ultimately preferred not to involve certain allies in the operation.

At the November 17 meeting of the Politburo of the Central Committee of the BCP held after the Hungarian Uprising had been crushed, Pencho Kubadinski's call was heeded: the number of Interior Ministry troops was increased, so-called "Armed Military Labor Groups and Units" were formed and issued weapons and ammunition, the labor camps were reopened, where once again "hostile and criminal elements most threatening to the order and security of the country who have taken up residence in Sofia and other large cities in the country [were] imprisoned," and so on.[36] The Hungarian Uprising of 1956 became the first major bloc-internal crisis, whose repercussions were felt in all the Eastern European nations.

Bulgaria and the Third World

After the end of World War II, there was a noticeable upsurge in national independence movements in colonized countries in Asia and Africa. These movements had already begun to arise in the prewar period. The principles of self-determination declared during the war, on the one hand, and the difficult economic situation most of European colonial states found themselves in after the war on the other created auspicious conditions for the collapse of the global colonial system. The processes of decolonization developed within the context of a sharp international opposition between the two political blocs: the Eastern Bloc, controlled by the USSR, and the Western bloc, defended by the USA. In the transition of former colonies into independent states, the communist bloc saw an excellent opportunity to weaken the capitalist states' international positions and to expand communist influence on a global scale. To this end, the Soviet Union and its satellites began offering strong support to independence movements in the colonial world, especially those with a left-leaning orientation. This support most often took the form

Foreign policy and the Cold War 215

of supplying arms, securing finances, and providing material and political support for so-called revolutionary organizations. Bulgaria also actively participated in this policy, which was mapped out by Moscow. Thus, for example, in the early 1960s the Bulgarian state managed to secretly supply the illegal Algeria Front for National Liberation with a huge quantity of arms in its struggle against France.[37]

Having obtained their political independence, many of the new African and Asian states, in their desire to secure more economic independence from their former rulers, sought closer ties with the Eastern Bloc, announcing that they would follow the socialist path of development. As a result, they began to enjoy a series of trade and credit concessions in their relations with Comecon countries. In addition, they also received direct financial aid through the so-called Moscow Fund. This was a mechanism for financing communist movements around the world. The fund's resources were collected via annual contributions that had been set for each of the Warsaw Pact countries. Bulgaria dutifully paid its share until 1988, when it ceased its payments due to the severe hard-currency crisis near the end of the communist regime.

Besides carrying out Soviet orders to support global revolutionary processes, Bulgaria, in its relations with Third World countries, aimed to find a solution to some important economic problems. On the one hand, the Bulgarian leadership hoped through these contacts to secure much-needed cheap raw materials for its constantly developing industrial base, while on the other hand, they hoped to find lasting markets for Bulgaria's industrial products, which otherwise could not compete on free world markets.

At the end of the communist period, Bulgaria maintained diplomatic relations with 116 countries around the world, and, despite the fact that the regime considered this a major recognition of Bulgaria's international importance, in reality the economic situation did not look at all positive in hindsight.[38] Even if they did initially achieve success on a given Third World market, Bulgarian industrial products had difficulty maintaining long-term positions within those markets. The products' low quality, as well as the lack of repair facilities and spare parts, caused these countries to gradually reject Bulgarian offers in favor of those from Western Europe. Moreover, the Bulgarian leaders' expectations of significant imports of cheap raw materials were also disappointed. Many of the new states did not offer goods attractive to Bulgaria, or those that did required processing and significant investments, which the Bulgarian state was in no position to make. Overall, trade volumes were not large, and in most cases, despite the clearing agreements, the resulting trade balances were heavily in Bulgaria's favor – Bulgarian exports were met with very small reciprocal imports, and the balance was made up in the form of debts to Bulgaria; collecting on these debts became ever more uncertain as time went on.

The only trade relations that turned out to be more lively and long-lasting were those with certain Arab countries, which were most interested in Bulgaria's weapons supplies. A significant quantity of Bulgaria's trade was

216 *The times of high Stalinism*

established with Iraq, Libya, Algeria, and Syria. But even with these countries, Bulgaria's profits were far from assured. The majority of Bulgarian exports were made possible through lines of credit offered by the Bulgaria government to its partners, but, due to the fact that these countries were frequently involved in armed conflict (external or internal) or simply due to bad governance, they often fell into bankruptcy, which forced Bulgaria to restructure old debts and open new lines of credit.

Bulgaria had especially notable trade imbalances with countries such as Cuba, Mongolia, Mozambique, Ethiopia, Nicaragua, Vietnam, and Afghanistan. In order to support the pro-communist regimes in those countries, significant quantities of industrial and agricultural goods were exported once again via interest-free or low-interest loans. Again, following the policy of offering economic and political support, Bulgaria often imported goods from them at higher than market prices.

As a result of this foreign policy toward developing countries, which was driven above all by ideological aims and not by economic expediency, by 1989 Bulgaria was owed nearly $US2.8 billion, at a moment when the country itself was deeply indebted to Western banks.[39] In March 1990, Andrey Lukanov's government was forced to declare a moratorium on repayment of the foreign debt due to the complete exhaustion of the country's currency reserves.

Notes

1 *BKP, Kominternât i Makedonskiyat vâpros (1917–1946)*, vol. I, I. Bilyarski and I. Burilkova (eds.), *Arhivite govoryat No. 4*, vol. II, Sofia, 1999, pp. 1102–1103; at p. 1109.

2 For more details, see K. Paleshutski, *Yugoslavskata komunisticheska partiya i Makedonskiyat vâpros (1919–1945)*, Sofia: BAS, 1985; L. Panayotov, K. Paleshutski, and D. Michev, *Makedonskiyat vâpros i bâlgaro-yugoslavskite otnosheniya*, Sofia: St. Kliment Ohridski, 1987; G. Daskalov, *Bâlgaro-yugoslavskite politicheski otnosheniya 1944–1945*, Sofia: Hristo Botev, 1989; M. Lalkov, *Ot nadezhda kâm razocharovanie: Ideyata za federatsiya v balkanskiya Yugoiztok (1944–1948 g.)*, Sofia: b. d. i., 1993; D. Michev, *Makedonskiyat vâpros i bâlgaro-yugoslavskite otnosheniya (9.IX.1944–1949)*, Sofia: St. Kliment Ohridski, 1994; V. Angelov, *Hronika na edno natsionalno predatelstvo: Opitite za nasilstveno denatsionalizirane na Pirinska Makedoniya*, Sofia: Gergana, 2004; N. Veljanovski, *Makedonija vo jugoslovensko-bugarskite odnosi, 1944–1953*, Skopje: Institut za natsionalna istorija, 1998.

3 Y. Baev, *Sistemata za evropeyska sigurnost i Balkanite v godinite na Studenata voyna*, Sofia: Damyan Yakov, 2010, pp. 37–39.

4 Angelov, *Hronika*, p. 72.

5 *BKP, Kominternât i makedonskiyat vâpros (1919–1946)*, vol. II, I. Bilyarski and I. Burilkova (eds.), Sofia: DA "Arhivi," 1999, pp. 1268–1271.

6 TsDA, f. 1B, op. 5, a. e. 25, l. 123.

7 Angelov, *Hronika*, p. 271.

8 This refers to territories along the western Bulgarian border which were taken away after World War I.

Foreign policy and the Cold War 217

9 E. Kalinova, "Balkanskata politika na Bâlgariya – predizvikatelstva ot zapad i ot yug (1944–1989)" in *Izsledvaniya po istoriya na sotsializma v Bâlgariya (1944–1989)*, vol. II, ed. E. Kandilarov, Sofia: Fondatsiya "Fr. Ebezt," TsIPI, 2010, pp. 712–813, at p. 719.

10 T. Sandu, *Histoire de la Roumanie*, Paris, Perrin: 2008. Cited in the Bulgarian edition: *Istoriya na Rumâniya*, Sofia: Riva, 2010, p. 294.

11 *Berlinskata (Potsdamskata) konferentsiya na râkovoditelite na trite sâyuzni dârzhavi – SSSR, SASht i Velikobritaniya, 17 July–2 August 1945 g. Sbornik dokumenti*, Sofia: Partizdat, 1987.

12 Iskra Baeva and Elena Kalinova, *Sledvoennoto desetiletie i bâlgarskata vânshna politika*, Sofia: Polis, 2003, pp. 77–78.

13 Baeva and Kalinova, *Sledvoennoto desetiletie i bâlgarskata vânshna politika*, p. 147.

14 Cited in Baev, *Sistemata za evropeyska sigurnost i Balkanite*, p. 44.

15 Lyubomir Ognyanov, *Diplomatsiya na sâvremenna Bâlgariya*, Shumen: Episkop Konstantin Preslavski, 2006, pp. 36–38.

16 For more details, see Gospodinka Nikova, *SIV i Bâlgariya (1949–1960)*, Sofia: Otechestven front, 1989.

17 Nikova, *SIV i Bâlgariya*, pp. 32–45.

18 The so-called London Protocol of October 22, 1951, was adopted to accept the two countries into NATO. The decision came into force, however, only on February 18, 1952, after the parliaments of all the member countries had ratified the agreement.

19 Baev, *Sistemata za evropeyska sigurnost i Balkanite*, p. 59.

20 Mark Kramer, "Stalin, Soviet Policy, and the Consolidation of a Communist Bloc in Eastern Europe, 1944–1953," *Divinatio*, 31 (2010): 53–100.

21 Vitka Toshkova, *SASht i Bâlgariya, 1919–1989: Politicheski otnosheniya*, Sofia: Sineva, 2007, pp. 266–267.

22 Cited in Ognyanov, *Diplomatsiya na sâvremenna Bâlgariya*, p. 109.

23 R. Todorova, "Bâlgaro-amerikanski otnosheniya (1949–1959)," *Istoricheski pregled*, 3 (1992): 30–46.

24 M. Karasimeonov, *OON i Bâlgariya*, Sofia: Profizdat, 1975, pp. 56–78.

25 For more details, see N. Dolapchiev, *Bulgaria, the Making of a Satellite: Analysis of the Historical Developments, 1944–1953*, Rio de Janeiro: "Foyer Bulgare, Bulgarian Historical Institute," 1971.

26 D. Koen, *Evreite v Bâlgariya 1878–1949*, Sofia: Fakel-Leonidovi, 2008, pp. 317–319.

27 Sh. Shealtiel, *Ot rodina kâm otechestvo: Emigratsiya i nelegalna imigratsiya ot i prez Bâlgariya v perioda, 1939–1949*, Sofia: St. Kliment Ohridski, 2008, pp. 356–360.

28 For more details, see D. Gadzhev and N. Baruh, *Polet 4H-AKS*, Sofia: Trud, 2003.

29 Ognyanov, *Diplomatsiya na sâvremenna Bâlgariya*, p. 119.

30 G. Markov, *Zadochni reportazhi za Bâlgariya*, Sofia: Profizdat, 1990, p. 414.

31 TsDA, f. 1B, op. 5, a. e. 231, l. 32.

32 TsDA, f. 1B, op. 5, a. e. 231, l. 34.

33 TsDA, f. 1B, op. 5, a. e. 233, l. 114.

34 TsDA, f. 1B, op. 5, a. e. 233, l. 114.

35 Baev, *Sistemata za evropeyska sigurnost i Balkanite*, p. 175.

36 For more details, see M. Semkov (ed.), *1956 "Prekrasniyat povod": Dokumenti za otrazhenieto na Ungarskata revolyutsiya v Bâlgariya*, Sofia: Ungarski kulturen institut, 2006, pp. 94–252.

218   *The times of high Stalinism*

37 H. Hristov, *Imperiyata na zadgranichnite firmi: Sâzdavane, deynost i iztochvane na druzhestva s bâlgarski uchastie zad granitsa 1961–2007*. Sofia, Institute for Studies of the Recent Past/Ciela, 2009, pp. 20–21.

38 Kalinova and Baeva, *Bâlgarskite prehodi, 1939–2002*, p. 217.

39 Martin Ivanov, Tsvetana Todorova, and Daniel Vatchkov, *Istoriya na vânshniya dârzhaven dâlg na Bâlgariya 1878–1990: Treta chast*, Sofia: Bulgarian National Bank, 2009, p. 256.

Part II

From sheepish de-Stalinization toward the consolidation of the regime and its penetration into everyday life

11 After Stalin

Political processes within "real socialism"

News of Joseph Stalin's death, which was officially announced on March 5, 1953, was greeted as the greatest possible tragedy that could befall the communist movement and as an apocalyptic event of global proportions. In this respect, the reaction from the political elite in Sofia did not differ from that in Moscow or in any of the other capital cities in the Soviet camp. A week of mourning was declared, and a nationwide campaign to pay final honors to the deceased leader began, which sometimes took on bizarre and hysterical forms. All signs indicated that one of the most bereaved people in Bulgaria was the leader of the country's official delegation to Stalin's funeral: Vâlko Chervenkov. This was to a certain extent due to the fact that his whole conscious life as a communist was tied to the study, popularization, theorization and implementation of Stalinism at all levels and stages of his political career. The other, no less fundamental reason was that his personal future began looking less and less clear. Since Chervenkov had cultivated the unerring reflex for coordinating his every political step and thought with Stalin, the lack of a clear heir to the "great leader" made holding on to his position of power in the future an increasingly difficult task. The situation was further complicated by the extremely contradictory signals coming from the Kremlin. Chervenkov's participation in the funeral from the tribune of the Lenin–Stalin Mausoleum also did not bring him further clarity as to who the "new boss" there was. The power struggle that had begun, fueled by the Russian elite's instinct for physical survival, transformed into an alliance between key figures from the Politburo of the CPSU against Stalin's sinister Interior Minister and Deputy Premier, Lavrentiy Beria. After the latter was executed by firing squad in July 1953, a triumvirate of sorts installed itself in power, consisting of Prime Minister, Georgiy Malenkov; the new First Secretary of the Communist Party, Nikita Khrushchev; and the Chairman of the Supreme Presidium of the Soviet Union, Kliment Voroshilov. Even though the inclusion of Voroshilov was little more than a symbolic gesture toward a veteran Bolshevik and a declaration of loyalty to old values, the basic problem with leadership clearly had not been solved. Beria's physical elimination at first allowed the Soviet system's monstrous "distortions" to be blamed on him, such that the temporary liberalization being undertaken at the time did not

222　*From de-Stalinization to regime consolidation*

seem anti-Stalinist. The first signs of the "loosening the noose" appeared while Beria was still alive. On April 1, 1953, the so-called Voroshilov Amnesty was declared, in which more than 1.2 million people were freed – according to official statistics, this constituted around half of the political prisoners, criminals and camp inmates within the gulag system.[1]

These first signs of the "softening" of the regime in the USSR were a clear enough signal for Chervenkov. At the Plenum of the Central Committee of the BCP in July, where the official interpretation of what had happened to Beria was provided, a course of timid liberalization was adopted. The General Secretary himself criticized the work of the so-called "punitive organs," declaring the existence of camps as a sign of arbitrariness and noting that the number of death sentences issued was enormous. He even menacingly waggled his finger at such "perversions" and at the people who stood behind them.[2] His speech was a clear signal to the various "bodies" and following a long-standing, tacit reflex, the Bulgarian authorities also announced an amnesty. As early as August, the first 853 inmates were released from the camp in Belene, while on September 5, the camp was closed down by a Politburo resolution. The number of prisons in the country was also drastically reduced from nineteen to eight. The regime of internal resettlement was also lifted for the nearly 26,000 Bulgarians who had been forcibly interned in this manner. Of course, in Bulgaria, just as in the Soviet Union, not all the "enemies of the people" were released. The most dangerous were not granted amnesty, while nearly 500 of the inmates from Belene, who were imprisoned there without being convicted, were "handed over to the judicial system." With that, the regime clearly showed that it would continue to keep track of transgressions committed against it, while even those prisoners and camp inmates who were released found themselves permanently labeled as a "hostile contingent" which would be "preventatively reimprisoned" every time domestic or international shockwaves roiled the system.[3]

However, the timid thaw after Stalin's death did make some open forms of labor protest possible. One example of this was the tobacco workers' strikes that broke out in Plovdiv and Haskovo during May 1953.[4] They were focused above all on the seasonal nature of such employment and the correspondingly low wages in the branch. This blow to the proletarian government was extremely unexpected, since in the BCP's official history and in the stereotypical notions held by its functionaries, tobacco workers, especially those in Plovdiv, were seen as a constituency that was traditionally loyal to the party. The working-class and revolutionary biography of one of the party's leaders, Anton Yugov, was tied precisely to that city and that sector of the labor market. Moreover, this was actually the second strike initiated by the same people who had already protested in 1947. The strikers touched a sore spot, and the authorities responded by harshly punishing the organizers. The fact remains, however, that as a result of this strike the problem of seasonal employment was solved.[5] The law for creating stability in the workforce within enterprises, which had been copied directly from Stalinist legislation

After Stalin 223

and which in practice reduced workers and employees to little more than serfs of such enterprises, was abolished. At the same time, an illegal anarchist group in Sofia made an attempt to blow up the monument to Stalin in the Borisov Gardens.[6] Although the attempt was unsuccessful and only slightly charred the monument, this act of desecration was of great symbolic significance. Similar processes were also taking place beneath the surface within the Communist Party itself.

A timid thaw in Bulgarian society

In early 1954, Vâlko Chervenkov, accompanied by Rayko Damyanov and Georgi Chankov, visited Moscow yet again. Although Khrushchev and Malenkov had not yet resolved the question of CPSU leadership, both of them were in agreement that the Bulgarian party and state leader's "cult of personality" had to be abolished, which meant the removal of all of Chervenkov's busts, bas-reliefs, statues, and so on. The measures "recommended" by the Kremlin to this effect also included the separation of the posts of Party Leader and Prime Minister, which Chervenkov had combined up until that moment. Following this "exchange of opinions," the position of "general secretary of the Central Committee of the BCP" was abolished at a plenum on January 26, 1954, while Chervenkov, who had occupied it up to that point, invented the post of "leader of Politburo affairs," despite the fact that such a position did not exist within the by-laws of the Communist Party.[7] Here Chervenkov made his first serious political misstep in keeping the post of Prime Minister for himself and formally giving up leadership of the party. His second mistake, which also turned out to be fatal to his future political career, was his choice for new First Secretary of the Central Committee. At that time, Chervenkov was clearly operating under the assumption that his handpicked First Secretary would be a figurehead, while the overbearing and clumsy "leader of Politburo affairs" would continue pulling the strings. The person he chose for the role of "straw man" was the Central Committee's secretary for agricultural questions and the youngest member of the Politburo: Todor Zhivkov.

The former partisan turned state leader was born in the village of Pravets near present-day Botevgrad on September 7, 1911. According to his own claims, he joined the communist movement and took part in a Marxist youth circle while still a high-school student in Botevgrad. In fact, it must be noted that practically his entire pre-September 9 biography is based solely on his personal memories, told and retold on various occasions, which were later transmitted and written down by others. Again, according to Zhivkov himself, he was expelled from high school due to a student strike, but instead of going back to his home village, in 1929 he found himself in Sofia, where he managed to enroll in a printing school. While studying, he also worked as a typesetter.[8] Since it was precisely this job that legitimized him as a member of the proletariat and hinted at parallels with Georgi Dimitrov's biography, in the years

224 *From de-Stalinization to regime consolidation*

following his ascent to power, this fact from his past was broadcast far and wide. The truth is, however, that his typesetting job did not secure him a sufficient salary, so he turned to waiting tables as an additional source of income.[9] In 1930, he joined the communist youth organization, while from 1932 on he was a member of both the legal Workers' Party and also the illegal BCP. As early as the following year, he was elevated to the position of party coordinator for one of the outlying neighborhoods of Sofia. In 1936 and 1937, he served for three months a year on a military construction brigade. The rest of the time, he worked as a regional coordinator for the BCP in two Sofia neighborhoods. His first run-ins with the police date from this time. In the years after Zhivkov's fall from power, hypotheses were bandied about that during this period he had been recruited by the head of the tsarist political police, Nikola Geshev, that he was in fact an agent provocateur within the Communist Party, and so on. The truth is that during this time, most communist activists were interrogated and forced to sign declarations repudiating their communist convictions. After being released from prison, most of them went back on these signed declarations and reverted to their old communist activities. In the years of the Stalinist purges, hundreds such people were subjected to party-internal "investigations," as a result of which some of them were labeled as agent provocateurs and killed or convicted, while others escaped with less harsh, party-internal penalties. Zhivkov fell into the second category. One well-known hypothesis claimed that he had destroyed his own police dossier on September 9, 1944, but recently it has come to light that a huge portion of such police dossiers were seized by the Soviet occupying forces and were carefully studied by the NKVD. Subsequently, some of these materials about "tsarist" agents in the previous era were sent back to Bulgaria and used as grounds for convicting those individuals. The fact that over the years nothing of this sort has been discovered about Zhivkov among the materials in Sofia or those in Moscow largely proves the groundlessness of this hypothesis.

In the years immediately preceding World War II, Zhivkov's life underwent a series of changes. With the help of his future life partner, Dr. Mara Maleeva, he graduated from high school as a private student, and even enrolled in the Law Department at Sofia University. Although there is no information indicating that he ever took any exams, from this moment on, law became his calling; his future appearances on the world stage as a statesman and constitutionalist were to some extent related to this sphere of knowledge. A key turning point in his life was his marriage to Maleeva in 1939. Until the beginning of the war, he accompanied his wife, who was sent to various parts of Bulgaria as a district medical officer, while Zhivkov himself remained without a clear profession. His lack of a solid career and constant work in those villages allowed him to become a highly respected backgammon player, while he also took part in amateur theatrical productions. It was precisely during this period that their daughter Ludmila was born in Govedartsi on July 26, 1942. According to her father, she was named after the Soviet sniper-heroine, Ludmila Pavlichenko, who was popular in communist circles at the time.[10]

After his daughter's birth, Zhivkov once again settled in Sofia and reestablished his connections with his old party comrades. Although the brief partisan period of his biography was widely ridiculed during his rule, it must be admitted that during his relatively short stay in the Balkan Mountains he managed to carve out strategic positions for himself, which he would subsequently use to his advantage during the decisive assault against the old regime. In 1942, Zhivkov became one of the secretaries of the Sofia Regional Committee of the BWP. In this capacity, he was also assigned to serve as a representative of the "Chavdar" partisan division. Within this organization, he worked under the illegal codename "Yanko." Such duties allowed him to shuttle between the partisan groups, Sofia and the surrounding villages, ultimately playing the role of savior in a number of critical situations. His work with "Chavdar" was also the source of many of his long-standing personal friendships with some of the partisans whom he later promoted to the highest leaderships ranks within the BCP and the state. Such friends included the division commander Dobri Dzhurov, who would later serve for many years as Defense Minister and a member of the Politburo; Yordan Yotov, another member of the Politburo; Dimitar Stanishev, Secretary of the Central Committee of the BCP, and so on. The division's expansion during 1944 and its adoption of the bombastic appellation "brigade" came about with Zhivkov's personal participation and was yet another bonus in his partisan biography.[11] This secured him a place among the ranks of those who would be tapped for direct participation in the coup being planned in Sofia. A series of late writings about Zhivkov's life insisted that an operations bureau had existed which was subordinate to the main headquarters of NOVA (*Narodoosvoboditelnata vâzstanicheska armiya,* whose acronym in Bulgarian spells "new" and means people's liberation revolutionary army) and which was headed by Zhivkov, who was assigned the task of seizing power in the capital.[12] Whether such a "bureau" really existed and what exactly its functions were is highly debatable, but the fact remains that Todor Zhivkov directly took part in the seizure of power in Sofia and was among the first to infiltrate the police directorate, which had been abandoned by its security forces.

On September 10, 1944, his name figured among the earliest appointments made by the new Interior Minister, Anton Yugov. Zhivkov received the rank of lieutenant-colonel and the post of chief inspector within the directorate of uniformed militia.[13] The bloody days and nights of September and October 1944 are some of the least known and vaguest episodes from his biography. Zhivkov chose the well-known Slavyanska Beseda Reading Room in central Sofia as his headquarters.[14] It was used as a transit point for the arrest and execution of "former people." At Zhivkov's headquarters, the "dirty work" was done by the likes of future generals Mircho Spasov, Grigor Shopov, and Slavcho Radomirski. They would invariably hold posts as Deputy Minister of Internal Affairs until well into the late 1980s. From there, detainees would be transported out of Sofia under the cover of night and shot.

226   *From de-Stalinization to regime consolidation*

Zhivkov himself clearly did not show great affinity for police work; as early as October 1944 he resumed his former post as Secretary of the Sofia Regional Committee of the BWP(C). It was in this capacity that Zhivkov was selected as a candidate member of the Central Committee of the BWP(C) in the days between February 27 and March 1, 1945, when the Eighth Expanded Plenum – the first official party forum after the communists has seized power – took place. Under the new political conditions, this post guaranteed him access to key figures within the Communist Party and assured his place in the ranks of its supreme nomenclature. Given his relatively high-ranking posts, he was also included in the BWP(C)'s candidate lists for the elections for the Twenty-Sixth Parliament; in November 1945, he also became an MP. From that moment on, he would remain an invariable member of parliament for the next forty-four years.

In early 1948, Zhivkov became Secretary of the Sofia City Committee of the BWP(C). This leadership post in the largest organization within the Communist Party opened up new networks and horizons to him. That same year, he also assumed the duties of mayor of Sofia. At the Fifth Congress of the BCP in December, he was made a full member of the Central Committee.[15]

The purge of the BCP leaders, which had began with the case against Traycho Kostov, offered Zhivkov an opportunity to further advance his career. He was precisely the person who, in the name of the Sofia BCP organization, submitted the first demand to the Politburo that Kostov be expelled from the party. The court hearings during the trial, which took place at the Military Club building in December 1949 and which were once again under his leadership, were attended by a vocal propagandistic group of "outraged honest workers" who insisted on the harshest possible punishment. Such services assured Zhivkov a place in the Bulgarian delegation to celebrations marking Stalin's seventieth birthday in December of the same year. Over an exceptionally short period of time, his career skyrocketed. During the following year, he was recruited as a candidate member of the Politburo and at the same time was made Central Committee Secretary in Charge of Collectivization within the Country. His handling of the so-called Kula Uprisings in the spring of 1951 earned him full membership in the Politburo as well. His access to these two posts – one within the Politburo, the body that made the basic political decisions, while simultaneously serving as a Central Committee secretary, which allowed him direct contact with and control over the party apparatus – placed him in an exceptionally favorable position to take over the leadership post within the party. He himself claimed that as soon as he entered the Politburo, he joined the anti-Chervenkov faction led by Foreign Minister Vladimir Poptomov and further consisting of Encho Staykov, Dimitâr Ganev and Georgi Damyanov. After Poptomov's death in 1952, he even headed up this group, according to his own claims.[16] However, Zhivkov's real opportunity to make moves against Chervenkov came only after Stalin's death. The fact remains that Chervenkov continued to consider him a loyal and harmless apparatchik who would keep carrying out his sinecural role in the future as well. At the Sixth Congress of the BCP (February 25–March 3, 1954), Todor Zhivkov was elevated to First Secretary of the Central Committee at Chervenkov's suggestion. The latter continued to be the true puppeteer, however – at least in his own mind.

During the period following Stalin's death, when communist leaders throughout the Eastern Bloc were waiting for clearer messages from Moscow, such imitative reshuffles of party elites took place in the other Soviet satellites as well. In such processes, prominent Stalinist leaders were forced to accept dualistic power-sharing arrangements or to surrender their posts to second-tier functionaries who were considered less threatening. Thus, in Hungary, the ultra-Stalinist leader Mátyás Rákosi was replaced with the less emblematic Ernő Gerő, while in Poland, the old communist leader Bolesław Bierut was sent to enjoy a "well-deserved rest" by his successor Władysław Gomułka. The tie between the old Czechoslovakian Comintern veteran Klement Gottwald and his erstwhile protector in the Kremlin could be described as "karmic." After catching a cold at Stalin's funeral, he got pneumonia and died. His natural political heir, Antonin Novotin, truly personified the cosmetic nature of the changes within Eastern European communist parties at the time. In East Germany and Romania, where the old Stalinist leaders managed to hang on to power, they were nevertheless forced to perform self-criticism or to "return to the principles of collective leadership," to borrow a characteristic phrase from party-bureaucratic-speak.[17]

Meanwhile, in Sofia, the communists who had been convicted during the Traycho Kostov trials and who later received amnesty and were freed from prison were gradually rehabilitated by the party and also joined the ranks of those who were disaffected and embittered against the "leader." As early as the autumn of 1954, some of them had been completely pardoned, while sentences were substantially reduced for another group. In October 1955, yet another group of imprisoned communists was set free. Some of the so-called Traycho Kostovites were not pardoned, however, since, in the words of Interior Minister Georgi Tsankov, "they behaved badly in prison and demonstratively declared that they were unjustly convicted."[18] Despite this, on the very eve of the April Plenum of the Central Committee of the BCP, Zhivkov assigned Tsankov the task of preparing new investigations into these people and proposing that they be released. At the same time, the charges against Traycho Kostov concerning "criminal connections" with Yugoslav and Anglo-American agents were also dropped.

Many high-ranking army officers who had been repressed were also restored to party membership and granted leadership positions. They included the generals Ivan Kinov, who was appointed as First Deputy Minister for the People's Defense; Slavcho Trânski, restored as head of the Military Academy; Boris Kopchev; Zdravko Georgiev; Dencho Znepolski; Stoyan Trendafilov; Ivan Radonov and others.[19] Some were extremely shaken by what had happened to them and preferred to maintain a low profile, while others resolutely joined the ranks of those seeking party-internal justice and revenge.

228   *From de-Stalinization to regime consolidation*

When Nikita Khrushchev visited Sofia on his way back from Belgrade in June 1955, his statements signaled to many of the key figures within the BCP leadership that changes were afoot. It became clear that on the one hand Khrushchev was emerging ever more clearly as the likely winner in the war for control over the Kremlin, while on the other hand, if this were truly the case, Chervenkov's chances for retaining power were dwindling. Khrushchev seems to have chosen Zhivkov during this very visit. The two men were similar in a number of ways: both had been seen as outsiders by their one-time party bosses; they had both literally risen "out of nowhere"; they were more or less on the same intellectual level; indeed, at times they looked strikingly alike. Khrushchev's encouraging attitude in Sofia gave Zhivkov the confidence to undertake concrete steps to eliminate Chervenkov. The latter's long course of medical treatment in Moscow in early 1956 only fueled his delusions that he could win the trust of the new Soviet leader. In fact, the exact opposite occurred – his absence from Bulgaria at that moment gave forces within the Politburo an opportunity to seriously regroup before the impending changes.

The 1956 April Plenum of the Central Committee of the BCP and its consequences

At the beginning of 1956, four separate camps took shape within the upper echelons of the BCP. The first of them was headed by Todor Zhivkov, while figures such as Encho Staykov, Dimitâr Ganev, and others also gravitated toward this group. The second strong faction was that of Anton Yugov and Georgi Chankov. Because the former had been removed from the post of Prime Minister in 1948, he had earned the halo of "victimhood" to a certain extent, even though he had continued to participate actively in the country's government. Both he and Chankov were deputy prime ministers with extensive cabinet experience and hence could lay claim to certain "competencies." At that point, the coalition between the two men looked unshakable – and this was precisely the source of their strength. The third group was Chervenkov's circle. Its ranks were steadily thinning in lockstep with the messages coming from Moscow. Rayko Damyanov remained within this faction longer than most, but in the end he too switched to the winning side. A fourth group also existed, which could provisionally be called the "faction of old and disaffected veterans." Second-tier figures such as Dobri Terpeshev, Radenko Vidinski, the generals Yonko Panov and Boris Kopchev, as well as others, joined its ranks. They all had good reason to hate Chervenkov, but they could not fathom how people like Zhivkov, Chankov and Yugov, who had supported Chervenkov's methods and decisions during his whole time in power, could now suddenly take up the role of the bearer-banners leading the charge for change. In this sense, this group was not protesting against Chervenkov personally but against the status quo as a whole, which automatically turned all that gravitated toward this faction into outsiders. On the very eve of Chervenkov's fall from power, Zhivkov made a tactical alliance with the Yugov–Chankov group. He suggested that Yugov take the post of Prime Minister, while Chankov serve as First Deputy Prime Minister. The offer seemed advantageous, since it would mean a promotion for both men, while in exchange Zhivkov wanted to keep his leading post within the party – freed, however, from Chervenkov's tutelage. Thus, when Khrushchev undertook his de-Stalinization campaign in earnest in February 1956, a solid majority opposed to Chervenkov had already been established within the Bulgarian communist ruling elite.[20]

From February 14 to February 25, the Twentieth Congress of the CPSU was held in Moscow – the first such forum to take place since Stalin's death. Alongside the topics typically on the agenda of such a state event, a report by Nikita Khrushchev entitled "On the Cult of Personality and Its Consequences" had also been included at the very end.[21] As later became clear, even during the preceding discussions within the Soviet Politburo (which was known as the "presidium" at that time), Khrushchev's plans faced intense opposition. He, however, had calculated that he could hold on to power only by increasing the anti-Stalinist pressure on his opponents and by gradually labeling them as "defenders of the cult." When his comrades advised him not to criticize Stalin, he replied, "If we don't tell the truth at the Congress, we will be forced to tell it at some time in the future. Then, however, we won't be giving speeches, but will be under interrogation."[22] Khrushchev's speech was a striking document condemning Stalin and Stalinism. It came like political bolt from the blue for listeners, who until that moment had been completely convinced of the grandeur and purity of Stalin's image. Despite the fact that the speaker left out important facts and circumstances and claimed that the Soviet system had survived these Stalinist distortions and was returning to "Leninist principles," the effect was exceptionally significant not only within the Soviet context but also for the international communist movement.[23]

Chervenkov was the leader of the Bulgarian delegation at that large-scale propaganda event. When the actual report was read, he was not feeling well and was not in attendance. When Rayko Damyanov later informed him of what he had heard, the Bulgarian leader could not believe it. He first attributed it to his trusted agent's poor command of Russian. Later, however, it turned out that even Damyanov with his poor language skills had understood perfectly well.[24] Despite this, Chervenkov, like some of the other Eastern European leaders who had been placed in power by Stalin, still did not make the connection between this new phase in the process of de-Stalinization and his own ability to remain in power. For this reason, following the Congress, Khrushchev and the other members of the Politburo were forced to hold bilateral meetings with the leadership of each of the satellite countries and to offer them "recommendations" on how to proceed. When the Bulgarian delegation was called to Moscow in March, Chervenkov no longer had any allies within the Russian Politburo. His surprise was even greater when he heard himself being sharply and directly criticized by none other than Khrushchev himself. He was blamed for the insufficiently rapid de-Stalinization of the BCP. And at the end of the meeting, when the Soviet leader turned to the Bulgarian

230   *From de-Stalinization to regime consolidation*

delegation and asked who would report on its behalf on the "conclusions and lessons from the Twentieth Congress," Chervenkov raised his hand – as did Todor Zhivkov from the other end of the table. When the remaining members of the delegation were asked who would make the report, they all unanimously pointed to the First Secretary. Zhivkov's exposé essentially repeated what Khrushchev had already said, containing ruthless personal criticism against the now former "leader" and expressing his resolve to officially confirm the new status quo within the party elite.[25]

This official confirmation came about during the April Plenum of the Central Committee of the BCP, held from April 2 to April 6, 1956, in what is today Sofia City Hall. The main report was given by Todor Zhivkov and was entitled "The Twentieth Congress of the CPSU and Its Lessons for Our Party." It generally repeated what had been said in Moscow two weeks earlier; however, the tone was even sharper in some respects. The entire blame for the "cult of personality" was pinned on Chervenkov personally, while the remaining functionaries were criticized without being specifically named. In fact, no other figure from the communist elite was singled out concretely. At the same time, even at the meeting in Moscow, Khrushchev had declared that it was not good for the Bulgarian communists to be completely deprived of Chervenkov's "rich experience" and competence. This was a signal to the marionettes in Sofia that, unlike the preceding period, when such practices ended in the physical elimination of the scapegoat, in this case the changeover should take place slowly and gradually, guaranteeing the fallen leader, as well as those who would come after him, that he would retain at least some of his status. As an experienced apparatchik, Chervenkov also realized that under such conditions his only chance to survive politically, if only partially, was to publicly "eat crow" by performing the most extensive "frank self-criticism" possible, making an open declaration accepting the new status quo and expressing his desire to cooperate with the new powers-that-be. On the whole, that was the spirit of his two statements at the plenum. Almost all speakers (out of a total of thirty-four) leveled accusations at him, while in some cases a desire for personal retribution could be felt – primarily from those who had passed through "the nine rings of hell" at the hands of State Security and who were later "rehabilitated" under the new circumstances and were finally coming face to face with one of the main culprits responsible for their personal suffering. Some of the speakers also raised the question of the personal guilt of the remaining members of the Politburo during those years and insisted on widening the circle of those being punished. That was the nature of the statement made by Yonko Panov, who publicly questioned why Todor Zhivkov of all people was playing the role of arbitrator and why "a person with middling potential" had been placed in the leadership position. The First Secretary and his faction within the Central Committee, however, were prepared for such a turn of events. Zhivkov and his supporters had set themselves the task of softening the tone of the criticism in their statements and limiting the circle of those affected, on the one hand, while on the other hand, in the plenum hall, their goal was to constantly rebut and hinder such anti-Zhivkov insinuations.[26] During the plenum itself, which lasted five days, Zhivkov was forced to make an additional trip to Moscow for further consultations on the course of action and above all to discuss the question of personnel.

In the end, the plenum decided to "suggest to Parliament" that Vâlko Chervenkov be relieved of his duties as Prime Minister and that he be appointed Vice-Chairman of the Council of Ministers (i.e. the number of deputy prime ministers would be increased from five to six). Anton Yugov was "recommended" as his replacement. The number of Central Committee secretaries was also increased from three to five. In this way, the most advantageous positions within the government were offered to key figures within the winning factions at the plenum. Since the criticisms leveled at certain members of Chervenkov's inner circle were very serious (especially with respect to Interior Minister Georgi Tsankov), the decision was made to create a party-internal commission headed by Central Committee Secretary Dimitâr Ganev, which would investigate all complaints from Communist Party activists concerning the arrest, interrogation, and degradation of repressed functionaries. This was meant to suggest that everything had not been definitively resolved and, depending on the commission's "findings," further reshufflings of power positions could take place. In this way, the winners warded off in advance various factional attempts to oppose the "April line" that had been taken. In the spirit of the plenum's "recommendations," on April 17, Parliament voted to replace the head of state. It is a curious coincidence that on the very next day, Moscow announced the dissolution of Cominform.

We can make the generalization that the April Plenum represented the final phase that the process of Stalinization within the BCP was allowed to take. In other words, this political "window-dressing" instead of sincere changes demonstrated the impossibility of having an open conversation about the past and present of the Communist Party and the inability to blaze a trail toward a true reform, rather than just an imitative one. Developments over the following months only further confirm this statement.

The BCP leadership faced difficulties even in the process of "transmitting" the new April course of action to its own local structures. Some of its functionaries, as well as rank-and-file party members, truly began to believe that this new phase represented a conscious and sincere desire for change and not simply a hollow act in which the elite merely pretended to be interested in their opinion. This was the reason why unusually bold statements and demands for an even broader process of de-Stalinization were made at a series of party meetings held in April and May. In this spirit, both Dobri Terpeshev and Kiril Dramaliev sent separate reports to the Politburo, demanding that an Extraordinary Party Congress be called to openly discuss such problems.[27] This unusually critical spirit could also be felt in a series of editorial articles published between April 18 and May 5 of that year by Vladimir Topencharov, editor-in-chief of *Fatherland Front*, the second most important newspaper

232 *From de-Stalinization to regime consolidation*

in Bulgaria after the official party mouthpiece, *Rabotnichesko Delo*. These and other pieces in the same newspaper, as well as others in the humorist weekly *Stârshel* (*Hornet*), demanded freedom of speech, sharply criticized well-known practices from the recent past, and expressed the hope for a true reform of Bulgarian society.[28]

This wave of party-internal discontent from "below" was parried by successful countermeasures taken by the supreme leadership. On May 20, *Rabotnichesko Delo* published an editorial article "On the Correct Action of the Party against Petty-Bourgeois Dissipation." It set a clear boundary between "constructive criticism" and "petty-bourgeois elements" and unambiguously declared that freethinking would no longer be tolerated. The editor-in-chief of *Fatherland Front* was fired, while party-internal sanctions were levied on higher-ranking communist functionaries who were critically minded.

The tactic Zhivkov had adopted of "walking the thin line" between condemning the cult of personality on the one hand and engaging in reform-minded, party-internal criticism on the other turned out to be the only possible course of action that could salvage his own position and that of the BCP elite at that moment. They stayed this course during the subsequent September Plenum of the Central Committee (September 6 and 7, 1956), where the results of the "investigations" by Dimitâr Ganev's commission were presented. On this basis, decisions were made to "partially rehabilitate" Traycho Kostov but also to simultaneously punish the open opponents of the "April Course" – as the generals Yonko Panov, Yanko Kostov and Boris Kopchev were labeled. Inquisitors and sadists from various levels of State Security, against whom shocking evidence had been collected, were punished with a mere "scolding."[29]

In analyzing the "April Thaw," what is striking is that all expressions of freethinking were made by staunch communists and that they did not go beyond the boundaries of party-internal discussion. This can be explained by the relatively successful, draconian measures that had been taken against any and all types of "enemies" in the preceding years, which nipped in the bud any thought of resistance or even of expressing an independent position. For this reason in 1956, which was such a red-letter year for Eastern Europe, expressions of discontent with the Bulgarian regime that came from beyond the ranks of the Communist Party itself can be counted on the fingers of one hand. They were primarily expressed through the galvanization of rural resistance to the "second mass collectivization" that had begun in the spring of the same year. The activities of the poet Yordan Ruskov stands out among expressions of opposition. As early as 1953, he published two issues of the illegal newspaper *Svobodno izkustvo* or "Free Art." During the time of the Hungarian Uprising, he wrote a poem "Cry for Freedom," which called upon Bulgarians to follow the Hungarians' example, and circulated mimeographed copies of it in Sofia and Plovdiv. Despite State Security's attempt to unmask the anonymous dissident as early as 1953, his activities remained secret until as late as 1959. In the meantime, he was accepted as "reliable" by the authorities and was even sent to a youth festival in Moscow. He returned from there with the poem "Lethal Moscow." In total, he was the author of more than 200 poems "with hostile content." He was finally discovered and convicted to seven years in prison, while his property and literary works were confiscated.[30]

Interior Minister Tsankov, in his report to the collegium of the Interior Ministry on the events in Hungary, informed them about the general activization of "anti-popular elements" and an increase in the writing of slogans, pamphlets, threats and so on. As proof of this, he cited the lawlessness demonstrated by people who greeted one another with the traditional phrase "Christ has risen!" on Easter.[31] While there were undoubtedly stirrings of discontent during this period, we must also take into account the fact that one of the characteristics of the repressive institutions at the time was their propensity for seeing "enemies" even where none existed and thus constantly overestimating the true scope of such discontent. For this reason, the measures taken by Bulgarian State Security during the time of the Hungarian Uprising were also more preventative in nature, rather than being a response to broad societal discontent with the system. The labor camp in Belene was reopened as early as autumn of that same year. Waves of arrests took place in Sofia and other larger cities; some of the detainees were sent to Belene or forcibly resettled in different areas of the country.[32] Such preventative reaction on the part of the regime would be repeated in the future every time shockwaves roiled the system in various parts of Eastern Europe. Whenever a hypothetical possibility arose for such unrest to spread to Bulgaria, the filing cabinets filled with the dossiers of stigmatized "enemies of the people" would be subject to renewed interest on the part of omnipresent State Security.

Todor Zhivkov's seizure of absolute power

When Zhivkov was confirmed as party leader in 1956, his claim to the top leadership position was not indisputable. At that stage, he had secured the support of the Yugov–Chankov group, but it was clear to everyone that the fight to win Moscow's trust would continue. This was the reason that he began a complex and intricate game to gradually eliminate his real and potential rivals and to slowly refill their positions with people who were reliable and personally devoted to him. In the spirit of the measures that had been taken against critics of the "April Line," one of his main detractors at the plenum was removed from power that very same year. With a resolution on June 7, 1956, General Yonko Panov was relieved of his duties as Deputy Defense Minister and Head of the Political Bureau of the Army, while General B. Kopchev, Head of the Army's Home Front, was likewise dismissed. Other lower-ranking army commanders were also demoted, as they were suspected of having ties to that party-internal faction.[33]

The decisive battle for sole power within the CPSU finally took place in 1957. During June, the Presidium of the Central Committee (i.e. the Politburo)

234 *From de-Stalinization to regime consolidation*

voted to dismiss Khrushchev from his post as First Secretary. However, with the support of Zhukov, who arranged for airplanes to fly Central Committee members in to Moscow from thousands of kilometers away, he succeeded in securing a majority at the plenum that was called immediately thereafter. At this meeting, the "anti-party group consisting of G. Malenkov, L. Kaganovich, and V. Molotov, as well as D. Shepilov, who has joined them" was politically shattered, while the individuals mentioned were blocked from any real participation in the government.[34]

Khrushchev's newly solidified position in the Kremlin gave Zhivkov new confidence, so he decided to eliminate Chankov as a potential rival for the leadership position. This blow took the latter completely by surprise, since he also enjoyed Yugov's support. At the July Plenum held in 1957, which was meant to "transmit" the official interpretation of events in Moscow to the members of the Central Committee, the agenda also included an item entitled "discussion of the behavior and errors of Comrade G. Chankov." As the Deputy Prime Minister in Charge of the Economy, Chankov was held responsible for the "rationing strategy" that had been imposed since 1953. Even though this system had essentially been handed down by Khrushchev, the "blame" for it and for the "delayed pace of socioeconomic development" was pinned on Chankov. He himself was removed from the Politburo, while a "recommendation" was made to Parliament that he be dismissed from the Council of Ministers. The Plenum also stripped the abovementioned Yonko Panov and D. Terpeshev of their Central Committee membership, accusing them of "revisionism."[35]

At the same plenum, these high-ranking positions were filled by veterans who had held posts in differing levels of the BCP leadership during the Stalinist period but who had subsequently been dismissed for various reasons. In this way, Dimitâr Ganev and Boyan Bâlgaranov ended up in the Politburo, while Zhivkov's close associates Mladen Stoyanov and Dimitâr Dimov were made candidate members.[36]

An important ace up the new leader's sleeve was the Committee of Active Fighters Against Fascism and Capitalism, which was created in 1959 following his suggestion.[37] This organization classified "active fighters" into four categories based on to their contribution to pre-1944 underground communist movement; in this way, the new communist elite was subject to additional hierarchization and was further differentiated from the non-elite. The extension of the system of privileges to these people's children was an exceptionally important move in Zhivkov's struggle to win party support "from below."[38] He built himself a "praetorian guard" of sorts, whose members had a personal and familial interest in keeping him in power. For this reason, protests against him from local functionaries and structures became ever weaker and more muted.

One of the few exceptions in this respect was the so-called Kufardzhiev group. Kufardzhiev himself was a trade-union secretary, while the other six people in his faction also had "pre-revolutionary" credentials within the

After Stalin 235

Communist Party. On June 1, 1960, they sent an open leader to the members of the Central Committee of the BCP, expressing their consternation about the hypocrisy of a large portion of the party elite and about the total disconnect between reality and their past and present outlooks. In closing, it made an appeal for a "critical discussion" of the actions of various key figures, including Todor Zhivkov, Vâlko Chervenkov, Georgi Tsankov, Mitko Grigorov, and Boris Velchev. As the names mentioned indicate, they were concerned with very different figures who had quite dissimilar political profiles. Obviously, the group had a completely unrealistic idea about the mechanisms and key figures involved in the BCP's decision-making process, as well as a utopian vision of "party-internal democracy" and the ways in which change could come about. The consequences of this letter came after an uncharacteristic delay during which time attempts were made to discern which of the existing factions these heretofore-unknown party reformers were or could be in contact with. Finally, on March 3, 1961, a special plenum was called to address the question. At this meeting, the letter was characterized as "factionalism" and "Yugoslav-style opportunism." Zhivkov's old enemies Yonko Panov and Dobri Terpeshev were indentified as the instigators behind the group. This was the decisive blow against them. They, along with those who had signed the letter, were expelled from the BCP, fired from their jobs and forcibly resettled.[39]

Incidentally, when analyzing the factional struggles within the BCP during this period and expressions of opposition to Zhivkov, it must be mentioned that the Kufardzhiev group is the only one who criticized him "from the right" – with all the caveats such a definition entails, of course. The group's gesture could be seen as a naive attempt to provoke discussion and reform within the upper echelons of the Communist Party. All the other criticisms, attempts at collusion and conspiracies against Zhivkov stemmed from orthodox, neo-Stalinist and Maoist positions. Zhivkov's next moves were aimed precisely against this latter type of opposition to the "April Line." Just like his earlier moves, they, too, resulted from the political course taken up by Khrushchev. Zhivkov used the next wave of criticism against the "cult" in Moscow at the 22nd Congress of the CPSU in 1961 to complete the process of purging the "old guard" from the Bulgarian Politburo.

Perhaps the most emblematic member of this old guard was Chervenkov himself. His decline on the larger political stage was progressing too slowly, thus the First Secretary decided to speed up the process. At the plenum held on November 28–29, 1961, to discuss the most recent CPSU Congress and the "lessons to be learned from it," Zhivkov again gave the main report. His presentation devoted extensive space to criticism of Chervenkov's "doctrinaire viewpoints," accusing the latter of "not having abandoned distorted working methods." Following a well-known script, Chervenkov himself not only agreed with these conclusions but also engaged in self-criticism yet again. At Zhivkov's suggestion, he was removed from the Politburo, while a "recommendation" was made that Parliament relieve him of his governmental

236 *From de-Stalinization to regime consolidation*

duties, leaving him only with his Central Committee membership. This last honor was stripped from him the following year. On November 4, 1962, one day before the opening of the Eighth Congress of the BCP, an Extraordinary Plenum of the Central Committee was called to discuss one basic agenda item: "Personal Conclusions about the Immediate Perpetrators behind the Crude Distortions of State Security Bodies and the Trampling of the Rule of Law during the Period 1949–1956." In fact, the central attack here was aimed at Yugov and his group within the communist ruling elite. Todor Zhivkov once again gave the main report, in which he suddenly "realized" that both Yugov and his successors to the post of Interior Minister – Rusi Hristozov and Georgi Tsankov – as well as their respective deputy interior ministers, were to blame for the "distortions" during the Stalinist period, in solidarity with the others who had already been declared culpable. Following Zhivkov's suggestions, they were all removed from the Central Committee along with Vâlko Chervenkov, while the latter was also expelled from the BCP. The justification for this was:

> the creation of a situation within the party and the country that was foreign to Marxism-Leninism, for gross violations of socialist law and heavy damages incurred to the party and state, for his anti-party behavior after the April and November Plenums of the Central Committee, for actions aimed against the party line and against the unity of the party.[40]

The Plenum "recommended" that the others not go to the party congress that would be opening the following day. Rayko Damyanov was also advised to tender his own resignation. Furthermore, the Plenum decided to recommend that Parliament select Todor Zhivkov as Prime Minister. On November 20, Bulgaria's supreme legislative body once again unanimously accepted this suggestion. Thus, after a series of complex and intricate moves, the state government and the BCP had not only a new sovereign but also a new type of political leader whose persona was extremely different from the image of the leader that had been formed during the Dimitrov–Chervenkov era. What turned out to be the most significant features of this new leader were his demonstrative populism, lack of principles, and unscrupulousness, which guaranteed his survival in a broad range of situations.

The First Secretary had long been gearing up for this final battle with his political opponents. Slowly but surely in the years following the April Plenum, he had promoted new people at various levels within the party; these newcomers were primarily provincial communist functionaries who owed their progress above all to Zhivkov himself and for this reason were personally loyal to him. As early as 1959, in connection with the new administrative-territorial division of the country into twenty-eight districts, the formation of new district committees of the BCP and their corresponding bureaus began. Zhivkov used this opportunity to install "his people" as first secretaries. Some of them were also immediately included in the Central Committee as well. New Zhivkov supporters were also selected to replace the Politburo members removed during 1962; Mitko Grigorov and Stanko Todorov played a central role along this new group of appointees. Even at lower levels, only trusted people were promoted to positions of power: Tano Tsolov, Pencho Kubadinski, Dobri Dzhurov, Zhivko Zhivkov, Lâchezar Avramov, Nacho Papazov, and Ivan Prâmov. All of them were younger, with less experience as apparatchiks and for this reason they naturally accepted Todor Zhivkov's absolute leadership. As far as the old party veterans were concerned, some of them became "happy retirees" or could still be formally found holding high-ranking, yet essentially sinecural posts. A small handful of them enjoyed a renaissance of sorts, including Boyan Bâlgaranov, Todor Pavlov, Ivan Mihaylov, Petko Takov, and the emblematic Tsola Dragoycheva, who remained part of the communist ultra-elite until the fall of the regime and who in a certain sense – due to her physical and political longevity – became the personification of that regime.[41] Zhivkov created a suitable environment for nourishing his own absolute power and for giving rise to the most monstrous forms of governmental corruption.

Undoubtedly, the reasons and mechanisms that allowed Zhivkov to maintain his grip on power for decades will continue to intrigue both researchers and new generations in the future. One of the most important among them was party-internal and was tied to his personnel policy within the BCP. To secure his power, Zhivkov would rapidly elevate and equally rapidly demote high-ranking functionaries. This particular mechanism was also related to another approach employed by Bulgaria's party and state leader: when he removed someone from the highest echelons of power or when he was battling yet another real or imagined faction within the Communist Party, he never went to extremes – i.e. he did not physically eliminate or use violence against his opponents. In fact, his strategy was precisely the opposite. In a great majority of cases, Zhivkov guaranteed a cozy, respectable post for the demoted official and let him retain his privileges. The only thing required of him was to recognize very well what had happened and to have no pretensions of being a decision-maker anymore. Some of these "reeducated" people were later reappointed to some political post, albeit of a lower rank. For this reason, during the whole period of his government, party-internal opposition to Zhivkov was weak and lethargic. Without support from Moscow, such opposition stood no chance of success.

Factional struggles and conspiracies within the BCP during the 1960s and the early 1970s

Even after the Twentieth Congress of the CPSU, Krushschev continued to face growing hostility from various international communist leaders toward his attempts to dismantle Stalin's cult of personality. The first to express such discontent were the Chinese, and especially Mao Tse Tung. In order to smooth over such differences, an international conference was held in

238 *From de-Stalinization to regime consolidation*

Moscow in 1957 for representatives of the communist and workers' parties of the world. In this way, the Soviet leadership wanted to demonstrate its new relationship to the other communist parties, which was different from the relationships that had been established within Comintern or Cominform, which had been closed down the preceding year. Although the conference passed without any particularly notable scandals, the differences between various figures within the international communist movement remained. The Soviet side expected to benefit from the international "rehabilitation" of Tito and from welcoming the Yugoslav communists back as part of the "brotherly family." However, both Tito and Mao refused to change their positions. This made it necessary to hold a new conference in 1960. There, the Soviet and Chinese leadership had a public falling-out. This time, Beijing's stance was also supported by the Albanian dictator, Enver Hoxha.[42] From that moment on, a third "Maoist" tendency appeared within the international communist moment (following the second tendency, which was Titoism). Despite possessing numerous specific characteristics, Maoism transformed into a strange brand of neo-Stalinism within the Eastern European context. Thus, the most retrograde forces within the various communist parties began to express their sympathies for the "Chinese path." The party-internal opposition to Zhivkov during the 1960s and 1970s also based their political platform and expectations on Mao.

Khrushchev's removal from power in October 1964 also fed the hopes of a number of key figures within the BCP that Zhivkov would lose the Kremlin's support and that this would turn out to be fatal for him. The new conservative leadership in Moscow headed by Leonid Brezhnev, however, was in no hurry to make changes to the ruling elites in its satellite states. At that stage, it was content to test whether the loyalty of the various Eastern European leaders was to Khrushchev personally or to Moscow in principle. This greatly simplified Zhivkov's task within the new political climate. If any consistency and logic can be found in his political moves at all, it is in his attitude toward the Soviet Union. His first and foremost principle was strict adherence and obedience to Moscow's will. He understood very well his own role in transmitting that will and clearly realized that this was the only way to maintain his grip on power.

The party-internal coup against Khrushchev inspired the neo-Stalinist and pro-Chinese opposition to Zhivkov to begin preparing for a military coup against him. At the heart of this conspiracy were former commanders of "Gavril Genov Partisan Brigade" from the Vratsa region, including Central Committee member Ivan "Gorunya" Todorov; the military commandant of Sofia, General Tsvyatko Anev; the former First Secretary of the Vratsa Regional Committee, Tsolo Krâstev; and Colonel Ivan Velchev. In early 1965, the army generals Micho Ermenov and Lyuben Dinov were recruited to the conspirators' cause, as was General Dimitar Georgiev from the Interior Ministry. Besides the military personnel, the conspiracy also included the ex-Secretary of the Central Committee of the BCP Boris Taskov. The conspiracy was uncovered, however, when its members attempted to recruit yet another general. State Security began an elaborate operation to trap the conspirators. Even though they were all experienced in such intrigues and did not speak in enclosed spaces, agents placed recording devices in their military caps. Since almost all of them were in uniform, the government was able to gather quite accurate intelligence about their plans. On April 8, 1965, the authorities moved in to arrest the conspirators. Gorunya killed himself when an attempt was made to apprehend him – at least that was the official version of events. The remaining participants in the plot were arrested, with some receiving fifteen-year prison sentences.[43] Some of their co-conspirators, however, avoided arrest. Within the lower ranks of various army and police structures, and especially within Communist Party organizations in the Vratsa region, the conspirators' followers remained at large; they continued to staunchly oppose Zhivkov, as they were deeply convinced of the "revisionist" nature of the leader and his regime.

Some of the conspirators who had not been discovered during State Security's previous investigation formed the core of the so-called "second center" against the Zhivkovists, which functioned during 1967 and 1968. Its key figures once again came from the military, this time holding lower ranks, as they were mainly colonels. The conspirators' political "padding" consisted of the illegal Blagoev–Dimitrov Communist Party, which managed to attract around a hundred communist Stalinists into its ranks. Those involved in the plot included Colonel Mihail Doktorov, as well as Ivan Mladenov and Nayden Naydenov. In 1968, the group was discovered and its most active conspirators and officers were given prison sentences, while the others were punished administratively and expelled from the BCP.[44]

More indirect attempts to depose Zhivkov were also made at the highest level, but they involved trying to convince Moscow of the necessity for his removal. The primary figure in such plots was Mitko Grigorov, who in 1962 was elevated to the rank of second-in-command within the party hierarchy. At the Eighth Congress, he was initially declared Zhivkov's deputy for party affairs and in the Secretariat of the Central Committee. However, his attempt to conspire with the Russians behind his boss's back turned out to be an unwise and ill-judged move. At the following Ninth Congress during 1966, at the last minute he was not included among those being "proposed," and, as a result, he was not chosen for the Politburo, nor was he included in the Secretariat of the Central Committee.[45] This example, as well as others that followed, showed clearly how "ephemeral" the position of Todor Zhivkov's second-in-command really was. In practice, he had a vested interest in making sure that such a position either did not exist or that this unofficial post was frequently rotated between various holders. After Grigorov's removal, Stanko Todorov briefly took his place. He remained one of the few high-ranking communist apparatchiks who managed to hold on to his key positions almost until the very end. After his promotion to Prime Minister in 1971, the post of Zhivkov's second-in-command was filled by Boris Velchev. He, however,

240 *From de-Stalinization to regime consolidation*

lasted in this lofty position only until 1977, when he was also sent to enjoy a "well-deserved rest."

The last conspiracy against Zhivkov was hatched in 1972, again by neo-Stalinist factions. It is known as the *pârvenetskoto shushukane* or "The Pârvenets Whispering" and involved communists from the Plovdiv region who were dissatisfied with the First Secretary. They had gathered in the village of Pârvenets near Plovdiv to celebrate the sixtieth birthday of the local veteran Todor Kordovski. On this occasion, he was awarded the order of "Hero of Socialist Labor," and at first glance, everything seemed to be playing out according to the rules. His birthday celebration, however, turned out to be a pretext for gathering together yet another group of communists who were dissatisfied and who in a certain sense had suffered under Zhivkov's functionaries. They included the former Central Committee member and First Secretary of the Plovdiv District Committee Todor Zvezdov and the former political commissar of the Antonivanovtsi Partisan Brigade, General Slavcho Gilin, among others. The star among them was the former Prime Minister, Anton Yugov, who was greeted enthusiastically as the natural leader of those who had gathered. The "Whispering" itself actually consisted of several speeches, which sometimes directly and sometimes obliquely criticized Zhivkov and his working methods and expressed what were more likely desires rather than concrete intentions for the "termination of the situation that had been created within the party." On that very same night, all of those that had taken part in the "celebration" were arrested, and some of them were forcibly resettled for several years. A special resolution by the Central Committee of the BCP stripped these would-be conspirators of all state medals and honors and expelled them from the party.[46]

In this case, as in similar situations, however, Zhivkov did not show himself to be extremely vengeful when it came to his opponents. This was especially true when it came to Chervenkov. After the latter was expelled from the BCP, in 1966 the Politburo discussed his request "for the reestablishment of his party membership." Since it was decided that at that moment such a move could be interpreted incorrectly by the public, the request went unanswered. Three years later, however, in 1969, his membership was restored, and he was even given credit for "constant party service." This stemmed from the conclusion that "his behavior since 1962 had been loyal," and with that, he regained some of the privileges that had been his due, which he continued to enjoy until his death in 1980.[47]

Zhivkov took a similar attitude toward Yugov. In 1984, he was re-awarded the title "Hero of Socialist Labor" in connection with the fortieth anniversary of September 9. In 1989, on the forty-fifth anniversary of the same event, he was awarded the rank of "Hero of the People's Republic of Bulgaria."[48] The privileges he and his family had enjoyed were reinstated. The other participants in the "whispering" were also granted such partial rehabilitation. One of the paradoxes of the late history of the BCP is the fact that after Zhivkov was deposed and especially after the Extraordinary Party Congress

After Stalin 241

that was called in January 1990, the so-called Zhivkovists were expelled from the party, while the former Stalinists who were still alive, including Yugov, Chankov, Rusi Hristozov, Georgi Tsankov and others, were "rehabilitated" and recognized by the new socialist reformers.

The Zhivkov Constitution of 1971 and the leader's new cult of personality

The Tenth Congress of the BCP was held from April 20 to April 25, 1971. The forum was orchestrated as a large-scale, lengthy and festive event taking place in commemoration of the eightieth anniversary of the founding of Dimitar Blagoev's Bulgarian Social Democratic Party, of which the Communist Party considered itself the direct descendant. However, there were several additional reasons for this exceptional pomposity, including the plan to adopt a new party platform "for building a developed socialist society," as well as the presentation of the latest set of "directives for the development of the People's Republic of Bulgaria during the Sixth Five-Year Plan," approval of the decision to adopt a new constitution that would correspond to "the stage in building socialism that our country now finds itself on," and so on.[49] Last but not least, the Congress was held on the eve of the sixtieth birthday of the party and state leader, Todor Zhivkov, who saw this as convenient grounds for presenting himself as the most prominent figure in the history of the communist movement in Bulgaria. According to official statistics, 1,558 delegates participated in the Congress as the designated envoys of the BCP's 669,476 total members.[50]

In Zhivkov's report and in the new program that was adopted, the phrase *razvito sotsialistichesko obshtestvo*, or developed "socialist society," was established as a term meant to explain the stage in the process of building the communist future that Bulgaria had reached at that time. According to the authorities, this new stage inevitably called for a corresponding constitution as well. As part of the flurry of Congress-related activities, the regime also undertook a "nationwide discussion" to prepare a preliminary draft of a new constitution. One significant factor that helped push this idea toward implementation was Zhivkov's desire to enshrine his name in history as a constitutionalist, alongside the fathers of the Târnovo Constitution and the "leader and teacher" Georgi Dimitrov. In fact, this idea had been around for some time. It was put forth for the first time in 1958 in connection with preparations for the Seventh Congress of the BCP, which was touted as "the congress of victorious socialism." At that time, a special commission was created under Zhivkov's leadership to prepare a draft of a new constitution. For a long period of time, however, work on it was suspended due to more pressing concerns. Work was resumed on the new constitution only after 1968. In early 1971, it was discussed in turn by the Parliamentary Constitutional Commission, the Politburo, and at the Plenum of the Central Committee of the BCP in March of the same year. To adopt this fundamental piece

242 *From de-Stalinization to regime consolidation*

of legislation, the regime used a new approach that differed from constitutional practice until that time. This was the so-called "nationwide discussion," which, in fact, became an orchestrated campaign to noisily praise Zhivkov and his governance. According to official statistics, 6,000 meetings were held around the country to discuss the draft constitution; at these meetings, 15,000 amendments to various parts of the text were suggested. In the end, the constitution was adopted by not only a unanimous vote in Parliament but also via a referendum held on May 16, 1971. Again according to official statistics, 99.7 percent of eligible voters took part in the referendum, with 99.66 percent of them voting in favor of the new constitution.[51]

Unlike previous constitutions and drafts for such legislation, Bulgaria's new basic law also included a preamble, which explained the motivations behind its creation. From a purely syntactical point of view, its structure is very curious, since it is more than a page long yet consists of only a single sentence. It begins with the words "We, the citizens of the People's Republic of Bulgaria," followed by a long list of motivations, reasons, and stipulations for creating the legislation, including the principles upon which it is based, and so forth, and ends with the declaration "we have adopted this constitution." In this preamble and in the main body of the constitution, the Soviet Union and the "Soviet Army-Liberator" are mentioned four times.[52] The regime's claim to speak in the name of the people is nothing new, but it must be noted that the use of such a stylistic construction to express the collective voice of the Bulgarian citizenry represents a new height of propaganda.

Beginning in Article 1, the constitution speaks of "the leading role of the BCP in society." Further on, the classic principle of the separation of powers is replaced by the phrase "the unity of state power." It is personified by the new governing body – the *Dârzhaven sâvet*, or "State Council," whose powers are far greater not only than those of the Parliamentary Presidium that had existed until that point (in analogy to the Presidium of the Supreme Council of the USSR), but also of parliament and the government itself. The Chairman of the State Council was, in fact, the head of state (even though this institution had been envisioned as a collective body) with exceptionally wide-ranging powers. Indeed, this was a post that Zhivkov had created for himself. One important characteristic of this body was that the number of its members was not specifically stated. This gave the Chairman the opportunity to further "co-opt" figures whom he might consider useful at any given moment, while being able to quietly dismiss others.

One important innovation introduced in the constitution was a new interpretation of the notion of property ownership within Bulgaria. It was explicitly stated that the country's economic life was based on "public ownership of the means of production," while the types of ownership included: "state (national) property, cooperative property, property belonging to public organizations, and personal [*lichna*] property."[53] Thus, the existence of private (*chastna*) ownership is officially renounced, while a new type of property is introduced: that of public organizations. Moreover, additional emphasis was placed on the role of various formal organizations within the country's political system.[54] Some of these organizations – the state Agrarian Union (BANU), the Fatherland Front (the largest organization for currying support for the regime among the masses), and the Komsomol were explicitly mentioned in various articles and were assigned functions that they were already carrying out in any case.

It can definitely be said that the so-called Zhivkov Constitution indeed provided a true reflection of the state of Bulgarian society at the beginning of the 1970s. It officially formalized the status quo that had already been established in practice and also provided an opportunity for further strengthening Zhivkov's sole grip on power and expanding his cult of personality. On July 9, 1971, he was unanimously elected as Chairman of the State Council, and Georgi Traykov, the leader of the state Agrarian Union who had until then served as Chairman of the Parliamentary Presidium, was tapped as First Deputy Chairman. Stanko Todorov was chosen to fill Zhivkov's vacated post of Prime Minister.[55] However, this change did not have any effect on state policy or on the government's functioning, since Zhivkov continued to be directly in control of all such processes. Similarly, later leadership changes within the Council of Ministers – such as in 1981, when the post of Prime Minister was assumed by Grisha Filipov, and again in 1986, when the latter was himself replaced by Georgi Atanasov – also did not fundamentally affect the county's course.

Todor Zhivkov's absolute power within the BCP and the state was also reflected in the rapid development of his cult of personality. This, in fact, was one of the basic aspects of public life in Bulgaria during the 1970s and 1980s. Large-scale outbursts of this cult occurred around his jubilee birthdays – in 1971, 1976, and especially in 1981. While it found expression in all public spheres, this cult reached its most grotesque form in artistic interpretations of the dictator's role in the pre-1944 resistance movement. "Yanko," who had heretofore been undistinguished in his partisan exploits, began being touted as one of the leaders of the illegal communist movement, the true savior of the Bulgarian Jews, and so forth. He became the main character of the films *Osmiyat* (*The Eighth*) and *Eshelonite* (*The Echelons*). The documentary film *A Man of the People*, which was created in honor of his seventieth birthday, is especially notable for its panegyric tone.

Literature from that time was extremely rich with similar examples. Poets such as Venko Markovski, Georgi Dzhagarov, Lyubomir Levchev, Aleksandâr Gerov, Anastas Stoyanov, Nino Nikolov, Lilyana Stefanova, and many others put their names and talent behind such laudatory works. A large portion of this unctuous poetry about Zhivkov was published in the infamous collection *April Hearts*.[56] The poems in this volume, which were interspersed with poetry in praise of Georgi Dimitrov and Vâlko Chervenkov, convincingly impress upon the reader the notion of the time of communism as a chronotope in which time's linear passage is of no significance. On the

244   *From de-Stalinization to regime consolidation*

occasion of Zhivkov's seventieth birthday, an extremely luxurious album telling Zhivkov's life story was prepared under the title *Son of the People, Son of His Time*. The album's text hews to a genre model borrowed from hagiographical literature.[57]

Some of the authors of this panegyric verse were members of Zhivkov's inner circle, which was known as "the hunting party." This group functioned as an unofficial advisory panel that used hunting expeditions as an informal opportunity to have personal contact with the dictator and to discuss "current domestic and international issues." The group's stalwarts included the Chairman of the Bulgarian Academy of Sciences, Angel Balevski; the literary figures Pantaley Zarev, Georgi Dzhagarov, and Emiliyan Stanev; and the actor Stefan Getsov. The poet Lyubomir Levchev, the artist Velichko Minekov and others were later recruited into this clique.[58]

Zhivkov gradually began appointing members of his family to posts at various levels within the government. His daughter Ludmila's career was the most dizzying example of such a trend. Within a short period of time, she was elevated to chair the Committee for Culture, was made a member of the Bureau of the Council of Ministers, and, from 1979 on, was also a member of the Politburo. Given that sixty-six was the average age for members within the party's supreme body, the inclusion of the not-yet thirty-eight-year-old functionary was a clear example of Zhivkov stepping completely beyond the boundaries of what had until then been standard practice, even within the context of the permanent system of personal connections to the leader that had characterized the BCP's entire postwar history.[59] At the same time, Zhivkov's wife was appointed General Director of the Committee for Television and Radio. Her uncle was given the highest scholarly rank of "Academic" and was made First Deputy Minister for the People's Health. Thus, even after Ludmila Zhivkova's death in 1981, the dictator's family remained well represented within the highest levels of government, as a joke that was popular at that time shows: "What is a vicious circle? Todor Zhivkov awarding his son Vladimir Zhivkov the Order of Ludmila Zhivkova."

Old foreign policy with a new voice

Since the second half of the 1950s, the Bulgarian party leadership and Todor Zhivkov in particular were the most zealous defenders of the purity of Marxist-Leninist teachings and the most vigilant with respect to threats of "revisionism" within communist circles. Since the Polish Communist Party and the new Polish leader Władysław Gomułka showed themselves to be freethinkers to a certain extent, at various Polish-Bulgarian meetings, the Bulgarian representatives did not miss a chance to express their disapproval of "revisionism" as a matter of principle during bilateral talks. Thus, at a meeting in Poland between Zhivkov and Gomułka in 1958, immediately following the host's report, the Bulgarian communist leader directly raised the question of "the state of the ideological front in Poland and the struggle against revisionism." Gomułka declared that there was "not enough time" for him to give a well-argued response and turned straight to economic questions.[60]

The Bulgarian party leadership played a similar role in the case of Albania. Enver Hoxha's month-long visit to Bulgaria during 1959 and Todor Zhivkov's reciprocal visit to Tirana in October of the same year in no way foreshadowed the turn of events that would begin in the middle of the following year. At the meeting of communist and workers' parties held in Moscow in 1960, where the Soviet–Chinese conflict erupted at full force, the Albanian leaders firmly took the side of the Chinese.[61] Zhivkov, of course, once again categorically supported the Kremlin. During the bilateral Bulgarian–Albanian talks that had been scheduled to take place within the framework of the meeting, Hoxha refused to even meet with Zhivkov due to the latter's sharp personal attacks on him. During the following year, the Bulgarian communist leader even sent Khrushchev a "Plan for a Proposal to the Political Consultative Committee of the Warsaw Treaty Organization" to expel Albania from the organization. It turned out, however, that the treaty did not stipulate any procedure for expelling members, thus the proposal was not submitted for this reason.[62] Officially, Tirana terminated its participation in the organization on its own, and after Warsaw Pact troops invaded Czechoslovakia in 1968, Albania for all practical purposes left the Eastern Bloc.

Since 1964, Bucharest had also proved to be an "internal dissident" within the Soviet camp, although its rebellion took on a milder form. With a special resolution adopted during April, the Central Committee of the Romanian Workers' Party declared the equality and autonomy of the individual members of the international communist movement. It also attempted to strike a balance between the Chinese and Russian positions. The death of Gheorghe Gheorghiu-Dej in 1965 and the selection of Nicolae Ceauşescu to succeed him deepened the rift between the Soviet and Romanian positions, without leading to an open break, however.[63] During the whole period until the fall of both regimes, the Bulgarian communist leader always categorically took the side of the Soviet Union. However, Bulgarian criticism of Ceauşescu's "revisionism" were more tempered, since a definitive break with the Romanians would not have been advantageous to either the Bulgarian or the Soviet side.

In addition to using political declarations and diplomatic means, the Zhivkov regime also supported Soviet foreign policy financially – namely through the unofficial "Moscow Fund," to which all Eastern European satellite states annually contributed. The Kremlin determined the amounts of such contributions. This secretive fund was earmarked to assist leftist pro-Marxist movements in their struggle for power as well as to support communist regimes in the Third World or simply to financially stimulate the Western European communist parties. After his fall from power, Zhivkov testified in court:

246 *From de-Stalinization to regime consolidation*

When I assumed the post of General Secretary of the Central Committee, I was told that Bulgaria had to contribute $300,000 annually. This started during the Khrushchev era. Once, the Soviet Ambassador came to me and said that the Central Committee of the CPSU in Moscow had created a secret fund which all socialist countries contributed to in order to support communist parties and revolutionary parties in the Western capitalist countries and in developing nations. The amount set for us was $300,000–350,000. It had to be delivered in convertible currency. Dollars were brought to me from the bank. The cashier of the Central Committee brought them. After that, I called in the Soviet Ambassador [. . .] and turned them over to him. He didn't count it, because the money had been wrapped up by the bank. And that's how it went for a few years, before I decided not to bother with that business anymore and assigned the task to Dimitâr Stanishev, who was Secretary of the Central Committee and was in charge of ties to the brotherly com-parties. After a while, he reported to me that our contribution had been increased, I don't remember how much exactly – to 400 or 500,000 dollars.[64]

This practice continued for twenty-nine years: from 1959 until 1987. The total amount Bulgaria paid into the secret "Moscow Fund" during this period was $11,620,000. Besides this sum, targeted subsidies were also released to various communist parties via Politburo resolutions, while a number of regimes in the Third World with dubious international reputations also received official state loans.[65]

The Bulgarian party and state leader once again stood staunchly behind Moscow during the Prague Spring of 1968. With growing alarm, communist leaders from the whole Eastern Bloc watched the deep political and economic transformations in Czechoslovakia, which had begun at the start of that year and which aimed at building "socialism with a human face." When the new party head Anton Dubček and the leadership of the Czechoslovakian Communist Party were called to Moscow for "consultations" on May 4 and 5, 1968, they were met by accusations not only from Leonid Brezhnev but also from the other Eastern European leaders, with one of the "hawks" being none other than Todor Zhivkov. Even before the meeting, he announced his position to the Soviet leader: "we should do everything possible, including putting ourselves at risk, but we must not allow counterrevolution to break out in Czechoslovakia and be lost to us . . . We must be ready to act with our armies."[66] The Czechs' and Slovaks' "shilly-shallying" at the meeting only increased the hostility of their counterparts from the Political Consultative Committee of the Warsaw Treaty Organization. On July 14, a new meeting of elites was called at the Kremlin, this time without Dubček, at which a "brotherly letter" was formulated to the leadership of the Czechoslovakian Communist Party, which yet again warned of the risk of counterrevolution and the eventual consequences this would have on the entire bloc. At the next meeting of Eastern European party leaders in Bratislava on August 3 of the same year, the Soviet leader "informed" his colleagues of his foreign-policy doctrine:

> Each communist party is free to apply the principles of Marxism-Leninism and socialism within its own country, but it is not free to deviate from them, if it wishes to remain a communist party . . . The weakening of any link in the international system of socialism directly affects all socialist countries and they cannot look upon this with indifference."[67]

In the end, on August 21, 1968, Warsaw Pact troops (excluding Romania) invaded Czechoslovakia. Bulgarian was the only participating country that did not share a common border with Czechoslovakia. Bulgarian sent two motorized infantry divisions (from Elhovo and Harmanli) with a total of 2,164 men. They entered Czechoslovakian territory through the USSR, after first undergoing specialized training.[68] The first division was deployed in the vicinity of Prague, while the second was active in Slovakia. Throughout the entire course of operations, the two Bulgarian divisions suffered only two casualties; however, the moral consequences of the country's participation in this act are far graver.[69]

Bulgaria and the end of the Cold War

Beginning in the early 1970s, there was a change in the international "climate." This was related to the "Helsinki Process," which outlined important steps to be taken in limiting the arms race, reducing the tension between the two blocs and encouraging mutual commitment to policies for protecting and respecting human rights. On November 10, 1972, the Finnish government officially invited leaders of all European nations, the United States and Canada to begin multilateral negotiations in order to "improve" the international climate. In July 1973, the first meeting of foreign ministers from the invited countries took place (Albania alone refused to participate), where the Organization for Security and Co-operation in Europe (OSCE) was essentially established. Even before the Helsinki conference, the countries from the Eastern Bloc held a series of consultative meetings involving politicians and specialists in order to coordinate their positions. Initially, they saw all of this as yet another round of empty speeches that would help them pull the wool over the outside world's eyes, which is why they did not see accepting the obligation to defend human rights and economic and cultural cooperation as any particularly threatening trap. This is also the reason that in the end, on August 1, 1975, all of the Eastern Bloc countries signed the "OSCE's Final Act."[70] Among its various principles, the most important turned out to be the so-called "Third Basket" issues, which included defense of human rights and fundamental freedoms, including the freedom of conscience, thought and speech, as well as people's right to self-determination and equality. Precisely this basket gave rise to the Helsinki Movement in defense of human rights

248 *From de-Stalinization to regime consolidation*

during the following year, which quickly gained steam and found supporters even to the east of the Iron Curtain. The leaders in Czechoslovakia, Poland, and Hungary (and to a lesser extent in the other communist countries) quickly found themselves facing an increasing number of informal parties, clubs, committees and so forth. Despite the fact that the authorities all over Eastern Europe took the usual measures for dealing with such expressions of opposition, the obligations taken on in Helsinki nevertheless to some degree prevented them from resorting to wider-scale repression. The consistent line taken by the American President Jimmy Carter's administration, which involved protecting human rights on a global level and exerting diplomatic pressure not just in principle but as a means of resolving specific humanitarian problems, was of particular importance for this policy of "clearing the air."

Ronald Reagan's arrival in the White House in 1981 set off the final cycle of confrontations within the Cold War era. His much-touted Strategic Defense Initiative, the deployment of new missiles in Europe, the sharp increase in the US defense budget and so on clearly testified to his intention to further erode the economies of the Eastern Bloc countries by forcing them to participate in the arms race.[71] At first, the Soviet leadership got caught up in this spiral, since a series of rapid changes at the highest levels within the Kremlin clearly did not allow for a more long-term analysis and for a more sober assessment of the deepening structural imbalances between the two blocs. It was only after Gorbachev came to power in Moscow that the Soviets slowly began to grasp this reality.[72]

On October 11 and 12, 1987, Gorbachev and Reagan met in Reykjavik. This meeting marked the start of a new round of negotiations at various levels concerning the reduction of strategic nuclear weapons. On December 8 of the same year, the two heads of state signed a treaty for the elimination of intermediate-range nuclear missiles. The beginning of this new cycle of Soviet–US negotiations had long-lasting effects on their bilateral relations and on the general easing of tension around the world. The progress made at such summits, however, was not sufficient to offset the general processes of decline within the international communist system, which had been further accelerated by Gorbachev's *perestroika*. Soon the regimes in Eastern Europe would begin falling like dominoes in a process of disintegration that was initially instigated and controlled by Moscow. However, once it spread into an unprecedented implosion of the whole bloc, Moscow stood aside for the first time and impassively watched these events unfold.

Notes

1 V. A. Kozlov, *Nepoznati SSSR. Sukobi naroda i vlasti 1953–1985*, Belgrade: Rossica 2, 2007, pp. 73–77, 102–104.
2 Lyubomir Ognyanov, *Politicheskata sistema v Bâlgariya 1949–1956*, Sofia: Standart, 2008, p. 188.

After Stalin 249

3 P. Stoyanova and E. Iliev, *Politicheski opasni litsa: Vâdvoryavaniya, trudova mobilizatsiya, izselvaniya sled 1944 g.*, Sofia: b. d. i., 1991, pp. 131–133 and 148.

4 D. Dochev, *Provintsialniyat totalitarizâm: Part 1 (1944–1964)*, Plovdiv: Narodna biblioteka "Iv. Vazov," 2007, p. 272.

5 TsDA, f. 1B, op. 6, a. e. 1787, l. 50–61.

6 V. Topencharov, *Besove na moeto vreme*, Sofia: Bulvest – 2000, 1993, p. 156.

7 Ognyanov, *Politicheskata sistema v Bâlgariya*, pp. 74–76.

8 T. Zhivkov, *Memoari: Sofiya – V. Târnovo*, Veliko Tarnovo: Abagar, 1995, pp. 44–66.

9 I. Baeva, *Todor Zhivkov*, Sofia: Kama, 2006, p. 11.

10 Zhivkov, *Memoari*, p. 130; L. Levchev, "Lyudmila Zhivkova ili plamâkât na vârha: Opit za biografichen ocherk," in *Mislete za men kato za ogân*, Sofia: Partizdat, 1982, p. 11.

11 Zhivkov, *Memoari*, pp. 106–107.

12 Sl. Petrova, *Hronika na DevetoSeptemberyskata sotsialisticheska revolyutsiya: June–September 1944*, Sofia: Partizdat, 1984, p. 388 and many others.

13 L. Ognyanov, *Dârzhavno-politicheskata sistema na Bâlgariya 1944–1948*, Sofia: Standart, 2006, p. 25.

14 Petrova, *Hronika na DevetoSeptemberyskata sotsialisticheska revolyutsiya*, p. 388.

15 Baeva, *Todor Zhivkov*, p. 20.

16 Zhivkov, *Memoari*, p. 182.

17 Tony Judt, *Postwar: A History of Europe since 1945*, London: Penguin Press, 2008. Cited in the Bulgarian edition: *Sled voynata: Istoriya na Evropa sled 1945 g*, Sofia: Ciela, 2010, pp. 342–350, 487–488.

18 Ognyanov, *Dârzhavno-politicheskata sistema na Bâlgariya*, p. 59.

19 Ognyanov, *Dârzhavno-politicheskata sistema na Bâlgariya*, p. 151.

20 Marcheva, *Todor Zhivkov*, pp. 67–86.

21 Dr. Draganov, *V syankata na stalinizma: Komunisticheskoto dvizhenie sled Vtorata svetovna voyna*, Sofia: Hristo Botev, 1990, p. 105.

22 N. Borsukov, "Kak sozdavalsya 'zakritыy doklad' Hrushchova," *Literaturnaya gazeta* (February 21, 1996), p. 11.

23 R. Service, *Comrades: A World History of Communism*, Stanford, Calif.: Stanford University Press, 2007. Cited in the Bulgarian edition: *Drugarite: Svetovna istoriya na komunizma*, Sofia: Bard, pp. 459–460.

24 Vladimir Topencharov, *Besovete na moeto vreme: Kladenetsât na spomenite*, Sofia: Bulvest 2000, 1993, p. 214.

25 Ognyanov, *Dârzhavno-politicheskata sistema na Bâlgariya*, p. 87.

26 Y. Zarchev and M. Tsutsov (eds.), *Aprilskiyat plenum na TsK na BKP: Pâlen stenografski protokol*, Sofia: Atlas pres, 2002.

27 Ognyanov, *Dârzhavno-politicheskata sistema na Bâlgariya*, p. 92.

28 Topencharov, *Besovete na moeto vreme*, pp. 219–234.

29 TsDA, f. 1B, op. 5, a. e. 199, l. 22–32.

30 DA Plovdiv, f. 55, op. 15, a. e. 13, l. 41–43; Fotev, G., *Dâlgata nosht na komunizma v Bâlgariya*, Sofia: Iztok-Zapad, Sofia: 2008, pp. 382–384.

31 AMVR, f. 1, op. 5, a. e. 143, l. 8–12.

32 AMVR, f. 1, op. 5, a. e. 143, l. 8–12.

33 Ognyanov, *Dârzhavno-politicheskata sistema na Bâlgariya*, pp. 154–155.

34 Draganov, *V syankata na stalinizma*, p. 116.

35 Elena Kalinova and Iskra Baeva, *Bâlgarskite prehodi, 1939–2005*, Sofia: Paradigma, 2006, pp. 138–140.

250 From de-Stalinization to regime consolidation

36 Al. Vezenkov, *Vlastovite strukturi na Bâlgarskata komunisticheska partiya 1944–1989*, Sofia: Institute for Studies of the Recent Past/Ciela, 2008, p. 141.
37 TsDA, f. 1 B, op. 5, a. e. 391.
38 TsDA, f. 1 B, op. 35, a. e. 801; Notice from the Presidium of the National Assembly No. 104 (December 29, 1959).
39 Kalinova and Baeva, *Bâlgarskite prehodi, 1939–2005*, p. 141.
40 TsDA, f. 1B, op. 5, a. e. 554, l. 140.
41 Vezenkov, *Vlastovite strukturi na Bâlgarskata komunisticheska partiya*, pp. 140–143.
42 Draganov, *V syankata na stalinizma*, pp. 155–160.
43 Y. Bonov, *Legendarniyat Ivan Todorov – Gorunya*, Vratsa: IK "S boichki i srichki," 1994; Ts. Anev, *Spomeni i razmisli na edin "gorunovets,"* Sofia: S boichki i srichki, 1996; Iv. Bakalov, *Prevratadzhii ot pârvo litse: Zagovorite sreshtu Todor Zhivkov*, Sofia: Milenium, 2008, pp. 15–76.
44 M. Doktorov, *V shvatka s oktopoda: "Vtoriyat tsentâr" v borbata protiv zhivkovistite 1965–1968 godina*, Sofia: Bâlgari, 1993.
45 N. Yahiel, *Todor Zhivkov i lichnata vlast*, Sofia: M-8-M, 1997, pp. 205–206.
46 T. Zvezdov, *Politicheska izpoved*, Plovdiv, b. d. i., 1994, pp. 100–102.
47 Ognyanov, *Dârzhavno-politicheskata sistema na Bâlgariya*, p. 82.
48 T. Tashev, *Ministrite na Bâlgariya 1879–1999*, Sofia: Professor Marin Drinov, 1999, p. 530.
49 *Istoriya na BKP*, Sofia: Partizdat, 1976, p. 713.
50 *Istoriya na BKP*, p. 713.
51 V. Metodiev and L. Stoyanov (eds.), *Bâlgarski konstitutsii i konstitutsionni proekti*, Sofia: BAS, 1990, p. 55.
52 Metodiev and Stoyanov, *Bâlgarski konstitutsii i konstitutsionni proekti*, p. 56.
53 Metodiev and Stoyanov, *Bâlgarski konstitutsii i konstitutsionni proekti*, p. 60.
54 While "private property" still existed as a term in the first communist constitution from 1947, the text from 1971 substituted it with "personal property" referring to belongings and production used solely to meet the personal and family needs of the owner, thus evading the political incorrectness of private property and its capitalist and bourgeois connotations.
55 *Istoriya na BKP*, p. 714.
56 *Aprilski sârtsa: Antologiya*, Varna: G. Bakalov, 1981.
57 *Sin na svoya narod, sin na svoeto vreme*, Sofia: Partizdat, 1981.
58 L. Levchev, *Ti si sledvashtiyat*, Sofia: Trud, 1998, pp. 306–307.
59 K. Metodiev, "Bâlgarskiyat prehod: generatsionen diskurs," *Ponedelnik*, 7–8 (2010): 79–92, at p. 81.
60 Baev, *Sistemata za evropeyska sigurnost i Balkanite v godinite na Studenata voyna*, p. 179.
61 Service, *Drugarite*, p. 466.
62 Service, *Drugarite*, p. 183.
63 Sandu, *Histoire de la Roumanie*, p. 316.
64 Hristo Hristov, *Todor Zhivkov: Biografiya*, Sofia: Institute for Studies of the Recent Past/Ciela, 2010, p. 251.
65 Hristov, *Todor Zhivkov*, p. 252.
66 Cited in Kalinova and Baeva, *Bâlgarskite prehodi, 1939–2005*, p. 179.
67 Cited in: Judt, *Postwar*, p. 489.
68 For more details, see Iskra Baeva, *Bâlgariya i Iztochna Evropa*, Sofia: Paradigma, 2001, pp. 124–143.

After Stalin 251

69 I. Skalova, *Uchastieto na Bâlgariya v smazvaneto na Prazhkata prolet 1968*, Sofia: Stigmati, 2010.
70 Yu Kashlev, *Helysingskiy protsess, 1975–2005: Svet i teni glazami uchastnika*, Moscow: Izvestiya, 2005, pp. 93–98.
71 M. Sarotte, *1989: The Struggle to Create Post-Cold War Europe*, Princeton, NJ: Princeton University Press, 2009, pp. 54–58.
72 R. Medvedev, *Sovetskiy soyuz poslednie gody zhizni: Konets sovetskoy imperii*, Moscow: Labirint, 2010, pp. 45–47.

12 The course toward accelerated economic development and reform of the economic model

The crisis in the socialist system in 1956 was caused primarily by the desire for greater freedom in public life and in foreign policy; however, significant economic and social factors were also at play. Ongoing deprivation, the low standard of living and constant shortage of crucial goods that continued even ten years after the end of World War II fueled discontent among the working and rural populations in central European socialist states and forced the rulers in the USSR to back away from some of the basic economic postulates of Marxist-Leninist theory. For example, the communist authorities gave up on mass collectivization in Poland, and slightly later allowed the development of private economic initiatives in Hungary.

In search of new economic priorities

The Bulgarian state and party leadership, personified by Todor Zhivkov, evaluated the events of 1956 and decided that the best way to solve these problems was not to make significant changes to the Bulgarian political and economic system, but rather to deepen the country's ties to the Soviet Union on the whole. Given the difficulties Moscow was having keeping control over the communist world, Sofia figured that a demonstration of loyalty, accompanied by guarantees that Bulgaria would not create any problems for its "comrades from the CPSU," could be used as a means for gaining a more privileged position within Comecon's division of labor and for securing concessions from the Soviet authorities that would allow for Bulgaria's accelerated economic development. Indeed, the Soviet ruling circles did change their opinion that Bulgaria should develop its agriculture and light industry as a priority; despite the country's shortage of raw materials and lack of significant energy sources, it was decided that Bulgaria would develop large-scale industrial enterprises in metallurgy, machine-building and the chemical industry. The Bulgarian government was promised yet another large loan of 200 million rubles. At the Eighth Comecon session in 1958, albeit with some reservations and amendments, the participants agreed to allow Bulgaria to expand exports from its machine-building and metalworking industries to the socialist bloc. The development of these sectors was also imposed as a basic directive in

Bulgaria's Third Five-Year Plan, which was adopted during the Seventh BCP Congress held from June 2 to June 7, 1957.[1]

In order to implement this ambitious industrial program and to improve the supply of consumer goods for the population, the Bulgarian government focused its efforts on increasing the country's foreign loans. By the end of the 1950s, Bulgaria had secured several investment and commodity loans from communist states with a total value of 792,764,200 rubles.[2] The size of Bulgaria's debt to fellow Comecon countries reached 176 percent of its annual export to these countries, while the annuities totaled 30 percent of that same amount. This data testifies to the enormous pressure placed on the Bulgarian economy and the country's export capabilities.[3]

If we trace Bulgaria's trade balance with the Comecon countries during the second half of the 1950s, the situation appears even more critical, while the prospects for reducing this significant debt look absolutely grim. With the exception of 1957, which ended with a positive trade balance, all the other years from 1955 to 1959 ended with significant trade deficits for Bulgaria. Over these five years, the deficit accumulated through trade with socialist countries totaled 449.7 million leva.[4] This deficit in the balance of payment was primarily covered by long-term loans from Comecon member states and to a lesser extent appeared as liabilities on the country's clearing balance. In other words, in order for Bulgaria not only to balance its trade with the socialist countries but also to begin paying off its significant debts, it would have to at least double its exports to Comecon over the course of five to six years – and that is assuming the level of imports would remain the same. Clearly, it would have been impossible to implement such a scheme without sending major economic, financial and social shockwaves through Bulgarian society.

Besides the fact that the Bulgarian manufacturing sector was not in a position to allocate such a large quantity of goods for export, Comecon's adoption of the foreign-trade price system for payments between the various member countries also turned out to have a very adverse effect on Bulgaria's foreign trade. This principle was adopted in 1958. That very same year, as a result of unfavorable differences in the prices of imported and exported products, the Bulgarian state suffered damages of around 280–300 million convertible leva.[5]

To escape from this hopeless situation, the Bulgarian government, in the person of Todor Zhivkov, was forced to find a political solution to the country's financial and economic problems. On November 2, 1960, the Bulgarian Politburo adopted a resolution asking the Soviet government for a new long-term loan of 650 million rubles in order to pay off the equipment for the Kremikovtsi metalworks and the Maritsa Iztok power plant.[6] At the Moscow meeting of communist and workers' parties, which was held the same month, Khrushchev rewarded Bulgaria for yet another demonstration of loyalty to the USSR by agreeing to provide significant financial aid to the country.[7] A loan of 600 million rubles was released to the Bulgarian state, while the country was allowed to postpone 210 million rubles in payments

254 *From de-Stalinization to regime consolidation*

to cover the principal and interest on its earlier financial obligations.[8] This aid package, which amounted to a total of 810 million rubles, was the largest loan the Soviet Union had ever given. Moreover, the size of the loan was almost equal to the total amount that Bulgaria owed to the other communist countries. This consolidation of loans allowed the Bulgarian government to solve some of the problems wracking its economy in the late 1950s and also helped guarantee an accelerated rate of development. The downside of this approach was that it created the sense that in the future the country could rely on unlimited Soviet support, which further deprived the Bulgarian economy of the stimulus it needed to improve its functioning and to manufacture competitive products.

In the late 1950s, Bulgaria maintained a high rate of industrialization; it also devoted significant efforts to modernizing its agricultural sector through the widespread introduction of mechanization. Unlike the beginning of the decade, these economic processes were now implemented with fewer restrictions on the Bulgarian population's consumption. Attempts were even made to improve living standards. However, a massive investment program that was more palatable to the average Bulgarian could only be carried out at the price of rapid and significant accumulation of foreign debt, which only further increased the country's economic and political dependence on the socialist bloc and especially the Soviet Union.

Communist Bulgaria's first debt crisis (1960–1964)

Beginning in the mid-1950s, Bulgaria's foreign-trade contacts with developed Western European countries increased markedly. This was due to the overall upswing the global economy was experiencing. The economic and financial consequences of World War II had been fully overcome, manufacturing was showing consistent annual growth, and Western European and North American societies were experiencing a previously unseen boom in consumption.[9] The thaw in the political climate between the capitalist and communist social systems also contributed to the reestablishment of more active economic relations between the western and eastern halves of Europe. The socialist states, for their part, had overcome the autharchic attitudes imposed after the war and openly expressed their desire for more extensive contact with capitalist countries.

Bulgaria specifically needed to expand trade with developed Western countries to support its program of accelerated industrialization, which required not only a significant flow of raw materials but also more advanced technologies and equipment. Official reports on goals achieved during the Third Five-Year Plan indicate an average annual increase in industrial production of more than 23 percent, which is almost twice as large as that reported during the Second Five-Year Plan.[10] The creation of a significant industrial base while lacking the necessary supply of local materials for processing, combined with the country's scarce energy sources, caused the development of Bulgarian industry to be enormously dependent on imports. A steady supply of the necessary resources for this accelerated process of modernization could not be secured solely through exports from the Comecon countries. Moreover, the intention to produce competitive, high-quality goods required more modern machines and equipment, as well as higher quality raw materials, most of which the Bulgarian economy could not acquire through "the primary avenue of trade" (i.e. trade with socialist countries). We must also not forget the communist leadership's undeniable desire to raise the population's living standards and thus to curtail unrest of the sort that had rocked Poland and Hungary. However, to achieve this goal, the Bulgarian state – in addition to everything else – also had to improve its supply of higher quality consumer goods, some which were also secured through imports from developed Western countries. Of course, this incentive was not a primary motivation for the government's foreign-trade policy, yet it nevertheless played a role in the reestablishment of more active contacts with the West.

One telling example of the growing trade between Bulgaria and Western countries was the almost fivefold increase in such trade over the course of just five years: from around US$45 million in 1954 to over US$200 million in 1959.[11] However, a major problem stemmed from the fact that, starting in 1956, the trade balance with developed Western countries inevitably ended with a significant deficit for Bulgaria. The rate of import growth markedly outstripped that of export. Despite all the efforts made to impose new economic policies, Bulgarian exports remained essentially traditional: the country primarily exported agricultural goods, and minimally processed ones at that (tobacco, grains, vegetables, fruit and pulp, oleaginous seeds, animal products, as well as ores and ore concentrates). In return, Bulgaria imported machinery, metals, chemical products, various types of cloth, and consumer goods from Western countries. The list of items traded shows that the exported goods commanded significantly lower prices on international markets in comparison to the imported products. In order to balance its trade with developed countries, the Bulgarian economy would have needed to abruptly increase the quantity of its exports; however, unlike its industry, Bulgaria's agricultural sector, which provided the country's basic goods for export, showed no significant increase during the Third Five-Year Plan. Animal husbandry even experienced a slight decline.[12] Moreover, according to the trade agreements it had signed, Bulgaria had taken on the obligation to export a significant quantity of agricultural products to the Comecon countries as well, with which it had also accumulated a large trade deficit. Given this situation, it was clear that Bulgarian agriculture was in no position to produce the quantity of goods necessary to cover the country's ever-increasing import demands.

The problem could not be reduced merely to quantity but had also to take into account quality, since Bulgaria could not offer a sufficiently rich assortment of goods that would bring sizable returns. It was practically impossible for the country to balance its trade with the West by abruptly curtailing its imports, since such a move would seriously threaten the country's industrial

256 *From de-Stalinization to regime consolidation*

activities, which were highly dependent on the import of raw materials, energy and equipment. The negative trade balance also grew as a result of the fact that other socialist countries frequently did not fulfill orders for industrial raw materials, which forced Bulgaria to make up for such shortages by resorting to unplanned imports from Western Europe, which further reduced the country's already scarce supplies of convertible currency.[13] Last but not least, another factor that significantly increased Bulgaria's imports was the fact that its economic leaders' main concern was fulfilling the Five-Year Plan at all costs, which usually was more easily accomplished by increasing imports of high-quality materials and machines from the West (i.e. "the secondary avenue of trade").[14]

As a result of the specific nature of Bulgaria's economic development and the serious difficulties the country faced in foreign trade with Western states, from 1955 onward Bulgaria ended up with a significant trade deficit every year. Data from the BNB indicate that the country was facing a very serious problem that was becoming ever more difficult to solve (see Table 12.1).

Thus, the accumulated deficits amounted to a total of 951.6 million leva, while, at the end of 1959, the Bulgarian state's net liabilities in capitalist currency had reached 871.8 million leva. According to the official exchange rate between the leva and the dollar at the time, which was established by the BNB, the debt amounted to nearly US$115 million.[15] Servicing this debt presented a considerable burden, given the limited opportunities for expanding Bulgarian exports to Western markets. This large foreign-trade deficit was mainly covered through the use of short-term loans provided to the Bulgarian government and its foreign-trade companies, primarily to facilitate ongoing imports. Bulgaria was granted loans almost exclusively from the two Soviet banks: Banque Commerciale pour l'Europe de Nord (known in Bulgarian documents as Eurobank), whose headquarters was in Paris, and the Moscow People's Bank, based in London. Despite being subsidiaries of Gosbank in Moscow, these two banks carried out hard-currency operations that followed international standards; i.e. they used standard market interest rates and strictly required payments on specific dates.[16]

The Bulgarian government adopted a series of measures to solve its currency problems. According to the corrected plan, Bulgaria's foreign trade during 1960 was expected to result in a positive balance of 105.2 million

Table 12.1   Bulgaria's trade balance (1955–1959) in millions of leva.

Year	Deficit
1955	−20.4
1956	−155.6
1957	−85.4
1958	−90.5
1959	−599.7

Accelerated economic development and reform 257

convertible leva. The problems kept mounting, however, despite such party decisions. As early as March 1960, the BNB's short-term obligations amounted to approximately US$129.4 million. This required that urgent new changes be made to the currency plan, reducing anticipated imports from capitalist countries by US$13.8 million, while increasing Bulgaria's export to those countries by US$13.6 million. Despite the alarming size of the country's foreign debt, the Bulgarian economy was not in a position to provide sufficient goods for export so as to be able to improve the country's trade balance. Even the expected increase in exports during the autumn months of the year did not come to pass, hence the negative trade balance with Western countries remained. Some payments coming due were covered with new loans, which only further complicated the country's currency problems. Once again, the Soviet Union was forced to release additional funds in hard currency in order to meet Bulgaria's need to import supplies and raw materials.

The fact that Bulgaria had been facing the same foreign-trade problems over the preceding seven to eight years did not weaken the state leadership's resolve to undertake export expansion within Western Europe. In this respect, they once again set unrealistic goals, planning to pay off debts of over US$60 million to the two Soviet banks by the end of 1964. However, the actual results quickly showed that if some other solution was not found, the country's debt would soon run completely out of control. Data from the BNB on increases to Bulgaria's debt are extremely alarming. Calculated in new leva (after the monetary reform undertaken in 1961, which entered into force on January 1, 1962, in which one new lev was equal to ten old ones), the size of Bulgaria's short-term loans was growing very quickly: December 1962, 136 million leva; June 1963, 187 million leva; and September 1963, 199 million leva. The country's clearing liabilities and long-term loans (from other socialist countries) had also increased. Including these obligations, the total amount of debt grew from 650 million leva in December 1962 to 880 million in September of the following year (see Fig. 12.1).

Faced with the impossibility of controlling its growing debts in convertible currency, the party and state leadership looked toward the easiest solution, which was also emerging as the only possible one: selling the state's gold reserves.[17] This idea was discussed as early as 1960, but it initially ran afoul of legal regulations within the country that prohibited the export and sale of its gold reserves. The situation became so untenable, however, that the leadership was forced to circumvent the law. This was done by announcing that the gold held by the BNB did not constitute the state's reserves, even though there was no other gold in the country. In fact, permission was requested from the Soviet state bank. On personal orders from Todor Zhivkov, the sale of Bulgarian gold began, with the Soviet banks in Western Europe acting as middlemen. From 1962 to 1964, 23.5 tons of gold, which constituted almost the entirety of the country's reserves, were sold in several batches. At the end of 1964, the BNB's yearly report indicated that barely 2.1 tons remained. The funds raised by these sales were used to pay off part of the country's debt.

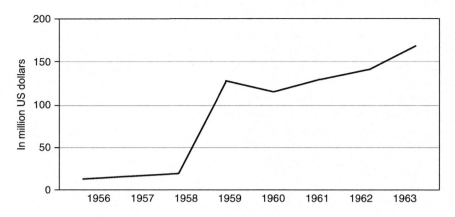

Figure 12.1 Bulgarian foreign debt in US$ million (1956–1963).

Along with the sale of gold, the country's leaders also resorted to yet another round of negotiations with the CPSU, which agreed to defer some of the payments due to the Moscow People's Bank and Eurobank and also to pay for some of the Bulgarian goods exported to the Soviet Union in convertible currency. As a result of these financial operations and negotiations, by the mid-1960s the Bulgarian government had managed to stabilize its position with respect to servicing the country's foreign debt. However, the need to fundamentally reform the Bulgarian economy so as to make it more profitable and competitive was growing ever more urgent.

The first timid attempts at reforming the economic model (1963–1968)

When their attempts to find an escape from the crisis yielded unsatisfying results, the Bulgarian communist elite gradually realized the necessity of implementing what they considered a significantly more radical program of economic reform. Without a doubt, the reform attempts that were being unveiled in the USSR and the GDR at the same time played a decisive role in fomenting this idea. The similarities between the Bulgarian reforms of 1963 to 1966 and the "original plan" published by Soviet economist Evsei Liberman in *Pravda* in September 1962 were so great that some Western authors have even claimed that the USSR used Bulgaria as a "testing ground for these changes."[18] Todor Zhivkov would later openly admit that the BCP had deliberately delayed the practical introduction of the "New System for Planning and Managing the National Economy" in order to wait for the "theoretical elaboration" provided in the program adopted at the Twenty-Second Congress of the CPSU.[19]

From the beginning of 1963, the brainstorming process about how to reform the economy accelerated noticeably. The May Plenum of the same year developed directives for the "new system" and thus formally launched the first wave of economic reforms. In January, they were adopted by the Politburo, and, on April 1, 1964, they began to be experimentally applied to a series of enterprises in various sectors.

This switch from the "great leap forward" and the "acceleration" strategy toward reform was accompanied by multilayered struggles between various groups within the party leadership. Behind their public façade of unity, a complex, multifaceted battle was playing out within the Politburo. We cannot overlook the enormous political significance Todor Zhivkov placed on these changes, since at that point he had not yet completely consolidated his power. The reform program he introduced at the May session of the Central Committee (1963) did not meet with the approval he was undoubtedly hoping for. His opening speech before the plenum was not published, while the promulgated resolution contented itself with repeating decisions that had already been made public. Paul Johnson even considers this experimentation with the new system to be an attempt on the part of the Zhivkovists "to present the Politburo with a fait accompli." The Zhivkov faction achieved only partial success, however. To opponents of the changes, "the endless string of experiments looked like part of a general strategy to postpone any such changes." The reform program was finally published in December 1965 under the title *Theses*.[20]

The testing of the "new system" began in April 1964 and involved a series of enterprises from industry, construction, trade, transport, and agriculture. According to official data, the experimental production units achieved better results than those operating on the classical Stalinist model. In 1965, for example, the former showed a 34 percent growth in profits as compared to the previous year, in contrast with only 16 percent growth in the non-reformed enterprises. The two groups' *obshtestvenata proizvoditelnost na truda* or "social productivity" – the measure of economic units' competitiveness – grew by 15.6 and 4.9 percent, respectively.[21] Given the experimental units' clearly better results, during 1965 whole sectors and sub-sectors began functioning according to the "new system."

The two Central Committee Plenums held in November 1965 and April 1966 made crucial contributions to the development of the reform plan. The "Basic Provisions for the New System of Planning and Managing the National Economy" which they discussed set out many of the milestones for subsequent economic changes implemented in the country all the way until November 10, 1989. At both plenums, however, opponents of reform offered serious resistance to the planned innovations. Before the November Plenum of 1965, Georgi Petrov and Evgeni Mateev held a heated, hours-long debate in Todor Zhivkov's office. Zhivkov refrained from making any comments whatsoever, but on the next day he nevertheless delivered his report to the Central Committee. The important April Plenum of 1966 was delayed twice, and, according to Paul Johnson, even there the reform program was "seriously called into question," since it was only given the status of "basic guidelines,"

260 *From de-Stalinization to regime consolidation*

while the Politburo was assigned the task of making the necessary further changes.[22]

"The Basic Provisions for the Subsequent Development of the System for Managing Our Society" were adopted in their final variant by the July Plenum in 1968. They systematically laid out a minimalistic variant of the reform program, which would remain practically unchanged for the following quarter-century. Its basic benchmarks were:

> *Planning:* In the future, it stipulated a fundamental change in planning methods. Instead of the entire plan being released from the top down, as had been the case until that point, the State Committee for Planning would henceforth only define the macro-framework – the proportions, economic structure and the control numbers[23] for the Five-Year Plan. On the basis of the framework prepared by the State Committee for Planning, the various enterprises would put together their own "counter-plans." The goal of the counter-plans was to discover additional resources, while the tasks deriving from these counter-plans necessarily had to surpass the state targets. During the final phase, the State Committee for Planning would combine all the counter-plans into an annual plan for the country. In this way, the plan was to be developed not only from the top down but also from the bottom up.
>
> The administrative methods used to implement the plan (oversight by the ministries and punishment in cases of noncompliance) would in the future be replaced by a "scientifically based system of guiding and regulating norms and indicators." Rather than requiring everyone to do everything, the State Committee for Planning would now indentify a limited group of mandatory indicators, while the rest would be left up to the production units' free economic initiatives. In the 1966 version, "Basic Provisions" stipulated four mandatory indicators:
>
> 1. the production volume of basic items (in the form of a state order);
> 2. a limit on capital investments with a list naming the basic projects and the deadline for their being brought into operation;
> 3. limits on certain basic raw materials and supplies;
> 4. the amount of hard currency to be earned from export and a limit on the amount of hard currency available for production-related imports.

However, the basic indicators, limits and norms established at the July Plenum of 1968 were double those proposed two years earlier. The new indicators (which were, in fact, a continuation of the old model) included: limits on certain basic raw materials that were in short supply; specification of the maximum size of the salary fund; and tasks meant to further technical progress (technological innovations) and so on.[24]

Contract System: This was supposed to bring about the desired decentralization of the planning process. In areas that remained outside the State Committee for Planning's regulation (i.e. outside the scope of the mandatory indicators), enterprises would have the right to enter into contracts which would allow them to defend their own interests. For example, in cases where a certain raw material or part needed for production could be obtained in more than one place, the producer could choose between various "offers," and thus an organic element of competition would be introduced into the system. Also, if an enterprise failed to comply with its contractual obligations, the injured party could hold them responsible and seek damages. Thus, instead of administrative punishment "from above" for non-compliance, firms would be sanctioned in accordance to the damages stipulated in the contract's clauses.

Self-sufficiency: This was seen as the main way to restrict loses within the economy. Self-reliance (the withdrawal or significant restriction of state subsidies) was supposed to become a basic principle of economic self-sufficiency. The "new system" tried to force all enterprises "to cover their production and other expenses with funds it received from its production or services, in this way securing a pure income both for itself as well as for society."[25] Enterprises would now be able to make new investments and pay salaries only if they turned a profit. However, the plan did not stipulate a procedure for the bankruptcy and closure of inefficient production units, thus self-sufficiency was never fully imposed.

Remuneration for Labor: The salary fund of a given production unit would be formed on the basis of the profits made after production expenses, taxes and loan interests had been deducted. According to the 1966 variant, the salary fund consisted of "the residual quantity" (profits *minus* expenses), but according to the "basic provisions" adopted by the July Plenum, it would be further controlled by centrally determined norms regarding the maximally acceptable salary expenses for every 100 leva of profits.

The Investment Process: To increase the effectiveness of capital investments, in the future they would have to be financed not centrally from the budget but rather primarily with the firms' own funds or through bank loans (or both). It was expected that in this way, economic entities would be motivated to take on only investment projects with real future perspectives for profit, since they themselves had supplied the financing for them, rather than the money being given gratis from the state. However, strategic sectors (heavy industry, mining, energy, and several others) were exempted from this general rule; in those cases, capital investments would continued to be made as in the past, with funds released from the budget. In all other industries, reinvested profits would become the main source for investments.

262 *From de-Stalinization to regime consolidation*

Bank Control: Bank loans (along with reinvested profits) would be the second basic resource for financing capital investments. The previous practice of no- or low-interest loans would be replaced by "economically grounded interest rates," which would stimulate the efficient use of funds received. By granting loans, the bank would earn the right (and the responsibility) to oversee the quality of the investment projects proposed, thus displacing the old, corrupt practice of politically motivated (and irrational) capital investments. The idea was that the bank (BNB) would have a vested interest in only financing quality projects with good future outlooks for profitability, because otherwise it would not recover the funds it had loaned out.

Prices and price formation (economic levers): According to the "basic provisions," adopted by the July Plenum of 1968, prices would play a "primary role" in the new system of managing the national economy. Instead of a system of centralized and often arbitrarily decreed prices set by the State Committee on Prices, the new program declared its intention to take pricing levels and interrelations on the international market into consideration when setting prices in the future. However, this declaration also explicitly emphasized that international prices "would not be used mechanically in the formation of new wholesale prices for industrial production." That is, global prices would only be used as a reference, but "when necessary," the Bulgarian state would continue to subsidize the selling price of certain goods and materials.

Limited price liberalization was planned, with the state reserving the right to establish the prices of basic goods. Besides being determined centrally, however, the new plan allowed for some prices to be set through "free" negotiations between economic agents (through the contract system) within the framework of minimum and maximum prices fixed by the government (known as "limit prices"). For one very limited group of goods, firms would have complete freedom in price formation.

Economic Self-government: "Extending socialist democracy within the conditions of the new system" was supposed to lead to the expansion of a company's economic independence and the management's rights and competencies on the one hand, as well as contributing to the increased participation of labor collectives in the management of an enterprise, on the other. The party committed itself to transferring part of its "alienable" oversight functions to other elected bodies. The models for some such bodies were borrowed from neighboring Yugoslavia's economic committees, which were supposed to be created within every economic organization. The leaders of a given enterprise were obliged to implement the Production Committee's decisions and to take their proposals into account.

Presented very briefly above, these reforms were quite limited and did not constitute a radical break with the earlier practices within the

Accelerated economic development and reform   263

"command-administrative system," in which all economic activity followed instructions from the center (i.e. from the party–state). Overall, the Bulgarian reform program differed quite substantially from the Hungarian, Czechoslovakian, and Yugoslav models. In an interview, one of the active participants in the preparation of the "basic provisions" later announced, "The new system was a completely useless and absolutely self-contradictory mechanism. It didn't guarantee any market reforms . . . The whole thing was one big fraud."[26] According to Zhivkov's longtime adviser, Niko Yahiel, "The changes that were made in Bulgaria at that stage did not go beyond the system that had been established here, however. They were reforms to the system itself. They did not affect its essence and did not provide for a change in the system."[27]

Even in this extremely minimal variant, however, the planned program of changes raised serious concern among the party elite. Between 1967 and 1968, the Politburo reconsidered the Bulgarian reform program. Criticism of the "new system" was made on expert and political grounds even during 1967, but a true change in course occurred during the Central Committee Plenum held in July 1968. This change led to greater centralization of planning mechanisms and restricted the role of the counter-plans; the number of mandatory indicators was significantly increased (from four to eight); the maximally allowed profit was differentiated depending on the sector; and the right to set free and floating prices (within a fixed range) that had been promised earlier was revoked in practice. The newly created Ministry of Supply and State Resources (founded in December 1968) was granted a monopoly over the distribution of raw materials, supplies and fuel, and for all practical purposes limited the parameters of interenterprise contracts. Despite the widely advertised adoption of economic self-sufficiency, the practice of "planned loses" and budget subsidies for loss-producing enterprises and sectors continued (what the prominent Hungarian economist János Kornai calls "soft budget constraints").[28] Without being officially rejected, the reform plan was fundamentally revised and made pointless in practice.

Most scholars accept the argument that the Soviet invasion to suppress Prague Spring in 1968 was the reason that economic changes were nipped in the bud.[29] However, a simple chronological analysis is enough to discount this supposed "Czechoslovakian connection." The Prague Spring first began gaining steam only after pro-reform enthusiasm had already begun cooling off in Bulgaria in 1967. It can be assumed that for Todor Zhivkov, economic reforms were simply yet another chessboard upon which he skillfully played out his gambit. With the definitive liquidation of the "internal opposition," Zhivkov lost interest in actually implementing this promised course of reforms, which would surely be painful.

Substitutes for reform (1968–1976)

Having abandoned the path of reform, the Bulgarian communist leaders sought strategies to compensate for the many flaws in the old Stalinist

264   *From de-Stalinization to regime consolidation*

command economy in a "less painful" and more ideologically palatable way. Thus, at the end of the 1960s and the beginning of the 1970s, the consolidation of industrial capabilities, the changed structure of the economy, and the scientific-technical revolution (electronification and computerization), as well as collaboration with – with an eye to a future merger with – the USSR all became surrogates for reform.

The concentration of production

The benchmarks for the new course were set at the September Plenum of 1969. The forum's resolution emphasized the fact: "Accelerating the process of concentrating production and scientific-technical research [. . .] is the main condition for the subsequent development of the economy."[30] At first glance, this idea seems feasible. The planned economy presumes and even stimulates the consolidation of various capabilities into gigantic economic units. It must be noted that similar process were taking place at the same time across the whole Eastern Bloc. In the USSR, for example, industrial and production associations were formed; in the GDR, associations of nationalized enterprises and combines were created; in Poland, large industrial complexes took shape; while in Romania, industrial centers were founded.

In practice, the policy of "concentration and specialization" had begun to be imposed in Bulgaria as early as the end of the 1950s and the beginning of the 1960s. However, an essential step in that direction was made with the adoption of the joint Decree No. 50 by the Central Committee of the BCP and the government in November 1968 (only four months after the July Plenum!). The document set out in detail the functions of the consolidated *dârzhavni stopanski obedineniya* (DSO, or "state economic unions"). The industrial enterprises making up the DSO would only formally retain their legal and economic independence. These new mastodons were given sweeping powers to manage the activities of their subordinate economic units by controlling their labor expenses, raw materials, and energy; by distributing centrally received resources; by approving changes in production; by entering into contracts with other economic units; by making decisions about new investments, modernization of production; and so on.[31] The thousands of enterprises that existed at the end of the 1960s were united into 120 DSOs, while at the end of 1970, their numbers were reduced again by half to sixty-four.

An important step in the process of concentration was the creation of the agrarian-industrial and industrial-agrarian complexes (known as APK and PAK [*promishleno-agraren kompleks*], respectively) in the early 1970s. The idea had been discussed at the July Plenum of 1968, and by the end of that year, five experimental APKs had been created. After nearly two years of tests, in April 1970 the Central Committee decided that the new organizational form would be applied to the entire agricultural sector. Over the course of twenty months, the 744 existing TKZS and fifty-six state agricultural enterprises were united into 161 APKs and PAKs. On average, these complexes were comprised

Accelerated economic development and reform 265

of 274,000 decares of land and 6,500 employees.[32] It was envisioned that the APK/PAK would undertake "production-territorial shifts so as to create large-scale blocks of a single crop, enormous stock-breeding enterprises, large-scale specialized fodder depots, and wholesale depots for raw materials for the food industry, regardless of the boundaries between the individual enterprises."[33] They would also have common warehouse spaces, a unified transport system, shared repair facilities, agrochemical centers, modern processing points, and so on.

Through this "reform," the model of DSO concentration was introduced into Bulgarian agriculture. Structurally, the APK/PAK replicated the state economic unions, while their component TKZS and state agricultural enterprises still retained their independence. In analogy to DSOs, councils of representatives from the united units were created within the APK, which had the right to coordinate activities and solve certain general problems. The horizontal (in terms of territory) integration of agricultural units that was carried out was seen as merely the first stage in consolidating the sector. In November 1973, the next step was taken toward a vertical integration of units with related production activities, even though those units might be from different sectors or different regions of the country. The Central Committee Plenum decided to establish a national agrarian-industrial complex as a "body of state management" for agriculture and the food and tobacco industries.[34] In the great majority of cases, however, such vertical consolidation remained on paper in party resolutions and was not put into actual practice.

Despite their contradictory results, these complexes, which had been tested within agriculture, were also adopted in other sectors of the economy. In a policy document entitled "General Directions for Improving the Management of the Economy During the Seventh Five-Year Plan," the party presented its vision for future forms of economic organization.[35] Yet another wave of consolidation would come about through merging the sixty DSOs into a dozen national economic complexes. Instead of mechanically gathering separate economic units together under shared management, as had been the case previously, through "reforms" within the framework of the DSO, organization would shift toward "closing the entire production cycle for the preparation of a given finished or relatively finished product."[36] The first national economic complexes were founded at the end of that year in the chemical industry. Several months later, identical decisions were made regarding Bulgaria's other industrial sectors as well. Eleven national economic complexes were created in place of the nearly sixty previously existing DSOs.[37]

With the strategy of economic concentration that was undertaken during the second half of the 1960s, the BCP was attempting to improve its control over economic processes in the country. By uniting thousands of enterprises under a dozen or so "caps," the bureaucracy significantly simplified its own task of keeping watch over and directing the production process. The formal "lowering" of the level at which economic decisions were made (i.e. it was lowered from the level of ministries to the DSO, APK and national economic

266 *From de-Stalinization to regime consolidation*

complexes but not to the level of the enterprises themselves), without undertaking a fundamental reform of the planning and investment mechanisms, could not compensate for the rationality lacking within the communist economy. "Old apparatchiks who were used to receiving orders and passing them on down the line" were appointed to positions in the new intermediate units.[38] They continued to function bureaucratically, not taking the initiative. Instead of replacing the ministries and curbing the administrative apparatus, the APK and national economic complexes simply replicated the central governmental bodies.

Attempts at a structural transformation of the economy

The structural transformation of Bulgarian industry carried out during the 1960s and 1970s was in large part a result of the long since forgotten twenty-year plan. Silently abandoned in 1963, just a year after its formulation, this megalomaniacal project for economic "acceleration" nevertheless identified the basic priority sectors into which massive funds (by Bulgarian standards) would be poured over the following years. The four industrial "whales" making up the foundation of the twenty-year plan, which was adopted at the Eighth Congress of the BCP in 1962, included energy, (black) metallurgy, machine-building and the chemical industry.[39] According to official statistics, between 1960 and 1970, the primary funds, i.e. assets for all of Bulgaria's industry, increased by 3.7 times on average, while in the priority sectors this rate of growth was considerably higher: 9.7-fold for metallurgy, 6.5 for the chemical industry and 4.2 times for machine-building. Only energy failed to meet the goals set by the Eighth Congress, as the growth of its assets remained below average at 3.5. Significant investments in sectors identified as priorities led to proportional increases in their production as well. If the year 1957 is taken as a baseline, general industrial production grew by 590 percent in 1970, while metallurgy showed a 1,300 percent rise, while machine-building and the chemical industry both boasted elevenfold increases.[40] During this period, "structurally definitive" enterprises such as the nitrogen fertilizer factory near Stara Zagora, the Maritsa Iztok power plant, the Kremikovtsi metallurgical combine, Neftochim near Burgas, the semi-conductor factory in Botevgrad, the thermoelectric power plant in Ruse, and others, were brought into operation. As a result, black metallurgy's share in the specialized structure of industrial production grew from 1.1 to 3.1 percent between 1960 and 1970, while machine-building increased from 12.4 to 20.2 percent; the chemical and rubber industry grew from 3.7 to 7.5 percent. Despite significant efforts, however, even the official "economy history" of Bulgaria was forced to admit that "on the cusp between the 1960s and the 1970s [the country's industrial structure] was still defined by comparatively greater production in the food and tobacco, tanning and textile industries."[41]

These unsatisfactory results drove the political leadership to lay their stakes on ever greater "acceleration" in the priority sectors during the 1970s.

Accelerated economic development and reform 267

One-third of all actual investments between 1970 and 1977 were directed at these branches, while their relative share of overall industrial production rose from 30 to 38 percent, approximately equal to that of the food and tobacco, tailoring-textile, and tanning industries (whose share fell from 41.3 percent in 1970 to 36.1 percent in 1977).[42] This gradual transformation of sectors in the domestic economy is due both to the priority earmarking of budget funds for such privileged sectors, as well as to the increasing attention being paid to the so-called "scientific-technical revolution."

The scientific-technical revolution

The Central Committee Plenum held in September 1969 declared the scientific-technical revolution to be one of the primary "super keys" capable of unleashing economic rationalization. Initially, Bulgaria's hopes for the technological modernization of industry were pinned on powerful scientific research centers that were supposed to implement the "integration of science and production."[43] A special joint decree, No. 39, of the Central Committee and the government was also issued "For the Accelerated Introduction of Scientific-Technical Achievements into Production."[44]

Along with this "consolidation" of science, Bulgaria was also counting on collaboration with the USSR to overcome its technological backwardness. Even as early as 1961, Zhivkov had announced: "we cannot answer the big questions of technical progress on our own . . . [for which reason] we need to firmly tie ourselves to the Soviet Union and to dig in there with both hands."[45] Practical steps in this direction were taken at the July Plenum (1973), which adopted "Basic Directions for the Development of Comprehensive Cooperation with the USSR during the Period of Building a Developed Socialist Society in the People's Republic of Bulgaria," as well as during Brezhnev's visit to Bulgaria in September of the same year.[46] These expectations were fulfilled in 1978–1979, when the Kremlin released a significant number of licenses and technologies crucial for Bulgaria's industrial sectors free of charge.[47] For example, the ES-2020 central processor and radio navigation receivers were developed and adopted into industrial production with Soviet participation.[48]

In the mid-1970s, the Bulgarian authorities decided to concentrate modernization efforts in several priority sectors. This plan for technological innovation was developed in detail in a special document adopted in early 1976. The basic task of the program "For the Accelerated Development of Several Strategic Tendencies within the NTR of the People's Republic of Bulgaria" was to implement the "sweeping electronification of the national economy . . . and on this basis to achieve high levels of quality and efficiency." They hoped to bring about this "turning point" by concentrating future investments in several key sectors seen as the "engines" of the NTR: electronics, robotics, chemistry and biology.

Despite a series of successes (e.g., within the framework of Comecon, Bulgaria managed to establish itself as the primary country where electronics

268   *From de-Stalinization to regime consolidation*

were developed), the country's basic goal – to make "fundamental process in the modernization of its capabilities" – was not achieved.[49] In his report before the January Plenum in 1976, Ognyan Doynov expressed the party leadership's concern over the sluggish introduction of technical achievements even in sectors in which the country showed good potential. Todor Zhivkov's assessment before the Politburo in September 1977 was even more critical: "Significant achievements in science and technology are being implemented sluggishly in production and are insufficient to meet the modern requirements of the NTR."[50]

The example of the adoption of 24-megabyte memory devices in the 1970s is highly indicative of the problems facing technological innovations in the context of a planned economy. As Ognyan Doynov put it: "While we were taking the second step and introducing 24-megabyte disks, the leading firms had already gotten significantly ahead of us. They were constructing and mastering the production of several generations of new high-density devices and were already manufacturing integrated disk modules."[51]

The second foreign-debt crisis (1973–1978)

After nearly a decade of relative calm on the "economic front," at the very end of 1973 the Politburo was faced with an abrupt deterioration in the state of the country's economy. The reason for this deep global recession was the Arab–Israeli War (also known as the Yom Kippur War, since Arab forces invaded Israeli territory on this major Jewish holiday) in October 1973. Military operations in the Near East led to a sudden jump in prices for many raw materials on the international market. The most onerous such leap was the price of oil, which quadrupled. The economic crisis this war set off in developed Western countries severely restricted Bulgarian opportunities for export to the "secondary avenue of trade" and reduced its income in convertible currency.

The long-term contractual trade obligations among the Comecon countries initially insulated Bulgaria from the spike in oil prices. Between 1974 and 1977, the PRB continued to receive Soviet oil at prices that were considerably below average market values.[52]

However, the Bulgarian political and economic elite did not use this "grace period" of low oil prices from the Kremlin rationally to reduce the wastefulness of the Bulgarian economy, which did not use resources efficiently. Despite the fact that the Politburo adopted various economization plans "by the truckload" in the mid-1970s, the country's technologically obsolete industrial sector continued to consume 1.5 to 2 times more raw materials per unit produced than the international norm.[53] Bulgaria's energy expenditures were "20 to 25 percent higher than in more advanced countries." Bulgarian industry's energy efficiency ratio did not exceed 25–26 percent, while in the case of metals, this figure rose to 40 percent.[54]

Emboldened by the Soviet oil cushion, the Bulgarian party leadership developed yet another ambitious and extremely unrealistic hard-currency plan for 1975. The Planning Committee predicted a 26 percent increase in exports to non-socialist countries in comparison to 1974. As could be expected, given the economic recession that had gripped the entire world, instead of ending the year with a positive payment balance, as predicted, the country faced a deficit of almost 700 million convertible leva.[55] By counting on unrealistically high revenues from export, this overly optimistic hard-currency plan provided grounds for a proportional increase in imports and in practice widened the country's foreign-trade gap. As a result of such reckless steps, in the first two years of the crisis alone and despite enormous price reductions from Moscow, Bulgaria's negative trade balance exploded to over 1.3 billion convertible leva.

Such a deficit could be financed either by attracting foreign funds (in the form of loans from the USSR or the West, or both), or through savings, which would mean sacrificing the rate of growth and redirecting most available resources toward balancing the trade deficit. High economic growth was one of the planned economy's sacred cows, however, while reducing it to levels more logical given the financial crisis would mean curtailing investment projects that had been trumpeted far and wide by the party propaganda machine (expansion of the industrial facilities in Devnya and Neftochim-Burgas, etc.), sharply reducing imports (both of machines and technologies, as well as of consumer goods), and accelerating exports (redirecting part of the production that would otherwise satisfy the needs of domestic industry and the local population). Such a stabilization program would have a significant social cost and would require political audacity and vision, which the members of the Politburo clearly lacked.[56] Instead of heading down the path of painful reforms and corrections, they started down what appeared to be the much easier path of increasing the foreign debt.

At first glance, the strategy of *growth-cum-debt* looked much more rational that the *deflation-minus-debt* scenario, especially given the fact that after the recession which the leading Western economies had fallen into interest rates on loans fell sharply while Comecon member countries became some of the international banks' most sought-after clients. Thus, "without realizing it," Bulgaria began accumulating debt. Over the course of five years, its debt increased sixfold from 1.254 billion convertible leva in 1973 to 6.083 billion convertible leva in 1978.[57]

This runaway foreign debt in hard currency soon brought Bulgaria's economy face to face with the very real threat of bankruptcy. During 1976–1977, it was already clear that foreign loans, rather than helping to solve the country's payment balance problem, were merely adding fuel to the fire and widening the imbalance. As a result of serious flaws within the planned economy, a significant portion of resources borrowed from abroad were invested inefficiently. Bulgaria's liabilities in hard currency jumped drastically, without this bringing about a tangible increase in the country's potential to service the loans it had taken out. On the contrary, it soon became clear that the size of the debt was growing significantly faster than the trade gap itself. This meant that more and more new loans were being taken out to pay off

270 *From de-Stalinization to regime consolidation*

old obligations and interest. As Bulgaria's foreign debt grew, Western banks' enthusiasm for extending the country new lines of credit waned. In 1977, the country entered a downward spiral leading toward financial collapse.[58]

The end of 1976 and the beginning of 1977 were a watershed moment in the development of Bulgaria's second debt crisis. The *growth-cum-debt* model kept running into ever more snags that threatened to lead the country into insolvency. The growing number of refusals for new loans from Western banks and corporations forced the Politburo to come up with some alternative if it wanted to avoid bankruptcy.

The urgency of the situation caused the BCP leadership to adopt several extreme measures. After nearly a decade in the deep freezer, the economic reforms planned between 1964 and 1966 but never implemented were again given the green light (the second wave of reforms will be discussed in greater detail below). In the summer of 1977, a new budget for the following year was developed that stipulated 150 million leva in cuts to capital investments and a subsequent contraction in the rate of economic growth (from 7 to 9 percent in 1974–1975 to 6 percent). Measures were also taken to reduce imports by 1 billion leva and to stimulate exports, especially to developed capitalist countries. In October 1977, the Hard Currency Commission was created, which was headed by Todor Zhivkov personally.[59] Attempts were made to restructure the foreign debt to a certain extent by "replacing" some loans from Western banks with a loan from the USSR. To this end, Moscow released 115 million convertible rubles to Bulgaria in May 1977.

This wide array of measures – reduction of investments and expenses, decrease of imports, greater oversight of hard-currency balances through the specially created Hard Currency Commission – had mid-term and long-range effects. However, the critical foreign-debt situation required an immediate and radical solution. Only the USSR could provide this much-needed "first aid." The BCP already had experience from the previous hard-currency crisis of the 1950s and 1960s, and, without being particularly alarmed, it turned again to the Kremlin for help. However, the latter did not rush to deploy the "Soviet debt parachute" for the Bulgarian party leadership, which had acted so imprudently. Bulgaria's initial demarche in December 1977 was met coldly in Moscow, and, as could be expected, Prime Minister Alexei Kosygin and his deputy Nikolay Baybakov criticized the Bulgarian delegation for the fact that Bulgaria had set rates for economic growth that were far too high, making enormous capital investments in metallurgy rather than developing its electronics and computing-technology sectors, arguing that it was not making maximal use of its available resources. Requests for an increase in imports of Soviet energy resources were also turned down, with doubts being expressed that Bulgaria really needed such large quantities. Demonstrating market-minded thinking that was astonishing in a Marxist-Leninist, Kosygin openly declared that "factories whose production cannot be sold should not be built."[60]

The decisive breakthrough regarding Bulgaria's requests – a new investment loan, a significant increase in oil deliveries, and a ten- to fifteen-year

Accelerated economic development and reform 271

deferment on Bulgarian payments to the USSR that were coming due – was made only during Zhivkov and Brezhnev's meeting in the Crimea in the summer of 1978. The First Secretary of the BCP openly informed the Soviet leader that "the situation had already become untenable," and unless the questions raised by Bulgaria were answered, "we don't know what we'll do, we're simply paralyzed."[61] The following part of Todor Zhivkov's exposé is extremely indicative of the exceptionally close relationship that had sprung up between the two leaders:

> In this case, no particular sacrifices on the part of the Soviet Union are necessary: it simply needs to sit down and solve the problems [. . .] you must act like you would with *any one of your republics* [author's emphasis]. If, for example, I were a member of the Politburo of the Central Committee of the CPSU and if in Bulgaria something was going wrong economically and it were to the detriment of the Soviet Union – I would suggest that the Bank and Gosplan [i.e. the State Planning Committee] of the Soviet Union step in and take charge of the situation.[62]

As strange as it may seem, these appeals had an effect, and the previously frozen negotiations moved forward. Brezhnev once again took up the role of the "generous uncle helping out his younger and poorer nephew."[63] To implement the decisions made in Yalta, a new round of talks between Nikolay Baybakov and Tano Tsolov were held in Varna on September 14–16, 1978, at which the Soviet side promised to deliver three nuclear reactors, to provide assistance in the modernization of the Lenin and Kremikovtsi metallurgical combines, and to increase exports of strategic raw materials and imports of Bulgarian machine-building products. The most crucial issue for Bulgaria was resolved in the spring of 1979, when the two countries signed a special agreement, according to which Bulgaria would received 400 million convertible rubles each year in 1979 and 1980, in the form of "price allowances" meant to stimulate production and export to the Soviet Union of Bulgarian agricultural, food and tobacco, and light industrial products; the USSR would also arrange the salary payments for Bulgarian workers in the USSR (in the Komi Republic and elsewhere) and cover accommodations for Soviet tourists in Bulgaria.[64]

The significant financial aid Bulgaria received, as well as the increased supplies of Soviet fuel and raw materials (the majority of which were re-exported from Bulgaria to Western countries in exchange for convertible currency), quickly allowed the country's payment balance to improve and gradually brought the debt crisis under control. As early as 1979, the foreign debt began falling, and by the early 1980s the problem was almost eradicated. Just as in the 1960s, Bulgaria overcame the second currency crisis as well, thanks to "decisive help" from Moscow. Even though such a solution might seem like the most painless route possible from an economic point of view, it had a disastrous effect since economic reforms that had been planned for decades were never actually put into practice. The Kremlin's help allowed the

272 *From de-Stalinization to regime consolidation*

BCP to continue its policy of half-hearted, toothless reforms. These indirect subsidies from Moscow only further coddled the Bulgarian economy, which, due to its planned nature, was not particularly robust to begin with. The moment such help was reduced or cut off, as happened in the mid-1980s, Bulgaria would suddenly find itself lacking any means to stave off disaster and would be forced to declare bankruptcy (i.e. the moratorium on foreign debt declared by Andrey Lukanov in March 1990).

"The new economic mechanism" (1979–1980)

The deepening debt crisis due to the chronic inefficiency of the centrally planned economy breathed new life into ideas about reforms. The Politburo, however, embraced such transformations with poorly disguised reluctance and only after all other alternatives had clearly been exhausted. The several-year-long grace period from the global economic crisis that Bulgaria had enjoyed was incorrectly interpreted by the party leadership as an opportunity to yet again avoid the bitter pill of economic reform.

Several small reform "breakthroughs" in the sphere of planning were made at the July Plenum of 1976 and at the National Party Conference of 1978. After nearly a decade hiatus, the old practices of counter-plans (under the new name of "engineering projects") and bottom-up planning were revived.[65] The true "return" to economic reforms began with the March Plenum of the Central Committee in 1979. Using the language of the time, it was "historic" in many respects. For the first time since 1966, the political elite was championing a more or less total program of reforms to the basic economic mechanisms. The New Economic Mechanism that was discussed by the Politburo in February 1979 and by the Central Committee during March of the same year was based on six key ideas:

1. Decentralization of planning through the reduction of mandatory indicators (from eight to five).
2. Decentralization of managerial processes, with some of the decisions being left to the individual production units.
3. Stimulation of "strong interest among producers to seek out concrete, optimal solutions for the most effective use of land and equipment, for the most frugal outlay of materials, finances and labor resources."
4. Increase in "the role of prices and contracts – as a means for economic influence in the compilation and development of counter-plans [. . .] and as economic regulators of the interrelations between economic organizations in the process of implementing the plan."
5. Introduction of "maximum limit prices" and "the systematic modification of wholesale prices with an eye to keeping them congruent with international prices." However, it also stipulated the creation of a "price regulation fund" that would stimulate production through "systematic discounts and premiums on the unified state purchase prices."

Accelerated economic development and reform   273

6. Salaries would once again be drawn from residual funds left over after all mandatory deductions and payments to the centralized funds (that of the budget and the DSO) had been made. From this moment onward, funds for salaries would not be guaranteed but would have to be earned."[66]

Just as during the 1960s, now, too, the BCP "decided" to launch these changes only after the Kremlin had begun preparations to publish a joint decree by the Central Committee and the government on the New Economic Mechanism in July of the same year.[67] This time, too, it was not so much the hard-currency stagnation and the deepening economic crisis as it was the BCP's characteristic mimicry of the Soviet Union that tipped the scales in favor of reforms.[68] The true depth of this resuscitated zeal for reform activities can be judged from the jargon preferred by the Politburo at the time. The term "reform" was conveniently replaced by the euphemistic phrase "the New Economic Mechanism," while "improvement" was substituted for "change."

Between 1979 and 1981, the second package of reforms was expanded with several more components complementing the six basic ideas that were formulated at the March Plenum of the Central Committee. At the national meeting for party, state, economic and public officials held in January 1980, Todor Zhivkov presented a special report, "For the Consistent Application of the New Economic Mechanism in All Spheres of Public Life." The document introduced several new reform ideas that were absent or only noted briefly during March 1979:

- Economic self-sufficiency must be applied not only "to the country as a whole, but also to every economic organization, every unit, every brigade, and every individual worker."
- In addition to prices and contracts, other things such as profit, loans, taxes, salaries, premiums, hard currency and so on would be considered as possible levers that could be used to influence economic processes.
- Administrative coordination (i.e. control over the economy by the administration) would be replaced by "control via the lev and the loan."
- Limited private initiatives would be allowed in some "nonstrategic" sectors such as agriculture and the service industry.
- Every producer would have the opportunity to sell his products directly on the domestic and foreign markets, without necessarily going through the state trade organizations.[69]

This new package of reform measures very closely resembled those put forth in 1965–1966. However, certain aspects that had been accentuated in the earlier proposal were missing in the new formulation, including investment policy, economic self-governance (workers' committees), and the contract system. The partial liberalization of foreign trade and loosening of restrictions on private initiatives in some sectors represented steps forward. While the "Basic Provisions" from the mid-1960s spoke of "maintaining the state monopoly

274   *From de-Stalinization to regime consolidation*

over foreign trade" and for allowing certain exceptions in which some producers would directly come into contact foreign partners only "under the guidance and control of the Ministry of Foreign Trade," only a decade later the authorities were already declaring their willingness to allow "every producer to reach the consumer on his own, both on the domestic and on the foreign market."

At first, the New Economic Mechanism was applied experimentally to agriculture (March 1979), while in May of the same year it was extended to cover foreign trade, and in January 1980 it was to be introduced in "all spheres of public life."[70] However, the party continued to make decisions in a reality parallel to that of the true situation in the country. In the second half of 1980, nearly a year after the triumphant announcement of the new economic experiment, Politburo member Ognyan Doynov admitted to his colleagues from that body: "In essence, two economic mechanisms, two economic approaches are now functioning within our economy [. . .] Since the old approach and the old mechanism has not disappeared, while the new one has not been imposed in all spheres [. . .] We are still in a period of diarchy with respect to economic approaches."[71]

By the end of 1982, the situation had not changed fundamentally. In Zhivkov's own words, "in practice, [the New Economic Mechanism] is now being applied only in brigades, it has not yet fully covered enterprises, factories or unions."[72] Even on the level of brigades, however, "The job has not been fully carried out. In many cases it has been applied mechanically, formally, superficially. There are many brigades still working as before."[73] Thus, the Central Committee decided to once again give a fresh start to the changes, this time beginning from January 1, 1983. After a new round of reformist talk at the November Plenum of 1984, Zhivkov declared, "as of January 1, 1985, we will switch over to the total experimental application [of the New Economic Mechanism] throughout the entire economy and in all spheres of our development."[74]

In essence, the second reform program of 1979 turned out to be a short-lived flare of enthusiasm to make changes within the framework of the classical command system. It is very difficult for the unaided eye to see its results, for which reason historiography has unanimously given it a poor assessment.[75] Several price "corrections" were adopted in the hopes that they would be "brought in line with international prices" (November 1979, December 1980, September 1985). Work was begun on a new labor codex, although its adoption was postponed. The parameters of the strictly controlled private initiatives in agriculture and services were broadened. The normative framework for creating joint ventures and for foreign investments in Bulgaria was liberalized in February 1980. The economic recovery of the early 1980s for all practical purposes froze the new experiment, whose implementation was postponed numerous times. However, it must be noted that the second wave revived faded ideas for reform. Unlike the "retreat" following the first wave that occurred in the late 1960s and early 1970s, in the early 1980s

Accelerated economic development and reform 275

the reformist atmosphere persisted; innovative initiatives were delayed but not "taken off the table" entirely. The cliché of the "New Economic Mechanism" remained part and parcel of the party's propaganda arsenal. Despite lacking any specific practical dimensions, reformist talk gradually created an atmosphere of greater tolerance toward change, which contributed to the growing "acceptance" of such changes on the part of the public and the party.

Economic or political restructuring: Zhivkov with/versus Gorbachev

It is almost impossible to discern the precise border between the second and the third waves of reform, which took place in the late 1970s and in the second half of the 1980s, respectively. Even in the absence of any real changes after 1979, the debate over the "new mechanism" did not die down. Renewed interest in reform was closely tied to the global recession that arose in the early 1980s and the crisis in Bulgarian agriculture during the summer of 1983.[76] These two events, along with the "changing of the guard" in the Kremlin, which dragged on for months between 1981 and 1983, jumpstarted the third and final attempt to repair the economy's command-administrative mechanism.[77] The Politburo's January Plenum of 1984 replaced the heretofore somnolent tempo of reforms with a much denser schedule of changes: "We have reached a stage," Zhivkov said at the forum, "when we can no longer delay solving the problem of the political system, because it is already causing difficulties [. . .] All the measures we have taken to implement the new economic approach are based on the political system. It is the wall which is now preventing us from solving certain problems."[78]

Admitting the necessity for fundamental transformations within the "superstructure" (i.e. the political system) would become one of the key characteristics of the third wave of reforms. Moreover, changes to the political system were perhaps the most essential distinguishing feature setting the third wave apart from previous reform attempts, which were ideologically shallow. During 1965–1966, the topic of political reform arose in the debate but remained outside the core of the "minimum reform plan" under discussion. In the mid-1980s, however, albeit in fits and starts, this idea would take up a lasting place amidst the new reform cycle's priorities. It would even lead to a cooling of relations between Zhivkov and Gorbachev and to accusations that Sofia had gone too far in its ideas for "distinguishing the functions of the state and the party."

At their meeting in Moscow in October 1987, the General Secretary of the CPSU sharply noted that "*perestroika* without the party and democracy without the party was impossible." Zhivkov, however, would continue trying to defend his stance that "it was necessary to eliminate the situation in which the party was also synonymous with state governance."[79] Over time, however, Zhivkov would become ever more open to abandoning this "specifically Bulgarian version of perestroika." Almost at the end of his rule, in his same old menacing tone, he again reminded the Politburo: "we cannot give the Council

276 *From de-Stalinization to regime consolidation*

of Ministers ideology [. . .] Second, we cannot give hand over the party and its development to anyone else." In what turned out to be his last meeting with Gorbachev in late June 1989, Zhivkov declared: "What worries me about what is going on [in the Soviet Union] is the fact that the restructuring of the political system is blatantly outstripping the restructuring of the forces of production [. . .] We should hardly take the same steps as you have taken."[80]

By this point, the earlier distribution of roles had been reestablished: Zhivkov was once again the conservative, the man from the older generation who was "worried" about overly radical changes to the "superstructure." His role-switching game was surely a carefully considered strategy. After he realized that there was no future for him in playing the zealous reformer extraordinaire – on the contrary, in doing so he ran the risk of blaspheming against party dogma – he quickly returned to his old modus operandi. Twenty months after Zhivkov and Gorbachev's meeting at Kremlin in October 1987, the roles had been completely reversed.[81]

Until now, conventional readings of the clash between Zhivkov and Gorbachev have argued that Zhivkov's "July Conception" and his proposal for limited changes to the "superstructure" brought about the sharp conflict between the two party leaders.[82] In fact, such conflicting ideas about reform were used merely as a smokescreen to disguise the real problems, which can be attributed to personal and generational clashes and not so much to ideological divergence. To Gorbachev, Zhivkov was clearly a member of the older generation who would soon have to be sent to enjoy a "well-deserved retirement."[83]

In this shadow theater, however, none of the actors showed his true intentions. This was why the criticism aimed at Bulgaria in October 1987 regarding its ever-closer ties with the West (including accusations that the country was becoming a "mini-Japan" or a "mini-Federal Republic of Germany") and concerning fundamental changes to the political system should not be seen as evidence of radical differences over which direction the reforms should take. Thus formulated, Gorbachev's accusations are merely a fig leaf covering the Kremlin's disapproval and a sign that Zhivkov no longer ranked among Moscow's favorites; these remarks also set into motion the scramble within the Bulgarian Politburo for the heir who would inherit Zhivkov's post. Needing public grounds for his conflict with the Bulgarian party leader, Gorbachev, who had previously announced himself in favor of "radical perestroika," quite cynically criticized Zhivkov, who was a conservative at heart, for his excessive liberalism. Over the course of that very telling meeting in late 1987, the Bulgarian General Secretary clearly realized that his "tricks" weren't going to work this time. The Kremlin's clear intentions, however, freed him from the need to continue playing the role of the super-reformist. Realizing that his attempts to "get under Gorbachev's skin" (as he had done with Khrushchev, Brezhnev, Andropov, and Chernenko earlier) would come to nothing, Zhivkov gave him a fitting answer: *if you don't want me to bother with political reforms, okay, that's perfectly fine with me!* He subsequently restricted himself to changes within the economy.

Notes

1 Nikova, *Sâvetât za ikonomicheska vzaimopomosht*, pp. 220–221.
2 Vachkov and Ivanov, *Bâlgarskiyat vânshen dâlg*, pp. 98–99.
3 In order to guarantee financial stability, experts believe that the foreign debt should not exceed 150 percent of export revenues, while annual payments should not exceed 15–20 percent of such revenues. See G. Minasyan, *Vânshen dâlg: Teoriya, praktika, upravlenie*, Sofia: Ciela, 2004, p. 133.
4 TsDA, f. 132, op. 1, a. e. 8, l. 73.
5 Nikova, *Sâvetât za ikonomicheska vzaimopomosht*, pp. 286–289.
6 TsDA, 1B, op. 6, a. e. 4295, l. 1–2.
7 Marcheva, *Todor Zhivkov*, p. 211.
8 AMVnR, op. 16p, a. e. 793, l. 3.
9 Patrice Touchard, Christine Bermond, Patrick Cabanel, and Maxime Lefebvre, *Le Siècle des excis: de 1870 à nos jours*, Paris: Presses Universitaires de France, 2002; cited in the Bulgarian edition: *Istoriya na sâvremennostta ot 1870 do nashi dni*, Sofia: Kama, 2005, pp. 35–37.
10 TsDA, f. 132, op. 1, a. e. 19, l. 78.
11 Vachkov and Ivanov, *Bâlgarskiyat vânshen dâlg*, p. 104.
12 TsDA, f. 132, op. 1, a. e. 15, l. 90–91.
13 TsDA, f. 132, op. 2, a. e. 82, l. 75.
14 Janos Kornai, *Economics of Shortage*, Amsterdam and New York: North-Holland, New York, c 1980; cited in the Bulgarian edition: *Sotsialisticheskata sistema: Politicheska ikonomiya na komunizma*, Sofia: Professor Marin Drinov, 1996, p. 324.
15 Vachkov and Ivanov, *Bâlgarskiyat vânshen dâlg*, p. 107.
16 Jean Rivoire, *Les Banques dans le monde*, Paris: Presses Universitaires de France, 1986, p. 106.
17 For a long time, the communist leadership and Todor Zhivkov personally categorically denied that the country's gold reserves had been removed from the bank and sold, but after the opening of the archives, this fact was fully proved and studied in detail. See Hristo Hristov, *Taynite faliti na komunizma*, Sofia: Ciela, 2007, pp. 49–60; Vachkov and Ivanov, *Bâlgarskiyat vânshen dâlg*, pp. 116–120; Avramov, *Komunalniyat kapitalizâm*, pp. 191–200.
18 Heinrich Vogel, "Bulgaria," in Hans-Herman Hohmann, Michael Kaser and Karl C. Thalheim (eds.), *The New Economic System of Eastern Europe*, London: C. Hurst & Co., 1975, pp. 199–222, at p. 218; George Feiwel, "Economic Development and Planning in Bulgaria in the 1970s," in Alec Nove, Hans-Hermann Hohmann and Gertraud Seidenstecher (eds.), *The East European Economies in the 1970s*, London: Butterworths, 1982, p. 238.
19 TsDA, f. 1B, op. 34, a. e. 30, l. 2.
20 Paul Johnson, *Redesigning Communist Economy: The Politics of Economic Reform in Eastern Europe*, New York: East European Monographs, 1989, pp. 96–97.
21 *Stopanska istoriya na Bâlgariya 681–1981*, Sofia: Nauka i izkustvo, 1981, p. 522.
22 M. Ivanov, *Reformatorstvo bez reformi: politicheskata ikonomiya na bâlgarskiya komunizâm. 1963–1989*, Sofia: Institute for Studies of the Recent Past/Ciela, 2008, p. 66; Johnson, *Redesigning Communist Economy*, p. 97.
23 Control numbers: the planned indicators for the quantity of goods to be produced, the maximum amount of capital investment, number of workers, rate of growth, etc., which were mandatorily imposed on enterprises.

278 *From de-Stalinization to regime consolidation*

24 TsDA, f. 1B, op. 58, a. e. 7, l. 58–62, 118–127.
25 TsDA, f. 1B, op. 58, a. e. 7, l. 62–65, 131–134.
26 Ivanov, *Reformatorstvo*, p. 75.
27 Yahiel, *Todor Zhivkov*, pp. 302–303.
28 Vogel, "Bulgaria," pp. 205–207; Johnson, *Redesigning Communist Economy*, pp. 97–99; J. F. Brown, *Bulgaria under Communist Rule*, London: Pall Mall Press, 1970, p. 172.
29 Kalinova and Baeva, *Bâlgarskite prehodi, 1939–2005*, p. 153; Iliyana Marcheva, "Opitite za ikonomicheski reformi v Bâlgariya prez vtorata polovina na XX v.", in *120 godini izpâlnitelna vlast v Bâlgariya*, Sofia: Gutenberg, 1999, pp. 288–300, at pp. 292–293; Richard Crampton, *A Concise History of Bulgaria*, Cambridge: Cambridge University Press, 1997, p. 198; Vladimir Migev, *"Prazhkata prolet – 68" i Bâlgariya*, Sofia: Iztok-Zapad, 2005.
30 TsDA, f. 1B, op. 58, a. e. 27, l. 160.
31 *Dârzhaven vestnik*, 89 (November 15, 1989).
32 Kalinova and Baeva, *Bâlgarskite prehodi, 1939–2005*, p. 157; Marcheva, *Opitite za ikonomicheski reformi*, pp. 293–294.; *Stopanska istoriya na Bâlgariya*, pp. 561–563.
33 TsDA, f. 1B, op. 58, a. e. 39, l. 73–77.
34 TsDA, f. 1B, op. 58, a. e. 91, l. 214–215.
35 On the exceptionally unsatisfactory results of the concentration with the agricultural sector and the introduction of APK, see John Alec Lampe (ed.), *The Bulgarian Economy in the Twentieth Century*, London: Croom Helm, 1986, pp. 206–209, and Marcheva, *Opitite za ikonomicheski reformi*, pp. 294–295.
36 TsDA, f. 1B, op. 35, a. e. 5423, l. 187–189.
37 TsDA, f. 1B, op. 66, a. e. 317, l. 1–2; Lampe, *Bulgarian Economy*, pp. 213–214.
38 George R. Feiwel, "Economic Development and Planning in Bulgaria in the 1970s," in Alec Nove, Hans Hermann Htshmann and Gertraud Seidenstecher (eds.), *The East European Economies in the 1970s*, London: Butterworths, 1982, p. 240.
39 *Istoriya na BKP*, p. 574.
40 *Stopanska istoriya na Bâlgariya*, pp. 497–498.
41 *Stopanska istoriya na Bâlgariya*, p. 501.
42 *Stopanska istoriya na Bâlgariya*, pp. 554–555.
43 TsDA, f. 1B, op. 58, a. e. 27, l. 15–18.
44 *Dârzhaven vestnik*, 73 (September 14, 1973).
45 TsDA, f. 1B, op. 5, a. e. 481, l. 111.
46 Kostadin Chakârov, *Ot vtoriya etazh kâm nashestvieto na demokratite*, Sofia: Trud, 2001, pp. 91–93.
47 Martin Ivanov, "Sâvetskata pomosht, 'spryanoto kranche' ot Gorbachov i bâlgarskata kriza ot vtorata polovina na osemdesette godini," in *Prelomni vremena: Yubileen sbornik v chest na 65–godishninata na profesor Lyubomir Ognyanov*, Sofia: Sv. Kl. Ohridski, 2006, pp. 840–854.
48 Yordan Mladenov, Ognemir Genchev, Ivan Dimitrov, and Petâr Totev, *Panorama na elektronnata promishlenost na Bâlgariya: Fakti i dokumenti*, Sofia: DBMr, 2003, pp. 74, 83.
49 Evgeni Kandilarov, "Elektronikata v ikonomicheskata politika na Bâlgariya prez 60-te-80-te godini na XX vek," *Godishnik na SU "Sv. Kl. Ohridski,"* Istoricheski fakultet, vol. 96–97, Sofia: UI "St. Kliment Ohridski," 2006, p. 454.
50 TsDA, f. 1B, op. 66, a. e. 886, l. 12.

Accelerated economic development and reform   279

51 TsDA, f. 1B, op. 65, a. e. 1, l. 22 and the following January plenum of the Central Committee in 1976.

52 In 1974, the oil received from the USSR was 70 percent cheaper than that sold on the international market, while in 1975 and 1976, it was 47 percent cheaper. Only in 1977 was the price differential reduced to 36 percent, yet despite this reduction it remained significant. Kate Crane, *The Soviet Economic Dilemma of Eastern Europe*, Santa Monica, Calif.: Project Air Force, 1986, p. 16.

53 In 1973, the National Program for Reducing Expenditures for Raw Materials was adopted. A year later, it was complimented by a decree for the more effective use of raw materials, fuel and energy. The July Plenum of 1976 ratified the new Complex Program for the Use of Secondary Raw Materials. The First National Party conference, held in 1974, also declared a "war on waste." See *Stopanska istoriya na Bâlgariya*, pp. 539–540, 542.

54 TsDA, f. 1B, op. 58, a. e. 113, l. 99–100.

55 TsDA, f. 630, op. 3, a. e. 14, l. 49. Payment balance: the remainder (in assets or liabilities) of all the country's hard-currency revenues minus all hard-currency payments made within the framework of the year. Part of the payment balance is the trade balance (import minus export), while its other constituent items include foreign direct investments, revenues from and payments of foreign debts, income and expenses from international tourism, transport and so on.

56 For more on the stabilization programs applied in socialist Bulgaria, see Roumen Avramov, *Pari i delstabilizatsiya v Bâlgariya 1948–1989*, Sofia: Institute for Studies of the Recent Past/Ciela, 2008, p. 339.

57 Vachkov and Ivanov, *Bâlgarskiyat vânshen dâlg*, pp. 159–161.

58 Hristov, *Taynite faliti na komunizma*, p. 262 and following.

59 Hristov, *Taynite faliti na komunizma*, p. 266.

60 TsDA, f. 1B, op. 66, a. e. 1176, l. 43.

61 TsDA, f. 1B, op. 66, a. e. 1373, l. 32.

62 TsDA, f. 1B, op. 66, a. e. 1373, l. 32.

63 Petâr Mladenov, *Zhivotât: Plyusove i minusi*, Sofia: Peteks, 1992, p. 185.

64 Vachkov and Ivanov, *Bâlgarskiyat vânshen dâlg*, pp. 180–182. Until 1986, the USSR would annual release to gratis assistance in convertible rubles, which, according to incomplete data, reaches a total sum of 2.9 billion rubles. Ivanov, *Reformatorstvo*, p. 274.

65 Ivanov, *Reformatorstvo*, pp. 95–97.

66 TsDA, f. 1B, op. 66, a. e. 1524, l. 12–13.; TsDA, f. 1B, op. 66, a. e. 1579, l. 26–27, 39–40.

67 Johnson, *Redesigning Communist Economy*, pp. 214–215.

68 Nikova is inclined to cite another original from which the Bulgarian second wave of reformed were copied. In her opinion, "the idea about the structural and other subsequent reforms were borrowed from Japan," while "the internal restructuring of the economy did not correspond either to that [of the USSR] or of Comecon." Nikova, Gospodinka, "Zhivkovata ikonomicheska reforma, perestroykata i startât na skritata privatizatsiya v Bâlgariya," *Istoricheski pregled LIX*, 5–6 (2003): 97–98.

69 TsDA, f. 1B, op. 66, a. e. 2140, l. 73 and following.

70 TsDA, f. 1B, op. 66, a. e. 2140.

71 TsDA, f. 1B, op. 66, a. e. 2617a, l. 150–151.

72 TsDA, f. 1B, op. 65, a. e. 57, l. 21.

280 *From de-Stalinization to regime consolidation*

73 TsDA, f. 1B, op. 65, a. e. 57, l. 25, 27.
74 TsDA, f. 1B, op. 65, a. e. 64, l. 3.
75 According to Crampton, the "grandiose scheme" of the new economic mechanism "had insignificant results." See Crampton, *Concise History*, p. 207; while, in Marcheva's opinion, "The reforms from the mid-1970s were one of the most conservative and stagnant set of reforms, through which the authorities [in Bulgaria] and Moscow tried to solve the pressing problems without addressing their true causes." See Marcheva, *Opitite za ikonomicheski reformi*, p. 294.
76 TsDA, f. 1B, op. 67, a. e. 2122, l. 93a–113.
77 In November 1982, after Leonid Brezhnev's death, Yuriy Andropov was elected General Secretary of the CPSU.
78 TsDA, f. 1B, op. 65, a. e. 62, l. 4–7.
79 TsDA, f. 1B, op. 68, a. e. 3272, l. 42.
80 TsDA, f. 1B, a. e. 3698, l. 60, 64.
81 TsDA, f. 1B, a. e. 3553, l. 65–69.
82 Yahiel, *Todor Zhivkov*, p. 343.
83 According to J. F. Brown, Gorbachev developed his "hostile attitude" towards Zhivkov as early as 1984, when he was sent to Sofia to dissuade Zhivkov from his planned visit to Bonn. J. F. Brown, *Surge to Freedom: The End of Communist Rule in Eastern Europe*, Durham, NC: Duke University Press, 1991, p. 186. According to Yahiel, the tension between the two men arose several years alter. Yahiel, *Todor Zhivkov*, pp. 307–316, 343–344.

13 Sovietization in the shadow of Khrushchev and the Brezhnev Doctrine

Over the years, only the reasons behind Bulgaria's stance as the most slavish Soviet satellite changed. While for Georgi Dimitrov and Vâlko Chervenkov the goal of such submissiveness had been to guarantee the full imposition of communist power in the country and to ensure their own physical survival during the Stalinist purges, in the mid-1950s Todor Zhivkov introduced a new aspect into Bulgaria's bilateral relations with Moscow. According to his arithmetic, it was "worth it" to sacrifice the county's political sovereignty, which was, in any case, fictitious, so as to reap gratuitous Soviet support for Bulgarian modernization. He had two important goals in turning the PRB into the most loyal Soviet satellite: to guarantee his own political longevity and to tip the balance of their bilateral relations in Bulgaria's favor. Such a choice, especially since it was made at a moment when China, Romania, and Albania bucked the USSR's smothering influence one after another, was unparalleled. There was no other Eastern European state so ready to sacrifice its own national sovereignty in the name of political (Zhivkov's preservation of his own position) and economic (no-string-attached aid) aims.[1] In one statement, especially directed at audiences in Moscow, Beijing and Bucharest, Zhivkov emphatically declared: "Our Romanian comrades, just like our Chinese comrades are talking about respecting sovereignty. The people understand 'sovereignty' as having something to eat, as living. That's what sovereignty is."[2]

The idea was to make Bulgarian into the sixteenth Soviet republic so as to secure cheap resources, low-interest loans, no-strings-attached financial aid, the transfer of technologies, and an enormous unpretentious market. In a country with traditionally strong Russophilic feelings, the political costs of such a move seemed negligibly low. Because, once again citing Zhivkov, "the Americans can't say anything more than what they're already saying: that we're satellites, that we're not an independent country."[3]

The first, still timid steps toward "closer ties, with the prospect of merging with the USSR" were made in 1962. In July of that year, Zhivkov felt out the mood in the Central Committee, hinting at an impending "full organic fusion of economies," albeit still within the framework of Comecon at that point, and not with the USSR.[4] In March 1963, the BCP approved

282　*From de-Stalinization to regime consolidation*

the Kremlin's directive for creating a unified planning body for the Comecon member states. Khrushchev saw this initiative as the first step toward the goal declared in the new program of the CPSU from 1961: "ever greater closeness between the individual national economies," and foreseeing in the future the creation of "a global communist economy," regulated by a single, unified plan.[5] The heated conflict that broke out with the Chinese and Romanian delegations at the Moscow meeting of Comecon's Executive Committee for Organization in July 1963, however, blocked attempts to strengthen Soviet control via Comecon mechanisms. Having ferreted out Khrushchev's secret intentions, which clearly could no longer be achieved within Comecon, Zhivkov launched a lightning-fast maneuver. Even before leaving Moscow, he felt out the Presidium of the Central Committee of the CPSU regarding an economic and political merger between Bulgaria and the USSR. Protocols from the meeting have not been preserved, but at the Plenum of the Central Committee of the BCP held only four days later, Zhivkov declared that he had been given the green light: "We raised this question, albeit in the form of a joke, and thus I came to understand that our Soviet comrades are not far from such an idea for closer collaboration."[6]

At the July Plenum of 1963, which was called "with obvious haste," the party leadership discussed "closer ties, with future prospects for a merger" with the Soviet Union.[7] In front of the audience, Zhivkov justified his initiative by citing the anticipated economic gains for Bulgaria. However, to all of those present it was clear that the campaign for Bulgaria to become the sixteenth Soviet republic was above all a personal public-relations drive on the part of Zhivkov. Encouraged upon receiving the Central Committee's support, in August 1963 Zhivkov presented the Politburo with theses for a letter to Khrushchev that would already discuss the form of the impending union – as a confederation or as a federation. Many of the party leaders feared, with good reason, that the initiative would cement Zhivkov as the permanent leader of the country for years to come and hence refused to support the letter.[8] Zhivkov, however, would not allow anyone to stand in the way of his wonderful opportunity to join in Khrushchev's scheme for the "confederation of the Soviet bloc."[9] He "elegantly" sidestepped the Politburo's reservations by calling a Special Plenum of the Central Committee in December 1963. There, the majority of old communists "with Stalinist temperaments" met his proposal for "closer ties, with future prospects for a merger" of Bulgaria with the Soviet Union with enthusiastic applause.[10] Radenko Vidinski and Rada Todorova tearfully admitted that "they had been dreaming of this moment for many long years," while Todor Pavlov insisted that there was no need whatsoever to put the question to the people in the form of a referendum.[11] Before this decisive plenum in October 1963, Zhivkov and Stanko Todorov had made one final trip to Moscow to sound out the situation there; Khrushchev once again announced his support for the initiative, saying: "I agree with your proposal!"[12]

At the December Plenum of the Central Committee of the BCP, a special letter to Khrushchev was prepared, requesting "closer ties, with future prospects for a union between the People's Republic of Bulgaria and the USSR."[13] It turns out that Zhivkov's initiative fit in perfectly with the Soviet leader's idea of a "unified socialist family." Khrushchev developed this notion in detail during his meeting with the Bulgarian party leader in February 1964. According to Zhivkov, the most suitable form for the future integration would be a confederation between Bulgaria and the USSR, with the former retaining all of its state institutions. "Of course," he continued, "under such circumstances there would be closer coordination in the functioning of the Foreign Ministry, in national defense and so on." This is precisely what the Chinese, Romanian, and Albanian communist parties were opposing, while Zhivkov's voluntary proposal gave Khrushchev an ideal opportunity to begin integration despite their opposition.

Tracing the chronology of the first attempt to make Bulgaria into the sixteenth Soviet republic shows just how manipulative attempts to downplay the initiative after the fact have been. In his memoirs, for example, Zhivkov would later claim that his proposal was merely a symbolic gesture, since he knew the USSR would not accept it. In essence, he attempted to argue that Bulgarian sovereignty was never truly under threat and that, in exchange for a "few pretty phrases," Bulgaria received enormous economic benefits from the USSR.[14] This interpretation would be repeated later in other memoirs, as well as in certain historical studies.[15] It has been claimed that with this clever move Zhivkov secured a 300-million ruble loan, as well as technical assistance for constructing several large factories.

Exactly ten years after his first attempt, Zhivkov decided to repeat his "tried-and-true recipe" from 1963 to 1964.[16] In July 1973, a plenum of the Central Committee of the BCP was convened that was formally dedicated to the party's international activities, but its true task was actually to discuss the country's bilateral relations with the Soviet Union. At this forum, the Central Committee adopted "Basic Directions for the Development of Comprehensive Relations with the Soviet Union," which revived the initiative to make Bulgaria the sixteenth Soviet republic. Clearly, just as in 1963, Zhivkov had again managed to discern which way the winds were blowing in Moscow, because his offer again received support from the Kremlin. In September 1973, the Central Committee of the CPSU sent a special letter in reply, while Brezhnev cut short his vacation in the Crimea and personally visited Sofia. According to Zhivkov's close adviser, Niko Yahiel, the "high point" of the visit was the meeting between the two heads of state at the Voden residence. Zhivkov did everything possible to create a particularly warm and friendly atmosphere. Before that, Brezhnev had been greeted by frenetic crowds on the Sofia streets, and he was honored for the first time with the title "Hero of the People's Republic of Bulgaria" (he would later be awarded the same title two more times, in 1976 and 1981). At the Voden

284 *From de-Stalinization to regime consolidation*

hunting lodge, Dimitâr Metodiev and Brezhnev recited poetry by Bulgarian and Russian poets.[17]

Zhivkov's unexpected offer fit very well with the Brezhnev Doctrine, which had been proclaimed in 1968 and which envisioned limited sovereignty in relations between the USSR and its satellites. The proposal came at a time when the Kremlin was seriously considering reforms within Comecon and the Warsaw Pact which would further strengthen Soviet control over Eastern Europe. For Brezhnev, as Lâchezar Stoyanov argues, "this surprising voluntary suggestion was valuable in so far as it could influence the position of the remaining socialist countries as well." After a warm reception in Moscow in November 1972, the Bulgarian party leader began nursing hopes that this time he would succeed in establishing himself "as a new Georgi Dimitrov" – i.e. as a mouthpiece for Soviet policy, in exchange for the corresponding political and economic perks, of course.[18] Or, as Stanko Todorov openly admitted: "Relations between Bulgaria and the Soviet Union are a prototype for cooperation between the peoples in communist society."[19]

By trumpeting this "unique Bulgaro-Soviet cooperation," Zhivkov managed to secure a series of concessions from the USSR.[20] The data is incomplete, but according to some assessments, between 1979 and 1985 alone, Bulgaria received 2.9 billion rubles in gratis aid.[21] This refers to price allowances for export to the Soviet Union of Bulgarian agricultural, food and tobacco, and light industrial products; as well as to the USSR's compensation for the salaries of Bulgarian workers in the USSR; and for accommodations for Soviet tourists in Bulgaria. To this end, 520 million convertible leva were released annually during 1979–1980, while this amount was subsequently reduced several times over, reaching 150 million in 1986.[22] Besides direct aid, the Soviet Union supplied Bulgaria with important strategic raw materials (oil, gas, ores, etc.) at preferential prices that were considerably lower than those on international markets. In certain years such as 1974, this subsidy was equal to as much as 70 percent of the global price, while during almost half of this period it hovered around and above 50 percent.

Of course, these Soviet gestures were not at all "gratis" but rather came with heavy strings attached. They were cleverly balanced out by the Kremlin through the use of various mechanisms. This is why the 2.9 billion rubles (or US$3 billion) in Soviet aid in the late 1970s and early 1980s were almost nullified if we add to the balance the considerable sums required from Bulgaria for the purchase of Russian weapons, for the financing of mining and transport capabilities within the territory of the Soviet Union, and so forth. Not surprisingly, evidence of such deals is scarce, but a letter from General Dobri Dzhurov to the Warsaw Pact Marshal Dmitriy Ustinov that was preserved in the Politburo archives sheds some light on this dark side of Bulgaro-Soviet relations. From the letter it becomes clear that according to agreements Bulgaria had entered into, the country was obligated to import "special goods" with a value of 1.244 billion rubles (of which 1.006 billion ruble's worth were from the USSR) between 1981 and 1985. The amounts subsequently increased to 1.656 billion rubles during 1981 and 1982.[23] A second important means of "balancing" Bulgaro-Soviet relations were agreements for Bulgaria to participate in the building of mining or transport capabilities in the USSR. Given the lack of sufficient data about Bulgaria, Polish economists' calculations about their country's situation, which was similar to the Bulgaria's, are very valuable. They have calculated the People's Republic of Poland's share in building the Orenburg and Polotsk pipelines in the Soviet Union added an additional 37.1 percent to the basic price at which energy resources were purchased.[24] In 1985, the Long-Term Program was signed, which stipulated that, "the Bulgarian side will participate in the construction of gas pipelines and oil industry infrastructure within the territory of the USSR."[25] The scheme had been used numerous times before as well. In this way, the Orenburg gas pipeline, the Vinnitsa–Albertisha power transmission line, and the lumber industry in Komi were developed during the 1970s.[26] The Long-Term Program obligated Bulgarian to take part in two projects which were enormous, given the size of the country's economy – the Yamburg gas field and the Krivoy Rog metallurgical complex – by investing a total of 1.7 billion convertible rubles and more than US$500 million. Moreover, these sums had to be paid significantly before the promised resource returns from the projects – gas, oil, and steel – would be received.[27]

Whether and to what extent Sofia managed to take advantage of the voluntary surrender of its sovereignty is a difficult question to answer without full access to the Soviet archives. Nevertheless, in academic literature, attempts have been made to quantify the material gains received by Bulgaria in return for playing the role of Moscow's most loyal satellite. Models developed by Michael Marrese and Jan Vaňous, as well as by Kate Crane, show that the increase of "gratis" aid to Bulgaria was due not so much to the country's surrender of its national sovereignty but rather to its great backwardness and poverty in comparison to the other Comecon member states.[28] According to Crane, even though "the Soviet Union took into account political factors [as well]" in defining the size of its aid, "there is no clear evidence that the size of the indirect trade subsidies was used as a political instrument to gain political concessions" (see Table 13.1).[29]

After holding third place during the 1960s and the early 1970s, Bulgaria moved up into second place after 1973–1974. It turns out that the sacrifice of sovereignty was not "rewarded" by Moscow with more or cheaper resources. On the contrary, according to these calculations, during the 1960s, the exact opposite was the case. Between 1960 and 1964, when Zhivkov was making his push for "merger," every Bulgarian paid US$33 in indirect trade subsidies to the Soviet Union, while between 1965 and 1969, when the idea had been rejected, this figure fell to US$24 per capita.[30] It was only in the mid-1970s (and only briefly) that Zhivkov managed to hit upon the right approach to the Soviet leadership and to Brezhnev personally.

In time, after the initial enthusiasm with which Moscow greeted Bulgaria's voluntary proposals, the interest in such a "merger" there waned. Zhivkov,

286 *From de-Stalinization to regime consolidation*

Table 13.1 Classification of Comecon member states according to the amount of Soviet aid received.

Relative position in terms of received support	1960–1978 (Marrese and Vañous 1983)	1970–1984 (Crane 1986)
1	GDR	GDR
2	CzSSR	Bulgaria
3	Bulgaria	CzSSR
4	Hungary	Hungary
5	Poland	Poland
6	Romania	Romania

Source: K. Crane, *The Soviet Economic Dilemma of Eastern Europe*, Santa Monica, Calif.: Project Air Force, 1986, p. 22; M. Marrese and J. Vañous, *Soviet Subsidization of Trade with Eastern Europe*, Berkeley, Calif.: Institute of International Studies, 1983, p. 85.

however, with astonishing insistence, continually reminded the Kremlin of the agreements from 1963 to 1964 and 1973 and constantly hinted that Bulgaria was ready to give up its national sovereignty. Having recognized the importance of maintaining "special relations" with the Soviet leader, Zhivkov attempted to use the model that had worked in 1973 and 1978 with every subsequent General Secretary of the CPSU. The elevation of the young and pragmatic Mikhail Gorbachev was a new challenge to the aging Bulgarian party leader, who had still not lost his taste for power. Using his well-honed scheme, he attempted to ferret out Gorbachev's "weakness" and to support him on that front as zealously as possible.[31] The new boss of the Kremlin was cut from different cloth, however. It was inappropriate for Zhivkov to "kiss him, as he had Khrushchev and Brezhnev."[32] Working on the principle of "short reckonings make long friends," which he had declared as early as 1985, Gorbachev showed that initiatives such as those in 1963 and 1973 would no longer fly in Moscow. Thus, Zhivkov started talking about *reforms* instead of *merger*. In July 1985, he composed and delivered his "Considerations" on urgently needed economic and political changes to the Soviet leader. His goal was not only to recommend himself as a passionate adherent of *perestroika* but also to show that he had the necessary experience that could be of use to the General Secretary of the CPSU, who had just assumed the driver's seat. This time, however, Zhivkov miscalculated. It soon became clear that his letter had offended Gorbachev's "touchy sense of pride," and, without meaning to, he had sown the seeds of mistrust.[33]

The Soviet leader, of course, would not allow personal feelings to dictate his relations toward one of the USSR's most devoted followers in the socialist bloc. To Moscow it was clear that the old scheme – trading political loyalty in exchange for strategic resources and political guarantees for the party leader – was already too costly for the USSR's gasping economy. Besides, Gorbachev refused to impose Soviet hegemony with tanks. Within a few years, he drastically reduced gratis Soviet aid and arranged for the Bulgarian General Secretary, who was no longer of any use to him, to be replaced by communist leaders who were closer to the Kremlin.[34]

Notes

1 In a conversation with British Foreign Minister Geoffrey Howe, Zhivkov described relations in a rather boorish way: "Bulgaria is fine, because it has colonies, the biggest of which is the USSR." However, his explanation is not entirely nonsensical: Bulgaria paid for Soviet oil, gas and other raw materials with machines and equipment. Marcheva, "Perestroykata v Bâlgariya v svetlinata na modernizatsiyata," *Istorichesko bâdeshte VII*, 1–2 (2003): 79–98, at p. 84.

2 TsDA, f. 1B, op. 5, a. e. 584, l. 36.

3 Cited in Marcheva, *Todor Zhivkov*, p. 256.

4 TsDA, f. 1B, op. 5, a. e. 525, l. 186–187.

5 Cited in L. Stoyanov and Zh. Lefterov, "Politikata na BKP za prevrâshtane na Bâlgariya v sâvetska republika (Ot ideyni postulati kâm prakticheski deystviya). Chast 1," *Godishnik na Departament "Istoriya,"* NBU, vol. I, Sofia: New Bulgarian University, pp. 168–228, at p. 209.

6 TsDA, f. 1B, op. 5, a. e. 584, l. 37.

7 Stoyanov and Lefterov, "Politikata na BKP," vol. I, p. 215.

8 Zh. Zhivkov, *Krâglata masa na Politbyuro*, Sofia: Interpres '67, 1991, pp. 37–41; Yahiel, *Todor Zhivkov*, pp. 176–178.

9 Stoyanov and Lefterov, "Politikata na BKP," vol. I, p. 225.

10 Marcheva, *Todor Zhivkov*, p. 256.

11 Zhivkov, *Krâglata masa*, p. 45; Yahiel, *Todor Zhivkov*, p. 182.

12 Cited in Yahiel, *Todor Zhivkov*, p. 183.

13 Marcheva, *Todor Zhivkov*, p. 258.

14 Todor Zhivkov, *Sreshtu nyakoi lâzhi. Paralelni etyudi*, Burgas: Delfinpres, 1993, p. 66.

15 K. Chakârov, *Vtoriyat etazh*, Sofia: K&M, p. 124; Marcheva, *Todor Zhivkov*, p. 256; I. Baeva, "'Sblizhenieto' mezhdu Bâlgariya i Sâvetskiya sâyuz (1963–1973)," *Novo vreme, LXVIII*, 1 (1993): 89–106; I. Baeva, "Bâlgariya i Sâvetskiyat sâyuz sled Vtorata svetovna voyna: pragmatizmât na bâlgarskata pozitsiya," in *Bâlgariya i Rusiya prez HH vek: Bâlgaro-ruski nauchni diskusii*, Sofia: Gutenberg, 2000, p. 428; E. Kalinova, "Bâlgariya: 16–a republika na SSSR – Tova e mit!" *Trud*, October 29, 2010, p. 17.

16 L. Stoyanov, "Kato edin organizâm, koyto se orosyava ot edinna krâvonosna sistema (za Yulskiya plenum na TsK na BKP ot 1973 g.)," in *Mezhdunarodna nauchna konferentsiya Bâlgariya i Rusiya: Mezhdu priznatelnostta i pragmatizma*, Sofia: Forum "Bâlgariya – Rusiya," 2008, p. 659.

17 Yahiel, *Todor Zhivkov*, pp. 186–187.

18 Stoyanov, "Kato edin organizâm," pp. 663, 666. It alludes to the idea of the people's democracy, which was publicly defended by Georgi Dimitrov but had been previously thought up or at least permitted by Stalin.

19 Stoyanov, "Kato edin organizâm," p. 663.

20 TsDA, f. 1B, op. 35, a. e. 3665, l. 11. Todor Zhivkov's considerations on his upcoming visit to Moscow, presented to the Politburo in May 1985.

21 Yahiel, *Todor Zhivkov*, pp. 175–176. It must be noted that evaluations of such "aid" are quite contradictory in the scholarly literature. Some authors claim that the low- and no-interest loans amounted to US$3 billion, an amount of aid exceeded only by the GDR and Poland. Conversely, Marrese and Vatous calculate that such subsidies amounted to US $ 1.75 billion. See more on the various opinions in J. F. Brown, *Eastern Europe under Communist Rule*, Durham, NC: Duke University Press, 1988, p. 319.

288 *From de-Stalinization to regime consolidation*

22 TsDA, f. 1B, op. 66, a. e. 1707, l. 50–55; op. 68, a. e. 1180, l. 24.

23 TsDA, f. 1B, op. 67, a. e. 2492, l. 10–11.

24 J. Hylewski, "Rachunek efektywnoœci udzialu Polski we wspolnych inwestycjach energetycznych," *Studia ekonomiczne INE PAN*, 5 (1984): 284–296. Cited in V. Merkin, "Intra-COMECON Bargaining and World Energy Prices: A Backdoor Connection?," *Comparative Economic Studies*, 30 (4) (1988): 26–28.

25 TsDA, f. 1B, op. 68, a. e. 490, l. 84.

26 For the construction of the Vinitsa Electrical Grid, for example, the Bulgarian side was obligated to supply goods with a total value of 2.27 million rubles during the period of 1976–1979. See AMVnR, op. 33, a. e. 4592, l. 143.

27 TsDA, f. 1B, op. 68, a. e. 490, l. 84; Politburo meeting from August 1978 g.; AMVnR, op. 45–1, a. e. 72, l. 12. The Plan for the Initial Data on the Sixth Five-Year-Plan (1976–1980), for example, emphasizes that "an unusual feature of our participation in the joint construction of capacities within the territory of the USSR is that we will release the greater part of the loans within the first years of the period, while we will receive the raw materials and other goods at the end of the five-year-plan. This presents certain difficulties for our payments to the USSR." In fact, Bulgaria was receiving gas from the Yamburg Agreement almost until the end of the 1990s. Ivanov, *Reformatorstvo*, p. 280.

28 K. Crane, *The Soviet Economic Dilemma of Eastern Europe*, Santa Monica, Calif.: Project Air Force, 1986. M. Marrese and J. Vatous, *Soviet Subsidization of Trade with Eastern Europe*, Berkeley, Calif.: Institute of International Studies, 1983, pp. 72–73.

29 Crane, *Soviet Economic Dilemma*, p. 60.

30 Marrese and Vatous, *Soviet Subsidization*, p. 50.

31 Nikova, "Zhivkovata ikonomicheska reforma," p. 9.

32 I. Marcheva, "Za subektivniya faktor v sâvetsko-bâlgarskite otnosheniya po vreme na 'perestroykata' (1985–1989)," in *Mezhdunarodna nauchna konferentsiya Bâlgariya i Rusiya: Mezhdu priznatelnostta i pragmatizma*, Sofia: Forum "Bâlgariya – Rusiya," 2008, p. 702.

33 Marcheva, "Za subektivniya faktor," p. 703; Yahiel, *Todor Zhivkov*, pp. 307–310, 337–338.

34 Marcheva, "Za subektivniya faktor," p. 707; Nikova, *Zhivkovata ikonomicheska reforma*, pp. 122–123.

14 In search of a communist model of consumer society

After the Twentieth Congress of the CPSU, the regime in Bulgaria made efforts to reformulate the model for governance it had employed until that moment. The accelerated development of heavy industry, for which consumption had already been sacrificed for a decade, would give way to new, softer approaches that would guarantee society's political loyalty. To quote Georgi Markov, a contemporary of these changes: "The continual struggle between the fictions of ideology and the realities of life gave rise to important compromises."[1] The violence and fear from the first years of communist rule would be replaced by policies for "corrupting the masses," for courting them and focusing their attention on everyday concerns, rather than politics.[2] Battle cries were replaced with promises of satisfaction.[3]

In the late 1950s and early 1960s, the unspoken truce between the rulers and the ruled would outline the contours of the hypocritical consensus that was taking shape in Bulgaria after Stalin's death. The basic elements of this tacit contract included: the softening of the regime and its abandonment of mass terror (the concentration camps were closed in 1953 and a general political amnesty was declared in 1964); the loosening of the stranglehold on consumption, with Bulgarians being encouraged to gradually withdraw into the sphere of the individual and of material prosperity;[4] the population "gave up" open rebellion and "promised" to live (at least outwardly) within the framework of the rules set by the regime and (at least ostensibly) "agreed" to share its ideological obsessions.[5]

After 1956, it became clear that efforts to forcibly impose universal faith in communist ideals were not going to work. In the new context of the political thaw, the BCP would try to guarantee to population's obedience without terror and fear and would no longer require citizens to show sincere devotion to the party's ideological goals. From the beginning of the 1960s, declarative, conformist support for Marxism-Leninism was sufficient from the regime's point of view, as long as it was accompanied by a repudiation of all forms of open resistance. However, by turning the "gap between words and deeds" into a universal norm, this permissible form of mass hypocrisy eroded not only the economic but also the ideological foundations of the communist system. On the level of ideology, even the supreme party nomenclature recognized

290 *From de-Stalinization to regime consolidation*

the emptiness of the slogans it was forced to applaud publicly, while in the economic sphere, *Western* consumer standards were successfully transformed into a universally desired goal. Only two decades after the establishment of the communist regime, it would be completely emptied of content, while for the majority of Bulgarians "the material superiority of the other system" would be clear beyond a shadow of a doubt.[6]

Reasons for consensus instead of violence

What were the reasons that the regime decided to open the floodgates of consumption, which had previously been held tightly shut? The explanation given by the communist leadership itself was absolutely in step with the spirit of the times. Todor Zhivkov announced before the Central Committee Plenum of 1972:

> Due to underdevelopment of the material-technical base and our burden inherited from the past, we had to set aside more funds for industrialization, for the reconstruction of agriculture . . . Otherwise we would not have been able to move through this stage in our development . . . Given our current material and spiritual, as well as objective and subjective conditions, it is now not only necessary, but also possible, to confirm the achievement of a certain level of satisfaction of people's material and cultural needs as one of the main and immediate tasks in the development of production.[7]

To use the jargon of the regime, quantitative accumulations (industrialization) had led to qualitative changes (the ability to loosen the stranglehold on individual consumption). Other, far deeper motivations were clearly hidden behind this trivial explanation, which the First Secretary offered to members of the Central Committee. On the one hand, even the extremely conservative party leadership in Sofia could not refuse to follow the "course of production" announced by Moscow.[8] On the other hand, corrections introduced into the model of governance were the result of economic problems that had been growing ever more serious since the mid-1950s. Despite Bulgaria's decade-long effort to achieve hyper-rapid industrialization, the results remained modest, even according to official assessments. Between 1945 and 1956, the gross per-capita domestic product grew at an average annual rate of barely 1.5 percent, compared to a 7.3 percent annual rate of growth between 1934 and 1943. It is highly probable that the Politburo itself came to the conclusion that the economy had reached the limit, beyond which future development would "depend on the scale of consumption."[9] In a later statement, Grisha Filipov would shed a bit more light on the expected "side effects" of allowing consumption. Filipov emphasized the fact that, henceforth, the standard of living could not be seen only as a social question. In his opinion, "we need to conduct social policy in such a way as to more quickly develop the economy,

A communist model of consumer society 291

to strengthen the stimulating effect of the separate social measures being taken."[10] The increase in the standard of living was clearly seen as a stimulus for increasing the productivity of labor. According to the new rules, workers who completed more and higher quality work would receive higher wages, which they could in turn use to "buy" a better standard of living. Years later, Zhivkov would comment on this topic: "We can no longer look upon the socialist worker in such a limited way, as merely a creator of material and spiritual welfare. That worker also has his own specific needs, and society must create the material-technical base to satisfy them."[11]

Finally, by the mid-1950s, open resistance to the regime began visibly fading. The *goryani* movement was all but destroyed, the rural unrest in northwestern Bulgarian had been suppressed, and, after the West's obvious reluctance to support the Berlin Uprising of 1953 and the Hungarian Revolution of 1956, it had become painfully clear that the Americans would not be "coming" any time soon and that change would not arrive from the outside.[12] Moreover, with the completion of collectivization and with the great wave of migration from villages to cities picking up speed, a continually growing group of people was taking shape who had accepted the realities in the country but who *demanded* an improved standard of living in return for their political loyalty.[13] The population had settled down, and its efforts to "establish its urban mode of everyday life" took on epic proportions.[14] It is no coincidence that one of few Westerners who was deeply familiar with the subtle realities of Bulgarian totalitarianism, Richard Crampton, would later claim that alongside nationalism, "consumerism was the second easy path to increasing the regime's legitimacy."[15]

However, the question remains: Were the authorities consciously taking the initiative to firm up this consensus, or in backing away from the use of camps and overt violence, was the Communist Party simply trying to suppress future dissatisfaction? The first variant seems to have been indirectly accepted in the academic literature to date. However, extensive anthropological studies and observations by contemporaries from that period tip the scales in favor of the second alternative.[16] To put it another way, the Politburo followed behind, rather than blazing a trail before the social tensions that were rising up from beneath the surface. For a series of (economic and political) reasons, in the early 1960s the regime could not afford to continue the harsh propaganda battle against consumption that it had been waging until that point. What had been possible in the Stalinist years immediately after the war was impossible and even dangerous a decade later. Fifteen years after the September 9 coup, Bulgarian already knew that Coca-Cola was not an alcoholic beverage that American soldiers boozed themselves up with (as a popular newsreel from the second half of the 1940s had claimed). If until that point they had been kept "in the dark" about the growing wave of consumerism in the West by propaganda, or had been persuaded to sacrifice their standard of living for the good of higher political aims, during the 1960s and 1970s, such a strategy would no longer work. People were clearly aware of the enormous unsatisfied

292 *From de-Stalinization to regime consolidation*

consumer need that had accumulated and were unwilling to delay it anymore. They wanted refrigerators, personal automobiles, vacation tour packages, washing machines . . . The regime could no longer pretend not to notice their consumer desires.[17]

Mapping out the channels through which this mass "awakening to consumer desires" came about is a difficult if not impossible undertaking – all the more so because this "awakening" is a self-propelling process. Some of the channels stimulated others, which then united to unblock still others. However, all the paths that contributed to the creation of the image of a forgotten, yet yearned-for, consumerist socialism were due to intensified contact with the outside world. From the late 1950s and especially in the early 1960s, Bulgaria, along with the whole socialist bloc, gradually opened to the West. Diplomatic ties that had been broken off were reestablished, while English began to be studied en masse in Bulgarian universities. For technical and political reasons, foreign radio stations broadcasting in Bulgarian began to be more difficult to block out, while attempts to do so became less frequent. Bilateral trade grew sharply. Bulgaria's trade ties with developed Western countries jumped from 13–14 percent of its total trade before Stalin's death to almost 25 percent in 1968. The first imports of "capitalist" consumer goods were organized. Attempts were made to produce Renault cars using a French patent. Georgi Naydenov's Texim signed a licensing deal for the production of Coca-Cola.[18] Although still restricted to a chosen few, Western capitalism began to slip through cracks in the Iron Curtain. The leading "angels of communism" – the party nomenclature and their children – began illegally importing "nylon stockings, early tape recorders and washing machines, Italian shoes and German cars."[19] Four or five years later, tens of thousands of Bulgarian specialists, who had gone with their families to work in Arab, African and Latin American countries (including Algeria, Cuba, Angola, Ethiopia, Mozambique, Libya, Syria, Iraq, and others), followed in their lead.[20] Despite the fact that the state collected most of such workers' salaries, they were still able to save enough money to significantly broaden the client base for the Corecom hard-currency stores created during the 1960s.[21]

Without a doubt, the most important channel for "awakening" Bulgarian consumer desires was international tourism, which the country began developing in the late 1950s. The Black Sea and, to a lesser extent, Bulgaria's mountains became a laboratory for carrying out an enormous social experiment. In their tiny "Polish Fiats," Škodas, and Wartburgs, thousands of Polish, Czech and East German tourists annually brought forbidden and previously unknown consumerist temptations to Bulgaria. These Eastern Bloc tourists, however, were quickly overshadowed by the "real" Western tourists, who instantly had a shock effect on the average Bulgarian, similar to the waves a prison visitor makes among inmates.[22] Observing Westerners' seductive brilliance with "almost childlike amazement, bordering on rapture," the average Bulgarian, who had until recently lived under tight ideological

Table 14.1 Bulgarians who traveled abroad and foreign visitors to Bulgaria (1960–1988).

	1960	*1965*	*1970*	*1975*	*1980*	*1985*	*1988*
Bulgarians traveling abroad	60,765	207,912	305,118	675,228	756,631	533,367	505,118
In % of the whole population	0.8	2.5	3.6	7.7	8.5	6.0	5.6
Foreign visitors to Bulgaria in thousands	200.6	1083.9	2537.0	4049.0	5485.7	7295.2	8294.9

Source: Annual Statistical Book.

control, would begin nursing the "fatal conviction that one person is not equal to others unless he wears French pants, Italian shoes or an English sweater. To say nothing of radios, cassette tapes, refrigerators and cars."[23] Incapable of producing a living standard comparable to that in the West, the regime itself torpedoed the pillars upholding the truce between the rulers and the ruled, which were centered around everyday life and irrevocably sent this consensus sliding down the slippery slope of hypocrisy.

The paths to constructing a feigned consensus

Today it is difficult to imagine how greatly the softened and "domesticated" form of totalitarianism, which was gradually imposed in the late 1950s and early 1960s, differed from the regime's extreme early years.[24] After September 9, 1944, Bulgarian society had been forced to live under militarized Stalinism. And here we do not mean only the thousands of politically repressed families who were forcibly relocated to distant villages without the right to work and with no possibility for supporting themselves. The ration system in cities (which remained in place for eight years after the war, until 1953) and mandatory quotas of goods to be sold to the state in villages whittled consumption down to the "bare bones." Several unusually harsh droughts in the second half of the 1940s and the brutal sieve through which Moscow initially squeezed Bulgarian resources revived the specter of hunger. Georgi Markov's *In Absentia Reports* painted a grim picture of the empty stores on whose dusty shelves stood "only jars of jelly and marmalade." For every elementary item, "from an aluminum fork to a bike, a person had to wage a war through connections, bribes and schemes." Long lines of "professional waiters" wound in front of the frequently locked doors of shops; their folding chairs and knitting needles helped them while away the time until the "release" of "dog's delight" sausages or plain crackers.[25] Years later, Todor Zhivkov, in his typically gauche style, would tell a joke about how the Patriarch had awarded

294   *From de-Stalinization to regime consolidation*

him the Golden Cross of Christ for his great services to the church. For centuries, the church had struggled to impose fasting, while under Zhivkov's leadership, the BCP had imposed it en masse within a few short years.

In this joyless daily grind, cinema and soccer were the only permissible mass entertainments. But they too fell victim to "scientific aesthetic standards," which were militaristic and tasteless.[26] The whole population was called upon to make sacrifices in the name of the "bright future," while consumption was reduced to the biological minimum so that the necessary resources could be secured for the rapid development of heavy industry.[27] The problem was not so much the classic economy of deficits (à la Kornai), but rather the choice made by the political leadership in favor of forced economic growth. For almost twenty years, social prosperity was sacrificed on the altar of industrialization.

"The Great Easing," as Kristian Bankov calls it, was implemented in fits and starts in the late 1950s and the early 1960s.[28] The ostentatious asceticism that had been demanded while "pouring the foundations" began to be replaced by "concern for the person" and his "higher spiritual and material needs." The topic became a permanent feature of party documents and was discussed during at least a dozen BCP forums. As early as the April Plenum of 1956, the party proclaimed "raising the standard of living" as one of its basic tasks in the social sphere. Several years later, the Eighth Party Congress in 1962 would concretely outline its goals and announce that more resources would be directed toward the Consumption Fund, which was expected to grow 4.5 to 5 times over. The key July Plenum of 1968 introduced the topic of improving the standard of living into the plans for economic reform that had been discussed intensely since the early 1960s. The Tenth Congress of the BCP in 1970 and the "Program for Raising the Standard of Living" adopted by the December Plenum of 1972 definitively legitimized consumerism as an acceptable form of behavior from the ideological point of view. It became a practice that was not only permitted but desired by the regime as it would redirect social energy that had until then been focused on problematic aspects of consumption. This was why consumerism became "modern" and "new" and why the party set itself the goal of creating and cultivating a new type of (obedient) mass consumer.[29]

After unleashing consumerist desires, however, the authorities quickly had to defuse the Western models that were ever more easily slipping through the cracks in the Iron Curtain. To this end, propaganda attempted to shape mass taste via strict control over the design and quality of goods. According to the party, these goods could serve as the bearers of powerful messages to the consumer, for which reason they must necessarily be packaged in ideologically acceptable ways. After several consecutive interventions in the world of consumer goods during the 1960s, the Decembrist Program of 1972 took aim at particularly "dangerous" luxury goods, among others.[30] Their Western prototypes, which were slipping through the "wall" ever more frequently and becoming objects of mass admiration, gave rise to desires that were

A *communist model of consumer society* 295

slipping out of the party's control. To combat this, the entirety of Bulgaria's light industry was harnessed so as to "properly guide emerging consumer attitudes."[31] Thus, on holidays, the half-empty stores were stocked with Altay soda instead of Coca-Cola, with Inka coffee instead of Nescafé, or with blocks of soy-based sweets rather than fine milk chocolate. In the seaside resorts and some of the larger cities, "old-fashioned" restaurants began springing up like mushrooms – khan-style yurts, medieval Bulgarian-style residences, pubs fit for the legendary *haiduk* rebels from the mountains, windmills and so forth – all meant to replace the far more "dangerous" bars and discothèques.[32] In order to "improve the intonational environment," the authorities lent their support to Bulgaria's local pop-music scene, which, however, most contemporary listeners regarded as "total drivel."[33]

The whole problem lay in the inability of Bulgaria's so-called *industriya za choveka* or literally "industry of the person," i.e. the consumer-goods industry, to produce the necessary quantity and especially the quality of goods to maintain the consensus so desired by the party. Bulgarian analogs of Western products were often the butt of caustic jokes and ridicule. The stores remained half-empty, while waiting in line remained a "profession" until the very end of the regime. It turned out to be impossible for the Bulgarian planned economy to shift from being one-dimensional (focused on economic growth and heavy industry) to being two-dimensional (growth plus an improved standard of living) with respect to its goals. The industrial giants remained the pride and joy of the Bulgarian economy, while, to ease consumer needs, the authorities relied on techniques that were overly simple, such as "self-satisfaction" and mass production.

One year after the "Historic Plenum on the Standard of Living" in 1972, the Politburo gave the green light to a certain amount of liberalization within the agrarian sector. That was precisely where the regime's previous social policy had fallen particularly short. Securing sufficient agricultural products, and especially meat and dairy products, had turned out to be an impossible task for the economic and party leadership. The communist leaders were forced to resort to strictly controlled private initiative to combat this problem. Private farms were supposed to become an important means for "more fully satisfying the workers' needs."[34] Moreover, every district (*okrâg*) would henceforth have to supply the agricultural and animal products that it needed on its own. Several years later (at the end of 1977) it became clear that the district was too large an administrative territory, and thus *samozadovolyavane* or "self-satisfaction" would be limited to the newly created settlement systems (*selishtni sistemi*). Through "auxiliary farms organized by enterprises and military units" and experimental fields created by schools, local populations were supposed to solve their production problems on their own.[35] The report on the self-satisfaction system, which was discussed by the Politburo in 1982, shows that results were quite a bit more modest than initially hoped. The problem of production constantly lagging behind demand continued.[36] The self-satisfaction initiative adopted in 1977 was subject to a second assessment

296 *From de-Stalinization to regime consolidation*

in 1987. It became clear that during that decade the state had not managed to solve the relatively simple problem of organizing the purchase of goods produced by personal farms. A number of districts and settlement systems did not meet the quotas set by the plan. Many of the auxiliary farms "existed only formally, due to low interest in them on the part of the enterprises' leadership."[37]

At more or less the same time, several similar initiatives to increase the standard of living and guarantee "ever fuller satisfaction of workers' need" were unveiled. Production lines for mass-produced goods (known as *shirpotreba*) were created in almost every factory. As might be expected, this idea, too, was implemented without "enthusiasm" on the part of the factory leadership. A Politburo review would soon report that "these production lines are being developed as an end-in-themselves at our large firms, functioning just enough so the firms can report that they are also producing goods for popular consumption." This initiative even had a negative effect, since "valuable raw materials and resources are being wasted, while labor is being used ineffectively."[38] Instead of discontinuing the *shirpotreba* experiment, however, the party leadership issued a call "to organize ourselves and to develop our secondary production lines with the same seriousness and responsibility shown toward the primary production."[39]

In fact, all of these things – private farms, self-satisfaction, and the compulsory production of mass goods – speak to one and the same problem: the regime's complete inability not only to fundamentally raise the standard of living but also to fully guarantee the basic existential minimum required by the population. This is due to the fact that both the Decembrist Program, as well as the ever-growing consumerist desires in the country, were focused not on simple everyday necessities (meat, vegetables, household chemicals, etc.) but rather on complex consumer goods (television sets, washing machines, automobiles). At the same time, hardly 5 percent of the machine-building industry's production capability was aimed at everyday goods, while the production of consumer electronics (radios, televisions, gramophone players) was artificially "held back."[40] The extremely modest technologies that were mobilized to implement this ambitious social program reveal the complete impossibility of overcoming the genetic determinism of the planned economy (see Table 14.2).

Table 14.2 Distribution of the national income, 1952–1988.

	1952	1960	1965	1970	1975	1980	1985	1988
"Accumulation" Fund	23.8	27.5	28.3	30.8	32.8	26.9	23.8	25.3
"Consumption" Fund	76.2	72.5	71.7	69.2	67.2	73.1	76.2	74.4
Including population consumption	70.3	66.0	65.0	66.3	63.2	68.8	71.3	69.2

Source: Annual Statistical Book.

A communist model of consumer society   297

Bulgaria's unreformed economic system continued reproducing the classical strategy (forced growth) and priorities (heavy industry at the expense of light industry). Even into the 1960s, despite the announced change in policy, Bulgaria maintained one of the highest growth rates and rates of accumulation in the socialist bloc.[41] In this respect, the way in which discussion unfolded in the early 1970s about planned rates of growth until 1990 (and hence of investments made at the expense of consumption) is highly indicative. The initial variant suggested an annual growth rate of 7.5–8 percent.[42] However, Todor Zhivkov personally pressured the Politburo into supporting a significantly accelerated rate of 9 percent.[43] Six months later, the National Conception raised the bar still higher, recommending target rates ranging between 9–9.5 and 12–13 percent.[44] In its final variant, the Seventh Five-Year Plan (1976–1980) imposed an annual growth rate of 9.1 percent.

Thus, for a long period, the two-dimensional strategy announced in the early 1960s remained merely a good intention that could not be implemented. The reasons for this, however, do not lay solely with the Politburo's political short-sightedness and unrealistic ambitions. "Care for the person" also had to be put off due to the oil crisis that broke out shortly after the program was adopted. Only a few short months after the December Plenum of 1972, the party leadership was forced to quietly withdraw its noisily trumpeted plan for normalizing consumption. A series of price shocks on the international market forced the Politburo to cut imports and to rapidly expand its exports of consumer goods. Very soon it would have to revise the promise it had made in 1975 that in the future "goods for national consumption will be exported only after the demands of the domestic market have been satisfied."[45] The draft plan for 1979–1980 indicated that investments in Bulgaria's energy and raw materials capabilities were a priority, with "decisive preference" given to enterprises that would increase the country's hard-currency revenues. Residential and cultural-consumer construction "must be reined in to a certain extent . . . Bulgaria will not come to a ruin because of this for a year or two."[46] In several more documents from the late 1970s, the Politburo admitted that it was forced to "cease implementation of the December Program for a certain period" due to external reasons. Before the Central Committee Plenum of November 1978, Zhivkov stated, "We were not able to raise the people's living standards. We have reined them in for a whole five years now" (see Table 14.3).[47]

The task the Bulgarian authorities had set for themselves in the 1960s suddenly grew far more complicated in the early 1980s. "The Polish events" reminded them of the crucial need to maintain the consumerist consensus. The BCP's reading of the strikes organized by the Polish Solidarity movement is very indicative of the new political resonance social policy acquired after 1980:

One of the most important lessons of the Polish events is that such events, despite their specific conditions in the [People's Republic of Poland] are

298 *From de-Stalinization to regime consolidation*

Table 14.3 Implementation of the December Program.

	United Nations Norm	1980, December Program as planned	1976, actual report	1980, actual report	Expected growth, % (3)/(2)	Actual growth, % (3)/(4)
	(1)	(2)	(3)	(4)	(5)	(6)
Per capita						
Meat and meat products	80.0	75.0	59.3	61.2	20.9	3.1
Fish and fish products	12.0	10.0	n/a	6.9	n/a	n/a
Milk and milk products	260.0	250.0	184.2	259.0	26.3	28.9
Sugar and sugar products	32.0	36.0		34.7	n/a	n/a
Vegetables	180.0	160.0	92.5	93.8	42.2	1.4
Fruits (incl. grapes)	200.0	160.0	108.7	105.8	32.1	−2.7
Cotton fabric*	36.0	33.0	27.9	25.9	15.5	−7.7
Woven fabric*	7.0	6.0	49.0	4.6	18.3	−6.5
Per 1,000 households						
TV sets**	105.0	80.0	69.0	75.0	13.8	8.0
Refrigerators**	100.0	90.0	66.0	76.0	26.7	13.2
Laundry machines**	70.0	60.0	n/a	71.0	n/a	n/a
Automobiles**	40.0	30.0	20.0	29.0	33.3	31.0
Average growth						
Food and clothes					25.5	2.7
Technical equipment					24.6	17.4

Source: TsDA, f. 1B, op. 35, a.e. 5265, l. 22; op. 66, a.e. 2690, l. 17–18; op. 67, a.e. 668, l. 17–18.

All numbers are in kg except those marked with * which are in sq. m. and ** which are in number of units.

possible in any one of the other socialist countries . . . The shortcomings that have been tolerated in the planning and managing of the national economy led to the destruction of the economic balance [in Poland], to an insignificant increase in the effectiveness of the economy, and to a worsening supply of goods to the population.[48]

The two Politburo sessions held on the subject on October 24–25, 1980, would for a long time thereafter define the party's policy on living standards. The leadership outlined a series of steps that would avert the danger of the disintegration of the consensus as had occurred in Poland:

Certain questions concerning [our] policy, which immediately affect citizens' interests, require urgent measures. Above all, there is the question of securing the necessary goods and services for the population, especially those related to the category of the most essential goods and services . . . Plans and decisions have been made, obviously, but most of these extremely essential goods and services cannot be found.[49]

A few short weeks of Solidarity protests were enough to make the resuscitation of the consensus and the elimination of market shortages the communists' primary political task. A month later, Zhivkov would personally repeat the promise he had made earlier: "[We must] stop the export of all goods that are in short supply on our domestic market – meat, knitwear, furniture and so on. Our economy, our development and our trade balances are no longer in such a state to require us to export goods that are in short supply."[50]

After 1980, the fear of the political consequences of an unsuccessful social policy would leave a powerful mark on the BCP's overall strategy in the economic sphere. The dithering and modest measures of the 1970s would be abandoned. Resolutions for raising the standard of living began to be churned out. Later, even Prime Minister Georgi Atanasov would note, with good reason, that this was one of the Politburo's most widely discussed issues.[51] Stoyan Ovcharov states this even more concretely. According to his study of the period between 1983 and 1988 alone, the Bulgarian government adopted four ordinances and several resolutions aimed at "improving the state of the domestic market."[52] During the 1980s, the BCP sought to decisively increase the standard of living through investments in light industry (which would later be called "the industry for the person"), as well as through the restriction of exports and the expanded import of consumer goods. Statistics on automobile imports are a good indicator of the effectiveness of this new policy (see Table 14.4).

Table 14.4 Automobile imports, 1956–1988.

	1956	1960	1965	1970	1975	1980	1985	1988
Imports in absolute numbers	538	2,957	10,795	22,663	59,122	76,195	46,757	42,625
Western* (in % of all), %	4.5	12.0	6.1	2.4	0.7	0.1	0.3	0.0
Imported automobiles among 1,000 Bulgarian citizens	0.07	0.37	1.31	2.66	6.77	8.58	5.22	4.74

Source: Annual Statistical Book. Note: Imported from Western Germany and France, while only in 1956 imports from Austria and Italy are included in the estimates. * Import from Federal Republic of Germany and France; data for Austria and Italy is available only for 1956.

300   *From de-Stalinization to regime consolidation*

Against the backdrop of the simple practices of the 1970s, this new direction may seem far more meaningful; however, the actual picture on the ground turned out to be quite different. Capital investments in light industry were actually decreasing, which led to a contraction in the production of consumer goods. According to a report presented to the Politburo, consumer goods constituted 32.1 percent of Bulgaria's total industrial output during the Sixth Five-Year Plan (1971–1975), 30.8 percent during the Seventh (1976–1980), 30 percent during the Eighth (1981–1985), and 29.8 and 29.6 percent during 1986 and 1987, respectively. According to the report, this divergence between words and deeds resulted "above all from the investment policy imposed over the years. For years on end, investments made in the development of the consumer-goods industry were significantly smaller than what was actually needed."[53] As a result, the increase in the supply of consumer goods lagged significantly behind the growth in Bulgarians' incomes (32.8 percent as compared to 45.9 percent between 1981 and 1987). In other words, Bulgarian consumers had money, but nothing to buy with it, which led to a significant increase in savings. According to expert estimations, the Bulgarian population's unspent income grew annually by 4 to 6 billion leva, or approximately one-fifth of the national income generated in 1988![54]

From the outset, the government's investment model made it impossible for Bulgarian industry to satisfy consumer needs. According to Politburo data, in 1986 the consumer-goods industry produced only 50,000 different items, while at least 100,000 would be necessary to satisfy needs.[55] This is why imports turned out to be the only possible alternative. Unlike its response to the oil crisis in the 1970s, in the 1980s Bulgaria did not react to new economic challenges by quickly reducing imports. Despite the fact that serious debt and hard-currency problems were looming on the horizon, this time the party did not dare sacrifice consumption to pay off its sky-rocketing debt to the West, as Ceauşescu was doing in Romania at the same time, for example.[56] The plan for 1989 even allowed for 20 percent of all imported goods to be consumer products. Barter schemes and other exchange operations were also invented to satisfy the domestic market. The plan allowed for some of Bulgaria's uncollectible loans from developing countries to be paid for in consumer goods or raw materials for their production. One hundred million hard-currency leva were earmarked for the import of citrus fruits and for the delivery of medicine, spare parts and automobiles. Additionally, the government also set aside the necessary funds to rapidly establish 100 small firms and enterprises over the following two years in the consumer sector to produce goods for the population.[57]

Instead of improving, however, the situation seemed to be deteriorating over time. A study conducted by the Informational-Sociological Center of the Central Committee during the regime's final weeks showed that the population was highly critical of the domestic market. The overwhelming opinion was that it was "poor, hungry, and highly unstable." The shortage of more and more goods and services "seemed to be becoming a permanent characteristic."[58] Complex sociological tools were hardly necessary, however, to see how alarming the situation had become. After a visit to Africa, one of the BCP secretaries admitted, "For us, Zimbabwe is an unattainable ideal in terms of its domestic market," whereupon Zhivkov exclaimed in distress, "Have we really fallen that far!"[59]

Disintegration of the feigned consensus

The consensus's leaky consumerist center showed how unrealistic hopes had been that the communist system would be able to implement a multi-faceted economic strategy. The combination of qualitative and quantitative tasks, of forced growth and a high living standard, was clearly impossible within the framework of the communist state, and this undermined the very foundations of the feigned unanimity. The command economy showed itself to be lacking the necessary navigational equipment to orient itself within a world that was two-dimensional with respect to its goals. Instinctively, the system continued reproducing one and the same decisions in favor of forced growth: large investments in heavy industry at the expense of light industry. Communist Bulgaria's nearly three decades of experiments with consumption clearly show that the planned economy, political monopoly, and state ownership continually reproduced the very same classical "Stalinist" model of crushed consumption and disproportionate growth of the "Accumulation Fund."

There are other reasons for this as well. Ivaylo Ditchev has noted the regime's pervasive suspicion of everything that did not fit into the lofty narrative of the struggle for socialism; he calls this phenomenon "an ambivalent attitude toward consumption."[60] Certain material needs were considered "high," "rational," and ideologically legitimate, while others were denounced as "bourgeois holdovers." Unlike capitalist consumption, "socialist consumption must fit within some nonmaterial logic, in order to be ideologically legitimate."[61] Despite its structural importance to the consensus, consumption always teetered on the border between the "proper" socialist lifestyle and "bourgeois deviation."[62] Even as late as 1958, an accusation of "moral corruption" could still get you sent to the concentration camp in Belene. In a demonstrative campaign during that same year, more than 2,000 residents of Sofia were arrested for "wearing tight pants, short woolen coats with hoods or clothing that conformed to current local conceptions of Western-style clothing."[63] In 1962, a special decree was enacted against individuals "leading antisocial and parasitical lifestyles," which stipulated sanctions ranging from fines to prison sentences, while at the end of the same year, Zhivkov himself menacingly warned against "xenomania."[64] Just as in 1958, restaurants and nightclubs were again shut down in 1969 for playing "decadent" and "vulgar" music, while the Beatles were not allowed to perform at the International Youth Festival organized in 1968 in Sofia.[65] These examples are primarily from the 1950s and 1960s, but undoubtedly others can be found during the subsequent two decades of the regime.

302 *From de-Stalinization to regime consolidation*

This barren consensus, which was unable to produce a communist version of Western-style prosperity, instead gave birth to the hypocrisy that would decisively eat away at the ideological innards of "real socialism." Like a termite-ridden building which outwardly appears sound but internally is highly unstable, at the end of the 1980s all that would remain of the totalitarian state would be the empty shell of the feigned consensus between the rulers and the ruled. The floodgates of consumption, which had been opened but not satisfied, gave birth to "the most popular natural cult that has ever arisen in Bulgarian – the cult . . . to Western things."[66] After coming in contact with highly desired Western consumer icons, "the building of socialism" for most Bulgarians was transformed into a competition to possess more and more ideologically "non-safeguarded" goods. Slogans exhorting loyalty to Marxist ideals and moral purity were degraded to the point when they were little more than "fireworks that lit up the Bulgarian sky once or twice a year."[67]

As early as the mid-1970s, Georgi Markov claimed: "I personally don't know a single party member in Bulgaria, from the Chairman of the State Council down to the rank-and-file party member, who still believes in some communist ideal."[68] What the British Ambassador in Sofia had predicted in his farewell report in far-off 1963 had come to pass:

> We will not topple the regime all at once . . . but wider knowledge of the western way of life and government could convince Bulgarian society of the emptiness and isolation of their current system . . . Many Bulgarians do not support the regime, but they are too passive and too engaged in pursuing their own individual prosperity to openly express their hostility.[69]

The ritual worship of ideological gods whom no one believed in anymore would continue until 1989. Only a few days before the final collapse of the regime, Prime Minister Georgi Atanasov would be extremely frank: "With these shortages on the market, we will be toppled in two or three months."[70]

Notes

1 Markov, *Zadochni reportazhi*, p. 304.
2 I. Znepolski, *Bâlgarskiyat komunizâm: Sotsiokulturni cherti i vlastova traektoriya*, Sofia: Institute for Studies of the Recent Past/Ciela, 2008, pp. 222–223, 227–235.
3 Markov, *Zadochni reportazhi*, p. 305.
4 Znepolski talks about "malki teritorii zanemaren kontrol." See: Znepolski, *Bâlgarskiyat komunizâm*, p. 223.
5 Evgeniy Daynov summarizes the components of this "implicit social contract" as "prosperity in exchange for obedience." See E. Daynov, *Politicheskiyat debat i prehodât v Bâlgariya*, Sofia: FBNI, 2000, p. 332. See also Znepolski, *Bâlgarskiyat komunizâm*, p. 223.
6 A. Angelov, "Konsumativna kultura i stokovi proektsii na Zapada v sotsialisticheska Bâlgariya," unpublished master's thesis, Sofia, 2010.
7 TsDA, f. 1B, op. 35, a. e. 3688, l. 18–20.

A communist model of consumer society   303

8 D. Dimitrov, *Sâvetska Bâlgariya prez tri britanski mandata, 1956–1963: Iz arhiva na Forin Ofis za sâbitiya i lichnosti v Bâlgariya*, Sofia: BBS Bâlgarska redaktsiya, 1994, pp. 5–6.
9 K. Bankov, *Konsumativnoto obshtestvo*, Sofia: Lik, 2009, p. 218.
10 TsDA, f. 1B, op. 65, a. e. 1, l. 27. The January Plenum of 1976, which discussed and adopted the theses for the further implementation of the Decembrist Program. See statements made in the same vein by G. Tsonkov and I. Levi: G. Tsonkov, *Za nov sotsialisticheski bit: V pomosht na propagandistite na OF*, Sofia: Izdatelstvo na NK na OF, 1965, p. 3.; I. Levi, *Shiroko dvizhenie za nov sotsialisticheski bit: Materiali v pomosht na politicheskata rabota na OF*, Sofia: Izdatelstvo na NK na OF, 1969, p. 3.
11 TsDA, f. 1B, op. 68, a. e. 3052a, l. 177. Meeting of the Politburo from July 1987.
12 "If until 1956, the majority in Bulgaria nursed some illusions that change would come from the outside, the brutal suppression of the Hungarian popular uprising destroyed any last shred of such hopes." Markov, *Zadochni reportazhi*, p. 180. In the scholarly literature, the increased allowance of consumer goods is often seen as a "gesture" by the rulers to the ruled *after* stablilization has been achieved and not *for* the stabilization of the regime. E. Daynov, *Politicheskiyat debat*, pp. 302–303; Znepolski, *Bâlgarskiyat komunizâm*, p. 222.
13 This is also supported by the apathy the average Bulgarian displays in all sorts of situations, which was noted by the British Ambassador: "then he spends the summer in Varna, he demonstrates against Anglo-American aggression, listens to party speeches (but even Khrushchev's speech cannot move him)": Dimitrov, *Sâvetska Bâlgariya*, p. 41.
14 I. Elenkov, *Kulturniyat front: Bâlgarskata kultura prez epohata na komunizma – politichesko upravlenie, ideologicheski osnovaniya, institutsionalni rezhimi*, Sofia: Institute for Studies of the Recent Past/Ciela, 2008, p. 266. Kristian Bankov also explains this "permitted" consumption in a similar way: "The levels of industrialization that had been achieved after the first years of socialism began to presuppose new levels of consumption as well." See Bankov, *Konsumativnoto obshtestvo*, p. 219.
15 Crampton, *A Concise History of Bulgaria*, p. 203.
16 Creed, *Domesticating Revolution*, p. 301; Gruev, *Preorani slogove*, p. 362. See also the report by the British Ambassador from 1957: "this [improvement in the material standard of living] is due above all to the deliberate policy of the regime, which attempts to deflect demands for liberalizations by increasing the tempo of material concessions." Dimitrov, *Sâvetska Bâlgariya*, p. 19. Or a dispatch from 1960: "It is impossible to quantify the level of discontent, but it is far from negligible. I believe that it is extremely unlikely that the people would attempt to bring about change in governmental or party policies, but if the lack of foodstuffs worsens and people begin to go hungry, then the authorities will face difficulties and might be forced to make certain concessions." Dimitrov, *Sâvetska Bâlgariya*, p. 63.
17 Ivanov, *Reformatorstvo*, p. 209.
18 AMVnR, op. 26, a. e. 2589, l. 10–11; op. 27, a. e. 2831, l. 2–3; op. 22, a. e. 496, l. 2; *A Cold Coca-Cola during the Cold War*, BNT, 2005. A film by Damyan Petrov, Irina Nedeva, and Evgeniya Atanasova.
19 Markov, *Zadochni reportazhi*, p. 311.
20 Here we must also add the several thousand international drivers working for SO "MAT."

304 *From de-Stalinization to regime consolidation*

21 Elenkov, *Kulturniyat front*, pp. 256–257.
22 The metaphor once again belongs to Georgi Markov, of course. The exact quote is: "Just like a visitor to the prison, the foreigner from the West is a symbol of freedom, which means everything to most of the prisoners." Markov, *Zadochni reportazhi*, p. 323.
23 Markov, *Zadochni reportazhi*, pp. 308–309.
24 The term is introduced in Creed, *Domesticating Revolution*.
25 Markov, *Zadochni reportazhi*, pp. 66–67, 310.
26 Markov, *Zadochni reportazhi*, p. 69.
27 Bankov, *Konsumativnoto obshtestvo*, p. 222. Elenkov describes the phenomenon in the following way: "The old communist asceticism [should be understood as] the heroic extraction of raw materials from the bodies of laborers for the erection of the edifice of socialism." Elenkov, *Kulturniyat front*, p. 271.
28 Bankov, *Konsumativnoto obshtestvo*, p. 223.
29 Angelov, *Konsumativna kultura*, p. 10. Y. Boychev, *Povishavane blagosâstoyanieto na naroda: glavna grizha na BKP*, Sofia: Izdatelstvo na BKP, p. 73. There, the author tries to directly stimulate the desired consumerist behavior: "Socialist trade is called upon not only to secure for the population a regular supply of a sufficient quantity and varied assortment of goods, but also to cultivate within the population consumerist drives towards beautiful, modern and refined goods."
30 Elenkov, *Kulturniyat front*, pp. 241–262.
31 Angelov, *Konsumativna kultura*, p. 5.
32 Elenkov, *Kulturniyat front*, pp. 265–266. Ivan Elenkov describes the "ideological sabotage" of the Swedish disco Club 33 in the resort of Sunny Beach and how it was closed down by the secretariat of the Central Committee in person. Elenkov, *Kulturniyat front*, pp. 263–265.
33 Markov, *Zadochni reportazhi*, p. 330.
34 TsDA, f. 1B, op. 35, a. e. 4388, l. 11–36. Todor Zhivov's considerations on improving the work of the personal economy, adaopted by the Politburo in October 1973.
35 TsDA, f. 1B, op. 65, a. e. 18, l. 9–10; a. e. 19, l. 123–127. October Plenum of the Central Committee from 1977.
36 TsDA, f. 1B, op. 67, a. e. 859, l. 17–23. Politburo discussion of the Report on the Results from the System of Self-Satisfaction, February 1982.
37 TsDA, f. 1B, op. 71, a. e. 340, l. 10. Decision of the Secretariat of the BCP from April 1987.
38 TsDA, f. 1B, op. 65, a. e. 9, l. 22. July Plenum of the Central Committee from 1976.
39 TsDA, f. 1B, op. 65, a. e. 9, l. 23.
40 Nikova, "Zhivkovata ikonomicheska reforma," p. 114; Y. Mladenov, Ognemir Genchev, Ivan Dimitrov, and Petâr Totev, *Panorama na elektronnata promishlenost na Bâlgariya: Fakti i dokumenti*, Sofia: DBMr, 2003, p. 49.
41 According to one of the greatest experts on national balances in the socialist bloc, Paul Marer, in 1989 Bulgaria had an accumulation norm (investments as a percentage of the gross domestic product) of 33 percent, almost as much as during 1980 (34 percent). At the same time, in 1989, the United States earmarked 17 percent for investments, and the Federal Republic of Germany set aside 22 percent, just as much as France, which is known for its social policies. Paul Marer, Janos Arvay, John O'Connor, Martin Schrenk, and Daniel Swanson, *Historically Planned Economies: A Guide to the Data*, Washington, DC: World Bank, 1991, p. 49. The differences in the percentages between Marer's data and those in

Table 12.1 are due to the different methods of calculating the gross national product and national income.

42 TsDA, f. 1B, op. 35, a. e. 3591, l. 22–23. Politburo meeting from October 1972.
43 TsDA, f. 1B, op. 35, a. e. 3591, l. 84.
44 TsDA, f. 1B, op. 35, a. e. 4195, l. 2–4. Politburo meeting from July 1973.
45 TsDA, f. 1B, op. 58, a. e. 111, l. 10–14. Statement by Ognyan Doynov in front of the November Plenum of the Central Committee from 1975.
46 TsDA, f. 1B, op. 66, a. e. 1480a, l. 6. Politburo meeting from November 1978.
47 TsDA, f. 1B, op. 65, a. e. 26, l. 30. November Plenum from 1978.
48 TsDA, f. 1B, op. 66, a. e. 2617, l. 8–9, 16. Politburo meeting from October 1980, which discussed the specially introduced letter by Todor Zhivkov, entitled "Reasons for the Polish Events."
49 TsDA, f. 1B, op. 66, a. e. 2617, l. 28.
50 TsDA, f. 1B, op. 65, a. e. 37, l. 33. Statement by Todor Zhivkov in front of the December Plenum of the Central Committee in 1980.
51 TsDA, f. 1B, op. 68, a. e. 3379, l. 69. Politburo meeting from February 1988.
52 TsDA, f. 1B, op. 68, a. e. 3493, l. 19–20. Politburo meeting from September 1988.
53 TsDA, f. 1B, op. 68, a. e. 3493, l. 12–13, 28.
54 TsDA, f. 1B, op. 68, a. e. 3493, l. 12–13, 28. The national income for 1988 was 29.4 billion leva.
55 TsDA, f. 1B, op. 68, a. e. 2421, l. 17. Politburo meeting from November 1986.
56 TsDA, f. 1B, op. 68, a. e. 2421, l. 18.
57 TsDA, f. 1B, op. 68, a. e. 3493, l. 70–71. Politburo discussion of S. Ovcharov's report "On the Radical Turning Point in the Production of Goods and Services," September 1988; TsDA, f. 1B, op. 65, a. e. 92, l. 101–102. December Plenum of 1988.
58 TsDA, f. 1B, op. 71, a. e. 670, l. 20, 58. Decision of the Secretariat of the BCP of October 9, 1989.
59 TsDA, f. 1B, op. 68, a. e. 3526a, l. 430. Statement by Emil Christov before the Politburo, October 28–31, 1988.
60 I. Ditchev, "Usyadaneto na nomadskiya komunizâm. Sotsialisticheskata urbanizatsiya i krâgovete na grazhdanstvo," *Sotsiologicheski problem*, 35 (3–4) (2003): 33–63, at p. 43.
61 Venelinova, *Razkazi i obrazi*, p. 11.
62 Mineva, *Razkazi i obrazi*, p. 147.
63 Dimitrov, *Sâvetska Bâlgariya*, pp. 30–31.
64 Dimitrov, *Sâvetska Bâlgariya*, pp. 136, 147–150.
65 Dimitrov, *Sâvetska Bâlgariya*, p. 32; Elenkov, *Kulturniyat front*, pp. 264–265.
66 Markov, *Zadochni reportazhi*, p. 310.
67 Markov, *Zadochni reportazhi*, p. 306.
68 Markov, *Zadochni reportazhi*, p. 306. The British Ambassador offers a similar observation: "Propaganda has already [in 1958] become a repetition of worn-out clichés, which causes one to wonder whether their authors even expect anyone to believe them. This is probably the party's most obvious failure in Bulgaria." See Dimitrov, *Sâvetska Bâlgariya*, p. 41.
69 Dimitrov, *Sâvetska Bâlgariya*, pp. 30–31.
70 TsDA, f. 1B, op. 68, a. e. 3735, l. 74. Politburo meeting from August 1989.

15 Processes within society

The division of the public and private spheres

The Communist Party's total control over society and the complete usurpation of social space by structures under the regime's control continued throughout the entire communist period. However, from the 1960s onward, a gradual "thaw" took place, which led to a timid easing of ideological dogma and to the unofficial separation of the public from the private sphere. It was precisely in this fault line between official speech and the space of familial, friendly, and collegial circles that the first shoots of independence, the rudiments of civil society, sprang up. Of course, in the Bulgarian context, the term "civil society" must be used with certain caveats and with the understanding that even until the system's final collapse a clearly defined dissident movement never managed to emerge; the intelligentsia largely remained captive to the corrupting system of privileges. There was also an enormous shortage of publicly engaged individuals willing to openly express their opinions on social issues. This is the reason why expressions of free thought and disagreement with the status quo were generally the exception rather than the rule; they were also the work of a relatively small number of people and were doomed to remain isolated incidents. Almost all such statements came from the "artistic-creative intelligentsia" and remained within its closed circles. Contemporary historiography has established a relatively precise and full list of such acts, complete with descriptions.[1] It is more logical to search for the first shoots of civil society in the emergence of informal, urban social circles, youth groups and subcultures that formed around the "forbidden fruit" of Western music and the Western lifestyle. Unfortunately, even today this topic has remained outside the purview of scholarly studies, hence publications on this subject tend to be few and far between.[2]

Even during the Stalinist period, one of the basic ways to distance oneself from the regime was by telling political jokes. Such jokes gained such wide distribution that they began to function as a general metaphor for the distance between the average person and the rulers and also for the deep differences between official and nonofficial discourse. Unquestionably, joke-telling is a form of theatrical performance, and, as such, it requires an audience. In a number of cities, unofficial circles formed around talented authors and performers of such jokes, whose art acquired enormous power to expose

The division of public and private spheres   307

the true nature of the regime. The name and tragic fate of one of the most talented such joke-tellers, the Sofia-based musician and bohemian Aleksandâr Nikolov, better known by his nickname "Sasho the Sweetheart" (*Sasho Sladura*), has become closely associated with this practice. Because of the jokes he invented and told, he was sent to a concentration camp in Lovech in 1961, where he managed to survive for only eleven days before being brutally killed, as were hundreds of other internees.[3]

Another such legendary joke-teller was the Plovdiv-based architect Boyan Chinkov. In January 1964, he was publicly put on trial. Over the course of three days, the panel of judges heard testimony from a total of thirty-seven witnesses who had been present when jokes written by Chinkov had been told. Almost all the witnesses, who included his colleagues and listeners, attempted to exonerate him. However, due to the open trial itself, those who had not heard the jokes originally were able to learn them, pass them on, and retell them, thus, the trial had the polar opposite effect from that desired by the authorities. Chinkov was sentenced to five years in prison, but thanks to the intervention of French journalists, he was freed during September of the same year. Even at the moment he was informed that he was to be released, Chinkov joked, "Come on, now, boys, I had just solved my housing problem for the next five years!"[4]

Such jokes not only brightened people's bleak everyday lives, but for decades on end they also ridiculed the system, painting it as revolting and poorly functioning. Such jokes were not simply anti-communist; they were also a protest against the constant shortages and propagandistic lies. The majority of them were funny only in the context of the time. Political humor became not only a way of blowing off steam, but also developed into a true folk art and a unique "verbal graffiti" of sorts.[5] One of the primary characters in the genre, Todor Zhivkov, replaced the most famous Bulgarian literary archetype from the nineteenth century – Bay Ganyo (the personification of wiliness and shamelessness, the ultimate boorish parvenu), taking on his semantics and characteristics. This identification even went so far that the main character actually began associating himself with this image and telling jokes about himself. One of Zhivkov's favorite pastimes while drinking his morning coffee with his advisers was listening to the latest joke about himself. The double standard, however, remained in effect – Bulgarian courts continued to imprison people for "spreading jokes/rumors," even while their main character was popularizing some of the very same jokes.[6]

Young people were the other milieu that gave rise to an alternative to official social life. Beginning in the second half of the 1950s, informal circles sprang up around listening to and playing jazz, which had been banned. This gradually developed into a specific subculture, characterized by a certain type of clothing – long hair, tight pants, miniskirts, and so forth. The regime's alarm increased upon learning that even communist youth associations had begun organizing "dance parties," where "depraved dances were performed to the sounds of Western jazz music." According to some assessments, "the trend was

308 *From de-Stalinization to regime consolidation*

so contagious that once young people had danced modern dances and listened to Western music, they rejected tango and waltz as unsuitable for them."[7]

The year 1968, which was inarguably a dramatic one for all of Europe, was an important watershed in the process of forming alternative youth subcultures in Bulgaria as well. The Beatles, their music and their behavior became an example for young Bulgarians, as they were for millions of youth around the world, serving as the "petri dish" for the cultivation of a whole new ethos that rejected ideological dogmas and moralizing and that set freedom and love at its core. Even though the majority of visitors taking part in the International Youth Festival in Sofia in 1968 were leftists from all over the world, their way of life, clothing, songs, etc., changed the life of young people in Bulgaria. The Czechoslovakian delegation itself, through its behavior during the parade through Sofia's streets, clearly piqued the interest of young people in Sofia, as well as that of older, more open-minded people. There is no doubt that the Bulgarian rock group *Shturtsite* ("The Crickets"), which appeared the same year, also had an enormous effect on the formation of this new subculture. They, along with the band Signal, which arose slightly later, created hits that emotionally charged two generations of Bulgarians with such values. In fact, the hippie movement reached these geographical latitudes with a certain delay and with certain modifications. The rebellious subculture built on its foundations actually had more in common with the beatnik movement, even though its representatives preferred to call themselves *hipari* ("hippies").

The regime's reactions to such subculture phenomena were spasmodic and closely followed the example set by the USSR. Thus, Khrushchev's campaign against hooliganism, which was understood as a mixed criminal-political phenomenon, was the reason that this topic suddenly became widely discussed in Bulgaria and that all expressions indicating an alternative lifestyle subsequently became classified as "hooliganism." In the late 1950s and early 1960s, people accused of hooliganism ended up in camps in Lovech (for men) and in the village of Skravena near the town of Botevgrad (for women). After the camps were closed in 1962, "hooligans" were forcibly resettled from cities and interned for various lengths of time in distant parts of the country. For first offenses and less serious forms of alternative expression, the guilty parties would have their heads shaved (for wearing long hair) or would be sent home missing certain articles of clothing or with torn clothing (for wearing jeans or tight pants); girls would be sent home with chemical stamps on their legs (for wearing miniskirts) and so on. During the whole communist period, the regime as a rule tried to control not only public expressions of alternative thought but also the way adherents of such subcultures looked – from their hair to their clothing.

In March 1963, in front of a group of "representatives of the Soviet creative-artistic intelligentsia," Khrushchev gave one of his most damning speeches against the various types of critics of "socialist reality." Echoes of it appeared in Sofia a month later in Todor Zhivkov's speech against "the increase of bourgeois influence on Bulgarian culture," which was given to activists from "the

The division of public and private spheres 309

cultural front."[8] Since the Soviet leader's speech had included threats and direct accusations of homosexuality against certain artists, in Sofia a large closed trial was organized against Bulgarian representatives of the gay community. A similar trial with a large number of defendants also took place ten years later, in 1973.[9] These and a series of other events clearly demonstrate that Bulgarian public life aped Soviet political reality and shows the lack of any originality whatsoever in the exercise of power in Sofia. At the same time, however, the regime's identification of ever more milieus and groups within Bulgarian society as real or potential enemies clearly testifies to the fault line that had opened up between public and private space and to the "clustered" emergence of alternatives circles and social spaces that were not subject to party control. However, it must be noted that such circles were highly varied and specific phenomena, which had little in common with one another. While they did not constitute a homogeneous civil sector, they nevertheless served as a nourishing environment for the development of an underground and a counterculture of sorts.

One event from 1971 clearly demonstrated the widespread emergence of alternative values and interests within society, different from those trumpeted by communist propaganda and its high priests. Namely, this was the funeral of the talented Bulgarian soccer players Georgi "Gundi" Asparuhov and Nikola Kotkov, who were killed in an automobile accident. By chance, this tragedy happened to coincide with another somber event in the USSR: the official burial of the Soviet cosmonauts who had been killed in the line of duty. This second ceremony, which was widely covered in all Bulgarian media, was literally overshadowed by the massive outpouring of grief over the soccer players by hundreds of thousands of mourners. The free expression of sorrow by what was an enormous number of people by Bulgarian standards was practical evidence of a new value system, of a process for freely choosing idols that had taken place beyond the communists' control, proof of the reshuffling of hierarchies, and so on. This incident became a subject of discussion in the Politburo, where the blame was squarely placed on the Interior Minister, Angel Solakov. Here is what Todor Zhivkov had to say on the matter:

> What worries us is the funeral for the two athletes. We value these athletes, they are talented, but I don't know whether what Comrade Solakov has done would be allowed in any other socialist country, without the party and state leadership growing alarmed. More than 150,000 turned out at the funeral! Some comrades claim that this is the largest funeral Bulgaria has ever seen. Not even 150,000 people took part in Georgi Dimitrov's funeral procession."[10]

As a result of this incident, Solakov was removed from his post; however, this did not change anything.

Of course, it would be absurd to interpret this event as "oppositional." Neither the funeral, nor the overall increase in interest in soccer and in sports-fan culture could be seen as such. Given the state of Bulgarian society at the

310 *From de-Stalinization to regime consolidation*

time, however, sports were one of the few spheres of freedom where Bulgarians could openly express their emotions and feelings, and their likes and dislikes. With certain caveats, unofficial soccer fan clubs from this period could be seen as a type of subculture offering an alternative to official culture.

Any study of expressions of free thought among ever wider circles in Bulgarian society must note the important role played by listening to "enemy radio stations" – namely, "Voice of America," the BBC, Deutsche Welle, and other stations that broadcast in Bulgarian. Such stations influenced the formation of alternative counterculture, provided a platform for Bulgarian intellectuals who had fled beyond the Iron Curtain, and created a new type of public expression that was different from the official discourse. The radio DJs and their listeners established a unique form of contact that allowed their messages and broadcasts to reach a significant portion of the urban population. Individuals who made particularly valuable contributions to the formation of this alternative urban public forum included the writer Georgi Markov. His biography was particularly interesting since he was inarguably a talented person whose literary gifts had been highly valued by the regime. Moreover, Markov had managed to win the trust of Zhivkov himself and for a short time had been part of the revolving cast making up the dictator's informal "intellectual advisory staff," which was also known as "the hunting party." Like his other colleagues, despite of his lack of interest in hunting, Markov took part in these outings, at which the dictator revealed intimate sides of his character. Markov's closeness to Zhivkov made it possible for him to take the risk of expressing himself more freely, which won him popularity with wide strata of Bulgarian society. His plays *To Crawl under the Rainbow* and *Assassin in the Cul-de-sac* made particularly strong impressions and were criticized from an orthodox Marxist-Leninist viewpoint due to their liberality. In 1969, after Prague Spring had been crushed and another one of his plays, *I Am He*, had been pulled from the stage, Markov decided to take advantage of the dictator's benevolence while it still lasted and to leave the country legally. On the very same day the play was stopped during its internal premiere, Markov managed to leave the country to join his brother in Italy, before later settling in London. There some of his plays were performed on local stages over the following years, while in 1974 he won first prize for dramaturgy at a literary festival in Edinburgh. That same year, he began working in the Bulgarian section of the BBC, while also collaborating with Deutsche Welle. In 1975, Radio Free Europe began broadcasting his *In Absentia Reports*, a series of literary impressions and stories with strongly autobiographical elements. They made him exceptionally popular among an ever-expanding circle of people listening to "enemy radio stations." Information about him compiled by State Security and given to the Central Committee of the BCP states: "Markov's material is notable for its exceptional hatred and spite toward the socialist system in Bulgaria and toward the party and state leaders."[11] Zhivkov started nursing a particularly sinister grudge toward the writer in 1977, when Markov began reading a series of eleven fragments about their personal interactions

The division of public and private spheres 311

on Radio Free Europe. In them, he revealed the dictator's exceptionally primitive nature and his unscrupulousness, as well as his conceit and his lust for power. A true master with words, Markov also spoke of the purely human aspects of Zhivkov's character, which lent a particular realism to his works and strengthened the denunciatory effect of his message. All of this made him Zhivkov's personal enemy, and State Security began a "sharp action" (*ostro meropriyatie*) aimed at the writer's physical elimination. With the help of the KGB, a special umbrella was constructed that would fire a capsule of slow-acting poison. Markov was shot by this weapon on the Waterloo Bridge in London by an "unremarkable passerby" on Zhivkov's birthday in 1978. Four days later, the writer died of blood poisoning.[12] Georgi Markov's murder and news of the deadly "Bulgarian umbrella" led to a further deterioration of the regime's image abroad, which had already been highly negative. The writer's bizarre death, however, only brought him more international fame and added a European dimension to his biography and work.

Even though State Security organized several other demonstrative "sharp actions" against Bulgarian political immigrants to the West, it became ever clearer in the early 1980s that the regime's stranglehold on power was loosening yet again. The clearest evidence of this was the development of popular music. Groups appeared that did not merely imitate but actually parodied mass genres while at the same time trying to give their music a specifically Bulgarian flavor. Among such groups, Jendema is particularly notable. Beginning in 1985, this alternative culture also created its own annual "Woodstock" – the ritual greeting of the sun at dawn on July 1, originally in Varna, then later in the village of Varvara on the Black Sea Coast; this ritual was inspired by the song "July Morning" by Uriah Heep (and, more precisely, Ken Hensley).[13]

As of the beginning of Gorbachev's *perestroika*, a relatively small number of groups within Bulgarian society had been affected by the processes of the "thaw." However, there is one other phenomenon worth mentioning. The majority of Bulgarian proto-dissidents were not only members of the Communist Party but at certain stages in their lives they were also ideologically invested in its values. Such examples include Radoy Ralin, Boris Dimovski, Hristo Ganev, Nikolay Genchev, Ivan Radoev, and many others. The case of Zhelyu Zhelev, the first democratically elected President in post-socialist times, is in a certain sense similar, but more limited. The fact remains, however, that the closer a person was to the center of the action, the more protected he was from any eventual backlash and thus the freer he felt to express his disagreement.[14] This remained true of dissident expressions up through the end of the 1980s.

Notes

1 For more details, see N. Hristova, *Spetsifika na bâlgarskoto "disidentstvo": Vlast i inteligentsiya 1956–1989 g.*, Plovdiv: Letera, 2005; Vladimir Migev, *Bâlgarskite pisateli i politicheskiyat zhivot v Bâlgariya, 1944–1970*, Sofia: Kota, 2001; Vladimir Migev, *Prazhkata prolet '68 i Bâlgariya*, Sofia: Iztok-Zapad, 2005.

312 *From de-Stalinization to regime consolidation*

2 See in more detail certain publications by Karin Taylor, especially "Lennon, not Lenin: Youth between Socialist Discourse and Realities in Bulgaria of 1960s and 70s," doctoral dissertation, Graz, Philosophische fakultät der Universität Graz, 2004.
3 V. Stanilov, "Sasho Nikolov – Sladura," in Iv. Slavov, *Zlatnata reshetka*, Sofia: Sv. Kl. Ohridski, 2003, pp. 12–13.
4 D. Dochev, "Part I (1944–1964)," in *Provintsialniyat totalitarizâm*, pp. 317–319.
5 Vitsovete za komunizma – dzhazât na podtisnatite," *Dnevnik*, June 11, 2008.
6 Chakârov, *Vtoriyat etazh*, p. 101.
7 Dochev, *Provintsialniyat totalitarizâm*, pp. 320–321.
8 Migev, *Bâlgarskite pisateli*, pp. 204–207.
9 M. Gruev, *Komunizâm i homoseksualizâm v Bâlgariya (1944–1989)*, Anamnesis, http://anamnesis.info/broi1/scenes.htm (accessed on 18 June 2018).
10 Angelov, *Strogo sekretno*, p. 546.
11 Cited in Hristov, *Todor Zhivkov*, p. 279.
12 Hristov, *Todor Zhivkov*, p. 286.
13 Intervyu s antropologa R. Levi: "Dzhulaya e edna ot vrâhnite tochki na svobodata" [The July Festival is one of the tipping points of freedom].
14 Ivaylo Znepolski calls this "The Galileo Galilei Syndrome": *Bâlgarskiyat komunizâm*, pp. 305–310.

16 The ghosts of national communism and pressure on Muslim communities

The important, long-term consequences of post-1956 de-Stalinization included the definitive collapse of the idea of creating an international proletarian state; the process also spelled the end of the ideological rhetoric that had accompanied this idea. The international communist movement began to slowly and tacitly revise abstract Comintern-style internationalism, which had been based on the postulate of the universal brotherhood between the peoples of the world in the name of one universal goal: the triumph of the global proletarian revolution. To a certain extent, this change was due to a natural evolution within the ideological understandings of communist parties in all of the pro-Soviet regimes, which had recognized the hopelessly utopian nature of that goal. Once it became clear that such a goal was unattainable, most communist parties turned to the ever more important task of shoring up their own authenticity within their home country, emphasizing the teleological inevitability of their rule stemming from a centuries-old national tradition and, hence, their legitimacy, based on the laws of history. While most Eastern European communist parties embraced a similar nationalist change in message, this tendency was especially pronounced in the autocratic regimes in the Balkans. Every one of them must be examined individually, however. The specific features of the Bulgarian case must be recognized, since, unlike the regimes in Albania, Romania, and Yugoslavia, the BCP never took an anti-Soviet tone and never once assumed a position even slightly deviating from the Moscow line. Despite this, however, from the early 1960s onward, we can see clear signs of a return to the old, traditional Bulgarian nationalism, one that was above all hostile to its Balkan neighbors and their "infiltration" into the Bulgarian national body in the guise of various minority groups. The BCP's and especially Zhivkov's unwavering loyalty to the Soviet Union was to a certain extent rewarded in that Moscow allowed the regime in Sofia to exercise partial autonomy in its Balkan politics. This made it easier for Bulgaria to revive a series of prewar practices and stereotypes with respect to Bulgaria's neighbors and its ethnic policies. Since the old nationalism had been heavily discredited in the Communist Party's traditional rhetoric, it was replaced by "socialist patriotism." In the BCP's propaganda arsenal, this concept continued to be accompanied by the obligatory addendum "proletarian

314   *From de-Stalinization to regime consolidation*

internationalism," although the latter grew ever more devoid of meaning. When the mobilizing potential of the old progressive rhetoric seemed completely exhausted and the ideological gaps yawned ever wider, "socialist patriotism" turned out to be not only a fitting filler but it also served as a new glue aimed at national homogenization and a relegitimization of the regime, which was seeking a new image that was not only class-based but also nationally relevant. It must be noted that from the regime's point of view this new policy turned out to be exceptionally effective – the average Bulgarian easily recognized the old clichés, which successfully substituted for the communist utopia's lack of new horizons and lent a sense of inevitability to the new set of ideological and political imperatives.

Commenting on the debate about the coexistence between "practical communism" (real socialism) and nationalism and comparing it with similar processes in the other pro-Soviet regimes, Maria Todorova employs the concept of ideological nominalism – the revival of earlier nationalist discourse cloaked in terminology from the dominant Marxist-Leninist jargon. In this way, an escape from the contradiction between "a cosmopolitan universalist ideology and a particularist romantic belief" is found. Thus, unlike in the West and the Third World, "ethnicity, national and etatist communism trace a line in the historical development of Eastern Europe from the eighteenth to the twentieth century, forming something . . . like an (almost) uninterrupted nationalist continuum."[1]

Pressure and survival during the 1960s and early 1970s

The so-called "Revival Process" of the mid-1980s, which turned into a bloody clash that has been discussed at a series of international forums, had deep historical roots in the preceding decades. At the end of the 1950s, the regime's propaganda introduced the euphemism "cultural revolution" to denote its policy of forcible assimilation of Bulgaria's Muslim population. At first, this term seemed rather general and abstract, but it gradually began to be understood as a system of measures aimed at eradicating traditional Muslim clothing, along with the traditions and lifestyles associated with such garb. Thus, another term arose – *razferedzhavane*, which literally means "taking off the *ferece*," the term for the Muslim face veil – which emphasized the imposition of outward signs of communist modernism. The first attempts to forcibly replace traditional Muslim clothing date back to 1958, but such attempts were sporadic and related to celebrations marking the respective anniversaries of the communist seizure of power in Bulgaria and the October Revolution; after these incidents, the wearing of fezzes and *kyulyavs* (tall brown hats) by men and veils, *shalwars* (loose trousers), and *shamiya* (a kerchief that covers a large portion of a woman's face) was tacitly permitted.[2] In fact, this was one of the first examples of what would become a regular tactic of alternation between brutal, wide-ranging campaigns and temporary, partial retreats, which created a sense of constant confusion in the targeted group and raised unfounded hopes that the most recent campaign would be the last. The following year, 1959, a massive drive for *razferedzhavane* began, once again on the occasion of September 9, which was celebrated particularly actively since it was the fifteenth anniversary of the coup. Strict bans were imposed against covering women's faces, as well as on the wearing of *ferece* and *shalwars* for women, and fezzes and *kyulyavs* for men. Such bans were enforced primarily by posses that would patrol the streets and fields, arresting any women violating the ban. The offending articles of clothing would be publicly and demonstratively torn up, while men violating the new dress code would be driven from their workplace and so on.

At the very end of 1959, on December 30, the Ministry of the People's Health and Social Welfare issued a special memorandum which stated that the circumcision of young boys was being performed in an exceptionally primitive and unhygienic manner, which frequently led to complications. It also concluded that circumcision was unnecessary and harmful. Subsequently, medical institutions were instructed to strictly control the procedure in the future, making sure that it was performed only by doctors and medical personnel in medical institutions. Children were to be hospitalized for two to three days following the procedure.[3] Strict punishments were stipulated for those who had traditionally performed the circumcision ritual of *sünnet*. The licenses they had previously been issued were taken away, while the memorandum decreed, "The health authorities will pursue offenders and hand them over to the judicial system for criminal prosecution."[4] As can be seen, this decree aimed on the one hand at "modernizing" the practice and transforming it into a medically motivated operation, which would limit the chance of complications and infections. On the other hand, the reasons behind the above-cited memorandum are far from merely medical or hygienic. It was the first step toward the criminalization of circumcision. From that moment on, the regime would undertake a strong propaganda campaign against this ritual, one that would continue over the following decades.

On April 5, 1962, the Politburo of the Central Committee of the BCP adopted a special resolution, which was designed to "limit certain expressions of Turkish influence among Bulgarian Muslims, Gypsies and Tatars."[5] It stipulated that children from the aforementioned groups be placed in separate classes which did not contain Turks, that boarding schools also based on the principle of separation be created, that separate divisions be organized within the army, and so on. Local authorities were given the task of seeking out individuals who belonged to these ethnic/religious groups but who were registered as "Turks." Population registers were to be revised where necessary, such that these individuals' non-Turkish ethnic affiliation could be noted. Local authorities were also instructed to introduce a simplified administrative procedure for those who wished to change their names to Bulgarian ones, which did not require the court order that had previously been necessary. At the same time, local authorities were also charged with the task of "not allowing Bulgarian Muslims and Gypsies to move to settlements with a compact

316 *From de-Stalinization to regime consolidation*

Turkish population."[6] This new, differentiated approach, which distinguished between non-Turkish and Turkish minorities, laid the foundations of a policy of gradually "uniting" the separate, smaller Muslim groups with the so-called "Bulgarian socialist nation." For the first time, the question of changing the names of Pomaks (ethnic Bulgarians who profess Islam) became part of the agenda of the state's highest governing body. Despite the fact that the resolution's phrasing explicitly stated that such name changes would be made only "in the case of [the subject's] complete inward conviction and openly expressed individual desire," the cited document gave the "green light" to this new phase of assimilation.

The Politburo's directives were interpreted in different ways by the various regional structures of the Communist Party. While in the Central Rhodope Mountains (the Smolyan region), local authorities focused largely on the most active party functionaries and the local intelligentsia, to whom it was "hinted" that a name change would open up new personal and professional horizons, in 1964, local authorities in the Western Rhodopes (around Blagoevgrad) decided to undertake a sweeping, forcible campaign, which engaged the services of the police, State Security, so-called "voluntary militias," and all the local structures of the Communist Party. Certain villages were blockaded, while various other demonstrative actions were undertaken. The village of Ribnovo near Gotse Delchev put up the fiercest resistance. There, an open rebellion broke out against the forced name changes, which threatened to spread to the other communities in the region as well.[7] One important aspect of the events in Ribnovo was the fact that residents took their show of resistance beyond the village, transforming it into an organized expression on the part of the entire Pomak population. Moreover, they also sent delegations to the Central Committee of the BCP and to the Turkish embassy in Sofia. This was precisely what catapulted the case to national significance and compelled a response from the highest party leadership. In the end, a commission was sent to the region to investigate the incident and to report back to its superiors in Sofia. At this stage, the regime turned out to be ill-prepared to undertake such a wide-ranging renaming operation, thus it was forced to retreat. Meetings were held in the villages affected by the campaign, where it was explained that, in the end, a name was a matter of personal choice.

There is no doubt that the events in Ribnovo in 1964 slowed the implementation of a large-scale campaign to change names by seven or eight years. On the whole, however, such incidents did not fundamentally alter the policy being pursued. Albeit not as brutal, over the following years, pressure against Muslim religious identity nevertheless continued with full force. This pressure went hand in hand with serious capital investments in the region, aimed at creating permanent employment, bringing public services to communities, and raising the local standard of living. Ordinances issued by the Council of Ministers and the Central Committee of the BCP "For the Further Social-Economic and Cultural Development" of the Blagoevgrad (1968), Smolyan (1969) and Kârdzhali (1970) districts, respectively, played an important role in

Pressure on Muslim communities 317

this policy.[8] Overall, Zhivkov's skillful alternation between "the carrot and the stick" found one of its clearest applications in the case of Bulgaria's Muslim population.

The direct use of force, which had been employed by local functionaries in the Western Rhodopes, continued to be one possible approach considered by Zhivkov's circle, but, at that moment, they preferred to rely on possibilities for gradual change, which had not yet been exhausted. In this respect, the Smolyan party leaders' tactics turned out to be far more effective and unproblematic. During the second half of the 1960s, however, the difference between the two strategies gradually disappeared.

After this temporary retreat in the mid-1960s, the authorities reconsidered the means and possibilities for a new campaign to change names, this time one that would affect all Bulgarian Muslims. On July 17, 1970, the Secretariat of the Central Committee of the BCP resolved to continue working to improve the social status of Bulgarian Muslims while at the same time moving toward a change of names.[9] The campaign began that same year in the Smolyan region, before spreading east in 1971 and 1972 to the Madan, Rudozem, and Zlatograd regions, as well as west to the Devin and Dospat regions. Such actions followed the already well-rehearsed script, employing the same "pressure groups" that had been used during the time of *razferedzhavane* and the unsuccessful attempt at changing names in 1964. Teachers were almost without exception part of this campaign, both "locals," as well as outsiders that had been lured from other areas in the country by the petty privileges offered; they were joined by professional and volunteer party functionaries, Fatherland Front employees and propagandists, plainclothes and uniformed police officers, among others. As the Secretariat's resolution explicitly emphasized, the "principle of free will," which was considered ideologically legitimate, should be preserved – at least in cases where it could get results. In many places in the Eastern and Central Rhodopes, and especially in the Smolyan region, the campaign was carried out relatively painlessly and was even received positively, especially by the younger and middle generations.

But the further west in the Rhodopes the campaign spread, the fiercer the resistance against it grew. Such resistance was especially widespread in the village of Barutin near Dospat. The events in the village, in which two women were killed and dozens were beaten, imprisoned and forcibly resettled, served as an epilogue to the campaign in the Smolyan region, while at the same time developing into an even bloodier drama around name changes in the Velingrad, Gotse Delchev, and Razlog regions. The spread of the campaign to the Blagoevgrad district led to an abrupt rise in the number of individuals arrested and sent to camps. Most of them languished behind bars for years, without ever being convicted in a court of law. To deal with such a large number of detainees, the largest Bulgarian concentration camp, Belene, which was located on Persin Island in the Danube and which had been closed for a second time in 1959, was once again reopened.

318 *From de-Stalinization to regime consolidation*

In May 1972, the authorities were faced with serious mass resistance in the region of Yakoruda in the northwesternmost corner of the Rhodope Mountains. The local population's attempts to resist culminated in a truly desperate measure: approximately 400 men from the numerous small communities in the region coordinated their actions and decided to cross the crest of the Rila Mountains to reach the town of Samokov; from there, they would attempt to reach Sofia, where they planned to protest in front of the American and Turkish embassies. State Security found out about this plan only when the group was already high in the mountains. A complex operation was launched to "neutralize and detain" the men. The necessary "preventative measures" were taken with respect to the would-be protestors, who were all sent either home or were "forcibly resettled" with new names. One local died during this operation, while in the neighboring village of Buntsevo one of the leaders of the renaming campaign in the region was killed. New punitive operations were launched, while a closed trial was held against those responsible for the murder.[10]

The epilogue to the campaign to change the Pomaks' names came in March 1973 in the villages of Kornitsa, Breznitsa, and Lâzhnitsa in the Gotse Delchev region; these three villages had put up the fiercest resistance until that moment. Realizing that they were the last remaining holdouts and that the noose was tightening around them, the residents of Kornitsa began a round-the-clock vigil in the village square. The authorities were concerned that the three villages' actions might set a precedent similar to that of Ribnovo nine years earlier, which could influence the other communities in the region. Thus, the authorities decided to seize the village using military force. The operation was planned for March 28, 1973, at dawn and was led by the Interior Minister himself. During the operation, five villagers from Kornitsa and Breznitsa were killed and dozens of others were injured.

There is no doubt that the events in Kornitsa and Breznitsa in 1973 represent the culmination, and at the same time the epilogue, to the campaign to change the Pomaks' names. The authorities decided to teach a serious lesson to the three rebellious villages, hence the sentences subsequently handed down to participants in the uprising were extremely harsh. Eleven individuals were convicted, two of whom were sentenced to twelve years in prison. Dozens of others spent various periods behind bars without being officially convicted, while a large number of families were forcibly resettled.[11]

After the campaign to change the names of living had come to an end, the renaming of the dead began. In fact, this phenomenon arose in the course of the renaming process itself, when fictitious "Bulgarian" patronymics (which serve as middle names in Bulgaria) were given to people whose parents had passed away before the start of the campaign. "The renaming of the dead" also led to the eradication of all traces of old names on tombstones. In cases of relatively new graves, the municipal authorities required the deceased's families to obliterate the Muslim names; in cases of older graves, the tombstones themselves were completely destroyed. On the whole, this way of "dealing"

Pressure on Muslim communities 319

with the memory of the dead, the past and the symbolism it contained turned out to be one of the most traumatic aspects of the process.

"The Revival Process" from the mid-1970s through the 1980s

During the course of the campaign to change Bulgarian Muslims' names, the regime developed the term "Revival Process" and began including it in its political jargon. The official explanation for what was happening was that the process was, in fact, a "voluntary act" to revive the Bulgarian naming system that had been lost among this population during the Ottomans' campaign of forcible conversion to Islam centuries earlier. Over the course of time, however, this term began to be understood as denoting a whole system of propagandistic, ideological, and punitive measures whose goal was to convince society of the correctness of the policy being implemented and at the same time to send a serious message to those Muslims who had not yet reconciled themselves to their own "revival." Both eye-witness accounts from that time as well as Communist Party documents paint a picture of a large-scale, comprehensive process whose goal was to introduce pressure on the level of daily life, to make such pressure the norm and through this pervasive pressure to infiltrate the intimate world of family, kinship, neighborly, and friendly ties. Moreover, it aimed at instilling a new "identity modification" of sorts within the targeted population, which would erase religious and cultural differences and at the same time cultivate political loyalty to the Communist Party and the regime as a whole.

The Plenum of the Central Committee of the BCP, which was held on February 7 and 8, 1974, and which was dedicated to improving the party's ideological work, was a crucial event for the broad expansion of the Revival Process. The main report was given by Aleksandâr Lilov in his capacity as Zhivkov's newly elevated ideologue, which in practice made him the second-ranking figure within the party hierarchy. This forum essentially addressed the need to refresh the old ideological "bag of tricks," which had remained fundamentally unchanged since the time of Stalin. This plenum made it clear that the Communist Party's supreme leadership had realized that propagandistic rhetoric in its traditional form was losing its ability to mobilize society and was in need of a serious reinvigoration and overhaul. In this sense, the authorities expected that the subsequent shift of emphasis from class toward nation and "patriotic education" (as well everything hidden behind the latter term) could broaden support for the regime within Bulgarian society. This was also the main gist of Lilov's speech, in which the topic of "holding on to conquered territory" with respect to Bulgarian Muslims and expanding the party's influence on their consciousness through the introduction of "the new socialist calendrical-holiday system" held an important, if not central, place. In fact, replacing religion with Soviet and national content was nothing new to the regime. This substitution constituted an invariable part of its general policy of "atheistic education" and was seen as an important tool in acting upon

320 *From de-Stalinization to regime consolidation*

"the conservatism of the Muslim tradition." Translated into the language of the local party functionaries, it meant an intensification of measures banning the celebration of Muslim holidays, attendance at mosques, circumcisions and so on.[12]

The documents produced by the plenum did contain one new feature, however: "measures for the ideological-political assimilation of the population of Turkish descent."[13] In fact, from that point on, the regime's attitude toward the Turkish minority ever more closely resembled the policy it had pursued with respect to ethnically Bulgarian Muslims over the preceding decades. The model had been created, which the authorities would follow once again in the ensuing campaign to change the names of Bulgarian Turks. At the same time, the phrase "a unified socialist Bulgarian nation" was actively introduced into circulation in the early 1970s. Although it is still not entirely clear who coined the phrase, it closely corresponded to the idea put forward by Brezhnev in 1971 of "a unified Soviet people" as a "qualitatively different and higher form" of unification of the individual nationalities.[14] The phrase also expressed the Bulgarian communist leadership's vision of the future expansion of the Revival Process.[15]

In the early 1980s, pressure intensified against groups, families and individuals both outside of and within the regions densely populated by Turks. Growing numbers of Turks were forced to change their names in order to secure certain jobs (with the Interior Ministry, i.e. the police, as well as important business and party-related positions), to obtain construction permits or to receive new housing, change jobs, resettle or be employed in districts outside their birthplace.[16] This time, the renaming included not only the children but also the parents from mixed (Turkish–Pomak) marriages, meaning that both partners had to change their names, not just the Pomak spouse. This greatly increased the scope of those affected in comparison to similar campaigns in 1975.[17] Special commissions within regional administrations studied children's and parents' "family roots." From the spring of 1982 until the end of 1984, the names of approximately 50,000 people were changed, including a significant number of Muslim Roma.

This increasing pressure and the expansion of the name-changing campaign to include ever newer groups of Muslims also provoked a backlash. Underground Turkish groups began to form in many places, some of which developed into full-fledged terrorist organizations. The complex role played by the Turkish secret services in their emergence of such groups has yet to be adequately studied. However, one of their indisputable successes was the recruitment of ethnic Turks who collaborated with Bulgarian State Security; such operatives began preparing a series of terrorist attacks. Some of them predated the main campaign to change names in December 1984, while others were organized after this campaign. On August 30, 1984, explosive devices were simultaneously detonated at the Plovdiv train station and in the parking lot of the airport at Varna. The two attacks killed one woman and injured forty-four other people. The attacks shook up the deeply soporific atmosphere

Pressure on Muslim communities 321

in the country; during the entire course of the "Revival Process," these attacks were pointed out in propaganda as proof positive that the party had good reason to be concerned over the spread of Turkish nationalism.[18] On March 9, 1985, the same group organized an even larger-scale attack. Once again, two explosive devices were planted on the same day, one in a café in the central hotel in Sliven and the other in a car for mothers with children on the Burgas–Sofia train. The explosion at the Bunovo train station took seven lives, while dozens of others were injured. The group's final, albeit unsuccessful, attack was on the beach at the Black Sea resort of Druzhba (now known as St. Constantine). Thanks to the explosive device that had failed to detonate, State Security was able to unravel the plot, leading to the capture of four culprits. Three of them were condemned to death and executed.[19] Additional smaller, individual acts of sabotage were also staged by other Turkish underground organizations.

Until October 1984, it did not seem that the authorities intended to decisively extend their campaign to encompass all the Turks in the country. The government also did not officially reject their ethnic identity as "Turks." Two months later, however, things changed. Zhivkov's inner circle had made a radical decision, without any official report or shorthand record of such a resolution. The opinions of his unofficial advisers – who included the academicians Angel Balevski and Pantaley Zarev, the poet Georgi Dzhagarov, as well as Politburo members Pencho Kubadinski, Interior Minister Dimitâr Stoyanov, and the head of Zhivkov's cabinet, Milko Balev, and the Central Committee Secretary for Ideological Questions, Stoyan Mihaylov – leaned in the direction of more radical action. This was more or less the composition of the group when the decision was made to begin the intensive renaming campaign at the end of December 1984.[20] Lasting from late December 1984 until February 1985, this operation was well planned and thought out solely on the organizational/practical level, as could be seen from the way numerous groups were launched into action in full force, including all units of the administrative machine, the police, the Interior Ministry troops, even the border guards and other troops in some regions, party functionaries down to the lowest level, activists from various government organizations, other volunteers, as well as the intelligence and other services. Besides these groups, government bodies concerned with education, healthcare, trade and other activities were also engaged in the campaign.[21] Thus, in only two months, more than 800,000 people were administratively "processed" and given new passports. This meant preliminary preparation of hundreds of thousands of personal and other documents, at the same time as the old documents were being confiscated in order to obliterate former identities (including that of deceased fathers, mothers, grandmothers, and grandfathers).

The impersonal, grim rituals of administrative registration were almost the same as those employed during 1970–1973 with the Pomaks. In more than a few locales, they were again accompanied by the rattling of sabers and shots fired into the air; armored vehicles and tanks were brought into action,

322 *From de-Stalinization to regime consolidation*

while military marches and countless other methods were used to persuade, frighten or break the spirits of resisting Muslims. The entire procedure was typically capped off by a *horo*, or line dance, in the center of the village, which the "revivalists" and the "revived" were expected to perform together. Blood was once again spilled, which would take on both moral and symbolic as well as very real political significance during and after the "Revival Process." Collective protests and resistance were strongest in Benkovski, Gruevo, Momchilgrad, Dzhebel (near Kârdzhali), Krepcha and Golyamo Gradishte (near Târgovishte), Yablanovo (near Kotel), and elsewhere.[22] In certain places, demonstrators were fired upon, and some were killed; the first victim died on December 24 in the village of Mlechino near Ardino. The death of a seventeen-month-old girl, Tyurkyan, who died during a protest on December 26, 1984, near the village of Mogilyane in the Kirkovo municipality, received the widest public response. Other victims died as a result of the physical violence they suffered; hundreds were sent to camps preventatively or following acts of resistance, while still others were forcibly resettled to the interior of the country, either individually or with their families.[23] Just as during the renaming campaign from the 1970s, it has proven very difficult to indicate the exact number of casualties. On the one hand, this is due to the fact that the true cause of death was not indicated anywhere on victims' death certificates, while on the other hand, the majority of victims died later, as the injuries they suffered led to other illnesses or simply accelerated the progression of previously existing conditions. Estimates placing the number of victims at around fifty (including those who died during the May Events) seem realistic.

It is not the number of victims, however, that most clearly expresses the Bulgarian Turks' terrible suffering during the "Revival Process." The normalized practices of daily pressure on their cultural and religious identity turned out to have far graver consequences. In the spirit of the Orwellian "newspeak" adopted by the regime, the ethnonym "Turks" disappeared completely, replaced by phrases such as "Bulgarians with restored names," "Turkish-speaking Bulgarian Muslims," "citizens with troubled ethnic self-awareness," and so on. Speaking Turkish in public was forbidden, while offenders were fined various amounts. The authorities intensified their crackdown on various types of traditional clothing, Islamic religious rituals, and, in general, all forms of demonstrating "otherness."

Notes

1 Maria Todorova, "Ethnicity, Nationalism and the Communist Legacy in Eastern Europe," *East European Politics and Societies*, 7 (1) (1997): 135–154, p. 146.
2 Michail Gruev, *Mezhdu petolâchkata i polumesetsa: Bâlgarite myusyulmani i politicheskiyat rezhim, 1944–1959*, Sofia: Kota, 2003, pp. 202–204.
3 DA Blagoevgrad, f. 2B, op. 1, a. e. 583, l. 1–3.
4 DA Blagoevgrad, f. 2B, op. 1, a. e. 583, l. 3.
5 TsDA, f. 1B, op. 6, a. e. 4749, l. 15–17.

Pressure on Muslim communities 323

6 TsDA, f. 1B, op. 6, a. e. 4749, l. 15–17.
7 Gruev and Kalyonski, *Vâzroditelniyat protses*, pp. 52–55.
8 Bulletin No. 5 of the Central Committee of the BCP, August 1970.
9 *Decision of the Secretariat of the Central Committee of the BKP for further work on the national consciousness of Bulgarians of Muslim faith*, Sofia: July 17, 1970 (special edition), pp. 2–44.
10 Gruev and Kalyonski, *Vâzroditelniyat protses*, pp. 77–79.
11 H. Poulton, *The Balkans: Minorities and States in Conflict*, London: Minority Rights Publications, 1993, pp. 112–117.
12 A. Lilov, "Da izdignem ideologicheskata rabota na visotata na zadachite, postaveni ot Desetiya kongres i novata programa na partiyata za izgrazhdane na razvito sotsialistichesko obshtestvo," *Rabotnichesko delo*, February 11, 1974, continuation on February 15, 1974.
13 V. Stoyanov, *Turskoto naselenie v Bâlgariya mezhdu polyusite na etnicheskata politika*, Sofia: Lik, 1998, pp. 142–144.
14 Stoyanov, *Turskoto naselenie*, pp. 142–144.
15 Stoyanov, *Turskoto naselenie*, pp. 142–144.
16 Stoyanov, *Turskoto naselenie*, p. 156; E. Ivanova, *Othvârlenite "priobshteni" ili protsesât, narechen "vâzroditelen" (1912–1989)*, Sofia: Institut za iztochnoevropeyska humanitaristika, 2002, pp. 165–166.
17 Ivanova, *Othvârlenite "priobshteni,"* pp. 159–174.
18 P. Gocheva, *Prez Bosfora kâm vâzroditelniya protses*, Sofia: b. d. i., pp. 112–123.
19 A. Aleksandrov, *Zapiski ot sledstvieto: Spomeni i razmisli*, Sofia: Geya libris, 2010, pp. 84–90.
20 I. Yalâmov, *Istoriya na turskata obshtnost v Bâlgariya*, Sofia: Ilinda – Evtimov, 2002, pp. 392–400.
21 Yalâmov, *Istoriya na turskata obshtnost v Bâlgariya*, p. 396.
22 O. Halif and D. Tsankova, "Apokrifnata Yablanska epopeya: Apogeyat na sâprotivata sreshtu 'vâzroditelniya protses,'" *Sedem* (March 23–29, 2005); "Apokrifnata Yablanska epopeya II: Bâlgari i turtsi zaedno se vâzpraviha sreshtu diktaturata na Todor Zhivkov," *Sedem* (March 30–April 5, 2005).
23 *Istinata za "vâzroditelniya protses": Dokumenti ot arhiva na Politbyuro i TsK na BKP*, Sofia: Institut za izsledvane na integratsiyata, 2003, pp. 9, 185–188.

17 The church on the periphery of society

The communist period dramatically changed the traditional relations between the church and the state in Bulgaria. In the popular literature, the opinion can be found that the orthodox churches relatively easily accepted their subordination to the communist state due to traditional "caesaropapist" relations. Such an argument is highly exaggerated, however, and is difficult to support with historical facts – on the one hand, because traditional caesaropapism includes the presence of a "Caesar" who is Christian or who at least recognizes the role of religion, whereas such a figure does not exist within the totalitarian atheist state; while on the other hand, because in the early years of the communist period the higher clergy in the Bulgarian church made conscious and active efforts to defend their autonomy. It was only after the 1950s – when the communist state managed to win over the majority of the members of the Synod using alternating strategies of open repression and infiltration by agents – that the state began to demand active collaboration from the church along two basic lines: the distribution of "patriotic propaganda" among Bulgarian émigré communities and support for the communist system as a whole.

Christian churches: a struggle to survive under Stalinism

In theory, the Bulgarian communist state's relationship toward religious denominations was founded on the postulate the religion was incompatible with materialist communist ideology. In practice, religious policy in Bulgaria imitated measures taken in the Soviet Union after 1917, without reaching the extremes seen in the early Bolshevik period, such as the widespread destruction of churches. The goal of the communist state was to marginalize the various religious denominations to such an extent that they would become invisible to society without formally banning them.

The communist regime's attitude toward the Orthodox Church was most clearly expressed in the policy speech made by the communist dictator Georgi Dimitrov during celebrations marking the 1,000-year anniversary of the death of the most famous Bulgarian saint, St. John of Rila, at Rila monastery on May 26, 1946. In this speech, the communist leader did not hide his contempt for the church and outlined the main elements of the party's basic policy toward it: the church would receive the right to exist within the new society, but only because of its historical contributions to the preservation of the Bulgarian national identity. The speech clearly differentiated between "progressive" and "conservative" clergy, demanding the loyalty of the "progressives" and threatening the "conservatives" with punishment, even citing the repression against the Russian Orthodox Church immediately after the Bolshevik Revolution.[1]

In large part, the integration of the Orthodox Church into the communist state was aided by the traditional and widely held view of the church even before 1944 as a purely national institution that carried out the policy of the national state government. In addition to such historical grounds, this view of the church was also strengthened by the division of Bulgarian society into a Christian (Orthodox) majority and a Muslim minority, with Bulgarians usually self-identifying as Orthodox Christians, and ethnic Turks as Muslims. The communist state took advantage of this conception and turned it into one of the leading principles in its policy. The church was not formally shut down, but the attitude toward it was as if toward a dying institution, which could only function as a "national museum" or "cultural monument" – which is precisely what the monasteries and churches were turned into. It was precisely this narrow nationalistic conception of the church, along with active atheist propaganda, that formed the basis for the forced secularization of Bulgarian society. Despite the fact that the results of this secularization may be similar to the results of the secularization of every other modernizing society, in this case it is a question of a policy deliberately imposed by a totalitarian state, which did not allow for any other outcome besides the gradual "dying out" of the church and religion.

The main means used to implement this policy of marginalization of religious denominations consisted of formulating and legislating the principle of "separating the church from the state." This principle became the cornerstone of the 1949 Law on Religious Denominations, which proclaimed religious freedoms (at the beginning of each article) and then limited them (in the second sentence in each article). The Orthodox Church, as well as all the other denominations, was affected by the laws nationalizing urban property and agricultural land, which until then had been its basic source of income. An annual state subsidy was introduced to compensate for this financial deficit. The state proclaimed the principle of separation but at the same time deprived the large religious denominations of their basic sources of income and replaced them with state subsidies, whose "engaging effect" it greatly counted on. This concept of "separating the church from the state" also fulfilled an important propagandistic function – it was often used as an argument against those who criticized the lack of religious freedoms. The true goal of this principle was to separate the church from society and to draw a clearly demarcated boundary between the party and the church.

On a more tangible level, the policy of "separating the church from the state" found expression in the announcement during 1945 that civil marriage

326   *From de-Stalinization to regime consolidation*

was the only legally recognized form of marriage in the country, while religious marriage retained the status of a ritual, which could not be performed unless the civil marriage had been concluded first. The study of religion was eliminated from school curricula the same year. In 1950, the two existing seminaries were combined into one, which was moved from the center of Sofia to a distant monastery, while the Theology Department was removed from the state university and reorganized into a theological academy subordinate to the Holy Synod.

The wave of repression from 1944 until the mid-1950s affected all major religious denominations, even though different strategies were taken against them. The attitude toward the higher clergy (metropolitans and bishops) of the Orthodox Church was relatively mild, whereas the leaders of the other Christian denominations (Catholics and Protestants) fell victim to show trials and accusations of espionage. A significant portion of the parish priests from the Orthodox Church were repressed, being imprisoned in labor camps or sentenced to prison terms of varying length. They were among the victims of the first wave of repression that began immediately after the coup of September 9, 1944. The People's Court also did not pass over the clergy – according to the Legal Ordinance on Judgments by the People's Court, a total of 152 Orthodox clergymen were sentenced – thirteen to death, and another thirteen to life in prison.[2]

After a certain lull in persecutions, the stabilization of the new regime's international position during 1947–1948 was one of the factors allowing a new wave of repression to be unleashed against the opposition, including the church. The other, more important, reason was Moscow's failure to create an "Orthodox Vatican," which would be aimed against the Western states and which would include all Orthodox churches. After the failure of the plan in the summer of 1948, the Moscow Patriarchate and the other Orthodox churches lost their significance in Stalin's larger game. This was the reason for the new wave of repression against the Russian church, which automatically transferred to Bulgaria as well. The period immediately following the summer of 1948 until the death of Stalin was the most brutal with respect to the church in Bulgaria. This new wave of violence began on November 8, 1948, with the murder of one of the most influential, anti-communist members of the Holy Synod, the Nevrokop Metropolitan Boris, who was shot by a defrocked priest after the end of a liturgy. On the whole, however, the victims of the new wave of repression were again primarily parish priests. In the fall of 1948, the Committee on Church Affairs turned to local authorities with a request to prepare and send in written profiles of all parish priests. After generalizing from the data about them, the Committee divided the priests into eight categories based on their attitude toward the regime. Of 2,063 local priests, 1,600 were categorized as being negatively disposed toward the regime to some degree or other, while only 400 priests were declared to have a positive attitude toward the new government.[3] These characteristics were turned into grounds for the subsequent new campaign of repression, which led to at least 10 percent of all priests in the Bulgaria at the time being imprisoned or sent to labor camps.

In 1948–1949, the government seriously considered, but in the end rejected, the most radical ideas for repressing the higher clergy, including shutting down whole dioceses or imposing a "retirement age" on metropolitans. A milder yet nevertheless effective strategy was adopted, which concentrated on shattering the unity of the Holy Synod. Its members were divided into "extreme reactionaries" and those whose weaknesses and ambitions could be used by the government – they were labeled "progressive" and were put forth as the state's favorites. In the period of 1949–1951, negotiations were also held with the state concerning the new Statute of the Bulgarian Orthodox Church, which came into force on January 4, 1951. In the course of the negotiations, the Synod managed to withstand government pressure and to guarantee that metropolitans retain their status for life, which at that time was seen as an obstacle to direct government interference. In the end, the church's new statute, adopted in January 1951, preserved church traditions and the church's internal democratism, at least in theory. But by the end of communist period, these formulations had become little more than empty words.

Other Christian denominations were also targets of repression during this period. Bulgarian Protestants and Catholics fell victim to the classic show trials characteristic of the Stalinist period. Their leaders were accused of espionage, and some were condemned to death while others served prison terms of varying lengths. These trials had a serious and long-lasting negative effect on these communities throughout the whole communist period since their religious life was significantly curtailed, without ever being formally banned.

The leaders of traditional Protestant denominations were the victims of the first show trial. This trial lasted from February 25 until March 8, 1949, and included fifteen Protestant pastors as defendants. The leaders of various Protestant faiths were sentenced to life in prison: Vasil Zyapkov (of the Evangelical Cathedral and Chairman of the United Evangelical Churches), Yanko Ivanov (Methodist), Nikola Mihaylov (Baptist), and Georgi Chernev (Pentacostal). The remaining eleven defendants received prison sentences of varying length.

Why were representatives of non-traditional faiths the target of "judicial" terror in Bulgaria? On the one hand, the communist regime was not worried that the show trials against representatives of minority religions would lead to the alienation of large groups of believers. On the other hand, the reason can be sought in the particular circles and networks of contacts in which Bulgarian Protestants held sway. Arising in the second half of the nineteenth century as a result of missionary activity by pastors from the United States and Great Britain, Bulgarian Protestants managed to form tight communities during the 1920s and 1930s, which gradually began to spread from villages to include the active urban intelligentsia. The leaders of these communities were well-educated people who had extensive contact with foreigners, especially Americans and Englishmen, which made them suspicious in the communist authorities' eyes.

328 *From de-Stalinization to regime consolidation*

Almost all the pastors convicted during that trial served their full sentences. Only the life sentences were reduced to fifteen-year prison terms, as a result of which by the early 1960s all the Protestant pastors had been released. Some of them were even allowed to return to their pastoral duties but now in a completely changed political and social context in which the Protestant churches in Bulgaria were already carefully controlled by State Security. Of all those convicted in such trials, the brothers Haralan and Ladin Popov subsequently became the most prominent figures. After his release from prison in 1962, Haralan Popov was allowed to leave the country and emigrate, first to Sweden and later to the United States. Shortly thereafter, his brother also managed to leave Bulgaria illegally. From abroad, Haralan Popov created the organization Evangelism to Communist Lands and won great notoriety for his campaign in defense of religious freedoms within Eastern Bloc countries; Bulgarian State Security's constant interest in his "hostile" activities bears witness to this. Haralan Popov died in the United States in November 1988, several months after the Bulgarian authorities had allowed him to visit his homeland as part of the political framework of *perestroika*.

Among the representatives of various religious faiths in Bulgaria, those who suffered the worst fates were Bulgarian Catholics, both from the so-called Uniate Churches (the Catholic Church of the Eastern Rite), as well as from the Catholic Church of the Western Rite. They were also representatives of minority faiths, which made them convenient targets for communist repression. Although they were persecuted even in the earliest period of communist rule, trials against Catholics escalated in the summer of 1952, when forty priests, bishops, and monks were arrested during July. The trial ended in death sentences for Bishop Evgeniy Bosilkov of Nikopol and the priests Kamen Vichev, Pavel Dzhidzhov, and Yosafat Shishkov, who were executed on November 11, 1952. The other Catholic clergymen received prison sentences varying from three to twenty years. In the following years, the Bulgarian Catholic Church of the Eastern Rite avoided the fate of the other Eastern European Uniate Churches (which were shut down or merged with local Orthodox churches, the best example of this being Ukraine), but over the subsequent decades the organizational life of the Bulgarian Uniate Churches was reduced to a minimum. Trials against Catholics soured relations between Bulgaria and the Vatican for a lengthy period, while steps taken by the Vatican over the following decades to grant Bulgarian Catholics greater freedoms met with disapproval from the official state government in Bulgaria.[4] The full historical rehabilitation of Bulgarian Catholics came in 1998 when Bishop Evgeniy Bosilkov and three other priests were declared venerable martyrs of the Catholic Church by Pope John Paul II.

Elevation of the international status of the Bulgarian Orthodox Church

The Bulgarian Exarchate was established in 1870, during the final years of Ottoman rule in Bulgaria. At that time, it was officially acknowledged by the

The church on the periphery of society   329

Ottoman state, but not by the Ecumenical Patriarchate. In 1872, the latter declared the Bulgarian church schismatic; as a result, none of the other Orthodox churches maintained contact with it. Expectations that this question would soon be resolved were the reason that the Synod of the Exarchate was headed by a chairman ad interim, and not by an exarch after 1915. Immediately after 1944, the reason that the state supported the Bulgarian Exarchate's attempts to solve the problem of its international status lay in Moscow's plans to create a group of loyal churches and to use them on the international level. Moreover, the formal obstacles to reconciliation with the Ecumenical Patriarchate no longer existed; the first step toward this would be lifting the schism, with the ultimate goal being the elevation of the Bulgarian church into a patriarchate. On January 21, 1945, the Sofia Metropolitan Bishop Stefan was chosen as the new exarch; he was one of the most authoritative members of the higher clergy known as an active ecumenical figure, an opponent of the Bulgarian state's pre-1944 policy of close ties with Nazi Germany and a participant in the campaign to save Bulgarian Jews in 1943. His election as exarch provided new impetus for negotiations with the Ecumenical Patriarchate, which ended in success; on February 22, 1945, Constantinople officially lifted the schism and granted the Bulgarian Exarchate autocephalous status.

As the head of the church over the next three years, Exarch Stefan faced the difficult task of balancing the metropolitans' insistence that the church's autonomy be defended from government pressure with his desire to retain the support of the Bulgarian government and the Russian church in the drive to elevate him to Patriarch. At the same time, his election as exarch destroyed the absolute equality that had existed between the individual metropolitans on the Synod until that moment, while Stefan's desire to establish himself as the sole leader of the church earned him accusations of dictatorial behavior. Clashes between members of the Synod were skillfully exploited and fanned by the state, leading to a conflict whose resolution came about during the autumn of 1948.

In July 1948, Exarch Stefan went to Moscow to take part in the Moscow Meeting of Orthodox Churches, at which an unsuccessful attempt was made to create an "Orthodox Vatican."[5] The project failed because the other traditional Orthodox cathedras – in Constantinople, Alexandria, Antioch, and Jerusalem, supported by Athens – refused to back Moscow's idea, which would have meant recognizing the leading role of the Muscovite Patriarchate in the Orthodox world. At the meeting, Exarch Stefan took up Moscow's line, expecting in exchange to be enthroned as Patriarch during the meeting itself.[6] The negotiations with the Russian church on this question were kept secret from the Synod in Sofia, however, and it was only during the exarch's stay in Moscow that the Bulgarian state requested that the Synod approve Stefan's enthronement as Patriarch.[7] The metropolitans, however, silently refused to provide such a confirmation.

After Exarch Stefan's return from Moscow, the situation both on the political and the ecclesiastical levels had completely changed. Matters came to

330 *From de-Stalinization to regime consolidation*

a head during a stormy meeting of the Holy Synod on September 6, 1948, at the end of which the exarch tendered his resignation. He was counting on the element of surprise and hoped that his resignation would not be accepted either by the Synod or the government, which would further strengthen his position and his candidacy for patriarch. To his surprise, his resignation was unanimously accepted by the Synod on September 8, with the argument that he had displayed an "autocratic," "lordly" and "despotic" attitude.[8] Immediately thereafter, his resignation was also confirmed by the government. The former exarch was exiled to a village far from the capital, where he lived until his death in 1957. This led to a return to the synodal form of governing the church, which for the next five years was once again headed by the Chairman ad Interim of the Synod.

The approval of the new statute opened the way for the procedure for calling an Ecclesiastical National Council, which would declare the Bulgarian church a patriarchate and at which a patriarch would be elected. The statute stipulated holding a three-stage election process, in which parish boards of trustees would elect so-called diocesan electors, who on their part had the right to elect a new metropolitan in case a metropolitan chair became vacant, as well as to elect members of the Ecclesiastical National Council, which would vote for the new patriarch. These elections were held in 1952 and were carefully controlled by the government. Such activities, however, divided the metropolitans who were members of the Holy Synod into two clear camps: those who were loyal to the state's announced favorite for patriarch, the Plovdiv Metropolitan Kiril, and the opposition, which defended the idea of continuing the synodal governance of the church and delaying the election of a patriarch. The opposition held the majority until 1952, since it was supported by five of the nine members of the Synod. This made the election of a new Metropolitan of Nevrokop a crucial battle, in which the state and Metropolitan Kiril supported the candidacy of Bishop Pimen. His confirmation as metropolitan was blocked by the opposition on the Synod until December 30, 1952, when he finally officially assumed his new post as Metropolitan of Nevrokop. This evened out the votes on the Synod. State Security documents show that during that period, the Nevrokop Metropolitan Pimen was already a State Security collaborator whose code name was "Patriarch."[9]

Thus, the Ecclesiastical National Council finally came about, and it passed unproblematically from the point of view of the state. Called on May 8, 1953, the council first proclaimed the Bulgarian church a patriarchate, and then transformed itself into a patriarchal electoral council, which on May 10, 1953, elected the Plovdiv Metropolitan Kiril as the new Bulgarian patriarch. The decision was immediately acknowledged by Orthodox churches with close ties to Moscow. The Ecumenical Patriarchate, however, refused to approve this election, since its consent for elevating the status of the Bulgarian church had not been sought in advance. This again led to a cooling of relations with Constantinople, which were finally normalized on July 27, 1961, when the Ecumenical Patriarchate officially recognized the Bulgarian Patriarchate.

The church on the periphery of society 331

With the elevation of the status of the Bulgarian Orthodox Church and the election of the new patriarch, a new model of relations between the church and state in communist Bulgaria was imposed, a model personalized by Patriarch Kiril and the Chairman of the Committee for Church Affairs, Mihail Kyuchukov. The essence of this model lay in the state's readiness to support and increase the prestige of the Patriarch at the expense of the other members of the Holy Synod, by taking into consideration the Patriarch's opinions about the most important nominations within the church hierarchy. To further this goal, the state was also inclined to make small concessions to the opposition within the Synod, while at the same time continuing its active, atheistic propaganda campaign and its administrative restrictions on local clergy. In the years following Kiril's election as Patriarch, the opposition against him remained quite influential, since it included some of the most authoritative members of the Synod, but such opposition did not have the opportunity to reverse the overall course of church–state relations. Moreover, time was working against the opposition, as it was made up of elderly metropolitans, who over the course of several decades were gradually replaced by the next generation of clergy who did not have the authority to oppose the policies of the communist state.

The isolation of the Bulgarian Orthodox Church under Patriarch Kiril (1953–1971) and Patriarch Maxim

Paradoxically, isolation became the fundamental characteristic of the newly founded Bulgarian Patriarchate. The reason for this lay not so much in relations with the Ecumenical Patriarchate, which were once again deteriorating in the period before 1961, but rather was due to the fact that the Bulgarian Patriarchate fell under the full control of Moscow and the communist state. This isolation was a crucial factor in the Bulgarian church's subsequent marginalization, since it was imposed during the most critical phase of relations between the church and state, when opposition in the Synod was still strong, yet lacked external support. Whereas in the period before 1944, the Bulgarian church had been an active member of the ecumenical movement, in 1948 it supported Moscow and refused to take part in the founding assembly of the World Council of Churches (WCC). The Bulgarian Patriarchate's subsequent return to the WCC as a member in 1961 could not reverse its tendency toward isolation, since its ecumenical structures were controlled and directed by the state.

After Patriarch Kiril was elected in 1953, the authorities took it upon themselves to "support and strengthen his position and prestige," by turning him into a key figure in relations between the Holy Synod and the state.[10] Patriarch Kiril had been an authoritative member of the higher clergy even before 1944, thus he symbolized continuity within the church tradition. At the same time, the authorities continued to actively interfere with the election of the higher clergy; however, they carried out this policy carefully, taking the Patriarch's opinion

332 *From de-Stalinization to regime consolidation*

into consideration. During the 1950s and 1960s, this made it possible for the "reactionary" members of the Synod to be "naturally" replaced by a new generation of higher clergy that was considered more or less loyal to the regime.

During the 1950s and 1960s, several important reforms were carried out within the Bulgarian church, which influenced religious life over the following decades. At the end of 1968, the Holy Synod introduced calendrical reform, rejecting the Julian calendar, which was traditionally used by Orthodox churches, and adopting the so-called "New Julian Calendar" (which was, in fact, the Gregorian one), which was already used in secular practice, as well as by several Orthodox churches, including by the Ecumenical Patriarchate. According to archival documents, the goal of this reform was to support the Russian church's efforts to adopt the new calendar, in addition to facilitating the Bulgarian church's international contacts and ecumenical activity.[11]

Religious education, church publications and monasticism suffered severe blows during these years. In the early 1950s, the state imposed strict control over the Seminary and Theological Academy's study programs, and both educational institutions were filled with State Security agents. Publications of church literature were restricted to 1,600 pages annually, which were subject to censorship, as were the church's periodical publications.[12] In 1956, following orders from the Committee on Church Affairs, all religious libraries were "purged" of "reactionary books."[13]

The fate of Bulgaria's largest and most important monastery, Rila Monastery, was indicative of the state of the church as a whole. In 1961, the monastery was nationalized and turned into a museum.[14] In 1968, some monks returned to Rila; however, they were under explicit orders to perform church services only when the monastery was closed to tourists.[15] Throughout the whole communist period, there was an unwritten law against the construction of new churches in the country. Moreover, one of the indirect results of forced urbanization in Bulgaria was the decline of the church's system of parishes as a result of the abandonment of the old village churches. At the end of the 1950s, the state began keeping track of who visited churches, requiring employees of the Committee on Church Affairs to attend religious services and to inform the authorities in writing about who came to church, as well as to report on opinions expressed by the priests during services.

Patriarch Kiril died on March 7, 1971. The following day, the Politburo of the Central Committee of the BCP, acting on a suggestion from the Committee on Church Affairs, decided to support the Lovech Metropolitan Maxim as the candidate for Patriarch at the upcoming Ecclesiastical Council.[16] Four months later, Maxim was chosen as the new Patriarch at the Ecclesiastical Council held on July 4, 1971. The support of the Communist Party, however, provided grounds for his elevation to Patriarch to be questioned both at the time of the election itself, as well as in the early 1990s, and affected his entire tenure and his authority within the Synod.

Until the end of the communist period, he was forced to try to maintain a balance between the two factions within the higher clergy. The first consisted of the old metropolitans, whose goal was to preserve church tradition. The second faction was that of the metropolitans closest to the regime, who gradually became an alternative center of power. Paradoxically, the disunity among the higher clergy allowed the Synod to reestablish its collective character.

In the beginning of the 1970s, the Committee on Church Affairs ceased to be the main institution responsible for determining state policy toward the church, since that task was being assumed by the various departments within State Security to an ever greater extent. The new patriarch was not always consulted, even in the nominations of future metropolitans. This laid the foundation for the most serious conflict between the church and the state during the communist period, which unfolded in 1974 around the election of a new metropolitan of Vratsa. The state decided to support Bishop Kalinik as their "official candidate" in the elections, who was described as "a loyal and progressive clergyman [. . .] far more suited than the other bishops to carry out the specific duties Orthodox clergymen must fulfill in the church's domestic and international activities."[17] Despite expectations that Kalinik would be chosen, during the elections held on June 21, 1974, the diocesan electors proposed that the Holy Synod confirm Bishop Arseniy as the new metropolitan. This decision set off a true firestorm, with the Committee on Church Affairs going so far as to complain that the Patriarch had failed to take an active position in support of the "official candidate." In the end, the Synod was forced to acquiesce to state pressure; the election of Bishop Arseniy was annulled on fabricated grounds, while the diocesan electors were replaced. The new elections, which were held on November 10, 1974, went according to plan, and Bishop Kalinik was "elected" and confirmed as the new metropolitan of Vratsa.

The most important event during Patriarch Maxim's reign was the campaign to impose "civil rituals," which was marked by a new wave of administrative repression against parish priests. This campaign had its roots in the previous decade. In 1962, the state commissioned a massive sociological study on the population's attitude toward religion. The results were finally published in 1968 under the title "The Process of Overcoming Religion in Bulgaria."[18] According to the report, officially only 35 percent of the population declared themselves religious, with the majority of believers belonging to poorly educated and elderly social groups; they also largely included the rural population and women.[19] These results, however, contradicted data about the basic religious rituals that were being performed: 52 percent of all newborns were baptized in the church, 36 percent of couples had church weddings in addition to obligatory civil ceremonies, while the results for religious funerals were the most surprising, accounting for more than 80 percent of all funerals conducted.[20]

In response, the state issued a series of ordinances in the 1970s designed to restrict religious rituals. The campaign had two basic aims: first, to administratively impose civil rituals in the narrow sense of the word – civil marriages, civil "baptisms" and secular funerals – which had been created as replacements for the corresponding religious rituals. In the early 1980s, the campaign gradually

334   *From de-Stalinization to regime consolidation*

developed its second aim – the imposition of a "new socialist holiday system," whose goal was to abolish holidays rooted in religious tradition and to replace them with so-called "revised holidays."

The campaign was successful to a certain extent. According to statistics, in 1980, only 40.7 percent of newborns were baptized, while a mere 4.52 percent of marriages included a church ceremony. Religious funerals remained the most popular ritual, but even their numbers fell that year to 47.9 percent of all burials. At the same time, a series of state and academic institutions were assigned the task of inventing and imposing "revised holidays," whose basic goal was to replace the religious meaning of certain holidays, especially those from the paschal cycle. Another invention from that period was the practice of the one and only state television station broadcasting Western films or show programs on the evening before Easter (when most Bulgarians had traditionally gone to church), as was the idea of having children dye eggs on the first day of spring rather than on Easter.[21] Attempts were made to impose new holidays devoid of religious content at the same time as traditional church holidays were celebrated.

Local authorities were assigned the task of imposing the new civil rituals; as a result, parish priests were subjected to arbitrary administrative harassment that was difficult for the central authorities to control. In 1984, one official from the Committee on Church Affairs offered the following general recommendation at a special meeting with local officials: "the best thing a priest can do is to do nothing."[22] During the 1970s and 1980s, the policies from the preceding period remained in effect with respect to monasteries and churches. During the 1970s and 1980s, the state continued its policy of turning Bulgaria's large monasteries into museums; the Rozhen monastery, for example, also suffered this fate.

All of this provided grounds for Patriarch Maxim to be sharply criticized after 1990 for his failure to defend the church's autonomy during the communist era. Despite the fact that much of this criticism is fully justified, we must not lose sight of the fact that under the totalitarian conditions of the time, defending the church's autonomy was a nearly impossible task. By avoiding direct confrontation with the state, Patriarch Maxim personified the bureaucratic skills developed by the higher clergy during the 1970s and 1980s with respect to the communist state in order to partially preserve church tradition.

The Bulgarian Orthodox Church's international and ecumenical activities

The participation of the Bulgarian Orthodox Church in ecumenical organizations (such as the WCC, the Christian Peace Conference, and the Conference of European Churches) during the communist period was initiated, directed, and controlled by the state, primarily through State Security. If State Security was popularly described as a state within a state, then the ecumenical

The church on the periphery of society 335

activity of the church could be described as a church within a church. In this respect, the Bulgarian church was part of the larger Soviet aim to infiltrate the ecumenical religious organizations, to fill their leading positions with sympathizers of the Soviet system and, finally, to utilize these organizations for the purposes of communist propaganda, especially with regard to the so-called Third World countries.

The churches of Eastern Europe (with the exception of Catholic churches) joined the WCC in 1961. Proof that this occurred at the state's prompting is the fact that on February 22, 1961, the Bulgarian intelligence services sent a telegram to their agents abroad declaring the WCC an "object to be infiltrated" and ordering them to begin gathering information about it.[23] State Security likewise chose and sent the first Bulgarians participants to specialized ecumenical study programs abroad in the early 1960s; these same individuals subsequently became the leading ecumenical activists within the Bulgarian church.

Beginning in the early 1960s, the Eastern Bloc countries established a well-organized system for coordinating and unifying the action of their churches within ecumenical organizations. At the state level, this policy was coordinated by the Committees on Church Affairs, which regularly consulted with one another; at the level of the church, the Departments for Ecumenical and Pacifist Activities within the administrations of the respective participating churches were in charge of such coordination. The Leningrad Metropolitan Nicodemus (known at the KGB by his codename "Adamant") occupied the top of this pyramid during the 1970s.[24] Beginning in the early 1970s, his partner on the Bulgarian side was the Metropolitan Pancratiy of Stara Zagora, the leader of the Department for Ecumenical Activities within the Bulgarian Patriarchate, who had been recruited as a collaborator by Bulgarian State Security in 1971 under the codename "Boyko."[25] Thanks to its close relations with the Moscow Patriarchate, the Bulgarian church was able to establish itself as one of the most influential members of the ecumenical organizations; its greatest success in this regard was the 1979 election of Todor Sâbev as Deputy General Secretary of the WCC. Archival documents state that in this election, "the representatives of the Russian Orthodox Church, who prepared him extensively, deserve a great deal of credit."[26] Other archival data suggest directly after his election to the post of Deputy General Secretary, the Bulgarian secret services turned to the KGB with a request for assistance in helping Sâbev carry out his duties.[27]

The history of the Bulgarian diocese in North America and Australia is indicative of the communist authorities' utilitarian attitude toward the church. During the whole communist era, the Bulgarian authorities tried to impose their control over the Bulgarian churches in the United States, Canada, and Australia by restricting the spirit of democratism within them so as to be able to use them for propagandistic purposes.

Created in the late 1930s mainly by Bulgarian emigrants from the Macedonian outlands, the Bulgarian diocese in North America and Australia

336 *From de-Stalinization to regime consolidation*

from the very beginning was self-financed, which rendered it independent of the Bulgarian state. After 1944, anti-communist emigrants were elected to the parish boards of these churches, which only nominally accepted the jurisdiction of the Bulgarian Orthodox Church. Over the following decades, this was the reason that all metropolitans of this diocese, who were appointed from Sofia, were constantly forced to attempt to strike a balance between the emigrants' anti-communist sentiments and the communist government's desire to subordinate these churches to Sofia's plans. The impossibility of permanently maintaining such a balance led to several consecutive divisions of the diocese, which were encouraged and sometimes even instigated by the state.

In 1947, Bishop Andrey, who had been sent in 1938 to organize the diocese in America, was unanimously elected as metropolitan of the united Bulgarian eparchy. However, his sympathies for the anti-communists were the reason that his election remained unrecognized by Sofia until 1963. In that year, he decided to return to the jurisdiction of the Bulgarian Orthodox Church, causing half of the Bulgarian parishes that were dominated by Macedonian emigrants and anti-communist parish boards to break away into an independent diocese led by Archimandrite Kirill Yonchev. In 1964, Kirill Yonchev accepted the jurisdiction of the Russian Orthodox Church Abroad, which consecrated him as bishop. In 1977, Kirill, along with his whole diocese, went over to the Orthodox Church in America (OCA), which had received autocephalous status in 1970 from the Moscow Patriarchate. In this way, the Bulgarian religious community in America found itself divided into two equal halves, one of which accepted the jurisdiction of the Bulgarian Orthodox Church, while the other fell under that of the OCA.

In 1970, however, the diocese that had remained under the jurisdiction of the Bulgarian Orthodox Church further divided into two separate dioceses: one headquartered in New York, and the other in Akron, Ohio. This split was instigated by the communist state, which was trying to limit the influence of Metropolitan Andrey, whom it continued to view with distrust. Even after Andrey's death in 1972, the two separate dioceses remained in existence until the end of the communist period. The diocese in New York, which consisted of only a single parish, was headed by a metropolitan (initially Andrey, and later Yosif Dikov) who was respected by emigrants but whom the state distrusted. The metropolitan was to play the role of a façade before the émigré community, but he was, in fact, deprived of any real power. The center of Bulgarian religious life shifted to Akron, Ohio, where the diocese was administered by a bishop who enjoyed the state's trust. This diocese included all the other Bulgarian parishes in the United States, Canada, and Australia. The diocese led by Kirill Yonchev remained part of the OCA, even after Kirill's death in 2007.

The Western European diocese, unlike the churches in North America and Australia, did not pose problems to the Bulgarian state. The diocese was founded in the late 1970s and early 1980s with the support of Bulgarian embassies in the respective countries, which carefully selected members of parish boards of trustees who were loyal to the Bulgarian state.

Another institution abroad with difficult relations with the communist state was the St. George the Zograf Monastery on Mount Athos. Regarded spiritually as part of the Bulgarian Orthodox Church and inhabited by Bulgarian monks, the monastery is on Greek territory and under the jurisdiction of the Ecumenical Patriarchate. Under communism, the state saw the monastery as a national museum beyond Bulgaria's borders that contained important documents and manuscripts. The concept of monastic self-governance remained completely inconceivable and thus became a source of constant conflicts and arguments with the monastic order there. The state played favorites among the monks there, creating tension and personal conflicts within the monastic brotherhood itself. In response, some of the monks attempted to establish contact with Bulgarian emigrant communities and thus to counteract state pressure. Their attempt was unsuccessful, however, and in the early 1980s the state managed to impose its will on the monastery.

The monks' suspicions toward the Bulgarian state were not unfounded. In 1985, Bulgarian Intelligence Services arranged for the most important manuscript housed at the monastery – the *Istoriya slavyanobulgarska*, a work written in the late eighteenth century which is considered the cornerstone of the Bulgarian Revival – to be stolen and transported to Bulgaria. In the following years, the manuscript remained locked up in the head of the intelligence service's safe. The disclosure of this affair in 1996 stirred up a diplomatic and public scandal that threatened to damage Bulgaria's relations with Greece; for that reason, the decision was made to return the manuscript to the monastery. This scandal became symbolic of the failure of Bulgarian state policy with respect to Zograph monastery and undeservedly compromised attempts on the part of numerous well-intentioned scholars from the communist period to research Zograph's literary treasures.[28]

What were the results of the communist state's decades-long interference in the activities of the Bulgarian Orthodox Church and other denominations? The most visible results, which will take decades to overcome, include the decimation of the church's system of parishes and the discrediting of the higher clergy as a result of state meddling in ecclesiastical elections. From a statistical point of view, the most serious consequence is the sudden plunge in the number of parish priests – the total number of ordinary priests fell from around 2,500 in the mid-1940s to fewer than 1,000 in 1985. There has also been a significant, but not drastic, drop in the number of monks; the total number of monks and nuns fell from around 440 in the mid-1950s to 391 by the late 1970s. Rapid urbanization was also a factor in the marginalization of the church; this, together with the ban on the construction of new churches and the abandonment of village churches, led to the decline of the parish structure, which is the only possible foundation for influential and publicly visible church life. Another important consequence is the widely held utilitarian attitude toward the church, which is seen by the state and society as a

338 *From de-Stalinization to regime consolidation*

bearer of specific national values and interests, at the expense of its universal Christian mission.

From the communist period, we can cite examples both of bishops who tried to preserve the church's autonomy and tradition, as well as those who readily implemented state strategies meant to marginalize the church. However, the preservation of ecclesiastical tradition under the completely adverse conditions of the communist state has turned out to be insufficient for reviving the church and its public image in the post-communist period. Discord among the higher clergy came to the surface in 1992, when arguments about the legitimacy of Patriarch Maxim led to a schism, in which half of the sitting metropolitans refused to accept his election. Ironically, the leaders of this schism were precisely those metropolitans who had the closest ties to the communist state and its security services in the 1970s and 1980s, while much later it was officially confirmed that neither Patriarch Kiril, nor Patriarch Maxim were State Security informers as the schism supporters had claimed with respect to Maxim. Although it formally ended in 2002, for a long time the schism undermined attempts and hopes on the part of many believers to restore the authority and public influence of the Bulgarian Orthodox Church, which, like all other traditional denominations, found itself facing a whole series of new and previously unknown challenges after the fall of communism.

Notes

1 Georgi Dimitrov, "Rolyata i zadachite na bâlgarskata tsârkva," in *Sâchineniya*, vol. 12, Sofia: Izdatelstvo na BKP, 1954, pp. 186–189.
2 For more about repression during that period, see D. Kalkandzhieva, *Bâlgarskata pravoslavna tsârkva i "narodnata demokratsiya" (1944–1953 g.)*, Silistra: Fondatsiya "Demos," 2002, pp. 182–189.
3 AMVnR, f. 10, op. 9, a. e. 248.
4 Zh. Tsvetkov, *Razpyatieto: Sâdebnata razprava s deytsi na katolicheskata cârkva v Bâlgariya prez 1952 g.*, Sofia: n.p., 1994; Sv. Eldârov, *Bâlgariya i Vatikana 1944–1989*, Sofia: Logis, 2002, pp. 13–33.
5 T. Volokitina, G. Murashko, and A. Noskova, *Moskva i Vostochnaya Evropa: Vlasty i tserkovy v period obshtestvennyh transformatsiy 40-50-h godov XX veka*, Moscow: RAN/Russian Academy of Sciences, 2008, pp. 101–102.
6 Volokitina et al., *Moskva i Vostochnaya Evropa*, p. 100.
7 AMVnR, f. 10, op. 9, a. e. 225.
8 AMVnR, f. 10, op. 9, a. e. 204.
9 Arhiv na PGU, DS, f. 4, op. 5, a. e. 38.
10 The phrase was used by the Chairman of the Committee on Church Affairs, Mihail Kyuchukov, in 1955. AMVnR, f. 10, op. 9, a. e. 1024.
11 AMVnR, f. 10, op. 12, a. e. 359.
12 AMVnR, f. 10, op. 9, a. e. 1096.
13 AMVnR, f. 10, op. 12, a. e. 355.
14 AMVnR, f. 10, op. 12, a. e. 180.
15 AMVnR, f. 10, op. 12, a. e. 180.
16 TsDA f. 1 B, op. 35, a. e. 2040.

The church on the periphery of society 339

17 AMVnR, f. 10, op. 13, a. e. 660a.
18 *Protsesât na preodolyavaneto na religiyata v Bâlgariya: Sotsiologichesko izsledvane – Kolektiv pod redaktsiyata na prof. Zhivko Oshavkov*, Sofia: BAS, 1968.
19 *Protsesât na preodolyavaneto na religiyata v Bâlgariya*, p. 205.
20 *Protsesât na preodolyavaneto na religiyata v Bâlgariya*, p. 270.
21 AMVnR, f. 10, op. 13, a. e. 57.
22 AMVnR, f. 10, op. 14, a. e. 1198.
23 Arhiv na PGU, DS, f. 4, op. 8, a. e. 21.
24 K. Andryu and V. Mitrohin, *Taynata istoriya na KGB ili Arhivât na Mitrohin*, Sofia: Trud &Prozorets, 2001, p. 538.
25 Ya. Dimov, *Ne si pravi kumir (Ochertsi za bâlgarski tsârkovni deytsi)*, Vratsa: Poliprint, 1992, p. 187.
26 AMVnR, f. 10, op. 13, a. e. 652.
27 Arhiv na PGU, DS, f. 4, op. 8, a. e. 22.
28 Hristo Hristov, *Operazia 'Maraton': Istinata za Krazhbata na Paisievata Istoria ot Durzhavna Sigurnost v 'Zograf,'* Sofia: Ciela, 2012.

18 Processes within the culture of "real socialism"

Despite the lofty and dramatic calls for renewal after Stalin's death, which were proclaimed at both the Twentieth Congress of the CPSU and the April Plenum of the Central Committee of the BCP, there was no real change in the basic principles and structures governing Bulgarian culture that had been established at the dawn of communist rule. The Ministry of Culture, which was founded in February 1954, did not differ in terms of its structural organization from its predecessor, the Committee for Science, Art and Culture. It continued to function as one of the regime's central ideological institutions, while its standard agency-internal documents also remained unchanged, including organizational instructions, guidelines governing the internal structure and functioning of the Ministry's departments and units, its posts, bureaus, commissions, its regional and district councils for education and culture, regulations for the organization of artistic exhibitions, concerts, theatrical performances, public shows, as well as its censorship activities, and so on.

In early 1957, the Ministry of Public Education and the Ministry of Culture were combined into a single, new Ministry of Education and Culture. At first glance, here, too, we cannot speak of significant changes to its ideological foundations. Despite all that was written about the "April Breeze" at the time, the main images used in the official rhetoric filling the new institution's massive flood of documents were still the same old propagandistic and "politically educational" clichés that had constituted public discourse since the communist coup in 1944.

Nevertheless, the formula "closer to the people, closer to life" arose during this time, serving as a new nucleus for propaganda. It was an attempt to curry support among the newly forming social circles and cultural audiences, which were now different in terms not only of generation but also with respect to education, social status, and cultural attitudes. This shift of emphasis within propaganda gradually made it possible to roll out a new public language and official style of cultural communication – one that did not, however, even for a moment, cast doubt over the unified ideological essence of socialist culture.

Taking into account the years that had passed and the change in generations since the imposition of communist rule, the reworked ideological narratives shifted the emphasis away from the mythology of anti-fascist struggle that had been used to legitimize the communist regime, away the frenzy of the victorious revolution and the triumph of the people's retribution, as well as away from the trauma of the "cult of personality" years, and reoriented it toward the rising force of the "common man's" liberated labor within the dynamic construction of socialist society. The updated narratives reworked early communism's atavistic attachment to violence, death and vows of vengeance into purified reverence and quiet gratitude for the self-sacrifice of "every fallen hero" – proof of the righteousness of the party's historical deeds. Through the use of ideologically loaded films and literature, a new "propaganda of emotions" introduced novel discursive figures into culture: Emil Manov's 1957 novella *A Doubtful Case* introduced "the new positive hero," an ordinary worker who shrugs his shoulders at his own feats of heroism, as if to say "What's the big deal?!"; the 1968 film *The Prosecutor* painted a portrait of the young person hungry for truth, ready to defend justice to "his final breath," disgusted by his erstwhile comrades who had betrayed themselves and their own "youthful ideals"; the 1971 film *The Boy Is Leaving* introduced Bulgarians to the scoffing flock of high-school students with their tickets to life in hand, who don't want lofty rhetoric but moving and sincere experiences – "Just do it, boys!"; "the grassroots communist" from the 1963 film *There Is No Death* despises simple domestic bliss, middle-class morality and the consumerist temptations of the market, ultimately sacrificing himself under the reservoir wall, true to his call of duty, and so on and so on, ad infinitum. All of them can be seen as updated tools for general ideological and political mobilization, which remained invariably important to the communist authorities – they immersed "workers" in ideas, rather than the declarative slogans used earlier. These new tools aroused workers' innermost feelings, which were then transferred into an emotional attachment to the fundamental values of communist ideology. In this sense, it does not seem entirely justified to view the much-touted "thaw" in culture merely as a result of battles won by freethinking in its titanic clash with ideological obscurantism. In seeking to express the new "April Line," the authorities permitted the partial liberation of the ideological imagination, shifting and broadening the boundaries of official taste (albeit not without conflicts and victims); changes to the array of techniques that the institutional system for governing culture used to impose domination and control were closely related to this very process of broadening official taste.

Lyudmila Zhivkova and the new cultural policy: unified long-term cultural programs

After a series of institutional experiments and organizational reforms in the early 1970s, the basic features of what would become the most important change in cultural policy were already apparent: the conceptualization and introduction of "unified, long-term cultural programs." They constituted blueprints spanning considerable lengths of time and undeniably testify to

342 *From de-Stalinization to regime consolidation*

efforts to bring about urgently needed change in culture's social role. They included a new approach to the production and distribution of culture and thus can also be seen as the most important internal watershed in the history of the Bulgarian communist regime's cultural policy. Their emergence in the early 1970s reflected efforts being made to effectively gain control over the rapidly multiplying new social circles and cultural audiences that had arisen because of changes in the structure of society due to ongoing industrialization and urbanization. In these programs, the management of culture was no longer seen as the organization of one-off propagandistic events designed to pack a short-lived political punch; instead, cultural policy was viewed as the management of ongoing, differentiated social processes. In the context of the updated ideological narratives and the newly broadened boundaries of official taste, these programs aimed at stretching the social boundaries of an ideology that had been reworked with new motifs and making it accessible to more people, which also explains the wealth of various initiatives, their scope, their multifaceted orientation, and, last but not least, their high cost, in the literal sense of the word.

At the same time, these long-term programs also had another function: they made it possible for ideology to be combined with new cultural phenomena and the intelligentsia's contemporary creative experiments. Initiated by the highest rung of the cultural hierarchy – the Committee for Culture – the programs introduced themes that were associated with high, even elite culture, which presupposed the participation of all "artists," who would enjoy generous working conditions and be guaranteed access to renovated spaces for official, international cultural exchange. The programs reaffirmed artists' sense of belonging to a national "spiritual elite" – and this, in turn, strengthened the regime's firm conviction that it had not only forcible-political but also intellectual control over artists and that the party "led" them, in so far as it enjoyed their "unreserved support."

The programs united both the "public" and the "cultured person" of the 1970s and 1980s with the new ideological themes in socialist culture in a novel way. They were designed for "active users of culture," while their adaptability to new media broadened the programs' lifespan and increased the number of participants involved in them. The programs' multiplicity of forms, their eclectic content and mixed genres lent a more accessible, modernized form to the regime's ideological esotericism and were guaranteed to satisfy the "mass viewer's" desire to come into contact with works by the country's "spiritual elite." The programs were designed to bring about a fusion of sorts between all Bulgarians and to produce a new ideological homogeneity and cultural identity for "the developed socialist society."

Strictly speaking, the impetus for such programs and their actual beginnings were not directly tied to Lyudmila Zhivkova. However, her elevation to the post of chairwoman of the Committee for Culture in 1975, as well as the scope of the programs launched during her tenure, have made her name synonymous with socialist Bulgaria's new cultural policy. In 1972, "The Nationwide

Program for the Aesthetic Education of Workers and Youth" began to be developed. "The Long-Term, Complex Program for Elevating the Role of Art and Culture in the Harmonious Development of the Person and Society during the Construction Phase of the Developed Socialist Society" started in the mid-1970s, together with its two most famous subprograms: "Nicholas Konstantinovich Roerich" and "Leonardo Da Vinci." Such programs were an attempt to adapt the key values of Marxist-Leninist values to the cultural context of the 1970s; they were all based on the postulate that socialism was the proper atmosphere for true humanism, thus all great humanists from all preceding times and epochs could be seen as the spiritual forefathers of the communist ideology. In this spirit, later projects also included: the Banner of Peace international children's ensemble; the V. I. Lenin, Constantine-Cyril the Philosopher and Georgi Dimitrov programs; initial plans for the development of the Albert Einstein, Avicenna, Lomonosov, and Charles Chaplin projects, among many others. In order to understand how such programs were used as a tool for social control, as well as to show how such monumental self-representations were transformed into propaganda for the regime during the period of "real socialism" in Bulgaria, in the following section we will sketch out the largest of all such programs, which serves as a prime example of the new cultural policy: "The Program for Marking the 1,300th Anniversary of the Founding of the Bulgarian State," which would be observed in 1981.

The historicization of culture and the transformation of classical ideological postulates

The program marking the "1,300th Anniversary of the Founding of the Bulgarian State" can above all be seen as evidence of a crisis in the fundamental values of Marxist-Leninist ideology. The imposition of the "class and party-based approach into the evaluation of historical personages, events and phenomena" can be found even in its earliest variants. However, the more important thing, which had direct consequences for cultural policy over the following decade until the end of communism, was its "constructive" aspect. Through the Great Celebration, the program aimed to tie the entirety of Bulgarian history to communist mythology and symbolism and to create a national cult that included all the relics of Bulgaria's millennia-old cultural tradition, which were all seen as foreshadowing and contributing to Bulgaria's glorious communist future.[1]

"The Basic Principles for Celebrating the 1,300th Anniversary of the Founding of the Bulgarian State," which was presented in October 1976 by Lyudmila Zhivkova, as well as the subsequently derived "Preliminary Draft Concerning the Nature, Goals and Directions of Activity Connected with the 1,300th Anniversary of the Founding of the Bulgarian State," undeniably introduced new standards for the way official public performances were politically framed. The two documents can be taken as a dividing line marking a new format for political-ideological spectacles which was being established

344 *From de-Stalinization to regime consolidation*

and which categorically demanded a complete change in the social function of "nationwide celebrations," turning them from cyclically resuscitated bursts of propaganda and aggressive sloganeering, and from isolated cultural-educational campaigns in praise of the party's past struggles into support for an "ongoing process." They championed an approach which was "not compatible with the traditional idea of a one-off celebration," instead laying out a strategy that viewed a celebration as "the wide-ranging and complex programming of the spiritual and social life of the country." Indeed, these were the fully conscious and unambiguously articulated intentions expressed by the program's supporters.[2] In conceptualizing the celebration as encompassing the entirety of Bulgarian history, Lyudmila Zhivkova, when introducing these documents, argued that the basic foundation upon which the jubilee must be constructed was "measuring the significance of historical events with respect to their meaning for the future – as seen from the present point of view." Precisely this understanding made it crucially necessary for "the present stage of Bulgaria's development [. . .] to be very deeply, and not just formally, laid out and framed as the peak in the evolutionary development of the Bulgarian state." Zhivkova formulated the principle that would become the mainstay in the subsequently constructed conception: "through the combination of the trinity of past-present-future, [the program] must trace out the path traveled thus far, reaffirm all of our achievements in all fields as of 1981, and on this foundation, it must sketch out future prospects."[3]

As preparations for the Great Celebration progressed, a historicization of official culture was brought about, one that had long since reared its head but which was now clearly brought into focus. This meant constantly recalling the past in order to legitimize the socialist present. "Historicization" also meant the contrivance of a "performance" that would reconcile the great national historical narrative, the memory of the recent past that had not yet completely sunk into oblivion, and the academic discipline of history with the regime's current politics. It meant reconciling the history of Bulgaria with the history of the BCP as the final, crowning moment in that historical narrative, at the present moment and forever. "Historicization" meant giving a "performance," which would express the regime's deep roots in the past, its organic national lineage, and its absolutely unlimited future. A formula needed to be found which would write the anniversary narrative of the Bulgarian past – thirteen centuries of unbridled progress and upward movement – and which would declare the inevitability of Bulgaria's communist future from the lofty heights of its socialist present.

Inevitably, the anniversary celebration soon became out of touch with historical reality, hence the massive presence of art within the jubilee program. The aesthetic languages in use at that time were also filtered through anniversary-related ideology and propaganda, dissolving into the particular aesthetic pluralism of the "Zhivkova Era"; the diversity of artistic expressions so characteristic of that "epoch" took shape, although such expressions invariably confined themselves to the official, ideologized

Within the culture of "real socialism" 345

subjects and narratives. A vast number of "anniversary activities" crystallized around the jubilee's leading narrative – the legitimization of the genesis of communist power and the reaffirmation of the regime's rule in perpetuity – which could be interpreted as sub-narratives accompanying it: the construction of monuments marking the anniversary (the grandiose Founders of the Bulgaria State complex in Shumen, the Khan Asparuh Memorial in Tolbuhin [now Dobrich], the memorial to Tsar Samuil near Petrich, the Pantheon of Revivalists in Kotel, the Communist Party Headquarters on Buzludzha Peak, and, the crowning glory of anniversary-related architecture, the National Palace of Culture in Sofia, among many others). There were also museum exhibits (the number exceeded 3,000 in Bulgaria alone, with more than 800,000 artifacts on display), hundreds of artistic exhibitions, exhibits of old Bulgarian manuscripts and art, a sweeping anniversary-related publishing program, hundreds of theatrical performances as part of the programs "View toward the Centuries" and "Survey of Historical Plays," anniversary-related cinematic mega-productions on historical themes, including *Khan Asparuh*, *The Warning* (about Georgi Dimitrov and the Reichstag Fire Trial), *Man of the People* (a full-length documentary about Todor Zhivkov), and *The Strike* (about the coup of September 9, 1944), countless celebrations of Bulgarian literature, a "musical life enriched with more than 550 new anniversary-related events," an enormous international program including the exhibits "Thracian Art from Bulgarian Lands," "Medieval Bulgarian Civilization," "1,000 Years of the Bulgarian Icon," "Bulgarian Tales and Legends," "The Ethnographic Riches of Bulgaria," "The Treasures of Rila Monastery," and so on. Here we should also mention anniversary-related academic events, which lent content and pseudo-realistic substance to the jubilee's great meta-historical narrative: the First International Congress on Bulgarian Studies, the international conference "Bulgaria and the Balkans 681–1981," the international symposium "University-Level Study and Teaching of Bulgarian History at Home and Abroad," the international academic conference "Ties between Kievan Rus and Veliki Preslav," the international symposiums accompanying the exhibits "Bulgarian National Artistic Crafts," "Bulgaria – The Crossroads of Civilizations," "Bulgaria and the World," and so on. The so-called "specialized jubilee activities" – the production of commemorative signs and souvenirs – can be seen as an extremely profound reproduction of anniversary sub-narratives, since the items produced included highly prestigious distinctions (medals and badges of honor), the installation of jubilee symbols in locations within and outside various communities (on the outskirts of cities, along roads), commemorative coins, souvenirs, handicrafts, postage stamps, banners, certificates, flags, competitive prizes, posters, calendars, and pins. Even the Amnesty Law passed by Parliament during the jubilee year of 1981 must be viewed as part and parcel of this process. The list of examples goes on and on.

Anniversary-related activities completely structured "cultural life," giving it an inevitably collective "jubilee" appearance, coordinating workers' cultural

346   *From de-Stalinization to regime consolidation*

perceptions in accordance with the regime's dominant attitude and integrating them into the existing order. Despite their divergence from the archaic symbols of communism and their specific pluralism and diversity, the programs' techniques invariably reproduced its old functions: namely, the imposition of social control within Bulgaria's new, official, ideologically unified culture. After Lyudmila Zhivkova's unexpected death in July 1981, a new "unification of artists with the national-historical theme" became yet another basic ideological tool used to govern, which was accompanied by an abrupt return to the previous treatment of culture as nothing more than propaganda. This can be seen exceptionally clearly within the context of the campaign, which began in early 1985 to change the names of Turks in Bulgaria through the so-called Revival Process.

Crisis and mimicry in socialist realism: discursive tension

The first major crisis in communism, which was felt especially acutely in 1956, and the ongoing process of de-Stalinization called into question the foundations of socialist realism, which many saw as the aesthetic analog of the Stalinist regime. In Bulgaria, too, the discursive tension around the doctrine could be felt, especially in literary circles – albeit much more mildly than in Poland, Yugoslavia, Czechoslovakia, and Hungary. In 1957, accusations began to surface that "art had largely become abstract and dry dogmatism," that "socialist realism was gradually losing its realism, because in practice it sidestepped reality," that "on the basis" of socialist realism, "it was difficult to speak of the freedom of literary trends," and that "the realistic conception has tacitly given way to a creative practice that has taken us back to the sentimental-moralizing and dithyrambic verbiage of the past."[4] Some in the literary world were prepared to ignore the term "socialist realism," instead striving to undertake a revision of the doctrine; such a revisionist approach was gaining popularity in other Eastern European countries and focused on separating the problem of "worldview" from that of "method" and on abolishing the practice of equating aesthetic debates with class struggle. The idea of the *free choice* of method, style, school, and trends grew ever more popular.

The cultural climate in the PRB turned out to be ill equipped to handle such deepening differentiation and clear liberalization of the doctrine. Ideas concerning a Bulgarian revision of socialist realism were sharply criticized at meetings of the writers' union and in the press, which was dominated by anti-reformist opinions, while champions of such a revision found themselves gradually being marginalized. The claim was persistently made that the "weaknesses" in Bulgarian literatures "were in no way due to the method of socialist realism, as some are wont to believe."[5]

The Bulgarian–Czechoslovakian debate over socialist realism in 1957 remained emblematic of the epoch. In this argument, the dogmatic figure of Todor Pavlov was brought to the fore. He was a major name in Marxist-Leninist

Within the culture of "real socialism" 347

aesthetics, Honorary Chairman of both the Bulgarian Academy of Sciences and the Union of Bulgarian Writers, and a member of the Politburo of the Central Committee of the BCP; in short, he personified the connection between totalitarian power and culture in communist Bulgaria. In the debate, Czechoslovakian theorists and writers criticized Pavlov for lumping together opponents of communism and opponents of socialist realism; they accused him of "underestimating the creative individual and his right to freely choose his forms." In his texts, they found "tautological conclusions," hinted at "methodological dilettantism" and so on.[6] Essentially, the Czechoslovakian theoreticians were arguing for at least the relative autonomy of aesthetics with respect to ideology and politics. With much difficulty and following a fair amount of debate, the editors of *Literary Front* (Bulgaria's main literary publication under communism), thanks to the intercession of the Secretariat of the Writers' Union, managed to mount a defense of Pavlov by drawing Bulgarian critics who were staunch socialist realists into the debate.[7] From the mid-1950s until the 1980s, a peculiar discursive regime was upheld, in which official propaganda championed the rhetorically dubious claim that "true" socialist realism existed in Bulgaria, where it occupied a *neither–nor* position: it was neither "revisionist," nor "dogmatic."

To put an end to the intelligentsia's second-guessing of the doctrine, in 1958 a top-down discourse was put into circulation by none other than BCP First Secretary Todor Zhivkov himself, who at that point had still not managed to completely consolidate his power. At a meeting of the writers' union in April, Zhivkov cooled reformist enthusiasm by stating that the April Plenum "had not come to change the party line on the ideological front, on the front of literature and art" and that "the party line in the sphere of literature and art on the whole, regardless of certain weaknesses and mistakes, was nevertheless the correct line." As was to be expected, Zhivkov declared that socialist realism was homologous to the "theory" of Marxism-Leninism. Zhivkov also noted that recent "tendencies to reject socialist realism as a supposedly 'outdated' and 'narrow' method" had led to "serious confusion and rambling," as well as "to a lack of ideas and political apathy" and "to revisionist viewpoints" in the work of authors holding such opinions.[8] But alongside the edifying tone of the instructive discourse, the first notes sounding a "retreat" in the face of pressure from artistic practice could also be heard: "Because socialist realism makes it possible for all types and genres of literature and art and for a rich variety of styles, plots and themes to flourish."[9] Zhivkov also offered this more evasive and ambiguous declaration: "The party has never had and does not have any intention of regulating literature and art. Guaranteeing the correct political and ideological orientation of literature and art – that was and is the main concern of the party and its Central Committee."[10]

Zhivkov's speech held not only threats but also promises: The leader and the Communist Party would allow stylistic and thematic diversity and would back away from direct interference in art, reserving only the right to "orient" art politically; that is, they permitted a space of relative freedom for specific

348 *From de-Stalinization to regime consolidation*

artistic practices, while focusing instead on "cultural policy" as whole and on managing the "ideological front" (the organization of and principles behind the functioning of culture, the selection of leaders within the cultural sphere and so on). However, this promise remained unfulfilled up until the early 1970s. In keeping with tradition, Zhivkov personally headed up almost every campaign concerned with ideological oversight of the "cultural front" until the end of the 1960s. The two periods of partial liberalization in literature and art (1958–1962 and 1964–1968) were brought to an end by the communist leader's direct interference – through his open criticism of specific works and individuals no less. Zhivkov's speech before a conference of Komsomol members in Sofia in March 1969 put an end to the Bulgarian "thaw" in culture for all practical purposes.[11]

During the whole decade of the 1960s, it seemed as if the communist leader himself was struggling to draw the permissible boundaries within which literature and art's critical potential could unfold. Zhivkov's cyclical public outbursts against processes of liberation created a sense of insecurity and anxiety in the discursive regime within which socialist realism existed. In 1966, Zhivkov arrived at a relatively comfortable ideological formula that defined the permissible boundaries of criticism within communist Bulgaria. Once again in a speech before the writers' union, he championed the idea of "the two truths": the "greater truth" that "Bulgaria is building a socialist society, with new driving forces; that with every passing day our socialist achievements are reaffirmed, while the socialist social order is strengthened and perfected; that we are marching ahead toward communism"; and the "lesser truth" that "in Bulgaria, egoism, apathy, theft, conceit, careerism and bureaucratism can be found [. . .] expressions of a base morality [. . .] string-pulling [. . .] the truth of negative phenomena."[12] As a basic cause that had given rise to this "lesser truth," he pointed to a phenomenon that had been growing ever more visible since the 1960s and that could be defined as socialist consumerism. According to Zhivkov, a struggle must be waged precisely against expressions of this "lesser" or "secondary" truth, "while not forgetting the main thing: the events and facts within our reality must be examined in terms of their revolutionary development, and not from the viewpoint of petty-bourgeois radicalism and liberalism."[13]

Zhivkov attempted to revise the doctrine of socialist realism by eliminating the zone for criticism and calling upon "every artist" to do his utmost to help "liquidate the lesser truth" through "an active attitude toward reality." At the same time, he preserved the crucial socialist-realist idea of the "revolutionary development" of reality, which was set apart as a *meta-reality* ("greater truth") of sorts and which remained out of bounds to critical gestures and reflexes. In the following years, this formula was repeatedly tested in works of art through a true symbolic struggle, even while the border between "the two truths" began shifting and the zone of the "lesser truth" gradually grew, taking over ever-larger swaths of the *common* space of socialist literature and culture, which was in any case difficult to maintain.

Within the culture of "real socialism" 349

During the 1960s, this "change in proportions" was only hinted at in the emergence of the first "small theories," which were partially seen as *alternatives* but which were in fact *self-corrections* of socialist realism itself. In practice, they enriched and broadened the doctrine rather than replacing it. Faced with the impossibility of replacing or at least revising socialist realism *directly* and *completely* through public discussion or a common project, reform-minded artists continued to test the boundaries and buttresses of the doctrine – gradually, in a "private" way – via individual creative acts and group debates. New opportunities to make such alternatives public were constantly being sought. Perhaps this is why during this discursive phase of socialist realism (and not during the preceding, Stalinist phase) there were far more stopped films, banned performances, and seized books – because tendencies toward liberalization and reform in the artistic field were clashing with the anti-reformist reflexes of the institutions upholding socialist realism as the dominant doctrine.

The alternatives: vacillation and acknowledgment

Practically until the early 1960s, alternatives to socialist realism in literature and culture occupied the zone of *secret publicity*. Only after the fall of the communist regime did Bulgarian society find out about camp and prison poetry, most often composed "in the heads" of repressed authors, about the individual literary-political campaign launched by Yordan Ruskov, who in the autumn of 1956 distributed a poetic appeal in support of the Hungarian Uprising, or about the epigrams and lyrical descriptions of the regime's repressive machinery contained in the archives of the Zmey Goryanin and Yordan Kovachev.

Around 1956, two types of alternatives arose, which were essentially the results of attempts to reform socialist realism itself – indeed, the first self-corrective moves within socialist realism had begun to surface. Emil Manov's novella *A Doubtful Case*, Emiliyan Stanev's novel *Ivan Kondarev*, and other works tested the doctrine's normative boundaries "from the inside." Some of them became the targets of punitive measures, while others – following initial hesitation – were entirely acknowledged as politically correct and even "highly party-minded" works. The second type of alternative introduced a rhetorical style that would dominate ever-larger swaths of cultural territory over the coming years: a moderately anti-dogmatic criticism, proffered from the viewpoint of the *unrealized* communist ideal and projected onto a value-laden juxtaposition between "real communists" and "party bureaucrats."

The political thaw in the early 1960s stimulated an increase in alternative styles and artistic models. The doctrine found it ever harder to withstand the pressure mounting from art that had been created outside the norms of socialist realism. Sanctions imposed by official institutions and the censorship mechanism were growing less and less effective. Open terror had been abolished. The harshest repressive measures that had previously been used

350   *From de-Stalinization to regime consolidation*

against freethinking artists (imprisonment in camps, the organization of sham trials, and so on) were almost never invoked during this era. A growing number of people were prepared to pay the now lower price for an alternative lifestyle: being fired from work, expelled from the party, forcibly resettled, becoming the object of a public media campaign, having their professional development hindered, and so on.

More and more writers had found an "Aesopian language" which they used to engage in a specific type of allegorical criticism of the system. Other linguistic strategies were also employed (the language of folkloric-mythical sagas and poetic nonsense, among others), which ostensibly demonstrated sociopolitical neutrality but which often had a political effect when read or critically interpreted. This was the case with the poetry of Konstantin Pavlov and Nikolay Kânchev, which was removed from public circulation until the early 1980s. Thematic alternatives tied to antiquity and the Third Bulgarian Kingdom were also used to similar effect. Literature and especially poetry from the 1960s abounded with hints of social-moralistic maximalism, which laid the system's "weak spots" bare. Within the discursive tensions of the decade, these alternatives sometimes passed as socialist realism, while at other times they were savagely persecuted by pro-doctrine criticism and the institutions in charge of doling out sanctions. One telling example is the case in which the whole print-run of Ivan Dinkov's poetry collection *South of Life* (1967) was suppressed.

Individual theatrical productions also attempted to "overcome the standards of socialist-realist aesthetics, as well as inertia due to the asceticism of theatrical forms characteristic of that era."[14] Examples include *Improvisation* (by Valeri Petrov and Radoy Ralin, dir. by Grisha Ostrovski, 1962), *Abel's Mistake* (by Emil Manov, dir. by Asen Shopov, 1964), *The Poet and The Mountain* (by Ivan Teofilov, dir. by Leon Daniel, 1964), *Sky and Earth* (by Kliment Tsachev, dir. by Boris Spirov, 1964), *We Are 25* (by Nedyalko Yordanov, dir. by Asen Shopov, 1969), and others. At the same time, the state censors were hypersensitive to allegorical cinematic works such as *The Tied-Up Balloon* (dir. Binka Zhelyazkova, 1967) and *Monday Morning* (dir. Hristo Piskov, Irina Aktasheva, 1966); they even objected to critical sentiment directed at the "cult of personality" in *The Public Prosecutor* (dir. by Lyubomir Sharlandzhiev, 1968), refusing to let it appear in theaters until 1988.

In the 1960s, "retro tendencies" arose, which were indicative of the new regime within which cultural heritage found itself functioning. Literary and cultural names from before World War II that had been excluded from the official public realm began reappearing. The names of poets Atanas Dalchev and Aleksandâr Vutimski could once again be read on the covers of books, while Konstantin Gâlâbov, Ivan Radoslavov and other literary figures from the 1920s and 1930s began resurfacing in the book market as memoirists. Incidentally, besides the semi-official body of partisan memoirs, more memories of the "bourgeois" past between 1878 and 1944 began to be published during the 1960s, as well as works about the Macedonian liberation movement

Within the culture of "real socialism" 351

and other topics that had been taboo in the epoch of strict socialist realism. Of course, such texts were not unambiguous alternative artistic gestures; nevertheless, the increased number of such works stimulated the formation of an environment in which – as a counterbalance to the "contemporary theme" enshrined by socialist realism – "old" values not found within communist ideology were rehabilitated.

From the invisible turn during the 1970s and 1980s to the slow advance of alternatives

During the 1970s and 1980s, Bulgarian culture entered a phase during which a compromise was struck, which was expressed in the growing overlap between socialist realism and "socialist literature." Processes began to unfold in which socialist realism constantly adapted, broadened, grew more accommodating, milder, and more tolerant, so as to be able to encompass actual artistic practice. This, however, continually made the concept itself problematic, as it began losing its meaning.[15] During the final two decades of communist rule in Bulgaria, Zhivkov's criticisms of authors and works dominated by "pessimism and nihilism" and "twisted liberalism" in his 1966 speech could be applied to a host of other targets. Indeed, the 1970s and 1980s abound with such authors and works; however, they seem to have ceased to pose any particular problem to the authorities and official doctrine. Punitive measures were employed ever less frequently to defuse and neutralize such works.

Socialist realism was gradually forced to broaden its thematic and stylistic boundaries, to "accommodate" within itself every type of literature that decided to join its ranks, as long as the latter was not openly hostile to the totalitarian system and did not reject socialist realism itself. Critics were inclined to assimilate all other styles and phenomena that did not dispute socialist realism's dominance by broadening the "single method's" stylistic registers, by drawing these styles into traditional "politically correct" themes (for example, the so-called patriotic theme), and by including their authors in the well-established social hierarchies (through membership in artists' unions, the BCP or simply by "finding them a job").

But there was also another motive behind this new strategy. The reduction of the term "socialist realism" to a rhetorical sign and an empty password was dictated by the desire for the avant-garde or modernist style of authors with close ties to the authorities to be interpreted and reaffirmed as *socialist*. The doctrine was emptied of all principles to such an extent that an author had only to be a member of the BCP or at least be *approved* by the authorities for some reason to be able to retain his stylistic and thematic freedom, without having to worry about the principles of "method" being debated at round tables and discussions. Thus, socialist-realist art criticism began recognizing as "socialist artists" even individuals who in previous decades had been declared "unreliable" and even "hostile" to official art. Ideology was forced

352 *From de-Stalinization to regime consolidation*

to revise and rename the stylistic and figurative structures of avant-gardism and modernism in order to include them in the doctrine of socialist realism.

Todor Zhivkov's speech to the Third National Conference of Young Literary Artists in late 1977 is very indicative of this tendency. Despite the fact that at this same forum he delivered a line that would later become classic – "The spine of Bulgarian literature is political" – and reconfirmed literature and art's lack of autonomy in communist Bulgaria, it was not at all coincidental that in his speech he did not once use the term "socialist realism."[16] The authorities themselves had begun to realize that the doctrine's reputation had suffered and that it was growing more and more ineffective and unattractive for the purposes of propaganda. For this reason, instead of "socialist realism," the more general phrase "socialist literature and culture" began to be used with increasing frequency.

Despite the fact that uses of the term "socialist realism" were reduced to a minimum, the principle of "party-mindedness" – now further reduced to the principle of "leader-mindedness" – enjoyed a renaissance in this period after having been discredited in the "cult of personality" era of the 1950s. In the early 1980s, a new *hyper-personalization* of the image of the communist leader took place in various artistic practices. In 1981, the premature death of Lyudmila Zhivkova gave rise to a true posthumous cult, while Todor Zhivkov's seventieth birthday unleashed waves of personal devotion attested to in poetry collections and paintings, which crystallized most strongly in the abovementioned poetic anthology *April Hearts* (1981), instigated by the Union of Bulgarian Writers. Other collections with the same title appeared over the following years as well. Numerous Bulgarian poets combined mourning for the Daughter with displays of "gratitude for inspiration" toward the Father.[17] Fused in a strange duality, the two images – that of the Father and the Daughter – (re)constructed the phenomenon of the *political family*, both within real sociocultural life as well as within the figurative system of socialist realism.[18]

At the same time, alternatives within the literature and art of communist Bulgaria had a chance to develop their autonomy and to appear every more openly within the field of art. Their new-found publicity was accompanied by the discursive tension so familiar from the past; however, such works were ever more rarely banned outright but instead were drawn into debates designed to defuse their powerful messages. The ban on Blaga Dimitrova's novel *Face* and the strategy for discursively "packaging" Ivaylo Petrov's novel *The Wolf Hunt* are emblematic examples of these two approaches during the 1980s.

At the same time, alternative elements were making their way into most works of socialist realism. It became clear that not everything in a "socialist-realist work" was *socialist-realist*. More and more often, the public found contradictions in encounters between language and power in Bulgarian literature and culture; this became a source of constant confusion as to *where exactly* the borders of socialist realism lay – both within a given individual's oeuvre and even within a single work.

Within the culture of "real socialism" 353

In the poetry of Nikolay Kânchev, Konstantin Pavlov, Ivan Teolfilov, Ivan Tsanev, Ekaterina Yosifova, Binyo Ivanov, Georgi Rupchev, and others, as well as in the belletristic works of Zlatomir Zlatanov, Viktor Paskov, Krassimir Damyanov and others during the 1980s, we can find not so much names but rather linguistics models that definitively differentiate the alternatives to socialist realism, making it impossible for these models to be co-opted by the imitative communist ideology of the time.

As far as other art forms were concerned, alternatives to socialist realism appeared primarily in cinema – especially in screenplays by Georgi Mishev from the 1970s, which were characterized by their anti-philistine sentiment and their stark exposure of the existential desolation of the Bulgarian village (*Counting Wild Rabbits*, dir. Eduard Zahariev, 1973; *Villa Zone*, dir. Eduard Zahariev, 1975; *The Matriarch*, dir. by Lyudmil Kirkov, 1977). Films by Rangel Vâlchanov (*The Unknown Soldier's Patent-Leather Shoes*, 1979), Lyudmil Kirkov (*Short-lived Sun/A Short Spot of Sun*, 1979; *Orchestra without a Name*, 1982; *Balance*, 1983), and Hristo Hristov (*A Woman at 33*, 1982), despite addressing different topics and using different stylistic devices, fully overcame the schemata of socialist realism, managing to fulfill their sometimes invisible and imperceptible critical function within the artistic language itself. The strongest alternatives within Bulgarian culture from the 1970s and early 1980s clearly show the deepening of the already insurmountable split between language and reality, between existence and thinking about existence – a rupture that in the final years before 1989 would became an abyss. This is also confirmed by the fact that even the official state institutions charged with producing art also created works, which for the most part openly rejected socialist-realist postulates. The first appearances of *sots-art* and postmodern art at the end of the 1980s already laid the groundwork for the new language that would mark the changes in Bulgaria's literature and culture after 1989.

Notes

1 On the optics guaranteeing visibility and for an analysis of the events in "jubilee reality," it is necessary to explicitly underscore the significance of the study by Marla Susan Stone: *The Patron State: Culture and Politics in Fascist Italy*, Princeton, NJ: Princeton University Press, 1998; especially that part dealing with the celebration of the ten-year anniversary of the Fascist revolution in Italy in 1932.
2 TsDA, f. 405, op. 9, a. e. 263, l. 5. Protocol No. 6 from the meeting of the Leadership of the Committee for Culture, February 12, 1980, information about the state of the work on celebrating the 1,300th anniversary.
3 TsDA, f. 990, op. 1, a. e. 10, l. 45. Basic principles for the ideological content of the jubilee celebration of the 1,300th anniversary. 1976.
4 See the answers of writers Emil Manov and Emiliyan Stanev to a special questionnaire in "Razgovori i diskusii," *Plamâk*, 2 (1957): 46–47; see the words of critic Boris Delchev in: "Borba za revolyutsionna pravda," *Literaturen front*, 20 (May 16, 1957).

354 *From de-Stalinization to regime consolidation*

5 See the published version of the report from the annual meeting of the party organization of the Bulgarian Writers' Union: "Na borba za sotsialisticheski realizâm," *Literaturen front*, 11 (March 14, 1957).

6 See articles by the Czech participants in the debate in Frantishek Vrba, "Tsel i pâtishta," *Literaturen front*, 17 (April 25, 1957); Vladimir Dostal, "Estetikata na Todor Pavlov v dneshnata marksistka ofanziva," *Literaturen front*, 23 (June 6, 1957); Yan Tsiganek, "Estetikata v dvoumenie," *Literaturen front*, 25 (June 20, 1957); Irzhi Haek, "Da i ne," *Literaturen front*, 27 (July 4, 1957).

7 See the minutes from the meetings of the secretariat of the UBW, after which, following a sharp reaction from the offended T. Pavlov, actions were taken "to withdraw [from the debate] with dignity": TsDA, f. 551, op. 1, a. e. 89, l. 142–150, 205–206.

8 Todor Zhivkov, "Poveche mezhdu naroda, po-blizo do zhivota," in *Izkustvoto, naukata i kulturata v sluzhba na naroda*, vol. I, Sofia: Partizdat, 1965, pp. 183–186. Later, Zhivkov launches into personal – either clearly addressed or semi-anonymous – criticisms – of Emil Manov and Todor Genov, who had written and published "works that were unsuccessful in the political and artistic respect" (Zhivkov, "Poveche mezhdu naroda, po-blizo do zhivota," pp. 186–187) and against "certain of our current critics, who had struggled with quill and word to establish socialist realism in Bulgaria, and who today prefer either to keep silent or not to raise their voices in defense of socialist realism, against attempts to reject it, or else they have turned 180° and have begun repudiating that which they had earlier passionately endorsed" (Zhivkov, "Poveche mezhdu naroda, po-blizo do zhivota," pp. 194–195).

9 Zhivkov, "Poveche mezhdu naroda, po-blizo do zhivota," p. 185.

10 Zhivkov, "Poveche mezhdu naroda, po-blizo do zhivota," p. 197.

11 Todor Zhivkov gave the speech on March 16, 1969, in front of the HVI Accounting-Electoral Conference (*Otchetno-izborna konferentsiya*) of the Sofia Comsomol, but dedicated it entirely to problems of literary and artistic criticism.

12 Todor Zhivkov, "Za rabotata na Devetiya kongres na Bâlgarskata komunisticheska partiya," in *Za literaturata*, Sofia: Bâlgarski pisatel, 1981, pp. 240–242.

13 Zhivkov, "Za rabotata na Devetiya kongres," p. 248.

14 See *Teatralni naprezheniya. Gestus: Teatralen almanah*, Sofia: Fondatsiya "Ideya za teatâr," 2003, p. 19.

15 Mihail Nedelchev, "Sotsialisticheskiyat realizâm: Teoriya i praktika – Sâotvetstviya/ Nesâotvetstviya," in P. Doynov (ed.), *Sotsialisticheskiyat realizâm: novi izsledvaniya*, Sofia: Nov bâlgarski universitet, 2008, pp. 39–55, at p. 46.

16 Todor Zhivkov, "Borbata na naroda za svoboda, progres i sotsializâm: kostnata sistema na bâlgarskata literatura," *Plamâk*, 3 (1978): 3–15.

17 Characteristic lyrical elegies for Lyudmila Zhivkova were written by Lyubomir Levchev, Usin Kerim, Atanas Dushkov, and others, while panegyrics for Zhivkov were written by Aleksandâr Gerov, Lyubomir Levchev, Lilyana Stefanova, Lâchezar Elenkov, Nino Nikolov and others. See *Aprilski sârtsa*, Varna: Georgi Bakalov, 1981. See also the essay by Lyubomir Levchev, "Blagodarnost za vdâhnovenieto," *Literaturen front*, 36 (September 3, 1981).

18 On the problem of the political family, see Nikola Georgiev, "Semeystvoto: nachin na upotreba," in *Nova kniga za bâlgarskiya narod*, Sofia: St. Kliment Ohridski, 1991, pp. 7–49; as well as Plamen Doynov, "Uvod v politicheskoto semeystvo," in *Sotsialisticheskiyat realizâm*, pp. 295–306.

Part III

The collapse and peaceful withdrawal of communism in Bulgaria

19 The deepening crises and the paralyzation of the regime

Despite increasing stagnation in economic and social life and the party apparatus' apathy, Todor Zhivkov continued to nurse the hope that if he presented himself as an enthusiastic supporter of Gorbachev's reforms, he would manage (yet again) to retain his political post. His ambitions in this respect produced the "July Conception," which laid out yet another round of reforms. Following several years of contradictory attempts, the idea was to finally sketch out the basic contours of the new socialist model. The document adopted at the July Plenum (1987) allowed for the existence of various and formally equal types of ownership for the first time. In other words, private ownership would have the right to exist freely. According to recollections by Zhivkov's closest advisers, almost until the end of the regime, "he allowed private initiative to develop only in the services sector."[1]

Reform fever to the bitter end: from the July Conception to Decree 56

The July Conception was important in another respect as well, since the new program intended to "overcome the people's alienation from ownership and the means of production, which will transform them into a real actor in both government and management."[2] However, the attempt to award ownership to workers, who were officially declared the owners of the enterprises where they worked, met with silent indifference on the part of the "newly empowered."[3] Summing up the results of the campaign undertaken in 1987, Zhivkov admitted, "The act of placing socialist property under the management and control of workers' collectives has been carried out formally, sluggishly, and without producing any particular results."[4]

Clearly, half-hearted measures (the formal transfer of management, but not ownership) produced half-hearted results (alienation). The Politburo decided to make an ideologically risky move, suggesting not only that the management of businesses but their actual ownership be handed over to workers. The communist elite pinned what turned out to be its final hopes on "company organization based on the joint-stock principle," hoping that "in this way we can create a more complete and direct incentive for socialist workers and their collectives."[5] "The revolution from below," as Zhivkov called it, clearly had another aim – one that was not openly articulated. This new type of company organization allowed the central government to break up the intermediary links in the economy (the gigantic DSOs, national economic complexes, corporations, and associations). The company system, which was introduced at the December Plenum of 1988, was seen as a mechanism for shattering this intermediate level of the hierarchy, which had proved to be an obstacle to a series of economic reforms introduced from the center. It soon became apparent, however, that as it had been conceived the "company organizational system" would accomplish only one of the two tasks entrusted to it – it did indeed provide a detour around the intermediate structures blocking change within the economic system. But in order to overcome "alienation from ownership and the means of production," clear economic stimuli had to be introduced.

Several months had to pass, however, before the idea of using shares could make headway. Decree 56, which was adopted in January 1989 and which laid out very broadly the new conditions for doing business in Bulgaria, was nevertheless extremely reticent when it came to regulating this new legal form. Only legal entities could be the founders of joint-stock companies, while the acquisition of stock by citizens was put off for the future.[6] Only in July 1989, at a special discussion within the Politburo did it become clear that this process of "denationalization" would exclude the main industrial sectors, where the state would remain the single stockholder. The state would also retain a controlling interest (51 percent) in the electronics, chemical, and biotechnology industries, in leading branches of the machine-building, insurance, and construction sectors, as well as in several companies within the food and tobacco industry. The state's share was reduced only in the sphere of services, trade, and agriculture, but even then it did not fall below 20 percent. Only members of the respective labor collective could receive nominal shares in a company. However, each worker's share could not exceed 10,000 leva (or 1 percent of the company's capital). It was explicitly stated that "companies owned by citizens cannot acquire shares in joint-stock companies."[7] Zhivkov also particularly insisted on emphasizing the "worker-based" nature of such stock, or, as he would later call it, "our socialist-style stockholding."[8]

There was, however, one "special category" of people who would be allowed not only to own but also to manage the new firms, without having to meet the restrictive labor requirements:

> In forming the governing bodies of the self-managed companies in every sphere – in the material and spiritual spheres – older comrades who have already retired, as well as those who work in other spheres, can be included in the managing committee of companies and other economic organizations, *as long as they occupy the proper party positions* [my italics].[9]

The paralyzation of the regime   359

A short while later it would become clear that the party quota was expected to comprise "up to one-third of such steering committees," while its main task would be to become "a proxy for the state, without officially publicizing this."[10] In fact, the promise already given in late 1987 that "we are not creating a new type of property, but just a different way of managing this property" turned out not to be an "evasive maneuver" but rather a clear indication of the ideological boundaries within which Bulgarian communist reformism was trapped. Socialist ownership, as Zhivkov continued to insist, remained the "holiest of holies within our system."[11] For his part, Politburo member Nacho Papazov suggested that the stockholding system be used as a means of convincing people to "loosen their purse-strings and let us *take* [my italics], for example, 20 to 30 percent of the money that is now being hidden."[12]

In summary, even the most radical phase of Bulgarian *perestroika* did not manage to free itself from the burden of ideology. The changes introduced, albeit half-heartedly, were seen as a temporary retreat. The hope remained that things would turn around, and then, as had happened under Lenin's New Economic Policy, money that had been brought out into the open could be taken from would-be "speculators." Until then, however, the state would retain its unimpeded control over the economy. Sectors considered unattractive to the government, as well as money-losing enterprises, would be left to the pared-down sphere of private initiative. Only the responsibility for overcoming shortages within the economy and satisfying the need for consumer goods would be decentralized. Just as in the USSR during the 1920s, partially free private enterprise would be saddled with a job the state found itself incapable of fulfilling. However, the tempting pie of profit would be centrally confiscated by taxes reaching 70–80 percent, which would suffocate all businesses. By allowing only workers at a given enterprise to purchase stock in it, the company system clearly was not in any position to accomplish the tasks it had been saddled with.

In the end, the half-hearted and self-restrictive nature of changes to the economy not only failed to lead to improved performance but actually worsened the situation. They did, however, provide an opportunity for the more far-sighted and enterprising members of the communist nomenclature and State Security circles to begin to quickly register companies, including joint ventures with Western partners, in which their share was, in fact, the state's money, and to take out loans guaranteed once again with property that was technically not their own. In summarizing the results of these measures, the American economists Paul Gregory and Mark Harrison reached the conclusion that "the results of these partial reforms were worse than those of the unreformed system. Firms might want to avoid the arbitrary and often pointless interference of their higher-ups. However, those same firms cannot be granted independence if they are not subject to the discipline of market forces."[13] The sociologist Peter Berger has also commented on the reasons that attempts to create some kind of "market socialism" failed: "the transformation of industrial socialism through the introduction of market

360 *The collapse of communism in Bulgaria*

mechanisms will run up against economic limitations caused by the inability of the artificial market to reproduce the efficiency of the capitalist market ... No effective market economy can exist without private ownership of the means of production."[14] In practice, it turned out that the more reforms were imposed upon or imitated within the planned economic model, the more discrepancies arose, while ever greater conflicts and contradictions cropped up between the various segments and models.

The foreign-debt trap

The final debt crisis for communist Bulgaria began only after 1985, when the wave of debt moratoriums (in which countries such as Poland, Romania, Mexico, Argentina, and Brazil were allowed to postpone or terminate their payments) began to die down throughout the world and possible solutions appeared on the horizon (such as the Baker and Brady Plans). The BNB, after managing to reduce its debt by an average of 500 million leva annually over a six-year period (between 1979 and 1984), abruptly reversed this trend, and by 1989 Bulgaria's foreign debt was growing by 1.5 billion leva a year.[15] Recently declassified documents from Case Number 4 have shed more light on this dramatic reversal.

As of the summer of 1985, the dollar began quickly depreciating with respect to other currencies; within a year, it had fallen by more than a third since February 1985 (from 3:1 to 1.9:1 Deutschmarks to the dollar). This seemingly "insignificant" change had a catastrophic effect on Bulgaria's trade balance, due to the fact that Bulgaria traditionally exported in dollars but imported almost everything from Europe in Deutschmarks. Thus, the export of the same quantity of goods now resulted in profits that were 38 percent lower, while exports were 38 percent more expensive. The country's hard-currency reserves, which were held mainly in dollars and which had amounted to approximately US$1.4 billion by the mid-1980s, also depreciated by the same percentage. The poor quality and lack of competitiveness of Bulgarian exports did not allow export streams to be quickly redirected toward other, non-dollar markets. Thus, the combined effect of the devaluation of the US dollar on the Bulgarian economy amounted to a loss of nearly US$800 million during 1985–1986 alone.[16]

In addition, as of the autumn of 1985, the price of oil began to fall unexpectedly. After only five months, oil prices were already 60 percent lower than their previous peak. If we recall that the economic stabilization Bulgaria had achieved in the late 1970s and early 1980s was largely due to the country's re-export of Soviet oil, we can imagine the negative consequences Sofia suffered as a result of this change in the global oil market. According to later admissions by the then-director of the BNB, Vasil Kolarov, corrections to oil prices deprived Bulgaria of US$300–500 million in income annually.

Cheap oil set off a chain of bankruptcies that affected almost all of Bulgaria's debtors in the Third World. During the first oil crisis in 1973 and

The paralyzation of the regime   361

under pressure from Moscow, Sofia had begun seeking to diversify its oil supplies by activating its contacts with leftist and radical regimes in the Near East and Africa. The usual scheme involved Bulgaria exporting weapons on credit, which would then be paid for by importing fossil fuels from Iraq, Iran, Libya, Algeria, Nigeria, and other countries. The dried-up stream of oil revenues, however, upset the economies of Bulgaria's trading partners, who ceased making payments on their debts. In this way, Bulgaria ended up holding enormous and essentially uncollectable debts that amounted to US$2.8 billion.[17]

As a result of the combined effect of these global changes, after 1985 Bulgaria's hard-currency trade balances took a dramatic turn for the worse. However, the devaluation of the dollar, falling oil prices and the cessation of debt payments from the Third World would not have had such fatal consequences if the Bulgarian economy had been more flexible and had more reserves at its disposal. The planned economy is notoriously fragile in the face of external shocks. Reorienting the country toward new, altered conditions would require an interminably long period of rewriting economic plans, which would then have to be distributed to the individual enterprises. The purely technical time it would have taken to reorient Bulgarian exports toward non-dollar markets was so great that it largely rendered such an operation pointless. The typically low quality of Bulgarian products again discouraged manufacturers from seeking out new markets, which would have higher expectations with respect to quality. During the 1980s, only 15 percent of the 1,000 items Bulgaria exported to the West garnered hard-currency returns, i.e. they were exported at a price above the production cost.[18] According to an admission made by Trade Minister Hristo Hristov: "The unsatisfactory quality of our export products, which appears in many respects, is [. . .] one of the main reasons for the low quantity of exports to Western countries and for its decrease over the past years."[19]

A summary report by the Bulgarian embassy in London from this period offers a clear idea of the extremely low price margins that Bulgarian products were forced to maintain in order to compensate for their low quality: 3–15 percent for electric trucks, 18–20 percent for forklifts, 12–20 percent for universal metal-cutting tools, and 5–20 percent for food and tobacco products.[20] The party leadership tried to cover the growing trade imbalance by attracting external financing. However, since communist economies were traditionally hostile to direct foreign investments (within manufacturing companies, for example), bank loans were the only remaining option for filling the gap in the trade balance. Just as during the second half of the 1970s, the Politburo turned its attention precisely to such loans. Politically painful alternatives, such as reducing the rate of growth or making sacrifices in the social sphere, were not even discussed.

Bulgaria could no longer depend on Soviet support, either. The USSR itself was experiencing serious economic difficulties. Instead of providing loans, subsidies and oil to its satellite, as it had during the 1970s, Moscow now

362 *The collapse of communism in Bulgaria*

forced Bulgaria to pay off a significant portion of the debt it had amassed earlier than expected – in 1986, Bulgaria was forced to pay off loans from the International Bank for Economic Cooperation (IBEC), while in 1988–1989, it again paid off loans from IBEC and the USSR.[21] After 1986, the Kremlin not only stopped extending loans to Bulgaria to cover its trade deficit but even pressured its junior partner in Comecon into making significant net payments. Their exact amount cannot be determined at the moment; however, according to the yearly protocols for trade and payments between the two countries during 1988 and 1989, Bulgaria had to transfer nearly 600 million convertible rubles (approximately US$650 million at the official exchange rate) during each of those two years.[22]

The withdrawal of Soviet backing for Bulgaria's foreign debt considerably worsened the country's position. The extreme explosiveness of the situation, however, was due to a series of imprudent domestic decisions: the government's unrealistic hard-currency plans, inept management of the debt, hesitant and delayed implementation of economic reforms, and so on. Some of these problems have already been discussed above. The gap that opened in Bulgaria's trade balance after 1985 threw the party leadership into confusion. The Politburo and the government's economic team rushed to find Western lenders in order to balance their ever more lopsided foreign debts. The maturity structure of the country's debt clearly testifies to the panic that gripped the BCP leadership.[23] By the end of the 1980s, short-term obligations made up a significant portion of the country's loans and created an obstacle to servicing the foreign debt, one that could be surmounted only with great difficulty. Thus, according to the BNB's report, in 1989, "around half of [. . .] the debt consists of short-term financial and trade loans."[24] When numerous loans came due in quick succession during 1988–1991, these accumulated obligations set off the "debt bomb" that had been planted much earlier. Given that the country had an average annual export income of US$3 billion during the second half of the 1980s, servicing annual debt obligations of more US$2.5 billion (and in 1989–1990 of more than US$3 billion) was clearly far beyond the capabilities of the Bulgarian economy.

The party's delusion that with the help of foreign loans, the Bulgarian economy would be able to maintain its high growth rates without cutting into the population's consumption in the end led to a runaway increase in the foreign debt. Moreover, having experienced serious difficulties from at least the mid-1980s onwards, the Bulgarian economy was in no condition to absorb such a large flow of capital. Incoming foreign capital (at an annual average rate of US$1.5 billion between 1985 and 1989) did not generate analogous growth in the GDP (Gross Domestic Product) which would allow the loans to be serviced. Given a 3.6-fold increase in foreign loans in convertible currency between 1984 and 1989, the GDP at fixed prices grew barely 1.1 times, while for gross investments, this rate was only 1.13.[25]

At a certain point, however, even new loans ceased to be the solution. Given the ongoing global debt crisis, there was no creditor willing to lend

The paralyzation of the regime 363

such large sums for such short periods of time to an economy that was already seriously indebted. Having exhausted the debt roll-over option (the servicing of old liabilities through taking on new loans), Bulgaria was forced to turn to its reserves. According to a secret report by the BNB, in 1987 "part of the negative balance of payment was covered by hard-currency funds from the strategic hard-currency reserves."[26] Over that same year, US$570.5 million were spent to this end. Toward the middle of 1988, another US$300 million from the reserve was "redirected" to plug the hole in the trade balance. In less than a year and a half, the reserve was drained by more than half, from US$1.2 billion in December 1986 to US$580 million in May 1988.[27]

Plundering the fiscal reserves was a clear indication of the growing difficulties Bulgaria faced after 1986 in trying to finance its ongoing deficit in "the usual way" (i.e. through new loans). The regime's extremely risky decision to force Bulgarian Turks into exile in Turkey during 1989 decisively destroyed the country's trustworthiness in the eyes of Western financial institutions. In the early summer, *The Economist* and the *International Herald Tribune* published several articles about the "disintegrating Bulgarian economy." This news was grounds for "banks in a series of capitalist countries such as France, the United States, Great Britain, Switzerland, Holland and to a certain extent, West Germany and Japan, to essentially stop extending any new loans to the Bulgarian Foreign Trade Bank."[28]

After frittering away its currency reserves over the course of two years and exhausting the possibilities for new, revolving loans, Bulgaria was left with three possible choices: (1) turning to the creditor of last resort (the USSR); (2) paying the debt at the expense of consumption (the so-called "Romanian scenario" undertaken by Ceauşescu); or (3) negotiating with creditors to reduce the debt. As would become clear, the first choice was not actually a viable option. On the contrary, in the harshest years of the debt crisis (1988–1989), the Soviet Union had squeezed Bulgaria dry of some of its final resources. The second option was unacceptable given its huge social cost and the "Polish syndrome." After the rise of the Solidarity movement and the declaration of martial law in Warsaw, the political leadership in Bulgaria feverishly rejected any solutions that would "cost" the population dearly and hence threaten the regime's own survival. If during the 1970s the BCP could still allow itself to limit imports so as to pay off the country's foreign debt, in 1988, at the peak of the debt crisis, the Politburo was forced to make a decision to "increase the share of imported goods on the domestic market." Besides that, the plan for the same year called for "a significant decrease in exports, especially with respect to goods and services that are currently in short supply on the domestic market."[29] The third option was even more impossible. Despite censorship and informational blackouts, renegotiating Bulgaria's schedule of debt payments and pushing for their partial reduction would be an event that could not be hidden from the public. It would expose the huge problems that had been accumulating within the economy, shedding light on this ultra-secretive zone. In the eyes of the party leadership, making

364 *The collapse of communism in Bulgaria*

a deal with the International Monetary Fund (IMF) would be tantamount to publicly declaring the bankruptcy of the communist economy. For this reason, the members of the Politburo were "content" to merely discuss the possibility of submitting a request for membership to the IMF and the World Bank (the preconditions for starting talks for the reduction of the debt) several times. As could be expected, however, no concrete steps were taken in this direction.[30]

The communist elite's official attitude toward the country's increasingly serious debt problem is shocking in its absolute feebleness. The party and state leadership never managed to choose between the abovementioned possibilities. The Politburo was clearly in no condition to formulate a unified strategy for escaping the looming foreign-debt crisis, which it would then have to implement consistently. On the contrary, the Commission on Currency Problems, and hence the entire state apparatus, dithered between various alternatives: The country kept up its payments for a certain length of time by completely draining the currency reserves; extraordinary efforts were made to conceal the true state of the economy, in order to extend the revolving financing from Western banks for at least a few more months; groundless hopes were pinned on "miraculous" help from Moscow; and budgets for investments were cut (albeit insufficiently) in fits and starts, with cuts sometimes affecting funds for the technological renovation of production capabilities and sometimes targeting capital investments for improving the population's living standards. After the Politburo wavered between a series of contradictory and often mutually exclusive policies, declaring a moratorium on the debt became inevitable. Payments were stopped in March 1990 and with that the attempt to build a successfully functioning planned economy in Bulgaria also came to an end. It was an experiment that had ended in bankruptcy.

The collapse of the "Revival Process" and the intensification of Bulgaria's international isolation

Gorbachev's *perestroika* and its official Bulgarian replica in the form of Zhivkov's July Conception of 1987 placed the "Revival Process" in a wholly different domestic and international context.

"The winds of change" had led to the emergence of various dissident groups and proto-organizations, which to greater or lesser degrees included the question of human rights in their charters and declarations. In several cases, leaders and members of dissident associations helped Bulgarian Turks formulate their demands and tactics with respect to the government, as well as their declarations of protest addressed to Western media and human rights organizations.[31] Despite persecution, these "informal organizations" turned out to be catalysts for more far-reaching changes. Ankara, which from the very beginning of the campaign had tried to draw international attention to Bulgaria's violations of its Helsinki obligations, also officially stepped up its efforts. After attempting to raise the question at the annual meeting of the

The paralyzation of the regime 365

Islamic Conference, as well as at the Belgrade and Vienna meetings of the OSCE, Turkey prepared a new diplomatic offensive planned for the upcoming Paris meeting of the OSCE in May 1989 that was dedicated to human rights. This turned out to be an ideal opportunity for the downtrodden Turkish population in Bulgaria to remind the world of its plight, especially since interest in the situation had not died down in any case.[32] This set off the so-called May Events, which took the form of hunger strikes, mass protests, clashes with the police and special detachments created by the government; there were injuries and casualties on both sides of the conflict. The hunger strikes, some of which lasted until the end of May, grew into mass protests and demonstrations (especially on May 20 in the village of Pristoe near Shumen). There were protests by Bulgarian Turks in a number of places, but the largest such events were held between May 20 and May 31 in the regions of Kaolinovo, Dulovo, Isperih, Razgrad, Dobrich, Târogvishte, Shumen, Omurtag in northeastern Bulgaria, and Dzhebel in the Rhodopes. This turn of events, which caught the government off guard, convinced the leadership that their assimilation campaign had failed and caused them to return to their old strategy of forced emigration.

On May 29, 1989, Todor Zhivkov made a television and radio address that was printed the next day in newspapers and as a separate brochure. His long-winded speech in essence did not stray from the previously established course. Its basic message was that Turkey should open its borders to all Bulgarian citizens wishing to emigrate, who would be given that opportunity.[33] The Bulgarian–Turkish diplomatic row had reached a new, extremely tense phase.[34] "The Great Excursion" was a euphemism which began appearing in mass-media outlets and which reflected the official Bulgarian position that the people emigrating were, in fact, leaving the country only as tourists. At the conference in Paris, Foreign Minister Petâr Mladenov made a statement to that effect, blaming "certain foreign elements" for the unrest.[35] The government's behavior during the following extremely tense months once again showed they were coasting along on "revival" inertia.

Thus it came about that on June 3, Turkey opened its borders, setting off a massive wave of emigration that took place without any specially negotiated agreement between the two countries. "Emigration fever" spread among Bulgarian Turks, fueled by the two countries' propaganda campaigns as well as the tireless rumor machine, mutual negotiations, and pressure.[36] Panic, nationalistic sentiments, and xenophobia gripped the whole of Bulgarian society – a situation which at this point was welcomed by the Bulgarian government. In the meantime, the frantic rush to emigrate materialized in long lines for passports, vehicles loaded with whatever property the emigrants were allowed to take with them, the hurried sale of the rest of their belongings, usually for a pittance, including the exchange of apartments and houses for cars, which emigrants could use to transport their baggage. The roads leading to the Bulgarian–Turkish border were choked with columns made up of thousands of emigrants,

366 *The collapse of communism in Bulgaria*

carrying their humble possessions. Yet again, Bulgarian Turks found themselves playing the role of hostages in larger political games. These games, however, would ultimately lead to the fall of the Zhivkov regime, which the abovementioned maneuvers, as well as others could do nothing to save.[37] The collapse of the regime would also put an end to the "Revival Process." The scope of the "Great Excursion" again clearly demonstrates the failure of the Bulgarian government's assimilation campaign, which in its own way contributed to the ultimate discrediting of the ruling elite.

Between the beginning of the "excursion" on June 3 and the unilateral closing of the border by Turkey on August 21, 1989, approximately 360,000 people managed to emigrate; however, nearly 40,000 of them returned to Bulgaria before Zhivkov fell from power and before the three-month visas they had been granted expired.[38] It is no less important to note that nearly 400,000 more Bulgarian Turks had applied for passports, which means that, in total, more than 80 percent of Bulgaria's Turkish population had left or wanted to leave the country.[39] By the end of 1990, more than 150,000 (around 40 percent) of the emigrants had returned to Bulgaria. But they would find themselves in a country gripped by radical political changes that would gradually redefine their status as fully equal citizens.[40]

After Zhivkov fell from power on November 10, 1989, his successors "at the top" also inherited, alongside many other problems, a serious ethnic crisis in the country that had been brought on by the "Revival Process." After some hesitation, growing protests by Turks and Muslims demanding the return of their rights and their names hastened the party's decision to reject the revival policy and to place all the blame for it squarely on the toppled dictator and his inner circle. The formal end of the "Revival Process" came with resolutions at the Plenum of the Central Committee of the BCP on December 29, 1989, but it would be more accurate to say that they merely acknowledged the policy's serious and long-lasting consequences, not only for the regime but for Bulgarian society as a whole.

Making sense of the "Revival Process" and placing it within the larger social context is crucial for any analysis of the social and political nature of Bulgarian communism. It shows important structural differences between the regime in Sofia and the other Eastern European countries, with the exception of Romania. As has already been noted, it marked the final phase of a gradual nationalistic evolution, which slowly but surely shifted the emphasis from class back to nation. It was expressed in escalating suspicion, which grew into tension between Turks and Bulgarian, between Muslims and Christians, and, on the whole, between Bulgarians and non-Bulgarians, which materialized in several ways – in history and literature textbooks, through party/political propaganda, and through so-called "patriotic education" carried out by state organizations and especially the Fatherland Front. Thus, the "Revival Process" was actually designed above all to rally the Christian majority behind the regime's policies – and it must be said that in this respect it did achieve a certain level of success. This, in turn, made the consequences of the policy

The paralyzation of the regime 367

all the more grave and slowed the process of overcoming pent-up inter-ethnic tensions during the whole of the Transition period.

Perestroika-related processes in late-communist culture

Even though *perestroika*-related processes unfolded for only a very short time, they must be discussed here in order to understand the state of official Bulgarian culture immediately before the fall of communism, as well as due to the fact that they also left a mark on ideas about Bulgaria's cultural policy even after the end of the regime. With the start of *perestroika* (known as *preustroystvo* in Bulgarian, or literally "restructuring"), the regime's propaganda was filled with economic terminology that described new horizons for the utopian future and new vistas for human happiness under socialism. Bulgarian society would be restructured as a "self-governing system," whose basic cells would be independent "labor collectives"; these would be absolutely freely formed, and their stable economic foundation would consist of the socialist property that would be given to them "to manage and run," etc. – these were the first formulations of the planned economic liberalization of Bulgarian society under the party's unchallenged leading role and political supremacy.

The first concrete steps for changing the existing system for producing and distributing culture were taken after March 1988, in response to the first unambiguously dissident gestures made by influential Bulgarian intellectuals and coordinated mass acts of civil disobedience signaling open disagreement within the regime's policy. A series of meetings and two special Politburo plenums held before the autumn of 1989 would offer a more precise interpretation of the earlier, general formulations and would develop the regime's official answer concerning the necessary changes in culture. These key moments included the meetings of the Politburo on March 24 and 27, 1988, where the main ideas in Todor Zhivkov's report "Some Problems and Tasks Concerning Perestroika in the Spiritual Sphere" were approved; the Politburo meeting on May 26, 1988; the Plenum of the Central Committee held on July 19–20, 1988, and its resolutions "About Perestroika in the Spiritual Sphere"; the December Plenum of the Central Committee of the BCP on December 13–14, 1988, which identified company organization as the principle guiding the future existence of "self-governing organizations in the spiritual sphere"; the Politburo sessions in February 1989 and Zhivkov's meeting with "distinguished representatives from the sphere of science, culture and education" on February 20. The goal of all these meetings was to determine the acceptable "line of retreat" from the basic foundations of socialist society. During these sessions, the party elite discussed the permissible boundaries for economic initiatives within the sphere of culture and the free organization of intellectuals.

Three important documents which were approved by the Politburo on October 31, 1989, summarized the outcomes of these numerous high-level

368   *The collapse of communism in Bulgaria*

party and state discussions and offered an unambiguous interpretation of the meaning and content of the *"perestroika*-inspired" cultural policy that was imposed during the regime's final days. The "Decree for Economic Activity in Artistic Culture and in Publishing Activities" regulated the new conditions for economic activity and principles of company organization within "the sphere of spiritual production."[41] As part of the strategy to resolve the crisis in relations between the regime and artistic organizations, the document created conditions for "liberating artists" from the control of their own unions' leadership and allowed for their self-initiated and economically motivated collaboration with newly permitted companies within artistic and publishing spheres. The decree prescribed the conditions for a competition between such companies, while still guaranteeing a protected position for companies oriented toward state cultural policy. It confirmed the free determination of honoraria based on contracts with a direct client commissioning a work and free selling prices for all "spiritual valuables and services"; however, in certain cases it stipulated that the Council of Ministers, "with an eye to the complex domestic and international situation," would define a set level of compensation for certain particularly important types of artistic and performance work – including special publications, the creation and public production of special musical and dramatic works, and recordings of certain works on audio and video formats – which would regulate "the most important trends within the artistic-creative process." This essentially recreated the situation that had existed since the early 1950s, in which state control over honoraria forced artists toe the party line in cultural policy.

The second document was entitled "Economic Rules for Cultural Activity."[42] Its provisions covered state theaters, musical institutes, ensembles, reading rooms, libraries, museums, and groups for *hudozhestvena samodeynost* or "amateur artistic activity," and assigned new functions to the countless bureaucratic units within culture. Here, too, "due to the nature" of such activities, the most important source of financing in the future would be the state budget; however, funds would henceforth be dispensed through strict "results-oriented" selection based on the competing artistic programs such groups would develop and not simply in support of already existing structures, as had been the case up until that point. The "Economic Rules" guaranteed state management bodies a leading role in the "cultural process" through their right to determine the ratio between paid, unpaid, and partially paid commissions for "cultural valuables and services"; through the standardized and budgetary limits on financing and the scope of state commissions in national programs for culture; through the organization of competitions; through the state's predominant share in financial joint programs; through the introduction of fixed labor contracts for performers, as well as with the help of other economic means such as exemption from taxes, customs duties, fees, loan concessions, and so on.

"The Decree to Amend and Supplement the Law on Artistic Funds" was designed to undermine the leadership of the existing artistic unions, some of which in the final years of the regime had been sharply critical of the party leadership.[43] The document called for the managing boards of the artistic funds to become independent of the artistic unions' governing bodies. It stipulated that the boards carrying out the organizations' economic activities would become independent, competing companies, while the leadership of the artistic unions would have mainly aesthetic-artistic and critical authority.

Obviously, this planned "economization" of culture did not change in any way the party and state's leading position in the "management of the cultural process." It introduced economic and organizational accents into propaganda, which were aimed above all at undermining the cultural elite's social recognition. By exploiting vague liberal attitudes found in Bulgarian society at the time concerning the power of artistic freedom and individual talent, as well as faith in professionalism and in the miracle of the independent economic initiative, this "economization of culture" attempted to replace the fragile dissident criticism that was consolidating itself in the arts at that time with economic competition between "free organizations with a nonprofit goal." In the end, the "new economic regulators" and "new structures for self-governance in spiritual life" were called upon to carry out a new political distribution of real economic resources that would benefit politically constructed "free economic agents within the sphere of spiritual production."

Socialist realism as an abandoned fortress

In the final years of communism, Bulgaria entered a phase marked by the near total "concealment" of issues explicitly related to socialist realism and by its ultimate conversion into an empty catchphrase used to ritually acknowledge almost any artistic practice. All of communist Bulgaria's literature and culture had long since been declared *socialist*, but in the late 1980s, the topic of socialist realism remained marginalized even within the official public discourse. The process of completely draining the doctrine of any meaning through ubiquitous application was also accelerated by extensive use of the "patriotic theme." Lyudmila Zhivkova's cultural policy, which was characterized by exuberant declarations of collective Bulgarian identity as part of the ambitious celebration of the 1,300th anniversary of the founding of the Bulgarian state, unleashed the powers of state nationalism, especially following the Daughter's death. With the launch of the "Revival Process" in Bulgaria after 1984, the use of nationalist resources within communist ideology became radicalized and such elements reformulated into the "patriotic theme" within the doctrine of socialist realism. Books, plays, and films (including those by "assimilated" Bulgarian Turks with "restored names") tirelessly rehashed historical myths that served the propaganda of the "Revival Process."

The literature and culture of communist Bulgaria from the late 1980s also felt the pressure of perestroika and especially its element of *glasnost*, which had been proclaimed in Moscow. The reprinting of articles from the Soviet

370 *The collapse of communism in Bulgaria*

press in Bulgarian media – mostly about victims of Stalinism and unfairly repressed, forgotten artists who had until recently been banned – awakened analogous impulses in Bulgaria as well. There were almost no prominent artists left in Bulgaria who propounded the doctrine of socialist realism in their artworks. As Ivaylo Znepolski has noted, "the party ideologues were forced to maintain their strategy more and more through the use of generous financial support for specially commissioned works created by the literary-party nomenclature."[44] Artistic practices had demonstratively abandoned the doctrine and were expanding into other sociocultural forms, which stood at a categorically critical (and oppositional) distance from socialist realism. The emergence of *samizdat*, or underground self-publishing (such as the appearance of the illegal magazines *Bridge* and *Voice*, and the hand-to-hand distribution of censored and banned works) and the creation of the first free associations for members of the intelligentsia and the literati turned this alternative type of public space into a truly oppositional – as well as influential and popular – space for sharing strong criticism of the government. Thus, throughout the 1980s, there were signs (works not only from that period but also from the recent past) that sketched out the contours of an *alternative literature and culture*, while the elements of an *alternative literary public life* multiplied with the emergence of *samizdat* and informal literary groups and university seminars.

The final phase of socialist realism, even before November 1989, was actually a time of defeated socialist realism. The doctrine had been hollowed out – it was an abandoned fortress.

Notes

1 Yahiel, *Todor Zhivkov*, p. 340.
2 TsDA, f. 1B, op. 68, a. e. 3498, l. 17. The euphemism "overcoming the people's alienation from the means of production" actually masked the problems of employee discipline, production quality, and the enormous turnover/farce, ruefully captured in the phrase: "We pretend to work, they pretend to pay us" – all insurmountable within the framework of a centrally planned economy.
3 Iliyana Marcheva, "Perestroykata v Bâlgariya v svetlinata na modernizatsiyata," *Istorichesko bâdeshte*, 7 (1–2) (2003): 79–98, at p. 95 and following.
4 TsDA, f. 1B, op. 68, a. e. 3498, l. 15–17. On another occasion, Zhivkov expounds how the process of handing over property for private management is executed: "In agriculture, they told us straight out: well now, once upon a time you beat us so you could take the land; now, what do you want – to beat us again to return the land to us? But what happened in industry, it largely went over sluggishly." TsDA, f. 1B, op. 65, a. e. 91, l. 14–15.
5 TsDA, f. 1B, op. 68, a. e. 3541, l. 74.
6 *Dârzhaven vestnik* 4 (January 13, 1989). See especially Articles 34 and 35 of Decree 56 on Economic Activity.
7 TsDA, f. 1B, op. 68, a. e. 3698, l. 12–15, 21–24.
8 TsDA, f. 1B, op. 68, a. e. 3541, l. 72.
9 TsDA, f. 1B, op. 68, a. e. 3541, l. 89.

The paralyzation of the regime   371

10 TsDA, f. 1B, op. 68, a. e. 3553, l. 7.
11 TsDA, f. 1B, op. 68, a. e. 3252, l. 70 and following.
12 TsDA, f. 1B, op. 68, a. e. 3252, l. 14–15.
13 Cited in Avramov, *Pari i delstabilizatsiya v Bâlgariya*, p. 299.
14 P. Bârgâr, *Kapitalisticheskata revolyutsiya: Petdeset tvârdeniya za prosperiteta, ravenstvoto i svobodata*, Sofia: Ciela, 1998, pp. 224–225.
15 In 1985, the country's foreign debt in convertible currency was $US4.1 billion, while in 1987 it reached $US7.5 billion, and in 1989, it had already surpassed $US10 billion.
16 Hristo Hristov, *Taynite faliti na komunizma*, Sofia: Ciela, 2007, p. 375.
17 Vachkov and Ivanov, *Bâlgarskiyat vânshen dâlg*, p. 229.
18 TsDA, f. 1B, op. 66, a. e. 2094, l. 25.
19 AMVnR, op. 40, a. e. 517, l. 43.
20 AMVnR, op. 42, a. e. 1039, l. 24–28; price margin: here, the reduction of the price below that of the world market, to guarantee the sale of lower-quality goods.
21 The International Bank for Economic Cooperation was one of two banks belonging to the Council for Mutual Economic Assistance (Comecon), which financed investment and other projects in the Comecon member states.
22 TsDA, f. 136, op. 81, a. e. 1072, l. 3–4; op. 82, a. e. 102, l. 3–4.
23 Maturity structure: the time frame for repayment of a country's foreign debt.
24 AMVnR, op. 36, a. e. 376, l. 74; *BNB: Godishen otchet za 1990*, Sofia: BNB, 1991, p. 39.
25 Calculated based on *BNB: Godishen otchet, 1990*, Sofia: BNB, 1990, pp. 75–84; and Angus Maddison, *The World Economy: Historical Statistics*, Paris: OECD, 2004, pp. 93–100.
26 TsDA, f. 132, op. 15, a. e. 1, l. 23–25.
27 TsDA, f. 132, op. 15, a. e. 1, l. 23–25.
28 TsDA, f. 132, op. 15, a. e. 1, l. 1–2.
29 TsDA, f. 1B, op. 68, a. e. 3493, l. 52.
30 TsDA, f. 1B, op. 68, a. e. 3476, l. 306.
31 *Istinata za "vâzroditelniya protses": Dokumenti ot arhiva na Politbyuro na TsK na BKP*, Sofia: Institut za izsledvane na integratsiyata, 2003, pp. 36, 50–54, 103, 106; "DPS – portret v dvizhenie. Ot nelegalna organizatsiya do parlamentaren tsentâr," *Standart*, June 5, 1993.
32 See, for example: Amnesty International, "Bulgarien: Inhaftierung von ethnischen Türken und Menschenrechtsaktivisten, February, 1989," *Amnesty International Jahrbuch*, Sofia: Amnesty International, 1989, pp. 425–428.
33 *Istinata za "vâzroditelniya protses,"* pp. 38–44. (The unity of the Bulgarian people is the concern and the destiny of every citizen in our dear homeland. Statement by the Chairman of the State Council of the People's Republic of Bulgaria Todor Zhivkov on Bulgarian Television and Bulgarian Radio – May 29, 1989).
34 For Bulgarian–Turkish relations and the international aspect of the "Great Excursion," see Stoyanov, *Turskoto naselenie*, pp. 207–214.
35 Kalinova and Baeva, *Bâlgarskite prehodi, 1939–2005*, p. 244.
36 *Istinata za "vâzroditelniya protses,"* pp. 87, 89, 97, 103, 107, 113, 115–116, 120, 129.
37 Kalinova and Baeva, *Bâlgarskite prehodi, 1939–2005*, pp. 246–257.
38 For the "Great Excursion," its social composition, and various evaluations of the intensity and scale of the emigration wave and the subsequent stream of returnees by the end of 1989, and after that until the end of 1990, see: Stoyanov,

372 *The collapse of communism in Bulgaria*

Turskoto naselenie, pp. 204–214; U. Byuksenshyutts, *Maltsinstvenata politika v Bâlgariya: Politikata na BKP kâm evrei, romi, pomatsi i turtsi*, Sofia: MTsPMKV, 2000, pp. 176–182; *Etnicheskiyat konflikt v Bâlgariya 1989*, Sofia: Sociologicheski arhiv, Partizdat, 1990, pp. 106–112; D. Vasileva, "Bulgarian Turkish Emigration and Return," *International Migration Review*, 26 (2) (1992): 342–353.

39 Y. Baev and N. Kotev, "Izselnicheskiyat vâpros v bâlgaro-turskite otnosheniya sled Vtorata svetovna voyna," *Mezhdunarodni otnosheniya*, 2 (1994): 59–60.

40 Stoyanov, *Turskoto naselenie*, pp. 214–233; V. Stoyanov, "Po trudniya pât kâm vâzrazhdaneto: bâlgarskite turtsi i myusyulmani v otvoyuvane na maltsinstvenite si prava," in *Aspekti na etnokulturnata situatsiya v Bâlgariya: Osem godini po-kâsno*, Sofia: Asotsiatsiya AKSES i Izdatelstvo "Otvoreno obshtestvo," 2000, pp. 190–205; K. Kertikov, "Etnonatsionalniyat problem v Bâlgariya," *Bulgarian Quarterly*, 1 (1992): 76–120.

41 TsDA, f. 1 B, op. 68, a. e. 3799, l. 119. Decree for economic activity in artistic culture (draft). October 1989.

42 TsDA, f. 1 B, op. 68, a. e. 3799, l. 18. Report by Y. Yotov, Politburo member and secretary of the Central Committee of the BCP. October 26, 1989.

43 TsDA, f. 405, op. 11, a. e. 131, l. 62. Information about the restructuring of artistic funds. September 25, 1989.

44 Ivaylo Znepolski, "Literaturna publichnost i politika," in *Ezikât na imaginerniya prehod*, Sofia: Bâlgarska sbirka, 1997, p. 12.

20 The limits of the communist model and an evaluation of the regime's social policy

Today, ordinary Bulgarians nostalgic for the past, as well as historians of the communist period, note that it was a time of the peaceful construction of the country's industry, a time of security and equality. The quintessence of this attitude can be found in Todor Zhivkov proud proclamation from the 1980s, "We built two Bulgarias!" meaning that under socialism the country had taken a huge leap forward. These words seem to have retained their magical effect, since even today they evoke the same wild applause as they did at the high-level party forum where they were first uttered. Moreover, sociologist Andrey Raychev recently went so far as to correct the General Secretary, adding that actually far more than two Bulgarias were built – we could even speak of three or four . . . Indeed, the formal foundations for such a claim do seem to exist. "Despite all the problems, mistakes, aberrations and difficulties," we read in a history textbook,

> from 1944 until 1989, a significant industrial base was built in Bulgaria. In comparison to 1939, it produced far more textiles, cigarettes, paper, metals, coal and other industrial goods. The machine-building, metallurgy, electronics and chemical industries underwent intense development. Bulgaria remains one of the world's leaders in the manufacturing of electric trucks and forklifts. Its munitions industry has found a stable international market. Agriculture experienced a significant increase in the production of animal and plant products.[1]

According to the statistics cited, overall industrial production in 1989 grew by 103 times compared to 1939, agriculture grew by a factor of 2.65, and construction expanded fourteen times over.[2]

How can we explain these statistics, which at first glance appear very impressive? In two ways: We must first recall Bulgaria's humble starting point. When industry has not been developed in a country, the construction of even a single factory increases the statistical indicators many times over. This is a phenomenon characteristic of poorly developed countries. In such cases, growth rates are normally far higher than in developed countries. For example, the average annual growth rate of national incomes around the world between 1971 and

374   *The collapse of communism in Bulgaria*

1975 was 3.9 percent, while in Comecon member countries it was 6.4 percent and in Bulgaria 7.8 percent – a statistic that made the country one of the fastest-growing in the world.[3] On the other hand, this quick growth, as we have already seen, was also due to the extensive accumulation of various elements of production: capital, cheap labor, and total mobilization (i.e. workers' extreme physical efforts and the cult glorifying this), which all came at a high human cost. Bulgaria's growth remained relatively high for quite some time, but there was nothing exceptional about this. If in the short term, communist industrialization appeared efficient, in the mid-range this effect dwindled and soon petered out. It was precisely this initial spurt of intense development that caused Khrushchev to challenge the West to a peaceful competition between the systems in the early 1960s and even to declare that during the 1980s the Soviet Union would have already built communism. Precisely this same optimism was gushing forth in Zhivkov's statement about "the two Bulgarias."

We must also ask to what extent the official statistics from the communist era can be trusted. The various sources we have consulted indicate different, often fundamentally contradictory data. Moreover, the primary sources upon which these publications were based are often missing. Thus, the attempt to objectively evaluate communist Bulgaria's economic growth also runs up against the problem of the quality of the data itself. This problem is not confined to Bulgaria; researchers studying the Soviet economy also find themselves facing the same difficulty. It is well known that under communism statistics were readily used to serve the purposes of domestic and international propaganda. No effective mechanism for oversight and control existed within the country – nor did anyone have any interest in carrying out such oversight. Statistics were usually prepared on the basis of what had been planned in advance, while afterwards it was not the real production level but rather the projected one that was reported as the "result." It is also well known that accounting reports from enterprises and the ministries in charge of various sectors inflated their successes and growth levels in order to further professional and financial ambitions, thus in most cases we can assume that the data was falsified in one way or another. Official statistics automatically reproduced this dubious information, as a rule not taking into account inflation or price changes that would affect the production levels determined within the five-year plans.[4] For all of these reasons, economic data from the communist era must be used very carefully. But let us assume for the moment that such data deserve our trust and that the levels of growth indicated were actually real.

And so, returning to Todor Zhivkov's words: "We built two Bulgarias!" This phrase essentially compares Bulgaria to itself; it is almost like saying that a twenty-year-old is twice as tall as he was when he was five. When a claim is made in this way, we cannot form any real idea of an individual's actual growth with respect to his schoolmates. The same holds true in the case of economic growth. What is being compared are not two autonomous national economies but rather two different points in the economic trajectory

The limits of the communist model 375

of one and the same national economy, which cannot serve as the basis for an objective evaluation. It is natural for a half-century of peaceful development to lead to certain changes in a country's economy; otherwise, we would have to entertain the possibility that a society with zero-percent growth could exist, permanently frozen at its starting point. Bulgaria certainly increased its wealth during the communist period, but how can we discern whether these achievements were sufficient, whether the country developed to its fullest potential, and, most importantly, whether these gains were worth the price. By comparing Bulgaria from 1939 or 1944 with Bulgaria from later periods, we preclude the possibility of forecasting what the country's economic growth might have been if its economic model had not been changed from capitalism to communism.

However, the comparison between Bulgaria of 1939 or 1944 and Bulgaria of 1980 is not particularly valid for another reason as well: such development took place in fundamentally different contexts. Over the intervening decades, the world witnessed several technological revolutions that led to the electronic era. The worlds of 1944 and 1980 were completely different, not only with different possibilities but also with different dynamics. Accelerated economic development was a universal post-World War II phenomenon, not confined to the European continent – the German and Italian "economic miracles" were repeated in many other parts of world. Asian countries are typical in this respect, as their annual growth rates remained between 10–15 percent for quite an extended period. Thus, the communist economy should not be examined with respect to its own starting point but rather within the context of what was going on around the world during the same period.

A true evaluation of the economic growth achieved by Bulgaria's communist regime can be made only by comparing the development of other countries that followed a different economic model. The best choices for such a comparison are neighboring countries and those similar in terms of population, territory, or natural resources, such as Greece, Yugoslavia, Portugal, Finland, and Ireland, for example. I am not aware that any such comparative studies have been conducted in Bulgaria or about Bulgaria, but I am familiar with the results of a similar study about the Soviet Union – conducted outside of its borders, of course – that compared its growth with that of nearly 100 other countries around the world with similar levels of investment and education for the period of 1960–1989, i.e. the period after the initial positive effect of intensive growth had waned. The conclusions are telling: the Soviet Union's economic achievements rank among the lowest in the world.[5] We can presume that the truth about Bulgarian growth is not radically different, since the USSR served as its economic model.

Precisely such a comparison with other (more or less distant) countries brings to the fore the issue that is difficult to grasp within a closed, self-referential system: what price was paid for the gains made? And what remained unaccomplished, despite the ostensible rate of development? In one of the numerous recent chronicles of the former regime's successes, we read,

376 *The collapse of communism in Bulgaria*

"Under communist rule, the national income increased sixteen times over, while the gross domestic product increased twenty-six times over."[6] Taken by themselves, these results sound impressive. The problem arises, however, when we start asking why has the standard of living remained relatively low if these statistics are true. Here, of course, we find ourselves facing a problem that only the most experienced economic historians are prepared to solve: which monetary unit should be used as the basis of these calculations? Should we use the so-called golden Bulgarian lev from before the war, or the wartime currency, or the lev that was sharply devalued after the war, or the inconvertible and officially greatly overvalued lev from the communist era, which itself underwent several changes in value . . . We merely note this problem, since we cannot find any explanations of the methodology used in the abovementioned calculations; however, that is not even the most fundamental problem. The more important question is why, with such solid assets to its name, did Bulgaria sink into economic crisis in the late 1980s and accumulate a foreign debt that the country was absolutely incapable of paying off? This was debt which the system needed to function but which it was in no condition to service.

Clearly, the problem cannot be solved by citing various figures and percentages, nor can it be reduced to describing the industrial base that was created. Instead, we must examine this industrial base's expediency and the way it functioned. Simply reporting the quantitative output of industrial production does not make clear the most important thing: the degree to which this production was effective and saw realization on the market. Today, most assessments of the communist economy agree that a large portion of Bulgaria's industrial giants generated losses. Even though they produced goods, they did not generate profits; hence, they not only failed to contribute to the country's wealth but actually undermined it. They existed for the sake of prestige (and for the sake of official reports) and guaranteed jobs, which was important for the policy of full employment that was trumpeted in propaganda. Another large percentage of enterprises, given their lack of competitiveness, found themselves without a market for their products once the undemanding Soviet market had been lost. Thus, a significant portion of the industrial capabilities built turned out to be ends in themselves, production for the sake of production. This was production that did not generate profits and that hollowed out the domestic product, leaving it with no real content. This low rate of return on investments in no way justified the enormous social sacrifices that had been demanded. The growth achieved by the communist regime was not accompanied by a sufficient increase in the standard of living; moreover, its economy continued to function at a deficit until the very end of the regime. People got by in their everyday life by gaming the system – by developing a parallel market or creating informal networks. The consequences of the Soviet path of development have proved impossible to overcome in the nearly twenty-seven years after the changes in 1989. Bulgaria remains the poorest country in the European Union with a per capita GDP of €6,000, while the

The limits of the communist model   377

average for the twenty-eight member states is €26,900 – and this at a growth rate of 4.1 percent compared to the 1.5 percent average of the twenty-eight member states.[7]

This evaluation shows that the success of forced communist industrialization was primarily limited to the sphere of social engineering – a tactic that in the end turned against the regime itself.

A social policy "in service of the people"

The communist regime's social policy, which supposedly fulfilled the promise of equality and social justice, was based on two fundamental principles: redistribution and leveling. Centralized planning and financing allowed for the gradual passage of the necessary laws and the redirection of funds toward social programs. This, in turn, led to an increased standard of living for groups that had been the most socially disadvantaged and underdeveloped in prewar times. Communist social policy demands a more detailed study; here we will limit ourselves to briefly recounting the standard social benefits that the new government guaranteed to its citizens. First, we must mention the constitutionally enshrined right to work, which, combined with the policy of forced industrialization and massive state investment, gradually eradicated unemployment, which has traditionally been the scourge of undeveloped countries. Widely propagandized trade-union rights guaranteed the strict observation of the standard workday and outlawed child labor.[8] Reasonably priced cafeterias were set up in factories and administrative departments, which were subsidized by the respective enterprises. A broad network of kindergartens and vacation complexes for workers on the seaside and in the mountains was created, serving nearly the whole population. Paid annual vacation was also introduced. Pensions paid 60 percent of the salary a worker had received over three consecutive years of their choice, as long as they had worked for twenty-five years and had reached the age of sixty for men or worked twenty years and reached the age of fifty-five for women. Pensions were also gradually introduced for members of agricultural collectives, a practice previously unheard of in villages. This allowed elderly people to maintain at least a minimal standard of living. Some of these new social benefits resulted directly from the "peaceful competition between the systems" championed by Khrushchev. Thus, in Bulgaria, too, the length of the workweek was shortened for purely propagandistic purposes, even though the country had not met the necessary economic preconditions for such a move. Despite chronic shortages of various goods, the standard of living in the 1970s had already surpassed that of the 1940s. Incidentally, the competition between the communist and capitalist systems directly led to a general improvement in the social climate and an elevated standard of living in the West as well. The welfare state constructed in Western Europe after the war can in certain respects be seen both as a move to strengthen the home front in case of a Soviet invasion and as a response to the communist regime's

378 *The collapse of communism in Bulgaria*

propaganda about social policy, which activated the leftist and trade-union movements and increased pressure on Western governments.

The Bulgarian population was guaranteed free and equal access to state healthcare, which did not require any type of individual health insurance. In comparison to the prewar and wartime periods, this represented a giant step forward. Many new hospitals were built while medical clinics were opened in smaller communities. Mandatory, free-of-charge check-ups for all citizens were introduced, while infant mortality rates plunged. As the years passed, however, the quality of health services in Bulgaria began to significantly lag behind the postwar standards achieved in other countries. The material conditions in most hospitals, as well as their hygiene, left much to be desired. Mortality rates for the most serious illnesses remained high, while pharmacies did not have access to quality medicines. They depended mainly on Bulgaria's newly created domestic pharmaceutical industry, which was in no position to respond to the population's actual needs, despite imports from other socialist countries.

Education was declared a basic priority and was considered the regime's fundamental achievement in the social sphere. A massive campaign was undertaken to eradicate illiteracy, as such rates were high among the elderly rural population, despite the fact that mandatory primary education had been imposed by the Târnovo Constitution, which had been adopted in 1879 shortly after Bulgaria's liberation from the Ottoman Empire. During the 1930s, mandatory education was extended to include most of the population, which was required to attend school from ages seven to fourteen.[9] In 1946, 75.6 percent of the population was literate, including 85.5 percent of urbanites and 72.3 percent of rural inhabitants. In the 1950s, the government began building and operating an extensive system of schools, which would serve most rural regions, while mandatory education was extended until the age of fifteen and now included minorities as well. New universities were founded in the larger cities around the country, leading to a significant increase in the number of university students, professors, and academic researchers. The regime did much to further the education of the "masses," namely the children of workers and villagers. Residents of underdeveloped economic regions on the country's periphery were given preferential admission to universities. The regime was working on the assumption that once it became educated the working class would take control of its own destiny and compensate for the lack of qualified specialists, thus the regime would be less dependent on the "bourgeois professionals" who had been temporarily recruited. Hundreds of thousands of young people from poor families were given opportunities they had never had before.[10] But alongside this "opening" of the universities, a parallel "closing" was occurring. Universities were deprived of their autonomy, which had never been questioned, not even during the most dramatic years of the war and armed conspiracy in Sofia. University deans and the academic staff were now party figures installed "from above," often political emigrants returning from the Soviet Union. Hundreds of "unreliable" students were expelled, while

The limits of the communist model 379

the experienced prewar professors were removed (with few exceptions) and were replaced by incompetent party comrades. It was only during the 1960s, with the emergence of a new generation of instructors, that things partially improved, but almost until the end of the regime only young people who had received a note certifying their "reliability" from the local Fatherland Front organization were allowed to apply to a university.[11] Professors were hired at the universities only after their candidacy had been approved by the Science and Education Department of the Central Committee of the BCP.

The regime also provided cultural benefits to broad strata of the population that had previously been deprived of them: It expanded the network of traditional reading rooms (which served as something like community centers), organized film projections in villages, arranged visits to theaters and concerts for workers' collectives, and so on. Access to theater, opera, concert halls, and books, which had been associated with material and cultural privilege in the past, was democratized when the government removed culture from the market and placed it under state patronage. The communist regime rolled out an enlightenment project that was essentially motivated by class and propaganda but that was in any case beneficial to the whole population. This was also confirmed by annual statistics, which were cited with relish in party documents and which are pointed to nostalgically by contemporary critics of the democratic state's reduced financing for certain cultural activities. Communist cultural policy was made possible not only by investing significant funds but also by introducing the principle of leveling: if, in terms of cost, access to cultural benefits became almost symbolic, this was because the salaries paid to artists, musicians, doctors, lawyers, engineers, economists, professors, and scientists were also symbolic. Highly qualified labor and unskilled manual labor were evaluated in one and the same way. The "coefficient of differentiation between incomes in absolute terms was 0.975 for workers, 1.011 for the intelligentsia, and 1.081 for agricultural laborers."[12] These statistics show the damage that was done to specialists and people involved in intellectual labor. This leveling of the prestige and payment for various categories of labor could also be seen in the diminishing gap between living standards and satisfaction of material needs, which led to a gradual homogenization of society and its transformation into a mass industrial society with a low level of organization and material security. At the same time, these processes imposed certain limits on individual development, not allowing for the formation of a highly qualified elite, and kept specialists in a state of social dependence, requiring tastes to be adapted to the mass standard.

The lower rungs of society received a series of benefits that improved their everyday life. An ambitious construction plan was unveiled, which led to a significant increase in the amount of housing available at low prices and with correspondingly low quality. The immediate results of this plan were the panel-block complexes forming the newest neighborhoods of the growing communist cities, which provided shelter to several large waves of migrants. This is also one of the reasons for Bulgaria's high rate of home

380 *The collapse of communism in Bulgaria*

ownership. Incidentally, these statistics are not an exceptional achievement, since the most recent comparative statistics within the borders of the European Union show that the same high percentage of home ownership can also be found in countries such as Greece, Portugal, and Spain; thus, we find that this is a phenomenon characteristic of less developed and poorer southern European countries where home ownership is a symbolic guarantee of social survival. Here we should also mention a series of new benefits to the basic standard of living: mass electrification, central heating in the larger cities, private bathrooms, telephone service, an expanded water-supply network, and so on. Such benefits reached ever-wider segments of society and were affordably priced. For the numerous poorer groups within society, these constituted significant social achievements, representing an image of social advancement that remained uncontested until the very end of the regime. Compared to living standards in developed countries, all of these measures satisfied needs on a rather humble level, but for most of the beneficiaries, this constituted a serious step forward. The "socialist culture" of free time and mass vacationing also developed along the same lines. The regime took care to expand – albeit it at slower tempos – the mass's purchasing power, since precisely such promises of quick prosperity lent it legitimacy. Todor Zhivkov had grown ever more aware of this fact, since in the final years of the regime he resorted to taking out significant foreign loans to satisfy domestic consumption and maintain a living standard that had become impossible for the national income, which was growing ever more slowly, to sustain.

This social policy largely explains the regime's resilience and longevity. In exchange for a life deprived of freedom and individual initiative, it offered the abovementioned compensations, creating conditions in which most people could live, if not proudly and independently, at least securely and tolerably to some extent. Moreover, given communist Bulgaria's closed society, they were not familiar with other living standards that could be used as a basis for comparison. (Later, in the late 1970s and early 1980s, when the borders gradually opened and the number of people who had traveled to the West increased, the difference would start to stand out, and the regime's base of support would begin to shrink.[13]) The fact remains that almost until the end of the regime, there were no mass demonstrations of discontent; workers' strikes like those in Poland seemed unthinkable, both in Bulgarian villages and factories. Dissatisfaction arose solely in intellectual circles, but even this did not call into question the regime's principles but rather criticized the mediocrity and pettiness of the functionaries in charge of the cultural sphere. But this does not mean that the "average Bulgarian" simply did not feel any particular need for freedom and willingly traded it for a minimum level of security. In fact, something far worse occurred: the regime's principles penetrated deeply into people's innermost psyche and shaped them according to its model. After the fall of the regime on November 10, 1989, alongside the loss of social status and the destruction of lifestyle stereotypes (a life marked by a slow pace and little stress, which lulled one into a routine), this internalization of the regime's principles formed the basis for "retro nostalgia."

Sources and uses of nostalgia

The change of 1989 was reflected in various expressions of nostalgia for the recent past, which certain observers use to relativize assessments of the communist period. But nostalgia is not a simple phenomenon; instead, it has varying sources and different faces. This is why it seems more precise to speak not of nostalgia but of nostalgias. Another key point in understanding this phenomenon is the fact that nostalgia is not a mass phenomenon; it did not arise immediately after the democratic change but appeared in connection with enormously unrealistic expectations and the disappointment that followed them. The sources of this disappointment also varied. In every societal change there are losers, but the change after the fall of the Berlin Wall was a radical change to the system and hence tied to a widespread displacement of positions. Communism had carefully constructed its own social base, weaving a huge network of supporters. This network initially consisted of thousands of people with little education, whom the regime brought up from the bottom of the social ladder and placed at the center of society. They were rank-and-file representatives of the party in all spheres of life: factories, agricultural collectives, universities, academic institutions, trade, healthcare, administration, the court system, apartment blocks, neighborhoods, villages, cities, and so on. This multitudinous army, in exchange for its contribution to securing total control of society, enjoyed significant gains and privileges. But the power structure collapsed unexpectedly, and they (and the members of their families, we must add) felt immediately affected – they lost not only their privileges but also the social status they had been given. Psychologically, it seems understandable that they are turned fully toward the past. The stranger thing is that among them we find newly minted "red richies" – their material wealth is not enough to compensate for their lost influence and sense of class superiority. In this group, nostalgia draws its strength from the vehement rejection of democratic practices.

The second social group generating nostalgia is made up of people who welcomed the fall of communism but who are marked by the social passivity inherited from it. Their nostalgia is tied to a mistaken understanding of democracy as a system that would quickly solve all of their problems. Their nostalgia stems from a lack of readiness for a free life and from a lack of knowledge about the world and the society communism entrapped them in. Having left behind a life characterized by a slow tempo and minimal stress that lulled them into routines, these people were shocked by the collision with new realities that demanded other qualities in order to build a successful life – the ability to take the initiative, overcome struggles and compete . . . Individuals from this group begin to value in hindsight the security and calm of communism, the humbleness of life under social leveling, but they do not

382 *The collapse of communism in Bulgaria*

forget the arbitrariness and the lack of freedom. They are disappointed by the present, yet they do not wish to return to the past. For them nostalgia is a dream of a simple and predictable life, a giving themselves over to the charm of a lost time, a "Marcel Proust" syndrome of sorts.

The third category of people includes older and elderly people who are not in a position to take advantage of the new opportunities the democratic changes have presented and who would find it difficult to change their way of life. They are primarily retirees, but also the inhabitants of small villages and border regions that have been most affected by the collapse of socialist heavy industry, people with educations who have lost their jobs . . . They have low incomes and, despite the various mechanisms for social support, find it difficult to cope with the new market situation. The ever-growing social inequality makes them ever more prone to reminiscing about the "security" of everyday life under communism.

In recent years, nostalgic commentaries by young people, who express the desire to revise the negative assessment of Bulgaria's communist period, have also been increasing. They have not lived under communism and have no personal experience of it. Their position draws on arguments from two different sources, which often overlap. Observations of this age group show that most often, although not always, their opinion is based on that which Paul Ricoeur calls "indebted memory." These are young people who have grown up in families connected in one way or another with the former regime and who associate their personal or familial success entirely with it. These young people remain true to their parents' memories. This behavior cannot be defined precisely as nostalgia, since it is not dictated by attachment to specific practices of the communist state but rather to abstract principles of the communist idea, removed from any particular bearer. A second source for this nostalgic discourse also plays an important role – the idea of a new leftist project promoted by this social group. The new Bulgarian leftists, under the influence of radical leftist movements in the West, reject the politics of global capitalism and the hollowing out of liberal democracy, seeking an alternative in some form of resurrected communism. However, this return to strict ideology and utopianism is most often conceived of as a double alternative – both to capitalism and to the distorted Soviet form of communism. The basis for such behavior can be found in accumulated social dissatisfaction in need of an outlet it can be channeled into.

All the forms of nostalgic behavior or nostalgic discourse mentioned here are fueled by one common source: the post-communist political parties' speculation with the actual difficulties people face, with the aim of achieving some political gain. Such speculation recycles the political narrative of "good socialism," which takes care of the little people. For example, at a campaign rally in the provinces during spring of 2017, the chairperson of the Bulgarian Socialist Party (the direct descendant of the BCP) uttered the following telling phrase: "Democracy took many things away from us – it took away our healthcare, our education, our security, but it gave us the freedom to think, to have an opinion and to fight for our rights." This statement is not based on a real comparison of the state of healthcare, education, and security in the communist period and the present but rather on an idealized picture of the past and the abstract principles of social utopia. But this deceptive discourse also shows something else: an attempt to channel politically fueled nostalgia by removing it from the realm of its experiencers' private contemplation and harnessing it for active political practice. Most voters, however, recognized the switch these words attempted to make, and, despite favorable pre-election prognoses for the upcoming election, the Socialist Party suffered a defeat. This fact may sketch out the boundaries for the political exploitation of nostalgia.

Justice and solidarity in the communist *état-providence*

Let us return to the question posed above concerning the link between the communist regime's political nature and its social policy. We accepted the fact that social benefits possess some degree of autonomy from any given political system, since to a certain extent they could not help but be implemented over the course of time. The same or similar benefits were introduced sooner or later in countries with different political systems: Soviet Russia, Fascist Italy, Nazi Germany, the welfare states in Western Europe and the United States. But we cannot ignore the fact that the political nature of the Bulgarian regime left its mark not so much on the form of social policy as on its fundamental principles and on the way social rights were exercised; the political nature of the regime also defined the place of social rights within the system of human rights as a whole.

To this end, let us recall how the idea of social security developed and was imposed in Europe over the past two centuries. In the late nineteenth and early twentieth centuries, with the advance of the industrial revolution, technical progress and the abrupt growth of the factory proletariat and the service sector, a new idea about the relations between society and the state was gradually accepted. Sociologists have defined this process as "the invention of the social." Émile Durkheim's book *The Division of Labor in Society* marked an important new stage in this process.[14] He contributed to the significant evolution of then-existing notions about society by showing that the social division of labor increases dependencies between people not only due to the fact that individuals are equal but also because they perform mutually complementary roles within the social system. This pushes the state toward exercising a new type of power which is based on the concept of solidarity. Solidarity ceases to be "mechanical" and becomes "organic." And society's organic solidarity is more significant that a voluntary contract between individuals, in so far as it is grounded on the division of labor, which in its essence means the distribution of social functions. Following the French Revolution, the big question was how to harmonize the *principle of solidarity* (the idea that society owes a debt to its members) and the *principle of responsibility* (the idea that every

384　*The collapse of communism in Bulgaria*

individual is their own master and responsible for making their own way); in other words, it was a question of how to coordinate a right with a type of behavior. This division between the right to social support and the principle of individual responsibility presumes that the sphere for exercising solidarity cannot be clearly defined in principle but rather remains organic. This is why the idea of imposing the practice of mandatory insurance was eventually arrived at, as it more successfully combines individual initiative with solidarity. "Insurance allows every individual to take advantage of the advantages of the many, while leaving them free to exist as individuals. This seems to reconcile the two antagonistic concepts – society and individual freedom."[15] The practice of insurance allows social problems to be acknowledged as involving risks that require compensation and not as resulting from a preexisting injustice that requires a fundamental change to society. The universalization of the principle of insurance acted as a sort of *moral* and *social transformer* of society, in so far as it functioned as an invisible hand of security and solidarity, without requiring people's deliberate efforts. In this sense, insurance functions as an institution of the social contract. Beginning in the second half of the nineteenth century, the state and insurance would be transformed into two mutually complementary institutions for reducing social insecurity.[16] The state's interference in the sphere of the social arose from this dual evolution in viewpoints: the subsequently acknowledged right to organize unions and strike, the regulation of labor negotiations, laws on work-related injuries and so on.[17] Even then, the tendency emerged to view the state as the "total insurer" – Rosanvallon quotes Émile de Girardin, who in 1850 expressed the view that the state was becoming a sort of earthly equivalent of divine providence (*Providence terrestre*). This early intuition suggests an idea, which, slightly paraphrased, would later leave its mark on a whole era. However, the appearance of the concept of the *état-providence* (i.e. the state as provider, the state as savior, the state as mother of all) would have to wait until the end of World War II.[18]

After World War II, in France, Great Britain, the Scandinavian countries and later Germany, as well as the United States to a certain extent, the economic and social spheres which had previously been seen as separate would no longer be viewed as conflicting. The concept of social insurance would give way to the concept of social security and the related concept of social rights. The social sphere made increasing economic growth possible, while economic growth allowed for the more just distribution of the fruits of such growth within the social sphere. "The welfare state necessarily arose in order to tame liberal capitalism and thanks to the redistribution of wealth along state lines, to incorporate a larger portion of the social classes in it. This process was assisted by the exceptional development of production capabilities and in the large growth in production."[19] The *état-providence* is historically seen as part of a reform movement whose goal was the redistribution of expenses while the way it was carried out was based on the principle of universality. However, its history is not so straightforward and consistent. It had to overcome both

The limits of the communist model   385

the tacit resistance of employers as well as a series of political biases. And, although society remained far from the proclaimed principles of social equality and justice, as a result of the establishment of such a policy, Western Europe overcame social insecurity in a very short time, and "fear of what tomorrow might bring" essentially disappeared. Unemployment dropped drastically, and the state guaranteed jobs, health insurance, vacations, and free education.

However, the concept of justice itself is very complex; thus, analysts of social processes have turned their attention to the traditional opposition between *commutative* and *distributive justice*. Commutative justice is formal justice based on equal rights. It rests on the principle of reciprocity and corresponds to the maxim *to each according to his abilities*; that is, it is based on the rule of just desserts – everyone receives the equivalent of what he contributed. Distributive justice is a corrective to commutative justice, it seeks to be "real." It is based on redistribution between the rich and the poor and corresponds to the maxim *to each according to his needs*. This latter phrase must not be interpreted in light of Marxist theory concerning the second stage of building a communist society, when all needs will be completely satisfied. In this case, it is a question of guaranteeing that people's basic needs will be met, allowing them to avoid despair and maintain their human dignity. It aims not at erasing but at lessening inequality and softening the sense of injustice and alienation. Whereas commutative justice can function without political mediation (on the basis of the contract or individual insurance), distributive justice assumes the intervention of state institutions. The opposition between these two types of justice is overcome in practice in the welfare state through actualizing the principle of solidarity. Solidarity becomes a sort of compensation for differences, in so far as the sharing is a positive act. The sharing of risks is at once a standard for justice and a procedure for solidarity.[20]

In Bulgaria before September 9, 1944, the problem of balancing the principle of individual responsibility and solidarity in social policy could be observed in its classical form. At the same time, following Europe's example, the idea of solidarity began gaining ground as it was recognized as necessary for coordinated actions to mutually secure insurance payments and pension funds. However, this principle had not spread throughout the entire working population. Solidarity was expressed most clearly within the bounds of individual professional communities or among state employees and was largely tied to the principle of individual responsibility. The principle of commutative justice continued to dominate, and large parts of the population (especially those involved in agriculture) were not included in the insurance system.

After September 9, 1944, all existing professional insurance funds were nationalized and their assets were poured into a single general fund, which from that point on was supposed to cover the entire population – that is, both those who had insured themselves and those who had not insured themselves previously. This could formally be construed as a gesture of social solidarity if the insured had taken the initiative themselves or had at least been asked

386 *The collapse of communism in Bulgaria*

for their agreement in principle. But due to the way this act of redistribution was implemented, it was fundamentally devoid of justice, since the concept of solidarity only has meaning in so far as it is an expression of free will. Of course, the funds that were amassed by force turned out to be hopelessly insufficient given the increased number of beneficiaries (despite withholdings from salaries that were paid into the obligatory Workers' Social Initiative Fund that was created immediately after the coup). Over the years, the common insurance fund would continually be shored up with funds from the state budget. The principle of individual responsibility was abolished, while the communist state introduced the principle of solidarity, with the state itself taking on the full responsibility, in so far as it proclaimed itself its main subject and guarantor.

The principle of commutative justice was at least formally allowed to continue functioning at full force. Marxist social theory itself postulates that in the stage of building the socialist society, individuals' rewards should be directly proportionate to their contribution to society's gross product. It is founded on the principle of *to each according to his abilities*; however, the regime undermined this principle from the very beginning and made it pointless in practice. Career advancement for personnel both in the administrative and production sectors did not truly depend on demand and the market, while on the personal level an individual's contribution as a worker or his competency was not the deciding factor but rather his party membership, loyalty to the regime, family background, and personal contacts. In short, everything functioned according to the logic of structural corruption that has been described previously in this book. Communist universality was developed on the basis not of class cooperation but rather class antagonism, on exclusion from the social community and the establishment of new privileges.

This fundamentally changed the principles not only of distributive justice but also of solidarity. The same notions within two different social and political contexts (the liberal and communist variants of the *état-providence*) reveal their differing contents. It would be difficult to say of Bulgaria that social solidarity was based on the principle of redistribution, since the state was not a mediator between contracting individuals; instead, in its capacity as the holder of all resources, it is the single distributor of public funds. In distributive justice, political mediation provides the mechanism for taking from the rich (through taxes and insurance obligations, and through a general policy of subsidization) and giving to the socially disadvantaged in the form of insurance, social services, and assistance in the case of unemployment, illness or disability. But within communist society class inequality is impossible by definition; no one can say who is rich and who is poor, even though people can see the differences in living standards and lifestyles. Consequently, the criteria for distribution are based not on consciously adopted principles and decisions made by specific individuals but rather are imposed "from above" and are an element of state ideology. This undermines the very foundations of the principle of solidarity. Communist society, which declares itself the most unified society in terms of its social sphere, is, in fact, not built on gestures of solidarity but rather on forced leveling.

Here is an example from the sphere of cultural politics, which is most often pointed out as an exceptionally successful case of the principle of social equality being fulfilled. Above we already mentioned the significant investments that transformed expensive forms of high culture (opera, ballet, performances of classical music, and theater) into events accessible to wide strata of the population. In this respect, we could call attention to a series of curious cases: the maintenance of a state symphonic orchestra in a rather small city with a limited audience, which performed several monthly concerts for an admission fee of 2 leva when the real value of the ticket exceeded 100 leva. This cultural policy was made possible through a "top-down" decision to implement the accepted principle of the "aesthetic elevation of the masses" and its corresponding slogan "Culture – close to the people!" regardless of a specific social group's need for various types of cultural practices. In such an undertaking, the professional musicians themselves are nothing more than regular workers carrying out a job; it was not their decision to "go down" among the masses, even if some of them might sincerely wish to do so. Their gesture of solidarity toward those whose taste has not had the opportunity to develop is made impossible or slips by unnoticed due to the very way the decision has been made.

In assuming the status of universal benefactor, the communist state appears as the only subject of justice and solidarity – a subject that swallows up all other subjects, depriving them of the right and possibility for autonomous acts of solidarity. John Rawls, in his now classic book *A Theory of Justice*, emphasizes that the principle of justice is realized in the combination of mutual disinterest (i.e. given a difference in incomes, the willingness to also accept a difference in contributions to funds for collective welfare) and that which he calls "the veil of ignorance" (i.e. uncertainty about which individuals will benefit most from the established system of benefits).

> This ensures that no one is advantaged or disadvantaged in the choice of principles by the outcome of natural chance or the contingency of social circumstances . . . This explains the propriety of the name "justice as fairness": it conveys the idea that the principles of justice are agreed to in an initial situation that is fair.[21]

The situation in the communist state is the polar opposite: individuals begin developing strategies not toward others but rather with respect to the state or party functionaries in change of distribution, with the goal of influencing their decisions and their direction of money from common funds. Social solidarity between individuals and groups loses ground to competition, as long as there is sufficient proof that the distribution of benefits in most cases depends on a subjective evaluation and often also on the incompetence of those who have usurped the privilege of doing the

388 *The collapse of communism in Bulgaria*

distributing. The condition arises in which the principle of social solidarity is degraded and replaced by self-seeking strategies benefiting an individual or group.

Social benefits and the social corruption of the masses

The communist regime's social policy was used both as a basic tool for maintaining the consensus that had been achieved as well as an instrument for the social corruption of the masses. In this case, how should we view the results of this policy – as social demagogy or as true social gains? Taken at face value, the social benefits listed above do not necessarily figure within the characteristics of a totalitarian system; however, it turns out that they are one of the things that make it possible. On the other hand, must we accept the argument that there is no direct link between the political nature of a regime and the principles of its social policy? It seems that we can speak of a certain autonomy in the social sphere in so far as labor rights and living standards in and of themselves reflect ongoing, widespread tendencies which are directly tied to technological developments. All of the social benefits listed above, as well as many others, can be found in one form or another in the modern Western welfare state as well. They are no longer burdened with the ideological connotations that were so starkly visible in earlier periods but rather have become part of the accepted system of social rights. Such rights, in turn, were a result both of active demands by organized labor as well as of influential strikes and political reform movements that were gaining steam. One argument that social benefits under communist rule did not stem wholly and directly from the system's nature can be found in the fact that they did not disappear with the end of the regime but have continued in one form or another under the new political system.

We find interesting confirmation of this fact in the Federal Republic of Germany immediately after World War II.

> Overtime pay, vacation and Christmas bonuses, family allowances, disability pensions, laws protecting small business owners, the abolition of a series of conditional privileges from the Weimar Republic with an eye to increasing equality, the introduction of previously unknown paid leave and vacation for workers, support for families and for encouraging the birth-rate, a retirement policy aimed at breaking the link between age and poverty, an increase in days off and holidays, a tax exemption for those with the lowest income, a tax reduction within the agricultural sphere, the introduction of mandatory minimum insurance contributions (widows and orphans were exempt from such payments), an increase in pensions and many other moves that had contributed to the popularity of national socialism can be seen in a series of benefits that would later mark the Federal Republic.[22]

The limits of the communist model 389

Some of these social benefits were difficult to maintain in the first years immediately after the war, but the emerging German democracy did not dare get rid of them. The Reich's social policy also sketched out the basic contours of the pension system that the Federal Republic managed to implement only after 1957.

But on the other hand, both in the Third Reich, as in communist Bulgaria, social benefits were not won through union struggles, nor were they a result of competing political projects – they were given as privileges to buy the loyalty and support of the people. The Reich's social policy was accompanied by a policy of mass murder, which turned the people into an accomplice of the regime and also led to an intensified sense of collective guilt after the war. National Socialism sought to fund its social programs through external expansion, conquest, and the pillaging of other nations; however, the communist regime in Bulgaria did not have that option, which is why its social policy was oriented toward internal expansion, toward the conquest and subjugation of Bulgarian society. In the Bulgarian case, the role of the Jews and the Nazis' "lower races" was played by the bourgeoisie or simply any wealthier and more active person, regardless of his political stripes. Things did not stop there, however: as the analysis of forced industrialization shows, communist economic expansion, which followed the Soviet recipe, used the people themselves as a basic resource, treating them as "human material" that the regime could do with as it wished. In the end, both totalitarian systems exchange social benefits for political support. The price the Germans paid was blind loyalty and participation in crimes; the price the Bulgarians paid was ostensible loyalty and turning a blind eye to crimes. Following Gotz Aly, we can describe this situation as "a policy of social corruption." Communist Bulgaria's social policy was at once a means of buying citizens' loyalty and a propagandistic act.

By depriving people of the right to individual initiative and ignoring personal interest (public interest completely swallows up the private), the regime not only created the preconditions for raising the standard of living in a "non-labor-related" way but also changed the entire attitude toward work. Formerly prestigious (communist propaganda had tried to make work prestigious in the years of postwar reconstruction, amidst the frenzied promotion of the Stakhanovite movement), work became transformed into a burden and practically a duty, into a marker of low status, the absolute opposite of free time. Unable to enjoy any true gratification from their work, people became disinterested and turned their backs on their labor, instead concentrating their attention on their free time. Boris Groys points out the ambiguous meaning of the notion of freedom. In the West, people are exceptionally active and are working all the time, establishing themselves through their work. If the construction and expression of human individuality are tied to external constraints that must be overcome through creative realization, then under communism people are deprived of true individuality or possess only a very small amount of individuality to differentiate them.

390 *The collapse of communism in Bulgaria*

What does it mean to be free? To have free time! To simply do nothing. Today it is frequently said: people in Eastern Europe were freed from communism. But under communism they had much more free time and hence much more freedom. Nobody made any particular effort. For that reason the whole endeavor itself wasn't particularly efficient, but that has nothing to do with freedom. On the contrary: in the West, people are much more subject to external constraints. Hence the West's greater efficiency.[23]

People who are deprived of the responsibility and who are not in control of their own destiny become undemanding of themselves and others. Their interest is focused on the only possible form of freedom, that of free time, and that which could fill it: material acquisitions, pleasure, consumption. Sociologists from the 1960s and 1970s wrote volumes on the consumer society in the West, which was based on hyper-production and the hyper-supply of goods on the market; however, the paradox is that the most malignant consumerist mentality arose in the East, in the communist societies with their low-quality production of consumer goods and their permanent shortages. Over time, people came up with ever newer and various ways of avoiding the regime's ideological constraints, and living with them became a sort of routine. They withdrew into themselves, into circles of friends or colleagues and were satisfied with a relatively unattractive, yet easy life. During various attempts by the regime to "reform itself," Bulgarians generally adopted the attitude that any change was for the worse. And in most cases, this was true. An internal disinterest in change arose, which was particularly advantageous for the regime but which also led to its downfall.

There is also another aspect to structural corruption: it is also a result of individuals' legal status and the social relations established on the basis of this status. This began the very day after the communists took power, when the future "people's republic" was sketched out as a society in which there was not equality before the law, since some were privileged due to their social backgrounds and their contributions to the struggle against the previous regime. If, according to the popular saying, "poverty is no vice," then the rural and urban masses discovered that poverty, alongside active support for the new authorities, was a quality they could cash in on. Thus began the formation of a society based on "ours" and "theirs," on "included" and "excluded." Literally having just descended from the mountains with guns in hand, the partisan units occupied Sofia as a hostile "bourgeois" territory. They were soon joined by their families, relatives, and fellow villagers, who came flowing in from all corners of the country to take up the newly vacated positions within the state administration – usually without the necessary educational qualifications. They were hostile toward any successful and wealthy person; for them, "bourgeois" was synonymous with "fascist" and hence was an "enemy" who needed to be put in his place. This is the key that ordered the life of the new hegemonic class. The newly adopted housing

The limits of the communist model 391

law stipulated that "needy families" would be accommodated in homes that were judged to be larger than the established norms required to meet their owners' needs. And despite the formal existence of a housing distribution directorate with its corresponding regional commissions and housing courts, a literal hunt for desirable housing began. Armed groups would roam the city center, take a liking to a certain apartment, and submit a housing request to the local commission, but they often forcibly took up residence on their own. Later, through the widespread practice of resettling "hostile elements" to the provinces or sending them to prisons and camps, significant spaces for "expansion" were freed up in the city's center. The prosaic interpretation of the slogan from Marxist theory about "expropriating the expropriators" was reflected in the settling of "victors" in the wealthy's homes and appropriation of their property. The same criteria held in the system for distributing food rations in the period of postwar shortages. Distribution was made "on the basis of the type and number of (legally established) social and productive categories within the population, the characteristics of its lifestyle and its accidentally arising needs." The population was divided into five social categories. The first category, which received the most rations, included party and state leaders, while the fifth category encompassed "unproductive" urban classes.

This was only the beginning of a process that, contrary to common logic, continued to expand and deepen in the years after the Communist Party's complete consolidation of power and when food shortages had been more or less overcome. The clearest expression of this structural corruption can be found in the nomenclature system, which was imported from the Soviet Union. The new hegemonic class drew its power, its prestige, its ideology, and its habits from the very idea of "ownership by the people." In Mikhail Voslenski's analysis in his classic two-volume work *Nomenklatura: The Soviet Ruling Class*, he focuses on appropriation (theft) on the basis of the unmediated instrumentalization of relations. The process of appropriation on the part of the nomenclature is not, as Marx's classic analysis of class relations would frame it, a result of direct ownership of the means of production but rather stems from the nomenclature's leading position in society and its control over distribution. The nomenclature uses its position as the ruling class to appropriate the people's property.[24]

This happened on the path toward implementing a smooth system for the use of privileges dependent on an individual's position in the Communist Party and administration. One's position in the government determined one's "contributions" and hence the benefits deserved – all of this was embedded in the term "rights holders." In the chapter about the State Security system in the present book, the mechanism for making use of such privileges is described in detail. A special division within State Security, the Department for Safety and Protection, catered to the high-ranking party and state nomenclature, supplying material privileges to these "rights holders" in addition to security services. Special supplies of goods and products not available to normal citizens were secured for the nomenclature; special stores with limited access

392   *The collapse of communism in Bulgaria*

were opened or Western goods were ordered; luxurious villas and apartments were built that were not subject to the normative limitations (12 m³ of living space per person); two housekeepers paid by the state were supplied, as well as unaccounted entertainment allowances that exceeded by tenfold the average annual income in the country; special hotels were built on the seaside and in the mountains, while hunting lodges were also maintained at state expense. The nomenclature was not subject to the legal limitations affecting average people; they could exchange up to half their salary in levs for Western currency (for ordinary citizens it was a crime to possess Western currency whose source could not be accounted for). The nomenclature and their families traveled to the West without restrictions (ordinary citizens were protected from the influence of the bourgeois way of life). They had access to Western cars (ordinary citizens had to wait more than ten years to purchase a Moskvich or Lada). Courts and the public prosecutors were subordinated to party politics, thus the nomenclature was untouchable by the law.

Over the years, the pyramid of the privileged progressively expanded from top to bottom, although the benefits still varied great in form and quantity. The typical beneficiary of these privileges was socially marked and recognized as an "active fighter against fascism and capitalism." This term did not arise in the first years after taking power but to some extent was engendered by the attempt to deflect the growing dissatisfaction in some communist circles against what was called "the betrayal of the ideals of equality and equity," i.e. the newly established privileges for the high-ranking party nomenclature and the tendency toward its "bourgeoisification." The "unity of the party" supposed a certain sharing of this wealth. In 1945, the Union of Partisans was established in Sofia – we do not have precise data about how many people were members. Even today there continue to be arguments about the number of communist fighters during the period of 1941–1944. Depending on the source, membership estimates range from 3,000 to 7,000. The partisan movement did not succeed in reaching a scale that would have been an actual threat to the previous regime, but, as is noted in this book's introductory chapter, "In fact, the significance of the partisans grew palpably after September 9, 1944, when the cadres who would run the country on the local and mid-levels – and who would also carry out the new government's repressive policies – were selected mainly from their ranks" (see p. 47). It can hardly be expected that most of them waited for someone's blessing or permission to solve their material problems during the "revenge period"; however, official recognition in a union gave their high-handedness a legal form.

Only in October 1947 was the Union of Fighters against Fascism and Capitalism founded; its by-laws significantly expanded the circle of people (and actions) that contributed to the new regime. People who had supported the partisans and Communist Party activities were now recognized as "fighters," while the temporal framework was expanded to include the decades before the war. At first, this recognition was not accompanied by specially regulated privileges but rather was carried out via individual arrangements and networks; however, it fell far short of including everyone who felt that their contribution should be "valued." When the grand figures of Bulgarian Stalinism, Georgi Dimitrov and Vâlko Chervenkov, who had spent their ideologically formative years as emigrants to the Soviet Union, left the national stage and local communists took control, things changed. The relations between the party leadership and the party's rank-and-file members became more prosaic; bombastic rhetoric gave way to a direct negotiation of claims. On June 1, 1959, the First Secretary of the Central Committee of the BCP, Todor Zhivkov, presented to the party's politburo a report entitled "On Arranging for the Social, Material and Everyday State of Active Fighters against Fascism and Capitalism." Here the adjective "active" appeared for the first time. "Thus, the new privileged class in Bulgaria was institutionalized in practice. The people dubbed it 'the red bourgeoisie.'"[25] In this way, in the impending battle for party leadership, Zhivkov managed to win over to his side those active parts of the party that had felt neglected and forgotten. In exchange for material benefits, he won supporters and loyalty. These "active fighters" themselves were not equal but were split into four categories:

1. those killed in battle, condemnded to death (regardless of whether the sentence had been carried out or not) and those who were partisans for more than one year;
2. participants in the partisan movement for more than six months, political prisoners and political emigrants;
3. and 4. supporters and all other participants in the anti-fascist struggle, participants in the September Uprising of 1923 who were killed and repressed in the "White Terror" of 1925 after the attack on St. Nedelya Church, political prisoners and those repressed for political reasons after the Soldiers' Uprising in 1918 and so on.

According to the new ordinance, the privileges which "active fighters" enjoyed were strictly regulated:

- a people's (state) pension;
- an extra allowance added to salary;
- priority in job appointments;
- priority in applying to the university;
- special medical services;
- free vacation complexes;
- priority in obtaining housing and purchasing automobiles;
- free city transit pass;
- free pass/access to city bath.

Of course, those partisans who were in Sofia and thus closer to the seat of power were also closer to privileges, and this engendered further tension between participants in the partisan movement in various parts of the country.

394 The collapse of communism in Bulgaria

Partisans from the Chavdar unit, which had been active in the Sofia region and with which Todor Zhivkov had been associated were especially privileged; many of them later were recruited into the high-ranking party and state leadership. Resentment grew among groups associated with the larger and more effective partisan detachments such as the Anton Ivanov unit in the Rhodope Mountains or the Gavril Genov unit in Vratsa. Given their contributions to the struggle, they felt unfairly undercompensated. The first informal networks for support and mutual supply in Bulgarian communist society formed around participants in various partisan units. Later such networks were also formed on a different basis: professional affiliation, economic interest or ideological likemindedness.

Zhivkov attempted to reduce the tensions that had arisen between these group by playing the role of an "auctioneer" of state power, distributing posts and increasing their privileges. His strategy turned out to be effective. On August 25, 1969, twenty-five years after the communists seized power, a document entitled "Improving the Material and Social State of Revolutionary Cadres" was approved, which increased pensions for "active fighters." On January 1, 1970, an addition was made to the Law on Retirement, establishing a lower retirement age for "active fighters": fifty-five for men and fifty years for women with at least fifteen years of work experience. In addition, privileges for "active fighters" were also passed along to their children: they were accepted into high schools and universities with a minimal entrance exam grade of 3 (in a scale where 6 is the highest mark). But even those who did not successfully pass the exam were accepted into a given educational institution after special permission from party organizations. Later, "active fighters'" privileges were passed along to their grandchildren as well, while some of the party leaders adopted their own grandchildren to ensure this transfer of privilege. For example, Todor Zhivkov himself adopted his late daughter's child, even though the girl's father was still alive.

In one interview after the change of November 10, 1989, Kostadin Chakârov, one of Todor Zhivkov's trusted advisers, shared his own experience of running up against the "active fighters'" networks. In the early 1960s he was First Secretary of Komsomol in Plovdiv, Bulgaria's second-largest city. Thus he was involved in the job appointments of young specialists. In seeking the reasons for difficulties in governance and production, he was struck by the incongruity between the young people's level of preparation and the jobs they were entrusted with. He ordered a review of the five higher-education institutions in Plovdiv and established that those students with the poorest marks included precisely those young people who relied on their fathers' and grandfathers' privileges. In an attempt to improve production results, he began to deviate from the prevailing party-class criteria for career development and began to suggest promoting qualified young people from normal families, without clearly realizing that he was impinging on the interests of the powers-that-be. This provoked strong reactions in party organizations at the city and regional level. He was accused of

The limits of the communist model 395

promoting "fascists." He was forced to explain his actions in person in front of Tano Tsolov, one of the secretaries of the Central Committee of the BCP, insisting that in his job-appointment policy he had been guided solely by state and economic interests. His arguments were rejected. "You have dared to encroach on our blood" – this was the active fighters' decisive argument. Kostadin Chakârov was removed from his post and banished from Plovdiv. In the meantime, however, he had become a doctoral student at the High Party School in the capital. There he established powerful connections, and after a decade he once again found himself in the game. He was assigned a few tasks related to problems the head of state himself was working on. He put enormous effort into these tasks – "delicately, quietly, and humbly." Todor Zhivkov liked his work and allowed him into his inner circle. Chakârov took advantage of this. Encouraged by another powerful adviser to Zhivkov and once again taking a risk, he again raised the question of the relationship between people's qualifications and the criteria for career advancement. "I was thinking to myself – what if he tosses me out, what if he says 'our blood.' But you know what Zhivkov did? He listened to me carefully, taking notes on a white sheet of paper . . . This happened in 1974. He was silent for a moment and told me: 'Look, my boy, I listened to you carefully, and I agree with your every word. But they are very strong, how will we take away their privileges? They'll topple me.' Just imagine, Zhivkov, the dictator, the vicious tyrant, saying in the 1970s: 'How can I hurt my comrades, they'll topple me, tell me what to do?' "[26] This episode is not only evidence of the deep roots of corruption within society but also of the fact that all attempts to root it out were doomed.

Which is why, contrary to all normal biological laws, over the years the number of "active fighters" grew exponentially, and the appetite for privileges spread to the masses. Permanent commissions were established in regional and city committees of the BCP to approve new candidates for this title. The procedure required written testimony from three people who attested to the candidate's revolutionary activities. In the 1960s, the number of "active fighters" was 30,000. By the late 1970s it had grown to 70,000, while by the mid-1980s there were already 240,000. All sorts of candidates began appearing – it was a veritable machine for securing privileges for relatives and friends. Legends are told about this system: A person was recognized as an "active fighter" when out of purely humanitarian concerns he gave two loaves of bread to hungry partisans who were being pursued, or a person who in 1944 had been eleven years old . . . There was also a popular anecdote from this time concerning a certain prominent "active fighter": "He was half-underground – he was in hiding, but no one was looking for him."

But there was also another, even greater expansion of the circle of the privileged. It included all members of the Communist Party, whose rank-and-file membership was also constantly growing. In the 1980s, membership reached almost 1 million people, out of a total population of 8 million. All of them had priority in job appointments, in taking important posts in the

396   *The collapse of communism in Bulgaria*

administration or in industry, in academic careers; they were the most likely to be allowed to travel abroad, etc.

The horizon of opportunity for the average person was completely blocked. In a poor country with limited resources, where private initiative was forbidden, privileged access on the part of some to basic benefits such as housing, a car, healthcare or education (in some university disciplines up to 50 percent of the students were enrolled with privileges, i.e. despite poor marks), as well as to goods necessary for the normal functioning of everyday life meant limited access or shortages for others. This situation was accompanied by people's deep conviction of the unfairness of the mechanisms and criteria for recognition and distribution, which had nothing to do with an individual's actual qualities and contributions. We must also add the injustice with respect to people denied rights: there were whole categories defined as "former people" or "hostile contingents" who were denied access to the university; they were forbidden from holding even the lowest-ranking posts; they could not travel abroad, etc. However, needs are needs, and these people gradually learned to cope with many of the limitations and deficits. Of course, this meant the establishment of another kind of "unofficial" corruption, which was a direct replication of the system of privileges and which resulted from limited resources, bans and a heartless administration. The corruption of the masses that pervaded the whole fabric of socialist society is a mirror image of the corruption at the top.

This situation was summarized in a secret party-internal document. In 1985, the Informational-Sociological Institute of the Central Committee of the BCP, an internal structure that was not publicly advertised, presented the results of a broad research study on the topic "Tips and Bribes in Our Society: Their Nature, Distribution and Consequences."[27] The results were classified, and the report was printed in only sixteen copies, since officially there was no corruption in socialist society, thus such problems could not be discussed publicly. But clearly the leadership had begun to grow seriously concerned about the scope of the phenomenon and its consequences. Comparing the data with the results of another study conducted five years earlier, the authors concluded that "from generation to generation there has been a steady and gradual increase in the tolerance for tips, liberalism toward their socioeconomic and moral assessment has increased, and a resigned attitude toward them has expanded and deepened." According to 77.8 percent of those polled, tips had become an "endemic phenomenon in almost all service sectors, social life and all levels of society." As a fully anonymous and nonpublic means for securing present advantages and as a guarantee of expected advantages in the future as well, tips "are degenerating into something compulsory/deteriorating into violence."

Tips (defined by the report as "spontaneous and voluntary overpayment") as a corrupt practice affected people's everyday life and constituted a deal between those who have control over a certain social resource in short supply and those who want to make up for the lack of basic necessities created by

The limits of the communist model 397

this shortage. It encompassed all spheres of everyday life: trade in foodstuffs, domestic appliances, home renovations, delivery of construction materials, imported goods, truck and taxi transport, automotive repair services, home furnishings, tailoring services, and so on. But it also spread to the sphere of social services: healthcare (securing access to a good doctor, paying a nurse to look after a patient), education (private lessons, presents for teachers), administrative services, and especially the legal system. Moreover, tips as a private relation between individuals was transformed into a means for settling organizational and business-related questions (for deliveries for raw materials to firms, for stocking restaurants with the necessary products) . . . The report establishes the commonly held conviction in society that the resolution of crucial personal and often social questions as well was becoming ever more difficult or even impossible without connections, persuasive intercession by an intermediary, and not without the functionary in question receiving his due.

In connection with this, it should be noted that "the expansion of tips from a mutual relationship between citizen and service personnel to a mutual relationship between officials within socialist organizations is one of the most serious reasons for tipping to transform into bribery." Of those polled, 76.8 percent replied that in Bulgaria bribes existed in all spheres of life. Bribes were most often used to skirt official administrative procedures, for the purchase of an apartment, residential buildings, villas and garages, for construction-renovation, for automotive transport and other services, for appointment to posts involving material, financial and administrative-managerial responsibility, in order to be sent to work abroad, for the issuance of fake university diplomas, for getting a driver's license, for proof of disabilities (in order to receive an added pension), for purchasing a car, for gaining admission to the university, for winning tax exemptions, for medical care and access to difficult-to-obtain medicines, for arranging a lighter military-service assignment and so on. "Bribes work their way up through the hierarchy, being accepted by powerful representatives of the authorities and the government, making their demoralizing influence ever stronger."[28]

This situation generated widespread corruption, which we can call *structural corruption*, in that it stems directly from the nature of social relations and the mechanism for making political decisions. It appears both on the institutional level and in the behavior of individuals. On the institutional level, structural corruption is tied to the monopolistic nature of authority – the hyper-centralization of decision-making in the economic and social spheres and the planned economy.

In the meantime, reality was changing, and the regime's "top-down" programs for economic development began to fail to address economic realities – in so far as they had ever managed to fully liberate themselves from the voluntarism of the Stalinist five-year plans and from the temptations of the "great leap forward." Personnel working within the real economy knew very well that these top-down plans were most often unrealistic, but they could not openly oppose them and ostensibly accepted them, frequently even showing

398 *The collapse of communism in Bulgaria*

enthusiasm, knowing that not only the evaluation of their work but also their entire career and welfare depended on gratifying the higher-ups' expectations. Their strategy of cunning was made easier by the fact that the central leadership was in no position to oversee all of Bulgaria's industrial and economic operations, nor even, at the end of the day, the implementation of the plan itself. And, since many of the institutions and individuals within the chain of command for distributing directives and reporting on results were connected, the practice of falsified and reassuring reports became routine procedure. (Precisely this mechanism lies at the heart of the doubts expressed above about the veracity of official statistics from the communist period.) In order for such a falsification operation to be safe, a broad network of participants must be established, often including individuals from all levels of production and the state administration – from the ordinary engineer to the director of the enterprise to the regional party and state structures to the respective ministers . . . Thus, over long periods, the tendency developed to work around the top-down plans and norms. Analysts of the Soviet-style economy have noted that concentrating all the social power in the hands of the party was accompanied by a progressive degradation in the mentality and behavior of party cadres and in practice led to the erasure of the boundary between what was legal and illegal. Everyone who was threatened by punishment for failing to fulfill unrealistic norms was forced to go beyond the established boundaries in order to survive. That is, they stood de facto outside the law, but not outside the system, in so far as this tactic was well known, a public secret that was in no one's best interest to reveal. We are compelled to entertain the hypothesis that this situation was deliberately maintained, with an eye to "socially creating a sense of guilt" at all levels, which made the government's task of keeping people under control much easier. The party elite reaped great advantages from this state of affairs: it placed everyone in a legal gray area. "The interiorization of repression is one very rarely mentioned dimension of Soviet citizens' everyday life."[29]

Structural corruption on the level of individuals, the ordinary cogs within the gigantic machine, is of a different nature, which we defined above as the "buying of loyalty." However, the mechanism allowing for this purchase requires some clarification. The reduction of people to extras in someone else's show, as well as the disparity between the social prosperity trumpeted in ideological discourse and the real standard of living, feeds mass apathy and disinterest in the results of one's labor. No one feels responsible for their own situation, or rather, they are left with the feeling of having been tricked by unrealizable promises. From the economic point of view, the system becomes ever less efficient, a problem that is closely tied to the devaluation of the person and the blockage of their creative abilities. Ubiquitous bans and limitations, as well as absurd norms, force citizens to constantly feel as if they are outside the bounds of what is permitted, yet at the same time it also gives them a false sense of personal satisfaction that they have had the opportunity or wherewithal to escape the dangers lurking everywhere around them. This

The limits of the communist model 399

excludes any possibility for sincere and voluntary cooperation between the individual and the state. Alongside the growth of egoism and the tendency to withdraw into the family, the lack of interest and ability to unite to achieve common goals also increases.

The ethics of asceticism from the 1950s had long since become dusty exhibits in the museum of the revolution, and calls for a "socialist consciousness" had lost their mobilizing force. The only formula for preserving the regime's legitimacy and the façade of a basic, established consensus turned out to be what was known as Hungarian "goulash socialism," which also appeared in a more humble Bulgarian version. This meant artificially maintaining a satisfactory standard of living based on low (nonmarket) prices for basic foodstuffs and everyday services, as well as expanding social funding for consumption at the cost of increasing domestic and foreign national debt. The ruling communist elite were growing ever more fearful of unpopular measures.

In a recollection about Zhivkov, the dictator's political assistant Kostadin Chakârov recounted the following episode. When Yuriy Andropov became General Secretary of the CPSU, he noted the problematic spread of irresponsibility within the state economy and decided to launch an offensive to improve workers' discipline. The methods he chose reflect his mentality as a former head of the KGB: he sent groups of uniformed and plainclothes police officers out among the population to conduct inspections of restaurants and stores. They stopped people on public transportation and on the street, demanding their identification, questioning them about where they worked, what their official work time was and so on. Violators were fined, sometimes quite harshly. With this action, the state reasserted its claim as the one and only employer. The results of Andropov's initiatives were not made public, but even if any results were achieved they were certainly only temporary. The interesting thing about this case is that since during that time, all of Moscow's initiatives were automatically and uncritically reproduced in Bulgaria as well (the KGB–Bulgarian State Security hotline worked tirelessly), similar campaigns were launched in Bulgarian cities. Citizens, and above all certain intellectuals close to the regime, expressed their displeasure at such methods, which resurrected the half-forgotten specter of police terror from the 1950s and early 1960s. Upon hearing of this (Chakârov claims that the Interior Ministry's initiative had not been approved by the party leadership, which seems highly unlikely, but let us accept the author's account for the moment), Todor Zhivkov ordered that such activities be suspended immediately. "We don't believe we can take such action here in Bulgaria. He was furious, but when he calmed down, he admitted: 'What idiot hasn't figured out yet the people are governed by *meze*.[30] The people want *meze* on the table. To hell with everything else."[31] This memory evoked particularly fond emotions in Zhivkov's former helpmate, who did not stop to think that the price paid to purchase the people's goodwill and obedience in this way was the moral corruption of the people themselves. *Meze* in exchange for obedience – that was the government's formula. Of course, Andropov's initiative, just like that

400 *The collapse of communism in Bulgaria*

of his Bulgarian lackeys, was equally as unacceptable and ineffective. It was the act of a feudal lord, of a boss who holds all the stock in the enterprise known as the USSR (and the PRB, respectively), of an owner who is prepared to resort even to violence to make people work, instead of asking himself why they refuse to allow themselves to be exploited.

Today the temptation has arisen to explain this state of structural corruption within a historical-cultural framework, since it is more difficult to make sense of a concrete situation in and of itself. In order to be understood in its full complexity, it needs to be placed in the context of tradition and inscribed within the processes of the *longue durée*. According to the historian Nikolay Genchev, the phenomenon described above is related to a deep historical flaw within the Bulgarian character. He defines it with a concept popularized in the second half of the nineteenth century by the revolutionary and publicist Zahari Stoyanov: *bizhirdisvane*. Due to centuries of slavery and ignorance, and due to a lack of real prospects for normal development, the Bulgarian has developed a type of behavior that has become constant and typical despite the changing times.

> He is not interested in the shared, in the public, or at best ostensibly takes part in public life out of a sense of decorum. The Bulgarian looks after his own best interest, trying to scrounge whatever he can: he wants to secure a comfortable life for himself, to have a nice house, a good wife, healthy children, to make money and to save for "a rainy day," to avoid antagonizing the powers-that-be [. . .] to be loyal and if possible close to those in power, because in Turkish times, just as in the communist era, this behavior brought jobs, money, security, they are "holding both the bread and the knife," [as the old Bulgarian saying goes] . . . Thus, the Bulgarian's historical life philosophy seems to have prepared him for communist reality, and while our generation and one or two after it may have broken the rule – i.e. earnestly championed the revolution and the "bright ideals of communism" – suddenly things fell back into their proper place. It became clear that communism was a hoax, that it was stupid to chase chimeras, that its ideals were stillborn, that only practical everyday life remained, which can't be lived without a home, bread, and normal human interactions.[32]

While there is certainly a dose of truth in this distressing statement, this view in and of itself presupposes interpretations that go beyond national psychology. It is not difficult to draw out and justify other characteristics of the Bulgarian national psyche by citing other facts, events or individuals. Beyond this debate, whose origins remain unclear, we find it far more important that a series of other nations in Central and Eastern Europe also reached basic consensuses with respect to their respective regimes' principles and the corresponding behavior they required, without sharing Bulgarian *bizhirdisvane* or only partially sharing it, since the phenomenon of adjusting

The limits of the communist model   401

to the powers-that-be is not unknown to any nation (we need only recall the mass collaboration during the Nazi occupation of Europe). This is why the causality must be reversed: the Bulgarian national mentality did not prepare the nation for communism, which would mean that Bulgarian behavior is completely determined by the past and that we are its prisoners, but rather that communism itself honed and brought to the fore the negative, antisocial aspects of the Bulgarian national mentality, which were potentially present in the Bulgarian's historical existence, without always being the dominant traits and which did not necessary become the shared norm.

The consensus established in the 1960s around the principles of the communist regime and which lent it a veneer of stability were not grounded in the mass's ideological convictions, nor, even stranger still, in their political confidence in the party's ruling bureaucrats, but rather it was based on a generalized form of corruption that encompassed the whole of society. And even though it was generated by the party elite who created the model, it affected each and every individual without exception, in so far as their everyday strategy for survival and advancement was based on adapting to and inscribing themselves within the framework set out by the regime. Regardless of their opinions or objections to the government's policies and initiatives, people strove – by constantly making compromises and coming to agreements – to accomplish their petty, individual everyday goals which guaranteed them relative security and professional advancement, but which at the same time neutralized them not only politically, but also morally. On the other hand, however, neither "structural" nor "petty" corruption turned out to be a promising foundation for the consensus sought by the regime, as the collapse of communism showed.

Social rights and their internal erosion: an element of communist Bulgaria's final crisis

The essential difference between a liberal-democratic and a communist regime lies in the fact that in the latter, social rights, which are in principle collective, are juxtaposed against individual rights and freedoms. Moreover, social rights can only exist when individual rights are limited. This is why in the end even the social rights themselves become hollowed out and do not fulfill citizens' expectations. We have already mentioned that doing away with unemployment in communist Bulgaria resulted directly from the constitutional proclamation of work not only as a right but also as a duty. This essentially distorted policy in two ways. On the one hand, it caused the artificial creation of more full-time positions in various economic units than were actually needed (hidden unemployment), and on the other hand it also led to growing disinterest in the results of one's labor, alienation from labor, and, in the end, social apathy, which made Bulgarian industry itself inefficient and noncompetitive. Young specialists were required to complete a mandatory tour of duty (*razpredelenie*) upon graduating from the university. Under this system, new graduates were sent around the country to fill various positions,

402 *The collapse of communism in Bulgaria*

being forced to work wherever the state felt it there was a need (except those who, via scheming or connections, found a way to weasel out of this duty). In this way, the lack of a free labor market and the failure to fill positions through competition turned work into a constraint that could halt talented specialists' professional development for years on end and deprive society of highly qualified experts.

Let us also examine education, which, as we noted above, the new rulers declared a fundamental priority and a sphere whose achievements must necessarily be accounted for. Universal, free, and mandatory education up to a certain level was a success, as was the strong state support for advancement in scientific or cultural spheres. But if we focus on how well the communist system rooted out illiteracy, we must keep in mind the different content which we, under contemporary conditions, attribute to that concept. Today, we usually take the term "illiterate" literally, meaning people who cannot read and write, who sign with an X, with thumbprints and so on. However, sociology has defined a contextual type of "secondary or functional illiteracy," which became particularly evident after the changes in late 1989, when the political and social realities required citizens to take an active position on current events and to show personal initiative and responsibility. This illiteracy affects people who are formally able to read and write and who in rare cases even hold diplomas from higher educational institutes. This type of illiteracy is tied not to quantitative knowledge but rather to its quality, to the values a person absorbs during their education, the cultivation of emotions, the formation of attitudes, the acquisition of civil and political culture. These are precisely the criteria by which the educational systems are judged in developed countries. And it is precisely on this level that the flaws in the Bulgarian educational system during the communist era loom large, providing grounds to speak of a process that developed mass secondary illiteracy and produced people who are not culturally, psychologically or even practically prepared for life under democratic conditions.

The communist campaign to raise the population's level of "literacy" was carried out in tandem with the mandatory acquisition of unnecessary and often downright unscientific knowledge, which – from the earliest preschool age to the end of university studies – allowed for the crude imposition of ideology and for the assimilation of the world and society through the prism of this ideology alone. These impenetrable ideological filters left their mark on Bulgarians' mastery of history, literature, the arts, economics, ethics, and even the natural sciences, such as biology or cybernetics. University programs were overloaded with mandatory pseudo-disciplines, for which many departments employing a large number of faculty were opened: "The History of the Bulgarian Communist Party," "The History of the Communist Party of the Soviet Union," "The Foundations of Marxism-Leninism," "The Political-Economics of Socialism," "Historical Materialism," and so on. At the same time, contemporary, international developments in the social sciences and humanities were completely left out of such curricula; indeed, such fields were banned, and contact with such knowledge was criminalized. Hundreds of pseudo-scholars were engaged precisely in the task of filling the heads of schoolchildren, college students, and adults with various forms of party-influenced "education" and mandatory ideological postulates. This fact minimized the effect of the entire educational process. The educational system did not produce thinking citizens – it mainly pumped out obedient subjects. As early as the 1950s and 1960s, a sudden drop in the level of knowledge in a series of spheres could be discerned, along with a general "dumbing down" of society.

Over the subsequent decades, the ideological framework for education in Bulgaria remained unchanged, but a certain opening up of the system allowed for active, seeking individuals to go beyond the boundaries of officially regulated norms. Books by Bulgarian authors or in translation that said something slightly different from the party line were already enjoying large print runs. Yet another shortage cropped up: a shortage of good books, i.e. those that had avoided playing the propagandistic role that was usually imposed on them. Taking advantage of formal gains in the sphere of education (especially the study of Western languages), many Bulgarians managed to develop various individual strategies which grew ever more difficult for the state to directly control, even though the field where such autodidacts could apply this accumulated knowledge was not particularly large. In any case, for communist subjects, who were deprived of the chance to be real economic and political actors, science and culture gradually became a compensatory realm of relatively free individual choice and hyper-investment in one's personal development – this came with a price, however, such as the use of "Aesopian language" and constant cat-and-mouse games with the censorship institutions. This fact also explains foreign observers' claims about the high level of Bulgarians' cultural knowledge and professional competency after the fall of communism. However, there was something that individual curiosity and effort alone could not compensate for: we only became painfully aware of the flaws in the moral and social construction of the personality later, upon witnessing the infantile ideas put forth – especially by the new political elite – about freedom, democracy, ethics, and economic initiative. The failures of democratic reconstruction stem above all from failures in the "personal factor" from communist times. Despite new horizons, changes to the dominant mentality have remained relatively modest; the damage done to the several generations that grew up under communism is deep-seated and cannot be overcome merely by a formal rejection of direct ideological indoctrination. Universal education cannot possibly compensate for the enormous damage done, which the writer Atanas Slavov, who emigrated to America after the fall of communism, calls "the destroyed value system." Communism erased the differences between the educated and the uneducated person, between the honest and the corrupt person, between the foolish and the intelligent person, reducing social structure to the opposition "ours vs. theirs." And in order for the biggest fool to become the most important person, Slavov

404 *The collapse of communism in Bulgaria*

continues, "communism had to destroy the value system that Bulgarians held. The average Bulgarian (before September 9, 1944) may have been slightly ignorant, but he had a clear system of values. This system was completely destroyed and people were socially uprooted."[33]

By the end of the 1980s, it had become all too clear that the broad spectrum of social rights guaranteed by the communist state were becoming ever more formal and that their low quality could not meet individuals' needs or contemporary global standards. The system's internal exhaustion, along with the regime's crumbling legitimacy, caused the erosion of the principles of social policy which the regime itself had imposed: the principle of individual responsibility was trampled and the principle of commutative justice was distorted, while the principle of distributive justice was used by people to their own advantage. This led people to indirectly associate the exercise of social rights with corruption and generated an antisocial mentality whose consequences could be keenly felt during Bulgaria's rocky transition to democracy.

Notes

1 Lyubomir Ognyanov, "Bâlgarskata ikonomika v nay-novo vreme," in *Istoriya i tsivilizatsiya za 11 klas,* Sofia: Prosveta, 2002, pp. 293–301, at p. 297.
2 Dimitâr Ivanov (ed.), *Ot deveti do deseti,* Sofia: IK "Zahari Stoyanov," 2004, pp. 151–152.
3 Lyubomir Ognyanov, "Razvitie na sotsialisticheskoto obshtestvo v Bâlgariya, 1958–1982," in *Kratka istoriya na Bâlgariya,* Sofia: Nauka i izkustvo, 1983, pp. 423–463, at p. 459.
4 François Benaroya, *L'Économie de la Russie,* Paris: La Decouverte, 2006, pp. 42–45.
5 William Easterly, Stanley Fischer, "The Soviet Decline: Historical and Republican Data," NBER, Working Paper, No. W 4735. Cited in Benaroya, *L'Économie de la Russie,* p. 28.
6 Ivanov, *Ot deveti do deseti,* p. 155.
7 Republic of Bulgaria, National Statistical Institute, *Realen BVP nag lava ot naselenieto i temp na prirast,* Sofia: National Statistical Institute, 2017.
8 Similar laws were adopted by governments before September 9, 1944, but their restrictions on trade-union activities and opposition on the part of employers, as well as reduced enforcement often led to their violation. On this question, see the general picture offered by Rumen Daskalov in *Bâlgarskoto obshtestvo 1878–1939,* vol. II, Sofia: Gutenberg, 2005, pp. 301–315.
9 Dimo Donkov, "Razvitie na osnovnoto obrazovanie v Bâlgariya ot 1878 do 1928 g.," in *Materiali za izsledvane na uchebnoto delo v Bâlgariya,* No. 7, Sofia: n.p., 1928. Cited in Daskalov, *Bâlgarskoto obshtestvo,* pp. 362–364.
10 In *Vâpreki vsichko: Moyata politicheska biografiya,* Sofia: Kolibri, 2005, Zhelyu Zhelev recalls what a major event his earning of a university diploma in philosophy was for his home village in the 1960s. He was the first college graduate the village had ever produced, and this not only was a source of common pride but also brought him exceptional prestige within the small community.
11 A similar picture of various privileges (i.e. acceptance without competing or taking exams) in enrolling at the university can be found in Pepka Boyadjieva's

The limits of the communist model   405

book, *Sotsialnoto inzhenerstvo: Politiki za priem vâv visshite uchilishta prez komunisticheskiya rezhim v Bâlgariya*, Sofia: Institute for Studies of the Recent Past/Ciela, 2010.

12 Ivanov, *Ot deveti do deseti*, p. 582.

13 One of Todor Zhivkov's political advisers testifies: "Consumption grew significantly, but people didn't want just any old consumption at that, but individual consumption. With improved taste, no less. Their model was Western goods. This comparison became the most powerful weapon against dictatorship. Every Western item carried within itself a propagandistic charge that destroyed and made the psychological system of socialism in the eastern European countries highly vulnerable. People would say, 'Look at the two Germanies: one makes Mercedes, the other Trabants!'" K. Chakârov, *Vtoriyat etazh*, p. 174.

14 Émile Durkheim, *De la division du travail social*, Paris: Félix Alcan, 1893.

15 François Ewald, *L'État-providence*, Paris: Grasset, 1986, p. 177.

16 Pierre Rosanvallon, *La Nouvelle Question sociale: Repenser l'état-providence*, Paris: Seuil, 1995, pp. 26–27.

17 On the history of social policy and social rights, see Marie-Therese Join-Lambert (dir.), *Politiques sociales*, Paris: Dalloz, 1994, pp. 27–46.

18 Even before the French Revolution, Rousseau made this appeal: "Let the homeland, therefore, show itself as the common mother of all citizens." Pierre Rosanvallon notes that this is why the modern welfare state owes more to Rousseau than to Marx.

19 Join-Lambert, *Politiques sociales*, p. 33.

20 Join-Lambert, *Politiques sociales*, p. 56.

21 John Rawls, *A Theory of Justice*, Cambridge, Mass.: Harvard University Press, 1971, p. 22.

22 Gotz Aly, *Comment Hitler a acheté les Allemands: Le IIIe Reich, une dictature au service du people*, Paris: Flammarion, 2005, p. 31. Original title: *Hitlers Volksstaat*, Frankfurt: S. Fischer Verlag, 2005.

23 Boris Groys, *Politique de l'immortalité: quatre entretiens avec Thomas Knoefel*, Paris: Maren Sell Editeurs, 2005, p. 141.

24 Mikhail S. Voslenski, *Nomenklatura, der herrschende Klasse der Sowjatunion*, Vienna: Molden, 1980.

25 Pencho Kovachev, "240,000 aktivni bortsi se radvat na privilegii prez 1980 g.," *24 chasa* (September 11, 2011). We owe the summarized chronology of this phenomenon to this article.

26 Oral history archive of the Institute for Studies of the Recent Past, F. 2, op. 24, a. e. 15, l. 18–19. Maya Stoyanova, Conversation with Kostadin Chakârov, former adviser to first secretary of the Central Committee of the BCP, Todor Zhivkov, until the end of the regime in 1989, Sofia, April 29, 2011.

27 TsDA, F. 1B, op. 55, a. e. 527, l. 1–46: ISTs na TsK na BKP, "Bakshishite i podkupite v nasheto obshtestvo – harakter, razprostranenie i posleditsi," *Zlobodnevni problem, Signalen byuletin No. 4*, July 1985. Top secret. The subsequent data are quoted from Ivan Elenkov, *Orbiti na sotsialisticheskoto vsekidnevie*, Sofia: Institute for Studies of the Recent Past, 2018, pp. 241–270.

28 TsDA, f. 1B, op. 55, a. e. 527, l. 1–46.

29 Gérard Duchêne, "L'Officiel et le parallèle dans l'économie soviétique," *Libre*, 7 (1980): 151–188.

406 *The collapse of communism in Bulgaria*

30 Translator's note: *Meze* is a Turkish loanword in Bulgarian, meaning "appetizer" or snack, but since it is almost invariably accompanied by brandy, it is also associated with good food and good company around the table.
31 K. Chakârov, "Zhivya za naroda si . . ." in *Dârzhavnikât i chovekât: Todor Zhivkov v spomenite na sâvremennitsi*, Sofia: Fenomen – 21, 2001, p. 253.
32 Nikolay Genchev, *Spomeni: Izbrani proizvedeniya*, vol. V, Sofia: Gutenberg, 2005, p. 292.
33 Atanas Slavov, *Evropeyskata tsivilizatsiya e nashiyat torf, a ne izbor: Asparuh Panov, razgovarya s Atanas Slavov po sluchay negovata sedemdesetgodishnina*, Sofia: Grazhdanin, 2000.

21 Gorbachev's *perestroika* and its influence on processes in Bulgaria

The new Soviet leader, despite belonging to a completely new generation from his predecessors, had followed the career path of a typical party apparatchik: thanks to his exceptional diligence, he had risen through the ranks of the provincial and Kremlin bureaucracy. Despite the fact that both of his grandfathers had fallen victim to Stalin-era repression – one for his participation in a rightist-Trotskyite group, and the other for being a *kulak* – the grandson managed to build an impressive Komsomol career in his native Stavropol region, and in 1952 he also became a member of the CPSU.[1] However, his viewpoints were essentially formed during the Khrushchev thaw and thus show deep disappointment and shock over the revelations made in 1956. Like Krushchev, Gorbachev deeply believed in the correctness of Leninist teachings and in the possibility for socialism to be just and humane. This is the reason why in the early period of his rule, his statements and speeches frequently included calls "for a return to Leninist principles" and "for more socialism"; a return to slogans and rhetorical devices from the period of de-Stalinization can also be noted. To paraphrase the Hungarian philosopher and dissident Ferenc Feher, who described the late Kádár regime as "applied Khrushchevism," Gorbachev's early years in power can be characterized as "enlightened Khrushchevism."[2]

After taking power, Gorbachev gradually changed his rhetorical style. In late 1987, he began speaking of the "socialist market" for the first time.[3] Gradually, however, he had reached the conclusion that in order to reform the economy, society had to be reformed, and in order to reform society the party itself had to be reformed. The call for *glasnost* – which comes from the word *glas* or "voice" and literally means "openness" or "publicness" – was the first step in his plans to that end. *Glasnost* was initially put into practice through a new wave of disclosures about Stalinist repression and crimes from the past, without, however, sullying the cult of Lenin or shaking the ideological foundation of the system as a whole. It very quickly became clear, however, that *glasnost* was not merely a "superstructural" phenomenon but could crucially affect the lives of millions of people. On April 26, 1986, one of the four nuclear reactors in the Ukrainian city of Chernobyl exploded, releasing radiation into the atmosphere that was 100 times greater than that of Hiroshima and

408 *The collapse of communism in Bulgaria*

Nagasaki combined.[4] Since this was not the first nuclear disaster in the USSR, the authorities followed their old practice and preferred to keep silent about the event. Two days later, the Russian News Agency nevertheless mentioned "by the by" that such an incident had occurred. Before this announcement, as well as after it, no measures were taken to inform the civilian population about how to respond or to minimize harm to citizens. However, once the radioactive cloud had already spread over half of Europe, on May 14, Gorbachev was forced to make an official announcement acknowledging only part of the truth and calling for international assistance.[5] The Chernobyl disaster seriously shook Soviet society and made citizens painfully aware of the irresponsibility, hypocrisy, and cynicism of the whole Soviet state and party bureaucracy, which had attempted to cover up the incident without concern for the lives and health of millions of people.

When the new Soviet leader assumed control of the Kremlin, he found in Sofia one of the most conservative communist regimes in the whole Eastern Bloc. Zhivkov had personally ruled the party–state for more than thirty years, and all signs indicated that he had no desire or intention to "restructure" himself. Zhivkov's government suffered from an exceptionally negative international reputation due to the ongoing scandal around the murder of the writer Georgi Markov by Bulgarian State Security and growing suspicions of Bulgarian involvement in the assassination attempt against Pope John Paul II in 1981. The recently suspended campaign to forcibly change the names of Bulgarian Turks had additionally tarnished the regime's already sullied image. This put both Moscow and other allies in the exceptionally awkward position of having to justify and downplay Bulgaria's flagrant violation of the Helsinki Accords before the international community.

When Gorbachev first began *perestroika*, Zhivkov, led by inertia from his many years in power, announced his support and transferred Soviet practice to Bulgaria as he had done in the past. In Bulgaria, too, talk of Stalinist crimes was permitted to a certain extent, while portraits of members of the Bulgarian and Soviet Politburos were removed from public places, and objects named after Ludmila Zhivkova were quietly rechristened.[6] The Bulgarian authorities also followed in the Soviet example when it came to the Chernobyl disaster on April 26, 1986, taking belated, contrite measures. Ordinary Bulgarians were officially informed about the incident only on May 2 – one day after the population was ordered to stand outside in the rain for mass May Day celebrations. Only as late as May 4 did the government finally organize a meeting where steps to protect the population were taken.[7] Overall, during the whole early period of *perestroika*, Zhivkov tried to copy exactly what Gorbachev was doing in Moscow. Despite this, it gradually became clear to him that he was unwanted. When the changes in the Soviet Union began to threaten the foundations of the system, Zhivkov decided to take matters into his own hands. The Bulgarian dictator was still not ready for an open confrontation with Gorbachev; however, his intentions were to undertake a reform program whose planned changes would not undermine his own power.

Gorbachev's *perestroika* and Zhivkov's *perestruvka*

A Bulgarian joke circulating at the time claimed that the basic difference between the USSR and Bulgaria was that while Gorbachev was carrying out *perestroika* there, in Bulgaria Zhivkov was carrying out *perestruvka* – a play on the Bulgarian word *prestruvka* meaning "a feigned action, or pretending to do something." This anecdote clearly shows that the Bulgarian population was not fooled by Zhivkov's reform program and saw it for the empty imitation it was. One of the clearest examples of Zhivkov's sham reformism was the July Conception from 1987, which was adopted at the corresponding Plenum of the Central Committee of the BCP. In theory, it called for changes to the economy, the social sphere, and the administration that were quite sweeping in comparison to previous reform attempts. Only in the political sphere did they remain purely symbolic and on the whole did not challenge the Communist Party's monopoly on power. Zhivkov's attempt to outflank Gorbachev "from the left" – i.e. by being a more radical reformer than the Soviet leader himself – led to a conflict with the latter, even if on the surface, both sides continued spouting the clichés of Bulgarian–Soviet friendship.[8] Nevertheless, in August of the same year, the Bulgarian party and state leader launched his "conception." The first reforms were made to the administration. The twenty-eight districts (*okrâzi*) that had existed until then were abolished, and nine large regions (*oblasti*) were established in their place (including the so-called Sofia City region). Many interpreted this act as an attempt by Zhivkov to concentrate power and to place exceptionally reliable people in key positions around the country. Some of the cities chosen for new regional centers were extremely unsuited to such a role, while the selection criteria remained unclear. For example, the newly created Razgrad region included Ruse, the largest industrial and cultural center in northeastern Bulgaria, while the Lovech region subsumed far more important urban centers such as Pleven, Târnovo, and Gabrovo. Similarly, the Haskovo region included the much more important city of Stara Zagora. Even the "Settlement Systems" created in 1977 were abolished and the system of municipalities (*obshtini*) was revived. In any case, the officially proclaimed goal of this reform – the reduction of bureaucracy and administration – was not accomplished. Moreover, the number of people employed in the administrative sector was constantly increasing. A series of ministries were also combined and restructured on similar grounds. All of this, accompanied by the wide-ranging organizational and bureaucratic activities tied to the Revival Process and the related change of an enormous number of personal and official documents, created complete institutional chaos. The administrative reform required new elections for regional, municipal, and local people's councils. In some of these elections, which were held in 1988, more than one candidate ran for the first time in more than forty years. Curiously, where this occurred, both candidates were nominated by the Fatherland Front; hence, they were

410 *The collapse of communism in Bulgaria*

either both communists or both agrarians, since a competition between the two parties was still not allowed.

As early as 1988, attempts were made to experimentally introduce limited market mechanisms into certain individual companies. Academic institutions for economics were saddled with this task, while the government even signed a contract with the large consulting firm Price Waterhouse to experiment with "injecting" market elements into the planned economy. This attempt ended in complete failure, as the results a year later showed. The reason for this was that the ruling elite continued to view the market as a sort of "crutch" to support the planned economy and not as a fundamentally different economic model. The Bulgarian government, in its official reasons for dissolving the contract, however, wrote that in order to accomplish their task, the consultants had asked for data that were either strictly confidential or were simply impossible to supply.[9]

The abovementioned failure does not mean that the Zhivkov regime collapsed thanks to its economic bankruptcy alone. Just like the Soviet model, the Bulgarian system was coasting along on deep-seated inertia, thus its destruction could have dragged on for years. The chronic deficit of goods it created was also nothing new for Bulgarians. In this sense, the average Bulgarian, who had grown used to deprivation and permanent scarcity, did not see this crisis in the late 1980s as a particularly unusual or urgent situation. This was the reason why dissatisfaction in Bulgaria remained limited primarily to the intelligentsia and on the whole was expressed far more mildly than in the central European countries. The communist regime in Bulgaria fell only thanks to external factors – just as it had been established. For this reason, the average Bulgarian was largely caught off guard by the fall of the regime.

The "grand era of the intelligentsia" and the late Bulgarian dissident movement

In the second half of the 1980s, a circle of writers, scholars, and intellectuals gradually formed in Bulgaria who were increasingly autonomous from the Communist Party and the regime as a whole. This proto-dissident nucleus consisted mainly of members of the Communist Party or people who had been close to it in the past; however, precisely such associations gave them more creative independence and freedom to speak and act. Younger people, including environmentalists and human-rights activists emboldened by Gorbachev's *perestroika*, gradually joined this circle. Thus, the autonomous circle consisted of a diverse mix of people with differing ideological convictions – and most often with no clearly formed viewpoints at all – who were united by their dissatisfaction with the status quo and desire for change. Unlike Poland, Hungary or Czechoslovakia, for example, the Bulgarian dissident movement had no deep historical roots. It lacked shared memories of dissident events during 1956, 1968, and 1980. It also lacked the support of the working classes and the rural population, which would have given it a mass dimension and made it representative of Bulgarian society as a whole. Yet, despite these failings, by the end of the 1980s it was a fact among the intelligentsia that could not be ignored. The sense of a new mission was most clearly expressed in an article published in 1988 by the philosopher Zhelyu Zhelev entitled: "The Grand Era of the Intelligentsia." The article essentially argued that Gorbachev would succeed only if he relied on the intelligentsia and its critical energy and potential. At the same time, it declared the necessity for a union between the reformist wing of the Communist Party (the article spoke solely about the Soviet Union, but the subtext made it clear that it was directed above all at the Bulgarian situation) and the real intelligentsia. It also expressed the hope that Gorbachev would not repeat Khrushchev's mistake; the latter, fearing for the very foundations of the system, began suffocating and persecuting the intelligentsia. The article recalled that this was precisely what had precipitated his fall from power.[10] Zhelev's article was essentially a call for cooperation between the Bulgarian intelligentsia and the still rather vague circles within the Communist Party itself that were opposed to Zhivkov. He urged these two groups to come together in the name of reform and two create bridges between them, not more distance. However, the regime took steps in the exact opposite direction. As early as the fall of 1987, three professors and one associate professor were "preventatively" expelled from the BCP organization at Sofia University for having officially criticized the Communist Party. The campaign in their defense launched by some of their colleagues, as well as the Western scholarly community, created precisely the right public atmosphere and conditions for the emergence of an organized dissident movement.[11]

Gradually, individual public figures and circles of freethinkers began creating various informal associations and making statements in the name of such organizations. The first such group was the Independent Association for the Defense of Human Rights in Bulgaria, which was founded in January 1988. It differed from later dissident formations in the total absence of BCP member (or former members) among its ranks. The members of this group, as well as their basic platform, clearly demonstrated its distinctly anti-communist nature. The association was the brainchild of two Bulgarian emigrants in France who had formerly been political prisoners: Alfred "Freddie" Foscolo and Petâr Boyadzheiv.[12] They contacted Iliya Minev – the person who held the dubious distinction of having spent the longest time behind bars in communist Bulgaria, who was living in the town of Septemvri at the time. Known as "the Bulgarian Nelson Mandela," Minev had spent a total of thirty-three years in prison. The other members of the group were also names well known to State Security. According to State Security intelligence, seventeen of the association's twenty-five members were former political prisoners.[13] The association prepared and broadcast a "Call for the Defense of Human Rights in Bulgaria" on "enemy radio stations." Gradually, a large number of Pomaks (Bulgarian Muslims) and Turks, who were fighting against the Zhivkov

412   *The collapse of communism in Bulgaria*

regime's assimilation policy, also joined the group and subsequently founded a special Muslim section within the association.[14]

The second dissident organization, whose profile differed greatly from that of the Association, was the Public Committee for the Ecological Protection of Ruse, founded on March 9, 1988. As early as autumn of the previous year, women and mothers from the Danubian city had begun demonstrating against toxic chlorine fumes from a large chemical factory on the Romanian side of the river that had been polluting the Bulgarian city. A screening of the documentary film *Breathe* by director Yuri Zhirov, which was dedicated to the issue, served as impetus for the founding of the committee. The writer Georgi Mishev became Chairman, while the Committee also included some public figures closely tied to the regime, including the artist Svetlin Rusev, choreographer Neshka Robeva, the prominent scholar Krâstyo Goranov and others, in the hopes that in that way the group would not be forcibly dispersed.[15] The inclusion of Sonya Bakish – the wife of the longtime Communist Party "second-in-command" and Politburo member Stanko Todorov – also served a similar preventative and symbolic purpose. Zhivkov's political cronies responded by expelling some of the committee members, including Bakish, from the BCP. In response, her husband resigned from the Politburo – but not from his post as Speaker of Parliament.[16]

Over the following months, dissident organizations began cropping up one after the other: the Committee for Religious Rights, Freedom of Conscience and Spiritual Values; Committee 273 (referring to Article 273 in the Bulgarian Penal Code, which was usually used to convict political prisoners); as well as the independent trade union Podkrepa ("Support"). The regime was particularly alarmed by the founding of the Club in Support of Glasnost and Perestroika in Bulgaria on November 3, 1988. It was chaired by Zhelyu Zhelev but also included many other publicly influential Bulgarian intellectuals, including the writers Blaga Dimitrova, Radoy Ralin, and Valeri Petrov; the artist and animator Anri Kulev; the playwright and director Boyan Papazov; as well as many others.[17] The majority of participants were members of the Communist Party, including five former partisans from the communist resistance movement in 1944. The authorities responded with individual threats to the club's members and sympathizers. Some of its activists were arrested while others were expelled from the BCP. Despite such repression, however, the regime found itself facing organized resistance for the first time in decades. The group soon won international recognition. During French President François Mitterrand's visit to Sofia on January 19, 1989, members of the Club were invited to an official breakfast with him.

In the autumn of 1989, the newly created dissident organization Ecoglasnost (Ecological Openness), which had grown out of the Ruse Committee, organized a wide-ranging campaign against two government projects, Rila and Mesta, which aimed at diverting the course of the Mesta River and using it to supply water to Sofia and the Sofia region. Signatures also began being collected for a petition. On October 26, the authorities arrested the

Perestroika *and its influence in Bulgaria* 413

organizers; however, the campaign was being followed and publicized by Western journalists, thus the arrests had the opposite effect than the regime intended: this action strengthened the campaign rather than crushing it. On November 3, Ecoglasnost organized a protest march on Parliament to deliver the petition, which included more than 11,000 signatures. This, in fact, turned into the first and only mass demonstration against the regime before Zhivkov's fall from power. On the whole, the dissident movement in Bulgaria remained anemic, in part due to in the combination of anti-communist activists and communist *perestroika* supporters within it. The authorities recognized perfectly well the contradiction between the people who wanted to destroy the system and those who were trying to reform it from within and thus preserve it. Thus, the government focused its efforts precisely at exploiting this disconnect. We must also not underestimate the fact that the dissident movement was in large part cleverly "directed" by the huge number of State Security collaborators who managed to infiltrate it. The repressive apparatus, including State Security, was initially not psychologically prepared to accept the existence of informal organizations. However, its traditional methods of threats and blackmail began to lose their effectiveness in the new conditions. The State Security system was also deeply confused by the contradictory signals coming from Moscow and from the Bulgarian party leadership. Evidence of such confusion can be found in statements made at a meeting of the Interior Ministry leadership about the operative situation in the country on February 13, 1989. At this meeting, one of the directors of State Security declared,

> We need greater clarity from the party leadership. Will we allow such things [dissident expressions]? If we won't, I believe, and am in full agreement with Comrade Musakov, that we need to go on the offensive. If such things will be allowed to exist in some form, then our tactics will also have to find their proper place – we will send our people to lead and guide the subsequent direction of such groups. I believe we are now fighting a series of petty battles, one by one. We need clarity from above on this question.[18]

Since instructions failed to come from above, in the end State Security began taking two basic types of action: first, the abovementioned policy of infiltrating the informal associations with its own agents, and second, discrediting such groups in the eyes of ordinary Bulgarians by taking advantage of the nationalist hysteria that had gripped the country after May 1989 and painting such organizations as "pro-Turkish."

The simple truth is that dissident organizations did not topple Todor Zhivkov. It is equally true, however, that they created the social climate that made such a change possible. At the very end of the regime's existence and especially around the May Events in protest against the Revival Process, dissident groups gained strength from parallel actions by Turks who were also protesting. These two movements began mutually supporting each other,

414 *The collapse of communism in Bulgaria*

providing additional grounds for some of the ruling elite to take direct action to remove Zhivkov from power. Fissures that had appeared within Bulgarian society were also transferred to ruling circles, thanks to family and friendly ties between members of the informal associations and high-ranking party leaders, as well as due to clever prompts from Moscow.

The November 10 coup and Todor Zhivkov's removal from power

As of 1989, the world was no longer the same as it had been during the Cold War. Gorbachev's *perestroika* had entered its critical phase. One by one, the old communist leaders were forced to give up power by the more reform-minded or simply by the younger wings of their own parties. The first to do so was the Czechoslovakian communist leader Gustav Husak in 1987. While giving up his post as party leader, he nevertheless retained the presidency, thus guaranteeing that his retreat would be at least somewhat gradual. Later, Zhivkov would try to make the same move, but it would be too late. The following year, the Hungarian leader János Kádár would make his exit under pressure from reformist circles within his own party. His death in 1989 during the course of Hungary's peaceful revolution held symbolic significance, marking the end communism as well.[19] The Bulgarian dictator also decided to undertake similar maneuvers to "outflank" the growing opposition. As early as November 4, 1988, he tendered his resignation to the Politburo. However, no one in his circle believed that his intention to resign was sincere. This move could easily be interpreted as a preventative measure on Zhivkov's part to feel out the party leadership's mood; any sign of eagerness to see Zhivkov go would likely lead to the removal of such "impatient" Politburo members. For this reason, his associates unanimously rejected his resignation and even began trying to convince him that the party and the state needed him now more than ever. Satisfied by what he heard and with a fair amount of condescension, Zhivkov withdrew his resignation.[20]

Beginning in the spring of the following year, a destructive chain reaction was set off within the international communist system. The Polish communists' catastrophic loss in the country's first multiparty elections and the opening of Hungary's borders with the West had a domino effect on the remaining Eastern Bloc countries. Hundreds of thousands of East Germans began "pouring" out of the system's no longer "hermetically sealed" borders. This placed the remaining regimes in a dilemma: Should they follow the example of Poland and Hungary or distance themselves and fall into even greater isolation? In May of the same year, Bulgarian Turks began demonstrating in dozens of places in eastern Bulgaria, demanding that their names and rights be restored. Once the regime finally realized that its assimilation campaign had failed, on May 29, Todor Zhivkov announced that the country would be opening its borders and that everyone would be free to go where they wished. This brought about the enormous wave of emigration to Turkey that was described in previous chapters.

Perestroika *and its influence in Bulgaria*   415

In July, the penultimate meeting of the Political Consultative Committee of Warsaw Pact member states took place in Bucharest. Gorbachev refused to meet with Zhivkov personally outside the official meeting. Instead, he held a confidential conversation with Foreign Minister Petâr Mladenov and Defense Minister Dobri Dzhurov. At the meeting, he made it clear that Zhivkov was no longer an acceptable option for him. Even though the Bulgarian dictator found out about the meeting through his own channels, he was no longer in a position to take the traditional countermeasures he had in the past.[21] In the autumn of 1989, Gorbachev once again evaded Zhivkov, who wanted to visit Moscow "for consultations." This was a signal to the people in his inner circle to distance themselves from him one by one. The first to do so was his longtime "right-hand man," Stanko Todorov, the Speaker of Parliament. On October 24, 1989, Foreign Minister and Politburo member Petâr Mladenov distributed an "open letter" to the BCP leadership, which harshly blamed Zhivkov for the general crisis the country was in. Two days later, he tendered his resignation.[22] "Moscow's man" within the party leadership, Andrey Lukanov, also openly declared his opposition to Zhivkov. At Lukanov's urging and largely realizing that he had no other choice, Prime Minister Georgi Atanasov, who was also a Politburo member, also declared his opposition to Zhivkov at a critical moment. Behind them stood the powerful Soviet Ambassador in Sofia – the KGB general Viktor Sharapov. As it turned out, immediately preceding Zhivkov's removal from power, Sharapov negotiated with him in the name of the conspirators.[23] The first of Sharapov's meetings with Zhivkov where his withdrawal from power was discussed was held on November 3, coinciding with the first public demonstration in Sofia, which applied additional psychological pressure on him.[24] One of the countermoves Zhivkov had thought up in response to the conspiracy was to propose replacing Prime Minister Atanasov with Petko Danchev, his fellow villager from Pravets, who was currently serving as Deputy Prime Minister. He hoped to do so at the party plenum scheduled for November 10, thus winning some extra time.[25] However, such a major change "at the top" in Sofia still could not come about without Moscow's blessing – and Sharapov had no intention of helping Zhivkov. On the contrary, at Sharapov's urging, Politburo members Dobri Dzhurov, Yordan Yotov, and Dimitâr Stanishev – all three had been his brothers-in-arms in the Chavdar Partisan Brigade – paid Zhivkov a visit on November 8. In a semi-friendly manner, they tried to convince him that he had no other option but to resign. The last maneuver the dictator made was an attempt to retain his post as Chairman of the State Council as a sort of guarantee that his removal from power would be gradual.[26] In an ironic twist of fate, at a Politburo meeting held on November 9, the group accepted the resignation which Zhivkov had tendered a year earlier and which Georgi Atanasov had carefully preserved. The Plenum of the Central Committee of the BCP held the next day was designed to officially confirm this change. Until the very end, Zhivkov attempted to counter the arguments being made and to retain at least his state post as Chairman of the National Council. The news that the Berlin Wall had fallen only hours earlier applied additional psychological pressure

416 *The collapse of communism in Bulgaria*

on the communist elite. It had become clear even to his staunchest supporters that Zhivkov's time was up – now they had to hurry to try to salvage what remained of their power. Under the clever guidance of Atanasov, who chaired the meeting, Zhivkov's resignation was accepted with one vote against it, while Petâr Mladenov was selected to take his place as Party Chairman. The decision was also made to relieve Zhivkov of his post as Chairman of the State Council. On November 17, the new party leader was also chosen as the head of state.[27]

The party-internal coup of November 10, 1989, put an end to Todor Zhivkov's thirty-five-year reign. While the coup's organizers saw it as a means of preserving the system by sacrificing its most anachronistic representative, it very soon became clear that this event held a far greater significance. It set off the domino-like collapse of the totalitarian state, such that preserving the status quo in any form whatsoever proved impossible. For this reason, it essentially put an end to the communist regime that had ruled Bulgaria for more than forty-five years.

Notes

1 Official website of Mikhail Sergeyevich Gorbachev: www.gorby.ru/gorbachev/biography/ (accessed June 8, 2018).
2 Ádám Takács, "Totalitarianism as an Atmosphere: Morality and Mentality in Hungary under the Kádár Regime," *Divinatio*, 31 (2010): 113–123.
3 Judt, *Postwar*, p. 656.
4 Chenobilskaya tetrady, https://medium.com/usaid-2030/remembering-the-worlds-worst-nuclear-disaster-33359ed71863 (accessed June 2018).
5 Chernobil: 20 godini po-kâsno, http://bglog.net/Vestnik/6061 (accessed June 8, 2018).
6 Dimitâr Ludzhev, *Revolyutsiyata v Bâlgariya 1989–1991: No. 1."Nezhnata" 89–a i neynoto vreme*, Sofia: D-r Ivan Bogorov, 2008, pp. 21–23.
7 Hristov, *Todor Zhivkov*, pp. 304–305.
8 Kalinova and Baeva, *Bâlgarskite prehodi, 1939–2005*, pp. 228–229.
9 Rumen Avramov, *Pari i de/stabilizatsiya v Bâlgariya 1948–1989*, Sofia: Institute for Studies of the Recent Past/Ciela, pp. 279–280.
10 Zhelyu Zhelev, "Velikoto vreme na inteligentsiyata," *Narodna kultura*, 38 (July 22, 1988).
11 Ludzhev, *Revolyutsiyata v Bâlgariya*, pp. 25–26.
12 AMVR, f. 1, op. 12, a. e. 937, l. 44. (delo No. 37/1989, vol. 1) (Analytic general summaries of the state of the country in 1988).
13 AMVR, f. 1, op. 12, a. e. 937, l. 41.
14 Z. Ibrahimova, "Pomnya studa i straha, koito byaha skovali vsichko – i pâtishtata i dushite ni. Dialog," *Niderlandiya*, 50, February 2009, pp. 7–11.
15 Veselina Antonova and Detelina Kamenova, *Demontazh: Edna balkanska istoriya ot kraya na XX vek*, Ruse: Avangard print, 2008, pp. 61–74.
16 Iskra Baeva, "Iz istoriyata na bâlgarskoto disidentstvo – Obshtestveniyat komitet za ekologichna zashtita na Ruse i vlastta," *Izvestiya na dârzhavnite arhivi*, 76 (1998): 33–53.
17 Ludzhev, *Revolyutsiyata v Bâlgariya*, p. 57.

Perestroika *and its influence in Bulgaria* 417

18 AMVR, f. 1, op. 12, a. e. 917, vol. 2, l. 14.
19 Judt, *Postwar*, p. 671.
20 Hristov, *Todor Zhivkov*, p. 604.
21 Chakârov, *Vtoriyat etazh*, pp. 70–71.
22 Mladenov, *Zhivotât*, p. 323.
23 Zhivkov, *Memoari*, pp. 615–638.
24 G. Milushev, *Po koridorite na vlastta*, Sofia: Intra book, 1991, p. 13.
25 Hristov, *Todor Zhivkov*, p. 609.
26 Bakalov, *Prevratadzhii ot pârvo litse*, pp. 83–148.
27 Boris Traykov, *10 November: Prevratât*, Sofia: Trud, 1999, pp. 110–117.

22 The beginning of the Great Transition

After the bloodless coup against Todor Zhivkov, the new leaders of the BCP – Andrey Lukanov, Aleksandâr Lilov, and Petâr Mladenov – enjoyed a high level of public trust. In their initial plans, they seemed to have assigned the "informal associations" the role of supernumeraries. Their job was to support reformers against conservatives within the BCP, without being allowed to become a real public force.[1] However, after organizing several mass demonstrations, human chains, protest marches and strikes (on November 18, December 10, December 14, and December 26, 1989) in Sofia, the newly founded Union of Democratic Forces (UDF; Sâyuz na Demokratichnite Sili [SDS]) managed to establish itself as a party to the unfolding debate about Bulgaria's future. The UDF's participation in the National Round Table held from January 3–May 15 of 1990 contributed enormously to legitimizing the group as a political force. Thanks to live broadcasts on television, "people could see and understand what kind of people these newly-hatched, bearded and long-haired politicians were, who were calling for the BCP to be removed from power."[2]

The establishment of the UDF (rather than one of the dozen other parties that were multiplying like mad at the time) as the opposition resulted from the furtive yet growing support its leaders received from the second main architect of the "Great Transition": the streets. The demonstration on December 14, 1989, which was initially planned as a human chain of students around Parliament to demand the abolition of Article 1 of the communist constitution, for the first time addressed subjects that had previously been taboo. That demonstration gave rise to slogans that still sound heretical even today: "Down with the BCP!" and "For peace, send the BCP to Siberia!" among others. At times during this emotionally intense event, the protestors seemed on the verge of storming Parliament; however, the leaders of the UDF did not allow this. On an improvised sound system, they called on the crowd to disperse, to go home "to see and hear how Bulgarian television and radio inform you about free will in Sofia."[3] This most likely prevented bloodshed, since the nearby streets were held by armed units of the National Guard. We can see just how explosive the situation was from a line the head of state (and future president elected from the BCP) Petâr Mladenov let slip that

The beginning of the Great Transition   419

same night: "We'd better roll out the tanks!" Both on December 14 as well as years later, the leader of the UDF at the time, Zhelyu Zhelev, did not discount the possibility that the communists might resort to the use of force: "In such cases, the rulers' fear and confusion is particularly dangerous. In such moments, they can make very reckless decisions."[4]

Today, it is difficult to say with certainty whether tanks (or at least the National Guard) would have been called out or whether storming Parliament would have radically hastened the Transition in Bulgaria. It is clear, however, that without December 14, 1989, the changes would have occurred even more slowly, while the Round Table likely would have had more than two parties. Sensing support from the street, the UDF leaders blocked attempts by the BCP to demand the presence of a "third force" at the talks, namely the communist state's social organizations: the Komsomol, trade unions, the Fatherland Front and so on. The opposition, which was less than a month old, managed to formulate and impose several extremely important conditions: the right to publish a newspaper, a building to use as a headquarters, and regulations guaranteeing their access to the national media. Since the question of an office turned out to be exceptionally difficult for the authorities to resolve, the first meeting of the Round Table was suspended prematurely and only restarted once the UDF had received its building at 134 Rakovski Street.

Although it has been much debated in hindsight, the National Round Table played an enormous role in helping the opposition maintain the strategic upper hand it had gained after December 14. Feeling threatened, the former BCP, which had in the meantime changed its name to the Bulgarian Socialist Party (BSP), tried to rewrite the agenda, which had been dictated by the opposition. According to Zhelev's vivid description, "in order to take revenge on and frighten the capital city, the BCP's provincial nomenclature (surely not without prompting from Sofia) bussed in thousands of nationalists who raged in downtown Sofia for an entire week."[5] At that moment, Bulgaria seemed to be sliding toward a "Yugoslav scenario." However, the beginning of the Round Table moved the debate back into the realm of politics: abolition of Article 1 of the Constitution, the dissolution of State Security, and the disbanding of party organizations in workplaces. The battle around disbanding communist cells in companies and administrative institutions was especially fierce. The UDF was forced to demonstratively walk out of the Round Table session and to organize a month-long protest campaign to achieve that end.[6]

The most important decision made by the Round Table, however, was the creation of a "series of consensually accepted documents which form the basis of the political system in post-communist Bulgaria."[7] After several months of debate, an agreement was reached to hold elections for a GNA by the middle of the year (July 10), using a mixed voting system. Despite the fact that the UDF had already taken the strategic upper hand from the BSP and with support from the streets had dictated the agenda for the changes, the coalition's inexperience and chaotic structure took its toll. The UDF made both large and small mistakes, which perhaps dictated not only the outcome of the elections

420   *The collapse of communism in Bulgaria*

but also the events of the following several years. The decision to hold elections for a GNA rather than simply for a regular national assembly (i.e. parliament) resulted from the UDF's extreme optimism and the series of opposition electoral victories in the former Eastern Bloc. Bulgarian's "greenhorn" dissidents did not have a good grasp of the mood in the country and hoped through such an electoral victory to "catch up with and even surpass" the more advanced countries in Central Europe.[8] A mistake that seems more trifling on the surface was their failure to insist on redrawing the boundaries for the individual electoral regions. As the head of the UDF election headquarters later admitted, the party had no idea how important this issue was, and when it finally realized it, the borders were already fixed.[9] The UDF also paid almost no attention to the accuracy of voter rolls, which later turned out to be hopelessly inaccurate.[10] It also turned out to be quite risky to hold the elections in June, and not in September, as some of the older parties in the UDF's "blue coalition" (such as the agrarians and the social democrats) had insisted. This series of mistakes, a poor understanding of the situation outside of Sofia, and a clumsy election campaign led to unexpectedly low electoral returns for the opposition, which found itself in second place with 144 MPs (36 percent), far behind the majority of 211 seats won by the BSP (53 percent). Although it was highly tempting (and justifiable) to refuse to recognize the election results, the UDF was forced by external pressure to accept its defeat. With an absolute majority in the GNA, the former communists seemed to have regained the upper hand.

However, an "energetic minority" took shape in Parliament and used street pressure over the course of five months to rearrange the pieces of the political puzzle. Citizens in Sofia and the larger cities were extremely shocked by the UDF's electoral loss, which gave rise to informal protest networks. Students began a sit-in at Sofia University, a tent town dubbed "The City of Truth" cropped up in front of the Communist Party headquarters in Sofia, and many of Sofia's main intersections were blocked by acts of civil disobedience.[11] Broadcasts of the so-called "tank tape," in which Petâr Mladenov called for tanks to be used against demonstrators on December 14, 1989, between the two rounds of voting for the GNA gave the "street" new cause and impetus to continue its struggle. The awkward justifications offered by Mladenov, who had in the meantime been elected President, only confirmed the opposition's claims that "communist lie" and that they were ready to use force against the citizenry. The "tank line" immediately led to a list of demands from the protesting "blue mob," who called for Mladenov's resignation, the resignation of the director of Bulgarian National Television, Pavel Pisarev, and a verification of election results. In response to mounting pressure, the President was forced to resign on July 6, 1990. Less than a month later (on August 1, 1990), the GNA chose Zhelyu Zhelev to take Mladenov's place. Contrary to expectations, these two victories did not quell the wave of civil disobedience that had gripped Sofia and Bulgaria's larger cities. Instead, the opposition's demands grew more radical with every passing day. In August 1990, a campaign was launched to remove communist symbols from public buildings. The ultimate focus of this drive was

The beginning of the Great Transition 421

the red star hanging over the Communist Party Headquarters in Sofia. On the square in front of it, two protestors, Plamen Stanchev and Father Ambarev (an Orthodox priest), doused themselves with gasoline and threatened to set themselves on fire if the star was not removed in a matter of hours.[12] On television, the poets Yosif Petrov and Radoy Ralin called on the BSP to save "a human life." The news stirred up emotions, and an ever-larger crowd gathered on the square. The escalating tension ended in protestors storming the party headquarters. In a matter of minutes, the building went up in flames, while the police and security guards supposedly guarding it remained suspiciously indifferent. Later the BSP explained this with the police's unwillingness to shed blood, while the UDF argued it was a deliberate communist plan to justify the imposition of martial law.[13]

As a result of the fire at the party headquarters, the "City of Truth" was forcibly dismantled and barricades were set up at intersections. The "energetic minority" in Parliament, however, enjoyed the continued support of the streets and was able to influence the GNA session that was under way. Survey results show that the UDF's fiery and energetic struggle had managed to win over ever-greater numbers of voters in the provinces, who until then had remained passive. In the middle of August 1990, 40 percent of respondents now declared their support for the UDF, while two months later a whole 46 percent of respondents said they would have voted for the UDF – 15 percent more than would have supported the former communists.[14] In November 1990, the UDF introduced a motion of no confidence against the BSP cabinet's economic policy. The government survived, but the country's two trade unions – Podkrepa and the Confederation of the Independent Syndicates in Bulgaria (Konfederatsia na Nezavisimite Sindikati v Bâlgariya) – proclaimed Bulgaria's first ever nationwide strike. The streets were once again seized by the ever-growing "energetic minority," with demonstrators blocking intersections. On November 29, 1990, Prime Minister Andrey Lukanov was forced to resign along with his entire BSP cabinet. A caretaker government headed by Dimitâr Popov was established, in which the UDF controlled the Ministry of the Economy, while the Interior Ministry was in the hands of opposition supporter Hristo Danov. Over the course of six months, thanks to the pressure from the "energetic minority," the UDF managed to take control of the main institutions in the country, while its electoral support reached nearly 50 percent, as opposed the barely 30 percent support for the BSP.

Notes

1 According to one person present at the "mythical" meeting organized by Lukanov with representatives of the dissident movement: "He [Lukanov] told us some things about the 'coup,' read a letter from Petâr Mladenov to the Politburo [. . .] and called upon us to support the reformers within the BCP." Petâr Beron, *Zhivot li be da go opishesh*, vol. II, Sofia: Geya-Libris, 2004, p. 252.

422   *The collapse of communism in Bulgaria*

2 Zhelyu Zhelev, *Vâpreki vsichko: Moyata politicheska biografiya*, Sofia: Kolibri, 2005, p. 321.
3 Zhelev, *Vâpreki vsichko*, p. 301.
4 Zhelev, *Vâpreki vsichko*, p. 305.
5 Zhelev, *Vâpreki vsichko*, p. 306.
6 M. Spasov, *Sâzdavaneto na SDS 1988–1991*, Sofia: Gutenberg, pp. 120–134, 143–146.
7 E. Daynov, *Politicheskiyat debat*, p. 350.
8 Kalinova and Baeva, *Bâlgarskite prehodi, 1939–2005*, pp. 259–260.
9 Petko Simeonov, *Golyamata promyana 10.HI.1989–10.VI.1990: Opit za dokument*, Sofia: Otechestvo, 1996.
10 According to later claims made by experts, the voter rolls included at least 500,000 "dead souls" or slightly less than 8 percent of all voters in elections on June 10, 1990. Spasov, *Sâzdavaneto na SDS*, pp. 204–205.
11 Nasya Kralevska, *Bez zaglavie: Rushiteli i stroiteli na Bâlgariya*, Sofia: Iv. Vazov, 2001, pp. 233–260.
12 Nikolay Todorov, *VII Veliko narodno sâbranie zad kadâr*, Sofia: Hr. Botev, 1993, pp. 79–80.
13 Spasov, *Sâzdavaneto na SDS*, pp. 232–237; A. Semerdzhiev, *Prezhivyanoto ne podlezhi na obzhalvane*, Sofia: Hr. Botev, 1999, pp. 426–461.
14 Daynov, *Politicheskiyat debat*, pp. 407, 411.

Timeline of the People's Republic of Bulgaria

September 1, 1939 World War II begins.

September 15, 1939 Bulgaria declares neutrality.

December 1939–January 1940 Elections for the Twenty-Fifth Ordinary National Assembly.

February 16, 1940 A cabinet led by Prof. Bogdan Filov is appointed.

September 7, 1940 With German mediation, the Treaty of Craiova is signed, under which Romania returns to Bulgaria the territories of South Dobrudja, annexed by Romania in 1913 after the Second Balkan War.

November 1940 The Bulgarian government rejects the offer of the Soviet Union for a cooperation pact that would allow the establishment of Soviet military bases in the country.

March 1, 1941 Bulgaria joins the Tripartite Pact.

April 19–20, 1941 Bulgarian troops enter the historically disputed territories of Vardar Macedonia (Yugoslavia) and Aegean Thrace (Greece).

June 24, 1941 The Central Committee of the BWP adopts a course of military resistance to the Bulgarian government.

November 25, 1941 Bulgarian joins the Anti-Comintern Pact.

December 12, 1941 Under pressure from Germany, the Bulgarian government declares war on the United States and Great Britain, calling the declaration "symbolic."

June 5, 1942 The United States declares war on Bulgaria.

July 17, 1942 The Fatherland Front announces its political platform.

February 22, 1943 The newly established Commissariat for Jewish Affairs signs an agreement with Germany for the deportation of Jews from the newly annexed territories in Greece and Macedonia to Nazi concentration camps.

March–May 1943 A joint initiative by Bulgarian MPs, the Bulgarian Orthodox Church, and a significant portion of the public succeeds in saving Bulgarian Jews in Bulgaria proper (but not in the annexed territories) from deportation. After months of unrest, Tsar Boris III cancels the planned deportation.

August 10, 1943 The National Committee of the Fatherland Front is established.

August 28, 1943 Tsar Boris III dies.

424 *Timeline*

September 9, 1943 The Twenty-Fifth Ordinary National Assembly elects Professor Bogdan Filov, Prince Kiril of Preslav/Bulgaria and General Nikola Mihov as regents of the underage Tsar Simeon II.

September 14, 1943 A cabinet led by Dobri Bozhilov is appointed.

End of 1943–Beginning of 1944 Mass Anglo-American bombardment takes place, destroying large parts of Sofia and other Bulgarian cities.

June 1, 1944 A cabinet led by Ivan Bagryanov is formed with the goal of appeasing the nation and attempting peace negotiations with the Allies.

August 26, 1944 The Central Committee of the BWP decides to adopt a course toward a coup d'état.

September 2, 1944 A new government led by pro-Allies Konstantin Muraviev is formed.

September 5, 1944 The Soviet Union declares war on Bulgaria despite Bulgaria's ongoing diplomatic relations with the USSR throughout the war and its refusal to send troops to the Eastern Front. Almost simultaneously, but independently, Bulgaria declares war on Germany.

September 8, 1944 Soviet troops enter Bulgaria.

September 9, 1944 A coup d'état is carried out, and a government of the Fatherland Front led by Kimon Georgiev replaces the government of Prime Minister Konstantin Muraviev. Professor Venelin Ganev, Tsvyatko Boboshevski and Todor Pavlov are appointed as regents.

September 17, 1944 The Fatherland Front government publicizes its political program.

September 30, 1944 The Fatherland Front government issues a decree for the creation of the so-called People's Court, which would "bring to justice those responsible for Bulgaria's siding with Nazi Germany in World War II."

October 1944 Under pressure from the victorious Allies, Bulgarian troops and administration begin to withdraw from Aegean Thrace and Vardar Macedonia.

October 8, 1944 Bulgaria joins the military offensive against Germany. In an effort to block the withdrawal of German troops from Greece, the Bulgarian army begins Operations Niš and Stratsin-Kumanovo in Yugoslavia.

October 16, 1944 The Bulgarian army begins Operation Bregalnitsa-Strumitsa in Yugoslavia.

October 25, 1944 The Bulgarian army begins Operation Kosovo in Yugoslavia.

October 28, 1944 An armistice between Bulgaria and the Allies is signed in Moscow.

December 1944–April 1945 The People's Court is active across Bulgaria, handing down a total of 9,155 sentences, including 2,730 death and 1,305 life sentences.

January 1945 Under pressure from the Soviet administration in Bulgaria and the BWP(C), Georgi "Gemeto" Dimitrov, the leader of the BANU, and Kosta Lulchev, leader of the BWSDP, who were both critical of the Fatherland Front government, are replaced with Nikola Petkov and Dimitar Neykov, respectively.

Timeline 425

January 21, 1945 Archbishop Stefan of Sofia is elected Bulgarian Exarch.

February 22, 1945 The schism between the Bulgarian Exarchate and the Ecumenical Patriarchate of Constantinople, declared in 1872, is officially lifted.

January–March 1945 The first communist concentration camp for political opponents of the regime is opened near Gara Sveti Vrach.

March 6, 1945 The Bulgarian First Army begins its defense of the Drava Valley and Transdanubian Hills (a.k.a. Operation Drava).

March 29, 1945 The Bulgarian First Army begins Operation Mura, eventually reaching Vienna.

June 17, 1945 Divisions of the Bulgarian First Army are welcomed back in Sofia with a ceremony.

September 7, 1945 The BANU, the BWSDP (United) and the Democratic Party are legalized as members of the opposition.

November 18, 1945 The first postwar elections, to elect the Twenty-Sixth Ordinary National Assembly, are held. The opposition, protesting the electoral law and timeframe, refuses to take part. The Fatherland Front, the only party to run for Parliament, wins the elections.

March 12, 1946 The GNA passes the Land Reform Act.

March 31, 1946 A second government of the Fatherland Front led by Kimon Georgiev is formed.

August 9–10, 1946 The BCP (at this point and until December 1948, the party is still called the BWP(C)) holds its Tenth Plenum, dedicating it to "the Macedonian question." In preparation for establishing a Yugoslav–Bulgarian Federation, the notion of the "cultural-national autonomy" of the Bulgarian region of Pirin Macedonia is introduced.

September 7, 1946 The Bulgarian monarchy is put to a referendum and abolished. According to government sources, 96 percent of votes are in favor of a republic.

September 15, 1946 The PRB is established. Vasil Kolarov is elected its first Provisional Chairman.

October 27, 1946 Elections for the Sixth GNA are held, with the goal of devising a new republican constitution for the country.

November 22, 1946 A third Fatherland Front government, led by communist leader Georgi Dimitrov, is formed – the first overtly communist postwar government.

February 10, 1947 Bulgaria signs the Paris Peace Treaty.

June 5, 1947 Nikola Petkov, leader of the opposition, is arrested and beaten in the Bulgarian Parliament.

July 30–August 1, 1947 Bulgaria and Yugoslavia sign the Bled Treaty, which outlines the road to a future federation between the two countries.

August 1947 The BANU is outlawed. Its leader, Nikola Petko, is sentenced to death.

September 1947 The BWP(C) and eight other European communist parties co-found Cominform, with headquarters in Belgrade.

426 *Timeline*

October 1, 1947 Bulgaria and the United States restore their diplomatic relations.

November 27, 1947 Bulgaria and Yugoslavia sign a "friendship, cooperation and mutual assistance" pact.

November 1947–July 1948 Bulgaria and the other Eastern European countries sign bilateral "friendship, cooperation and mutual assistance" pacts, a first step toward an integrated Eastern Bloc.

December 3, 1947 Bulgaria's new republic constitution (a.k.a. the Dimitrov Constitution) is adopted by the National Assembly.

December 11, 1947 A fourth Fatherland Front government, led again by Georgi Dimitrov, is formed.

December 23, 1947 The Industry and Mining Nationalization Act and the Banking Sector Nationalization Act are passed in Parliament.

February 1948 No longer in need of a cover-up, the Communist Party transforms the Fatherland Front into a state-funded mass organization, which supports the regime.

June 28, 1948 The Yugoslav Communist Party is expelled from Cominform. In the ensuing conflict, Bulgaria sides with Stalin, which puts an end to the special relationship between Bulgaria and Yugoslavia and the idea of a Balkan federation.

September 6, 1948 Exarch Stefan resigns as head of the Bulgarian Exarchate.

September 1948 The BWSDP (Fatherland Front) merges with the BWP(C).

Summer of 1948 Forcible mass collectivization of agricultural land and property has begun.

April 1948 Dimitar Gichev, leader of the opposition BANU Vrabcha 1, is put on trial.

August 1948 The BWSDP (cf. entry dated September 1948) merges with the BWP(C).

October 1948 The BANU (Fatherland Front) officially accepts "the leading role of the Communist Party in society" and assumes the role of a junior governmental partner.

November 1948 Kosta Lulchev, leader of the opposition BWSDP (United), is put on trial.

November 29, 1948 Bulgaria and Israel establish diplomatic relations.

December 1948 At its Fifth Congress, the BWP(C) renames itself the BCP.

January 1949 Bulgaria becomes a founding member of the Council for Mutual Economic Assistance (Comecon), based in Moscow.

February 18, 1949 Bulgaria's first five-year economic plan (1949–1953) is adopted.

February 26, 1949–March 8, 1949 Fifteen Protestant pastors are put on trial, receiving sentences varying from life imprisonment to a year on probation.

February–March 1949 The Radical Democratic Party and Zveno disband, marking the end of the multiparty system in Bulgaria.

Timeline 427

Spring 1949 The Belene concentration camp for political opponents of the regime – the largest in the country – is created on the Danubian island of Persin.

May 15, 1949 The first postwar regional elections are held, which are also the first elections under a one-party system.

July 2, 1949 Prime Minister Georgi Dimitrov dies in a sanatorium in Moscow. On July 10, his body is laid inside a purpose-built mausoleum in the center of Sofia, where it remains until 1990. Vasil Kolarov becomes Prime Minister.

December 1949 Traycho Kostov, until recently the Communist Party's second-highest-ranking member, is subject to a Stalinist-style show trial and sentenced to death on allegations of anti-Sovietism, leftist sectarianism and espionage. His conviction and execution mark the beginning of BCP's campaign against "enemies with a party ticket"/"enemies within the party's ranks."

January 23, 1950 Vasil Kolarov dies. Vâlko Chervenkov succeeds him as state and party leader.

February 20, 1950 The United States breaks off diplomatic relations with Bulgaria.

November 8, 1950 Vâlko Chervenkov is elected General Secretary of the Central Committee of the BCP. His cult of personality reaches its zenith.

January 4, 1951 A new Statute of the Bulgarian Orthodox Church is adopted.

October 3, 1952 A group of Catholic priests and monks are put on trial: Evgeniy Bosilkov, Bishop of Nikopol, and three other priests are sentenced to death. They are executed on November 11, 1952.

March 5, 1953 Joseph Stalin's death is announced.

May 1953 First attempts to shake off the terror that has gripped society: tobacco workers go on strike in Plovdiv, the protest is quelled; an anarchist attempts to blow up the monument to Stalin in Sofia.

May 10, 1953 A Council of the Church and the People restores the patriarchal rank of the Bulgarian Orthodox Church and elects Archbishop Kiril of Plovdiv as Bulgarian Patriarch.

September 1953 The Belene concentration camp is closed down.

January 26, 1954 Vâlko Chervenkov resigns as party leader but retains the post of Prime Minister. On his suggestion, Todor Zhivkov is elected as General Secretary of the BCP.

June 1955 Soviet leader Nikita Khrushchev visits Bulgaria for the first time. Todor Zhivkov succeeds in winning his confidence.

December 14, 1955 Bulgaria becomes a member of the United Nations.

February 14–25, 1956 The Twentieth Congress of the CPSU takes place in Moscow, prompting a first wave of de-Stalinization in the USSR, which is echoed, in a more subdued form, in Bulgaria.

February–March 1956 A second wave of agricultural collectivization takes place.

March 1956 The politburos of the Bulgarian and Soviet communist parties discuss the fate the regime's strongman Vâlko Chervenkov.

428 *Timeline*

April 2–6, 1956 The April Plenum of the Central Committee of the BCP denounces the personality cults of Joseph Stalin and Vâlko Chervenkov.

April 17, 1956 Vâlko Chervenkov loses his post as Prime Minister and is replaced by Anton Yugov, an ally of Zhivkov.

October 31, 1956 A plenum of the Central Committee of the BCP denounces the "counterrevolution" in Hungary.

November 2, 1956 Bulgaria pledges its support for the quelling of the Hungarian Uprising. The events in Hungary provoke a new wave of violence and stagnation in the country.

November 17, 1956 The Belene concentration camp is reopened for preventative incarceration of "subversive elements."

July 1957 The July Plenum of the Central Committee of the BCP dismisses Georgi Chankov, who is Todor Zhivkov's key potential rival, from his position as Deputy Prime Minister.

June 2–7, 1958 The Seventh Congress of the BCP officially declares the "socialism has prevailed in Bulgaria."

March 24, 1959 Diplomatic relations between Bulgaria and the United States are restored.

August 27, 1959 The Belene concentration camp is closed down for the second time. Some detainees, labeled as "incorrigible recidivists," are sent to the "labor groups" in Lovech (men) and Skravena (women), which are notorious for their inhuman conditions and numerous cases of murder.

1959 Agricultural collectivization is completed.

1959 Administrative and territorial reform: the country is divided into twenty-eight regions, which, with minor changes, remain in place to this day.

November 1962 Anton Yugov is ousted as Prime Minister. Having cleared his path to absolute power, BCP General Secretary Todor Zhivkov takes control of the government as well.

November 5–14, 1962 Following the Soviet example, the Eighth Congress of the BCP adopts "The Big Leap" political program, under which Bulgaria would arrive at communism by 1980.

March 1963 The March Plenum of the Central Committee of the BCP denounces the notion of "a separate Macedonian nation" in Bulgaria.

December 1963 A secret plenum of the Central Committee of the BCP decides to present Moscow a proposal for "a course of closer cooperation and, eventually, a merger of the PRB with the USSR."

November 5, 1963 The Kremikovtsi metallurgic plant, the largest industrial complex in the Balkans, opens near Sofia.

1964 The government attempts to change the Turko-Arabic names of ethnic Bulgarian Muslims (Pomaks) in the region of Pirin Macedonia as part of an assimilation campaign. The campaign is aborted after a rebellion.

1964–1965 Former resistance movement commander and member of the Central Committee of the BCP Ivan "Gorunya" Todorov and Sofia garrison commander Tsvyatko Anev attempt to oust Todor Zhivkov. The coup is exposed and thwarted by the counterintelligence services.

August 21, 1968 Bulgarian troops take part in the quelling of Prague Spring in Czechoslovakia within the framework of the Warsaw Pact.

March 7, 1971 Patriarch Kiril dies.

April 20–25, 1971 The Tenth Congress of the BCP adopts a political program "for the building of a mature socialist society."

May 18, 1971 A new constitution (known as the Zhivkov Constitution) is adopted. A new higher institution, the State Council, is created, and Todor Zhivkov becomes its first Chairman. The party leader is now also the head of state, a post which until then had been held by the Speaker of Parliament. Zhivkov concedes the post of Prime Minister to Stanko Todorov.

July 4, 1971 A church council elects Archbishop Maxim of Lovech as Bulgarian Patriarch.

November 29, 1972 Long-term émigré political leader Georgi "Gemeto" Dimitrov dies in Washington.

December 1972 A plenum of the Central Committee of the BCP adopts a course toward "an accelerated improvement of the living standards of the population."

1970–1973 An assimilation campaign succeeds in changing the Turko-Arabic names of ethnic Bulgarian Muslims.

September 1973 At a meeting with Leonid Brezhnev, Todor Zhivkov renews his offer of merging Bulgaria with the Soviet Union.

August 1, 1975 Bulgaria signs the Helsinki Accords.

September 7, 1978 The Bulgarian secret police assassinate writer and dissident Georgi Markov in London. The case acquires international notoriety as "The Umbrella Murder."

1981 Nationwide celebrations of the 1,300th anniversary of the founding of the First Bulgarian Kingdom take place across the country, blending communist ideology with nationalism. Lyudmila Zhivkova, the organizer of the festival program, dies on July 21, in the middle of the jubilee year.

1981 Grisha Filipov replaces Stanko Todorov as Prime Minister.

August 30, 1984 In response to a name-changing campaign, Turkish activists carry out terrorist attacks at Plovdiv's Central Railway Station and Varna Airport. One woman dies, dozens are injured.

December 1984–February 1985 The government embarks on a campaign to change the names of Bulgarian Turks as part of an official assimilation program known as the "Revival Process."

March 9, 1985 Turkish activists carry out terrorist attacks at Bunovo railway station and in Sliven, killing thirty people.

1985 A general political thaw begins, prompted by Mikhail Gorbachev's rise to power in the Kremlin and his plans for comprehensive reform, known as *perestroika*.

1986 Georgi Atanasov becomes Prime Minister.

April 26, 1986 A nuclear accident occurs at the Chernobyl nuclear power plant in Ukraine. The contamination affects Bulgarian territories, but the

430　*Timeline*

authorities, worried about the USSR's reputation, conceal the news from the population.

July 1987 The July Plenum of the Central Committee of the BCP adopts policies in line with Gorbachev's *perestroika*. But, unlike Gorbachev, who puts political reform first, Zhivkov places emphasis on economic reforms.

January 16, 1988 The Independent Society for Human Rights Protection, the first dissident organization in Bulgaria, is founded, with Iliya Minev as Chairman.

March 8, 1988 The Civil Committee for the Environment Protection of Ruse is founded.

October 19, 1988 The Spasenie Christian Union for the Protection of Religious Rights, Freedom of Conscience and Spiritual Values is founded.

November 3, 1988 The Club for Support of Glasnost and Perestroika in Bulgaria is founded in a lecture hall at Sofia University.

1988 The first *samizdat* magazines, *Glas* and *Most*, are published.

January 26, 1989 The State Council's Decree No. 56 allows for limited private economic initiative.

February 11, 1989 The independent Podkrepa Trade Union is founded by Konstantin Trenchev.

May 1989 Large-scale protests by the Turkish population against the government's "Revival Process" take place in northeastern Bulgaria.

June–August 1989 A mass emigration wave of Bulgarian Turks (commonly known as "The Big Excursion") takes place. More than 300,000 people leave the country, prompting Turkey to close its border unilaterally on August 21.

October 24, 1989 In an "open letter" addressed to the party elite, longtime Foreign Minister and Politburo member Petâr Mladenov harshly denounces Zhivkov, starting a battle for reforms inside the party.

November 3, 1989 The first large-scale anti-government demonstration in forty years takes place in Sofia in support of an environmental petition addressed to the National Assembly. The demonstration is dispersed by police and its organizers are arrested.

November 10, 1989 Under strong pressure from the Soviet Union, a plenum of the Central Committee of the BCP ousts Todor Zhivkov from all his posts. Petâr Mladenov is elected General Secretary of the BCP and Chairman of the State Council.

November 18, 1989 An anti-communist rally attended by thousands takes place in Sofia.

December 7, 1989 The UDF, a coalition of dissident organizations and restored pre-1944 parties, is founded. Zhelyu Zhelev, a philosopher and Chairman of the Club for Support of Glasnost and Perestroika in Bulgaria, is elected Chairman of the Coordinating Council of UDF.

December 10, 1989 The first large-scale rally of the newly created UDF takes place in Sofia, marking the beginning of the era of street politics.

December 14, 1989 A large-scale rally outside Parliament demands the abolition of Article 1 of the Constitution of the PRB, which guarantees the

Communist Party its political monopoly. The enraged crowd threatens to storm Parliament, forcing MPs to promise to meet their demand.

December 29, 1989 A plenum of the Central Committee of the BCP denounces Zhivkov's "Revival Process."

January 20, 1990 Todor Zhivkov is arrested and put on trial.

January 3–May 15, 1990 The political conditions for a transition to democracy are negotiated at round-table discussions between the ruling Communist Party and the opposition.

January 4, 1990 Leaders of the Turkish minority in Bulgaria found their own political party: the Movement for Rights and Freedoms.

June 1990 The BSP, successor to the BCP, wins the Seventh GNA elections.

July 6, 1990 President Petâr Mladenov (BSP) resigns under street pressure.

August 1, 1990 Opposition leader Zhelyu Zhelev becomes the first democratically elected President of Bulgaria.

November 29, 1990 Prime Minister Andrey Lukanov (BSP) resigns under street pressure. A cabinet of experts, nominated by the UDF and the BSP, is formed under the leadership of Dimitar Popov, an unaffiliated judge. Bulgaria embarks on a long and difficult transition to democracy.

Leading historical figures from the period

Andrey, Metropolitan Bishop (1886–1972). Orthodox clergyman. In 1929, he was ordained as bishop and awarded the ecclesiastical title "Velichki." In 1937, he was sent to organize the Bulgarian Eparchy in America. In 1947, he was selected as metropolitan bishop of the new Bulgarian Eparchy in America and Australia, but the authorities in Sofia prevented the Holy Synod of the Bulgarian Orthodox Church from acknowledging this election. In 1963, Andrey and his entire eparchy accepted the jurisdiction of the Bulgarian Orthodox Church, a move that met with resistance from some of the parishes. In 1969, the Bulgarian Eparchy in America and Australia split into three; Andrey remained metropolitan of the New York Eparchy until his death.

Georgi Atanasov (1933). Born in the village of Pravoslaven in the Plovdiv region. From 1965 to 1968, he served as First Secretary of the Central Committee of the Komsomol. In 1966, he also became a member of the Central Committee of the BCP. In 1977, he was made a secretary of the Central Committee of the BCP. In 1986, he became Prime Minister, while the following year he was also made a member of the Politburo. He was one of the organizers of the party-internal coup against Todor Zhivkov on November 10, 1989. In February 1990, he was forced to resign under public pressure. After his fall from power he spent a short time in prison.

Ivan Bagryanov (1891–1945). Politician and statesman. He began his career in the military, participating in the Balkan Wars and World War I. In the postwar years, he grew close to Tsar Boris III and sympathized with the agrarian regime. After the military coup of 1923, he withdrew to his home region and worked to introduce modern agricultural methods. When the non-party regime was established in 1938, he joined the government, occupying the post of Agricultural Minister in several cabinets. Shortly before Bulgaria joined the Tripartite Pact, he resigned from the government. During the summer of 1944, as the political crisis in Bulgaria deepened, he agreed to lead the government and tried to conclude an armistice with the United States and Great Britain; however, this attempt was blocked by Soviet diplomacy. After the coup of September 9, 1944, he was arrested and sentenced to death by the People's Court.

Leading figures from the period   433

Tsar Boris III (1894–1943). The last Bulgarian tsar (1918–1943). He ascended to the throne after the abdication of his father, Tsar Ferdinand I, who was blamed for Bulgaria's disastrous loss in World War I and the subsequent economic crisis. In the first years of his reign, Boris did not actively participate in governing the country, but, beginning in the mid-1930s, he gradually established control over the state government. During World War II, he was forced into an alliance with Germany, but until his death he refused to allow Bulgarian troops to actively take part in military operations. He contributed significantly to saving the Bulgarian Jews within the country's borders. He died of a heart attack on August 6, 1943, only days after a tense discussion with Hitler in Berchtesgaden.

Boris, Metropolitan Bishop of Nevrokop (1888–1948). An Orthodox clergyman ordained in 1930 as the Bishop of Stobi and elected as Metropolitan of Nevrokop in 1935. After 1944, he established himself as one of the most staunchly anti-communist members of the Holy Synod, for which reason he was killed on November 8, 1948, following a church service. His murder marked the beginning of a new wave of repression against the clergy.

Evgeniy Bosilkov (1900–1952). Catholic clergyman. In 1934, he was ordained as a parish priest in the village of Bârdarski Geran, and in 1947 he was elected and ordained as the Catholic Bishop of Nikopol. Along with other Catholic clergymen, he was put on trial and sentenced to death on October 3, 1952. The death sentence was carried out on the night of November 12/13, 1952. In 1998, he was proclaimed "Venerable" by Pope John Paul II.

Dobri Bozhilov (1884–1945). Financier, politician, and statesman. During the economic and financial stabilization of Bulgaria that began in the second half of the 1930s, he occupied important financial positions: Director of the BNB and Minister of Finance. After the death of Tsar Boris III he became Prime Minister, but he could not find the strength and courage to break the alliance with Germany. After the coup of September 9, 1944, he was arrested and sentenced to death by the People's Court.

Titko Chernokolev (1910–1965). Born in Târgovishte, he was a BCP member from 1930 and a political prisoner and concentration-camp inmate in the period before 1944. At the time of the September 9 coup he was leader of the communist Young Workers' Union. From 1949 to 1951 he was a member of the Politburo of the Central Committee of the BCP. As Agricultural Minister in 1950 and 1951, he was directly responsible for collectivization. Due to disagreements with Vâlko Chervenkov in 1951, he was removed from all his posts and arrested. He was released from prison after some time, without ever having been charged, but he was in practice banned from taking part in politics. After Chervenkov was removed from power in 1956, Chernokolev gradually resumed his party work, albeit not on such a high level. From 1962 until his death, he served as Minister-Without-a-Portfolio under Todor Zhivkov.

434 *Leading figures from the period*

Vâlko Chervenkov (1900–1980). A communist functionary, he joined the communist movement immediately after World War I, becoming part of its radical wing. He supported the idea of an armed uprising in the autumn of 1923, and later he helped organize a series of political assassinations in Bulgaria. He was sentenced to death *in absentia* for these activities and was forced to flee the country in 1935, settling in Moscow. In 1926, he entered into a common-law marriage with Georgi Dimitrov's youngest sister, although they were never officially married. He displayed an impressive mastery of Leninist-Stalinist teachings and was soon appointed Director of the Lenin International School. During World War II, he led the BCP's Foreign Office in Moscow and served as General Director of the Hristo Botev radio-station broadcast from the Soviet capital. In these capacities, he implemented Soviet policies and BCP decisions – and continued doing so after his return to Bulgaria. After Georgi Dimitrov's death, he took control of the Bulgarian party leadership and became the autocratic ruler of the country. Under his reign, the wave of communist terror unleashed in 1944 also spread to members of the Communist Party. After Stalin's death, he was forced to relinquish leadership of the party, retaining only the post of Prime Minister. In April 1956, he was removed from all official governmental posts by a man he had considered his loyal supporter: Todor Zhivkov.

G. M. "Gemeto" Dimitrov (1903–1972). Politician, leader of the agrarian movement; one of the leaders of the leftist agrarian organization BANU – Aleksandâr Stamboliyski. In the second half of the 1930s, he was a vocal opponent of Tsar Boris III's nonparty regime. He was openly opposed to Bulgaria joining the Tripartite Pact in February 1941; with the help of British diplomats in Sofia, he unsuccessfully tried to organize a coup. He left Bulgaria shortly thereafter and established the Bulgarian National Committee in Egypt. After the Fatherland Front seized power, Dimitrov returned to Bulgaria but quickly clashed with the communists, as he opposed their domestic platform. Soviet occupying forces helped orchestrate Dimitrov's removal from the BANU leadership post; he was placed under house arrest. He managed to escape and left the country with the help of American diplomats. In 1947, Bulgarian courts sentenced him to life in prison *in absentia*. In the United States, Dimitrov led the largest Bulgaria emigrant organization, whose goal was to topple the communist regime in Bulgaria.

Georgi Dimitrov (1882–1949). A prominent communist functionary, he had been a member of the social-democratic movement since the beginning of the twentieth century, while during the war years of 1912–1918, he was an MP from the ranks of the "narrow socialists." After World War I, he joined the radical wing of the Communist Party, and in 1923 he supported the Comintern idea of organizing an armed uprising in Bulgaria. After the revolt was put down, he left the country, doing various jobs for Comintern. In March 1933, he was arrested in Germany and charged with helping set fire to the Reichstag. In the subsequent trial in Leipzig, Dimitrov mounted a brave defense, enjoying the strong support of the USSR and the international communist movement. After the end of the trial, he settled in Moscow, where he was later elected Secretary-General of Comintern. In the following years, he implemented Stalinist policies with respect to the other communist parties, which included the liquidation of some such parties (such as the Polish Communist Party in 1937). After the end of World War II, he returned to Bulgaria and strictly carried out Moscow's instructions for imposing a Soviet-style regime in the country. Toward the end of his life, he lost Stalin's trust and died while in the USSR undergoing medical treatment.

Kiril Dramaliev (1892–1961). Communist functionary and politician. Born in Sofia, he graduated in German studies and got his Ph.D. in Munich. He became a member of the BCP in 1921. In the early 1940s, he was active as a representative of the BWP(C) in the National Committee of the Fatherland Front. After September 9, 1944, he was Chairman of the Union of Education Workers (1945–1947) and served as Minister of Public Education under Georgi Dimitrov, Vasil Kolarov, and Vâlko Chervenkov (1947–1952). He was Ambassador to Poland (1952–1954) and the GDR (1956–1958).

Dobri Dzhurov (1916–2002). Born in the village of Vrabevo in the Lovech region, he became a member of the Komsomol while still a student at the seminary, and in 1938 also joined the BCP. In 1942, he went underground and became commander of a partisan unit later known as the Chavdar Brigade, in which Todor Zhivkov also briefly took part. After the September 9 coup, he briefly worked for the Interior Ministry but later dedicated himself to an army career and graduated from the staff college in Moscow. From 1962 until 1990, he served as Minister of the People's Defense. He attained the highest rank in the Bulgarian army: army general. In 1977, he became an invariable member of the Politburo of the Central Committee of the BCP. He was a member of Todor Zhivkov's inner circle. In 1989, he turned against Zhivkov and actively helped remove him from power.

Grisha Filipov (1919–1994). Born in the village of Kadievka, Ukraine, to a family of Bulgarian communist emigrants to the USSR, he returned to Bulgaria in 1936 and became a member of the BCP in 1940. He was a political prisoner until 1944. After the September 9 coup, he studied economics in Moscow. In 1966, he became a member of the Central Committee of the BCP. In 1971, he became a secretary of the Central Committee of the BCP, while from 1974 until 1989 he served as a member of the Politburo as well. He was Prime Minister from 1981 to 1986. One of Todor Zhivkov's closest supporters, he was expelled from the BCP in 1990.

Bogdan Filov (1983–1945). Scholar, politician, statesman. Until the second half of the 1930s, Professor Bogdan Filov worked exclusively on academic research in the sphere of archeology and Thracian studies. His political career began with the establishment of the nonparty regime in Bulgaria, when he was appointed as Minister of Education in 1938. In February 1940, he replaced

436 *Leading figures from the period*

the longtime Prime Minister, Georgi Kyoseivanov. His drive to peaceably revise the terms of the Neuilly Treaty met with great success. In September 1940, Romania returned Southern Dobrudzha to Bulgaria. A fervent supporter of Bulgaria's alliance with Germany, on March 1, 1941, Filov signed the agreement making Bulgaria part of the Tripartite Pact. After the death of Tsar Boris III, he was appointed regent. After the communists seized power, Filov was arrested and sent to the USSR; he was subsequently returned to Bulgarian and sentenced to death by the so-called People's Court.

Venelin Ganev (1880–1966). Scholar, lawyer, politician. In the early twentieth century, he joined the Radical Democratic Party, and as a representative of that party he was part of T. Teodorov's broad coalition government following World War I. He was also a member of the Bulgarian delegation to the Paris Peace Conference in 1919. During World War II, he did not approve of the government's policies and joined the communist-backed Fatherland Front. After the coup on September 9, 1944, he was included in the Regents' Council, which governed in the name of the underage Simeon II. However, the regency's activities were under the absolute control of the communists. Critical of the communists' repressive policies, Ganev joined the opposition. After the opposition was crushed, he was sent to the prison camp in Dryanovo.

Ivan-Asen Georgiev (1907–1964). Communist activist and diplomat. After September 9, 1944, he was the first Head Secretary of the Interior Ministry. In 1946, the intelligence services sent him as an adviser to the Bulgarian embassy in Paris, where he remained until 1948. From 1956 until 1961, he was Deputy Head of the Bulgarian UN mission in New York. In 1962, he was elected as Chairman of the International Institute of Space Law. In 1963, he was accused of espionage and sentenced to death. According to the case against him, he had been recruited by American intelligence in 1956.

Kimon Georgiev (1882–1969). Military officer and politician. He served as an officer in the Balkan Wars and World War I. As a close confidant of the Military Union, he took part in the organization of three coups (June 9, 1923; May 19, 1934; and September 9, 1944). In May 1934, he headed the government installed after the coup and abolished the democratic political system in Bulgaria. He abolished the Târnovo Constitution and outlawed the political parties' activities. His cabinet did not last long, falling from power in early 1935. In 1943, he joined the communist-dominated Fatherland Front coalition, and, after the coup of September 9, he again became Prime Minister. Even though he was ostensibly a representative and leader of the Zveno Circle within the coalition, in fact, while serving as Prime Minister until 1946, he strictly carried out the communists' and the Soviet occupying forces' commands. In the subsequent fifteen years, he occupied various posts within the communist government.

Dimitâr Gichev (1893–1964). Politician and activist in the agrarian movement. As a very young man he joined Stamboliyski's Agrarian Union and was engaged in anti-war activities during World War I, for which he was sent to prison. In the mid-1920s, he became head of the moderate wing of the agrarian movement, BANU Vrabcha 1. During World War II, he declared his opposition to Bulgaria's alliance with Germany, but refused to join the communist-dominated Fatherland Front. He was part of Konstantin Muraviev's cabinet, which broke ties with Germany. After the coup on September 9, 1944, he was convicted by the so-called People's Court. A year later, when the Bulgarian government was under pressure from the United States and Great Britain to hold free elections, Gichev was freed and joined Nikola Petkov's oppositional BANU. After the legal opposition was crushed, he was sentenced to life in prison in 1948. In 1960 he was freed and died four years later.

Dimo Kazasov (1886–1980). Writer, journalist and politician. Born in Tryavna, he graduated from high school in Ruse in 1904 and got a law degree from Sofia University in 1918. He was a Marxist, BWSDP supporter, a "broad socialist" and member of the central leadership of that party, and an MP from its delegation in the Eighteenth Parliament during 1919–1920. He took part in the coup of June 9 in 1923 and became Minister of Railways, Post and Telegraphs (1923–1924) in Aleksandâr Tsankov's government. He was one of the founders of the Zveno political circle. After the coup of May 19, 1934, he assumed the post of Minister Plenipotentiary in Belgrade (1934–1936). He became a member of the National Committee of the Fatherland Front in 1943. After the coup of September 9, 1944, he headed the newly founded Ministry of Propaganda. He also served as Minister of Information and Art (1945–1947). He was director of the Main Directorate for Publishing Houses, the Printing Industry and Trade in Printed Works (1950–1953).

Kiril, Bulgarian Patriarch (1901–1971). Orthodox clergyman. In 1936, he was ordained as Bishop of Stobi, while in 1938 he was elected Metropolitan of Plovdiv. He actively participated in the campaign to save Bulgarian Jews from deportation to death camps in 1943. After the coup in 1944, he was arrested but was released in March 1945. On January 4, 1951, he was elected Vice-Chairman of the Holy Synod, and during the Third National Ecclesiastical Council held May 8–10, 1953, he was chosen as the first Patriarch of the restored Bulgarian Patriarchate.

Vasil Kolarov (1877–1950). Communist functionary and one of the few highly educated Bulgarian communists – in the early twentieth century, he got a law degree in Switzerland. After World War I, he was chosen as Secretary of the Central Committee of the BCP. In 1922, he became General Secretary of Comintern. The following year, he arrived in Bulgaria to convince Bulgarian communists to organize an armed uprising against the government that had overthrown Stamboliyski in a military coup. After the September Revolt failed, he retreated to Yugoslavia and later returned to Moscow. Once Georgi Dimitrov rose to international prominence following the Leipzig Trial, Kolarov was forced to cede the leadership of Comintern to Stalin's new favorite. After

438 *Leading figures from the period*

the end of World War II, he returned to Bulgaria and joined the government as Speaker of Parliament. He led the Bulgarian delegation to the Paris Peace Conference in 1946. In 1949, he was an active participant in the denunciation of Traycho Kostov, in hopes of eliminating a serious opponent in the power struggle within the Communist Party, which had been brought on by Georgi Dimitrov's clearly deteriorating health. After Dimitrov's death, however, he still did not manage to take control of the party, since Stalin preferred Vâlko Chervenkov.

Traycho Kostov (1897–1949). He joined the communist movement after World War I. Due to his illegal activities during the 1920s, he was tried and sent to prison. In 1931, he became a member of the Central Committee of the BCP. During World War II, he took part in the communist resistance but was caught in 1942 and received a death sentence, which was later commuted to life in prison. After the September 9 coup, he was freed and became Deputy Prime Minister in the Fatherland Front government, but he was in fact one of the most powerful figures in the country. In 1947, he actively participated in the campaign to crush the legal opposition, but he himself later fell victim to the Communist Party's repressive policies. Due to several timid attempts by Kostov to preserve Bulgaria's economic independence from the USSR, at least in part, Stalin personally set the campaign against him in motion. At the end of 1948, he was accused of anti-Sovietism, removed from all his governing duties and put on trial. He was sentenced to death under trumped-up charges that he had conspired against "the people's government" and had worked on behalf of the Americans. His trial marked the start of a mass purge within the ranks of the Communist Party, aimed at imposing the unquestioning sovietization of the country.

Georgi Kyoseivanov (1884–1960). Politician, diplomat and statesman. Over the course of twenty years, he held various diplomatic posts in a series of European capitals. From the autumn of 1935 until early 1940, he headed several nonparty cabinets. His foreign policy was moderate and reserved; he managed to bring about the repeal of the military restrictions imposed by the Treaty of Neuilly, strengthened diplomatic ties to Yugoslavia, and largely defused the anti-Bulgarian attitude within the Balkan Pact. From 1940 onward he served as Minister Plenipotentiary in Bern; after the communist coup in Sofia, he refused to return to Bulgaria and died in Switzerland.

Kosta Lulchev (1882–1965). Politician. He assumed leadership of the Social Democratic Party in the mid-1920s. After the coup of September 9, 1944, he attempted to maintain the social democrats' independence within the Fatherland Front, which caused the communists to launch an attack on him. In 1945, he and Nikola Petkov formed the legal opposition in Bulgaria. After the opposition was smashed in 1947, he was sentenced to fifteen years in prison.

Leading figures from the period 439

Georgi Markov (1929–1978). Writer and dissident. After working as a writer and screenwriter in Bulgaria, he left the country in 1969 and began working as a journalist for the BBC, Deutsche Welle and Radio Free Europe. His brilliant and passionate reports established him as one of the most prominent and influential critics of Bulgaria's communist regime. He died on September 11, 1978, after being shot with a poisoned pellet from a "Bulgarian umbrella" on September 7. The assassination was organized by the First Main Department (intelligence) of Bulgarian State Security.

Maxim, Bulgarian Patriarch (1914–2012). Orthodox clergyman. He was ordained as bishop in 1956 and elected Metropolitan of Lovech in 1960. At the National Ecclesiastical Council held on July 4, 1971, after Patriarch Kiril's death, Maxim was elected Patriarch of the Bulgarian Orthodox Church.

Petâr Mladenov (1936–2000). Born in Urbabintsi (present-day Toshevtsi) in the Vidin region. He was the son of a communist partisan killed in 1944. He became a member of the BCP in 1964. In 1971, he became Foreign Minister as well as a member of the Central Committee of the BCP. He was one of Bulgaria's longest-serving foreign ministers, holding the post until 1989. In 1977, he was made a member of the Politburo of the Central Committee of the BCP. He was one of the organizers of the party-internal coup against Todor Zhivkov. On November 10, 1989, he was elected General Secretary of the Central Committee of the BCP and Chairman of the State Council of the PRB. After the latter post was abolished, he also became the first President of the PRB. He was forced to resign on July 6, 1990, after intense pressure from the opposition.

Konstantin Muraviev (1893–1965). Politician and statesman. He graduated from the military academy and served as an officer in the Balkan Wars and World War I. After being discharged from the army, he joined the BANU and quickly rose through the party ranks, joining the government in spring of 1923. Later he became a minister in the National Block government from 1931–1934. During World War II, he declared his opposition to an alliance with Germany. In the critical days in the late summer of 1944, he headed a government that lasted only a few weeks, but in that short time he managed to break ties with Germany and declare war on that country. Three governments in which Muraviev took part were toppled by military coups (1923, 1934, and 1944). After September 9, 1944, he was arrested and sentenced to life in prison by the so-called People's Court. He was interred in various prisons and camps until 1961.

Nikola Mushanov (1872–1951). Politician and statesman, leader of the Democratic Party. He was Prime Minister of Bulgaria during the Great Depression (1931–1934), and the economic and financial policies he introduced were not particularly effective. A military coup removed him from power; over the following years, he constantly agitated for the return of con-stitutional freedoms and the restoration of the democratic, multiparty regime.

440 *Leading figures from the period*

During World War II, he openly opposed the alliance with Germany. He was a member of Muraviev's democratic cabinet, which broke ties with Germany. After the communists seized power, Mushanov was thrown in prison and convicted by the People's Court but was released a year later due to US and British pressure on the Bulgarian authorities to hold free elections. He revived the Democratic Party and assumed an openly anti-communist position. After the legal opposition was crushed in Bulgaria in 1947, he was once again arrested, imprisoned in various places around Bulgaria, and killed in 1951.

Krustyo Pastuhov (1875–1949). Politician and activist in the social-democratic movement. After World War I, he took part in Teodor Teodorov's broad coalition government. After 1934, he publicly argued for the restoration of the Târnovo Constitution, while during World War II he was a vocal opponent of the alliance with Germany. As a champion of democratic principles, he refused to join the Fatherland Front coalition proposed by the communists. After the coup of September 9, 1944, he declared his opposition to the dictatorship imposed by the communists and the Soviet occupying forces in Bulgaria, which made him a serious enemy of the regime. He was sentenced to five years in prison in 1946 because of two articles published in an opposition newspaper, and was strangled in his cell in the Sliven Prison in 1949.

Dimitâr Peshev (1894–1973). Lawyer and politician. Until the 1930s, he worked as a judge, prosecutor, and lawyer. With the establishment of the nonparty regime in 1935, he joined the government as Justice Minister. He was an MP from the governing majority and deputy speaker of the Twenty-Fourth and Twenty-Fifth Parliaments. In 1943, he undertook a parliamentary and public campaign to save the Bulgarian Jews. After the coup of September 9, 1944, he was arrested and sentenced to fifteen years in prison by the so-called People's Court for "fascist and anti-Semitic activities." A year later, thanks to the intercession of Jews close to the communist government, he was freed. He died in poverty.

Nikola Petkov (1893–1947). Politician and activist in the agrarian movement. His father Dimitâr Petkov was a close associate of Stefan Stambolov and was one of the founding fathers of modern Bulgaria after independence, serving as prime minister in the early twentieth century. In the late 1920s, Nikola Petkov joined the agrarian movement. During World War II he led the Agrarian Party, and in 1943 he supported the communists' idea of founding the Fatherland Front. After the coup of September 9, 1944, he participated in the Fatherland Front government as Deputy Prime Minister. He gradually came into conflict with the communists, and in the summer of 1945 he left the government and led the legal opposition to the regime. In 1947, after signing the Paris Peace Treaty, the Communist Party went on the offensive against the opposition. Nikola Petkov was sentenced to death on trumped-up charges and was executed on orders from Stalin.

Stoyan Savov (1924–1992). He began working in the political intelligence services immediately after September 9, 1944. He was the head of the First Main

Leading figures from the period 441

Department (intelligence) within State Security during 1972–1973, after which he was appointed Deputy Interior Minister in charge of intelligence activities. He committed suicide in 1992 immediately before the beginning of a trial in which he was accused of destroying the writer Georgi Markov's dossier.

Grigor Shopov (1916–1994). Communist activist and politician and longtime Deputy Interior Minister (1967–1989). After 1973, he served as first Deputy Interior Minister and head of State Security. He was one of Todor Zhivkov's trusted agents, through whom the latter could control the security forces.

Aleksandâr Stamboliyski (1879–1923). Politician and statesman, leader and ideologue of the agrarian movement in Bulgaria. During World War I, he was categorically opposed to Bulgaria entering the conflict. He was convicted and thrown in prison for his anti-war activities. He was granted amnesty at the end of the war, and later, during the autumn of 1919, he was elected Prime Minister in a decisive electoral victory. In this capacity, he signed the Neuilly Peace Treaty on November 27, 1919. Domestically, he undertook a program of radical social reforms. He was removed from power by a military coup and killed several days later.

Stefan, Exarch (1878–1957). Orthodox clergyman. In 1921, he was ordained as Bishop of Marcianopolis (modern-day Devnya) and the followed year as elected Metropolitan of Sofia. He established himself as one of Bulgaria's most authoritative clergymen, with broad-ranging ecumenical connections. In 1943 he actively participated in the campaign to save Bulgarian Jews from deportation to death camps. On January 21, 1945, he was elected Exarch of the Bulgarian Exarchate but on September 6, 1948, he resigned from this post. After his resignation, he was exiled to the village of Banya near Karlovo, where he remained until his death.

Dimitâr Stoyanov (1928–1999). Communist activist and politician. After September 9, 1944, he first worked for Komsomol and became Secretary of the Central Committee of the Dimitrov Communist Youth League (1958–1961). He served as Secretary (1961–1971) and First Secretary of the Regional Committee of the BCP in Veliko Târnovo (1971–1973). From 1973 to 1988, he was communist Bulgaria's longest-serving Interior Minister. In additional to his ministerial post, he was also selected as a member of the Central Committee of the BCP in 1976, and later made a member of the Politburo and a secretary of the Central Committee of the BCP (1988–1989).

Stanko Todorov (1920–1996). Born in the village of Klenovik near Radomir, he became a member of the BCP in 1943. During the party's underground years he came into contact with Todor Zhivkov and remained one of the latter's closest associates until the very end of the 1980s. In 1952, he became Agricultural Minister under Vâlko Chervenkov and remained in that post until 1957. In fact, the forced collectivization of land was completed under his leadership. In 1954, he became a member of the Central Committee of the

442 *Leading figures from the period*

BCP, while in 1957 he became one of the secretaries of the Central Committee, becoming a member of the Politburo as well in 1961. From 1959 to 1966, he served as Deputy Prime Minister in the governments of Anton Yugov and Todor Zhivkov. From 1971 until 1981, he also served as Prime Minister. In the late 1980s, his relations with Zhivkov cooled, and in 1988, he resigned from the Politburo. He was one of the organizers of the party-internal coup against Zhivkov on November 10, 1989.

Damyan Velchev (1883–1954). Military officer and politician. He served as an officer in the Balkan Wars and World War I. In 1919, he was one of the founders of the illegal Military Union. As one of its leaders, he took part in the coups of 1923 and 1934. After military officers were removed from Bulgaria's government, in the autumn of 1935 he attempted to organize a conspiracy against Tsar Boris III. He was sentenced to life in prison but received amnesty in 1940. Velchev was among the main organizers of the coup on September 9, 1944, which brought the communist-dominated Fatherland Front to power. He became Defense Minister but could not manage to shield the army from communist influence. In 1946, he became a nuisance to the communists and was removed from the government; the authorities "neutralized" him by sending him to Switzerland as Minister Plenipotentiary. He was recalled a year later but refused to return to the country.

Kirill Yonchev (1920–2007). Bulgarian and American Orthodox clergyman. In 1941, he was ordained as a monk and sent to Bachkovo monastery. In 1946, he emigrated to the United States and was appointed parish priest at St. George's Church in Toledo, Ohio. He led the opposition against Metropolitan Andrey's decision to accept the jurisdiction of the Bulgarian Orthodox Church in 1963. In 1964, along with some Bulgarian communities in America, Yonchev accepted the jurisdiction of the Russian church abroad, which made him a bishop. In 1977, he and his whole eparchy accepted the jurisdiction of the OCA and was appointed Archbishop of Pittsburg and of the Bulgarian diocese of the OCA. He remained in this post until his death.

Anton Yugov (1904–1991). Born in the village of Karasuli in Greek Macedonia, he became a member of the BCP in 1928. Between 1934 and 1937, he lived in the USSR and studied at the International Lenin School. After his return to Bulgaria, he became a member of the Politburo of the Central Committee of the BCP. In 1941, he assumed the leadership of the Military Faction of the Central Committee of the BCP in charge of the underground communist movement in the country. He played an active role in the coup on September 9, 1944, and was appointed Interior Minister that very same day. He was also one of the leaders and organizers of the wave of killings and repression that swept the country in the first months after the coup. He remained in the post of Interior Minister until 1949, when he became Deputy Prime Minister, first in Vasil Kolarov's government, then in Vâlko Chervenkov's. After the April Plenum of the Central Committee of the BCP in 1956, he was promoted to

Prime Minister and remained in that post until 1962, when he was removed from power by Todor Zhivkov and excluded from political life. In 1972, he was even expelled from the BCP.

Zhelyo Zhelev (1935–2015). Bulgarian philosopher, dissident and politician, born in the village of Veselinovo in the Shumen region. In 1982, he gained national notoriety for his book *Fascism*, which made very clear allusions to the similarities between fascist and communist dictatorship. He became one of the leaders of the Bulgarian dissident movement at the end of the 1980s. In 1989, he headed the newly formed opposition coalition, the UDF. On August 1, 1990, he was appointed Temporary President of the Republic of Bulgaria. After winning the presidential elections in 1992, he remained in that post until 1997. He is the author of a series of scholarly works and memoirs.

Lyudmila Zhivkova (1942–1981). Daughter of the first party and state leader Todor Zhivkov and the doctor Mara Maleeva. She received a history degree from Sofia University in 1965, a degree in art history in Moscow in 1970, and studied at Oxford in the early 1970s. She briefly served as Deputy Chairman of the Committee for Friendship and Cultural Ties Abroad (1971–1972) and the Committee for Art and Culture (1972–1975). After that, she chaired the Committee for Culture and later also became a member of the Politburo of the Central Committee of the BCP. As Chairwoman of the Committee for Culture, Lyudmila Zhivkova established a new cultural policy whose effects lasted until the fall of the regime.

Bibliography

Avramov, Dimitâr. *Letopis na edno dramatichno desetiletie: Bâlgarskoto izkustvo mezhdu 1955–1965 g.* [*Chronicle of a Dramatic Decade: Bulgarian Art Between 1955 and 1965*]. Sofia: Nauka i izkustvo, 1994.

Avramov, Rumen. *Komunalniyat kapitalizâm. Iz bâlgarskoto stopansko minalo* [*Communal Capitalism: From the Bulgarian Economic Past*], vol. III. Sofia: FBNK/TsLS, 2007.

—— *Pari i de/stabilizatsiya v Bâlgariya 1948–1989* [*Money and the Destabilization of Bulgaria 1948–1989*]. Sofia: Insitute for the Study of the Recent Past/Ciela, 2008.

Baeva, Iskra. "Aprilskiyat plenum: predpostavki, problemi i posledstviya" [The April Plenum: Preconditions, Problems and Consequences]. *Novo vreme*, 81 (2006) (6–7): 137–146.

—— *Todor Zhivkov*. Sofia: Kama, 2006.

Bakalov, Ivan. *Prevratadzhii ot pârvo litse. Zagovorite sreshtu Todor Zhivkov* [*Coup Participants in the First Person: Conspiracies against Todor Zhivkov*]. Sofia: Milenium, 2008.

Bâlgariya i Rusiya prez XX vek: Bâlgaro-ruski nauchni diskusii [*Bulgaria and Russia during the Twentieth Century: Bulgaro-Russian Scholarly Discussions*]. Sofia: Gutenberg, 2000.

Bankov, Kristian. *Konsumativnoto obshtestvo* [*Consumer Society*]. Sofia: LIK, 2009.

Bârgâr, P. *Kapitalisticheskata revolyutsiya: Petdeset tvârdeniya za prosperiteta, ravenstvoto i svobodata* [*The Capitalist Revolution: Fifty Claims about Prosperity, Equality and Freedom*]. Sofia: Ciela, 1998.

BNB: Godishen otchet [*BNB: Annual Report*]. Sofia: BNB, 1990.

Bochev, Stefan. *Belene, skazanie za kontslagerna Bâlgariya* [*Belene, a Story about Bulgarian Concentration Camps*]. Sofia: Fondatsiya "Bâlgarska nauka i izkustvo," 2003.

Boychev, Yordan. *Povishavane blagosâstoyanieto na naroda – glavna grizha na BKP* [*Improving the Welfare of the People: The BCP's Main Concern*]. Sofia, Izdatelstvo na BKP, 1971.

Boyadzhieva, Pepka. *Sotsialnoto inzhenerstvo. Politiki za priem vâv visshite uchilishta prez komunisticheskiya rezhim v Bâlgariya* [*Social Engineering. Politics for Acceptance in Institutes for Higher Education during the Communist Regime in Bulgaria*]. Sofia: Institute for Studies of the Recent Past/Ciela, 2010.

Brown, James Franklin, *Eastern Europe under Communist Rule*, Durham, NC: Duke University Press, 1988.

Bibliography   445

—— *Surge to Freedom: The End of Communist Rule in Eastern Europe*, Durham, NC: Duke University Press, 1991.

Brunnbauer, Ulf, *"Die sozialistische Lebensweise": Ideologie, Gesellschaft, Familie und Politik in Bulgarien (1944–1989)* [*"The Socialist Way of Living": Ideology, Society, Family and Politics in Bulgaria (1944–1989)*], Weimar: Btshlau, 2007.

Chakârov, Kostadin. *Vtoriyat etazh* [*Second Floor*]. Sofia: K&M, 1990.

—— *Ot vtoriya etazh kâm nashestvieto na demokratite* [*From the Second Floor to the Inrush of the Democrats*]. Sofia: Trud, 2001.

Chervenkov, Vâlko. *Za izkustvoto i kulturata* [*On Art and Culture*]. Sofia: Bâlgarski pisatel, 1950.

Chichovska, Vesela. *Politikata sreshtu prosvetnata traditsiya* [*The Policy against the Enlightenment Tradition*], 2nd edn. Sofia: Gutenberg, 2010.

Crampton, Richard, *A Concise History of Bulgaria*. Cambridge: Cambridge University Press, 1997.

Crane, Kate. *The Soviet Economic Dilemma of Eastern Europe*, Santa Monica, CA: Project Air Force, 1986.

Creed, Gerald. *Domesticating Revolution: From Socialist Reform to Ambivalent Transition in a Bulgarian Village*. Pennsylvania, PA: Pennsylvania State University Press, 1997.

Daynov, Evgeniy. *Politicheskiyat debat i prehodât v Bâlgariya* [*The Political Debate and Transition in Bulgaria*]. Sofia: Fondatsiya "Bâlgarska nauka i izkustvo," 2000.

Dimitrov, Dimitâr. *Sâvetska Bâlgariya prez tri britanski mandata, 1956–1963: Iz arhiva na Forin Ofis za sâbitiya i lichnosti v Bâlgariya* [*Soviet Bulgaria during Three British Mandates, 1956–1963: From the Archive of the Foreign Office about Events and People in Bulgaria*]. London: BBC Bâlgarska redaktsiya, 1994.

—— *Sâvetska Bâlgariya prez tri britanski mandata, 1964–1966: Iz arhiva na Forin Ofis po vremeto na pârviya britanski poslanik Uylyam Harpâm* [*Soviet Bulgaria during Three British Mandates, 1964–1966: From the Archive of the Foreign Office during the Time of the First British Ambassador William Harpham*]. London: BBC, 1999.

Dimitrov, Georgi. *Dnevnik. 9 mart 1933–6 fevruari 1945* [*Diary. March 9, 1933–February 6, 1945*]. Sofia: Sv. Kliment Ohridski, 1997.

Dochev, Donko. "Part 1 (1944–1964)." In *Provintsialniyat totalitarizâm* [*Provincial Totalitarianism*]. Plovdiv: Narodna biblioteka "Ivan Vazov," 2007.

Doynov, Plamen, ed. *Prinudeni tekstove: Samokritika na bâlgarski pisateli (1946–1962)* [*Forced Texts: Self-Criticism by Bulgarian Writers (1946–1962)*]. From the series "Cherno na byalo. Literaturen arhiv na NRB [Black on White. Literary Archive of the People's Republic of Bulgaria]." Book 1. Sofia: Ciela, 2010.

—— *Bâlgarskiyat sotsrealizâm 1956, 1968, 1989: Norma i kriza v literaturata na NRB* [*Bulgarian Socialist Realism 1956, 1968, 1989: Norm and Crisis in the Literature of the People's Republic of Bulgaria*]. Sofia: Institute for Studies of the Recent Past/Ciela, 2011.

Draganov, Dragomir. *V syankata na stalinizma. Komunisticheskoto dvizhenie sled Vtorata svetovna voyna* [*In the Shadow of Stalinism: The Communist Movement after World War II*]. Sofia: Hristo Botev, 1990.

Elenkov, Ivan. *Kulturniyat front. Bâlgarskata kultura prez epohata na komunizma – politichesko upravlenie, ideologicheski osnovaniya, institutsionalni rezhimi* [*The Cultural Front: Bulgarian Culture during the Communist Era – Political Management, Ideological Foundations, Institutional Regimes*]. Sofia: Institute for Studies of the Recent Past/Ciela, 2008.

446 *Bibliography*

Ewald, Francois, *L'État-providence* [*The Welfare State*]. Paris: Grasset, 1986.

Feiwel, George. "Economic Development and Planning in Bulgaria in the 1970s," in Alec Nove, Hans-Hermann Höhmann, and Gertraud Seidenstecher (eds.), *The East European Economies in the 1970s*, Cologne: Butterworth-Heinemann, 1982, pp. 215–252.

Fotev, Georgi. *Dâlgata nosht na komunizma v Bâlgariya* [*The Long Night of Communism in Bulgaria*]. Sofia: Iztok-Zapad, 2008.

Genchev, Nikolay. *Izbrani istoricheski trudove* [*Selected Historical Works*], vol. V. *Spomeni* [*Memoirs*]. Sofia: Gutenberg, 2005.

Gruev, Mihail. *Preorani slogove: Kolektivizatsiya i sotsialna promyana v Bâlgarskiya severozapad (40-te–50-te godini na XX vek* [*Replowing the Field Boundaries: Collectivization and Social Change in the Bulgarian Northwest (1940s–1950s*]. Sofia: Institute for Studies of the Recent Past/Ciela, 2009.

Gruev, Mihail, and Aleksey Kalyonski. *Vâzroditelniyat protses: Myusyulmanskite obshtnosti i komunisticheskiyat rezhim* [*The Revival Process: Muslim Communities and the Communist Regime*]. Sofia: Institute for Studies of the Recent Past/Ciela, 2008.

Hristov, Hristo. *Sekretnoto delo za lagerite* [*The Secret Case of the Camps*]. Sofia: Ivan Vazov, 1999.

—— *Taynite faliti na komunizma* [*The Secret Bankruptcies of Communism*]. Sofia: Ciela, 2007.

—— *Todor Zhivkov. Biografiya* [*Todor Zhivkov: A Biography*]. Sofia: Institute for Studies of the Recent Past/Ciela, 2010.

Hristova, Nataliya. *Spetsifika na bâlgarskoto "disidentstvo." Vlast i inteligentsiya 1956–1989* [*The Specific Characteristics of the Bulgarian "Dissident Movement": Power and the Intelligentsia 1956–1989*]. Plovdiv, Letera, 2005.

Istoriya na Bâlgarskata komunisticheska partiya [*A History of the Bulgarian Communist Party*]. Sofia: Partizdat, 1984.

Isusov, Mito, and Yordan Zarchev (eds.). *Aprilskiyat plenum na TsK na BKP. Pâlen stenografski protokol* [*The April Plenum of the CC of the BCP: Full Stenographic Report*]. Sofia, Atlas-pres, 2002.

Ivanov, Martin. "Goryanskoto dvizhenie v Kyustendilsko i Gornodzhumaysko po sâdebni dokumenti ot Arhiva na MVR" [The Goryani Movement in the Kyustendil and Gorna Dzhumaya Regions According to Court Documents from the Interior Ministry Archives." *Demokraticheski pregled*, 27 (9) (1994): 119–140.

—— *Reformatorstvo bez reformi. Politicheska ikonomiya na bâlgarskiya komunizâm 1963–1989* [*Reformism without Reforms: A Political Economy of Bulgarian Communism 1963–1989*]. Sofia: Institute for Studies of the Recent Past/Ciela, 2008.

Johnson, Paul. *Redesigning Communist Economy: The Politics of Economic Reform in Eastern Europe*. New York: East European Monographs, 1989.

Join-Lambert, Marie-Therese (dir.). *Politiques sociale*. Paris: Ed. Daloz, 1979.

Kalinova, Evgeniya, and Iskra Baeva. *Bâlgarskite prehodi (1939–2005)* [*Bulgarian Transitions (1939–2005)*]. Sofia: Paradigma, 2006.

Kolarova, Rumyana, and Dimitâr Dimitrov (eds.). *Krâglata masa: Stenografski protokoli 3 yanuari–15 may 1990* [*The Round Table: Stenographic Reports January 3–May 15, 1990*]. Sofia: Biblioteka 48, 1998.

Levi, Izidor. *Shiroko dvizhenie za nov sotsialisticheski bit. Materiali v pomosht na politicheskata rabota na OF* [*A Broad Movement for a New Socialist Way of Life: Materials in Support of the Political Work of the Fatherland Front*]. Sofia: Izdatelstvo na NK na OF, 1969.

Bibliography 447

Maddison, Angus. *The World Economy: Historical Statistics*. Paris: OECD, 2004.

Marcheva, Iliana. "Opiti za ikonomicheski reformi v Bâlgariya prez vtorata polovina na XX vek" [Attempts at Economic Reforms in Bulgaria During the Second Half of the Twentieth Century]. In *120 godini izpâlnitelna vlast v Bâlgariya* [*120 Years of Executive Power in Bulgaria*]. Sofia: Gutenberg, 1999.

—— *Todor Zhivkov: pâtyat kâm vlastta – Politika i ikonomika v Bâlgariya 1954–1964* [*Todor Zhivkov: The Path to Power – Politics and Economics in Bulgaria 1954–1964*]. Sofia: Kota, 2000.

—— "Perestroykata v Bâlgariya v svetlinata na modernizatsiyata" [*Perestroika in Bulgaria in Light of Modernization*]. *Istorichesko bâdeshte*, 7 (1–2) (2003): 79–98.

—— "Za subektivniya faktor v bâlgaro-sâvetskite otnosheniya po vreme na 'perestroykata' (1985–1989)" [On the Subjective Factor in Bulgarian-Soviet Relations During the 'Perestroika' Period (1985–1989)]. In *Mezhdunarodna nauchna konferentsiya: Bâlgariya i Rusiya – Mezhdu priznatelnostta i pragmatizma* [International Scholarly Conference: Bulgaria and Russia – Between Gratitude and Pragmatism]. Sofia: Forum "Bâlgariya – Rusiya," 2008.

Marer, Paul, Janos Arvay, John O'Connor, Martin Schrenk, and Daniel Swanson. *Historically Planned Economies: A Guide to the Data*, Washington, DC: World Bank, 1991.

Markov, Georgi. *Zadochni reportazhi za Bâlgariya* [*In Absentia Reports about Bulgaria*]. Sofia: Profizdat, 1990.

—— *Kogato chasovnitsite sa spreli. Novi zadochni reportazhi za Bâlgariya* [*When the Clocks Stopped: New In Absentia Reports about Bulgaria*]. Sofia: P. K. Yavorov, 1991.

Marrese, M. and J. Vatous, *Soviet Subsidization of Trade with Eastern Europe*. Berkeley, Calif.: Institute of International Studies, 1983.

Merkin, Victor, "Intra-COMECON Bargaining and World Energy Prices: A Backdoor Connection?" *Comparative Economic Studies*, 30 (4) (1988): 25–51.

Metodiev, Momtchil. *Mashina za legitimirane: Rolyata na dârzhavna sigurnost v komunisticheskata dârzhava* [*The Machine for Producing Legitimacy. the Role of State Security in the Communist State*]. Sofia: Institute for Studies of the Recent Past/Ciela, 2008.

—— *Mezhdu vyarata i kompromisa. Bâlgarskata pravoslavna tsârkva i komunisticheskata dârzhava (1944–1989)* [*Between Faith and Compromise. the Bulgarian Orthodox Church and the Communist State (1944–1989)*]. Sofia: Institute for Studies of the Recent Past/Ciela, 2010.

Migev, Vladimir. *Kolektivizatsiyata na bâlgarskoto selo (1948–1958 g.)* [*Collectivization of the Bulgarian village (1948–1958)*]. Sofia: Stopanstvo, 1995.

—— *Bâlgarskite pisateli i politicheskiyat zhivot v Bâlgariya 1944–1970* [*Bulgarian Writers and Political Life in Bulgaria 1944–1970*]. Sofia: Kota, 2001.

—— *Prazhkata prolet '68 i Bâlgariya* [*Prague Spring '68 and Bulgaria*]. Sofia: Iztok-Zapad, 2005.

—— *Polskata kriza, "Solidarnost" i Bâlgariya (1980–1983)* [*The Polish Solidarity "Crisis" and Bulgaria (1980–1983)*]. Sofia: Sv. Kliment Ohridski, 2008.

Mladenov, Yordan, Ognemir Genchev, Ivan Genchev, and Petar Totev. *Panorama na elektronnata promishlenost na Bâlgariya: Fakti i dokumenti* [*A Panoramic View of the Electronics Industry in Bulgaria: Facts and Documents*]. Sofia: DBMr, 2003.

Nikova, Gospodinka. "Zhivkovata ikonomicheska reforma, perestroykata i startât na skritata privatizatsiya v Bâlgariya" [Zhivkov's Economic Reform, Perestroika and

448 *Bibliography*

the Beginning of Secret Privatization in Bulgaria]. *Istoricheski pregled*, 59 (5–6) (2003): 92–125.

Nove, Hans-Hermann Hohmann and Gertraud Seidenstecher (eds.), *The East European Economies in the 1970s*. London: Butterworths, 1982.

Ognyanov, Lyubomir. *Politicheskata sistema v Bâlgariya 1949–1956 [The Political System in Bulgaria 1949–1956]*. Sofia: Standart, 2008.

Ogoyski, Petko. *Zapiski po bâlgarskite stradaniya [Notes on Bulgarian Suffering]*, vol. II. Sofia: Jusautor, 2008.

Petersen, Roger, *Resistance and Rebellion: Lessons from Eastern Europe*. Cambridge: Cambridge University Press, 2001.

Rosanvallon, Pierre, *La Nouvelle Question sociale: Repenser l'Etat-providence*. Paris: Seuil, 1995.

Semerdzhiev, Petâr. *Narodniyat sâd v Bâlgariya 1944–1945: Komu i zashto e bil neobhodim [The People's Court in Bulgaria 1944–1945: For Whom and Why Was It Necessary]*. Sofia: Izdatelstvo Erusalim, 1997.

Service, Robert. *Comrades! A History of World Communism*. Boston, Mass.: Harvard University Press, 2007.

Sharlanov, Dino. *Goryanite: Koi sa te? [The Goryani: Who Are They?]* Sofia: Prostranstvo i forma, 1999.

Simeonov, Petko. *Golyamata promyana 10.XI.1989–10.XI.1990: Opit za dokument [The Great Transition November 10, 1989–November 10, 1990: An Attempt at a Document]*. Sofia: Otechestvo, 1996.

Spasov, Metodi. *Sâzdavaneto na SDS 1988–1991 [The Creation of the UDF 1988–1991]*. Sofia: Gutenberg, 2001.

Stopanskata istoriya na Bâlgariya 681–1981 [The Economic History of Bulgaria 681–1981]. Sofia: Nauka i izkustvo, 1981.

Stoyanov, Lyubomir. "'Kato edin organizâm, koyto se orosyava ot edinna krâvonosna sistema' (za Yulskiya plenum na TsK na BKP ot 1973 g.)" ["Like a Single Organism, Fed by a Single Circulatory System" (on the July Plenum of the CC of the BCP of 1973)]. In *Mezhdunarodna nauchna konferentsiya Bâlgariya i Rusiya: Mezhdu priznatelnostta i pragmatizma [International Scholarly Conference: Bulgaria and Russia – Between Gratitude and Pragmatism]*. Sofia: Forum "Bâlgariya – Rusiya," 2008.

Stoyanov, Lyubomir, and Zhivko Lefterov. "Politikata na BKP za prevrâshtane na Bâlgariya v sâvetska republika (Ot ideyni postulati kâm prakticheski deystviya)" [The BCP's Policy of Transforming Bulgaria into a Soviet Republic (from Ideological Postulates to Practical Actions): Part 1]. *Godishnik na Departament "Istoriya,"* vol. I [*Yearbook of the History Department*]. Sofia: New Bulgarian University, 2007, pp. 168–228.

Tsonkov, Geno. *Za nov sotsialisticheski bit. V pomosht na propagandistite na OF [For a New Socialist Way of Life: In Support of the Propagandists of the Fatherland Front]*. Sofia: Izdatelstvo na NK na OF, 1965.

Vachkov, Daniel, and Martin Ivanov. *Bâlgarskiyat vânshen dâlg 1944–1989: Bankrutât na komunisticheskata ikonomika [The Bulgarian Foreign Debt 1944–1989: The Bankruptcy of the Communist Economy]*. Sofia: Institute for Studies of the Recent Past/Ciela, 2008.

Verdery, Katherine, *What Was Socialism, and What Comes Next?* Princeton, NJ: Princeton University Press, 1996.

Bibliography 449

Vezenkov, Aleksandâr. *Vlastovite strukturi na Bâlgarskata komunisticheska partiya 1944–1989* [*The Power Structures of the Bulgarian Communist Party*]. Sofia: Institute for Studies of the Recent Past/Ciela, 2008.

Vogel, Heinrich, 'Bulgaria,' in Hans-Herman Hohmann, Michael Kaser and Karl C. Thalheim (eds.), *The New Economic System of Eastern Europe*, London: C. Hurst & Co., 1975, pp. 199–222.

Yahiel, Niko. *Todor Zhivkov i lichnata vlast: Spomeni, dokumenti, analizi* [*Todor Zhivkov and Personal Power: Memories, Documents, Analyses*]. Sofia: M-8-M, 1997.

Yosifov, Kalin. *Totalitarnoto nasilie v bâlgarskoto selo (1944–1951) i posleditsite za Bâlgariya* [*Totalitarian Violence in the Bulgarian Village (1944–1951) and the Consequences for Bulgaria*]. Sofia: Sv. Kliment Ohridski, 2003.

Zhelev, Zhelyu. *Fashizmât* [*Fascism*]. Sofia: Narodna mladezh, Izdatelstvo na TsK na DKMS, 1982.

—— *Vâpreki vsichko: Moyata politicheska biografiya* [*Despite Everything: My Political Biography*]. Sofia: Kolibri, 2005.

Zhivkov, Todor. *Za literaturata* [*On Literature*]. Sofia: Bâlgarski pisatel, 1981.

—— *Sreshtu nyakoi lâzhi: Paralelni etyudi* [*Countering Certain Lies: Parallel Etudes*]. Burgas, Delfinpres, 1993.

—— *Memoari: Sofia-Veliko Târnovo* [*Memoirs: Sofia-Veliko Târnovo*], Sofia: Abagar, 1995.

Zhivkov, Zhivko. *Krâglata masa na Politbyuro* [*The Round Table of the Politburo*]. Sofia: Interpres 67, 1991.

Znepolski, Ivaylo. *Ezikât na imaginerniya prehod* [*The Language of the Imaginary Transition*]. Sofia: Bâlgarska sbirka, 1997.

—— *Bâlgarskiyat komunizâm. Sotsiokulturni cherti i vlastova traektoriya* [*Bulgarian Communism: Sociocultural Features and the Trajectory of Power*]. Sofia: Institute for Studies of the Recent Past/Ciela, 2008.

—— (ed.). *Totalitarizmite na XX vek v sravnitelna perspektiva* [*The Totalitarianisms of the Twentieth Century in a Comparative Perspective*]. Sofia: Institute for Studies of the Recent Past/Ciela, 2010.

Index

Note: Page numbers in **bold** indicate a table. The letter 'n' following a page number indicates an endnote

Abdul Hamid II, Sultan 31
Academic Council 190, 191
Africa 177, 214–15
Agrarian Party 67, 100, 129
agrarians 41, 44, 56, 66, 68, 70, 73, 128–9; *see also* Bulgarian Agrarian National Union (BANU)
agriculture 31, 113, 117, 122, 123, 255; agrarian-industrial complexes 144, 264, 265–6; collectivization 135–44, 142–4; control of 370n4; equipment purchase 135; growth 373; *kolkhoz* model 127; liberalization 295; private and collective 126–30; quota system 133–4
Aktasheva, Irina 350
Albania 177, 244–5, 209, 211, 247, 283
Alexander I, Prince 29, 30
Alexander III, Tsar of Russia 29
Allied Control Commission (ACC) 62–3, 68–9, 77, 203n20
Ambarev, Father 421
anarchists 223
Anarcho-Communist Federation 70
Andrey, Bishop 336
Andropov, Yuriy 182, 280n77, 399–400
Angelov, A. 304n29
anti-Semitism 41, 56, 212
apathy 303n13, 347, 348, 357, 398, 401
April Uprising (1876) 60
architecture 344
Arendt, Hannah 6, 85
army: and BCP 65–6, 227; and elections 70; and foreign intelligence 182; Military Intelligence 176, 180–1, 182; modernization of 35; post World

War II 76; post-World War II 71, 73; purges 102; repression of 61; World War II 61, 63–4, 106, 109
Arseniy, Bishop 333
Arsov, Boris 180
art 199, 201, 202, 352
arts 197; *see also* culture
Asenovgrad 140, 151, 152
Asparuhov, Georgi "Gundi" 309
Atanasov, Georgi 243, 299, 302, 415, 416, 432
Austro-Hungarian Empire 30
Avramov, Roumen 154n1

Baeva, Iskra 154n1
Bagryanov, Ivan 47, 48, 432
Bakish, Sonya 412
Balev, Milko 321
Balevski, Angel 244, 321
Bâlgaranov, Boyan 234
Balkan Alliance (1911) 32
Balkan Pact (1953) 35, 37–8, 210
Balkan Wars 30, 32
Balkans, borders 29, 75
Baltic States 38–9
banking 31
Bankov, Kristian 294, 303n14
banks: Bulgarian National Bank (BNB) 108, 110, 112, 114, 121, 256, 257, 262, 360, 362, 363; International Bank for Economic Cooperation (IBEC) 362; World Bank 364
Bârdarski Geran 139–40
Barev, Tsenko 211
Barnes, Maynard 67
Barutin 317

Baybakov, Nikolay 270, 271
Beatles, The 301, 308
Bennett, John 211
Berger, Peter 359–60
Beria, Lavrentiy 122, 221–2
Biryuzov, General Sergey 64, 65, 67, 69, 77, 114
black market 133, 134
Blagoev, Dimitar 239, 241
Blagoevgrad 316–17
Boboshevski, Tsvyatko 57
Bochev, Stefan 170
Boev, Histo 176–7
books 196–7, **196**, 199, 350–1, 352, 369, 403
Boris III, Tsar 34, 38, 41, 46, 97, 433
Boris, Metropolitan Bishop of Nevrokop 326, 433
Bosilkov, Bishop Evgeniy 326, 328
Botev, Hristo 22, 23
Boyadzhiev, Petâr 411
Bozhilov, Dobri 46, 47, 433
Brannik ("Defender") organization 41, 56
Brezhnev, Leonid 238, 247, 270, 283–4, 320
Brezhnev Doctrine 18, 176, 284
Breznitsa 318
bribes 397; *see also* corruption
Brown, J. F. 280n83
Bulganin, Nikolay 123
Bulgarian Academy of Sciences 193
Bulgarian Agrarian National Union (BANU) 14, 66–8, 70, 72, 76, 77, 80, 100, 129, 243
Bulgarian Communist Party (BCP):
and 1944 government 47–8, 49;
and BANU 129; beginning of 100;
Central Committee 43, 47, 58, 95, 96, 136–7, 140, 143, 166, 206, 213–14, 225, 227, 230–1, 232, 236, 240, 241, 259, 264, 265, 272–3, 283, 290, 316, 317, 319, 366, 367, 396, 409, 415; and Comecon 281–2; committees 234, 342; Congresses 117, 243, 294; criticisms of 234–5; and culture 195; and debt 270, 360, 362; Decembrist Program (1972) 294–5; de-Stalinization of 229–30, 231–2; and economy 115, 258–9; and Edict No. 56 17; and education 163, 192; expulsions from 100–1; factional struggles and conspiracies within 237–41; and Fatherland Front 14, 199; general

secretaryship abolished 223; and Great Transition 419; growth 395–6; HQ fire (1990) 421; and hierarchy 185; and *kolkhoz* system 127; opponents 99–100, 181, 227, 413; political regime 44; and political repression 57–9; and political transformation 20–5; and power 12–13, 96, 160, 289; purges 102, 140; reform 18; Round Table 20, 21; and socialism 21–2; and socialist realism 198, 199; Sofia City Committee 225; Soviet criticism of 99; and sovietization 156–7, 158–9, 313; Stalinization process 231; and standard of living 299–300; and State Security 169, 172; and violence 33
Bulgarian kingdom 28, 31
Bulgarian Labor Party 45
Bulgarian Labor Social Democratic Party 45
Bulgarian Social Democratic Party 241
Bulgarian Socialist Party (BSP) 382–3, 419
Bulgarian state, reestablishment (1878) 29
Bulgarian Studies 345
Bulgarian Workers Party (BWP) 47
Bulgarian Workers Party (Communists) 65–6, 67, 68, 72, 73, 77, 79, 100, 111, 116, 128, 165, 65, 66, 72
Bulgarian Workers Social Democratic Party (BWSDP) 67, 72, 77, 99–100
Bulgarian Workers Social Democratic Party (United) 68, 70, 72, 76, 77
bureaucracy 409
Burgas 47, 49
Byrnes, James 76

capitalism 17, 160, 200
cars 291, **299**, 392
Ceauçescu, Nicolae 245, 300, 363
censorship 78, 195–7, 199, 349
Chakârov, Kostadin 394–5, 399
Chankov, Georgi 228, 229, 234, 241
Chernobyl nuclear explosion (1986) 407–8
Chernokolev, Titko 130, 136, 140–1, 433
Chervenkov, Vâlko 84, 99, 103–4, 122, 123, 140, 141, 142–3, 159, 164, 165, 166, 171, 198, 201, 221, 223, 226–7, 228, 229–31, 235–6, 240, 243, 434
Cheshmedzhiev, Grigor 45, 67
children 23, 315, 343, 394
China 177, 237, 238, 245, 281, 282, 283

452 *Index*

Chinkov, Boyan 307
Cholakov, Professor Stancho 73, 190
churches 31, 325; Bulgarian Orthodox
Church 28, 46, 157, 324–7, 328–38;
Catholic 326, 327, 328; Exarchate
31, 157, 328; Protestant 326, 327–8;
Russian Orthodox Church 325, 326,
336; St. Nedelya's church, Sofia 33;
see also Exarchate
Churchill, Winston 38, 62, 207, 208
cinema 243, 341, 345, 350, 353, 369, 412
civil rights 18, 71, 210
civil society 17, 306
class struggle 94, 100, 132–3, 386;
see also middle class; working class
Cold War 79, 96, 208, 247–8
collectivization 126–45, 130–7, 291,
357–8 and social change
Comecon 119, 123, 209, 252, 253, 267,
268, 269, 281–2, 284, 371n21
Cominform 99, 231
Comintern 45, 87, 88, 156, 197
Committee for Science, Art and
Culture 197
communism: conditions for 36;
experiences of 1–2, 6–11; historical
sociology of 8; interpretation of
4–5; and political debate 4; and
post-communism 3–4; spread of
78; transformations within 5–6;
withdrawal of 5
communization 157
concentration camps 6, 15, 71, 141, 149,
170–1, 214, 289, 308; Belene 18, 100,
170, 171, 222, 233, 317; Lovech 186n2;
Sveti Vrach 59, 170
consensus 399, 400; constructing
293–301; disintegration 301–2; need
for 290–3
constitutions: abolition of (1934) 34;
"Dimitrov" Constitution (1947) 76,
78–9, 93–4, 165, 193, 195; Fatherland
Front government 55; Târnovo
Constitution (1879) 29, 33, 49, 57,
58, 73, 378; Zhivkov Constitution
(1971) 241–4
consumerism 9, 289–302, 390;
Decembrist Program 294, 296, **298**
cooperatives 121, 137, 143–4
Corecom stores 291
corruption 9, 16, 90, 386, 388, 389, 391,
395, 396, 397–9, 400
Council of Foreign Ministers (CFM) 74

Council of Ministers 59, 61, 65, 103,
127, 130, 136, 140, 170, 173, 191, 193,
194, 195, 197
counterculture 309, 310
counterrevolution 214
coups 3, 20, 30, 33, 34, 55, 66, 111,
239, 414–16
Courtois, Stéphane: *The Black Book of
Communism* 4
courts 60, 135, 226, 307, 392; People's
Court 13, 58–9, 65, 81n13, 116,
192, 326
Crampton, Richard 280n75, 291
Crane, Kate 285, **286**
Creed, Gerald 138
Croatia 151, 155n12
cult of personality 96–7, 104, 171, 172,
213, 223, 229, 230, 243, 350, 352
cultural revolution 314
culture 193–5; democratization of 379,
387; and *perestroika* 367–9; and "real"
socialism 341–6; socialist realism in
197–202; *see also* counterculture
currency 110, 113–14, 121, 183, 215,
256–8, 269, 360; exchange rate 110,
112, 120, 256, 362
cynicism 17, 408
Czechoslovakia 5, 10, 35, 143, 209, 212,
227, 248, 346, 347, 414; Prague Spring
(1968) 5, 15, 20, 246–7, 263

Damyanov, Rayko 223, 228, 229, 236
Danchev, Petko 415
Dannecker, Theodor 45
Danov, Hristo 421
Daynov, Evgeniy 302n5
debt 110, 216, 254–8, 268–72, 300,
360–4
Defense Ministry 65, 181, 182
democracy 29, 34, 56–7, 68–9, 78,
382–3; "the people's democracy"
13–14, 70–1, 92–3, 94–5, 117, 140;
see also elections; referendums
Democratic Party 45, 57, 72
demonstrations 413, 418
denationalization 358
Department for Economic
Counterintelligence 183
Dertliev, Dr. Petâr 76, 160
de-Stalinization process 6, 13, 187n7,
229–30, 231–2
Dikov, Yosif 336
Dimitrov, Bozhidar 178

Dimitrov, G. M. "Gemeto" 41–2, 66–7, 72, 211, 434; G. M. Dimitrov Brigade 150, 151

Dimitrov, Georgi 14, 44, 60, 80, 84–97, 103, 104, 157, 158, 159, 164, 165, 166n8, 198, 206–7, 209, 243

Dimitrova, Blaga 352, 412

Dimitrova, Roza 90

Dimov, Dimitâr, *Tobacco* 201

Dinkov, Ivan, *South of Life* 350

diplomats 177

dissidents 18, 19, 181, 182, 232–3, 306, 311, 364, 367, 410–14, 420

Ditchev, Ivaylo 301

Dobrudzha *see* Southern Dobrudzha

Doktorov, Colonel Mihail 239

Doynov, Ognyan 268, 274

Dragalevtsi 145

Dramaliev, Dr. Kiril 45, 190, 213, 231, 435

Dubcek, Anton 246

Dupnitsa 47

Durkheim, Émile, *The Division of Labor in Society* 383

Dzhagarov, Georgi 243, 244, 321

Dzhurov, General Dobri 225, 237, 284, 415, 435

Eastern Rumelia 29, 30

Ecoglasnost organization 412–13

economy 106–23, 252–76, 374–7; Accumulation Fund 120, **296**, 301; Five Year Plans 117, 118, 120, 241, 253, 254, 256, 260, 297, 300; growth 362; Long-Term Program 284–6; post-World War I 35; reforms 17, 357, 359–60, 410; Soviet model 14–15, 16, 27n29, 31, 34, 209; top-down plans 397–8; Transition 20; *see also* Comecon; consumerism

education 378–9; agricultural 128; "Fatherland Front notes" 192–3; higher 162, 192–3; ideological 402–3; laws 193; modernization 189–93; "patriotic" 319–20; religious 326, 332; World War II 41; *see also* schools; universities

elections 14, 34, 38, 68, 69–70, 71, 76, 77, 225, 409–10, 419–20; *see also* referendums

Elenkov, Ivan 304nn27, 32

elites 16, 18, 27n29, 162

émigrés 178–80, 211, 212, 365–6

Engels, Friedrich 95

entertainment 294; *see also* film; music; nightclubs; sport

equal rights 56

European Union 376–7

families: and control 8, 10, 23, 57, 100, 102, 138, 152, 283, 352, 319, 320; political; resettlement of 149, 212, 318, 322

farms 295, 296; cooperative (TKZSs) 127, 129, 131, 133, 135–6, 137–9, 143, 144, 149, 264, 265; *see also* agriculture

fascism 39, 58, 196, 353n1

Fatherland Front 14, 31, 44–5, 48–9, 55–60, 64–8, 69, 70–1, 73, 75, 76, 77–81, 92, 93, 96, 100, 106, 111, 113, 115–16, 127, 136, 157, 165, 189, 194, 195–6, 243, 409–10

Federation of Rural and Urban Workers 76

Ferdinand, Prince (later Tsar Ferdinand I) 31, 433

Filatov, General 168

Filipov, Grisha 243, 290–1, 435

Filov, Professor Bogdan 38, 41, 46, 435–6

financial sector 99, 121; *see also* banks; treasury bonds

Finland 38, 39, 46, 207, 247–8; Helsinki Accords 247–8, 364, 408

food 59, 111, 119, 122, 142, 171, 303n16, 391

foreign policy 205–16, 244–7, 291

Foscolo, Alfred "Freddie" 411

Foucault, Michel 7

France 2, 3, 34–5, 38, 41, 77, 178, **299**, 304n41; *see also* Paris

Fromkin, David 208

Ganev, Dimitâr 226, 228, 231, 232, 234

Ganev, Professor Venelin 57, 436

Genchev, Nikolay 311, 400

General Workers' Professional Union 100, 194

Genov, Gavril, "Gavril Genov Partisan Brigade" 238–9

Genov, Todor 354n8

Georgiev, Ivan-Asen 177, 436

Georgiev, Kimon 45, 49, 55, 72, 75, 436

German Democratic Republic 9, 19, 143, 161, 174, 209, 227, 264, 414

Germany, 3, 18, 34, 35, 37, 38, 40, 43–4, 61, 64, 112, 109, 133, 389

454 *Index*

Germany, West 178, **299**, 304n41, 363, 384, 388–9
Geshov, Ivan 32
Gheorghiu-Dej, Gheorghe 214, 245
Gichev, Dimitâr 45, 81, 436–7
Giddens, Anthony, *The Constitution of Society* 7
Girardin, Émile de 384
glasnost (openness) 17, 407, 412
Glavinchev, Lev 58
Glavlit 197
gold reserves 257
Gomulka, Wladyslaw 227, 244–5
Gorbachev, Mikhail 12, 17, 248, 275, 276, 286, 407–8, 411, 415
goryani ("mountaineers") movement 149–53, 291
Gotse Delchev region 316, 317, 318
Gottwald, Klement 227
Grâbchev, Dimitâr 184
Grand National Assembly (GNA) 419, 420
Great Britain 30, 34–5, 37–8, 39, 41, 43, 48, 60–1, 64, 70, 71, 75–6, 79, 206, 211, 327, 363, 384; *see also* London
Great Depression (1929–1933) 33–4
Great Powers 28, 30, 32, 35, 36, 37, 75–6
"Great Transition" 418
Greece 32, 35, 39, 61, 62, 75–6, 108, 155n9, 177, 206, 208, 209–10, 337, 380
Gregory, Paul 359
Grigorov, Mitko 235, 237
Groys, Boris 389
Gullino, Francesco 180
Gyaurski, Marian 152, 154n2
Gypsies 315–16; *see also* Roma

Harrison, Mark 359
healthcare 378
Heath, Donald Reed 210–11
Heym, Stefan 19
Hitler, Adolf 35, 37, 40, 43, 97n1
holidays 319, 320, 334, 377; *see also* tourism
homosexuality 309
hooliganism 308
housing 379–80, 390–1, 392
Hoxha, Enver 209, 238, 245
Hristov, Hristo 180, 353, 361
Hristozov, Rusi 89–90, 168, 236, 241
human rights 247–8, 364–5, 411
humor 307; *see also* jokes
Hungary 5, 10, 15, 39, 46, 82n25, 143, 207, 209, 210, 211, 212, 227, 407, 248,

252, 248, 210; Uprising (1956) 213, 214, 303n12
Husak, Gustav 414
hypocrisy 302, 307

Ignatov, Assen 186
Iliev, Petâr 55
illiteracy 378, 402
incomes **296**, 300, 373–4; *see also* salaries
independence 28, 31
industrialization 290, 377
industry 14, 31, 99, 116–18, 120–1, 122–3, 252–3, 254, 264–7, 268, 269–70, 300, 373
inflation 110–11
inheritance 126, 146n2
insurance 383–4, 385–6
intellectual life 16, 18, 199; *see also* culture
intelligentsia 28, 160, 182, 308–9, 342, 367, 380, 410–14; proletarian 162, 163, 192, 193
Interior Ministry 65, 102, 168, 172, 173, 181, 182, 185, 413
International Monetary Fund (IMF) 364
internationalism 313–14
"iron curtain" 208
Islam 17, 319; *see also* Muslims
Italy 39, 46, 177, 207, **299**, 353n1
Ivanov, Tsveti 72

Japan 39, 43, 81n10, 178, 363
Jarosz, Professor Dariusz 147n49
Jendema 311
Jews 41, 45–6, 59, 163, 212, 389
John Paul II, Pope 408
Johnson, Paul 259–60
jokes 306–7
journalists 57, 69
justice 385–6, 404
Justice Ministry 65

Kádár, János 414
Kaganovich, L. 234
Kalinik, Bishop 333
Kalugin, Oleg 179
Kânchev, Nikolay 350, 353
Kârdzhali 316–17
Kasabov, Konstantin 152, 154n2
Kashev, Iliya 184
Kavala 75
Kazasov, Dimo 45, 194, 437
Khrushchev, Nikita 13, 122, 143, 214, 221, 223, 228, 229, 234, 237, 238, 253, 282, 283, 308, 374, 411

Kinov, General Ivan 227
Kintex company 183
Kiril, Bishop (later Patriarch) 46, 330, 331, 332, 437
Kiril, Prince 46
Kolarov, Vasil 75, 80, 84, 101, 103, 113, 360, 437–8
Komsomol 243, 348
Kopchev, General Boris 227, 228, 232, 233
Kordovski, Todor 240
Kornai, János 8, 263
Kornitsa 318
Kostov, Doncho 48
Kostov, Traycho 89–90, 93, 101–2, 115, 116, 142, 165, 210, 211, 226, 227, 232, 438
Kostov, Vladimir 180
Kostov, General Yanko 232
Kosygin, Alexei 270
Kotkov, Nikola 309
Kotsev, Vasil 179
Kozloduy 139
Krâstev, Tsolo 238
Kubadinski, Pencho 214, 237, 321
Kufardzhiev group 234–5
Kula 140, 153, 226
kulaks 131, 132, 133, 134, 143
Kulishev, Georgi 75, 114
Kunev, Trifon 72–3, 76
Kuusinen, Wille 94
Kyoseivanov, Georgi 34, 37, 38, 438

labor, social division of 383
"labor front" 159
labor market 401–2
labor-reeducation camps 59; *see also* concentration camps
Latour, Bruno 8
Lavrishchev, Alexander 48
Law in Defense of the Nation 41, 56
Law on Inheritance 146n2
Law on Labor Land Ownership 128–9, 130
Law on Nationalization 132
Law on Religious Denominations 325
Law on Retirement 394
Law on the Organization of Bulgarian Youth 41
Law on the Sanitation of Villages 128
Law on the State Gendarmerie 56
Laws on Higher Education 193
Lefort, Claude 96
leftists 308, 382

Legal Ordinance for the Defense of the People's Government 59
Lenin, Vladimir Ilyich 95
Leshnikov, Ivan 150
Levchev, Lubomir 243, 244
Liberal Party 29
libraries 199, 332, 368
Lilov, Aleksandâr 319, 418
literacy 378–9
Litvinov, Maksim 37
loans 110, 111, 119, 120, 253–4, 262, 300, 363
London: émigrés 211; murder of Georgi Markov 179–80, 311
London Protocol (1951) 217n18
Lovech 152, 409
Lukanov, Andrey 21, 22, 272, 415, 418, 421
Lulchev, Kosta 67, 81, 438

Macedonia 31, 32, 33, 36, 42, 46, 61, 63, 73, 150, 205–7, 350
macrohistory 11
Maleeva, Dr. Mara 224
Malenkov, Georgiy 122, 221, 223, 234
Manov, Emil 350, 354n8; *A Doubtful Case* 341, 349
Mao Tse Tung 237
Maoism 238
Marcheva, Iliyana 280n75
Marer, Paul 304n41
Marinov, General Ivan 55
Markov, Georgi 179–80, 213, 289, 302, 303n12, 304n22, 310–11, 439; *In Absentia Reports* 292, 310
Marrese, Michael 285, **286**, 287n21
marriage 325–6, 333
Marx, Karl 9, 95
Marxism-Leninism 6, 36, 96, 164, 165, 193, 195, 200, 247, 314, 343
Mateev, Evgeni 259
Maxim, Patriarch 332–3, 334, 338, 439
memory 2–3
Metodiev, Dimitâr 284
microhistory 11
middle class 8, 164, 350, 390
migration 16, 18; *see also* émigrés
Mihalchev, Professor Dimitar 64
Mihaylov, Ivan 237
Mihaylov, Stoyan 321
Mihov, General Nikola 46
Mikoyan, Anastas 159
militsia 58, 65, 67, 80, 135, 141
Minekov, Velichko 244

456 *Index*

Minev, Iliya 411
Ministry of Agriculture and Forestry 135, 136
Ministry of Culture 340
Ministry of Education and Culture 340
Ministry of Foreign Affairs 176, 194
Ministry of Foreign Economic Relations 176
Ministry of Foreign Trade 184
Ministry of Propaganda 193–4, 195–6, 202n16
Ministry of Public Education 190–1, 202n16, 340
Ministry of Supply and State Resources 263
Ministry of the People's Health and Social Welfare 315
Mishev, Georgi 353, 412
Mitterrand, François 412
Mladenov, Ivan 239
Mladenov, Petâr 365, 416, 418–19, 420, 439
Molotov, Vyacheslav 37, 40, 44, 62, 91, 234
monarchy, abolition of 73–4
monasteries 324–5, 332, 334, 337
Moshanov, Stoycho 48
Muraviev, Konstantin 48, 49, 59, 60, 439
museums 197, 325, 332, 334, 337, 344, 345, 368
Mushanov, Nikola 41, 45, 439–40
music 295, 301, 307–8, 311, 368
Muslims 313–22, 325, 366; *see also* Turks
Mussolini, Benito 39, 44

name changes place 316, 317–18, 320, 321
National Assemblies 70, 71, 74
national character 400–1
National Round Table 418, 419
nationalism 17, 313; Turkish 183, 321
nationalization 99, 116, 137, 164, 198–9; *see also* denationalization
National-Liberational Insurrectional Army (NOVA) 46–7, 225
NATO 209–10
Naydenov, Nayden 239
networks 8, 9–10, 32, 129, 137, 138, 151, 152–3, 158–9, 176, 182, 184, 327, 376, 381, 394, 420
newspapers 70, 72–3, 78, 157, 195, 199, 231–3
Neychev, Dr. Mincho 192
Neykov, Dimitar 67

Nicholas II, Tsar of Russia 31
Nicodemus, Metropolitan 335
nightclubs 301
Nikolov, Aleksandâr 307
Nikolov, Rayko 177
Nikova, Gospodinka 279n68
nomenclature 14, 16, 17, 20, 21, 89, 184, 291, 359, 370, 391–2
nostalgia 20, 22–3, 373, 381–3
Novotin, Antonin 227

Odrin (Edirne) 32
oil 268, 300, 360, 361
Organization for Security and Co-operation in Europe (OSCE) 247
Orwell, George, *1984* 19
Ottoman Empire 28, 32
Ovcharov, Stoyan 299

Palauzov, Mitko 23
Pancratiy, Metropolitan 335
Panov, Yonko 228, 230, 232, 233, 234, 235
Papazov, Boyan 412
Papazov, Nacho 237, 359
Paris 180, 177, 365
Paris peace conference (1946) 74–5
Paris Peace Treaty (1947) 79, 108–9
Parliament 420, 421
partisan movement 162–3, 225, 350, 390, 392, 393–4
Pârvanov, Georgi 178
"Pârvenets Whispering" 240
Pashov, Dr. Ivan 47
Pastuhov, Krâstyo 67, 72, 440
patriotism 313
Pavlov, Konstantin 353
Pavlov, Nikola 90
Pavlov, Todor 57, 282, 346–7
peasants 127, 131–2, 134–5, 136, 138, 145
Penal Code 412
Penelov, Ilko 196, 203nn18, 24
pensions 377
People's Republic of Bulgaria and Republic of Bulgaria compared 20–5
perestroika (restructuring) 12, 17, 20, 248, 275, 276, 286, 311, 328, 359, 364, 367–9, 408, 412, 414
Peshev, Dimitâr 46, 59, 440
Petersen, Roger 154n3
Petkanov, Konstantin 194
Petkov, Nikola 14, 45, 67, 68, 71, 80, 129, 149, 164, 440

Petrov, Georgi 259
Petrov, Ivaylo 352
Petrov, Valeri 350, 412
Petrov, Yosif 421
Petrova, Malina 89
Pimen, Metropolitan 330
Pirin 206, 207
Pirinski, Georgi 27n29
Pleven 140, 409
Plovdiv 29–30, 118, 140, 162, 222, 240, 320, 394
Poland 5, 10, 12, 35, 37, 99, 116, 143, 153, 209, 213, 244–5, 143, 227, 248, 252, 264, 285, 297–8, 299, 414
police 43, 59, 65, 68, 93, 169, 172, 225, 421; NKVD 104, 224; see also militsia
Politburo 89, 102, 136, 141, 170, 172, 173, 177, 185, 214, 226, 230, 240, 241, 253, 259, 263, 268, 270, 272, 275, 282, 290, 291, 295, 297, 298–9, 309, 315, 332, 357, 361, 364, 367, 415
Pomaks 316, 318, 321–2, 411–12
Popov, Dimitâr 421
Popov, Haralan 328
Popov, Ladin 328
Poptomov, Vladimir 84, 226
poverty 390
power stations 118
Prime Minister, post of 27n29, 31, 34–5, 38, 41, 46, 48, 75, 78, 80, 122, 123, 165, 191, 202n16, 210, 221, 223, 239, 243
prisoners: political 15, 48, 49, 58, 59, 72–3, 80–1, 100, 170, 171; of war 107
prisons 165, 171; see also concentration camps
professional associations 194
propaganda 13, 15, 68, 77, 78, 86, 87, 100, 104, 117, 118, 127, 130, 134, 158, 165, 178, 193–4, 242, 291, 305n68, 314, 319, 325, 340, 341, 343, 347, 377, 389; see also Ministry of Propaganda
property 242–3, 325, 357–9, 391; see also housing
publishing 196–7, 199, 344, 368, 370; see also books; newspapers
pubs 132, 295
purges 6, 55, 58, 59, 60, 65, 72–3, 84, 101–2, 115, 191, 226

Racheva, M. 67
Radical Party 57, 72, 77, 100
radio 43, 44, 55, 66, 71, 104, 138, 140, 149, 310–11, 411

Radomirski, Slavcho 224
Radoslavov, Ivan 350
Radoslavov, Vasil 32–3
railways 31, 61, 107, 111
Rákosi, Mátyás 88, 227
Ralin, Radoy 311, 350, 412, 421
ration system 134, 292
Rawls, John, A Theory of Justice 387
Raytchev, Andrei 8, 373
reading rooms 225, 368, 379; see also libraries
Reagan, Ronald 248
referendums 73–4, 242
refugees 33, 42; see also émigrés
regency council 46, 57
regions 409
religion 319, 333; see also churches; Islam
repression 10, 18, 59, 100–2, 149, 170, 174, 179–80, 181–6, 185
republicanism 73–4, 95
resistance 7–8, 13, 19, 24, 44, 55, 289, 412; Bulgarian Turks 17–18; goryani movement 15, 149–53; Muslims 322; villages 138, 139–41, 232, 316–19; World War II 3, 38, 40, 41, 42, 43, 46–8, 61; yatatsi groups 151, 152, 153
restaurants 295, 301
retirement 394
"Revival Process" 17, 173, 183, 186n2, 314, 319–22, 346, 364–7, 369, 409, 413
Ribnovo 316
Ricoeur, Paul 382
rituals 15, 22, 85, 302, 311, 315, 322, 326, 333–4
Robeva, Neshka 412
Roma 320; see also Gypsies
Romania 28, 32, 35, 39, 62, 143, 151, 155nn10, 12, 174, 207, 208, 209, 210, 211, 214, 227, 245, 264, 281, 282, 283, 300, 363
Rosanvallon, Pierre 384, 405n18
Rousseau, Emile 405n18
Rumelia see Eastern Rumelia
Ruse 47, 409, 412
Ruse Regional Agrarian Illegal Center 151–2
Rusev, Svetlin 412
Ruskov, Yordan 232–3, 349
Russia 3, 29, 30, 31, 161; see also Soviet Union
Russian Revolution (1917) 96
Russo-Turkish War (1878) 28–9, 41

458 *Index*

Sâbev, Todor 335
salaries 118, 261, 273, 291, 379, 392;
  see also incomes
Sanders, Irwin 145
Savov, Stoyan 173, 179, 180, 440–1
schools 31, 315, 378
science 193; "scientific-technical
  revolution" (NTR) 178, 267–8
Scientific-Technical Department 184
secularization 325
Sekelarov, Manol 102
Serbia 28, 30, 32, 61, 63
Sharapov, Viktor 415
Sharlanov, D. 154n2
Shepilov, G. 234
Shishmanov, Dimitâr 59
Shopov, Grigor 173, 224, 441
show trials 73, 80, 116, 135, 168, 170,
  326, 327
Silyanov, Evgeniy 166n1
Simeon, Prince (later King Simeon II)
  46, 57, 73
Slavov, Atanas 403–4
Slavov, Kiril 102
Sliven 151, 152, 153
Slovakia 39
Smolyan 316–17
Sobolev, Arkadiy 40
social democrats 56, 66, 68, 73, 105n11;
  see also Bulgarian Workers' Social
  Democratic Party
social exchange 9, 11
social policy 377–81, 388
social rights 384, 401–4
social security 383–8; *see also*
  welfare states
social structures 7, 403
socialism 21–2, 99, 100, 241, 399; "real"
  7, 10, 15, 18, 23–4, 314
socialist realism 197–202,
  340–53, 369–70
sociology 9, 16, 402
Sofia: BCP HQ 421; bombings of, World
  War II 44, 46, 47, 109; demonstrations
  80, 420; International Youth Festival
  (1968) 308; journalists 69; military
  coup (1944) 55; partisan occupation
  of 390–1; public life 309; St. Nedelya's
  church 33; Slavyanska Beseda Reading
  Room 224; Stalin monument 223;
  Union of Partisans 392; University
  420; water supply 412
Sofia City Region 409
Solakov, Angel 173, 309

solidarity 383–4, 385, 386–7
South Slavic federation 63, 109, 205–7
Southern Dobrudzha 36, 39, 42, 76
Soviet Union: aid from 284, 285,
  286, **286**; and Allied Control
  Commission 69; anti-Semitism 212;
  bi-lateral agreement (1947) 209;
  and Bulgarian democracy 70, 71;
  Bulgarian dependence on 119, 120;
  and Bulgarian economy 252, 258,
  270–2, 276; Bulgarian emigrants in
  85, 89; Bulgarian loyalty towards 15,
  210, 213, 252, 253, 281, 285, 313; and
  Bulgarian State Security 168; burial
  of cosmonauts 309; CPSU Congresses
  13, 229, 234–5; and debt 361, 363;
  diplomatic relations 69, 214–15;
  dominance of 99; and economics
  123; economy 160, 258, 264, 375;
  German property transferred to 114,
  115; *glasnost* 407; hooliganism 308;
  influence of 41, 48, 49, 101; invasion
  of Bulgaria 55; KGB 174, 179,
  182; and Leipzig Trial 87; Moscow
  conferences 238; "Moscow Fund"
  245–6; and Paris Peace Conference
  (1946) 75; and *perestroika* 248, 276;
  police 104; Politburo 233–4; power
  struggles 121–2; and Prague Spring
  246–7; Red Army 3, 13, 39, 49, 164,
  205; and repression 59–60; and
  scientific-technical revolution 267;
  shooting down of South Korean
  airplane (1983) 212; and socialist
  realism 198; Stalinism in 5; trade with
  Bulgaria 112–13, 363; and "unified
  conspiracy" 169; and United Nations
  211; Voroshilov Amnesty 222; World
  War II 13, 36–7, 38–9, 40, 43–4, 47,
  48, 49, 61, 62; *see also* Russia
sovietization 156–66, 281–6
Spasov, Mircho 186n2, 224
sport 309–10
Stalin, Joseph 41, 62, 71, 80; and
  Bulgarian communism 92–3; and
  Bulgarian constitution 93–4; and
  Bulgarian village uprisings 140; and
  Chervenko 103; class struggle theory
  94; and collectivization 136; death 13,
  121, 221; and Dimitrov 85, 87–9, 91,
  95; Khrushchev's denunciation of 229;
  and Kostov 101; and socialist realism
  198; and South Slavic federation
  205; and sovietization 157; and Tito

101, 210; at Yalta Conference (1945)
207, 208
Stamboliyski, Aleksandâr 33, 128,
129, 441
Stamboliyski, Asen 76
Stambolov, Stefan 30, 31
Stanchev, Plamen 421
Stanev, Emiliyan 244; *Ivan Kondarev* 349
Stanishev, Professor Aleksandâr 59
Stanishev, Dimitâr 225, 246, 415
Stanishev, Sergey 27n29
State Committee for Planning 260
State Security system 76, 168–9, 170–86,
213, 233, 238–9, 310, 311, 318, 333,
334–5, 391–2, 411, 413
Stavertsi 139
Staykov, Encho 226, 228–33
Staynov, Professor Petko 64, 113
Stefan, Exarch 46, 329–30, 441
Stefanov, Professor Ivan 75, 102, 113
stereotypes 23, 380–1
Stoilov, Konstantin 31
Stola, Dariusz 8, 9
Stoyanov, Anastas 243
Stoyanov, Dimitâr 173, 179, 321, 441
Stoyanov, Lâchezar 284
Stoyanov, Mladen 234
Stoyanov, Petko 202n16
Stoyanov, Zahari 400
Stoychev, General Vladimir 63
strikes 118, 222, 421

Tanev, Georgi 173, 187n13
Tatars 315
taxation 41, 113–14, 115, 116, 131, 133,
137, 212, 359
technology 184, 296; "scientific-technical
revolution" (NTR) 177, 267–8
television 22–3, 334
Terpeshev, Dobri 228, 231, 234, 235
terrorism 33, 100, 149, 151, 164, 165,
320–1, 327
theaters 197, 350, 368
Thrace 32, 33, 36, 39, 40, 42, 46, 61
tips 396–7
Tito, Josip Broz 62, 83n54, 101, 157,
206–7, 210, 238
tobacco trade 119, 120, 255
Todorov, Gerasim 150, 153, 166n8
Todorov, Ivan "Gorunya" 238, 239
Todorov, Stanko 166n8, 237, 239, 243,
282, 284, 412, 415, 441–2
Todorov, General Vladimir 179, 180
Todorova, Maria 314

Todorova, Rada 282
Tolbukhin, Marshal Fyodor 82n31
Topencharov, Vladimir 231, 232
totalitarianism 6, 9, 13, 14, 19, 20–1, 84,
100, 104, 164–6, 198, 292, 302, 325
tourism 291, **292**
trade 31, 34–5, 112–13, 119–20, 183,
215–16, 253, 254–6, 274, 284–5, 291,
299, 361, 363
trade unions 194–5, 199, 377, 378,
404n8, 412, 421
Transition 10, 17, 20, 23, 24, 25, 92
Trânski, Slavcho 227
Traykov, Georgi 100, 243
treasury bonds 113, 114
Trendafilov, Stoyan 55, 227
Truman, Harry 208
Tsanev, Angel 173
Tsankov, Georgi 168, 227, 231, 233, 235,
236, 241
Tsar Krum (military organization) 73
Tseko, Bogdan "Boncho" 150
Tsolov, Tano 237, 271, 395
Tsonchev, Tsonyo 102
Turkey 28, 35, 155n9, 177, 209–10,
364–6; *see also* Ottoman Empire;
Russo-Turkish War
Turks, Bulgarian 17–18, 183, 322, 363,
364–6, 408, 411–12, 413–14; *see also*
Muslims
Turnovo 29

unemployment 377, 401
unification, national 30, 32, 42, 205,
206, 320
unions 21, 100, 151, 190, 194, 199,
200–1, 264, 265–6, 368–9, 392–3, 418,
419–20, 421; *see also* trade unions
United Nations 211
United States: and Bulgarian democracy
70, 71, 281, 291; Bulgarian intelligence
177; Bulgarian Orthodox Church
335–6, 432; and Bulgarian resistance
151; and Cold War 208; and "Helsinki
Process" 74, 247; investments 304n41;
loans 363; Marshall Plan 119, 161;
missionaries from 327; and Paris
Peace Conference (1946) 75; post-
World War II relations 79, 210–11;
social insurance 384; Strategic Defense
Initiative 248; truce with (1944) 48;
World War II 41, 43, 44, 62–3; Yalta
Conference (1945) 207
universities 192–3, 378–9, 420

460 *Index*

uprisings 28, 139–40
USSR *see* Soviet Union

Vaptsarov, Nikola 43
Varna 47, 93, 311, 320
Vatous, J. 285, **286**, 287n21
Velchev, Boris 27n29, 235, 239–40
Velchev, General Damyan 55, 61, 65, 70, 73, 442
Velchev, Colonel Ivan 238
Verdery, Katherine 132
Vidin 140, 153
Vidinski, Radenko 228, 282
villages: depeasantification of 145; destabilization of 149–50; living standards 128, 143; post-World War II 126; renaming of 316, 317–18; social change in 137–42, 144–5; uprisings 139–40; *see also* collectivization
violence, political 57–9, 70, 76–7, 135, 140, 169; "Revival Process" 17, 173, 183, 186n2
Vishinski, Andrey 71
Voroshilov, Kliment 221
Voslenski, Mikhail, *Nomenklatura: The Soviet Ruling Class* 391
Vrabcha BANU party 45, 57, 70
Vranchev, Petâr 55
Vratsa 22, 47, 140, 153, 239

war reparations 75, 76, 107–9, 115
Warsaw Pact 284, 415
Warsaw Treaty Organization 245, 246
welfare states 377–8, 388, 405n18; *see also* social security
Whitaker, Roger 145
women: inheritance of land 126; Muslim 314, 315; and protest 412; resistance by 139
Workers' Party 127
Workers Youth Movement 70
working class 94, 134, 341, 378; *see also kulaks*
World War I 32–3, 37; Paris Peace Conference (1919) 75; Treaty of Neuilly 35, 36, 39, 75
World War II 35–49; Anti-Hitler Coalition 44, 60, 61, 69, 74, 114, 156; Eastern Front 69; economic dimensions 106–10; Moscow Truce (1944) 61, 62–3, 64, 107–9; Nagykanizsa–Körmend Offensive 64; neutrality 37–41; Nuremberg trials

81n10; Potsdam Conference (1945) 207; Third Reich orbit 41–9; Third Ukrainian Front 49, 63, 106; Tripartite Pact 41; Tripartite Pact (1940) 39; Yalta Conference (1945) 207; *see also* entries for individual countries

Yahiel, Niko 263, 280n83, 283
Yakoruda 318
Yanev, Grigor 170
Yastrebino 23
Yonchev, Kirill 336, 442
Yotov, Yordan 225, 415
Yotsov, Professor Boris 59
youth: culture 307–8; nostalgia 382
youth organizations 100, 117–18, 159, 306
Yugoslavia 35, 36, 40, 42, 62, 63, 64, 66, 80, 91, 101, 106, 108, 109, 140, 143, 151, 158, 159, 205–7, 209, 210, 238; *see also* Macedonia; Montenegro; Serbia
Yugov, Anton 59, 66, 80, 166n8, 168, 213, 222, 224, 228, 229, 231, 236, 240, 241, 442–3

Zarev, Pantaley 244, 321
Zhelev, Zhelyu 311, 404n10, 412, 419, 420, 443; "The Grand Era of the Intelligentsia" 411
Zhendov, Aleksandâr 201
Zhivkov, Todor: background 223–7; BCP leadership 13, 16, 96, 164, 187n7, 228–9, 230–1, 233–7, 253, 408; and Brezhnev 271; and Bulgarian Turks 365; and collectivization 141, 142–3; and consumption 290, 291, 297, 299, 301, 380; and corruption 395; coup against 20; cult of personality 241, 242, 352; and culture 308–9, 351; and discipline 399; and economic reform 258, 259, 263, 273, 274, 275–6; and Hard Currency Commission 270; and Hungarian Uprising 213–14; and industrialization 122; and jokes 293–4, 307; on living standards 291; and Markov 213, 310–11; opposition to 181, 238, 239, 240–1; and partisan movement 393–4; and *perestroika* 367; poetry about 243, 352; power 243, 244; and reform 357, 358, 408–10; removal from power 3, 414–16; and renaming of villages 316;

and "Revival Process" 17; and sale of gold reserves 257; and socialist realism 198, 347–8; and Soviet Union 281, 282, 283, 285–6; and State Security 172; and technology 267, 268; "two Bulgarias" statement 373, 374–5; and "xenomania" 301
Zhivkov, Vladimir 244

Zhivkov, Zhivko 213, 237
Zhivkova, Lyudmila 224, 244, 342–3, 344, 346, 352, 369, 408, 443
Znepolski, Dencho 170, 227
Znepolski, Ivaylo 312n14, 370
Zveno (Link) political circle 45, 55, 68, 72, 77, 100, 111
Zvezdov, Todor 240

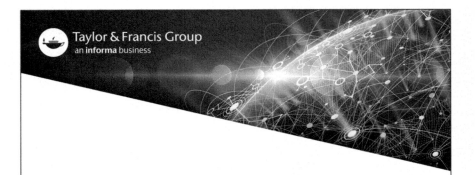